r.
in.
be

Le

λ

Ba
D

The Clergy Sex Abuse Crisis
and the Legal Responses

The Clergy Sex Abuse Crisis and the Legal Responses

James T. O'Reilly

Margaret S. P. Chalmers

OXFORD
UNIVERSITY PRESS

OXFORD
UNIVERSITY PRESS

Oxford University Press is a department of the University of Oxford. It furthers the University's objective of excellence in research, scholarship, and education by publishing worldwide.

Oxford   New York

Auckland   Cape Town   Dar es Salaam   Hong Kong   Karachi   Kuala Lumpur   Madrid
Melbourne   Mexico City   Nairobi   New Delhi   Shanghai   Taipei   Toronto

With offices in

Argentina   Austria   Brazil   Chile   Czech Republic   France   Greece   Guatemala   Hungary
Italy   Japan   Poland   Portugal   Singapore   South Korea   Switzerland   Thailand
Turkey   Ukraine   Vietnam

Oxford is a registered trademark of Oxford University Press in the UK and certain other countries.

Published in the United States of America by
Oxford University Press
198 Madison Avenue, New York, NY 10016

© Oxford University Press 2014

Library of Congress Cataloging-in-Publication Data
O'Reilly, James T., 1947- author.
The clergy sex abuse crisis and the legal responses / James T. O'Reilly, Margaret S. P. Chalmers.
  p. cm.
  Includes bibliographical references and index.
  ISBN 978-0-19-993793-6 ((hardback) : alk. paper)
1. Child sexual abuse by clergy—United States. 2. Child sexual abuse by clergy.
3. Child sexual abuse by clergy (Canon law) 4. Catholic Church—Clergy—Sexual behavior.
I. Chalmers, Margaret S. P. author. II. Title.
  KF1328.5.C45.O74 2014
  344.7303'276—dc23

2014017832

1 3 5 7 9 8 6 4 2

Printed in the United States of America on acid-free paper

Note to Readers

This publication is designed to provide accurate and authoritative information in regard to the subject matter covered. It is based upon sources believed to be accurate and reliable and is intended to be current as of the time it was written. It is sold with the understanding that the publisher is not engaged in rendering legal, accounting, or other professional services. If legal advice or other expert assistance is required, the services of a competent professional person should be sought. Also, to confirm that the information has not been affected or changed by recent developments, traditional legal research techniques should be used, including checking primary sources where appropriate.

(Based on the Declaration of Principles jointly adopted by a Committee of the American Bar Association and a Committee of Publishers and Associations.)

**You may order this or any other Oxford University Press publication
by visiting the Oxford University Press website at www.oup.com**

This work is dedicated to the memory of
Joseph Cardinal Bernardin
A source of inspired leadership, and a moral apostle
of prudence and forgiveness on this complex topic,
And to all of the innocent, faithful priests
who have continued to serve the people of God
throughout this time of great hardship and suffering,
As well as to all those clergy, religious, and laypersons
who have dedicated years of their lives
to cleaning up the mess that is this scandal.

CONTENTS

Preface   *xvii*

PART ONE: Context and Background
1. Introduction to a Complex Problem   *3*
    1:1 Understanding the Complex Dynamic Underlying the Legal Issues   *3*
    1:2 The U.S. Legal System Has No Perfect Answers   *5*
    1:3 The Church's Canon Law System Has No Perfect Answers   *7*
    1:4 The Clergy Sexual Abuse Lessons Are Useful in Other U.S. Faith
        Communities   *8*
    1:5 The Clergy Sexual Abuse Lessons Are Useful in Other U.S.
        Institutions   *9*
    1:6 The U.S. Lessons Are Useful to the Roman Catholic Churches in Other
        Nations   *10*
2. Understanding the Patterns of Clergy Abuse Litigation   *11*
    2:1 Introduction   *11*
    2:2 The Event   *11*
    2:3 Typical Post-Event Results   *15*
    2:4 Initial Reports   *16*
    2:5 Responses by Dioceses   *17*
    2:6 Contrasting External Legal and Internal Church Remedies   *19*
    2:7 News Media   *21*
    2:8 Significance of Prior Abuse Allegations   *21*
    2:9 Follow-Up Media Coverage   *22*
    2:10 Response by Local Law Enforcement   *22*
    2:11 Diocesan Review Boards   *24*
    2:12 Costs of Investigating and Defending Older Abuse Claims   *24*
    2:13 Fiscal Effects on Liabilities of the Diocese   *25*
    2:14 Financial Impacts on Income for the Diocese   *25*
    2:15 Insurer Responses   *26*
    2:16 Liabilities versus Assets   *26*
    2:17 Vulnerability of the Funds of Parishes   *26*
    2:18 Considerations of Bankruptcy   *27*
    2:19 Legislators' Roles on Limitations Periods   *27*
    2:20 Removal of the Accused Abuser Priest   *28*

PART TWO: Civil Litigation
3. Civil Litigation against Catholic Dioceses, Parishes, and Priests   *31*
    3:1 Individual Liability   *31*
    3:2 Litigation Begins   *31*
    3:3 Liability of the Diocese   *34*
    3:4 The Structure of "Employer Responsibilities" in the Church
        Context   *35*
    3:5 Determining Who Is the Employer under State Law   *36*
    3:6 Role of Parishes within a Diocese   *38*
    3:7 Discovery and Depositions to Gather Evidence   *39*
    3:8 Identifying Assets   *40*
    3:9 Pretrial Motions   *41*
    3:10 Attributing Liability to the Diocese   *41*
    3:11 News Coverage before Trial   *42*
    3:12 Pretrial Settlement Discussions   *43*
    3:13 Trial of a Sexual Abuse Civil Case   *43*
    3:14 Appeals   *44*
    3.15 Final Judgment   *44*
4. Participants in the Clergy Abuse Case   *47*
    4:1 Participants   *47*
    4:2 Victims   *47*
    4:3 Victim Advocates and Family   *48*
    4:4 The Accused Abuser   *49*
    4:5 The Diocesan Bishop   *50*
    4:6 Roles of the Vatican   *51*
    4:7 The Vicar for Clergy   *53*
    4:8 The Diocesan Staff Who Responded to Allegations   *54*
    4:9 The Liability Insurance Carrier   *55*
    4:10 The News Media Role   *55*
    4:11 Defense Counsel   *56*
    4:12 The Suspended or Dismissed Priest or Member of a Religious
        Order   *57*

PART THREE: Handling Abuse Claims
5. Delays and Limitations in Clergy Abuse Cases   *61*
    5:1 Exposing Weaknesses in the System   *61*
    5:2 Background   *61*
    5:3 Rationales for Limitations   *62*
    5:4 Delays and Tolling   *62*
    5:5 When the Period Begins   *63*
    5:6 Effects of Delay on Proof   *64*
    5:7 Frustrations   *65*
    5:8 Legislators' Responses to Reopening Limitations   *66*
    5:9 Courts and the Window Reopening Legislation   *69*

PART FOUR: Other Related Issues

6. Effects of Criminal Charges and Plea Agreements   *73*
    6:1 Criminal Law Context   *73*
    6:2 State Criminal Laws Applied to Clergy Abuse Cases   *74*
    6:3 Disincentives against Use of Criminal Charges   *75*
    6:4 The Criminal Prosecutor's Institutional Issues   *76*
    6:5 The Process of Criminal Prosecution   *76*
    6:6 Sentencing and Appeals   *78*
    6:7 Repeat Offenders   *79*
    6:8 Jury Nullification Defenses   *80*
    6:9 The Church's Altered Stance on Reporting Clergy for Criminal
        Prosecutions   *80*
7. Church Insurance and Abuse Claims   *81*
    7:1 Insurance Overview   *81*
    7:2 Coverage Disputes   *83*
    7:3 "Archeology" of Old Policies   *84*
    7:4 Was Sexual Abuse Covered as an Accidental "Occurrence"?   *84*
    7:5 Insurer Response to Sexual Abuse   *85*
    7:6 The Low Limits of Insurance Coverage   *87*
    7:7 The Primary and Excess Coverage Carriers   *87*
    7:8 Denial of Coverage for Known Offender Loss Events   *88*
    7:9 Pools and Retained Risk Groups   *88*
    7:10 Limitations on Insurance Claims Timing   *89*
    7:11 Exclusion of Coverage for Sexual Misconduct   *90*
    7:12 Vicarious Liability   *90*
    7:13 Broad Exclusions from Coverage after 1987   *91*
    7:14 Age of the Crimes and Age of the Insurance Contracts   *92*
    7:15 Diocesan Lawsuits against Insurance Carriers   *92*
8. Constitutional Issues   *93*
    8:1 Overview   *93*
    8:2 Constitutionality of Courts Overseeing Church Internal
        Discipline   *94*
    8:3 Bankruptcy and Criminal Rationales for Reviewing Internal
        Disciplinary Decisions   *95*
    8:4 Mandatory Reporting and the Religious Confessional Privilege   *96*
    8:5 No Special Immunities for Clergy   *98*
    8:6 Can There Be a Tort of Clergy "Malpractice"?   *99*
    8:7 Breach of Fiduciary Duty   *100*
    8:8 Post-Arrest Due Process Issues   *101*
    8:9 Conventional Statutes of Limitations Issues   *101*
    8:10 Statutory Reopening of Limitation Periods for Child Abuse
        Reports   *102*
9. Bankruptcy Issues   *103*
    9:1 Bankruptcy of a Diocese   *103*
    9:2 Operational Effects of Bankruptcy   *106*

9:3 Assets and Donor Relations   *107*
9:4 Assets of Parishes   *108*
9:5 Bankruptcy's Negative Effects on Dioceses and Donors   *110*
9:6 Bishops and Fraud   *112*
10. Mandated Abuse Reporting Issues   *113*
    10:1 Introduction   *113*
    10:2 History and Purpose of Reporting Statutes   *113*
    10:3 Operating Principles of the Abuse Reporting Laws   *116*
    10:4 Addition of Clergy to Mandatory Reporters   *117*
    10:5 The Connecticut Case Example   *118*
    10:6 The Kansas City Conviction   *119*
11. Evidence Privileges and Clergy Abuse Issues   *121*
    11:1 Conflicts with the State Law Clergy-Communicant Evidence
       Privilege   *121*
    11:2 Cross-Reference of Disclosure Statutes to Penitent Privileges   *125*
    11:3 Disclosure and Privilege as a Criminal Defense Argument   *126*
    11:4 What Are the Penalties for Not Reporting?   *127*
    11:5 Immunity for Clergy Members Who Report Child Abuse   *129*
    11:6 Instances of Conviction for Failure to Report   *130*
    11:7 Civil Tort Consequences from Not Reporting   *131*
    11:8 Immunity as an Incentive   *134*
12. Repressed Memory Inducement Cases   *135*
    12:1 What Is Repressed Memory?   *135*
    12:2 How Does This Theory Relate to Statutes of Limitations?   *136*
    12:3 Effects of the *Daubert* Standard   *138*
    12:4 Future of the Repressed Memory Cases   *138*
13. Fraud and Nondisclosure in the Assignment of Clergy   *139*
    13:1 Lawsuits Challenging Transfers of Abusers to Contact with
       Children   *139*
    13:2 The Role of Diocesan Concealment   *141*
    13:3 What the Data Shows   *143*
    13:4 How Priest Transfers Were Managed   *144*
    13:5 Priest Abuse Contrasted to Liability under Traditional
       Employment Law   *145*
    13:6 Concealment of Diocesan Knowledge of the Prior Accusations   *147*
    13:7 How Jury Decisions Would Be Made   *148*
    13:8 Transfers among Dioceses   *149*
    13:9 The Freedom of Religion Factor and the Judge's Role   *150*
    13:10 Charges of a Conspiracy of Silence   *152*
    13:11 Verdicts and Consequences   *152*
14. Defenses and Claims of Immunity   *155.*
    14:1 Overview   *155*
    14:2 Statutes of Limitations   *156*
    14:3 Diocesan Responses   *157*
    14:4 Presentation and Rebuttal of Evidence   *158*

14:5 Elements of the Damages   *158*

14:6 Emotional Injury Not Accompanied by Physical Harm   *159*

14:7 Privilege for Priest-Penitent Disclosures   *160*

14:8 Charitable Immunity from Larger Damages   *161*

14:9 Constitutional Defenses   *162*

14:10 Lack of the Bishop's Knowledge   *162*

14:11 Sovereign Immunity of Vatican Officials and the Pope   *163*

14:12 Absence of Diocesan Accountability for the "Rogue" Priest   *165*

14:13 Is a Countersuit Possible?   *165*

14:14 Default   *165*

15. Damages Issues   *167*

15:1 Overview   *167*

15:2 Prerequisites to Damage Awards   *167*

15:3 Prerequisites to Punitive Damages   *169*

15:4 Effects of Caps on Damage Awards   *170*

15:5 Awards of Plaintiff's Legal Fees   *171*

15:6 Church-Paid Counseling and Therapy as a Damage Element   *172*

16. Fiscal Impacts of Abuse Cases on the U.S. Catholic Church   *173*

16:1 Overview of U.S. Roman Catholic Church Finances   *173*

16:2 Uninsured Losses from Sexual Abuse Cases   *174*

16:3 Impact of Settlements and Verdicts   *175*

16:4 Impacts of Abuse Cases on Revenues   *176*

16:5 Effects of Liquidating Assets   *177*

16:6 Costs apart from Settlements   *178*

16:7 Lost Opportunities for Charitable Actions by the Catholic Church   *179*

17. Impact of Abuse Cases on External Relations of the Catholic Church   *181*

17:1 Why Would the Catholic Church Be Concerned about Its External Relations?   *181*

17:2 How Were Church Defenses in Abuse Cases Perceived?   *182*

17:3 What Audiences Have Mattered?   *183*

17:4 Legal Responses by the Church That Failed or Backfired   *184*

17:5 Successful Responses That Aid the Defense   *185*

17:6 "Fallout" from Clergy Sexual Abuse   *185*

18. Responses Vary Inside and Outside the United States   *187*

18:1 Overview   *187*

18:2 Central Vatican Authority over Bishops   *188*

18:3 Role of U.S. Conference of Catholic Bishops   *189*

18:4 Diplomacy and Vatican Litigation: Effects on the Universal Church   *189*

18:5 Fiscal Responsibility of Catholic Churches in Other Nations   *190*

19. The Church's Internal Big Picture—Governance and Law   *193*

19:1 Introduction   *193*

19:2 Role of the Canon Law Professional Community   *194*

19:3 Organizational Norms and Church Mindset   *195*

19:4 Vatican Initial Perceptions of the Crisis   196
19:5 International Church/State Interaction   198
19:6 Managerial Accountability Conflicts   199
19:7 The Church's Distaste for Haste   201
19:8 The Role of Cardinal Ratzinger in Cleaning Up the Mess   202
19:9 Moving Forward and Pope Francis   204
19:10 Canon Law   207
19:11 Governing Structures   208
19:12 Overview of the Code   209
19:13 Penal Aspects of Canon Law   209
19:14 Conflicts in Legal Values   210
19:15 Current Canon Law regarding Sexual Abuse   211
20. How Episcopal Culture Contributed to Administrative Failure   215
20:1 Understanding the Culture   215
20:2 Two Separate Issues   215
20:3 Diocesan Independence   216
20:4 Bishop Accountability   217
20:5 An Alternate Approach to Law   218
20:6 Ambivalence regarding Lay People   219
20:7 Resulting Frustrations   221
20:8 Isolation at the Top   222
20:9 Anti-Catholicism?   223
20:10 Secrecy and the Avoidance of Scandal   224
20:11 Consequences for Abuse Victims   225
20:12 The Role of the Diocesan Civil Lawyer   226
20:13 A Changing Culture   228
21. The Development of the Problem: 1950 to 2002   231
21:1 Introduction   231
21:2 The Learning Curve and the Standard of Judgment   232
21:3 The Years prior to the 1960s   232
21:4 What Happened in the 1960s?   233
21:5 The 1970s—The Peak of Abuse   235
21:6 Failure to Screen and Train Seminarians   237
21:7 The 1980s   239
21:8 What Was Happening with Victims   242
21:9 The 1990s   243
21:10 NCCB-Vatican Discussions   244
21:11 The NCCB Response   245
21:12 The Effects of an Accusation against Cardinal Bernardin   248
21:13 Post-1994   249
21:14 Summary   250
22. The Perfect Storm in Canon Law: What Went Wrong?   253
22:1 Overview   253
22:2 Remedies Previously Available in the 1917 Code   254
22:3 *Suspensio ex Informata Conscientia*   254

22:4 Other Instances in which a Bishop Could Act Unilaterally   *256*
22:5 Administrative Laicization Created, then Restricted   *256*
22:6 What Administrative Processes Were Available   *259*
22:7 Canonical Emphasis on Protecting Priest's Rights   *261*
22:8 American Canonists Had No Experience Conducting a Penal
    Trial   *263*
22:9 Difficulties with Investigations and Proofs   *265*
22:10 The Need for Victim Cooperation in a Penal Trial   *266*
22:11 The Canonical Penal Process Is Clunky, Vague, and Inefficient   *269*
22:12 Issues with Particular Canonical Requirements   *270*
22:13 The Law Itself Discourages Penal Trials   *270*
22:14 The Definition of a Minor   *271*
22:15 Prescription—the Canonical Statute of Limitations   *271*
22:16 Culpability   *273*
22:17 Treatment rather than Punishment   *274*
22:18 The Unwillingness of Bishops to Interact with Secular Enforcement
    Authorities   *277*
22:19 The Cumulative Effect   *278*
22:20 Summary   *279*
23. 2002 and Beyond   *281*
    23:1 Understanding the Events   *281*
    23:2 *Sacramentorum Sanctitatis Tutela, 2001*   *281*
    23:3 Boston and 2002   *282*
    23:4 The USCCB Meeting in Dallas, Texas   *283*
    23:5 The Charter and Norms   *284*
    23:6 The National Review Board   *286*
    23:7 The USCCB Office of Children and Youth Protection   *289*
    23:8 The USCCB's Committee for the Protection of Children and Young
        People   *290*
    23:9 The John Jay College Studies   *290*
    23:10 *Sacramentorum Sanctitatis Tutela*, 2010   *293*
    23:11 2011 CDF Circular Letter   *294*
    23:12 Anticipated Canonical Legislation   *294*
    23:13 Conclusion   *295*
24. The Particular Issues of Religious Communities   *297*
    24:1 Overview   *297*
    24:2 Background on Religious Orders   *298*
    24:3 Types of Religious Life   *298*
    24:4 Canonical Status   *298*
    24:5 Conflict between Orders and Bishops   *299*
    24:6 Membership   *301*
    24:7 Orders and Difficulties with Canonical Process   *302*
    24:8 Religious and the Norms   *303*
    24:9 The Norms Affecting Religious   *305*
    24:10 Transfers between Religious Houses   *306*

24:11 What about Non-clerical Members?   307
24:12 Penalties   307
24:13 Proactive Efforts   310
24:14 Summary   310

25. The Investigation and Pretrial Canonical Process   313
25:1 Canonical Sources for Procedure   313
25:2 Why Should the Church Conduct an Investigation?   314
25:3 Canonical versus Other Organizational Processes   316
25:4 The Roles of the Bishop   318
25:5 The Complaint   318
25:6 The Preliminary Investigation   320
25:7 Is the Alleged Act a "More Grave Delict"?   320
25:8 Is the Person a Canonical Minor?   322
25:9 Prescription   323
25:10 The Investigation   324
25:11 Who Conducts the Investigation?   326
25:12 When Is the Accused Notified?   328
25:13 Diocesan Review Board   330
25:14 What Are the Accused Cleric's Canonical Rights?   334
25:15 The Case Proceeds to CDF   335
25:16 The Bishop's *Votum* or Opinion   336
25:17 What Are the Congregation's Options?   336
25:18 Voluntary Return to the Lay State   337
25:19 CDF Takes the Case Itself   337
25:20 Automatic "*Ex Officio*" Dismissal   337
25:21 Judicial Trial   338
25:22 Administrative Process   338
25:23 Life of Prayer and Penance   341
25:24 Conclusion   342

26. The Accuser and the Canonical Process   343
26:1 Canonical Role of the Accuser   343
26:2 Important Disclosures   344
26:3 Full Procedural Transparency   344
26:4 Is the Accusation Covered by the Norms?   345
26:5 The Accusation Triggers a Formal Canonical Investigation   346
26:6 What Are the Accused Cleric's Rights?   346
26:7 Does the Accuser Get an Advocate?   347
26:8 What Is Done with the Accuser's Information   347
26:9 The Accuser's Rights   348
26:10 The Right to be Heard   348
26:11 Right to Reputation and Privacy   349
26:12 The Right to Assistance   350
26:13 Conflicting Processes   351
26:14 Conclusion   352

27. Canonical Penal Trials and Outcomes   353
    27:1 The Trial   353
    27:2 Who Constitutes the Court   354
    27:3 The Judges   355
    27:4 The Promoter of Justice   355
    27:5 The Canonical Notary   356
    27:6 The Auditor   356
    27:7 The Procurator/Advocate   356
    27:8 Experts   357
    27:9 Balance Re-Traumatizing of Victims with Rights of Those
        Accused   357
    27:10 Getting Started—Procedural Delays   358
    27:11 The Trial Begins   359
    27:12 Joinder of the Issues   361
    27:13 Discovery   362
    27:14 Psychological Records   366
    27:15 Witnesses, Depositions, and Hearings   367
    27:16 Publication of the Acts   371
    27:17 Concluding the Evidentiary Part of the Case   372
    27:18 Final Statements   372
    27:19 Rendering the Decision   373
    27:20 Trial Verdict and Sentencing   374
    27:21 Exoneration   375
    27:22 Verdict of Not Proven   376
    27:23 A Guilty Verdict   377
    27:24 The Appeal   377
    27:25 The Aftermath   378
    27:26 Conclusion   379
28. Limitations and Weaknesses in the Canonical Penal System   381
    28:1 Viability of the Current Canonical System   381
    28:2 What Is at Stake in This Process   382
    28:3 Inadequacies of the System   383
    28:4 The Juxtaposition of Canon and Civil Law   383
    28:5 Volume of Cases   385
    28:6 Overarching Assumptions   386
    28:7 Bishops   386
    28:8 Lack of Episcopal Accountability   388
    28:9 Judges   389
    28:10 Judicial Discretion   391
    28:11 Advocates/Procurators   392
    28:12 The Assumption That Timeliness Is Beneficial   395
    28:13 The Assumption of Witness Cooperation and Good Faith   395
    28:14 The Potential for the Lack of a Definitive Outcome   397
    28:15 The Inherent Problems with Dismissal   399

28:16 An Uncomfortable Question   *401*
28:17 Unreasonable Expectations   *401*
28:18 Conclusion   *402*
29. Clergy Abuse Issues in Non-Roman Catholic Denominations   *405*
29:1 Overview   *405*
29:2 How Other Congregations Have Responded   *405*
29:3 Other Denominations   *407*
29:4 Constitutional Issues and Cases of Non-Catholic Defendants   *407*

Chronology   *411*
Bibliography   *423*
Index   *433*

PREFACE

Two explorers entered the same large old attic by opposite stairs. This dusty attic of the ancient edifice had expanded in recent decades and was quite cluttered with packages not seen up in that attic in the past. One of the seekers was an older criminal law teacher with decades of experience as a church volunteer; his flashlight in the attic did not quite illuminate enough. At the other end, one of the best and brightest young canon lawyers flashed her light on the modern version of older rules and norms. Some of the attic's contents had been widely seen outside; others were buried deep in dust to avoid detection. Each recognized the other would see things differently; together, they could catalog the contents and report their findings to those below. Along the way they saw some things that are best left in the attic, while others very much needed to be cleaned out.

The reader is welcomed into the attic with us, as we study the legal aspects of the Roman Catholic Church experience with clergy sexual abuse in the United States. Like an attic, the Church has some memories that are put away, unpleasant to deal with, hopefully not to be seen again. Like explorers of that attic, we study, analyze, and synthesize for the reader so that these lessons are not to be forgotten in the Church of 2020 and beyond. The strength we can draw from learning about the process is actually enhancing the future of the Roman Catholic Church in its ability to deal more forthrightly with sexual abuse reports when they arise in the future, as they inevitably will.

There is a risk that we acknowledge. As three former advisors to the U.S. bishops wrote in a 2006 book: "Men and Women who have spoken up and questioned bishops have been accused of a catalogue of sins—from arrogance, misunderstanding, and disloyalty, to heresy."[1] We recognize that the subject matter of this text may result in our being accused of some or all of these.

As scholars and active participants in our Catholic Church, we offer you a series of informed insights into what our Church has learned and will continue to learn from the problem of clergy sexual abuse of minors. Writing a careful and well-reasoned book on this topic was not possible while the first wave of abuse cases was flooding the American Church in scandalous events. Writing a boringly deep treatise filled with minutiae is not possible as the legal issues have been changing as quickly as the news headlines change. Universal Church problems with clergy sexual abuse in

---

1. Thomas Doyle, A.W.R. Sipe & Patrick Wall, Sex, Priests and Secret Codes 289 (2006).

many nations, exposed and hotly debated in 2010, were the impetus for us to assemble this more readable yet more authoritative text.

We encourage readers to provide feedback so that we may share in your insights about this complex problem. No single answer can be given ex cathedra by laypersons, even with our backgrounds, and no law author has ever claimed to be infallible. With a spirit of humility and faith, we ask you to consider these lessons and consider how they may illuminate the events of the recent decades in the Catholic Church for future readers and for its future leaders.

Special thanks are due to veteran journalist William Burleigh, whose service on the National Review Board gave him an excellent perspective, and whose willingness to share time and concepts was a great help, though the ideas expressed in this text are those of the authors alone.

Professor O'Reilly thanks his family and his remarkably gifted coauthor, Dr. Chalmers, and greatly appreciates his student research assistants Charlotte Eichman, Andrew Cleves, and Meaghan Fitzgerald, for their months of assistance on this project. Professional law librarian Lauren Morrison provided excellent assistance for the sources and citations of this text, and her help is greatly appreciated.

Dr. Chalmers thanks Professor O'Reilly for inviting her to be a part of this project. Special thanks to all those canonists who took the time to share their wisdom, expertise, and resources, particularly Dr. Michael Ritty; Rev. John Paul Kimes; Rev. Paul Golden, C.M.; Rev. Patrick Lagges; and Rev. Gregory Bittner. Thanks to her husband, Jon; children David and Thomas; and her parents for supporting her during the duration of this project.

Prof. James T. O'Reilly, Cincinnati, Ohio
Dr. Margaret Chalmers, Greenville, South Carolina

PART ONE

Context and Background

CHAPTER 1

⌇

Introduction to a Complex Problem

1:1 UNDERSTANDING THE COMPLEX DYNAMIC UNDERLYING THE LEGAL ISSUES

The legal issues addressed in this text involve nuances of civil law, canon law, and external relations for the Roman Catholic Church in the United States and elsewhere. But we begin with the triggering event: the reality that a child was harmed, long before the particular case reached the trial court. This reality will keep our study of this tragedy in its proper perspective. At the base of our inquiry into that institution's experience has been a series of tragedies for individual children, the crime of sexual abuse with minors under the age of consent, with the tragic figures being not only the child victim but also the good priests of the worldwide institutional Roman Catholic Church.

American Catholics have experienced shock and a loss of trust as the 30-year, nationally publicized story of clergy sexual abuse has unfolded around them, and around their trusted pastors and bishops. This dismay has caused deep institutional damage to an important social institution: the Roman Catholic Church in the United States. The legal aspects of this damage are described and analyzed in this text. For those reading this work decades after the events depicted, we cannot do justice to the passions that this topic has evoked in the years 1980–2012, but the future reader can understand from some of the accounts of personal anguish and frustration, provided in the bibliography, that affected the contemporary Church as the problems were addressed in various stages.

The center of this tragedy is the child or teenager, and the complex dynamic of legal rights and responsibilities is built around the victimization of that central figure. Justice for the children and their families, as well as justice for the public and especially parents of other children, demands that the systemic reasons for the existence of clergy sexual abuse, the official responses of the dioceses and of the Vatican, and its aftermath be understood. Once the need for justice has been understood, the

Church as an institution needs to put effective systems in place at all 195[1] dioceses, to safeguard against further episodes that would be as painful as these incidents have been. Because only the Vatican can impose such requirements, the U.S. Conference of Catholic Bishops lacks the authority to compel Nebraska or Oregon bishops to comply with these standards.[2]

There was also an information gap, maintained by many bishops who wished to contain the public's awareness of the scandal. Readers of the world press in 2014 were shocked to learn that 400 priests had been defrocked in 2011–2012; these had been closely guarded secrets of the Curia before Pope Francis opened up more of the internal processes in 2013.[3]

Although most Americans today have heard of these efforts to limit the coverage and fallout, few understand how widespread these efforts had been. One diocese looked back 50 years and found credible accusations against 30 of its 372 priests over that time frame.[4] Though most abuse situations were not uncovered and the actors were not sent to treatment or into the criminal law system, a total of 1,624 U.S. Catholic priests received treatment between 1950 and 2002 for sexually abusing minors,[5] and more have been treated in the decade since; further, almost 3,400 incidents were reported in the peak year of sexual abuse reporting, 2002, when international negative publicity was drawn to the sexual abuse problem within the American branch of the Roman Catholic Church. In 2010, 505 credible allegations relating to 345 accused clergy were reported.[6] Experts estimate the average number of victims per priest-offender was about eight.[7]

As evidence of another far-reaching practice of containment, bishops were challenged by federal bankruptcy judges for hiding assets from creditors in clergy abuse cases.[8] Since 2004, $2,700,000,000 has been paid by U.S. dioceses due to clergy sexual abuse, largely on settlements and attorney fees.[9]

1. There are a total of 210 entities but 195 are dioceses. www.officialcatholicdirectory.com.
2. Dan Morris-Young, "Do Lawsuit Allegations Touch Diocese's Noncompliance Issues?," Nat'l Cath. Rptr. (Apr. 29, 2011).
3. John Heilprin, "Pope Defrocked 400 Priests in 2 years," Associated Press (Jan. 23, 2014) (260 in 2011, 124 in 2012, and 171 in the two years 2008 and 2009).
4. And 158 allegations were made against these 30 priests. Covington KY diocese, "A Report on the History of Sexual Abuse of Minors in the Diocese of Covington" (Aug. 18, 2003), on Web at covingtondiocese.org.
5. John Jay College Report to U.S. Conference of Catholic Bishops, The Causes and Context of Sexual Abuse of Minors by Catholic Priests in the United States, 1950–2010, at 80 (May 2011) (hereinafter "John Jay College Report").
6. Nancy O'Brien, "New Sex Abuse Allegations Down Slightly in 2010; Costs Continue to Rise," Cath. News Serv. (Apr. 11, 2011).
7. Thomas Plante, in Sin Against the Innocents 186 (2004).
8. "Chaos reigns, and given the deterioration in San Diego, threatens to exponentially accelerate." David Gregory, "Some Reflections on Labor & Employment Ramifications of Diocesan Bankruptcy Filings," 47 J. Cath. Legal Stud. 97, 116 (2008).
9. O'Brien, supra.

Because it asserts that it is the "universal Church," Roman Catholics in nations such as Ireland,[10] Belgium[11] and around the world must also recognize that they too will likely be confronting this problem, and they must develop effective prevention and remedial systems. Canada in 1989,[12] Belgium in 2010,[13] and Ireland in 2010–2011[14] showed that the consequences of the sexual abuse in one area could harm the reputation of the nationwide church.[15] As Pope Benedict told the news media in May 2010, "the greatest persecution of the Church comes not from her enemies without, but arises from sin within the Church, and that the Church thus has a deep need to relearn penance, to accept purification, to learn forgiveness on the one hand, but also the need for justice. Forgiveness does not replace justice."[16]

1:2 THE U.S. LEGAL SYSTEM HAS NO PERFECT ANSWERS

Child sexual abuse cases are not easily established beyond the reasonable doubt standard required in criminal law. Popular U.S. television dramas involving forensic experts and their crime-solving laboratories have filled the minds of the modern American jury pool with unrealistic expectations. Crime-solving by science seems to be much more feasible than the real standard that law enforcement officers must meet in the average prosecution of the average crime. And that impression is true, as the rise of rapid DNA sequencing and sample matching has irrevocably changed the centuries-old expectation that jury trials will be dependent on eyewitness testimony by credible witnesses.

That paradigm shift of proofs occurred in the 1990s; DNA from the Monica Lewinsky blue dress was a historical example of the scientific proof that can override denials in the classic "he said/she said" dispute. However, from the law enforcement perspective, the child sexual abuse claim that arrives in the police inbox as an offense from 10, 20, or 30 years before is the ultimate unprovable cold case.

There are no perfect legal answers for establishing the truth of clergy sexual abuse claims that occurred in years past—sometimes decades ago. Historically, the priest has been a respected source of informal authority within the community.

10. John Thavis & Sarah Delaney, "Irish-Vatican Summit on Sex Abuse Ends with Call for Courage, Honesty," Natl Catholic Rptr (Feb. 16, 2010); Tom Roberts, "Truth Must Be Told, Says Archbishop," Nat'l Cath. Rptr. 12 (Apr. 15, 2011).

11. Doreen Carvajal & Stephen Castle, "Abuse Took Years to Ignite Belgian Clergy Inquiry," N.Y. Times (July 12, 2010).

12. Stephen Rossetti, A Tragic Grace: The Catholic Church and Child Sexual Abuse 7 (1996).

13. Belgian Catholic Church "in Crisis," Irish Independent (Sept. 13 2010).

14. Id.

15. See e.g., "Priest Profoundly Sorry for Abusing Girl from Age of 11," Irish Independent at 1 (July 2, 2011).

16. Vatican Release, "Interview of the Holy Father with Journalists during the Flight to Portugal" (May 11, 2010), on Web at http://www.vatican.va/holy_father/benedict_xvi/speeches/2010/may/documents/hf_ben-xvi_spe_20100511_portogallo-interview_en.html.

If he denied under oath that the incident occurred, that denial would have had a determinative effect in previous decades. Today, the tarnished image of the priesthood that has emerged from decades of televised scandal reports makes it much less likely that the word of a priest would override that of an individual giving testimony about a past event of abuse. Cynicism about the credibility of Church leadership has reached a remarkable level in popular discourse. A Catholic legal scholar who is now a federal judge once warned bishops that juries and judges have been "poisoned" by the media coverage of the scandal.[17] An exhaustive study paid for by the American bishops[18] found that only 4 percent of priests had been accused of sexual misconduct, But this is not a matter of pride, but instead like a fire department whose members include 4 percent arsonists.

Innocence is a concept that cannot be determined in conventional criminal cases. The standard is that the prosecution has failed to prove its case "beyond a reasonable doubt," so acquittal does not mean that the crime did not occur. The same set of proofs about the same event can be tried to an acquittal in a criminal case and yet a victory for the injured person in a civil case, as the O.J. Simpson cases have demonstrated. The reputation of the Catholic Church in the United States has suffered adverse consequences stemming from at least four sources as a result of the abuse cases:

• from the fallout of the criminal prosecutions of priests and dioceses;
• from the fiscal wreckage of bankruptcy and massive settlements;
• from the public criticism of its defense strategy by respected journalists; and
• from the dislocation of past patterns of lay Catholics' allegiance and donations.

The Church continues to be powerful and still capable of providing religious and social benefits, according to its mission; however, the legal system's response to the abuse cases has shown that the Church is not "above the law" in any sense of the term.

Will other abuse claims arise after 2011? In August 2010, a prominent plaintiff's lawyer dismissed a potentially important case against the Vatican, because no other plaintiffs had come forward to join his clients' action. The plaintiff's lawyer told the media that "Virtually every child who was abused and will come forward as an adult has come forward and sued a bishop and collected money, and once that happens, it's over."[19] That attorney had represented more than 240 abuse victims who settled with the Louisville Catholic archdiocese for $25 million in 2003. His assessment reflects a general mood among plaintiffs' counsel that the most egregious cases have been identified and that there are relatively few remaining instances of past sexual abuse claims not yet asserted.

17. Patrick Schiltz, "The Future of Sexual Abuse Litigation," 189 America Magazine 8 (2003).
18. John Jay College Report, supra.
19. Dylan Lovan, "Plaintiffs Give Up Sex Abuse Case against Vatican," Associated Press (Aug. 10, 2010).

A report by John Jay College in 2011 made a similar assessment, but noted that the incidence of reports of cases is not a basis on which to conclude that these issues have been all exhausted.[20] The head of the largest Catholic diocese insurance pool predicted in 2011 that most of the claims that could be asserted from prior decades have, by 2011, already been made, and that as a result of the VIRTUS and other preventive programs against sexual misconduct, few of the persons who might engage in sexual misconduct in the Church or misconduct in today's parishes would avoid some degree of community awareness of their conduct. VIRTUS is a program training the adults who work with young people to avoid situations of possible sexual impropriety.

The question of whether a particular priest will reoffend with sexual contact after receiving discipline was studied by the bishops after 2002. Monitoring of the assignments and conduct of the offender priests was recommended, but in practice very few have been monitored (and of course, those who are dismissed have no further ties to, and cannot be tracked by, the Church).[21]

1:3 THE CHURCH'S CANON LAW SYSTEM HAS NO PERFECT ANSWERS

Responding to the abuse of power is never easy. The two levels of power at work in these abuse situations make it especially difficult to respond. The individual sexual predator who was a priest used his individual powers of persuasion to obtain sexual gratification from lewd acts with a child under the age of legal consent. This abuse of power violated Church law, civil law, and moral norms, standards about which that priest was considered a steward of God's law.

After the extent of the sexual abuse events became apparent, some number of bishops misused their special authority over the abuser priests to suppress general knowledge of the problem and to avoid dealing with the public scandal.[22] By doing so, they have damaged the foundation of trust built among the laity, the vast number of innocent priests, and their bishops.

Archbishop Diarmuid Martin of Dublin, Ireland, told a U.S. law school symposium that leaders of the Church had failed: "Were there factors of a clerical culture which somehow facilitated disastrous abusive behavior to continue for so long? Was it just through bad decisions by bishops or superiors? Was there knowledge of behavior which should have given rise to concern and that went unaddressed?"[23]

The Catholic Church has its own code of laws worldwide. Those laws are found in the Code of Canon Law as well as in the particular laws created by internal, local, and national Church legislation. While church entities are bound to follow the laws of the civil jurisdiction, where these exist, all members of the Catholic Church,

20. John Jay College Report, supra.
21. "Few Abuser Priests Monitored," Nat'l Cath. Rptr. 3 (July 23, 2010).
22. John Jay College Report, supra.
23. Archishop d. Martin, Nat'l Cath. Rptr. (Apr. 15, 2011).

including laity and clergy, are also bound to follow the laws of the Church, or face internal penalties. This has caused added complications and much misunderstanding in the Church's dealing with this issue.

Chapters 19 through 26 discuss the canon law issues in clergy sexual abuse cases. The reader will note that the separate canonical or Church internal system, which provides for the priest's accountability to the bishop or religious superior and the accountability of some bishops to the pope, did not function well to deter and then to isolate and then expel the abuser. The canon law system endures and is constantly being improved, but it has not fully answered the call for discipline and justice in recent decades.

1:4 THE CLERGY SEXUAL ABUSE LESSONS ARE USEFUL IN OTHER U.S. FAITH COMMUNITIES

The loss of trust and sense of alienation experienced within the U.S. Roman Catholic Church is seen in a lesser extent among other faith communities, including the Protestant and Jewish ones. Chapter 29 discusses the experiences of these other religious communities with their abuse incidents and how they are choosing to address the problem.

Other religious entities have a stake in the outcome of the cases and legislation that has been created to deal with the legal issues surrounding the abuse in the Roman Catholic Church, as well as any legal precedents set. To the extent that First Amendment constitutional protection aids all churches,[24] non-Catholic denominations may lose some of their constitutional protections against state interference if the Catholic sexual abuse cases yield precedents about remedies that override prior case law. There is also a new current of precedent in bankruptcy law that can have negative consequences for other denominations. In addition, the civil tort precedents concerning Catholic bishops' inadequate supervision or insufficient discipline may make some other religious institutions more vulnerable to damage awards.[25]

---

24. As to the limits of First Amendment protection for intra-church disputes, see e.g., Jones v. Wolf, 443 U.S. 595, 609 (1979); Gen. Council on Fin. & Admin., United Methodist Church v. Cal. Super. Ct., 439 U.S.1369, 1372 (1978); Presbyterian Church in the United States v. Mary Elizabeth Blue Hull Mem'l Presbyterian Church, 393 U.S. 440, 449 (1969).
25. The most articulate critic of those church abuse defenses that claim First Amendment privilege has been prolific in her warnings that others will be disadvantaged by the overuse of this defense. Marci Hamilton, "The Rules against Scandal and What They Mean for the First Amendment's Religion Clauses," 69 Maryland L. Rev. 115 (2009); Marci Hamilton, "The "Licentiousness" in Religious Organizations and Why It Is Not Protected under Religious Liberty Constitutional Provisions," 18 William & Mary Bill of Rights J. 953 (2010).

1:5 THE CLERGY SEXUAL ABUSE LESSONS ARE USEFUL IN OTHER U.S. INSTITUTIONS

Sexual misconduct is an unfortunate aspect of the spectrum of human weakness. Failings in the disciplinary oversight of "predator priests" by Catholic officials are discussed throughout this book, and more poignantly in the dramatic and empathetic sources listed in our bibliography.

A Catholic psychologist writing on the abuse cases commented that "the stabilized power of the Catholic Church is more evident to many people than is its sensitivity to human pain."[26]

The John Jay College Report on the clergy sexual abuse experiences likened the Roman Catholic Church to other hierarchical authoritarian entities, such as a police force.[27] The Report states that the existence of corruption at the lowest levels needs to be addressed and those responsible need to be removed swiftly; the failure to do both can damage the institution in the eyes of those from whom it must have respect. Priest or police candidates and trainees need to be selected out if they exhibit behavior patterns that show corruption would be tolerated or accepted. Once the higher officers or officials begin to tolerate illegal activity, the entire organization, whether it be the police force or the church, would now be in jeopardy of losing its moral authority to compel obedience.

One could argue more broadly that primary and secondary educational institutions and large youth organizations need to learn lessons from the bad experiences of the Church. However, as their arrangements are contractual, hierarchical allegiance is low, and there is an absence of both a solemn vow and strict adherence to a particular morality, those teachers differ greatly from the clergy. One lesson from the Church is nevertheless beneficial: it is clear that educational institutions whose leaders confront child sexual abuse, teach firmly against it, oversee protections for children, and prosecute each case quickly and decisively will have much less negative effects over the long-term than the repercussions felt by portions of the U.S. Catholic Church.

One could also argue that repeated failures by the American bishops to compel adherence to their collectively established norms of behavior, or to enact more stringent norms, can be compared to weaknesses inside a business conglomerate. If no central force or body pays close attention, multiple subsidiaries could react in divergent ways. A central headquarters that is slow and haphazard in its response to failures in its subsidiaries does a disservice to its owners and increases the risks of criminal prosecution of the entire entity and perhaps its senior management, including the potential for imposition of fines and imprisonment.

---

26. Dr. Margaret Miles, in A.W. Sipe, Sex, Priests and Power: Anatomy of a Crisis, at ix (1995).
27. John Jay College Report, supra.

1:6 THE U.S. LESSONS ARE USEFUL TO THE ROMAN CATHOLIC CHURCHES IN OTHER NATIONS

This book will demonstrate to other Catholic entities outside of the United States that they must study and benefit from the serious mistakes made by the U.S. Church leadership. Of the approximately 3,000 dioceses in the world, the Roman Catholic Church in the United States contains 195. The devastating effects on the public posture of the Church has had negative spillover effects in other nations as well. Italy,[28] Canada,[29] Belgium,[30] and other countries have had related problems of abuse. As the 2009–2011 visibility of sexual abuse claims in European churches has expanded,[31] these lessons gain in relevance.

For several years, extensive news coverage of the U.S. clergy sexual abuse events created the impression in the media that the misconduct of U.S. priests was in sharp contrast to the activities of priests in other nations. This also became the internal belief of priests and bishops in non–English-speaking countries. In retrospect, many dioceses in other nations had a comparable set of sexual misconduct events that were less visible and were mishandled, and that were deemed a "taboo" subject for public discourse;[32] these came to public attention long after the news stories of the U.S. experience. This comparability of errors has certainly not held good news for any parties involved. But it does suggest that for the future, decisions regarding the comparable issue by bishops in other nations in similar positions would be more productive if the Church leaders moved immediately to apologize, offer counseling, correct the flaws in supervision, expedite the investigation, and take other steps appropriate for their culture and in cooperation with their local law enforcement. There is much to be learned from the many mistakes made by the U.S. bishops.

28. Luca Bruni, "Italy Grapples with Priest Sex Abuse," Associated Press (Sept. 13, 2009) (late bishop who is being considered for beatification also alleged to have sodomized deaf student with a banana).

29. "Priest Charged with Multiple Sex-Assault Charges Back in Court in January," Quebec Post Media (Nov. 8, 2010).

30. Steven Erlanger, "Belgian Catholics Remain Anguished by Abuse," N.Y. Times (Sept. 19, 2010).

31. See e.g., Shawn Pogatchnik, "Abuse Charges Shake Europe's Catholic Balance," Associated Press (Mar. 14, 2010).

32. Bruni, supra.

CHAPTER 2

༄

Understanding the Patterns of Clergy Abuse Litigation

2:1 INTRODUCTION

To orient the reader to the chapters that follow, we offer in this one an abbreviated synopsis of the typical processes, events, and civil law steps that are likely to be taken when a clergy sexual abuse case arises prior to any ensuing litigation. Chapter 3 examines the civil litigation process, and later chapters address the canon law process. Generalizations about complex cases are inherently vulnerable to change, of course, but the reader will be better able to comprehend and navigate the remaining chapters with an understanding of a "typical" scenario of the ways in which these events, allegations, and liabilities evolve.

2:2 THE EVENT

We begin with an action: a priest's alleged sexual abuse of a minor occurs. This can be any kind of sexual contact, from touching, kissing, oral sexual contact, or intercourse. Sometimes there is physical pain or damage inflicted on the child or teen, but more often the damage is psychological and emotional. It has been estimated that several thousand young people were victimized; one study found it "reasonable to estimate that over fifty thousand young people were abused by priests" during the 1950–2002 period.[1]

What is considered sexual abuse? In 2002, the bishops defined the term to include "sexual molestation or sexual exploitation of a minor and other behavior by which an adult uses a minor as an object of sexual gratification," but this "need not be a complete act of intercourse" and it does not "need to involve force, physical

---

1. Mary Gail Frawley O'Dea, Perversion of Power: Sexual Abuse in the Catholic Church 6 (2007).

contact, or a discernible harmful outcome."[2] In this book we use this definition for sexual abuse, rather than the divergent terms used in state criminal law statutory language, which can vary widely.

The patterns in clergy sexual abuse cases are well understood by psychologists, sociologists, and others who study the reports, listen to the victims, and understand narratives in articles, video clips, interviews, books, etc. Our bibliography is replete with examples and personal narratives. The typical victim has been a male between 11 and 17 years of age, although girls and younger children of both genders have also been targeted.[3] The young person meets the clergy member in a church-related activity, as an altar server, recreational program user, or participant in a teen program or educational activity.

Millions of these interactions between priests and children occur each year, in the context of the priest's ministerial duties. In the overwhelming majority of these interactions, the meeting and involvement with the clergy member is positive, healthy, appropriate, and beneficial to the young people. As we focus our study on the number of sexual abuse cases, it is important to acknowledge at the outset that most clergy are good, stable, well-meaning, and even holy people. They are horrified by the acts of a small minority of priests. Most priests have entered the ministry to worship God and serve their communities; for these good men, the scandal has made their vocation much more difficult. One bishop has said: "It is particularly despicable and horrendous when such abuse is perpetrated by a person of trust, such as a priest."[4] This perspective is easy to overlook when dealing with the sad and terrible instances of abuse.

The exceptionally bad cases have involved intentional and deliberate predatory sexual behaviors. Oftentimes, these sexual interactions manifest themselves due to serious physiological flaws, sometimes coupled with substance abuse by the priest. Eight years after Boston's archbishop assigned a known pedophile priest to parish work, he sexually molested many children, and more than 30 filed claims against him.[5] When the parents of abused boys and their lawyer confronted a Louisiana diocese, they learned that the diocese had known of the priest's "problem for some time but thought it had been resolved."[6] These exceptional cases often begin with

2. U.S. Conference of Catholic Bishops, "Preamble, Essential Norms for Diocesan/ Eparchial Policies Dealing with Allegations of Sexual Abuse of Minors by Priests or Deacons" (Dec. 8, 2002), on Web at http://old.usccb.org/bishops/norms.shtml (hereinafter "Essential Norms").

3. John Jay College, Report to U.S. Conference of Catholic Bishops, The Causes and Context of Sexual Abuse of Minors by Catholic Priests in the United States, 1950–2010, at 9–10 (May 2011), on Web at http://www.usccb.org/issues-and-action/ child-and-youth-protection/upload/The-Causes-and-Context-of-Sexual-Abuse-of-Minors-by-Catholic-Priests-in-the-United-States-1950-2010.pdf (hereinafter "John Jay College Report").

4. Bishop Thomas Paprocki, "As the Pendulum Swings from Charitable Immunity to Bankruptcy, Bringing It to Rest with Charitable Viability," 48 J. Cath. Legal Stud. 1, 5 (2009).

5. Boston Globe, "Betrayal: Crisis in the Catholic Church" 35 (2003).

6. *Id.* at 37. (Father Gilbert Gauthe was sentenced to 20 years in prison.)

preparatory friendly steps that bring the young person into the priest's circle of friends. The priest intentionally lures ("grooms") the young person into a relationship of trust.[7]

As a National Association of District Attorneys project on child sexual abusers has noted:

> Through the grooming process, the child molester seeks out, befriends and manipulates a targeted victim. Similar to the adult courting process, the child molester "seduces" the child victim with attention, affection and gifts. Grooming is a gradual process and a skilled child molester takes care in laying a foundation of trust, love and friendship before escalating the relationship to a sexual one. Ultimately, the seemingly healthy relationship is only a farce used to take sexual advantage of a vulnerable child.[8]

In extreme cases, some priests used the religious factor as a cover for misconduct, such as the Connecticut priest who told victims "that performing oral sex on him was a special way of receiving Holy Communion from a priest."[9]

As the child continues to interact with the priest, gradual trust or emotional dependence evolves over months or years. Parents of the child support and endorse the priest's interaction with the child. Trust and dependency are fostered. In some cases, the child is introduced to alcohol, drugs, or pornography by the priest to lessen the child's natural resistance. Many of the books in our bibliography offer firsthand and interview examples of these patterns of sexual manipulation of the young person.

The interpersonal trust is then violated by the adult's sexualized conduct, including masturbation and intercourse. Along with the physical act, the priest's continued insistence upon secrecy in order to conceal the illicit actions builds up over time. Although some of the incidents were said to have been sudden events and resisted by the child, accounts of many other circumstances have shown a more nuanced acceptance by the confused child of the actions as the asserted physical manifestation of "closeness" or a showing of affection by the clergy member. Adult affection (and in some cases, alcohol, drugs, or pornography) eases the child or teen in their nonresistance to gradually accepting and participating in the sexual acts. The priest's authority of being the agent of God to the child makes these events especially reprehensible as the priest "can do no wrong." State laws regard the contact as criminal when actions by the priest trigger the state statutes for child abuse, battery, sexual abuse, or statutory rape.

---

7. See e.g., Doe v. Catholic Bishop for the Diocese of Memphis, 306 S.W.2d 712 (Tenn. App. 2008).

8. Candace Kim, "From Fantasy to Reality: The Link between Viewing Child Pornography and Molesting Children," American Prosecutors Research Institute Update 1, no. 3 (2004), http://www.ndaa.org/pdf/Update_gr_vol1_no3.pdf.

9. Frawley O'Dea, supra, 4.

A sexual event after some "grooming" of the youth is usually accompanied by an imperative order or plea for the child not to disclose what has happened. The clergy member's insistence on the child's acceptance of secrecy for the physical contact is used in court as a perverse indicator of the defendant priest's recognition that his use of the child for sexual gratification is wrong. Jurors hearing the child's testimony about the insistence on secrecy are likely to infer guilt and to convict the abuser. His oral or touching contact with the child may leave emotional or psychological issues, but the "secret" can be maintained if the child remains unwilling to disclose the event to a parent or adult friend. Exceptional cases would involve anal or vaginal bleeding from the physical effects of penile penetration, which are likely to be more difficult to conceal from parents, and so there is a greater risk to the abuser of detection through family questioning of the victim.

When the young person accepts the priest's claim that sexual contact is "our little secret that others wouldn't understand," or some other similar sentiment, the mental stress on the young person begins and, with continued patterns of sexual contact, is deepened. Further events of repeated sexual contact, in some cases, may occur in the church, in the rectory residence, in the school, in a car, at a youth camp, etc. The one-sided nature of the relationship extends to the abuser priest's ability to stage the sexual encounters with children in places with no witnesses. In numerous actual cases, the child's attempt to report the abuse is rebuffed; in one instance, the grandmother of a Minnesota boy slapped the child after he reported a priest's sexual advances, because of her belief that this could not have happened and the child must have been lying.[10] The pastor of an English church told a boy reporting oral sex with an associate pastor that the boy was "being silly" and that the pastor would tell his mother that the boy was acting up. After the pastor told the abuser, that priest threatened the boy into silence.[11]

Other resources demonstrate that for a child, physical attention and emotional empathy's grooming of the child's acceptance of an adult[12] can build a bond of trust with that adult. Playing with and touching the child might seem natural, up to a point. The fun aspects of being tickled and touched and wrestled may cause a child not to attach any significance at all to the contact. In some cases, the adult will be using this grooming to move that physical relationship, at a certain stage, on to oral, genital, or anal gratification of the adult, an act that surprises and confuses the naïve young person. These incidents of sexual conduct are not uniform events, and the amount of grooming by the adult may be reflected in the lack of alarm by the victim. The more intense or invasive the physical contact becomes, the more likely

10. Eller v. Diocese of St. Cloud, 2006 Westlaw 163526 (Minn. App. 2006). (The victim "told his grandmother what had happened, and his grandmother slapped him and instructed him to never again speak that way about a priest.")

11. Maga v. Birmingham Archdiocese (2010) 1 WLR 1441 and (2009) EWHC 780, cited in Laura Hoyano, "Ecclesiastical Responsibility for Clerical Wrongdoing," 18 Tort L. Rev. 154 (2010).

12. Dengler v. Doe, 2007 Westlaw 4183032, 1 (Cal. App. 2007). ("The perpetrator sexually groomed, abused and molested Dengler from 1978 or 1979 until approximately 1981.")

the child will protest to others about having been abused. It also becomes more likely that the child would recognize the unusual nature of that physical contact, and might disclose that it was uncomfortable to have the physical contact with the penis or anus as part of the interaction. Again, the bibliography offers first-person recollected stories of events from the perspective of the victim.

An aspect of clergy sexual abuse that is especially damaging to the child's sensibilities is the confusion between this priest's association with God and the very bad acts that the priest is doing to the child. The confusion that results, along with the demand for no disclosure of what has occurred, is psychologically impactful on the child's mind. Foreign courts have weighed heavily the nature of the abuser's status as representative of God to the child who is being molested.[13]

2:3 TYPICAL POST-EVENT RESULTS

Sexual gratification for the clergy person is the endpoint of the "use" of that young person. Secrecy from the child is a promise, made more serious by the role of the priest as the spiritual arbiter of God's commandments. The event ends, and the child returns home, or to camp or school. Or, a pattern may develop with hundreds of sexual incidents that can span over years. In one extreme example, the Illinois Supreme Court considered the liability of a religious brother who was charged with 900 sexual events.[14] Some victims immediately report the abuse, but most do not. The abuser may subsequently meet with the child and encourage the victim to remain quiet. The young victim's shame about the sexual nature of the act, confusion on the part of the victim about the attention and caring of the abuser, and other psychological factors that suppress the willingness to report the offense, all result in a strong deterrent effect against disclosure.

This book is not a medical or psychological treatment of the fallout from sexual contact, but we have listed many sources in the bibliography. We can generalize that secrecy, shame, and embarrassment play some role in the years of delay, as the child avoids pain by declining to make any disclosure of the abuse.

Gradually, manifestations of mistrust of authority and alienation by the young person become noticeable—he or she becomes withdrawn, secretive, frustrated— as the pattern of abuse continues. In many of the reported cases, physical changes will accompany the deepening depression or anxiety. Distancing the young person from the clergy member by means of family-related transfers or moves may occur, and this can inadvertently end the sexual opportunity for the priest. These location changes, such as the end of a summer camp season, typically end the sexual relationship, but the promise of secrecy drawn from the child by the priest can continue. The clergy person grows apart, perhaps to initiate a series of other relationships with other victims. Serial pedophile behavior could continue in this manner for years.

13. Hoyano, *supra.*
14. Clay v. Kuhl, 727 N.E.2d 217 (Ill. 2000).

Chapter 5 discusses the delay in victim reporting. Delayed reporting of past sexual abuse events may occur years or decades later, when events with certain mental triggers reduce the repressed shame and bring up discussion of the subject, including news media publicity about the similar offenses that are exposed nationally, or the arrest of the abusing priest amid revelations of similar offenses. The news accounts of clergy sexual abuse in the 1980s and 1990s prompted many past victims to break their silence. These inducements were highlighted by public notices in eight cities that the local Catholic diocese has declared bankruptcy and any claim must be made by a particular date, or be time-barred. Many different sets of incentives for belated reporting will affect the different situations of the abuse victims.

At a later point in time, the young person may disclose to adults that he or she was violated and feels affected by this past sexual event or pattern. The friend or counselor to whom this contact is disclosed then brings this to the attention of another adult, such as the child's parent or guardian. Some emotional response is to be expected; often this manifests itself as anger and distrust of the abusive relationship that has just been revealed.

In rare cases, there can be a violent response against the abuser that makes headlines and exposes the abuse.[15] If the victim is now an adult, the long-suppressed event can be revealed to a family member or counselor.

Prior to about 1985, when publicity about the serial pedophile priest Gilbert Gauthe in Louisiana exposed the situation, claims of abuse by a priest would have been discounted immediately by most of the Catholic adults who interacted with the child.[16] "It's your imagination, Father Ed is our friend, you must be making this up to get more attention!" The belated discovery by parents that the child had actually been abused is a shock. The realization can have a traumatic effect on the family group, especially if there had been a very religious household that welcomed the personal attention from the priest for their son. For the parents of boys, this attention by a priest for their son was often seen as promoting a religious vocation to the priesthood, and this twist on expectations by the predator priest made the abuse of trust seem even more egregious.

2:4 INITIAL REPORTS •

Events such as these sexual contacts with a priest appear to carry a shame and trauma that can remain secret for years. A few cases involving intensely physical intercourse have been reported immediately as a cry for help, but the majority are not revealed readily. So the timing of the exposure of sexual assault is delayed; if it is revealed, an external event draws it out as a past recollection. For example, when the national publicity was at its most intense in 2002, more than 3,300 reports of past sexual abuse were received by dioceses, far more than in years before or after.[17]

---

15. "Judge Orders Trial for Alleged Priest Attacker," Associated Press (Feb. 10, 2011).

16. *Eller v. Diocese of St. Cloud*, 2006 Westlaw 163526 (Minn. App. 2006). (Child was slapped for lying about the good priest).

17. John Jay College Report, *supra*, 75.

2:5 RESPONSES BY DIOCESES

At some point, the past act of abuse is reported to the diocese, or the superior of the religious order. The diocese will issue some response, hopefully in a beneficial and positive way to deal with the concerns of the person making the report. After 2002, national standards existed for how dioceses should respond to such disclosures, but not all dioceses followed them. Delay and hostility toward victims drove some dioceses' responses, while others were just not listening well. Damage control and "no immediate comment" would not counteract the community rumors when a priest was suddenly moved out of his parish. When cardinals' and bishops' internal documents have been disclosed in later lawsuits, the public following the story in the news media has been appalled by some of the Episcopal attitudes that appear so dismissive or so very defensive of the accused priests.[18]

Experts have observed that the past handling of sexual abuse allegations was "at best remarkably naïve."[19] Disclosure of the allegation of clergy sexual abuse to the diocese was, at a time before the mid-1980s, a shocking surprise. In the typical pre-1980s' instance: "The offending priest was remonstrated, sometimes given time to make a retreat (repent), and usually transferred to a different parish or parochial assignment."[20] In 2011, the head of the U.S. Conference of Catholic Bishops told the press: "We remain especially firm in our commitment to remove permanently from public ministry any priest who committed such an intolerable offense."[21] Today a one-strike-you're-out policy is on the books nationally as part of the Essential Norms, or Dallas norms, adopted in 2002 by the U.S. Conference of Catholic Bishops,[22] but it is not always followed in local dioceses. By the end of 2004, this Zero-Tolerance policy led to the removal of more than 700 priests from the ministry.[23]

Sexual abuse allegations were handled very differently in the years before the 2002 Dallas norms. Back then, it was more likely that the allegations would be treated with skepticism, and as a matter of intra-diocese "fraternal correction." After being told the news of a child's complaint, the accused priest would have been likely to issue an immediate denial of the sexual contact. Inquiries would avoid scandal by avoiding notification to police and other outside investigators. The bishop would be notified by diocesan staff, and as whenever abuse is reported, the vicar for clergy and the bishop would discuss their options. A scholar commented that the bishops of that era "demonstrated excessive generosity or credulity in

---

18. See e.g., Manya Brachear Pashman, "Papers Detail Decades of Sex Abuse by Priests," Chi. Trib. A1 (Jan. 22, 2014) (former Cardinal Cody wrote in a 1970 letter to an accused priest, which was disclosed in 2014: "I feel that this whole matter should be forgotten by you as it has been forgotten by me.... No good can come of trying to prove or disprove the allegations, and I think that you will understand this.").

19. Philip Jenkins, Pedophiles & Priests: Anatomy of a Contemporary Crisis 91 (1996).

20. A.W. Richard Sipe, Sex, Priests and Power: Anatomy of a Crisis 41 (1995).

21. Maryclaire Dale, "US Bishops Renew Vow to Oust Predator Priests," Associated Press (Mar. 24, 2011).

22. U.S. Conference of Catholic Bishops, supra.

23. Frawley O'Dea, supra, 139.

permitting an individual to reoffend repeatedly before taking decisive action."[24] The Chicago documents revealed in 2014 the letter of Cardinal Cody in 1970 that expressed a desire for no inquiries to be made: "No good can come of trying to prove or disprove the allegations, and I think that you will understand this."

Prior to the adoption of the Dallas norms[25] in 2002, the bishop could choose to send the alleged offender to a retreat or for psychological rehabilitation or other forms of separation from the parish in which the abuse allegation had occurred. The 2011 John Jay College report found that: "Bishops who held positions through the early 1990s pointed to the actions they had attempted but that did not succeed as causes of the 2002 crisis; such attempted actions included ineffective psychological treatment, inadequate processes to help priests leave the priesthood, and complex canon law processes for suspension."[26]

Times have certainly changed the way dioceses react. In most dioceses today, an accusation of sexual misconduct against a priest brings immediate investigation and a rapid suspension from the parish ministry until a definitive answer is found to the allegations. The diocese's risk management staff and lawyer(s) are notified. The case would then be referred to the members of the diocesan review board. Any case that the board deems to be a credible allegation[27] will result in suspension of the priest pending further investigation.

Once a report, such as an abuse victim's lawyer's "demand letter" has been received, the internal response by dioceses has changed even with regards to the accused priest. We speculate that for many years, individuals who alleged that a priest's inappropriate or illegal physical contact was undesired would have complained to the diocesan hierarchy of the church in writing or in person. Many of these informal reports were true, and many of the true reports were of criminal acts under canon law and state law. The person lodging the report would be told that the bishop would take care that the abuse would not occur again. The pre-2002 response employed remedies toward the priest such as reconciliation, admonition, and "fraternal correction" to deal with the incoming allegations. Some allegations resulted in admissions of guilt. Others were disputed in part, or categorically denied. The long-standing tradition of handling such conflicts internally within the Church's disciplinary process was flexible, whether or not it was successful in dealing with these sexual touching events. Increasingly, during the 1960s and 1970s, priests with known issues or problems (often left out of the records of the time) were sent to specific treatment centers in an attempt to fix the problem. (This pattern will be discussed in a later chapter.)

Today, these events would be called "credible allegations" and the suspension of the priest would result. A credible allegation is not a finding of guilt, but the conclusion of an initial review that shows the accusation "at least seems true."[28] The

24. Jenkins, supra, 91.
25. U.S. Conference of Catholic Bishops, supra.
26. John Jay College Report, supra, 76.
27. Zoe Ryan, "Pinning Down a Vague Term," Nat'l Cath. Rptr. (Apr. 29, 2011), 10.
28. Id.

effects of the finding about an allegation will be devastating to the priest, who loses his position, his home in the parish rectory, his local reputation, and his ability to expect other assignments. A prudent bishop has established a process to allow the priest who is under investigation to "respond to false allegations so that good priests inaccurately accused would not feel abandoned or forced into an isolated corner."[29] From 1993 to 2006, "over two dozen clergy suicides have been linked to the sexual abuse of minors."[30]

2:6 CONTRASTING EXTERNAL LEGAL AND INTERNAL CHURCH REMEDIES

The internal remedies available to the Church stopped cold when the criminal and civil law remedy processes commenced. Lawyers for dioceses counseled that records created for internal Church discipline, if there was any discipline, would have to be turned over to prosecutors and plaintiffs and could disclose damaging information. Improper physical contact between a priest and a young person is wrong in many dimensions, but many dioceses failed to provide the merciful and apologetic behavior that one might expect to be the response of Christians to a wounded child. Once the diocese engaged outside lawyers for the defense of high-stakes litigation, the possibilities for internal remedies and healing were shelved. As the 2004 National Review Board advised the U.S. bishops, "many dioceses and orders made disastrous pastoral decisions relying on attorneys who failed to adapt their tactics to account for the unique role and responsibilities of the Church."[31]

There are three human interactions to be considered with internal remedies: priest-victim, victim-bishop, and bishop-priest. Of these, the victim-bishop interaction seemed to have been the least pastoral, the least merciful, the most troublesome, and the most provocative of hostility, when viewed in hindsight.

To the classic Catholic view, when harm is done to a child by an adult, the ideal response toward the victim is pastoral—not a lengthy lawsuit, but a faith-filled process of counseling, forgiveness, and positive healing. Therapeutic, pastoral, healing interactions are very desirable when a grave breach of faith has occurred.[32] Redemptive healing from the consequences of sinful behavior begins with reconciliation and apology, and then through counseling and the sharing of views progresses to a healthier accommodation and forgiveness. "Fraternal correction" is one of the terms used in Catholic traditions for chastising a sinner; all religions have

---

29. Frawley O'Dea, supra, 142.
30. Id. at 140.
31. National Review Board for the Protection of Children and Young People, A Report on the Crisis in the Catholic Church in the United States, United States Conference of Catholic Bishops (Feb. 27, 2004), 120, on Web at http://old.usccb.org/nrb/nrbstudy/nrbreport.htm.
32. Several texts in our bibliography deal explicitly with these issues.

some form of mutual healing through discussion and shared forgiveness. But the legal system interrupts mutuality because it is adversarial by nature; the "healing" is only in the form of a cash payment in belated compensation.

Also to be considered is the relationship of the bishop with "his" priest, as the bishop is both father and brother to his priests. While the bishop could use "fraternal correction" with his brother priest, the bishop also must assure that natural justice is served and harm is remedied. By following proper procedure, the bishop is to assure that bad behavior is punished with penalties that both punish and attempt to reform the errant priest. The bishop should not put the priest in a situation that tempts him to reoffend, once there has been a credible allegation made by or for a child. And the bishop has an important responsibility to all the members of the diocese, not only to the priests. Although these are classic means of achieving mercy and justice for the Church, bishops often closed the door on the possibility of Christian interactions that would have brought mercy and mutuality. The Chicago documents released in 2014 showed one cardinal's insistence that no inquiry would be made of sexual abuse allegations, and that priest continued to be accused in later years of similar abuse patterns.[33]

The Vatican's letter to Irish bishops in 1997 told them not to adopt a policy of reporting child sexual abuse to the police.[34] For both "moral and canonical" reasons, the Congregation for the Clergy announced that all accusations must flow through internal channels of the Church. "Bishops who disobeyed, the letter said, may face repercussions when their abuse cases were heard in Rome. 'The results could be highly embarrassing and detrimental to those same Diocesan authorities.'" The Vatican subsequently shifted responsibility for abuse cases away from the author of that letter to another office, so in 2011 Vatican officials downplayed the significance of that 1997 letter. But the damage has been done: the appearance of a cover-up has deepened, and the beneficial opportunities for reconciliation were wasted.

Insiders who worked within the system have expressed great frustration: "The exposure of a myriad of cases in Boston and Los Angeles (more than five hundred) refines and demonstrates the extent to which the church bypasses and ignores its own guidelines, directives, law and wisdom."[35] The result of the bishops' actions was to leave the criminal law and civil law systems of harsh remedies as the only options for the victim of clergy sexual abuse, and his or her family. These remedies are adversarial by nature, with the predominant form of "healing" in civil cases a cash payment as compensation. The relations between the American bishops and the victims of clergy sexual abuse are going to be studied on other continents, in other religious denominations, and in future decades, as examples of how a faith community should not have responded.

---

33. Pashman, supra.
34. Laurie Goodstein, "Vatican Letter Warned Bishops on Abuse Policy," N.Y. Times (Jan. 18, 2011).
35. Thomas Doyle, A.W.R. Sipe & Patrick Wall, Sex, Priests & Secret Codes 202 (2006).

2:7 NEWS MEDIA

Although journalists did not create the clergy sexual abuse scandal, they did uncover its nuances and broadcast them unmercifully, to the harm of the American bishops. The story often begins very locally. The sudden removal and suspension of a local priest triggers wide discussion in the parish community: Why did Father suddenly leave us? Rumors of the alleged abuse may reach the local news media from various sources, after the priest is removed from a parish or school assignment and local rumors begin to unwind. Before the 2002 Dallas norms were adopted, and in some cases thereafter, the diocese would have historically gone into damage control mode with "no immediate comment."

The reporters then expand upon the few details of the current local story with background, perhaps including reports of other cases within the diocese (there often had been stories and rumors floating around about this priest), and cases of similar abuse in nearby dioceses and on the national level. Sex, money, court cases, power, hypocritical statements on morality by immoral priests, etc. are recurrent themes in the reporting of the clergy sexual abuse scandal. Attorneys seeking damages for victims have enabled remarkable insights into the actual words used by cardinals and bishops as the sex abuse reports were received but then discounted or disregarded.[36]

The diocese would respond that it has no comment "in order to protect the privacy rights of all parties." Reporters covering the criminal indictments of priests and an administrator in Philadelphia described Catholic parishioners' attitudes as discouraged and "caught in a wave of anxiety" that "sent the church reeling in the latest and one of the most damning episodes in the American church" in decades.[37] One Philadelphia victim said there are families who "don't know monsters live among them" because the archdiocese had "shielded the pedophiles."[38]

Step back from the harsh rhetoric and ask: What institution would wish for such a public image, when it must depend on that community's families to voluntarily send in the next generation of priests and voluntarily fill the next week's collection basket? There are lessons to be learned here.

2:8 SIGNIFICANCE OF PRIOR ABUSE ALLEGATIONS .

Lawyers would spot what others would not: any proof of diocesan knowledge of prior sexual abuse will empower the plaintiff to sue the diocese independently of suits against the priest. For example: the diocese that had known of Father Doe's unusual ways of showing affection for young altar boys in the rectory could be sued for the negligent assignment of Doe to the post that led him to molest this young

---

36. Pashman, supra.
37. Katharine Q. Seelye, "In Philadelphia, New Cases Loom in Priest Scandal," N.Y. Times (Mar. 4, 2011).
38. "3rd Suit Filed against Philly Archdiocese Heads," Associated Press (Mar. 16, 2011).

plaintiff. For a plaintiff's lawyer representing the abused child, this knowing act of negligence in assignments, made by the diocese, offers a cause of action that is much easier to prove than the claim of employer accountability for the priest's misconduct.

Reports of several past suppressed cases against the priest may be rumored to exist. Reporters will unsuccessfully ask the diocese for the personnel record of the accused priest. These requests are denied because canon law recognizes the right of the priest to privacy and the protection of his reputation. Later, in pretrial discovery of a civil case, the records may be revealed when they are officially found in the diocesan files or when the reports about cases are turned over to the plaintiff. Some cases of past allegations are received from various sources, and these are pursued by the attorneys retained by the aggrieved family.

Some of the past cases had been allegedly denied, suppressed, or settled by past diocesan administrators, resulting in suppression of the case and no action taken. Mishandling may have occurred through coercion to drop the complaint or by a small payment with a confidentiality promise in the settlement. Silencing the critic in the short term often rebounds in the longer term against the diocesan official who had insisted that the abuse be kept secret in return for the payment.

2:9 FOLLOW-UP MEDIA COVERAGE

Viewers and readers of the news media have short memories. So the follow-up story is a frequently utilized device during the many months that no action is being taken on pending criminal charges or civil lawsuits. The form of that follow-up may often take the "local angle." A diocesan bishop or administrators' recent actions handling alleged abuse cases, after the public dissemination of the Church's 2002 "Dallas norms," are more closely scrutinized in comparison to those national criteria. The diocese may be forced to respond to a wave of media inquiries: Why isn't the bishop acting like Cardinal X did in his archdiocese? Why isn't the bishop doing what the Vatican press release says will be done? Some non-actions by the local church leaders are found deficient by news media, with heavy comparison to other dioceses' responses toward similar allegations. This is especially devastating if the accused priest came from another diocese, where inquiries turn up other charges against that same priest. It is also a more serious problem when a number of similar abuse claims against the same priest arose after his transfer to a new venue.

2:10 RESPONSE BY LOCAL LAW ENFORCEMENT

In a small minority of abuse cases, local police are notified soon after the event, or immediately if a forcible rape has occurred, and the police will usually open a preliminary inquiry with interviews of the victim. Police and prosecutors had historically avoided charging priests with sex crimes unless the proof was overwhelming, but that is no longer the case. After an inquiry and an interview with the accused priest, who typically denies the charge and casts aspersions on the credibility of the alleged victim, the prosecutor makes a choice. Many past reports were filed away as unsubstantiated, and prosecutors would:

(1) decline to prosecute the case on basis of inadequate proof;
(2) decline because the delay in reporting exceeded the state statute of limitations (delay between action and report), as had been argued by the lawyers for the diocese; or
(3) arrest the priest on the basis of the victim's credible allegation.

If option (3) occurs, the allegation hits the news media before diocesan involvement in many cases. Cameras may show the monsignor outside the jail in handcuffs, or the local priest "doing the perp walk" into the courthouse for arraignment. The bishop is then asked for comment on the sexual abuse and is stuck in a lose/lose position with the news media speculating about "who knew what and when."

Reporters and police officers have a symbiotic relationship, as each shares intriguing information with the other. Priest arrests are rare and newsworthy events. The Church's delay in going to police in a particular case was typical; a priest who shot gay pornographic videos in his rectory with local boys was not reported to police for three months after the diocese acquired the video collection.[39]

Prosecutors' decisions in the past to shield the Church from harmful publicity are unlikely to remain secret today, as individual investigators recognize the news value of these abuse incidents.[40] As a scholar noted, the mid-1980s' change of direction was significant; "traditional qualms about embarrassing church authorities were increasingly questionable, and restraint that once seemed politically wise would now be legally dangerous."[41] It is probable that files about a now-"closed" inquiry, that relates to an abuse that had been too old to prosecute under state statutes of limitations, will "leak" to the press, condemning the accused priest and waving a red flag of negligence about the diocese to which that priest had voluntarily moved.

News about a priest who sought a voluntary transfer or reassignment, and then offended again, is particularly interesting to plaintiffs' counsel for victims in that later assignment. The negligence of the sending and receiving dioceses concerning this priest's character flaws or crimes will embolden the plaintiff's attorneys. A cluster of allegations about a priest who had been the alleged abuser of multiple children can result in a class action lawsuit or a series of coordinated trials by related groups of plaintiffs' counsel. The same number of sexual assaults in multiple dioceses aids the plaintiff's counsel in negotiating one diocese's defense team against another.

39. Jenkins, supra, 45.
40. Id.
41. Id. at 46.

2:11 DIOCESAN REVIEW BOARDS

The 2002 Essential Norms adopted for U.S. dioceses included the use of a review board to examine the available information and to make recommendations to the bishop, after the board had reviewed the records of that priest and of the alleged abuse. Members should have the professional backgrounds that enable them to make useful recommendations to the bishop. However, the board "is only as good as the cases a bishop puts before them," as an eminent Catholic legal scholar observed in 2011.[42] In several cases, diocesan boards were not given the full information or not told at all about reports about a problem priest. These omissions were not very well received by members of the involved boards, prompting some to resign as a result.[43] When a priest allegedly touched the genitals of a young man through his underwear, and the claim was made decades later, a New Jersey church review board drew criticism when that board dismissed the claim as not meeting the definition of sexual abuse, although the touching was "inappropriate."[44]

2:12 COSTS OF INVESTIGATING AND DEFENDING OLDER ABUSE CLAIMS

For a large institution of its size and scope, the Roman Catholic Church employs relatively few trained security officials. The cost to the Church to bring in outside contractors to investigate and defend old, "stale claims" of clergy abuse are significant. In a hypothetical example of a typical case, a credible report of elementary school students' sexual contact with a parish priest during the period 1966–1974 is received in 2011 from an adult among that group of victims, who demands compensation for psychological counseling to deal with the past traumatic events. Proof must be assembled to show that this accused priest had the capability and location assignment that makes the charge sound plausible. The priest may be dead, retired, or unwilling to be interviewed about the allegations. To reconstruct the 1966 parish school attendance list or the list of children going to sleep-away camp in 1973 may be nearly impossible.

The diocesan attorney will engage the services of an investigator. The results can be withheld from public disclosure under attorney "work product" privileges, because the investigator's findings were requested by the lawyer who is defending the diocese. Of course, withholding for pretrial advantages has the indirect consequence of stoking resentment of "just another church cover-up of scandals." When claims are paid in pretrial settlement, secrecy pledges are often used to prevent the

---

42. Joshua McElwee, "What's a Review Board to Do?", Nat'l Cath. Rptr. (June 10, 2011), 7.
43. Id.
44. Alan Cooperman, "Catholics Question Gray Areas of Abuse; Critics Say Some Priests' Misconduct Goes Unpunished under New Guidelines," Wash. Post (Nov. 30, 2002), A2.

victim from talking with others about the facts of the settlement. These have been widely criticized as indicative of a desire for a cover-up.

The settlement of claims poses an additional quandary. Too loose an acceptance of claims is seen as making the diocese an easy mark for demands for payment, while too tight a level of scrutiny of long-past events may sound like a cover-up and will lead to a lengthy trial. Refusing to settle may not be the best option for a diocese, even if it has some doubts about the belated reports, as news media have criticized dioceses for dismissing reports of sexual abuse because of time discrepancies in recall of those long-past events.

2:13 FISCAL EFFECTS ON LIABILITIES OF THE DIOCESE

Abuse case revelations may be the worst possible combination of factors for a diocese to face: an increase of large contingent liabilities, to be litigated without insurance, while receipts from donors are down and costs of investigation of older cases increase substantially. Chapter 16 covers these issues in more detail. The additional workload and payouts will strain the diocesan reserves, and in some cases, the size of the contingent liability exceeds the ability to pay even with all reserves and all current cash on hand. Facing these costs and liabilities, the decision regarding the sale of properties or the filing of bankruptcy may be intense.

2:14 FINANCIAL IMPACTS ON INCOME FOR THE DIOCESE

There is no clear comprehensive data available on the charitable gifts to dioceses, outside the confidentiality of the diocesan offices and the tax deduction monitoring by the IRS. If that data were available, it would likely reveal trends with selected dioceses showing a reduction in donations. These trends may roughly correlate to an index of trustworthiness or respect for the diocese that receives the funds. One might also look to the trends of actual Mass attendance, which is counted every October in every parish. A diocese that handles sexual abuse claims poorly may suffer, as compared to other dioceses with no similar problems. Chapter 16 addresses these issues in detail.

In the absence of definitive data either way, it is reasonable to accept the claims of other reviewers who speculate that clergy sexual abuse charges and a news media claim of a bishop's cover-up of "rogue priests" will lead to a reduction in the free-will charitable donations taken in by the diocese from Catholic donors. One donor may want to punish the Church as an institution. Another may insist on better diocesan disclosures of the actual facts as a prerequisite to stronger support. Donors who read about the controversy may begin to show wariness regarding contributions to the good works of the diocesan offices, aware that their gifts may be diverted from strictly charitable endeavors to the payments of settlements or other clean-up of prior problems. Europeans have a much more specific barometer of donor intent regarding church sexual abuse. As some European nations allow citizens to designate their church to receive a share of government aid, the scandals over clergy sexual abuse have led a certain percentage of taxpayers to remove their designation of the Roman Catholic Church as the recipient of the per-capita government payments. If a person resigns from the Church, by filling out a government form, the Church will receive less money. The U.S. Constitution prevents the government from "establishing" a particular religion, but in these European venues, we can more directly discern that the Church will be economically harmed by the resignations.

2:15 INSURER RESPONSES

Insurers who wrote liability coverage for the Church are inevitably asked to pay the costs of defense and settlements in these cases. But many carriers will deny coverage (1) post-1987 under the ISO's "abuse or molestation" exclusion discussed in Chapter 7, or (2) pre-1987 as outside the scope of coverage of agent/employee actions (intentional rogue acts contrary to employer norms are usually not covered). Chapters 7 and 16 discusses fiscal and insurance issues in further detail.

2:16 LIABILITIES VERSUS ASSETS

To those outside, the Roman Catholic Church appears to have fabulous wealth. To those on the inside, including the author who once chaired an archdiocesan pastoral council, the facade of wealth is a misperception, and the diocese does not usually have pockets as deep as a plaintiff's trial lawyer would anticipate. The assets of a diocese (including cash reserves, funds, surplus land, and saleable buildings) may be inadequate to cover the size of the contingent liabilities. As we have dug into the literature about the Church's response to these issues, we were perplexed by the very unusual accounting used in some dioceses. Some properties are valuable, yet some could not draw a worthwhile bid when put up for sale. Civil plaintiffs will certainly need the services of a skilled forensic accountant to discern the funds available within a diocese that claims it cannot afford to pay the settlement demanded or the verdict that is sought.

2:17 VULNERABILITY OF THE FUNDS OF PARISHES

In the majority of states, Catholic dioceses own parishes, schools, and other property as a "corporation sole" in which the bishop is the sole shareholder and hence the sole decision-maker. Parish fund accounts that appear to be held in an informal trust for purposes of that parish can be deemed part of the diocesan funds. Excellent studies on this issue provide great depth in this complex field.[45]

45. Nicholas Cafardi, "The Availability of Parish Assets for Diocesan Debts," 29 Seton Hall Legis. J. 361 (2005); Comment, "Separation of Church and Estate: On Excluding Parish Assets from the Bankruptcy Estate of a Diocese Organized as a Corporation Sole," 55 Cath. U. L. Rev. 583 (2006).

Because the parish assets or reserves are, in many dioceses, comingled with other diocesan accounts, they could be seized by a future bankruptcy trustee if the diocese declares bankruptcy. Shifting assets within a period of time before bankruptcy filings occur can be negated as fraudulent transfers; federal prosecutors dislike such shifts from the bankrupt estate when notified by creditors of the diocese that money has been hidden. Donors to the parish's weekly collection basket would be startled to know that their funds are taken away to settle sexual abuse claims in a distant part of the diocese. Donors might react by halting donations to the parish, which worsens the situation.

2:18 CONSIDERATIONS OF BANKRUPTCY

Bankruptcy has been filed by nine dioceses, and the effects have been harsh. The court orders the trustee to solicit all claimants to file their financial compensation claims. The trustee receives notice of past abuse claims, including the date(s) and the priests who are accused. The discovery of internal records may be much more intrusive than the bishop of the bankrupt diocese would prefer. Chapter 9 addresses these vulnerabilities of the diocese.

If a claim of past sexual abuse by clergy is not made within the time set by the bankruptcy court order, the claim may be precluded from any recovery. Chapter 9 discusses bankruptcy issues in further detail.

The trustee of the estate of the diocese will work with accountants to determine a plan for the liquidation of diocesan and parish reserve funds and for the sale of land and assets that may be required. Layoffs and the closure of some ministries may occur.

Even if we assume that a bankruptcy moves ahead smoothly on paper, the news media will jump on the shortcomings of the payment schedule that the trustee of the diocese has announced. The victims and their lawyers are bound to react that the diocese is "backing out of their responsibilities," hiding more documents, seeking to deny large verdicts to plaintiffs, etc.

2:19 LEGISLATORS' ROLES ON LIMITATIONS PERIODS

Criminal and civil laws often include a period of years during which the particular case can be brought in the courts. These statutes of limitations are intended for the more reliable and clear preservation of accurate memories by witnesses concerning facts and events that occurred in the past. When viewed in a more hostile light, however, a defendant's use of these time limits as a defense can appear to be a tool to shield those who raped or molested children as the accused can be protected from legal accountability as a result of the intended suppression of a child's report of abuse. Upset by news of church administrators' apparent suppression or mishandling of some older allegations, some state lawmakers have pushed for legislation to reopen the limitations period for certain crimes.

This state-by-state effort of plaintiffs and abuse survivor groups to create a look-back or "window" for older "suppressed" claims is debated, as well as opposed by lobbyists for the Church,[46] but may be passed into state legislation. These lobbying efforts result in attendant publicity, bringing in more claims of past abuse as news media in the state examines the multiple stories. In rare cases, the publicity may draw out the details of a predator who manipulated children into silence, leaving a case that can't be pursued because of the limitation period. This creates outraged complaints from news media and the voters, and outrage brings votes for changes in the statutes. For a more in-depth discussion of the issues surrounding statutes of limitation, see Chapter 5.

2:20 REMOVAL OF THE ACCUSED ABUSER PRIEST

The internal Church disciplinary process is discussed in Chapter 25. The process to "laicize" a priest is complex, so the decision to initiate the removal of the offender from his ministry is not made rapidly. Charges of sexual abuse may or may not remove an abuser from his status as a priest. If the case goes public, the priest is very likely to be removed from any ministry assignment related to children. As the removal of priestly status is a lengthy process, by the time these decisions are finalized, some of the accused may be dead or retired. The egregious offenders are likely to have been already laicized, even over their refusal to consent. The only priests left hanging in limbo with the Church are ones whose case has not been proven, or where there is some question about the veracity of the allegations. One way or another, given the current climate, it is unlikely that accused priest will ever function as a priest again, even if he is exonerated.

---

46. Patrick Schiltz, "The Future of Sexual Abuse Litigation," *America Magazine* (July 7, 2003), 8.

PART TWO

Civil Litigation

CHAPTER 3

✦

Civil Litigation against Catholic Dioceses, Parishes, and Priests

3:1 INDIVIDUAL LIABILITY

Sexual assault is both a crime and a civil tort. The award of damages against the abuser is based on a jury finding that: the preponderance of the evidence has demonstrated that the intentional tort of unconsented touching of the minor person has occurred; the young person has been harmed, and the actor does not have a legal privilege (i.e., a legitimate reason) for the touching, penetration, or other form of assault. (The Catholic Church's definition of "sexual abuse" does not require touching or harm.) Depending on the age of the victim at the time of the event, a defense of consent to sexual relations is unlikely to be accepted in the case of a civil damages case. In this chapter we recap the civil litigation process and liability defenses.

The amount of compensation in a sexual assault damage award is built upon physical and psychological treatment costs ("economic damages") and on the jury's assessment of the value of the emotional and related damage caused by the assault ("non-economic damages"). A damage verdict in the category of negligence or "intentional torts" applies. The law also allows "negligence per se" to be used in some cases, in which a direct violation of an applicable criminal law gives rise to a finding of negligent conduct by the priest. Punitive damages for intentional assaults might also impose a form of cash punishment on the diocese for inadequate supervision and on the priest for his egregious intentional assault on the victim.

3:2 LITIGATION BEGINS

After abuse is reported to a diocese, there are some informal interactions among the attorneys for the diocese, the victim, and the insurer (if any), regarding a potential settlement. There may be a settlement, but if agreement cannot be reached, a lawsuit would then be filed in state court near the residence of the plaintiff or the site of the event.

Alleged victims of clergy sexual assault have brought a wide range of claims in their various civil lawsuits. Plaintiffs filing a tort action could potentially claim any number of torts, including:

- assault;[1]
- battery;[2]
- intentional infliction of emotional distress;[3]
- negligent hiring or supervision of the priest;[4]
- tortious sexual abuse with fraudulent concealment of the abuse;[5]
- employer liability as *respondeat superior* for torts of the employee;[6]
- negligence per se for violation of the criminal statutes;
- breach of fiduciary duty in loco parentis;[7]
- misrepresentation if the bishop asserted no knowledge of past abuse;[8]
- failure to protect the child under a state duty of care;[9]
- negligent supervision of the priest by the bishop;[10] or
- the tort of "outrage."[11]

1. Rigazio v. Archdiocese of Louisville, 853 S.W.2d 295 (Ky. App. 1993) (assault is the unauthorized touching of a person, with or without injury).

2. See e.g., Dengler v. Doe 1, 2007 Westlaw 4183032 (Cal. App. 2007); Pritzlaff v. Archdiocese of Milwaukee, 533 N.W.2d 780 (Wis. 1995) (battery is a physical contact on the body of the person who sued).

3. See e.g., Restatement of Torts 2d 46(1) (1965) and Demeyer v. Archdiocese of Detroit, 593 N.W.2d 560 (1999) (this tort occurs when the defendant placed the plaintiff in serious emotional trauma).

4. Doe v. Catholic Bishop for the Diocese of Memphis, 306 S.W.2d 812 (Tenn. App. 2008) (this occurs when an employer has a duty not to keep agents who cause serious harms).

5. Clay v. Kuhl, 727 N.E.2d 217 (Ill. 2000); Dengler v. Doe 1, 2007 Westlaw 4183032 (Cal. App. 2007) (the unwanted sexual contact, or sex with a minor child, was concealed by the actor or employer).

6. Eller v. Diocese of St. Cloud, 2006 Westlaw 163526 (Minn. App. 2006) (the employer had a duty to prevent its agents from committing this offensive conduct).

7. Albright v. White, 503 S.E. 2d 860 (W. Va. 1998) (a person legally responsible for care of the minor child is liable when he or she is entrusted by the parents with control, and allows harm to occur to that child).

8. John Doe 1 v. Archdiocese of Milwaukee, 734 N.W.2d 827, 846 (Wis. 2007) (a false statement is made about the employer's knowledge of the actor's propensity to commit a crime such as assault).

9. Victor Schwartz & Leah Lorber, "Defining the Duty of Religious Institutions to Protect Others," 74 U. Cin. L. Rev. 11 (2005) (obligation in a state law requiring care was not met by the caregiver).

10. Martinelli v. Bridgeport Roman Catholic Diocesan Corp., 196 F.3d 409 (2d Cir.1999); Fortin v. Roman Catholic Bishop of Portland, 871 A.2d 1208 (Maine 2005) (duty of a higher level supervisor to monitor the conduct of the subordinate).

11. See e.g., Travis v. Ziter, 681 So.2d 1348 (Ark. 1996); Rigazio v. Archdiocese of Louisville, 853 S.W.2d 295 (Ky. App. 1993) (extremely offensive conduct toward a person that is more than mere negligence).

Many of the suits alleged several forms of sexual abuse had occurred and had been concealed at the insistence of the priest.[12] If there were multiple acts of sexual abuse, the law of most states recognizes that the period for filing suit begins on the last date on which the abuse occurred. The state laws allowing suits within a certain time period may be different for a suit by a minor child; some states allow the suit to begin within the permissible time period that begins when the child reaches the legal age of maturity, at 18 or older,[13]

Many states require the lawsuit to list the date of the specific event(s), specific actors, the consequential injuries, and the demand in dollars that the plaintiff is asserting. The filing of the lawsuit triggers a time period for the lawyers representing the diocese (and/or its insurance carrier) to file their responsive court documents, usually an answer that denies or claims a lack of knowledge of the allegations. The significant side effect of the filing of the lawsuit is typically the launching of publicity by the plaintiff, including media interviews with the plaintiff (and his/her parents if the complaint comes from a minor). News media coverage of clergy sexual abuse lawsuits has been extremely intense, and stories about the lawsuit filings are often nationally broadcast through wire service and network reports. Diocesan responses are usually a simple denial of knowledge, or refusal to comment. Disclosure during pretrial discovery of the actual words used by a cardinal or bishop makes front-page news with potentially damning results for the diocese.

Publicity brings on another inevitable "backlash" response: persons interviewed on camera at the Catholic parish, or the school or the religious congregation in which the alleged assailant served, will typically remember his good deeds, long service, great faith, etc. It can be expected that some parishioners will always vocally defend "their priest" against the allegations by a "greedy outsider." Some will discern bad motives in past activities of the priest; more will simply stop supporting that parish or the Catholic Church as a whole because of the abuse.

The lawsuit typically sparks some divisions in feeling about the priest that may soon appear in the parish, the neighborhood, or the community, with some siding with the young person ("I always worried about Father A") but many siding with the alleged assailant ("Father B was a great youth minister and would never have done this; this greedy lawsuit is all about money!").

Historians and sociologists will have to discern the long-term effect of these incidents on the retention of Catholic laity participation and the "loss of faith" by measures of Mass attendance and contribution levels. The impacts on seminary recruitment and enrollment for future priests and religious members is also a factor

---

12. A priest was alleged to have committed acts including "vaginal intercourse, anal intercourse, cunnilingus, fellatio, vaginal penetration with a vibrator, administration of enemas, . . . hypnosis, threats of physical violence, coerced prostitution and other lewd acts, physically striking plaintiff, and forcing Plaintiff to perform sexual acts with a police officer." Doe v. Maskell, 679 A.2d 1087 (Md. 1996).

13. Doe v. Howe, 626 S.E.2d 25 (S.C. App. 2005).

for future study, because family support for this vocation choice has been affected by the community awareness of the priest sexual abuse charges.

3:3 LIABILITY OF THE DIOCESE

Outside of the church setting, the employment tort litigation scenario is familiar: a rogue employee acts in a way that harms a third party; the employee, or agent, and the employer, or principal, are both sued; and the corporation denies liability because the employee acted outside the scope of employment. Lawyers familiar with principles of the law of agency and corporate attribution of liability face these cases every day.

Principal/agent relationships in the vertical hierarchies of senior executives, divisions, subsidiaries, etc., are well addressed in state tort law. Nonprofit corporation law is also well developed in most states, because of the issues surrounding leaders and volunteers. State corporation law regarding the attribution of a volunteer or an employed agent's misconduct has been articulated by appellate courts, as well as in Uniform Laws and Model Acts. The principle known as *respondeat superior*, which makes an employer liable for an employee's torts committed within the scope of the person's employment, will vary with each state's norms, but dioceses have vigorously denied that they had the aspects of control over an offending diocesan priest that would justify the application of liability to the diocese under the respondeat superior doctrine, or that of vicarious liability generally.[14]

But beyond the standard employer liability issues is the question of what the diocese knew about the sexual misconduct patterns and what it had actually done to protect this particular child from the known predator. For example, Bridgeport diocesan officials wrote in 1990 of a "developing pattern of accusations" of abuse by Father Charles Carr, but he was not suspended until 1995, later reinstated, and then finally removed in 2002, after which the diocese settled litigation for $12 million.[15] As apologetic bishops have written, "(W)e are the ones who, at times, responded to victims and their families as adversaries and not as suffering members of the church."[16]

The religious orders whose clergy commit abuse have also been held liable. In the Delaware Supreme Court decision about that state's 2007 clergy abuse provisions, there was held to be abundant evidence "including the Oblates' own records demonstrating prior knowledge of Norris' sexual abuse of children and his many other problems," so that the Oblates order may have violated the educational standard of care in their high school.[17]

14. Eller v. Diocese of St. Cloud, 2006 Westlaw 163526 (Minn. App. 2006); Aquilino v. Philadelphia Catholic Archdiocese, 884 A.2d 1269 (Pa. Super. 2005).

15. National Review Board for the Protection of Children & Young People, A Report on the Crisis in the Catholic Church in the United States 37 (2004) (hereinafter "National Review Board").

16. Bishop Blase Cupich, "The Bishops' Priorities," America Magazine 13, 15 (May 30, 2011).

17. Sheehan v. Oblates, 15 A.3d 1247 (Del. 2011).

3:4 THE STRUCTURE OF "EMPLOYER RESPONSIBILITIES" IN THE CHURCH CONTEXT

A prudent plaintiff's lawyer will recognize that the typical abuser-priest will not have sufficient individual funds to make for a successful civil action "target." In some cases, officials of the diocese knew of, and concealed, the misconduct of the priest, so they were legally accountable. Compensation should be available to a person who suffered the results of the abuse. In most instances, compensation is more likely to be available from the diocese, as it is likely to have insurance coverage and assets from which a settlement could provide the plaintiff with compensation.

The complex organization of the Roman Catholic Church hierarchy is often a challenge for the civil lawyer to understand.[18] But before one sues, understanding the issue of corporate form and accountability is essential. The reader is cautioned that each state has its own laws dealing with nonprofit entities. In states that have a cap on damage awards for nonprofit entities, the bishop will usually be sued along with the diocese, as an individual defendant, in an attempt to avoid the barrier of a statutory cap on damages against the nonprofit diocese as an entity.[19] The plaintiff in these cases is looking in pretrial discovery for evidence that the bishop or his staff's personnel director (often titled "Vicar for Religious") had personal knowledge of the misconduct by the priest. Knowledge would be the basis for a claim of individual liability by the bishop for failing to restrain the abusive activities or in some cases to knowingly assign the errant priest to a new parish where the plaintiff encountered that priest.

Lawyers familiar with nonprofit corporation defense in tort claims will consider the form under which the church as an entity is named in the lawsuit. A "corporation sole" is a state law structure for organizing an unusual limited liability structure such as a diocese. This form, allowed under many state laws, installs the bishop as the sole member and sole director of the corporation. It is a corporate form authorized under state laws to enable bona fide religious leaders to hold property and conduct business for the benefit of the religious entity. It allows a religious entity such as a diocese to be administered without a board of directors, ownership shares, or other diffusion of control common in corporate structures. The bishop personifies the corporation until he is replaced by the pope upon retirement, death, or resignation.

We assume in this chapter that a sexual abuse lawsuit or claim has been filed, and that the bishop did not have prior knowledge that the priest was likely to commit such a crime. If the bishop did have such knowledge of that priest's tendency toward sexual contact with minors, but had nonetheless moved the priest to another assignment in contact with young persons, the liability for negligence then becomes far more difficult to defend. Belated disclosures during pretrial discovery

---

18. See e.g., Doe v. Holy See, CV 02-430-MO (D. Or. 2011), on remand from Doe v. Holy See, 557 F.3d 1066 (9th Cir., 2009).

19. The Boston Globe Investigative Staff, "Betrayal: The Crisis in the Catholic Church," Boston Globe, at 48, 50 (2003) (hereinafter "Betrayal").

can be devastating to the diocese because of its impact on the potential pool of jurors, stimulating higher settlement offers. In one case, six bishops in three states allegedly knew of a priest's record of child abuse.[20]

3:5 DETERMINING WHO IS THE EMPLOYER UNDER STATE LAW

This section deals with the narrow question of whether a victim could sue on the basis that the employer bishop was accountable for the actions of the priest, leaving aside other causes of action. State labor and employment law will govern the civil tort attribution of liabilities to an employer. The context here is an individual priest's criminal, societally unacceptable act of physical abuse of a child. The diocesan lawyers will assert that this act is not only outside the scope of the priest's duties, but is contrary to the law and policy of the Church. The context may influence the way that a state court sees the status of the employer/diocese in its arguments. One also must weigh the impact on jurors of hearing about the priest's vows of obedience to his bishop, a concept of allegiance that is far stronger than the conventional employee's duty of loyalty to Wal-Mart or Citigroup. Some jurors will attribute the liability to the bishop because of this authority and will assume that such a direct oversight carries with it an implicit duty to prevent the clergy sexual abuse that happened in this victim's case.

Three models of state employment law may be chosen for analysis. The priest who committed the abhorrent assault could be treated as an:

(1) independent contractor;
(2) employee of the parish; or
(3) employee of the diocese.

For federal tax purposes, the priest is considered an independent contractor with the self-employed status that implies.[21] The plaintiff aims to impose tort liability on the diocese. If a priest is treated as an independent contractor under state law, plaintiffs could argue that this contractor has enjoyed "ostensible agency" to be viewed as the agent of the bishop; the negligent selection of that errant contractor may be a basis for recovery against the bishop who contracted for that person's services as a priest in that diocese. The diocese will argue that it did not direct the work of the priest in his errant decision to sexually molest the child, and that the priest acted badly, but his misconduct cannot be attributed to the contract-issuing diocese. These defenses are especially effective for the diocese where the priest is a member of a religious order, not a regular diocesan priest, so he would be out of the normal line of diocesan disciplinary authority.

20. Betrayal, supra.
21. Clergy self-employment is explained in IRS Publication 517, on the Web at http://www.irs.gov/publications/p517/ar02.html#en_US_2012_publink100033573.

If state law treats the priest as an employee of the parish, that approach can be used by the diocese to say that only the assets of the individual parish can be used to pay the judgment for damages. The specific facts of who assigned the priest to the parish, how long he was employed there, who wrote the paychecks, etc., will be debatable.

For a finding that the priest was an employee of either the parish or the diocese, the attribution of liability to the bishop as the ultimate employer will depend on the ability of the plaintiff's counsel to show (1) that the priest was ordained by the bishop for this diocese, X years ago; (2) that during this time he was assigned to this parish for Y years; and that (3) canon law and diocesan procedure designates the priest to accept reassignment from the bishop when needed, via the vow of obedience to the bishop for whose diocese the priest was "incardinated." Usually the diocesan newspaper lists the annual moves as "the bishop has assigned..." as another indicator of diocesan direction of the "employee." An annual retirement fund contribution and a W-2 tax form from the diocese may also be useful evidence of "employment" by the bishop. The case law of attributing abuse liability to a diocese has been extremely variable, making it difficult to draw one normative standard from the messy state case law.

The bishop's defense counsel attempts to distance the bishop from any finding of employer responsibility for actions of the accused abuser, in order to preserve assets of the diocese. This seeks to remove the diocese as a defendant, while acknowledging that the individual priest alone could be a liability target. Plaintiffs will assert that despite the tax arguments for independent contractor or parish-only status, it is the diocese that trains, accepts, ordains, assigns, and later reassigns the priest, so therefore the diocese should be held liable for "employer" status. That is not the end of the story, but it is a necessary part of the plaintiff's claim for diocesan funds to pay damages.

In an unusual aspect, the Church doctrine aspects of the religious vow helps the plaintiff; the obligation of the bishop to the priest under Church canon law serves as an important support for a plaintiff's claim that the bishop can be held liable for actions by the priest. But the First Amendment aspects of American constitutional jurisprudence warn the courts away from considering doctrinal matters.[22] So the diocesan defense lawyer is allowed to argue that the jury cannot be told of the obligations of obedience that canon law imposes on the priest-bishop relationship. Similarly, the plaintiff may assert "negligent selection" of a priest who should not have been ordained; this is analogous to a hospital's liability for negligent credentialing of a surgeon who is not competent for patient surgery because of some individual flaw that would predictably cause harm. This would be a creative claim for an astute plaintiff, but the assertion has not been thoroughly tested in case law.

Note that some courts have separated two causes of action: "vicarious liability for the claim of fraudulent concealment was separate and distinct from vicarious liability for [the priest's] alleged sexual abuse."[23] The Philadelphia grand jury

---

22. See e.g., Redwing v. Catholic Bishop of Memphis, 363 S.W.3d 436 (Tenn. 2012).
23. Picher v. Roman Catholic Bishop of Portland, 974 A.2d 286, 296 (2009).

evaluation of the fraudulent concealment illustrates the issue as it showed the decisions of the archbishops and their staffs regarding abuser priests.

State law of principal liability for agent misdeeds is helpful to the diocese as to the acts of sexual misconduct, but the laws do not help the diocese avoid liability on issues of negligent hiring, negligent training, and negligent supervision, all of which are potential claims against a bishop, as they would be against a secular business employer.

Most abuse cases settle. One could speculate that it is to protect the child from trauma, or perhaps to protect the Church from the bad publicity and risk of high-verdict costs that could be experienced from a full trial. During the trial, the plaintiff will typically introduce expert witness testimony as to the cause of the injuries, which include emotional and psychological problems. As the Delaware Supreme Court held in reversing a lower court's exclusion of a psychologist's testimony, this evidence is "necessary to establish the psychological baseline for the general types of emotional, mental, spiritual and physical injuries that survivors of childhood sexual abuse suffer," and this expert testimony would tend to prove causation of plaintiff's injuries.[24]

3:6 ROLE OF PARISHES WITHIN A DIOCESE

Most cases do not name the parish as a separate defendant, but some may do so if the abuser was an assistant and was subject to the direction of a more senior priest who served as pastor during the period of the abuse. Below the level of the diocese, each Catholic parish is an entity administered by the individual pastors, but under the "corporation sole" format, the parishes are officially part of one civil corporation rather than each being separately incorporated. This is very significant in today's liability situation. In many dioceses, funds for the operation of each parish are "banked" with the master account of the diocese, and attributed to each parish's needs after a "tax" for the central administration is deducted.

This allocation of unitary authority and common fund use worked quite well back in the day of solid authoritarian central governance, when there were few external challenges to the diocese. None of the advocates for this simple format could have foreseen the huge contingent liability that multiple sexual predators with multiple victims could impose on the diocese.

Today, the parish corporation might be created as a distinct financial entity. For the purposes of the sexual abuse crisis, dioceses that are set up as corporations sole have a much greater ability to pay damages, and much more difficulty in arguing that individual parish assets are not actually under the direct control of the diocese, than those parishes that are all separate corporations under state law.

The consequence of unitary governance under the bishop and comingling of funds works for the benefit of the tort plaintiff: all the money of all those institutions

24. Sheehan v. Oblate of St. Francis de Sales, 15 A.3d 1247 (Del. 2011).

that are part of the corporation sole are considered to be in the single fund that is deemed to be available for paying off the verdicts or settlements after the abuse tort actions are completed. Separately incorporated pension funds, hospitals, and ministries run by religious orders are not included. Sometimes the plaintiff will use a forensic accountant to trace the funds from which the pool of settlement money can be derived.

If the diocesan assets are not large enough for the liabilities, the corporation sole is forced into bankruptcy (see Chapter 9) and the bankruptcy trustee applies the state corporation statutes to determine that the parish funds are available to be allocated to creditors of the diocese as a "bankrupt estate."

It could seem unfair that the members and donors of one parish, several hundred miles from the abuser's parish, will lose their funds for maintenance, expansion, teacher salaries, athletic activities, etc., or even have their parish closed and its real estate sold, because of the abuser. The simplicity of the corporation sole bites the diocese where it really hurts, and so it indirectly dissuades laypersons from making donations to parishes, where that parish had no role in any of the misdeeds of the abuser, or no vote on decisions made concerning the diocesan handling of the abuse claims.

3:7 DISCOVERY AND DEPOSITIONS TO GATHER EVIDENCE

Soon after the filing of the suit, the diocese receives the requests for depositions of witnesses: the alleged assailant, the diocesan personnel manager known as the "Vicar for Clergy," the bishop, and former officials who have served at the time of the alleged physical contact. There will be very detailed requests for records, assuming that the plaintiff's lawyer is experienced or has studied the work of other attorneys in similar cases.

The "discovery" phase of a lawsuit often includes maneuvering to avoid certain disclosures. These could include "protective orders" to bar the challenger from seeing the confidential personnel files of priests, or the diocesan files that Church law categorizes as secret files. Mismanagement of files on priest personnel was a problem for plaintiffs: "Sometimes the existence of records is denied, only to be produced after repeated demands. In some cases, officials have even stated that the church does not keep personnel records or have a record retention policy."[25] It was also a problem for bishops and administrators who could not accurately account for the allegations: "Cardinal Law at one point put the blame for the transfer of predator priests in part on an inadequate filing system."[26] Disputes inevitably arise over which issues can be raised in questioning of the bishop; the First Amendment protects religious expression, such as the sacramental practices of a religious faith. But the scope of the privilege for "confessional" disclosures, or which documents

25. Thomas Doyle, A.W.R.Sipe & Patrick Wall, Sex, Priests & Secret Codes: The Catholic Church's 2,000 Year Paper Trail of Sexual Abuse 193 (2006).
26. National Review Board, supra, 111.

on what issues can be excluded from discovery, involve months of cross-arguments among the opposing lawyers. There may be motions for protective orders before or even during an extended deposition of the bishop.

The timing of a lawsuit often frustrates laypersons who are angry about the "too slow" court process. Neither side wants to have these ugly confrontations drawn out over years. The attorney for the plaintiff has a mounting set of bills and no income from the contingent-fee case until eventual settlement or verdict, so the willingness to settle ripens as the case gets older. The diocese has an interest in reducing the harmful publicity and avoiding trial. If the alleged offender is still a priest, he wishes to get his reputation cleared by a speedy trial that results in a jury verdict against the malicious accuser. The attorneys for the insurance carrier have some incentive to be paid by the hour for many hours; the insurance company has an interest in withholding payment for as long as feasible. In most clergy sexual abuse lawsuits during the 1990s and 2000s, other lawsuits against the same diocese for other alleged assaults were pending as the first suit was being handled, so there was a "vicious cycle" of perverse incentives: dioceses feared to settle the early cases at a figure so high that it would induce later plaintiffs to demand even higher figures in settlement.

3:8 IDENTIFYING ASSETS.

As an aside, the reader should recognize that it may be particularly difficult for a lawyer suing a Catholic diocese to compute the value of the assets from which the verdict or settlement would be paid, and this opaque financial picture sometimes hinders the resolution of the case. Suing a commercial corporation is easier, as financial reports are accessible and can be audited by a forensic accountant. An easy error can result: from the viewpoint of a plaintiff's lawyer with no prior insight into the way Catholic church finances operate, the Church has unlimited funds and the individual priest-actor has very little. The pursuit of the diocesan assets is not as simple as tracing a food company's net shareholder value. Chapter 16 describes these issues in depth.

Church funding is medieval, traditional, variable, and opaque. Dioceses are charitable corporations that own property and have multiple "burses" funds and accounts. Individual parish congregations own property and have funds and accounts. In some instances these parish assets are deemed to be "owned" locally, in other instances to be under the control and direction of the bishop. Individual diocesan priests have few restrictions on their ownership of property and funds, unlike priests of religious orders who take a solemn vow of poverty; but it is likely that a diocesan priest has few assets and little individual reserve of wealth from which to pay an individual judgment. (Some cases involve dead or retired priests.) Most Catholic schools, hospitals, and nursing homes are separately incorporated. They and the assets of the religious orders would be outside the asset-capturing powers of the bankruptcy trustee or the sheriff for purposes of paying a judgment against the diocese.

The Vatican and the U.S. Conference of Catholic Bishops have funds and property, but they are not likely to be amenable to lawsuits asserting damages in a local case such as a molestation allegation from a Tennessee parish.[27] Each of your authors have experience in church-funding issues; each concedes the complex picture one would see from the outside, as a potential plaintiff's lawyer dreaming of huge damage awards. But "piercing the corporate veil" will be a challenge to the average plaintiff's attorney in the circumstances of a diocese. The records of the local diocese are discoverable but the Vatican records might be shielded by federal statutory immunities. The case law in the Ninth Circuit came closest to allowing these records to be searched; but the independent national status of the Vatican as a distinct national entity invokes some of the protections of the Foreign Sovereign Immunities Act.[28]

3:9 PRETRIAL MOTIONS

Motions for dismissal will be filed in the course of the lawsuit. Most news reporters and lay observers view these as mini-trials, but they are not. The case is only dismissed in the event that the evidence is so weak that there is no way a jury could find liability, and the barrier is quite low. Dismissal is also possible in the event that a state law, such as the "statute of limitations," prevents an older incident from being litigated years after the event.[29] These are discussed in a following chapter.

Hearings on the Church's motions to dismiss sometimes will draw renewed publicity to the case, which has probably been out of the news media for months or years. Dismissal for procedural issues is sometimes regarded as a "vindication" for the priest or diocese, but the plaintiff's counsel will explain it as an unfair aberration that could allow the violator to escape responsibility, especially with the statutes of limitations barriers faced by plaintiffs.

3:10 ATTRIBUTING LIABILITY TO THE DIOCESE

The biggest substantive issue that a plaintiff's attorney must face is the attribution of responsibility of a diocese for the misconduct of an individual priest. The diocese will move to dismiss for failure to state a claim on which relief against the diocese could be granted.

In some states, dioceses cannot be held liable for the "rogue" priest who has violated his church oaths, church law, and pastoral duties, under respondeat superior concepts. To protect against infringement on First Amendment rights, civil courts are reluctant to delve into the religious hierarchy's discipline, mercy, absolution, and

---

27. Doe v. Holy See, 557 F.3d 1066 (9th Cir. 2009), applying 28 U.S.C. § 1605(a)(5) (2010).
28. 28 U.S.C. § 1605 (2010).
29. See Chapter 5 infra.

other forms of moral supervision of the clergy.[30] In other states, the common law's classic principal-and-agent relationship is applied; the diocese could be held to have been negligent if it had reason to know that the priest was a sexual predator before the priest was assigned to the site where the misconduct allegedly occurred. The diocese is liable because its "agent" at the parish level was known to be likely to cause harm to children. The plaintiff often argues both ways: either the diocese knew of the abuser's background and sent him into contact with the plaintiff, or the diocese negligently failed to supervise its agents when sent into jobs that offered contact with young persons.

This duty plays out in different ways in different contexts. The Washington courts held that a church did not have to have specific advance knowledge that the adult was a child molester before allowing children to be supervised and accompanied by that adult.[31] The Dallas archdiocese knew before it ordained Father Rudy Kos that he had pedophile tendencies; this knowledge resulted in a huge liability verdict from a Texas jury.[32]

Direct negligent "supervision" is often a part of the plaintiff's case against the bishop. Decisions on reassignments and transfers, made by the bishop or his Vicar for Clergy, are alleged to have facilitated the particular misconduct that is at issue in the case. Catholics sometimes refer to tempting scenarios as "the occasions of sin" to be avoided. Notice of a prior allegation against a priest did not stop some bishops from assigning the priest to youth-filled parishes or schools. In some cases, active concealment and cover-up are alleged to have occurred, going beyond mere negligence into conscious participation in the decisions that led to the incident.

3:11 NEWS COVERAGE BEFORE TRIAL.

The hearing of a motion for dismissal airs in open court, before reporters and cameras in some cases, and it features revelations (and sometimes videotape of the depositions) about the degree of the bishop's personal knowledge of the misconduct, and the degree of involvement by diocesan officials in transferring the priest around several assignments after notice of his misconduct. The news media (guided by plaintiff's counsel) will tend to play up the extent of diocesan knowledge and control, with a "how could they have sent him to minister to children. . . ." slant.

The defense of the diocese often denies that it had knowledge of the risk prior to the abuse, or asserts that as of the time of the incident, expectations were that the priest who had previous accusations against him later had been "cured" through

---

30. James O'Reilly & Joanne Strasser, "Clergy Sexual Misconduct: Confronting the Difficult Constitutional and Institutional Liability Issues," 7 St. Thomas L. Rev. 1 (1994).

31. N.K. v. Corporation of Presiding Bishop of Church of Jesus Christ of Latter-Day Saints, 175 Wash. App. 517, 307 P.3d 730 (2013).

32. Mary Gail Frawley-O'Dea, Perversion of Power: Sexual Abuse in the Catholic Church (2007).

intensive inpatient therapy.[33] Such religious personnel may have received intensive counseling and group therapy in specialized facilities in New Mexico, Missouri, or elsewhere.[34] The diocese might have been told that the therapy worked and the priest would not reoffend.

That rehabilitation then would be offered as the rationale for not treating the offense as a criminal matter. Video of the bishop's deposition responding to questions regarding duties to report child abuse, or to notify police, may be played in the courtroom on the day when the motions are argued.

3:12 PRETRIAL SETTLEMENT DISCUSSIONS

If "material facts" remain in dispute and motions for dismissal are not granted, then the case is scheduled for trial. Settlement negotiations intensify as the case comes closer to the date of the trial. Some judges insist that mediation or other forms of negotiation be used before trial. It is at this point that a decision needs to be made by the bishop: settle and bear the short-term publicity, or risk a jury verdict that could bankrupt the diocese. Because so many settlements contain confidentiality provisions, we speculate but cannot prove that the diocese apologizes to the victim in words negotiated by opposing counsel, that a payment is made from the insurer and/or diocese to the victim, and that the victim agrees not to discuss its settlement amount. Of course, not all settlements follow this pattern, but it is possible that many have done so.

3:13 TRIAL OF A SEXUAL ABUSE CIVIL CASE

Trial commences with selection of a neutral jury, and then moves to a jury hearing the evidence. After opening statements paint the conflicting pictures of liability, the plaintiff testifies and is cross-examined. The treating psychologist and physician describe the patient's adverse effects from the alleged contact, and the patient's needs. The defense presents its case of why the diocese should not be forced to pay damages. The cross-examination of the priest and the bishop will be newsworthy reports in the local media.

After the plaintiff's evidence is presented, the defense typically moves for directed verdict, arguing that there is not sufficient evidence from which a reasonable jury could find the diocese liable for the misconduct and the subsequent events in the alleged "cover-up." The plaintiff responds that each element of negligence has been shown, and that the case is ready for the jury to resolve the disputed issues. If the motion for a directed verdict is not granted, the defense puts on its case, then

33. This would presumably be group therapy, with individual psychological counseling as an inpatient.

34. These therapeutic centers have been very controversial, in retrospect, for their effects on the priest and on the community.

closing statements are made by each side, the jury is "charged" by the judge with instructions on state law, and the jury retires to deliberate.

Some last-minute settlement offers may be made at this time, as a "last roll of the dice." Each side's lawyer is now familiar with the look of the jury and the signals the jurors and judge may have given. Plaintiffs' counsel also have much more of their own law firm funds invested in the case at this point in time, assuming that they operate on a contingent fee basis. But offers and demands often vary greatly so no settlement might be achieved. The jury then returns its verdict, typical post-trial motions are made, and the news media report the outcome.

On the courthouse steps, if the plaintiff wins before the jury as most jury trials have been won, dueling press conferences may be held. The lawyer for the diocese may obliquely threaten to declare bankruptcy, if the verdict was large. The plaintiff's family and his or her attorney claims vindication and invites other "victims" to come forward. Broadcast "talk show" presenters will invite the victim and attorney to explain their successful verdict. The insurer, the diocesan attorney, and the bishop then meet to discuss the prospects for a successful appeal.

3:14 APPEALS

An appeal is filed by the diocese with an appeal bond, and another cash settlement offer is made. The plaintiff's counsel is likely to be more receptive to the larger settlement figure offered at this stage, as the emotional sense of closure and vindication has been achieved for the person affected. Settlement is discussed in more detail, and the insurance carrier may offer its amount of maximum coverage, together with further funds from the diocesan reserves. If no settlement results, the appeal is argued and decided; the plaintiff wins the amount awarded by the jury or is told to go through a new trial because of legal errors made in the course of the initial trial. The appellate court decision sometimes "borrows" legal principles from other states, extends prior case precedents in this state, or otherwise declares what the precedent of law should be in that state. Reviewing the actual appellate case law, some defenders assert that the trial court erred on First Amendment entanglement with religion; other defenders continue to fight the weakness of memories; others debate the admissibility of expert evidence; but virtually all hammer at the statute of limitations defense. Outcomes vary; until a U.S. Supreme Court case at some future date, we cannot predict one uniform appellate direction for these clergy abuse cases.

3.15 FINAL JUDGMENT

Unless the case has been settled, the final judgment after appeal is entered into the record, and a check in payment of the verdict and for certain court costs is paid by the defense to the plaintiff's lawyer (unless a bankruptcy has forced some lower amount in settlement). This may come from an old insurance policy covering the period of the sexual incident, from diocesan budget reserves, from a "tax" placed on the financial accounts of the parishes, from a pool of funds put up by other dioceses,[35] or from the sale of land or buildings. Payment is made and the case file is closed.

The successful plaintiff's attorney pays its bank for the loans that funded the lawsuit, and then gets new clients and files a new case, or others follow his or her lead and demand a larger settlement amount from the diocese.

35. See Chapter 8.

CHAPTER 4

cⱴɔ

Participants in the Clergy Abuse Case

4:1 PARTICIPANTS

It may be helpful for our understanding of the dynamics of the court proceedings to explain the likely players who will be involved in the clergy sexual abuse claims or lawsuits.

4:2 VICTIMS

The young person affected by the alleged abuse is first and foremost in the center of this set of circumstances. He or she is likely to have had friendly contact with the priest, involvement with activities together, and a sense of positive appreciation, in some cases affection, for the attentive concerns expressed by the priest. Other resources in the bibliography of this text can explain the psychological theory of interaction by sexual predators known as "grooming" the young person for the eventual request for sexual contact. These cases are rarely if ever a one-time rape by a stranger who happens to be a priest.[1]

The victims' accusations of clergy sexual misconduct are of two general categories: contemporaneous or recollected. If contemporaneous, a parent or guardian who learns of the child's or teen's allegation, soon after it has occurred, is likely to act promptly to contact police and the bishop of the diocese.

In some cases, the parent will meet first with detectives who are assigned to police sex crime units. The detectives will bring in a social worker specialist from the county or state juvenile protective services organization. The instances in which the parent of the victim went to the bishop to complain were at one time most

---

1. The 2011 U.S. Conference of Catholic Bishops–funded Report by scholars at John Jay College, described in Chapter 1 of this text, offers these evaluations of the patterns of abuse.

numerous, but we can speculate that the massive negative publicity the Church has received in recent years has changed this pattern. News media coverage about the Church would tend to deter parents from the prior patterns of communicating directly with bishops or their representatives.

In the second category of recollected abusive conduct, an adult who comes forward with an allegation of past sexual misconduct against a priest may be more sophisticated and is certainly more angry than the child that he or she once was. The adult charging that a priest had caused his or her past sexual abuse will, today, not likely contact the bishop directly. Today, these adults who once had been victims tend to speak through the civil law system with a lawsuit, which is likely to be the first time that the diocese learns of the alleged abuse. Or the adult victim may bring a criminal charge to the police, who may or may not be able to prosecute the case, because of the age of the offense relative to the statute of limitations for criminal charges of sexual assault.

We note for the reader that false claims of sexual contact have sometimes been made against priests for malicious reasons, and some from mistaken identities. The short-lived accusations against Cardinal Joseph Bernardin, later retracted, were an example of such false charges. But the majority of the cases that have reached the stage of a court trial have been supported by some evidence in the record. Prosecutors recognize cases of special political risk must be handled cautiously, and a weak case would be declined rather than risk news media criticism of the prosecutor's ill motives toward the Church.

4:3 VICTIM ADVOCATES AND FAMILY

If the victim is a minor at the time that the abuse is made known, then making this abuse known will be difficult. Emotional support for the young person should come primarily from the parents and other family members, but in a number of cases, the sexual predator selected the young person from the most dysfunctional background who appears most in need of the strength and affection that the clergy person promises.

For younger persons who disclose the abuse, it is likely to be an angry parent who directs the response to the reports of sexual conduct, if the report occurs soon after the event. The parents will be essential witnesses supporting the young person's claim of sexual abuse and the claim of damages. No general statement can be made about the motivations and feelings that bring the parent to the lawyer or the police with the complaint of sexual abuse; individual cases vary so greatly that we cannot generalize.

In the community there may be a victim's advocate program aligned with the local prosecutor, and/or a charity specializing in supportive guidance for victims of sex crimes. The more progressive dioceses have implemented the Dallas norms with an advocate for child protection who can assist the family if no other intermediary is involved.

4:4 THE ACCUSED ABUSER

The individual defendant in a church abuse case is the priest or religious ministry person, such as a religious brother or sister or nun, who is accused of sexual misconduct. The Catholic Church has three ranks of ordained clergy: bishops, priests, and deacons. Those clergy who are incardinated to (licensed to act in) a diocese can include persons with various titles, including auxiliary bishops, coadjutor bishops, monsignors (an honorary title for some priests), priests, and transitional or permanent deacons. All of them are accountable under their vow of "obedience" to the bishop of their particular geographic diocese.

There are two types of priests. Diocesan priests are assigned within a particular diocese. Religious[2] priests belong to an order such as the Jesuits. Approximately one third of U.S. priests are members of religious orders, not subject to a diocesan bishop as are the diocesan priests.[3] These priests are ordained in a religious order such as the Franciscans; they report to a religious "superior" such as an abbot, a prior, or a provincial superior. Depending on the institute, the leader may in turn report to the national or international head of his religious congregation. Abuse charges have been made against some of these priests,[4] with some orders settling with the claimants.

In the Roman Catholic tradition, an unmarried man becomes a priest only after completion of three steps: seminary training, the rite of Ordination (known as the sacrament of Holy Orders) to the diaconate and then to the priesthood, and the simultaneous acceptance by the bishop of that man as a deacon, then a priest of his diocese (known as the act of incardination). The majority of Catholic priests serve in dioceses, of which there are approximately three thousand internationally. Several hundred religious orders (Jesuits, Dominicans, and Franciscans are best known) have several thousand priests, about one third of U.S. priests. The authoritative annual book, *The Catholic Directory*, is an available guide to the dioceses, parishes, and other structures of the Church in the United States.

Priests can be assigned by bishops to be a "pastor" or associate pastor of a particular geographical parish; there are 18,500 parishes in the U.S. Church. Religious orders of priests could also be entrusted with the care of a geographic parish within a diocese. It is also possible for both diocesan and religious priests to work directly for the bishop in a specific administrative or judicial role, for example as Vicar General, Episcopal Vicar, or Judicial Vicar, or to run a particular office such as the diocesan education or outreach offices.

Deacons are males who have had theological training and are ordained as clergy but are not priests. "Permanent" deacons are often married and are career workers

---

2. "Religious" is a term of art used for a person who is a member of a religious order.

3. National Review Board for the Protection of Children & Young People, A Report on the Crisis in the Catholic Church in the United States 123 (2004) (hereinafter "National Review Board").

4. See e.g., Baselice v. Franciscan Friars Assumption BVM Province Inc., 879 A.2d 270 (Pa. App. 2005).

or retired men who perform some of the duties of the parish priest but are primarily ordained for service to the diocese and to the bishop. "Transitional" deacons are men who are in the process of becoming priests, and who are ordained to the office of deacon prior to their ordination as a priest. Deacons cannot perform some of the key sacramental tasks, such as consecrating the Eucharist, absolving sins, administering certain blessings, etc.

The religious orders allow their members to vote for a superior, who oversees the work of the order in a particular geography. In almost every male religious community, the leader is required by their statutes to be a priest. These priests perform managerial and administrative tasks for their order, for a defined period of time in that office,

Religious brothers (males with vows of poverty, chastity, and obedience who have not been ordained as priests) or religious sisters and nuns take consecrated vows after training by their respective religious orders, and are assigned to a "community," which may be a parish, a school, or a charitable or healthcare institution. The majority are active in their assigned community, while some are contemplative cloistered monks or nuns who live in monasteries. Sexual abuse cases against sisters or nuns have infrequently been brought in the United States, and there are no firm statistics on what percentage of claims involved religious women.[5]

4:5 THE DIOCESAN BISHOP

Another likely targeted defendant is the bishop for the diocese in which the abuse occurred. Bishops are clergy who have been selected and consecrated under Church law. Most bishops are heads of dioceses, and the diocesan priests owe allegiance to them by vows of obedience. There are approximately 3,000 dioceses worldwide, and when Vatican and other central administrators and diplomatic representatives of the pope are counted, there may be 3,500 bishops worldwide. A smaller number are appointed to larger city posts and are archbishops; an even smaller number, perhaps 80 worldwide, hold the rank of cardinal, and are eligible to vote in a "conclave" among the candidates for pope after the death of a sitting pope. There are also bishops called coadjutor or auxiliary bishops who are consecrated to assist the diocesan bishop in fulfilling his ministerial and administrative duties. Coadjutor bishops are specifically appointed to take over the role of the bishop when the incumbent retires; auxiliary bishops are appointed simply to aid the functions of the diocesan bishop, typically in a very large diocese.

Church law empowers the diocesan bishop to manage all affairs of the Church in a geographic area, identified under the name of the city in which the bishop's cathedral is located (e.g., Diocese of Cleveland). State law of nonprofit corporations defines the legal entity of the diocese (e.g., "Roman Catholic Bishop of Doeville, a corporation sole"). The diocesan priests who report to the bishop are said to be "incardinated" under his authority, but operate in their respective parish assignments

---

5. One Star v. Sisters of St. Francis, 752 N.W.2d 668 (S.D. 2008).

with considerable administrative autonomy as "pastors." The bishop has authority to assign, reassign, or withdraw a posting for a priest, though if a pastor objects to being moved from a parish, the pastor could appeal the bishop's decision, and then the bishop must conduct a formal process to move him. This process could end up being adjudicated by the Vatican.

When the review board selected by the U.S. Conference of Catholic Bishops studied the problems of concealment of clergy sexual abuse, they noted that some witnesses they interviewed revealed a chilling rationale for inaction: "[P]riests either explicitly or implicitly threatened to reveal compromising information about the bishop if the bishop took steps against the priest.... [A]ny priest who believes that there is a basis upon which he could be subject to blackmail should not allow himself to be elevated to bishop or placed in any other position of authority."[6]

The apologetic statements of some bishops have indicated their regret over the past assertions of "clericalism," an elite sense that bishops can have special rights over the needs of common people.[7] This is a policy disagreement over the exercise of power within the Church and not a legal issue. In 2011, a bishop observed that this past spirit of clericalism "is a direct violation of human dignity. In the case of child abuse, it is an attitude that has grown deaf to what the Scriptures tell us about the special place children have...When we realize how highly God holds children, it is hard to do anything but respect and cherish them and to abhor anything that uses and abuses them."[8]

4:6 ROLES OF THE VATICAN

But bishops do not have absolute authority under Church law; that is reserved for the pope. The total removal of a priest from duties as a priest requires the concurrence of the Vatican, acting for the pope. And while a priest who is a member of a religious congregation is assigned by his superiors to a post within a diocese, it is the superior and not the bishop who is responsible for the priest's activities and for his reassignment.

The case law and legal arguments have differentiated between acts of the bishop individually, and acts or failure to act by the bishop in his role as head of the diocese. Some bishops have resigned for sexual adventures with adults[9] and at least one with a minor boy.[10] If an allegation is made that the bishop had engaged in sexual abuse

6. National Review Board, supra, 111.

7. George B. Wilson SJ, Clericalism: The Death of Priesthood (2008).

8. Bishop Blase Cupich, The Bishops' Priorities, America Magazine 13, 15 (May 30, 2011).

9. The archbishop of Santa Fe resigned after prior adult female relationships were exposed. Boston Globe Investigative Staff, Betrayal: The Crisis in the Catholic Church 42 (Boston Globe, 2003).

10. The bishop of Palm Beach, Florida resigned after allegations of prior sexual misconduct were aired. "Palm Beach Bishop Admits to Sexual Misconduct, Resigns," Orlando Sentinel (Mar. 9, 2002).

with a minor, as has been the case in several instances,[11] the amended national Charter for the Protection of Children and Young People requires that the apostolic nuncio (the pope's ambassador to the United States) and local police be notified.[12]

A debate has continued under U.S. law about attaching tort liability to the pope, predicated upon the principal/agent relationship of the bishop and the pope.[13] Vatican oversight of the work of the dioceses is continuing, and every five years, every bishop must meet with the pope at the Vatican. But the Vatican has a complex relationship to the diocese,[14] not a straight line as in a major corporation dealing with a subsidiary company.[15] The Vatican has asserted, in briefs filed in defense of claims directly against it, that local bishops have autonomy and are not employees of the Vatican.[16] The outside counsel for the Vatican argued in one case that civil law norms of employee status were not met for bishops, because they are not paid or directly supervised on a daily basis by the Vatican, and that civil courts should avoid analysis of the Church doctrine of obedience because it would entangle the state in matters of religious doctrine.[17] That case was later settled. In another case in the Ninth Circuit, the Church argued that the priest was not selected, paid, or supervised by the Vatican, so the Vatican did not have liability under exceptions to the Foreign Sovereign Immunities Act.[18] Because the victim failed to allege the Vatican had day-to-day control of the priest, the plaintiff's claim was dismissed on remand.[19] However, plaintiffs' lawyer Jeffrey Anderson has concluded from two decades of suing the dioceses that "every single case demonstrates that control is at the top."[20] In an American abuse case, the bishop of Louisville was asserted to have a principal/agent relationship with the Vatican, in a controversial case arising in Kentucky.[21] That case was later abandoned for unrelated reasons, so the issue of Vatican adoption or initiation of policies remains to be resolved.[22]

11. Leon J. Podles, Sacrilege: Sexual Abuse in the Catholic Church (2008).

12. Dan Morris Young, "Bishops Tweak Child Protection Charter," Nat'l Cath. Rptr. 18 (June 24, 2011).

13. Doe v. Holy See, 557 F.3d 1066 (9th Cir. 2009).

14. For an experienced journalistic critic's view, see Jason Berry & Gerald Renner, Vows of Silence (2004).

15. A useful study is John Allen, All the Pope's Men 224 (2004).

16. John L. Allen, Jr., "Plaintiffs Drop Lawsuit against Vatican," Nat'l Cath. Rptr. 14 (Aug. 20, 2010).

17. Associated Press, "Vatican Defense Centers on Employment Status of Bishops and a 1962 Document," Wash. Post (May 18, 2010).

18. Doe v. Holy See, 557 F.3d 1066 (9th Cir. 2009), cert. den. 130 S. Ct. 3497 (2010).

19. Doe v. Holy See. 2011 Westlaw 1541275 (D. Or. 2011) (limited discovery allowed re: priest's laicization but not the removals of other sex-abuse priests.) (Vatican's defense attorney was T. M. Christ.)

20. Monica Davey, "A Frenzied Pace for Lawyer behind Vatican Suits," N.Y. Times (Apr. 27, 2010).

21. "Lawsuit Tests Relations between Bishops, Rome," 20 Cath. World Report 15 (July 2010).

22. Peter Smith, "Kentucky Plaintiffs Give Up Sex Abuse Case against Vatican," Louisville Courier-Journal (Aug. 10, 2010); Allen, "Plaintiffs Drop Lawsuit against Vatican," supra.

The issue of Vatican accountability for the actions of one individual priest has been raised but generally without success. Geographic distance, layers of hierarchical supervision, and an aggressive defense policy have made the attributions of responsibility to the Vatican quite difficult for the plaintiffs. It is possible that a future case with the right set of facts may lead to such an attribution of collective responsibility between the diocese and the Vatican, but as of 2014 no such decision has been achieved.

In some cases, the person who is the bishop responsible for handling abuse cases has acknowledged failures; an Irish cardinal said that he was "ashamed" of the role he played in forcing secrecy oaths on two boys who had described the crimes of a serial pedophile, and did not go to police.[23]

Whether justified by the facts or not, public anger in recent years has been directed to the bishops who led the Church during the critical decades. A psychologist member of the National Review Board said in 2010, "People are enraged by what they see as a coverup, by no high-ranking Catholic clergy being fired."[24] Resignations occurred but no "firing" was evident.

Chapter 14 on defenses addresses the ways in which the Vatican and its diplomatic status have been utilized in defense of abuse lawsuits.

4:7 THE VICAR FOR CLERGY

A third potential defendant is the priest who served as the diocesan personnel manager, often titled the "Vicar for Clergy." He is usually a veteran priest who has been an experienced and trusted aide to the bishop. This person can be named in the lawsuit as a codefendant to hold him accountable for the decision to transfer, assign, or reassign the errant priest, and naming him as a defendant aids in the event that the bishop denies he knew about the transfer(s) given to a priest after the past pattern of abuse became known.

This previously obscure administrative role is now a hot seat in the abuse-related litigation. Deposition and discovery requests are common. The criminal indictment and conviction of a Philadelphia priest, for his transfer of known predator priests, charged him with endangering the welfare of children.[25] He argued successfully that as he did not personally supervise children, he could not be charged with endangering them, and after 18 months in state prison he was granted a new trial.[26] Another Vicar for Clergy was granted immunity from prosecution for his

---

23. John Burns & Rachel Donadio, "Irish Cardinal Apologizes for Role in Abuse Scandal," N.Y. Times (Mar. 17, 2010).

24. Patricia Zapor, "Public Anger at Catholic Church over Abuse Prevails despite Changes," Cath. News Serv. (May 7, 2010).

25. Jon Hurdle, "Grand Jury: Archdiocese Covered Up Further Abuse," N.Y. Times (Feb. 11, 2011).

26. Maryclaire Dale, "Suit: Pa. Catholic Leaders Failed to Protect Kids," Wash. Post (Feb. 14, 2011); and see "People," Nat'l Cath. Rptr. 2 (Jan. 17, 2014).

testimony before a grand jury.[27] Many of the priests who had been criminally convicted were transferred among parishes in the months or years after allegations of sexual abuse became known, in a pattern that a Church critic described as "the church shuttled abusing priests among parishes and dioceses with no notice to families and the laity."[28] Holding the diocesan officials liable may or may not be viable, as the Philadelphia case will demonstrate.

Is this denial of responsibility genuine or artificial? Are the records of the diocese complete? Catalogued? In one place? "In some cases, [diocesan] officials have even stated that the church does not keep personnel records or have a record retention policy."[29]

4:8 THE DIOCESAN STAFF WHO RESPONDED TO ALLEGATIONS

When a claim of abuse is made, the person alleged to be responsible for the misconduct can be identified (or exonerated) at the local level, for example by a private investigator or police intervention. The report of the alleged abuse is sometimes made first by letter or visit to the bishop or the superior of the religious order. The responses vary, as the remainder of this book will demonstrate, and the worst diocesan responses were "cynical and callous" as the Philadelphia grand jury found in 2011.[30]

Typically, the bishop or superior will then bring the Vicar for Clergy for a meeting with the diocesan temporal affairs director and the diocesan civil and canonical legal advisors, who will be involved in deciding on the response. The decision within the diocese is solely that of the bishop, who may suspend the priest and begin the process of investigating the allegation. After the inquiry is completed, the bishop may deem the allegation unsubstantiated, or he may send the case to his diocesan review board to make a determination if the allegation is credible. The review board is to assess the allegations and to advise the bishop in "his determination of a cleric's suitability for ministry."[31]

The Church's systems for victim advocacy and the protection of persons making the allegations should be in place when the allegation first comes to the diocese. Education to avoid the crossing of boundaries is part of the ongoing remedial efforts.[32] Church protocols for handing new allegations of past sexual misconduct should presumably follow the patterns of diocesan compliance with the norms agreed to by American bishops at their 2002 meeting in Dallas.

27. Associated Press New Break, "LA Monsignor Called before Grand Jury" (Dec. 22, 2009).

28. Marci Hamilton, What the Clergy Abuse Crisis Has Taught Us, 195 America Magazine 17 (Sept. 25, 2006).

29. Thomas Doyle, A.W.R.Sipe & Patrick Wall, Sex, Priests & Secret Codes: The Catholic Church's 2,000 Year Paper Trail of Sexual Abuse 193 (2006).

30. Report of the Philadelphia County Grand Jury (2011).

31. Bishop Blase Cupich, The Bishops' Priorities, America Magazine 13, 14 (May 30, 2011) (suggesting need to clarify this directive).

32. Id. at 13, 14.

Because the norms were strongly suggested but not required of each bishop, some diocesan responses were much less effective or nonexistent. Some dioceses refused and continue to refuse to follow the norms (a reflection of their sense of autonomy from national governance), but most do so willingly.

The Philadelphia grand jury's 2011 report pointed out that the victim sometimes is left without an advocate during the Church's investigation, and in one case, the victim released his confidential mental health record to the diocese because he "mistakenly believed (staff) were his advocates."[33] Others such as the Milwaukee archdiocese have preprinted guides for use by the persons alleging that they were abused by diocesan priests.[34]

4:9 THE LIABILITY INSURANCE CARRIER

The most financially interested party when the claim is first filed is the insurance carrier whose liability policies had insured the diocese during the period when the alleged abuse has occurred. The Catholic Church had once been a desirable customer for underwriters; the insurers had a relatively small claims load in past coverages of diocesan liability, compared to their retail or manufacturing companies' insured accounts. Then the clergy sexual abuse allegations in the 1980s and 1990s produced a sudden rush of action to leave the church market before the revelations of sexual abuse brought out more claims.

This response led to a change in the standard liability insurance policies for churches. Led by the model forms created by the industry group ISO (the Insurance Services Office),[35] revisions to liability policies for churches since 1987 have excluded the claims of harm resulting from sexual abuse. Insurance carriers still are dealing with the older incidents being reported recently. The carriers may deny claims in some circumstances in which the insurer asserted that the diocese knowledge of the priest's propensity to abuse, arguing that the insurance was only for accidents, whereas the misconduct of this priest occurred to a degree that makes the sexual abuse more predictable to occur, and less of an accidental or unexpected harm. These are very fact-specific disputes.

4:10 THE NEWS MEDIA ROLE

The news media coverage of priest sexual abuse has been global, intense, and intriguing to watch...unless you care about the long-term consequences for the Roman Catholic Church. No participant in a clergy sexual abuse case can avoid the

33. Philadelphia County Grand Jury, Report on Archdiocese of Philadelphia 105 (2011).

34. Archdiocese of Milwaukee Metropolitan Tribunal, Trials According to the Canon Law of the Roman Catholic Church (2011).

35. See insurance Services Office website on the Web at http://www.iso.com/Products/Overview-of-ISO-Products-and-Services/ISO-s-Policy-Language-and-Rules.html.

sideshow of news media reporter questioning, often speculation, and one can sympathize with the many thousands of innocent priests whose personal integrity has been questioned from audiences seeing reports of the scandals. Critics can assert that the for-profit broadcast and newspaper coverage has boosted their audience's appetite for scandal, but at the cost of objectivity and balance. These discussions involve more of the moral and policy arguments which are beyond the scope of this chapter.

4:11 DEFENSE COUNSEL

"Good news and bad news" might be a brief characterization of the diocesan lawyer's response to the victim's report of abuse: there will be a response, and the victim will be invited to meet with the diocesan attorney at some point during the complaint review. At this stage the victim and/or parent might perceive the diocese as being part of the solution, capable of justly responding to the abuse case with appropriate action against the abuser. Unfortunately, we know that in many cases the victim and his or her family were misled, and the crimes were concealed in an "unholy alliance among Church officials, victims, and the attorneys."[36]

Legal defense notions may vary from the ideal. Digging into the plaintiff's background, often with diocesan counselors asking for signed releases before suit was filed, became a predictable defense tactic. The subpoenas by Church lawyers to therapists and abuse counselors caused a "firestorm of protests from survivors, victim advocates, and mental health professionals who perceived the deposition of therapists as an act of re-abuse."[37] There is no doubt that hardball tactics were employed to defend the bishop and diocese.

Lawyers will inevitably be involved when an incoming allegation of sexual abuse is received, because of the magnitude of the dollar risk to the diocese. Older patterns of bishops seeming to ignore complaints about the alleged offense produced frustration, litigation, and worse, scandal. In retrospect, those who complained early through Church channels fared worst of all. More complaints will be heard more carefully and handled through proper channels if the claimant's lawyer is involved (though there have been some bishops who have properly and compassionately handled these cases without lawyers). Documentation, detailed inquiries, review of personnel records, and interviews of those with some knowledge of the events surrounding the date(s) of the alleged abuse, are all benefits of attorney involvement. Some bishops in older times might otherwise have summarily dismissed the claimant's charge as unrealistic and unreasonable.

But the more aggressive defense lawyers and their bishop clients drew great antipathy from the news media, the victims, and the general public. An editorial

---

36. Boston Globe Investigative Staff, Betrayal: The Crisis in the Catholic Church 47 (2002).

37. Mary Frawley-O'Dea, Perversion of Power: Sexual Abuse in the Catholic Church 135 (2007).

in a Catholic journal expressed this well: "Telling bishops not to talk to victims or the press, not to apologize and not to pay for therapy until a case was settled, was not only un-Christian but legally counterproductive. Stonewalling and taking the offensive against victims angered both victims and the public, with the result that victims retained lawyers and juries wanted to punish the church with high damages."[38]

Ethics rules require a diocesan attorney to "zealously" protect the interests of the diocese. A fine line needs to be recognized: the diocese can counterattack against the claim of abuse, fight hard, and sometimes embarrass the claimant (and itself). But doing so will trigger the harshly negative backlash that worsens the situation. The best justification offered for "hardball" litigators' aggressive defense[39] was that such means were "necessary to protect the assets of the church in order to keep dioceses running."[40] The best reply came from the 2004 report of the bishops' National Review Board for the Protection of Children and Young People: "(M)any dioceses and orders made disastrous pastoral decisions relying on attorneys who failed to adapt their tactics to account for the unique role and responsibilities of the church."[41]

4:12 THE SUSPENDED OR DISMISSED PRIEST OR MEMBER OF A RELIGIOUS ORDER

So what happens to the priest who is accused? If the claim was of criminal sexual contact that had occurred shortly before the report to police, the priest would be arrested and charged. If the claim is of alleged sexual misconduct that occurred more than a few years before the report, prosecutors would probably not bring the case to indictment, because the statute of limitations period would have expired (e.g., three years for felonies). The bad publicity about the sexual offense would not itself trigger criminal charges, unless the charge came soon enough after the sexual misconduct to permit a timely criminal trial.

For any sexual abuse claim, the priest would be offered the opportunity to provide an explanation. Later chapters in this text describe the canon law steps of church investigation and church hearings. Under the 2002 Dallas norms of the U.S. Bishops Conference, officially titled "Charter for the Protection of Children and Young People," annual audits are performed of diocesan responses to sexual abuse allegations.[42] Each diocese may have its own program to implement the norms. Typically, the accused priest should be immediately transferred away from ministering around youths, or that may be done after the diocesan review board has

38. Editorial, "Victims," 189(9) America Magazine 3 (Sept. 29, 2003).
39. Donald Cozzens, Sacred Silence: Denial and the Crisis in the Church (2002).
40. Frawley-O'Dea, supra, 135.
41. National Review Board, supra, 120.
42. See Annual Report on Web at http://www.usccb.org/issues-and-action/child-and-youth-protection/upload/annual-report-on-the-implementation-of-the-charter-for-the-protection-of-children-and-young-people-2012.pdf.

found the claim to be credible. An accused priest/religious order member who is not in local police custody might be suspended from ministry. The investigation by church officials that could lead to removal from priesthood, called the "laicization" process, is discussed in Chapter 28.

After a claim has been received and investigated, the Essential Norms call for an inquiry, and if a claim is deemed credible the diocese is required to report the abuse allegation to the police. It may be that the police will not move ahead toward prosecution if the case would be dismissed in court as being beyond the statute of limitations. A civil damages claim is likely, and the diocese may want to have the abuser under sufficient church supervision for him to testify in the civil damages case. At a minimum, the diocese will want to have some contact, to assure itself that further abuse activities will be deterred, while the lengthy Vatican process of laicization is underway. If the 2010 reports are correct that about five thousand priests and religious brothers have been "credibly accused of sexually violating minors," then those who have been removed from contact with young people should be accommodated under some form of oversight or restricted assignments.[43] In 2011–2012, 384 priests were dismissed from the clerical state or "defrocked."[44] Later chapters deal with the issues of investigating priest personnel under canon law.[45] But it makes sense that the diocese should be able to contact the person who has been removed from ministry, at a minimum to address later allegations of similar abuse with other claimants. The diocese continues to pay the salary and living costs until the priest is dismissed, resigns, or is granted "laicization" (cessation of priest status) by the Vatican. This cost was approximately $10,000,000 in 2010.[46]

43. Mary Frawley-O'Dea, "Where Are the Perpetrators?," Nat'l Cath. Rptr. 28 (Aug. 20, 2010).

44. John Heilprin, "Pope Defrocked 400 Priests in 2 Years," Associated Press (Jan. 20, 2014).

45. Chapter 24, infra.

46. Nancy O'Brien, "New Sex Abuse Allegations Down Slightly in 2010; Costs Continue to Rise," Cath. News Serv. (Apr. 11, 2011).

PART THREE

Handling Abuse Claims

CHAPTER 5

༄

Delays and Limitations in Clergy Abuse Cases

5:1 EXPOSING WEAKNESSES IN THE SYSTEM

The greatest lesson for American civil law from the clergy sexual abuse scandal has been the revelation that our society's remedy for fighting predatory sexual misconduct by our most especially trusted adults is flawed. Our remedies in tort recovery, and to a lesser extent, in criminal prosecution of the predator, are blocked by the intersection of facts and law, here a long-lasting, shamed secrecy, and the states' barrier of the "statutes of limitations." These are laws that prevent civil injury (tort) or criminal abuse cases from being presented after a defined period of years has passed.

In many cases, clergy members who have violated public as well as moral law codes have managed to deter the child or teen from disclosing the facts of the abuse. Inducing the child to keep secret the past abuse or the pattern of dependency on the abuser often means that the delay serves the abuser's purposes: the state statute of limitations for remedies has passed by the time the abuse victim feels safe enough to make the report. The abuser escapes, and this frustration breeds a desire to allow for some retrospective remedy in these cases as a special exception.

This chapter deals with the civil law's statute of limitations in U.S. states. The Church disciplinary process has its own limitation system, modified in 2010 as a result of the abuse cases.[1]

5:2 BACKGROUND

Historically, the common law trials of tort (injury) claims were a search for truth regarding past events, where the litigating parties disagreed about who had done what

---

1. John Allen, Jr., "Vatican Revises Church Law on Abuse Cases," Nat'l Cath. Rptr. 1 (July 23, 2010).

in the event to cause harm. The conventional wisdom has been that statutes of limitations are a helpful discipline for the errors brought on by fading memories of witnesses.

Statutes of limitations have a useful role in most tort litigation. Before statutes were adopted, the common law line of court decisions did not decide on a uniform, specific number of years when damages claims were "too old" for the facts to be reliably remembered. (This was the era before computerized digital surveillance cameras, DNA, and similar truth-verification devices.) In the absence of a line of court decisions determining the age of memories within which lawsuit witnesses remained credible, state legislation was adopted to provide a fixed point when the age of a claim would reach its "limitations." That type of state statute would name the cause of action (e.g., assault, sexual misconduct, etc.) and the years allowed for the cases to be brought, and thereby would exclude the more aged cases that could no longer be brought in that state's courts.

5:3   RATIONALES FOR LIMITATIONS

Human experience with failures of accurate memory supports the common sense rationale for a decision limiting the older lawsuit claims to a certain period of years, before memories of eyewitnesses and participants fade. In the legislative bodies, enacting these civil statutes of limitations has reflected a form of compromise between defendants and their insurers, and advocates for the allegedly injured plaintiffs. If you are hurt, the law requires that you sue while the facts surrounding that injury are still well known. The legislature in many states selected two years for tort actions such as auto accidents or products liability calamities, as the statute of limitations for personal injury claims. Lobbyists for insurance companies worked diligently to protect these statutes from being lengthened or repealed, because a change that would extend the right to sue would mean more claims and more payouts. Today it is well settled that an act of physical injury, rape, forcible intercourse, etc. "starts the clock running" on the window of time for a lawsuit to be filed against the offender.

5:4   DELAYS AND TOLLING

Police who deal with the sex crimes field are aware that shame, confusion, mistrust, and avoidance of conflict can prevent some victims from reporting the encounter with the abuser. The police will decline to investigate an alleged rape that has occurred in the years past at a date earlier than the statute of limitations.

Courts that are faced with older claims of injury want to do justice. The legislative body has fixed the time for suits, so courts can use their prudent flexibility to determine when the clock starts ("accrual") for an injury event such as unlawful physical contact. The statutes dealing with delayed discovery apply to *accrual* of a cause of action, but do not *toll* the limitation period.[2]

2. Hearndon v. Graham, 767 So. 2d 1179 (Fla. 2000).

The courts also adopt case law about "tolling," or the suspension of the running of this exclusive period of time, when it is appropriate because of unusual events. Some courts have considered "equitable tolling." It was properly applied against a diocese when a teen reported sexual abuse by a religious school counselor, and the school agreed to pay for therapy but allegedly failed to disclose the counselor's history of misconduct and threatened a defamation suit if the plaintiff told anyone else about the abuse.[3] After passage of the statutory period, if these exceptions did not apply, the tort claims will be dismissed because of the statute of limitations.

5:5 WHEN THE PERIOD BEGINS

The "accrual date" for starting the two- or three-year period that is allowed by state law for lawsuits about an injury is the date of the wounding or harm, such as negligent leg surgery or an auto collision. But courts have recognized in medical injury claims an exception for belated "discovery" of who has caused the harm. Two surgeons operated inside the same hospital surgical room on January 10, 2011; only one is sued in a lawsuit in June 2012; on January 15, 2013, the injured person finally learns that it was the other surgeon who made the mistake, but by that time the two years have passed. In medical cases, the date when the plaintiff learned from a reliable medical source that his injury was caused by X's mistake, is the date on which the two-year statute has "accrued" for the lawsuit against X.

Shifting the accrual date can also be seen in cases of chemical toxic exposure; the date of "discovery" by reliable medical opinion that a patient's lung disease or cancer was caused by a product such as asbestos may be several years after the patient worked in the factory using that chemical. These cases boost the accrual date to the discovery date, not the date of actual exposure to the chemical.

The term "discovery" as an exception to limitations means "discovery that psychological harm occurring during adulthood was caused by an act of childhood molestation."[4]

A special feature of some, but not all, states' limitation statutes is the extension of the limiting statute's "accrual" for a child injury to begin when the child reaches the age of 18.[5] The "discovery" of what had happened as a child is deemed to be possible once the child becomes an adult. If the child was harmed at age 10, the two-year statute would begin to run when the child reached 18. For most physical injuries this does not matter; suit will be filed soon after the collision or assault has occurred. But where the child was shamed into silence or coerced to be quiet, there is an option in these states: their law allows the accrual to begin at age 18 and the window of time for litigation moves the closing "bar date" to age 20 (18 plus 2). In a few cases, the 20-year-old plaintiff has sued for sexual assault that occurred at age

---

3. Schauer v. Diocese of Green Bay, 687 N.W.2d 766 (Wis. App. 2004).

4. Roe 58 v. Doe 1, 120 Cal. Rptr. 3d 311 (Cal. App. 2 Dist., 2011).

5. Russell G. Donaldson, Annotation: "Running of Limitations against Action for Civil Damages for Sexual Abuse of Child," 9 A.L.R. 5th 321 (1993).

12. If that individual waited until age 25, his or her window of time for suing would expire. However, New Jersey moved the date to age 30.[6]

Some states have adopted a delayed discovery statute, under which the statute of limitations for claims based on injuries from sexual abuse begins to run once a reasonable person would know that he or she is injured.[7] Some courts have held that as a matter of law, one is injured if one is sexually abused.[8] But, as a matter of law, "a reasonable person under the legal disability of infancy is incapable of recognizing or understanding that he or she has been sexually abused,"[9] and therefore "the 6–year statute of limitations in the delayed discovery statute does not begin to run until the person reaches the age of 18."[10] Sometimes limitation periods begin when a person knew enough that he should have inquired about a particular exposure to risk, rather than continuing to accept the risk. Do parents of a sexually abused child have "inquiry notice" that they should have confronted the bishop for having assigned the priest with a record of past molestation to serve their parish and come into contact with their child? "A jury may find that there is a loud ring of truth to plaintiff's statement that he and his family never approached Diocesan officials to ask whether they had knowingly assigned to their church, to work directly with the parishioners, including young boys, a priest with a history of sexually molesting children, because it would never cross their minds that the church would do so." The court found that there is no duty of inquiry where there is no reason to suspect that the bishop had contributed to the injuries.[11]

5:6 EFFECTS OF DELAY ON PROOF.

Why does this timing issue matter? Clergy sexual abuse cases rarely have specific photographic or physical evidence that can be timed definitively. Children who have been seduced and molested are reticent to talk about it, according to child psychologists who have studied this phenomenon. Confronting the abuser will be difficult. A child is far less likely to be believed than is a prominent and trusted adult, such as the parish priest, in a non-provable situation of a "he said/he said" disagreement over what happened in the camp, in the school, or in the rectory.

Documentation of the facts of a sexual encounter between the priest and the young person is rarely easy; the analogy would be to the Monica Lewinsky blue dress stain, from which President Clinton's DNA was extracted to prove her claims of oral sex, but these rarely exist in the church cases.

6. N.J. Stat. Ann. 2C:1-6 (2007).

7. D.M.S. v. Barber, 645 N.W.2d 383, 389 (Minn. 2002).

8. Blackowiak v. Kemp, 546 N.W.2d 1, 3 (Minn. 1996).

9. Doe v. Archdiocese of St. Paul, 817 N.W.2d 150 (Minn. 2012).

10. *D.M.S.*, 645 N.W.2d at 389.

11. Matthews v. Roman Catholic Diocese of Pittsburgh, 67 Pa. D. & C.4th 393, 406, 2004 WL 2526794 (C.P. 2004).

In years before the current wave of awareness, if the parents and adults who heard the child's claim of sexual abuse had brought the complaint to church employees, these clerical misconduct complaints were likely to have been filed away in "secret" or nonpublic archives of the diocese, if they were recorded at all. Hopefully the diocese today would follow the "Essential Norms" and act promptly. So the patterns of clergy sexual abuse claims over many years have shown that the claim of past abuse often is aired in public much later, when the abused child grows up and for some reason has expressed a belated recollection of the incident.

5:7 FRUSTRATIONS

Courts and plaintiffs' lawyers have expressed frustration with the pattern of delayed disclosure and delayed litigation, but these frustrations did not produce a court exception granting a new accrual date for children who had been molested. It would require an action by the legislative body that wrote the statute of limitations to change the statute. Changes to legislation are required to be passed through the inertia that marks many state legislatures, and in the face of fierce opposition of church leaders. For example, Pennsylvania allows a minor child to sue until age 30, an increase from the prior age of 20, and this attracted some plaintiffs in the sexual abuse scandal of the Philadelphia archdiocese.[12]

Other plaintiffs expressed great frustration with the slow pace of disclosure of records from which bishops' actual knowledge could be discerned. In a Los Angeles priest sexual abuse case, $9,900,000 was paid to four claimants after the court ordered release of 12,000 pages of documents detailing the level of knowledge of Cardinal Roger Mahony. Mahony had been deposed in a case in which he addressed the claims against one priest; the priest told Mahony he had abused the boys but falsely stated he was receiving therapy. "And we found out later that he lived a huge lie all those years," Mahony said in the deposition.[13]

And the settlement tactics of some dioceses deepened the frustration of the victims. The pretrial mediation in a Wisconsin case disputed fraud allegations against the diocese for moving a known pedophile into further contact with young people; in mediation, the diocesan defenders "offered to donate $5,000 to charity if we would write a letter of apology for dragging the church through all of this." Ultimately the diocese paid $700,000 to settle before the trial commenced.[14]

12. "3rd Suit Filed against Philly Archdiocese Heads," Associated Press (Mar. 16, 2011).
13. Brian Roewe, "$10 Million LA Settlement First since Document Release," Nat'l Cath. Rptr. (March 29, 2013).
14. Marie Rohde, "Settlement Surprises Wisconsin Plaintiffs," Nat'l Cath. Rptr. 16 (Apr. 12, 2013).

5:8 LEGISLATORS' RESPONSES TO REOPENING LIMITATIONS

Amending state statutes of limitations to permit child abuse cases to be filed after expiration of the conventional period would represent a significant policy decision by state legislators to side with victims, over the interests of churches and especially the Roman Catholic Church. That these remedial expansion statutes were floated at all is significant.[15] That the bishops lacked sufficient political clout, after the clergy abuse scandals, to defeat these law changes, is itself a negative comment on the power of the hierarchy.[16]

Advocates for child victims pressed for the legislatures to open a window of time within which older claims could be filed.[17] Their arguments cited fairness considerations.[18] The changes in statutes were controversial.[19] Prosecutors actively urged the reopening of the limitations period.[20]

Legislators who campaign at church festivals and amid other church-sponsored events[21] are very familiar with the power of church leaders. Legislators see the real power of the insurance companies and defense law firms aligned with them. In California, a letter from the states' bishops was read throughout the state at every Mass on a particular Sunday. The letter complained that the legislature had opened a "window" for belated claims of sexual abuse that would cost huge sums; it asked Catholics to ask their legislators to oppose the law. This drew very widespread attention, not all of it favorable to the bishops; a nun criticized the letter as "another shameless and calculated public relations effort by the archdiocese to gain support for the church at the expense of the victims."[22] Some Protestants also opposed the change, This alignment of many pressures upon legislators puts the victim (and parent, in some cases) at a disadvantage. Many legislators were unwilling to change all of the presumptions in civil tort law for the benefit of a small set of claimants, and they preferred not to go against the power of the churches.

Also useful to the church argument about civil compensation claims was the U.S. Supreme Court's 2003 invalidation of a state criminal statute that reopened

---

15. Mary Gail Frawley O'Dea, Perversion of Power: Sexual Abuse in the Catholic Church 202 (2007).

16. Editorial, Nat'l Cath. Rptr. (July 2011).

17. Terry Carter, "Collaring the Clergy," 93 ABA J. 38 (2007).

18. See e.g., Marci Hamilton, Justice Denied: What America Must Do to Protect its Children (2008).

19. For background, *see* John Daly Cooney, "Determining When to Start the Clock: The "Capable of Ascertainment" Standard and Repressed Memory Sexual Abuse Cases," 72 Mo. L. Rev. 633 (2007); and Susan Heylman, "As States Suspend Time Limitations on Sex Abuse Suits, Clergy Cases Proceed," Trial 72 (Oct. 2007).

20. Maryclaire Dale, "Suit: Pa. Catholic Leaders Failed to Protect Kids," Associated Press (Feb. 14, 2011).

21. Your author, vice mayor of an Ohio city, attended 31 church festivals in a 2006 electoral race.

22. Karol Jackowski, The Silence We Keep: A Nun's View of the Catholic Priest Scandal 182 (2004).

certain types of criminal claims that had already expired, resulting in a prosecution against the individual assailant.[23] The court in *Stogner* held that a state law enacted after expiration of a previously applicable limitation period would violate the constitutional protection against ex post facto laws when it was applied to revive a previously time-barred criminal prosecution.[24] That case was not a civil suit and it did not involve clergy.

This was a criminal case, not a civil compensation lawsuit. Rejection of the California criminal law in *Stogner* forced other states to be more meticulous in their drafting of the set of claims that could be enforced retroactively in civil court.

Civil compensation legislation prior to that 2003 U.S. Supreme Court *Stogner* case was quite controversial. The California legislature re-enacted a provision of the childhood sexual abuse statute of limitations providing that earlier amendments to the statute were prospective in effect, while enacting a new limitations period of three years from discovery. This state law change did not revive causes of action that were time-barred under prior law and that had not been brought within the one-year claim revival period in 2003.[25]

The courts had earlier made several key decisions about these specific extension laws. The 1986 enactment of a special statute of limitations for childhood sexual abuse claims did not revive a former Catholic parishioner's time-barred third-party childhood sexual abuse claims against a bishop, in a case where the statute's revival and delayed-discovery provisions did not apply to third-party defendants.[26] A legislative "delayed accrual" statute represented a generous limitation period for adults who recognized that psychological injury or illness occurring after the age of majority was caused by the sexual abuse that occurred many years before. The California legislature had explicitly recognized that the sexual abuse victim's comprehension of harm can be delayed even to adulthood.[27]

Rather than carve out a particular subset of claims, and trying to respond to news media stories about unfairness in dealing with repressed recollections, a few states such as Delaware and California have enacted legislative proposals for a one-time "window" for accepting late claims of childhood sexual abuse. It was very hard to reach agreement on a "window" to reopen cases where the powerful force of the Catholic hierarchy opposed the selective nature of the extension. A Catholic legal scholar, later a federal judge, referred to the fight over this legislation as "a life-or-death issue" with stakes involving "hundreds of millions of dollars—dollars that could otherwise go to construct church buildings and educate students and

23. Stogner v. California, 539 U.S. 607 (2003).

24. Id., citing Collins v. Youngblood, 497 U.S. 37 (1990).

25. Cal. Code Civ. Proc. § 340.1(b)(2), (c) & (u) (2003); Doe v. Roman Catholic Bishop of San Diego, 178 Cal. App. 4th 1382, 2009 WL 3683192 (2d Dist. 2009), *opinion modified*, 2009 WL 3824392 (Cal. App. 2d Dist. 2009).

26. K.J. v. Roman Catholic Bishop of Stockton, 172 Cal. App. 4th 1388, 2009 WL 96261 (3d Dist. 2009).

27. Cal. Code Civ. Proc. § 340.1(2003) ; Shirk v. Vista Unified School Dist., 128 Cal. App. 4th 156, 26 Cal. Rptr. 3d 771 (4th Dist. 2005).

feed the hungry."[28] That 2003 statement was prophetic, as California opened the "window" for one year to permit older cases to be litigated, and a flood of cases arrived during the window period for older sexual abuse claims.[29]

Critics of the church hierarchy found the lobbying blitz to be "both predictable and sad: Church-employed wheel greasers in state capitols—the hired guns—defend the indefensible and resort to legal arguments rather than the imperatives of justice and mercy."[30]

Legislators in several states have opened the "window" for these belated claims of sexual abuse, and they have been castigated by the church leadership for their efforts. Some laws were killed by the church lobbyists. News media reports showed the political conflict in ways that were particularly harsh against the Church's position: critics said that, having hidden the known pedophiles who were moved to new assignments without notice of their misdeeds, the Church now resisted accountability in the civil compensation of its victims. Catholic legislators responded that bankruptcy would result from a flood of such belated claims, and no institution could reliably respond to decades-old allegations against alleged participants who had moved, aged to a state of incapacity to recall events, or died. This was a very messy debate that damaged the reputation of the Roman Catholic hierarchy.

Neutral legislators wished they did not have to vote either way: to be perceived as unfair to the alleged victims, or to be unfair to an important charitable institution. If procedural moves could not sideline the laws, and the legislation came up for a decisive vote, the typical state legislatures voted for opening the window of additional claims. This meant that the Catholic Church lobbying effort lost, and faced wider problems as the window of time for repressed sexual abuse claims was reopened for a defined period. A plaintiff's lawyer in Philadelphia praised the law and noted how much difficulty his client had experienced in deciding to go public with the story of his abuse. Because Pennsylvania allowed sexual abuse victims to have their cases accrue beginning no later than age 30, "I think we have a window of opportunity here...that the other suits have not had,"[31]

There was a price to be paid for defending the indefensible abusers. In the course of the legislative debate, the image of the Church's many other social welfare priorities may have been tarnished by its effort to shield the past acts of the priests. Once the window of time was opened, the statistical number of cases of abuse that were filed was several hundred. But the Church had incurred some publicity it would have preferred to avoid, and the controversy boosted news media and public recognition of the abuse cases among the citizens who would make up the future civil jury pool.

---

28. Patrick Schiltz, "The Future of Sexual Abuse Litigation," America Magazine 8 (July 7, 2003).
29. Editorial, "$660 Million," 134(14) Commonweal 5 (Aug. 17, 2007).
30. Editorial, "Money, Not Justice, Still Guiding Abuse Policies," Nat'l Cath. Rptr. 24 (Apr. 29, 2011).
31. Dale, supra.

5:9 COURTS AND THE WINDOW REOPENING LEGISLATION

Chapter 8 relates how the constitutionality of the statutes that permitted belated claims of sexual abuse to be asserted, a "window" to reopen past limitations, was resisted by church advocates who feared the volume of claims that would appear. In 2003, the U.S. Supreme Court held that certain of the criminal "window" reopening statutes would be an unconstitutional ex post facto punishment of a criminal defendant under certain circumstances.[32] States responded to this case with statutes that were tailored to avoid that constitutional problem.[33]

Opening the window led to the need to deal with hundreds of lawsuits extending over decades of time for dozens of alleged abusers, some of them dead and some retired. So when the Church lost in the legislative debates it asked appellate courts to reject the new statutes. Here again, the bad press was a remarkably negative consequence. The Delaware Supreme Court's 2011 opinion carefully dispensed with the claims of due process violation; the laws were upheld as the courts do not "sit as an uberlegislature to eviscerate proper legislative enactments," so it was the role of the legislators to decide whether delayed lawsuits could be extended by this "window" law.[34] "As a matter of constitutional law, statutes of limitation go to matters of remedy, not destruction of fundamental rights," Chief Justice Myron Steele wrote, holding that the law can be "applied retroactively because it affects matters of procedure and remedies, not substantive or vested rights."[35]

32. Stogner v. California, 539 U.S. 607 (2003).
33. See e.g., Cal. Code Civ. Proc. 340.35 (2003).
34. Sheehan v. Oblates, 15 A.3d 1247 (Del. 2011).
35. Id.

PART FOUR

Other Related Issues

CHAPTER 6

oⱮꜱ

Effects of Criminal Charges and Plea Agreements

6:1 CRIMINAL LAW CONTEXT

Much of this text deals with compensation to victims through civil court lawsuits. But the truth is that crimes were committed against young people, and criminal conviction and punishment has been properly applied in numerous cases. Some states have been more aggressive than others in applying criminal sanctions to the misconduct by clergy. Within the hierarchy of the Roman Catholic Church, decisions made about reassignment of clergy known or suspected of sexual misconduct may have been criminal offenses under state child-protective laws. Part of this story is reflected in the view of the U.S. Conference of Catholic Bishops' National Review Board in 2004: "The failure of Church leaders to recognize sexual abuse of minors as a crime, and not just the manifestation of a moral failing and psychological disorder, and to deal with it accordingly, has contributed enormously to the current crisis."[1]

The criminal law system has punished individual priests, and a Missouri bishop was convicted in 2012 of failing to protect children from a priest known to have had predatory behaviors, with arrests more likely and much more likely to be publicized.[2] Lengthy prison terms for clerics convicted of child sexual abuse have been imposed in Massachusetts, California, and other state courts. Shocking grand jury reports have drawn worldwide press coverage for the problems of the Church in Philadelphia, where the personnel director of a large archdiocese went to state prison for 3–6 years in a 2012 conviction for failing to stop a predatory pattern of

---

1. National Review Board for the Protection of Children and Young People, A Report on the Crisis in the Catholic Church in the United States 94 (2004) (hereinafter "National Review Board").
2. Janon Fisher & Jose Martinez, "Retired Brooklyn Monsignor, 78, Arrested for Alleged Criminal Sex Acts with Two Teen Boys," N.Y. Daily News (Oct. 15, 2011).

sexual misconduct by priests. Dozens of clergymen have been indicted or sent to prison for offenses against state law. Civil suits have followed criminal indictments or grand jury reports.[3]

The first criminal prosecution of an individual bishop occurred in Kansas City, Missouri, for failure to report a priest's sexual misconduct involving children.[4] Other bishops and cardinals have been implicated in failure to protect children, but because of death, senility, or departure for Rome, these crimes were never adjudicated. Several bishops have in some instances stood before the court to plead guilty on behalf of the diocese for failure to disclose child abuse, but not in their individual capacity.[5] In the Kansas City case, patterns of misconduct by the errant priest were well recognized, but inadequate attention was given, so the crime of failing to protect children was the focus of the indictment. Thomas Reese, S.J., a noted church historian said of the bishop's indictment: "This is historic...In terms of the Catholic Church, this is an extraordinary move which is going to signal that the times have changed. Neither people nor government are going to put up with any kind of activity that looks like a coverup."[6] And long-time psychology scholar A.W. Richard Sipe told the news media that: "This is a huge step that breaks the barrier of bishops being protected. This shows that bishops no longer are above the law."[7]

The existence of a criminal case is as much a matter of timing as it is for any other reason; the great majority of reports of priest sexual conduct have been delayed, as Chapter 5 relates, and cannot be prosecuted in criminal courts. The reader should not assume that the small number of criminal prosecutions means that the problem is small, but rather that the immediate reporting, arrest, and indictment of the priest is less frequent than it should be.

6:2   STATE CRIMINAL LAWS APPLIED TO CLERGY ABUSE CASES

As criminal law is a field of statutory law, the terms contained in criminal statutes have very specific meanings. Statutory coverage and the definitions of crimes will involve very specific elements of the court's criminal jurisdiction. The National Review Board made a good comment: "Many in the church failed to realize or appreciate that sexual conduct with an older minor is a criminal act. As a result...clergy abuse of minors was very rarely reported to the civil authorities."[8] The potential

---

3. See e.g., John P. Martin, "Ex- altar Boy Sues Priest, Archdiocese for Alleged Abuse," Phila. Inquirer (Oct. 19, 2011).

4. Judy Thomas, "Grand jury Indicts Bishop Finn, Diocese," Kansas City Star (Oct. 14, 2011).

5. "Cincinnati Archdiocese Pleads No Contest on Failure to Report," 189(19) America Magazine 4 (Dec. 8, 2003).

6. "Bishop Finn is Found Guilty of Failing to Report Child Abuse Suspicions", Kansas City Star (Sept. 6, 2012).

7. Id.

8. National Review Board, supra, 95.

criminal charges include assault, rape, criminal sexual contact with a minor, "enticing" a minor for sex,[9] sexual exploitation by a counselor,[10] and abuse of a child by a person in a "position of trust."[11] The California Court of Appeals in the Lopez case captures the bizarre religious dominance that concealed the criminal act by a priest on a young boy: "(D)efendant removed his own pants and placed Luis's hand on defendant's penis. Defendant then helped Luis remove Luis's pants and touched Luis's penis. Defendant masturbated himself. Then defendant told Luis to go to church and say 10 "Our Fathers" and God would forgive Luis."[12]

As discussed in the last chapter, long-standing "statute of limitations" policies are being reconsidered as a result of the long-delayed exposure of past predatory exploits of some priests. Chapter 5 discusses these limitation "reopeners" for specified "window" periods. If the laws that are barring older, delayed cases are modified, the result may be more priests on trial in more courts, for older offenses, facing much longer sentences. By the 2010s, public sentiment has shifted to embrace the prosecution of priests for sexual abuse crimes more than when criminal prosecution of abusing priests was a rare novelty in the 1980s.

6:3 DISINCENTIVES AGAINST USE OF CRIMINAL CHARGES

As the 2011 John Jay College study has observed, Catholic clergy traditionally had enjoyed a privileged status from law enforcement leaders, which made it unlikely that criminal penalties would be used against a priest in circumstances that would otherwise have resulted in immediate arrest. Testimony of clergy in sexual assault cases would typically have been given great credence by members of the community who sat on the jury.

Criminal cases with delays and conflicting proof pose a challenge to the criminal defense team; there is often a "he said-he said" dividing line, and there will rarely be witnesses with concrete evidence exhibiting the facts of the sexual contact with the young victim. The priest-penitent privilege reduces the ability of prosecutors to use some of the statements by the priest that the police have recorded in witness interviews.[13] Jury sympathies are likely to have been impacted by the scandals and news coverage of church problems, reinforcing the credibility of the child or adult who claims to have been assaulted.

9. See e.g., Conn. Gen. Stat. 53a-90a (2007), Del. Code tit. 11 § 1112a (2009), D.C. Code 22-3010 (2013), Fla. Stat. Ann. 787.025 (2012), Mass. Ann. Laws ch. 265 § 26C(2010), Wis. St. Ann. 948.07 (1987) ("enticing" means attracting a child for sex).

10. Iowa Code 709.15 (2014) (state laws may punish abuse in the context of a trusted counseling relationship).

11. W.Va. Code 61-8D-5 (2010), Colo. Stat. 18-3-405.3 (2013).

12. People v. Lopez, 166 Cal. App. 4th 1 (2008).

13. See e.g., State v. Orfi, 511 N.W.2d 464 (Minn. App. 1994) and Magar v. State, 826 S.W.2d 221 (Ark. 1992) (state law may bar the use in trial of statements made in a confessional setting to a minister or priest).

The situations vary from geographic area to area, but politics inevitably enters into the charging decision and especially into the decisions about plea bargains for jail terms. Criminal prosecutors fear a backlash from Catholic voters if the aggressive nature of the prosecution is seen as irrationally pursuing an inflated claim on weak evidence. It's more likely that pro-religion voters would react against a prosecutor's zeal than agnostic voters would act against a prosecutor's discretionary failure to indict. "Proof beyond a reasonable doubt" is a very high standard for the prosecutor if the priest adamantly insists that no sexual contact has occurred with this child or teen. Credibility of the child's (or later, young adult's) testimony is at risk in the "fresh" cases, while the credibility of the adult's recollection of long-past events is at risk in the "refreshed memory" cases of past abuse.

6:4 THE CRIMINAL PROSECUTOR'S INSTITUTIONAL ISSUES

The prosecutor's attitude toward the institutional aspects of the Catholic Church may make a difference. Is the Church a small minority in the larger community? Is the Church the dominant social hub for substantial ethnic communities who vote? The prosecutor is aware of the factors of available personnel, trial and investigatory expense, need for expert witness testimony, pretrial delay of a criminal trial, and likelihood of success at trial or on appeal.

The political risk of being perceived as an enemy of the Church is substantial in some states. The likelihood of an easy guilty/no contest/Alford plea may occur in some situations, as it did in Cincinnati,[14] but not where the priest and/or the diocese has asserted a vigorous denial that the abuse occurred. Speedy trial rights of the criminal defendant will apply to the case after the arraignment occurs, so often a prosecutor will delay charging until a full investigation has assembled a set of proofs that is very convincing. The older the case, oftentimes the more difficult it is to assemble convincing proof of guilt.

6:5 THE PROCESS OF CRIMINAL PROSECUTION

A report of child sexual abuse by an adult is significant in the criminal justice system. Because these reports are not of imminent or ongoing events, police will be assigned to ask questions and to gradually gather evidence to amass the "probable cause" that is needed to seek search warrants. Grand jury subpoenas and records searches will demand access to the diocesan priest personnel files.

---

14. "Cincinnati Archdiocese Pleads No Contest on Failure to Report," *supra*. (A plea that admits the prosecutor has sufficient evidence, but does not admit guilt, is an Alford plea, named for a U.S. Supreme Court decision. These have less impact in later civil cases, compared to guilty pleas.)

As in the United States, dioceses in Europe also experienced tough police searches to discover the incriminating records.[15] In Belgium, authorities raided the tomb of a late archbishop to find records that might have been buried with the late archbishop. This event was criticized as excessive and drew shocked criticism from the pope.[16] Simply chaotic and messy filing practices are evident in some dioceses, making it difficult to prove who knew what when about allegations of sexual misconduct. There is an inherent aura of mystery about religious hierarchical institutions, and the labeling of some documents "For the Secret Archives" sounds like a Dan Brown novel of sinister religious plots and cover-ups.

Witness testimony about long-past sexual misconduct may be difficult to manage. The experience of prosecutors is that the weaker the witness appears, the more he may jeopardize the prosecution's case by making concessions on cross-examination about what he or she saw— admissions that could open some doubt and harm the case.

Lawyers understand why some tactical measures are desired in criminal defense work. But the diocesan motives and policies often conflict with the exigencies of defending the cases. The charitable purposes of the diocese and the desire to have positive community relations among members of the parish, or parents of the school, are factors to be considered. What is done in the criminal defense effort will have an impact on tort suits as well.[17] The way that the lawyer defends a criminal case may not be compatible with the public image of charity, caring, and empathy that the parishioners expect from the institutional Church. If the case becomes a criminal defense of individual charges against the bishop,[18] it is likely that the defense will attempt to protect the bishop in an "all bets are off" strategy. However, the vigorous rebuttal of the victim's story is likely to alienate many Catholics. Years of negative revelations about sexual activities of a small percentage of priests have preconditioned media to disbelieve the priest.

A common form of police and prosecutor behavior is to select the several codefendants to indict in a mixture that will pressure the key defendant to settle. In the more typical case of robbery or fraud, a brother, wife, girlfriend, or parent of the shooter or fraud operator will be charged as accomplices, and the shooter will take a plea bargain to protect that other person from conviction. In the same way, prosecutors may offer the diocese a deal to plead guilty and pay an institutional fine, in return for the prosecution's willingness to drop the bishop as a codefendant. The Kansas City bishop's criminal case[19] was a rare case of actual adjudication of guilt.

The diocese and the bishop as an individual may face charges of failure to make a required report of suspected sexual abuse of a minor, and in some cases, of obstruction of a police investigation. Assuming that there is a desire to avoid individual

---

15. "Holy Father Deplores Police Methods in Raid on Belgian Church Headquarters," Cath. News Serv. (July 2, 2010).

16. Id.

17. See e.g., Martin, supra (indictment led to civil suit).

18. As occurred in Kansas City; see Judy Thomas, "Bishop Finn, Diocese Indicted in Abuse Case," Kansas City Star (Oct. 14, 2011).

19. Judy Thomas, "Bishop Finn, Diocese indicted in Abuse Case," supra.

jail time for the bishop, it would likely be agreed at the time of the diocesan guilty plea that the prosecutor will present the documents that had led to the charges. These documents will give the judge a basis for an allocution of responsibility by the defendant bishop, and reasons for a lighter sentence against him and a lesser penalty against the funds of the diocese.

The worst case would be a tangible documented paper trail or electronic message trail showing the bishop's knowing awareness of the child abuse patterns of that priest, followed by apparent cover-up activities on the part of the Vicar for Clergy or other diocesan official, followed by concealment of records that impedes the grand jury investigation of the abuse allegations. If the priest-abuser was dead or incapacitated by illness at the time of the trial, the bishop and the Vicar for Clergy would very likely be defendants.

6:6 SENTENCING AND APPEALS

Sexual misconduct by a priest that satisfies state criminal law criteria should result in a prison sentence equal to that which non-religious predators would receive. The guilty plea of an elderly, infirm priest may lead to a suspended sentence or probation with conditions. One of the worst serial pedophiles, Father Rudolph Kos, is serving a life term in Texas prison, and the original high profile abuser, Father Gilbert Gauthe, was sentenced to 20 years in prison.[20]

An example was the Cincinnati area, where serial rapist Father Earl Bierman had received a lengthy sentence for abuse actions in nearby Kentucky parishes, and other priests were charged with sex crimes and several were convicted and sentenced for their crimes. The television cameras were on as the Cincinnati archdiocese appeared in court, through Archbishop Daniel Pilarczyk, to plead as a criminal defendant in a group of cases asserting a failure to notify authorities of cases of child abuse. The court imposed a $10,000 fine for the five misdemeanor charges.[21] In Charlotte, North Carolina, Father Robert Yurgel was sentenced to nearly eight years in prison after pleading guilty to criminal sexual abuse charges in 2009. The victim was paid a settlement of $1 million from its insurance and would pay an additional $47,500 for counseling and medication for the now-adult victim.[22]

Dark shadows over the Boston archdiocese on the issue of criminal abusers sent several priests to prison and drove its cardinal into permanent exile at the Vatican.[23] Philadelphia commentators expected many more trials or plea bargains

20. Nicholas Cafardi, Before Dallas: The U.S. Bishops' Response to Clergy Sexual Abuse of Children 12 (2008).

21. "Cincinnati Archdiocese Pleads No Contest on Failure to Report," supra.

22. "Charlotte Diocese Settles Abuse Lawsuit for $1 Million," Associated Press (May 7, 2010).

23. Cardinal Law resigned in 2002 and his successor immediately fired the law firm that had been driving the defense of abuse cases, and began negotiations for a settlement of the outstanding claims.

as a result of its 2011 grand jury report. Criminal lawyers have spoken of more charges to come in several of the priest abuser cases. The scandal's criminal aspects have seized the public's attention over several years.

In the early days of the rare clergy sexual abuse cases, probation and suspended sentences were used. Sentencing to prison time was to be followed by "sexual predator" reporting. At the other extreme, a Boston predator priest with dozens of molestation complaints received a very long prison sentence but was killed by fellow inmates in 2003 in a Massachusetts prison.[24] The same fate awaited a Presbyterian minister dismissed for molestation and imprisoned, who was fatally stabbed in prison.[25] And a scholar in this field has observed that an ecclesiastical trial of a priest in Florence, Italy, held in the year 1570, ended with the priest beheaded and the choir boy victim whipped and exiled, but today's punishments are less severe.[26]

The issues that have been brought on appeal of clergy sexual abuse cases have been constitutional, jurisdictional, and statutory interpretation matters. The question of the constitutionality of the coverage of the state abuse-reporting statute under the facts of the particular case will be implicated in many appeals. The prosecution often argues that Church claims of confessional privilege are sometimes overextended and that a broader range of internal conversations between the priest and his bishop should be admissible. First Amendment arguments about the entanglement of the prosecution's criminal law power with the freedom to practice the inner discipline of a religion have been asserted. But when the diocese can be shown to have some knowledge of the events, its poor decisions about the future assignment of an abuser have made the diocese appear vulnerable to application of the same criminal standards as apply to other nongovernmental institutions.

6:7 REPEAT OFFENDERS

An aspect of clergy sexual abuse that has been both surprising and disturbing is the number of cases where, after detection and suspension, the priest was returned to ministry only to commit a later sexual abuse on a different child. The second time it becomes known, the bishop is embarrassed and ashamed that he had returned to duty a priest against whom there had been a substantiated claim of abuse.[27] In some cases, priests were repeatedly returned to ministry even after multiple "relapses" of abuse, and cycles of treatment and therapy, allowing a much greater number of children to be abused than would have happened if the bishop had removed the priest from ministry after the first allegation. As the bishop leading the 2010 effort

24. Shelley Murphy, "Insurer Files Countersuit against Archdiocese," Boston Globe B1 (Apr. 29, 2004).

25. Mark Chopko, "Shaping the Church: Overcoming the Twin Challenges of Secularization and Scandal," 53 Cath. U. L. Rev. 125, 133 n.33 (2003).

26. Stephen Rossetti, A Tragic Grace: The Catholic Church and Child Sexual Abuse 104 (1996).

27. Dennis Coday, "Costs of Abuse Scandal Becoming Clearer," Nat'l Cath. Rptr. 5 (Oct. 3, 2003).

of the U.S. Conference of Catholic Bishops said of the revised norms, "Claims often made by perpetrators in the past that they were contrite and would stop abusing are never again going to be taken at face value."[28]

6:8 JURY NULLIFICATION DEFENSES

An unusual twist on the clergy abuse cases should be noted. A child was molested on a weekend camping trip by a Jesuit priest. The abuse was reported years later as an adult, and a $625,000 settlement was paid in 1998. The Jesuit retired to a church rest home. In May 2010, the now-adult victim traced the priest to his current residence, and assaulted and beat the 65-year-old priest. The former victim, now attacker, was indicted for felony assault, and told the media that he hopes the jury will find the actions of 35 years before to be so reprehensible that he as the assailant is found not guilty.[29]

6:9 THE CHURCH'S ALTERED STANCE ON REPORTING CLERGY FOR CRIMINAL PROSECUTIONS

When a diocese learns of sexual abuse allegations today, it should follow the 2002 U.S. Conference of Catholic Bishops "Essential Norms" and report credible claims to local police. If there is credible evidence the matter should be turned over to the police for them to investigate.

The Church has changed policies on criminal investigation of abusers as a result of the fallout from the clergy abuse scandals. As recently as 1997, the Vatican blocked the Irish bishops from adopting a policy of "mandatory reporting" of suspect abusers to the police. The policy was rejected in an official letter to the Irish bishops because for both "moral and canonical" reasons, the bishops must handle all accusations through internal Church channels. Bishops who disobey, the letter said, may face repercussions when their abuse cases are heard in Rome. "The results could be highly embarrassing and detrimental to those same Diocesan authorities," the letter said.[30]

28. Blase Cupich, "Twelve Things the Bishops Have Learned from the Abuse Crisis," 209 America Magazine 8 (May 17, 2010).

29. Gillian Flaccus & Terence Chea, "Suspect Uses Beating Case to Publicly Shame Priest," Associated Press (Nov. 13, 2010).

30. Laurie Goodstein, "Vatican Warned Bishops Not to Report Child Abuse," Wash. Post (Jan. 18, 2011).

CHAPTER 7

༄

Church Insurance and Abuse Claims.

7:1 INSURANCE OVERVIEW

The liability insurance needed for a complicated and widely dispersed manufacturing or service company can be written by skilled agents for a sophisticated insurance carrier, who work from a database of losses by other companies in a similar business. The risks of fires, accidents, truck crashes, roof collapse, thefts, etc., can all be quantified and priced into the insurance bills. In a normal statistical year, a truck crash, a minor fire, and a slip-and-fall case might be claimed for that industrial customer.

But in the case of a religious institution, the underwriting of liability insurance is different in many respects from the liability insurance of a comparably sized corporation, and the clergy sexual abuse cases have made underwriters much more wary.[1] Sexual abuse settlements and verdicts have resulted in denials of coverage, refusals to issue new policies, and renewals with substantial cost increases.[2] Arguments about how many sexual abuse events constitute an "occurrence," and whether the occurrence is excluded from the policy, are unfortunately common in church liability claims.[3] As far back as 1994, the news media reported that large reputable insurers were denying coverage for sexual abuse claims and declining to renew or issue new policies for some Catholic entities.[4] Beginning at least in 1984, when insurance carriers paid $4,200,000 to settle nine abuse claims caused by one priest in Louisiana, the casualty insurers were aware that they had a problem.[5]

---

1. Caroline McDonald, "Sexual Abuse Coverage Can Be Found," 106(40) National Underwriter 18 (Oct. 7, 2002).
2. Douglas McLeod, "Church's Coverage at Risk," 36(25) Bus. Ins. 1 (June 24, 2002).
3. Roman Catholic Diocese of Brooklyn v. Nat'l Union Fire Ins. Co., 21 N.Y.3d 139, 991 N.E.2d 666, 969 N.Y.S.2d 808 (2013).
4. "Archdiocese of Milwaukee Sues Insurers on Sexual-Abuse Claims," N.Y. Times A10 (Dec. 27, 1994).
5. Mary Gail Frawley-O'Dea, Perversion of Power: Sexual Abuse in the Catholic Church 2 (2007).

Today, decades after knowledge of the clergy abuse scandals became widespread, the insurers continue to assert that these were intentional actions, not accidents. Injury was to be expected when the rogue priest was reassigned after an initial incident suggested a potential that the priest might be abusing minors. Negligent supervision remains a significant claim, and insurers decline to pay, apparently because few suits would be brought by a diocese in a sexual abuse case, and few insurers expect the diocese to find jurors receptive to such claims.[6]

There are hundreds of thousands of religious congregations of all types in the United States,[7] and Catholic facilities are the most numerous among the various religious affiliations. Catholic primary and secondary school sporting activities have a higher-than-normal risk of physical injuries compared to an adult maker of widgets. To the extent that a diocese operates the schools directly, not through independent corporations, risk management and control policies can reduce the liability exposure to a certain degree. If each parish school is separate and operates independently, the insurance carriers will probably seek to impose some form of mandatory risk management at a centralized level for those affiliated with the diocese. The underwriters of the insurance are aware that the school and youth activities of the parish are vulnerable to potential sexual abuse problems.

Sexual abuse by priests is, in historical perspective, a relatively rare claim, a "wild card" for insurance planners. An insurance expert commented in 1998: "Although incidents are relatively rare…any instance is like a crash of a jetliner—when it does happen, the results are catastrophic."[8] As will be the case for all forms of liability insurance, the events that will be compensated as covered "occurrences" are those for which the event is unexpected and causes harm, for which the insured may be liable.[9] For example, a 2007 settlement of sexual abuse claims by the Los Angeles archdiocese for $660 million included $227 million from insurance, largely from special coverage for sexual abuse claims.[10] Though rare, abuse was not unforeseeable. A report delivered to bishops by three experts in 1985 cautioned that "prior to the cancellation of coverage, a significantly higher actuarial value would be assigned to the risk, resulting in a significantly increased premium cost. One diocese that experienced insurance losses as a result of a priest sexually molesting children has been notified that the insurance premium shall increase more than 25 percent."[11] That was 1985; after a number of costly abuse settlements, the

6. Peter Swisher & Richard Mason, "Liability Insurance Coverage for Clergy Sexual Abuse Claims," 17 Conn. Ins. L.J. 355, 357 (2011).

7. Lynna Goch, "A Higher Calling," Best's Review 109 (Mar. 1998).

8. Id.

9. Jesse Cooke, "Beyond an Unfortunate 'Occurrence': Insurance Coverage and the Equitable Redress of Victims of Sexual Predator Priests," 36 Ariz. St. L.J. 1039 (2004).

10. Michelle Tsai, "Insurance for Sex Abuse," Slate (July 16, 2007).

11. Thomas Doyle, A.W.R. Sipe & Patrick Wall, Sex, Priests and Secret Codes: The Catholic Church's 2,000 Year Paper Trail of Sexual Abuse 162 (2006) (relating what the authors had described for bishops in 1985).

market for commercial coverage would soon after evaporate, leaving dioceses to form risk pools to bear their collective losses from abuse cases that conventional insurers refused to cover. This chapter will cover the issues concerning each step of how a church might seek an insurance policy to cover a reported abuse, ending in a discussion of how the risk pools operate and how risks are assured today.

7:2 COVERAGE DISPUTES

Courts had held in favor of coverage of policies that were in force at the time of the older cases, judging the "occurrence" by the "per plaintiff, per priest" model instead of treating each sexual contact as a covered event. This means that a predatory priest who forced a child to perform oral sex on 12 occasions has one occurrence, one coverage, not 12 events. That model would have applied the policy limits of payment to each child who had been allegedly abused by each priest. Where the molestation was a pattern of sexual events over several years, the insured portions for each year are treated separately, pro rata, across the several insurers who held coverage for each of those years.[12] Many interrelated coverage issues result.[13]

Several examples illustrate the difficulties involved. In the case involving the Winona, Minnesota, diocese, a priest who had five separate therapy sessions for his past molestations was again allowed to have contact with children, so the court held that the sexual abuse was a known event and not covered by the policy as an occurrence.[14]

Milwaukee had a similar denial of coverage upheld in court.[15] Boston archdiocesan officials fought their insurer for a year before settling; the archdiocese asserted the coverage during the years of abuse was up to $59.3 million with one insurer, and an additional $7.7 million during an overlap with another company's policy; ultimately the insurer paid $20 million of the $85 million global settlement with abuse victim claimants.[16] The insurer for the Fall River (Massachusetts) diocese had initially begun to defend sexual abuse claims, but then sued for a declaration that it had no duty to cover the diocese, asserting the diocese's failure to prevent the priest's contact with children was "so egregious and improper as to not be insurable as a matter of law."[17] This was settled.

12. Roman Catholic Diocese of Brooklyn v. Nat'l Union Fire Ins. Co., 21 N.Y.3d 139, 991 N.E.2d 666, 969 N.Y.S.2d 808 (2013).

13. Swisher & Mason, supra.

14. Dan Lonkevich, "Dallas Diocese Sues Insurers to Cover Verdict," 101 Nat'l Underwriter 3 (Aug. 4, 1997).

15. Marie Rohde, "Judge Rules Archdiocese's Insurance Not Liable for Fraud-Based Claims," Milwaukee J. Sentinel (Aug. 15, 2008).

16. Jonathan Finer, "Boston Archdiocese, Insurer Settle on Abuse," Wash. Post A8 (Mar. 8, 2005).

17. Dick Lehr, "Porter Case on Table, Church Insurer Backs Out," Boston Globe 31 (Aug. 20, 1992).

7:3 "ARCHEOLOGY" OF OLD POLICIES

Another problem concerns actually identifying which company had issued which policy with what exclusion, covering events as of what date. This would be the basis for allocating liability to each carrer in a multi-year abuse situation.[18] Matching carrier and type of liability is the beginning, not the end, of the "archeology" that the dioceses and churches must do to discern their specific coverage for older events. Church records may be sparse, and the retention of old policies may have seemed unnecessary.

7:4 WAS SEXUAL ABUSE COVERED AS AN ACCIDENTAL "OCCURRENCE"?

In general, diocesan liability insurance does not cover actions of the bishop, pastor, or priest himself committing an assault that intentionally provides some benefit to that individual. No accident occurred, and the intentional nature of the crime diminishes the claim for insurance coverage.[19] Sexual gratification of the individual priest did not inure to the benefit of the Church; it was a morally reprehensible act for a priest who had vowed celibacy, and, depending on the age of the individual sexual object, may also have been a crime.

The astute plaintiff in a civil case would avoid suing the priest, who probably has little money, and instead sue the diocese for negligence by the bishop and Vicar of Clergy for not preventing the foreseeable wrongful actions of the priest abuser.[20] Chapter 3 lists some of the causes of action available. The insurance carriers collectively fund an Insurance Services Office (ISO) to provide common language for multiple companies' liability policies. This ISO helped to draft the standard insurance policy language on the "ISO abuse and molestation exclusion"[21] and wrote it very broadly to reach many of these types of nontraditional claims.

The analogy may be that the individual bishop would not be covered with liability insurance if he intentionally attacked a member of the diocesan staff with a stick, and was sued for injuries. (Several bishops quit as a result of scandals involving sexual activities,[22] but this hypothetical is purely fictional.) An insurer's obligation to pay liability claims relates to injuries caused by accidental rather than intentional actions of the insured person. The reason this distinction is relevant to

---

18. Roman Catholic Diocese of Brooklyn v. Nat'l Union Fire Ins. Co., 21 N.Y.3d 139, 991 N.E.2d 666, 969 N.Y.S.2d 808 (2013).

19. Swisher & Mason, supra.

20. Shelley Murphy, "Insurer Files Countersuit against Archdiocese," Boston Globe B1 (Apr. 29, 2004).

21. New York: Insurance Services Office, ISO form CG-21-46-01-87, "Abuse or Molestation Exclusion" (hereinafter "ISO form").

22. Bishops from the dioceses of Palm Beach, Santa Fe, and Milwaukee resigned or retired under a cloud of sexual misconduct allegations.

this book is that insurance carriers are quite aware of the problems created by sexually deviant employee behaviors in healthcare, education, and other workplaces.

These risks can be classified as excluded or covered. What is different about the church situation is that prohibitions against sexual misconduct are directly part of the teaching mission of the religious institution, and that misconduct is expressly forbidden to members of that church community. Within a small number of cases, acts of intentional sexual abuse can be attributed to an intentional decision by a pastor or priest to contravene the explicit norms of the employer, and to seek personal sexual gratification with young persons in the church-owned camp, the rectory, or the gym locker room. The diocese, of course, has no benefit from that sexual gratification of the individual. It's no accidental occurrence; it's a crime.

Is the effect of the sexual contact covered or excluded? Usually, it is excluded in the specific policy or in the generic ISO endorsement[23] used by casualty insurance companies, as discussed below.[24]

7:5 INSURER RESPONSE TO SEXUAL ABUSE

Liability coverage for churches has been higher in cost and lower in competitive bids in recent years, and a "crisis in confidence" in the Catholic dioceses and institutions being covered has contributed to the wariness of insurers as a result of the publicity about the abuse cases.[25] Most diocesan accident and general liability policies contain the ISO exclusion so they cannot be used for abuse cases.[26] For the future, insurance carriers are pressing their diocesan clients to adopt screening, supervision, training, and other preventive policies. A Catholic risk pool created and stimulated the use of a standard video and print training system for all church volunteers and employees, called the VIRTUS training program, which has become mandatory training to be completed before adult volunteers or employees are allowed to have contact with parish or school children.

In today's climate of liability awareness, prevention of abuse is first, internal awareness and communication about risk is second, and responsive mitigation is third. Prudent dioceses will listen to complaints of suspected abuse, and will investigate, apologize, and pay for counseling and treatment, thereby reducing litigation over past abuse claims.[27]

The scenario is familiar to those in the sexual abuse treatment field. Assume that the diocese receives a report of sexual abuse by Father Doe at St. X parish; Doe was previously posted to St. Y and taught religion at Holy Z High School. The diocesan risk manager notifies the insurance carrier(s) whose liability policies were in

23. ISO form, supra.
24. Rohde, supra.
25. Edward Walsh, "Insurance a Worry for Catholic Church: Premiums Skyrocket, Old Policies Unreliable in Sex Abuse Settlements," Wash. Post A3 (July 10, 2002).
26. ISO form, supra.
27. McLeod, supra.

force when the alleged events occurred. There may have been multiple events with multiple children crossing the periods of coverage by multiple carriers. The claim by the diocese is to each carrier, for payment pro rata for the abuse that occurred over several years.[28] If the insurer does not deny coverage immediately, a claim file with a loss reserve is established by the insurance company, and the diocese will be visited by the claims representative to go through available documentation. It is very likely that the current carrier will deny coverage for lack of a present "occurrence." Instead, prior policy issuers would be liable (if any carrier is liable). The church's risk manager then must total up the years of the potential abuse actions claimed by the victims (e.g., sodomy in 1978, 1981, and 1985 with three boys in the same parish). The diocesan risk manager then must go through each of those years' policies and any other years' coverages for the full period of Father Doe's ministry. Claims notice about the sexual abuse claims must be given in writing to each of the carriers who wrote the primary and excess coverage for those years of 1978, 1981, and 1985. Each will respond with a demand for more information, and are likely to deny coverage,[29] so these sexual abuse claims mean that the risk manager's role becomes a very important diocesan function.

Father Doe's quite typical pattern among child sexual abusers is sadly common to the dioceses that have experienced similar misconduct. Each carrier will seek to limit its loss reserve and will press for details of Doe's career prior to that particular year of coverage. We can speculate these carriers will decline to bid for this diocese's business in future insurance bid periods. If they do accept the diocese as a client again, its premiums for future insurance contract costs will be far larger than before, if it can get insurance outside of a pool.[30] A pool is a shared loss enterprise where one diocese's payment to victims comes from the funds of all the dioceses in that pool. Unlike conventional investor-owned insurers, pool members have their own funds at stake and have incentives to monitor how careful each other diocese will be to avoid harm and therefore avoid payouts.

Many allegations of clergy sexual abuse that were asserted in the 1985–2005 period were made for older events that came to light long after they occurred.[31] The older insurance policies issued prior to the mid 1980s generally (with some exceptions) could be used to pay for the damages claimed during the coverage year,[32] if the insurer agreed, or if a court construed the ambiguities of coverage in a way that covered sexual abuse.[33] Cases had variable results, or were settled after litigation

---

28. Roman Catholic Diocese of Brooklyn v. Nat'l Union Fire Ins. Co., 21 N.Y.3d 139, 991 N.E.2d 666, 969 N.Y.S.2d 808 (2013).

29. Id.

30. Doyle et al., supra.

31. Examples in several texts and articles listed in the bibliography suggest that denial of coverage was likely to occur if the diocese had prior events with this priest. An example of prior notice is Michael Luo, "Cardinal Has a Mixed Record on Abuse Cases," N.Y. Times (May 5, 2010).

32. Elinor Burkett & Frank Bruni, A Gospel of Shame: Children, Sexual Abuse and the Catholic Church 205 (1993).

33. Walsh, supra.

between insurer and insured dioceses. This pattern ended with widespread use of the ISO endorsement after 1987.[34]

7:6 THE LOW LIMITS OF INSURANCE COVERAGE

Even then, with a finding of some coverage, the bad news is that the carrier's limits per "occurrence" were low in these older policies, probably a ceiling number such as $50,000, well below the amount a jury would award in an abuse case.[35] The argument has been made that the hierarchy failed to properly handle the abuse situation, and that the bishop often had sufficient knowledge of the priest's problems that he should have prevented further contact with children.[36] If the policy did not exclude all acts of abuse as of the time of the alleged event, then the carrier who held the coverage in a target year (e.g., 1984) may send a letter to the diocese offering a defense under reservation of rights. Early negotiation among the insurance company, the diocese, and the lawyer for the abuse victim may result in a larger loss reserve or an early tender of a share of the settlement, probably tendering the maximum available under that policy. It is possible in some policies that the aggregate amount of the losses claimed by a group of adults who had been molested as students in a Catholic school will trigger notice to the "reinsurance" carrier who held the excess coverage during the year(s) of the primary carrier's coverage.

7:7 THE PRIMARY AND EXCESS COVERAGE CARRIERS

The claim or demand for compensation is in recent years usually made by a formal compensation demand letter from a lawyer, and the legal process of defense takes over. The insurance carrier opens a file and assigns an internal "loss reserve." The insurance carrier may write to the diocese and disclaim any coverage of the event, for example because terms of the contract of insurance, as of the date of the alleged misconduct, had excluded criminal acts by employees from the coverage of the liability policy. Or the carrier may deliver to the diocese a letter called a "reservation of rights" that announces that the insurance company will initially offer the legal defense needed, but that the company reserves the right to decline coverage of the event when more of the facts are known. The excess coverage carrier will also be notified, if the cumulative amount at risk is alleged to go beyond the level at which the excess carrier is required to become involved in the coverage. For example, a base line policy amount for 1981 occurrences may have been limited to $100,000 with a $10,000 deductible. The excess policy amount might then be $100,000 to $2,000,000. So the excess carriers who wrote the added coverage in the 1980s may be startled to learn of its belated exposure.

34. ISO form, supra.
35. Walsh, supra.
36. Lonkevich, supra.

7:8 DENIAL OF COVERAGE FOR KNOWN OFFENDER LOSS EVENTS

In some cases, insurers have rejected coverage because the pattern of misconduct by the priest had made later molestations foreseeable, a "known loss."[37] The intentional act of the molester in repeating the sexual abuse with other young people makes it likely that the insurer will decline coverage of those abuse claims arising after the date when the diocese first had notice of the abuse.[38] The result may be litigation of diocese versus insurer in federal court while the filed documents are helpful to plaintiffs in victim versus diocese lawsuits.

Evaluation of the timing and value of direct or implied coverage is the primary task for the diocesan risk manager and his insurance representative. The ISO standard exclusion for abuse and molestation[39] began to appear in 1987, which affects the coverage and timing for older alleged incidents. Here, the recent history of such cases becomes important: if the incident that forms the basis for the lawsuit occurred before the church liability insurance policies excluded sexual conduct, as virtually all did after 1990, the insurance carrier will simply deny coverage and decline to pay for the defense of the claim. The diocese then will be fighting one incoming tort suit from a victim and perhaps multiple coverage-denial determinations.

7:9 POOLS AND RETAINED RISK GROUPS

There are also available pools of church-related entities that share the risks of sexual abuse claims through collective risk-taking; each diocese shares in paying losses. The pool excludes individual priest liability, and focuses solely on the diocesan liability exposure.[40] One can imagine the assets of 30 dioceses could each be tapped for 1/30 of the jury award to a member diocese that had been sued for negligence.

There are now over 60 dioceses and church entities that have entered the Catholic Mutual risk pool program.[41] The dioceses can buy insurance for sexual misconduct liability from the Catholic Mutual group.[42] Or they can enter the National Catholic Risk Retention Group that has 56 shareholders.[43] These groups have a strong incentive to reduce claims of abuse, and as a pool of diocesan funders, the risk retention entity is less eager to cut off one of its owner-dioceses by cutting that diocese out of coverage. The pool offers an excess liability layer for $3.5 million above the members' other insurance.[44]

---

37. McLeod, supra.
38. Walsh, supra.
39. ISO form, supra.
40. Joanne Wojcik, "Church Scandals Prompt Action," Bus. Ins. (Jan. 3, 1994).
41. See insurance website http://www.catholicmutual.org/Coverages/CUPII.aspx.
42. See id.
43. McLeod, supra.
44. See insurer group website www.catholicumbrellapool.org.

Commentators have noted the significance of this pool's tie-in with mandatory training programs to lower exposure to sexual abuse claims.[45] The VIRTUS program of the Catholic risk retention group[46] is required training for all those who are in contact with children under diocesan auspices. As mentioned earlier in this chapter, the VIRTUS program is a video-based training about the warning signs of abuse, how to prevent it, how to make a report, and how to respond to an allegation.[47] "Churches in effect have now acquired an external supervisory authority in the form of the insurance companies."[48] The companies make the coverage conditional upon these measures to reduce the incidence of future claims of sexual abuse.[49]

The use of a multi-diocese mutual pool is not an "out" and indeed it can drag down the assets of pool members. The Milwaukee archdiocese reported that "The [diocesan office] property currently carries a $4.65 million mortgage, which was taken out in 2006 to help pay the archdiocesan portion of a resolution of lawsuits filed by victims/survivors in California."[50] The reader should note the significance of this statement: Wisconsin diocese payments for California diocese liabilities are a result of pooling, and pooling is a result of the retreat by commercial insurers from the Catholic Church market, at least insofar as sexual abuse claims are concerned.

7:10 LIMITATIONS ON INSURANCE CLAIMS TIMING

Insurance also can be limited to those claims that are made during the time that the policy is active, as a "claims made" policy. Only a claim filed in the 365-day coverage period can tap into this year's coverage. So, for example, a person injured in a fall on the church's snowy sidewalk on March 1 would be making a claim in the same year during the summertime, allowing sufficient time to gather medical bills and other expenses. The claim is made on October 15 during the policy year, and so the company that wrote the policy will defend it as being within the covered period. The negligent failure to remove the ice and snow, if the state law requires that to be done, is the basis for liability claims.

The claim that is made in sexual abuse cases usually involves criminal sexual misconduct with a minor, and the act is concealed, quite intentionally, by the abuser. A decade or more then passes before the filing of the claim, so a "claims

45. Matt Kelly, "The Costs of Penance," 159 TIME 53 (Mar. 25, 2002).

46. John Allen, "Lessons Learned from Virtus," Nat'l Cath. Rptr. 8 (July 8, 2011).

47. And the VIRTUS program will be highlighted as an option for other nations facing similar problems: John Allen, "Vatican to Stage Major Symposium on Sex Abuse Crisis," Nat'l Cath. Rptr 23 (June 24, 2011).

48. Philip Jenkins, Pedophiles and Priests: Anatomy of a Contemporary Crisis 137 (1996).

49. McLeod, supra.

50. Information provided by the archdiocese noted that as to the archdiocesan offices, "The property currently carries a $4.65 million mortgage, which was taken out in 2006 to help pay the archdiocesan portion of a resolution of lawsuits filed by victims/survivors in California." Brian Olszewski, "Milwaukee Archdiocese Files for Bankruptcy Protection over Abuse Claims," Cath. News Serv. (Jan. 5, 2011).

made" policy excludes any later-filed claim. It is highly significant which type of coverage is being arranged. Some other policies include coverage for accidents that occurred during the year or a particular policy term, even though the injured person has not yet filed his or her claim by the end of that year.

7:11 EXCLUSION OF COVERAGE FOR SEXUAL MISCONDUCT

Insurance policies for institutions such as churches are written by casualty insurance companies, using standard form language. The ISO standard clauses were changed in 1987 to exclude abuse or molestation claims,[51] and these changed policies have been in effect for over 20 years now. When a claim for compensation is made, and a request for coverage and defense is made by the diocese, the diocese usually asserts that it did not know of the sexual contact as of the time the sexual abuse was occurring. The actions of the abusing priest are reprehensible and outside the scope of employment. The insurance company is certain to deny the claim on the basis that the ISO policy endorsement language fully excludes abuse or molestation cases.[52]

The Abuse or Molestation Exclusion is an endorsement attached to a policy, which expands or restricts its benefits or excludes certain conditions from coverage. "It is part of the contract to the same extent as if it were actually embodied therein. The policy and the endorsement are to be read together to determine the contract actually intended by the parties. Where provisions in the body of the policy conflict with an endorsement, the provision of the endorsement governs."[53]

The courts that have interpreted the ISO exclusion have found it to be clear and unambiguous.[54] This ISO exclusion "serves to exclude from coverage all classifications of damages arising out of incidents of molestation."[55]

7:12 VICARIOUS LIABILITY

Abuse and molestation are "intentional" acts, so they fall outside the standard commercial general liability policy coverage of bodily injury arising out of an "occurrence." Because the diocese is likely to be held vicariously liable for abuse committed by their church employees, the policy exclusion for intentional acts would not interfere with coverage for a diocese's vicarious liability. The ISO policy endorsement for sexual abuse eliminates coverage for an insured organization's liability in connection with abuse or molestation committed by someone other than that insured. The contract language is important. It applies to abuse and molestation

---

51. ISO Form, supra.
52. Id.
53. Harper v. Gulf Ins. Co., 2002 WL 32290984 (D. Wyo. 2002).
54. See e.g., Cmty. Action for Greater Middlesex County v. Am. Alliance Ins. Co., 254 Conn. 387, 757 A.2d 1074, 1082–83 (Conn. 2000).
55. Lincoln County v. Doe, 749 So. 2d 943, 946 (Miss. 1999).

incidents against "any person while in the care, custody, and control of any insured" committed by "anyone." That "anyone" includes priests who are employees, independent contractors, or visitors.

7:13 BROAD EXCLUSIONS FROM COVERAGE AFTER 1987

After wide use of the ISO language by insurance carriers, a very broad set of actions has also been excluded. The diocese could be sued for negligence in the inadequate screening of seminary applicants that allowed a person with a history of abusive behavior to become a priest and have charge of children. Those claims about selection are different from purely vicarious liability claims, as they allege actual negligence on the part of the diocese. Those claims are addressed in the second part of the exclusion, which applies to negligent "employment, investigation, supervision, or retention" of persons who commit abuse or molestation, for whose conduct the insured "is or ever was legally responsible."[56]

So courts have found that the specific, all-inclusive molestation exclusion bars coverage, and the exclusion is neither negated nor rendered ambiguous by the general severability clause in the insurance contract.[57] For example, a Catholic bishop lost a claim for coverage when the courts held that the sexual molestation exclusion unambiguously excluded coverage for negligent supervision claims against the bishop where a priest had molested a female parishioner.[58]

Where the Abuse or Molestation Exclusion applies to exclude coverage on the church's negligent failure-to-warn claim, the insurer does not have a duty to defend or indemnify the church.[59] And a claim of "negligent supervision" against a church was made after a woman was sexually assaulted by the pastor, but her claim that the church did not "warn or otherwise protect her" was held to be excluded by the 1987 endorsement.[60]

The Abuse or Molestation Exclusion is "drafted to exclude all coverage for sexual abuse, regardless of whether that abuse was caused intentionally (by the molester/employee) or negligently (by his employer)." The exclusion clarifies that no coverage is provided to employers for their negligence relating to any abuse or molestation. An employer's "duty to warn" is subsumed and implied within his "employment," "investigation," "supervision," and "retention" of a molesting employee."[61]

Efforts to deny accountability for parish priests as self-employed independent contractors are difficult to succeed in the face of possible sanctions motions.[62]

---

56. Harper v. Gulf Ins. Co., 2002 WL 32290984 (D. Wyo. 2002).
57. Caroff v. Farmers Ins. Co., 98 Wash. App. 565, 989 P.2d 1233, 1234 (Wash. App.1999).
58. McAuliffe v. N. Ins. Co., 69 F.3d 277 (8th Cir.1995)
59. Harper v. Gulf Ins. Co., 2002 WL 32290984 (D. Wyo. 2002).
60. Napieralski v. Unity Church of Greater Portland, 802 A.2d 391 (Me. 2002).
61. Harper v. Gulf Ins. Co., 2002 WL 32290984 (D. Wyo. 2002).
62. Martinelli v. Bridgeport Roman Cath. Diocesan Corp., 179 F.R.D. 77 (D. Conn. 1998).

7:14 AGE OF THE CRIMES AND AGE OF THE INSURANCE CONTRACTS

Insurance coverage for a defined occurrence at a defined date is usually unaffected by the age of the policies that covered those years. An act of abuse that occurred in the 1970s would be covered by the general diocesan liability insurance policy then in effect, a policy that probably did not expressly bar claims of sexual abuse or molestation. In some cases the insurance carrier is no longer in business. State insurance regulators may have forced older weak insurers to merge or otherwise to stretch their capital supply; tracing back to the 1950s'-era insurers may lead to a variety of successor companies, which presents a further complication in assembling a settlement package.

The historical benefit to the diocese of searching out old insurance policies becomes very evident. Psychologists recognize that the abuse patterns typically went on for several years, allowing the individual to perpetrate his crime, while two, three or more insurance policies were in effect. It is possible that those who have presented belated claims for abuse will be compensated by three different insurers under their respective policies covering those years. Prior to the ISO exclusion of abuse, the policies that applied earlier may have a long "tail" to late-reported events. Plaintiffs may be able to force the insurance carriers and the church organization or diocese to reach a settlement with contributions by those insurers. Experience with the insurance market strongly suggests that the insurance carriers will fight such a creative "stringing" of policy coverages.

7:15 DIOCESAN LAWSUITS AGAINST INSURANCE CARRIERS

Conflicts regarding coverage by insurance carriers have exposed more information about diocesan actions with abusive priests than the dioceses wished to have on the public record.[63] As the diocese is the plaintiff contesting the denial of coverage, it must demonstrate the underlying facts of the abuse in a way that is more transparent than usually preferred.[64] The paradigm case was the Fall River (Massachustts) diocese's knowledge in 1963 of suspicious behavior by a serial predator, James Porter. "The Fall River diocese replied that it could not have anticipated the 'social and legal changes' that resulted in the 1992 abuse claims, that its officials did not know the extent of Mr. Porter's abuse, and that there was a poor understanding of the consequences of abuse at the time."[65] The coverage case was settled in 1994.

63. Rohde, supra.
64. Swisher & Mason, supra.
65. McLeod, supra.

CHAPTER 8

⌒∿⌒

Constitutional Issues

8:1 OVERVIEW[1]

This book deals with a relatively narrow legal issue: the consequences of child sexual abuse by members of the clergy of a particular religion. This chapter deals with the principal constitutional issues that have arisen under this set of issues, which have been much discussed by commentators and courts.[2]

Churches, like all houses of worship, enjoy special constitutional protections, a freedom of religion, stemming from the First Amendment's protection against an establishment of one state religion.[3] The well-established doctrine of constitutional law contains a prohibition against the government becoming too "entangled" with the doctrine or practices of a religion. In this context, "entanglement with religion" means the claim that a particular legal remedy is too intrusive on the religious practices of a church. Government entanglement is an issue to be raised by the leaders of a church to protect their institutional interests. Entanglement is not, however, an individual defense for an accused priest.

State courts handling clergy sexual abuse cases have swept away most of the "entanglement" defenses as insubstantial, as articulated by the Colorado Supreme Court: "[a]pplication of a secular standard to secular conduct that is tortious is not prohibited by the Constitution."[4] In general, "civil actions against clergy members and their superiors that involve claims of a breach of fiduciary duty, negligent hiring

1. Professor O'Reilly expresses his appreciation for the excellent research work of Andrew Cleves, University of Cincinnati Class of 2012.
2. See e.g., Kelly W.G. Clark et. al., "Of Compelling Interest: The Intersection of Religious Freedom and Civil Liability in the Portland Priest Sex Abuse Cases," 85 Or. L. Rev. 481, 521 (2006) (judicial review of negligence in employment decisions requires application of the more neutral concept of foreseeability, and as such, religious doctrine per se is not implicated).
3. See e.g., Serbian Eastern Orthodox Diocese v. Milivojevich, 426 U.S. 696, 709, 96 S. Ct. 2372, 49 L. Ed. 2d 151 (1976).
4. Moses v. Diocese of Colorado, 863 P.2d 310, 320 (Colo. 1993).

and supervision, and vicarious liability are actionable if they are supported by competent evidence in the record."[5] The Florida Supreme Court has held that the First Amendment Establishment Clause does not bar tort causes of action for damages against a church that employed an abuser, because the imposition of tort liability "has a secular purpose and the primary effect of imposing tort liability based on the allegations of the complaint neither advances nor inhibits religion." A Connecticut court put it simply: "The Free Exercise Clause might well prohibit this court from interfering in the manner in which the Diocese supervised a priest's performance of Mass, or confession, but it certainly cannot prohibit this court from determining whether the Diocese should be liable for negligently allowing its employees to engage in sexual conduct with minor females."[6] The core inquiry will focus on whether the religious institution "reasonably should have foreseen the risk of harm to third parties. This is a neutral principle of tort law. Therefore, based on the allegations in the complaint, we do not foresee 'excessive' entanglement in internal church matters or in interpretation of religious doctrine or ecclesiastical law."[7]

8:2 CONSTITUTIONALITY OF COURTS OVERSEEING CHURCH INTERNAL DISCIPLINE .

When a religious body learns of sexual misconduct by a member of its clergy, and the religious body applies disciplinary measures, there may be some consequences to the civil or criminal law handling of the sexual abuse case. The Roman Catholic Church has asserted the broadest rationales for keeping prosecutors and plaintiffs from compelling the Church to produce its internal discipline records, but those arguments have generally been unpersuasive to appellate courts, who have ordered disclosure.[8]

Courts have generally held that there is no First Amendment violation in an inquiry into the following civil torts arising in abuse cases:

- negligent hiring, assignment, and retention;
- breach of fiduciary duty;
- fraud, fraudulent concealment, and conspiracy to conceal;
- negligent infliction of emotional distress;
- negligent misrepresentation; and
- negligent supervision.

A Massachusetts court that upheld a subpoena for records of Jesuit files on a particular Jesuit priest concluded that the court's examination of Jesuit documents

---

5. Id. at 321.

6. Givens v. St. Adalbert Church, 2013 WL 4420776 (Conn. Super. 2013).

7. Malicki v. Doe, 814 So. 2d 347, 364 (Fla. 2002).

8. See e.g., Roman Catholic Diocese of Jackson v. Morrison, 905 So. 2d 1213, 1238 (Miss. 2005).

regarding the priest in question did "not infringe on the Jesuits' autonomous decision-making with respect to [the accused priest]'s fitness, discipline, assignments, or any other aspect of his relationship with the Jesuits."[9]

8:3 BANKRUPTCY AND CRIMINAL RATIONALES FOR REVIEWING INTERNAL DISCIPLINARY DECISIONS

One tough case that was decided against Roman Catholic Church defenses was the bankruptcy court analysis of the privilege claims presented by an Oregon diocese that chose to file for bankruptcy in the face of the expense of settling abuse claims. For discovery purposes, the bankruptcy court forced diocesan officials to respond to deposition questions regarding church practices and policies, etc. The court held: "Evidence regarding diocesan 'patterns, practices, and policies' in regards to allegations of sexual misconduct with a minor by any priest while working in an Archdiocesan ministry assignment is relevant for discovery purposes to the negligence claims of various tort claimants" who were contesting the payout in a diocesan bankruptcy case.[10]

The Oregon bankruptcy court delved into church discipline because the diocesan officials allegedly had "knowledge of sexual misconduct of priests with minors, and knowledge about whether priests who engage in such behavior may safely be returned to ministry involving children, [which] bears upon whether debtor was negligent in how it handled allegations of abuse."[11] And the court looked to both past and present norms of clergy misconduct. "Although the relevant time frame for these claims is the time of the alleged misconduct, evidence of debtor's later policies could possibly lead to evidence that would be relevant to the claims of negligence or to establishing debtor's knowledge for purposes of extending the statute of limitations under [state law]."[12]

Ordinarily, churches' internal discipline policies would be deemed protected by the First Amendment, and would ordinarily not be disclosed in a civil case. But the act of probing policies was seen as valuable to the bankruptcy adjudication: "If, for example, evidence shows that debtor continued to reassign known pedophile priests to new parishes even after it knew that child molesters are likely to re-offend, that fact would provide some evidence that debtor's earlier reassignment was not merely a mistake or accident. Further, changes in policies after alleged abuse occurred could shed light on what the policies were at the time of the abuse."[13]

In the criminal law context, subpoenas for records showing the "internal workings" documents of a diocese were upheld on appeal, because the diocese was deemed

9. Society of Jesus of New England v. Commonwealth, 441 Mass. 662, 675, 808 N.E.2d 272, 283 (2004).

10. In re Roman Catholic Archbishop of Portland, 335 B.R. 815, 821 (Bankr. D. Or. 2005).

11. Id. at 821.

12. Id. at 823.

13. Id. at 823.

to be the "defendant's employer, for the purpose of gathering evidence in a criminal prosecution against defendant under the laws of Illinois. The State has neither expressed nor implied an aim to determine for itself whether defendant violated canon law, much less to override any determination of the Diocese on that point."[14]

And claims that internal discipline records were subject to priest-penitent evidentiary privileges were rejected in the Oregon bankruptcy case. "(T)he privilege extends to communications with clergy, not with other employees, agents, or officials of the church who are not clergy."[15] And "not all communications, even those made privately and in confidence, are subject to the privilege; only those confidential communications that are made to a clergy member 'in the member's professional character' are protected."[16]

A commentator presented another view: "The fact that Church administration would like to keep such documents confidential by claiming they are akin to information gained in the sacred confessional is beside the point. The information in these files is not given in a confessional context or even usually in a context that triggers the protections of Oregon's broad clergy-penitent privilege; accordingly, these files deserve no more protection than employee files of any other institution."[17]

As indicated in the Hosanna-Tabor case, the employment of particular ministerial employees is constitutionally protected in the employment context, but this does not relieve the religious institution from sexual abuse claims asserting a failure of proper supervision of ministers.[18] The better analysis of the impact of *Hosanna-Tabor* was the Connecticut view that a civil court could find liability for failure to warn the members of the new parish to which the alleged abuser was transferred, and the negligent supervision by the diocesan officials subsequent to that transfer.[19]

8:4 MANDATORY REPORTING AND THE RELIGIOUS CONFESSIONAL PRIVILEGE

Chapter 10 discusses in detail the conflicts concerning statutory and case law protections for confidential "confessions" received during religious counseling.

14. People v. Campobello, 348 Ill. App. 3d 619, 629, 810 N.E.2d 307, 315, 316 (Ill. App. Ct. 2004).

15. *Roman Catholic Archbishop of Portland*, 335 B.R. at 829.

16. Id.

17. Clark et al., supra.

18. Hosanna–Tabor Evangelical Lutheran Church & School v. EEOC, 132 S. Ct. 694, 706 (2012), and see Colomb v. Roman Catholic Diocese of Burlington, Vermont, Inc., United States District Court, No. 2:10–CV–254 (D. Vt. Sept. 28, 2012); Doe 169 v. Brandon, Court of Appeals of Minnesota, No. A12–1721 (Minn. App. May 28, 2013); Redwing v. Catholic Bishop for Diocese of Memphis, 363 S.W.3d 436 (Tenn. 2012); Givens v. St. Adalbert Church, 2013 WL 4420776 (Conn. Super. 2013).

19. Doe No. 2 v. Norwich Roman Catholic Diocesan Corp., 2013 Westlaw 387143 (Conn. Super. 2013).

CONSTITUTIONAL ISSUES (97)

The topic has been hotly contested in case law and by scholars.[20] This subsection focuses specifically on the constitutional aspects of that conflict between mandates for the reporting of abuse, and privileges for the secrecy of religious counselors' communications. This is a frequent controversy in clergy abuse cases.[21]

To be claimed "confessional" in a religious context, and therefore privileged from disclosure, these must be communications made in the role "as a spiritual advisor."[22] The Illinois appeals court applied the priest-penitent privilege "only to information that an individual conveys in the course of making an admission or confession to a clergy member in his capacity as spiritual counselor."[23] That court concluded that a privileged communication had to meet two following criteria to receive statutory protection: "1) made for the purpose of receiving spiritual counsel or consolation (2) to a clergy member whose religion requires him to receive admissions or confessions for the purpose of providing spiritual counsel or consolation."[24]

The Roman Catholic Church dioceses in the United States largely follow the Essential Norms adopted by the U.S. Conference of Catholic Bishops in 2002, as discussed in earlier chapters. Norm 11 establishes that the diocese/eparchy will comply with all applicable civil reporting laws and will cooperate in any investigation.[25] But the Church also took the lead, among all entities, in defending secrecy of communications received during religious counseling. As a priest-attorney wrote in a law review commentary, "[t]he Church regards communication under the seal of the sacrament of penance as absolutely privileged and will resist any attempt from a secular jurisdiction to impose a breach of such communication."[26]

The extent of the application of this "confessional privilege" does not necessarily engage the civil courts in intrusions upon the doctrine of a religion. The Massachusetts courts said that a court asked to enforce a subpoena for church records "can decide issues of relevance, burdensomeness, and the applicability of the asserted privileges without having to decide matters of religion or embroil itself in the internal workings of the (religious entity). Indeed, the only form of 'entanglement' with religion at issue in the motions to quash is a form that Talbot

---

20. See e.g., Clark et al., supra; Norman Abrams, "Addressing the Tension between the Clergy-Communicant Privilege and the Duty to Report Child Abuse in State Statutes," 44 B.C. L. Rev. 1127 (2003); Susan Vivian Mangold, "Reforming Child Protection in Response to the Catholic Church Child Sexual Abuse Scandal," 14 U. Fla. J.L. & Pub. Pol'y 155, 176 (2003); Julie M. Arnold, "'Divine' Justice and the Lack of Secular Intervention: Abrogating the Clergy-Communicant Privilege in Mandatory Reporting Statutes to Combat Child Sexual Abuse," 42 Val. U. L. Rev. 849, 886–88 (2008).

21. See e.g., Commonwealth v F.W., 465 Mass. 1, 986 N.E.2d 868 (2013).

22. Id. at 830.

23. People v. Campobello, 810 N.E.2d 307, 320, 321 (Ill. App. Ct. 2004).

24. Id.

25. Ladislas Orsy, S.J., "Bishops' Norms: Commentary and Evaluation," 44 B.C. L. Rev. 999, 1019 (2003).

26. Id. at 999.

and the Jesuits have themselves invited, namely, the court's consideration whether Talbot's communications qualify for protection under the priest-penitent privilege, G.L. c. 233, § 20A. Assessment of the applicability of that privilege does not lead to excessive government entanglement in religion."[27]

A religious privileged communication must satisfy all of the following elements: "1) it must be intended to be in confidence; 2) it must be made to a member of the clergy who in the course of his or her religious discipline or practice is authorized or accustomed to hear such communications; and 3) such member of the clergy has a duty under the discipline or tenets of the church, religious denomination or organization to keep such communications secret."

The facts of a particular abuse case may remove the context in which religious counseling or confession would be an issue. A New York case found no "counseling relationship...which the misconduct alleged was a part, such as might preclude an inquiry into the propriety of the priest's conduct as an excessive involvement in the philosophy of his religious community."[28] The court in a Colorado case found that the tort claims

> do not involve disputes within the church and are not based solely on ecclesiastical or disciplinary matters which would call into question the trial court's power to render a judgment against the defendants. Our decision does not require a reading of the Constitution and Canons of the Protestant Episcopal Church or any other documents of church governance. Because the facts of this case do not require interpreting or weighing church doctrine and neutral principles of law can be applied, the First Amendment is not a defense against (plaintiff)'s claims.[29]

8:5 NO SPECIAL IMMUNITIES FOR CLERGY

Courts are very aware of the sensitivity that they should not give special immunity to religious abusers compared to the commonplace adult sexual abuser. The First Amendment does not provide a shield behind which a church may avoid liability for harm arising from an alleged sexual assault and battery by one of its clergy members.[30] Giving a form of immunity to religious institutions in abuse torts "could risk placing religious institutions in a preferred position over secular institutions, a concept both foreign and hostile to the First Amendment."[31] As the Mississippi Supreme Court held: "For this Court to agree with the Diocese would require us to conclude that ecclesiastical principles could reasonably impose or suggest different

---

27. Society of Jesus of New England v. Commonwealth, 441 Mass. 662, 675, 808 N.E.2d 272, 283 (2004).

28. Jones by Jones v. Trane, 153 Misc. 2d 822, 828, 591 N.Y.S.2d 927, 930–31 (N.Y. Sup. Ct. 1992).

29. Moses v. Diocese of Colorado, 863 P.2d 310, 320 (Colo. 1993).

30. Malicki v. Doe, 814 So. 2d 347, 365 (Fla. 2002).

31. Id.

requirements for the protection of children from sexual molestation, than the requirements generally imposed by society. This we cannot do."[32]

Likewise, New York and North Carolina courts refused to establish an assumption that "a religious body must be held free from any responsibility for wholly predictable and foreseeable injurious consequences of personnel decisions, although such decisions incorporate no theological or dogmatic tenets," because this "would go beyond First Amendment protection and cloak such bodies with an exclusive immunity greater than that required for the preservation of the principles constitutionally safeguarded."[33]

The clash between religious and moral codes, and the allegation of sexual abuse of a child by a member of the clergy, underlies these appellate court views. "The Plaintiffs' claim...presents the issue of whether the Church Defendants knew or had reason to know of Privette's propensity to engage in sexual misconduct...conduct that the Church Defendants do not claim is part of the tenets or practices of the Methodist Church."[34] The analogy is more like that of a school board or college being held accountable for sexual misconduct of a teacher with a pupil. No special immunity is provided for churches and ministerial employees.

8:6 CAN THERE BE A TORT OF CLERGY "MALPRACTICE"?

There is no statutory definition of malpractice in the context of religious entities or practitioners, because the "practice" of one's religion is shielded by First Amendment principles. Thus, any express claims of clergy "malpractice" in tort would always involve entanglement: "It would be impossible for a court or jury to adjudicate a typical case of clergy malpractice, without first ascertaining whether the cleric...performed within the level of expertise expected of a similar professional..., following his calling, or practicing his profession within the community."

In contrast to skilled physicians or experienced attorneys, civil case precedents do not draw bright lines for the conduct of the "reasonable bishop." A court expressly rejected that claim: "Any effort...to instruct the trial jury as to the duty of care which a clergyman should exercise, would of necessity require the Court or jury to define and express the standard of care to be followed by other reasonable Presbyterian clergy of the community. This in turn would require the Court and the jury to consider the fundamental perspective and approach to counseling inherent in the beliefs and practices of that denomination. This is as unconstitutional as it is impossible. It fosters excessive entanglement with religion."[35]

32. Roman Catholic Diocese of Jackson v. Morrison, 905 So. 2d 1213, 1229–30 (Miss. 2005).

33. *Trane*, 153 Misc. 2d at 828, 591 N.Y.S.2d at 932; accord, Smith v. Privette, 128 N.C. App. 490, 495, 495 S.E.2d 395, 398 (N.C. Ct. App. 1998).

34. *Privette*, 128 N.C. App. at 495, 495 S.E.2d at 398.

35. Schmidt v. Bishop, 779 F. Supp. 321, 328 (S.D.N.Y. 1991).

Courts decline to engage in an analysis of the "right" way to provide religious counseling care, because to do so "inherently would entangle the civil judicial system in the religious merits of a minister's or church's implementation of its religious duties. In states like Colorado, the legislature has expressly evinced an intent to exclude religious ministers, priests, and rabbis from the statutory scheme which imposes liability upon psychologists for malpractice."[36]

8:7 BREACH OF FIDUCIARY DUTY

Unlike clergy malpractice, a breach of fiduciary duty claim against a church "does not run afoul of the Establishment Clause. The imposition of liability based on a breach of fiduciary duty has a secular purpose and the primary effect of imposing liability under the circumstances of this case neither advances nor inhibits religion." This is because the jury is not being called upon to interpret ecclesiastical doctrine. "Rather, the focus is on whether the Church Defendants had a fiduciary relationship with Doe giving rise to a duty and whether they breached this duty by failing to protect Doe from Evans. Moreover, the resolution of this dispute does not depend on 'extensive inquiry by civil courts into religious law and polity,'[37] or interpretation and resolution of religious doctrine. Thus, we foresee no excessive entanglement based on the allegations of Doe's amended complaint."[38]

In the analysis of other courts, setting the "duty" in selecting and retaining priests is tied in to the religious entity's faith norms rather than to conventional tort claims of negligent hiring of a business employee. "Questions of hiring and retention of clergy necessarily will require interpretation of church canons, and internal church policies and practices."[39] Because the court would be required to interpret internal church policies and practices—regarding an "inquiry into the decision of who should be permitted to become or remain a priest necessarily would involve prohibited excessive entanglement with religion"—claims of negligence predicated upon a "negligent hiring" theory were dismissed.[40] Other courts disagree: "rather than being restricted to consideration of a standard of care to be followed by clergy persons or other religious entities, a court or jury can, in some circumstances, measure a religious organization's or official's conduct by pre-existing secular standards of care to which all fiduciaries are held."[41]

When the tort law norm of "reasonable person" is applied to clergy sexual misconduct, the First Amendment prohibits claims against a religious entity for negligent hiring or retention, because such claims would require a court to develop

36. Destefano v. Grabrian, 763 P.2d 275, 286 (Colo. 1988).
37. Serbian E. Orthodox Diocese v. Milivojevich, 426 U.S. 696, 709, 96 S. Ct. 2372, 49 L. Ed. 2d 151 (1976).
38. Doe v. Evans, 814 So. 2d 370, 376 (Fla. 2002).
39. Isely v. Capuchin Province, 880 F. Supp. 1138, 1150 (E.D. Mich. 1995).
40. Id.
41. Martinelli v. Bridgeport Roman Catholic Diocesan Corp., 10 F. Supp. 2d 138, 146 (D. Conn. 1998), aff'd in part, vacated in part, 196 F.3d 409 (2d Cir. 1999).

a "reasonable cleric" standard of care, which would involve the interpretation of church canons and internal church policies.[42]

8:8 POST-ARREST DUE PROCESS ISSUES

After the arrest of a clergy member in a sexual abuse case, conventional due process protections apply for the preservation of his or her rights under U.S. constitutional law. None of the cases reported in the legal literature suggest any special immunity from criminal prosecution should apply to the status of religious defendants. Criminal prosecution for failure to report instances in which child sexual abuse is known or reasonably knowable from the circumstances can be pursued, as was the case for the Catholic bishop of Kansas City in a 2012 prosecution.

8:9 CONVENTIONAL STATUTES OF LIMITATIONS ISSUES

The fairness and due process safeguards for the accused in a U.S. criminal proceeding include the protection of statutes of limitations, the legislated decision that it would be unfair to prosecute a person in situations where the alleged crime occurred more than a certain number of years previously. Chapter 5 covers these constitutional issues in depth.

The issue of looking back at past abuse claims, in some cases by means of a new legislative "window" for time-expired sexual abuse claims, has been controversial. For example, the 2011 Delaware Supreme Court decision in *Sheehan* concerned a very old abuse case, brought to court decades later after the alleged harm. The court looked to the law as it was when the abuse occurred,[43] and the trial judge "determined applying anything other than the code in existence at the time of the alleged abuse would be a violation of due process, "[44] and "fundamental due process dictates that the scope of liability imposed by a retroactive law cannot substantially change the scope of liability existing at the time of the alleged abuse."[45]

The issue was one of timing for delayed reports of past sexual molestation. "If the current Delaware criminal code were found applicable, the sexual acts alleged in this case could fall within the definition of a criminal offense that did not exist at the time of the alleged abuse. The result would be to create a cause of action where none existed in 1962."[46]

---

42. L.L.N. v. Clauder, 209 Wis. 2d 674, 688, 563 N.W.2d 434, 441 (1997) (citing Pritzlaff v Archdiocese of Milwaukee, 194 Wisc.2d 302, 533 N.W.2d 780(1995)).

43. 10 Del. C. § 8145(a)(2009) states that "[a] civil cause of action for sexual abuse of a minor shall be based upon sexual acts that would constitute a criminal offense under the Delaware Code." Sheehan v. Oblates of St. Francis de Sales, 15 A.3d 1247, 1257 (Del. Feb. 22, 2011), reargument denied (Apr. 19, 2011).

44. *Sheehan*, 15 A.3d at 1257.

45. Id.

46. Id. at 1258.

8:10 STATUTORY REOPENING OF LIMITATION PERIODS FOR CHILD ABUSE REPORTS

One of the hottest due process debates in the clergy sexual abuse field has been the ability of state legislators to reopen the existing statutes of limitations in order to permit the prosecution of older cases of sexual abuse that had not been the subject of a timely report and timely prosecution. Chapter 5 covers these issues. Despite the controversy and public policy and constitutional arguments, most of the appellate review cases and commentaries have upheld such reopenings.

CHAPTER 9

cᴠⲟ

Bankruptcy Issues

9:1 BANKRUPTCY OF A DIOCESE

The American Catholic Church is "land rich and cash poor" and must depend on a constant stream of positive, accepting donors for the sustaining of its works of faith and charity. In its millennia of international challenges, the Roman Catholic Church as an institution has never faced the huge contingent liability of multiple punitive damage awards and large "global settlements" that it has confronted in the past three decades. The key word here is "contingent"; the Church cannot know with confidence how many child sexual encounters occurred, with whom, where, and in what years, and among those, how many will result in claims for money damages. As the bishop of Tucson explained after his diocese declared bankruptcy, there would be at least legal certainty; the federal bankruptcy court was objective and would provide "the best forum for fairly and equitably compensating all those harmed."[1]

The thought of a church entering bankruptcy is shocking, but the oddest aspect of the process for religious institutions is that they get the financial equivalent of what Catholic doctrine calls "general absolution." In the federal bankruptcy court, under Chapter 11 of the U.S. Bankruptcy Code, the diocese receives what it cannot otherwise achieve: a mandatory gathering of all claims against the diocese, from all past, present, and future claimants, with a stay of the active claims and suits that have already been asserted by persons who demanded compensation for past sexual misconduct.[2] Their individual tort claims are frozen until the bankruptcy court determines the amount to which all the normal suppliers and conventional business providers are due, and then the amount that this class of abused individuals may be entitled to receive, if abuse is actually proven. A person is designated to protect the interests of abuse claimants who have not yet made compensation

---

1. Bishop Gerald Kicanas, "Healing through Bankruptcy," 193(8) America Magazine 10 (Sept. 26, 2005).
2. Jennie Latta, "Bankruptcy and the Catholic Church," 191(17) America Magazine 18 (Nov. 29, 2004).

claims.[3] In practice, the opening of a bankruptcy case leads to the voluntary formation of settlement plans by the creditor committees. The committee of vendors who sold supplies to the diocese and those representing the retired workers, for example, will be separate from the committees formed of the abuse victims who seek compensation.

Having the bankruptcy court determine which claims will be paid, and which denied, proceeds from a set of factors that are different from the factors of conventional prioritization according to policy preferences or religious obligations.[4]

The bankruptcy court typically leaves the "debtor in possession," but it may appoint an examiner and may also appoint a trustee, who is paid to oversee the orderly payment of bills and the planning for a "workout" by the diocese. The examiner is assigned to find all the assets and to list all of the pending claims, so as to facilitate a compromise "workout" of the assets. A trustee, if one is appointed, has no religious function, but his or her control over expenditures may result, indirectly, in an important constraint on the operating decisions that can be made by the bishop. The court may allow a settlement in which a trust is created at a certain funding level; in the Tucson bankruptcy two trusts were created for the liquidation of certain properties owned by the diocese.[5] In the Portland bankruptcy, an attorney was designated to represent the interests of additional tort claimants who were not yet parties to the case.[6]

Bankruptcy is a federal court proceeding for the determination of which of a failed business's creditors will be paid, when a debtor's assets are exceeded by its current and contingent liabilities.[7] Churches can declare bankruptcy,[8] but they cannot be forced into involuntary bankruptcy.[9] Intriguing studies of the conflicts that have arisen and will arise in church bankruptcies have been studied by scholars.[10]

The colloquial term "going bankrupt," for "bills overwhelming income," does not apply to the clergy sexual abuse cases. These cases have contingent liabilities of a size that is unpredictable; depending on the activities of the alleged predator priest(s), the diocese may face a dozen or more claims that have a potential for jury awards of substantial compensatory and punitive damages. To aid the reader's understanding, we begin with a little background on the way that bankruptcy has been used when other multiple civil tort problems have been addressed.

---

3. In re Catholic Bishop of Spokane, 2010 WL 2560391 (E.D. Wash. 2010); In re Catholic Diocese of Wilmington, Inc., 484 B.R. 629, 57 Bankr. Ct. Dec. 90 (D. Del. 2012).

4. Confidential Claimant No. 87/204 v. Roman Catholic Church, 319 Fed. Appx. 566 (9th Cir. 2009).

5. Latta, supra, at 18.

6. In re Roman Catholic Archbishop of Portland, 661 F.3d 417 (9th Cir. 2011).

7. 11 U.S.C. § 101 et seq. (2010).

8. 11 U.S.C.A. §§ 101(8), 109(d) (2010); In re Miracle Church of God in Christ, 119 B.R. 308 (Bankr. M.D. Fla. 1990).

9. 11 U.S.C. § 303(a) (2010); United Church of the Ministers of God, 84 B.R. 50 (Bankr. E.D. Pa. 1988).

10. David Skeel Jr., "'Sovereignty' Issues and the Church Bankruptcy Cases," 29 Seton Hall Legis. J. 345 (2004).

The best modern analogy may be to the industrial companies that sold or used asbestos. A long-delayed death from asbestos-related lung diseases (asbestosis and mesothelioma) is a consequence of the human lung tissues being obstructed with tiny fibers that were inhaled while a worker used, installed, or removed the mineral product, asbestos. Companies that made products using asbestos became aware during the 1940s that lung damage could result from its use. Decades later, workers who were ill during the 1980s and later sued these companies for damages relating to the fatal lung disease, asserting that the illness manifested itself long after the actual exposure. So the litigant was making a claim that certain events many years before had caused injury. The companies that made the products were strong, viable makers of useful products and they paid all their bills regularly. But the prospect of paying thousands of individual claims, each claim being paid hundreds of thousands of dollars, was a real possibility. This presented the likelihood that at some future date, the total sum of all the company's assets and income would not equal the total payout for damages. Lawyers for the asbestos companies then advised their client companies to voluntarily enter bankruptcy as a form of orderly payment of the asbestos victims. The federal bankruptcy court "froze" all the claims.[11] Then the company's regular creditors such as its water or electric suppliers, and its litigation creditors including a committee of plaintiffs' lawyers handling asbestos claims, were able to negotiate a series of compromise settlements in which every valid injury claimant would get some payment, but something less than total compensation.

What is not clear is the "tipping point" that pushes a Catholic diocese into filing for bankruptcy. The tenth U.S. diocese to file for bankruptcy, Stockton, California, told its parishioners in September 2013 that $18,700,000 had already been paid to 22 claimants and more abuse claims were expected.[12] Such communications with the "people in the pews" are expected to cushion the blow of the news that their church has become unable to pay its bills. In prior bankruptcies there were comparable communications with donors and parishioners for the dioceses of Spokane, Tucson, Portland, Milwaukee, Davenport (Iowa), San Diego, Fairbanks (Alaska), Wilmington (Delaware). and Gallup (New Mexico).

When the Catholic dioceses with surprisingly large volumes of previously unknown abuse claimants examined their ability to pay damages to the young people who alleged that they had been harmed by clergy, the diocesan lawyers recommended a bankruptcy path similar to that of the asbestos companies. This was not an easy or welcomed outcome.[13] Normal creditors who supplied office supplies, for example, were creditors along with the abuse claimants. Abuse lawsuits were "frozen" by the automatic stay of the Bankruptcy Code,[14] regardless of the age of the claim or the length of time since the abuse, just as the older claimants

11. In re Johns-Manville Corp., 66 B.R. 517 (Bankr. S.D.N.Y. 1986).

12. Editorial, "Dark Days for Church," Stockton Record (Sept. 15, 2013).

13. John Jarboe, "Bankruptcy—The Last Resort: Protecting the Diocesan Client from Potential Liability Judgments," 37 Cath. Lawyer 153 (1996).

14. In re Roman Catholic Archbishop of Portland, 661 F.3d 417 (9th Cir. 2011).

for long-past inhalation of asbestos were frozen in those commercial bankruptcy cases. The effect of the process is to drive a settlement that receives the support of the majority of creditors; for purposes of this text, the secondary effect is to draw in all the claims at one time, rather than paying out each claim as it is filed.[15]

9:2 OPERATIONAL EFFECTS OF BANKRUPTCY

The bishop, in the role known to bankruptcy courts as the "debtor in possession," continues to conduct the normal work of the Church while his lawyer negotiates with the committee of the plaintiffs' attorneys. The goal was to bite the bullet, call in all the claims at once, and then sell assets such as land and liquidate longer-term investments such as seminary burse funds, and to work out a long enough payment schedule so as to effect a large enough settlement so that the bankruptcy court would accept the proposed dollar size and distribution formula of the settlement. A claims office would be opened for abuse claimants, and the plaintiffs who alleged that the diocese should compensate them for past abuse would present their grounds for claims to the neutral decision-maker. Because the public has a "weighty interest in public safety and in knowing who might sexually abuse children," the bankruptcy court could suspend payments to priests who had been accused of sexual misconduct.[16] The litigants and claimants who are current or future abuse plaintiffs would become part of the group of creditors who had claims which the bankruptcy court would recognize in the settlement.

The benefit to the diocese would be the "claim bar date," that is, extinguishment of future clergy abuse compensation claims that had not been filed in court before a certain fixed date. The bankruptcy order also ends claims for punitive damages or for willful and malicious injury, as these damages can be discharged entirely if the available assets in the asset pool are insufficient to satisfy all claims. Once confirmed in the bankruptcy court, the Chapter 11 reorganization plan defines all rights of the creditors, who receive only what is in the plan. So if the asset pool for the diocese is insufficient to satisfy claims that have higher priority than punitive damages, the claims may be discharged.

During the bankruptcy proceeding, the examiner appointed by the court estimates the debtor's likely damage liabilities.[17] This process of estimation is not res judicata as to causation and damages, but it does allow a goal to be set. This impacts on settlement negotiations. The process is used to define and limit the available asset pool from which claims are paid.

Further, the Bankruptcy Code provides a binding notice and bar date. This will establish a limitations period on claims that were viable (i.e., not time-barred) on the date the bankrtupcy case was filed. Those claims must be filed on or before the

---

15. Latta, supra, 18.

16. *Roman Catholic Archbishop of Portland*, 661 F.3d 417.

17. Confidential Claimant v. Roman Catholic Church, 2009 Westlaw 646253 (9th Cir. 2011).

bar date, or they will be discharged without payment, unless the estate had acknowledged the claim by listing it in a schedule (as it should have listed any abuse damages claim that has already gone to final judgment against the diocese). But if the statute of limitations has already run on the claim before the bankruptcy case is filed, the filing doesn't extend it.[18] The court may appoint an attorney as examiner of the abuse claims that were not filed before the bankruptcy proceedings began.[19] And some abuse victims may have been confused about whether bankruptcy revives older claims, and whether those claims could be asserted belatedly, after years had passed. For example, Delaware extended its statute of limitations by an additional two-year "window" and 175 suits were filed.[20] The notice requires any claims to be filed before the specific date when such claims are to be barred under bankruptcy law.

The official publication of the date by which claims must be made is a powerful tool; it cuts off any claims that have not yet been asserted.[21] So, according to a veteran bankruptcy lawyer, the bishop could publish a statement announcing to any and all current or future claimants: "Diocese 'X' has filed bankruptcy in the bankruptcy court of the district of 'X,' and any person having a claim resulting from the intentional or negligent injury caused by a person acting on behalf of or in the name of the Diocese is directed to file such claim by such and such bar date, and if not, it will be forever barred."[22]

To a lawyer, this process seems quite normal and logical. To the Catholic in the pew, it sounds shocking that their church could be "shut down" by a few lawsuits, even if the facts of the lawsuits were distressing. Press publicity about bankruptcy because of past sexual abuse is a very shaming, constraining defeat for the pride of the people served by that diocese, but the work of the Church continues. As described above, churches are not shut down by bankruptcy, just as insulation makers who had used asbestos in the past could continue to ship their products while arranging for future profits to be shared with the claimants. The church ordinarily might address the claims by selling buildings or its seminary, as Boston did, or part of its Catholic cemetery, as Cincinnati did. But when the bankruptcy court requires an accounting of all assets, the church may be called upon to "give 'til it hurts" in the disposal of available land or other assets.

9:3 ASSETS AND DONOR RELATIONS

Detailed accounting of the assets of the bankruptcy applicant is required, and the federal bankruptcy court severely punishes those who try to hide assets during a bankruptcy case. So the diocese is required to disclose the value of its land,

---

18. 11 U.S.C. § 1141(d) (2010).
19. In re Catholic Bishop of Spokane, 2010 Westlaw 2560391 (E.D. Wash. 2010).
20. Randall Chase, "Bankruptcy Filing Delays Church Sex Case," Associated Press (Oct. 20, 2009).
21. Id.
22. Jarboe, supra, 160.

buildings, and other fixed assets, and to disclose its cash reserves, long-term invest-ments, etc. Of course, public notice is made of the names of the known pedophile priests, and they can object to being listed and disclosed before a final adjudication of their claims of innocence.[23] This is very newsworthy and the news media can read the court filings on line via the federal court PACER system, to speed their reporting.

The delicate public communications task for the archdiocesan staff will be to continue to ask for donations while the donor community fears "paying my money to bail out the bishop for the benefit of some plaintiff's lawyer." Sale of large assets, such as the Boston archdiocese sale of its seminary grounds and other properties for $200 million to pay off sexual abuse claimants, was a painful penance for the loyal Catholic donors who never condoned or knew of the abuse.

9:4 ASSETS OF PARISHES

As explained in later chapters on canon law issues, the parish and the diocese have a very nuanced relationship. This canon law subtlety is not matched by any corre-sponding treatment in the state law of a "corporation sole," and federal bankruptcy law will follow these aspects of state law. Victims in clergy sexual abuse cases who sue dioceses "eye these parish assets because their inclusion deepens diocesan pockets."[24]

It is not acceptable in bankruptcy court for the petitioner, such as a diocese, to hide assets or disburse assets so that they cannot be found and counted in among the assets of the diocese.[25] Wealthy parishes have assets, but if the diocese is a "cor-poration sole" under state law, assets of the parishes are accessible by the trustee in bankruptcy, despite their temptation to segregate and withhold their funds. Ultimately the trustee will demand all of the assets that can be directly controlled under canon law by the bishop. These include the "bank" function of the diocesan treasury through which parish savings and investments are required to flow in some dioceses; Tucson learned a lesson after the bankruptcy experience showed the weakness of its system.[26] Although the corporate laws of the states may vary, it is more likely than not that federal bankruptcy law will reach into the assets of an individual diocese and an individual parish, and use the funding from both to help satisfy the claimants.

In diocesan accounting, there may be an inconsistency that affects the evalua-tion of the total asset value of the bankruptcy "estate." The treasurer of the diocese

23. In re Roman Catholic Archbishop of Portland, 661 F.3d 417 (9th Cir. 2011).

24. Daniel Marcinak, "Separation of Church and Estate: On Excluding Parish Assets from the Bankruptcy Estate of a Diocese Organized as a Corporation Sole," 55 Cath. U. L. Rev. 583 (2006).

25. See Fred Nafziger, "Bankruptcy Defeats," 194(11) America Magazine 11 (Mar. 27, 2006).

26. Kicanas, supra, 10.

may have operated an internal "bank" with individual accounts for each parish or each special grouping. For example, assume a local parish holds an annual fundraising festival that raises $60,000. At the end of each festival, the checking account is closed and the proceeds are forwarded to the diocese "bank" under the name of that parish. Is the $60,000 an asset of the diocese? Probably yes. The canon law issues of parish rights against the diocese are separate from the analysis of title and rights of ownership under federal and state laws.[27] Tucson's bankruptcy taught that diocese to change its informal central banking arrangements.[28]

Parishes have land, buildings, vehicles, and other assets. Parishes sometimes have bank accounts to pay for projects or for other purposes, titled in the name of the parish. Under state law, if the parish is separately incorporated, and its funds were not comingled in a funding structure run by the diocesan treasurer, an argument can be made under state law that its assets are not available to pay the debts of the diocese. Under canon law, each bishop is empowered to direct the actions of the pastor of each of his parishes. Determination by the bankruptcy trustee of the total value of the bankrupt estate may depend on who "owns" individual parish assets: the diocese or the parish?

For most parishioners who donated to (a hypothetical) St. Ann's Church for 50 years, it may come as a surprise to learn that the bishop could be pressed to sell the land and buildings to raise funds to settle the bankruptcy claims of a victim of a priest who never came to St. Ann's. These are the fine detail questions that arise when a "juridical" (Church law) question of authority comes into the rather unsympathetic process for examination of the debtor in federal bankruptcy court.[29]

All of the pending claims of abuse may not yet have been made, so that the embarrassing but necessary public advertisement would be made—deepening the public relations problem of the church—that anyone who had been sexually abused in the diocese by named priests or anyone else, would have to notify a certain attorney-trustee by a certain date, or be barred rom making the claim.[30] This is a newsworthy item that reminds the public of the diocese's crisis situation that led to bankruptcy.

Although a receiver is rarely appointed in institutional claims with an ongoing solvent entity such as a diocese, it is a remote possibility. Complexities of parish, school, and diocesan fund controls make it possible to overlook some money. Some states such as Wisconsin allowed separate corporations for each parish,[31] but dioceses that have chosen the corporation sole model leave all titles in the bishop.

Will a federal overseer of the diocesan finances be named by the court? The appointment of active Bankruptcy Trustees, who could request a federal fraud

27. Nicholas Cafardi, "The Availability of Parish Assets for Diocesan Debts: A Canonical Analysis," 29 Seton Hall Legis. J. 361 (2004).
28. Kicanas, supra, 10.
29. Catharine Pierce Wells, "Who Owns the Local Church? A Pressing Issue for Dioceses in Bankruptcy," 29 Seton Hall Legis. J. 375 (2004).
30. In re Roman Catholic Archbishop of Portland, 661 F.3d 417 (9th Cir. 2011).
31. Brian Olszewski, "Milwaukee Archdiocese Files for Bankruptcy Protection over Abuse Claims," Cath. News Serv. (Jan. 5, 2011).

prosecution for concealing assets, occur from time to time in individual bankruptcy cases. The situation becomes more complex for the lawyer representing a person who claims to have been sexually abused. The committee of creditors includes lawyers for these civil tort abuse claimants, whose claims are frozen during the bankruptcy process. The active pursuit of proof in these claims becomes somewhat more complicated as the settlement is more likely to be achieved. Historically, a bankruptcy filing by a diocese will have a significant impact to diminish the diocesan insurance carrier's willingness to settle older abuse, claims while the uncertainties of compensation for that abuse are exacerbated by the bankruptcy case.

In summary, the lesson of the multiple U.S. Catholic diocesan experiences with bankruptcy is to avoid it whenever possible. If it must happen, a prudent bishop will communicate what it actually means to the people in the pews, and accept the premise of civil law that all claimants in the bankruptcy claim process will be treated fairly, even those with sexual abuse allegations as the basis for their claims. They will be treated fairly in bankruptcy while the defense of civil litigation will continue.

9:5 BANKRUPTCY'S NEGATIVE EFFECTS ON DIOCESES AND DONORS

As of late 2013, nine Catholic dioceses in the United States had declared bankruptcy. This is a source of great shame and dismay, because of the harm that it is inevitably done to the social service ministry work of the Church. The loss of funding for social service projects is a result of the expenditure of diocesan reserve funds on compensation to those who have been abused.[32] For example, the 2011 bankruptcy of the Milwaukee archdiocese resulted after 190 cases were settled but the 16 outstanding claimants rejected an offer of $4.6 million in November 2010. Since 2002, the Milwaukee archdiocese has "sold property, liquidated savings and investments, eliminated ministries and services, cut staff by nearly 40 percent, and put all available real estate on the market in order to provide resources."[33] The poorest diocese in the United States declared bankruptcy in 2013 as it faced 20 sexual abuse lawsuits.[34]

A bankruptcy petition by a Catholic diocese is likely to contain admissions about the size and scope of the sexual abuse problem and the number of claims that have been filed against the diocese. The petition also may disclose the number of known abuse offenders and the number of incidents that have not yet ripened into actual legal claims.

32. Bishop Thomas Paprocki, "As the Pendulum Swings from Charitable Immunity to Bankruptcy, Bringing It to Rest with Charitable Viability," 48 J. Cath. Legal Stud. 1 (2009).
33. Olszewski, supra.
34. Mary Wisniewski, "Catholic Diocese of Gallup N.M. to Apply for Bankruptcy," Reuters Newsmax (Sept. 3, 2013).

The effect of taking the drastic step of filing for bankruptcy protection is a reaction to the realization that one or more priests abused multiple claimants, and the collective payment needed to settle these compensation demands is a liability that is greater than the total assets owned by the diocese. The results are distressing and quite messy for employees and programs of the diocese.[35] Because so many bankruptcies occurred before civil discovery depositions of Church leaders, plaintiffs were skeptical; one plaintiff's attorney said in 2013: "The bishop has done what we see all the other bishops do—they run to bankruptcy perhaps seeking financial protection but more importantly protection from the discovery process."[36]

The filing of bankruptcy by a Catholic diocese would draw fewer headlines today than it did in 2004 when the diocese of Portland, Oregon, declared bankruptcy, announcing that its contingent litigation liabilities from sexual abuse claims far exceeded its assets.[37] It had paid $53 million to settle 130 claims and faced an imminent civil damages trial date seeking $155 million for two plaintiffs.[38] That was major news, because it confronted the comfortable perceptions that the sexual abuse crisis was simply a passing disruption or distraction. In Wilmington, Delaware, for example, the church bankruptcy resulted in substantial cuts to the staff offices and to social service programs, which had been funded by the diocese of Wilmington. That diocese fought in bankruptcy court against claims by one of the priests who had been accused of abuse.[39]

Situations can go from bad to worse. The situation of bankruptcy generates emotional reactions among the church congregations and among the public. Will the church shut down 10 parishes in our city to sell the land? Perhaps. What hospital assets of the diocesan hospital are being sold? That is negotiable. Will the authority of the bishop be taken over by a court-appointed "receiver"? Probably not.[40]

In addition to the loss of flexibility and social service missions that the bankruptcy necessitates, the future expansion of the diocese to meet the needs of the suburban or ethnic congregations will be a significant loss. The building plans for suburban churches, which had been planned to keep pace with migration patterns in the metropolitan areas, will now have to be scrapped, and the land sold. Sales of hospitals, nursing homes, offices, and other facilities will be painful for those who have long supported the efforts of the archdiocese in those respective areas of service.

35. David Gregory, "Some Reflections on Labor & Employment Ramifications of Diocesan Bankruptcy Filings," 47 J. Cath. Legal Stud. 97 (2008).

36. Wisniewski, supra.

37. Manya Brachaer, "Bishops Conference Faces Twists in Picking Leader," Chic. Trib. 4 (Nov. 12, 2004).

38. Larry Stammer, "Oregon Diocese First to File Bankruptcy," L.A. Times A1 (July 7, 2004).

39. In re Catholic Diocese of Wilmington, Inc., 484 B.R. 629, 57 Bankr. Ct. Dec. 90 (D. Del. 2012).

40. Limitations on government control of the religious aspects would be founded in the First Amendment and implementing legislation such as 42 U.S.C.A. § 2000cc et seq. (2010).

Outside the doors of the cathedral, and outside the doors of the bankruptcy court, the potential future donors who are practicing Catholics may be tempted to lose heart and to feel alienated from the diocese. Loyal funding donors will be horrified and hesitant to donate. "Evil lawyers are draining Holy Mother Church's ability to perform its mission," as some would say. Why should a Catholic layperson donate money, which will then be paid to outside lawyers for alleged injuries that occurred decades before? A bankrtuptcy filing can relieve donor concerns by ensuring that current and future donations can be used for church programs and services, rather than payment on abuse claims. The obligations of the diocese are real, and despite the lack of popularity, bankruptcy may be the only manner by which the entire archdiocese can go forward to participate affirmatively in prudent Christian ministry.

Bankruptcy by a Catholic diocese has had long-term negative consequences, although perhaps not as bad as those that some had postulated. First Amendment issues of entanglement with the oversight of the bishop's decisions remain a matter of some concern that will have to be studied further.[41] Bankruptcy is not an answer to the fundamental issues of paying fair and just compensation to injured persons. Bankruptcy is a temporary bridge to reorganize the funding stream, so as to accommodate reasonable settlements of these pending claims for sexual misconduct.

9:6   BISHOPS AND FRAUD

Bankruptcy fraud can be punished as a criminal offense, but it is most frequently dealt with in criticism of the diocese during the bankruptcy hearings before the bankruptcy judge. In at least two of the diocesan bankruptcy cases, the diocesan bishop has been challenged directly for financial transactions. Cardinal Timothy Dolan requested Vatican permission to move $57 million in diocesan funds to shield them "from any claim or liability," when he dealt with the 575 claimants in abuse cases in Milwaukee, according to internal documents released in a bankruptcy case in 2013.[42] The federal judge in the San Diego diocesan bankruptcy criticized that diocese for misrepresenting its assets.[43] On top of the bad publicity that the diocese received for lawsuits against prior clergy abuse, the manipulation of assets during and before bankruptcy makes the image of the Church even more questionable, whether or not that suspicion is justified.

41. Angela Carmella, "Constitutional Arguments in Church Bankruptcies," 29 Seton Hall Legis. J. 435 (2004).
42. "Four years before the Archdiocese of Milwaukee filed for bankruptcy, then-Archbishop Timothy Dolan sought Vatican approval to move nearly $57 million in cemetery funds off the archdiocese's books and into a trust to help protect them from any legal claim or liability," Annysa Johnson & Ellen Gabler, "Milwaukee Archdiocese Releases Thousands of Pages from Priest Sex Abuse Files," Milwaukee J. Sentinel (July 2, 2013).
43. Bill Frogameni, "Where's the Money, Cardinal?," 18 Ms. Magazine 14 (Winter 2008).

CHAPTER 10

⌁

Mandated Abuse Reporting Issues

10:1 INTRODUCTION

Earlier chapters have addressed the civil and criminal ramifications of clergy sexual abuse. Disclosure of the fact that abuse of a child has occurred is required in many states. Society has made the collective decision, through state laws, that sexual contact by an adult with a minor should be prohibited and punished. State laws further require that child sexual abuse reports must be filed by some entities, and these state laws punish the suppression or conscious omission of reports of abuse. Are clergy members mandated to report, even if the report violates the secrecy of a religious sacramental confession? Coverage of these laws and the impact on clergy sexual abuse cases in the state courts are discussed in this chapter.

10:2 HISTORY AND PURPOSE OF REPORTING STATUTES

Before the 1960s, any person could report child abuse or neglect, but it was not mandatory as a matter of state law. As social consciousness about child abuse increased in the 1960s, more legislation was drafted to protect children.[1] In 1962, Dr. Henry Kempe published a groundbreaking article entitled "Battered Child Syndrome." The

---

1. Seth C. Kalichman, Mandated Reporting of Suspected Child Abuse: Ethics, Law, & Policy 13 (American Psychological Association ed., 2d ed. 1999); R. Michael Cassidy, "Sharing Sacred Secrets: Is It (Past) Time for a Dangerous Person Exception to the Clergy-Penitent Privilege?," 44 Wm. & Mary L. Rev. 1627, 1666 (2003). "Mandated reporting statutes were first enacted in the 1960s after research established that child abuse was a problem of widespread proportions likely to go undetected by law enforcement due to the age and vulnerability of its victims and a variety of other sociological factors."; Mary Harter Mitchell, "Must Clergy Tell? Child Abuse Reporting Requirements versus the Clergy Privilege and Free Exercise of Religion," 71 Minn. L. Rev. 723, 726–27 (1987). Beginning in the early 1960s public concern about child abuse was heightened, which led to legislative changes.

research concluded that child abuse was unlikely to be discovered by law enforcement because the young victims would abstain from reporting abuse. Dr. Kempe's
research had a profound effect on how state authorities attempted to protect children from abuse and neglect, and this eventually culminated in the enactment
of mandatory child abuse reporting statutes.[2] The federal Department of Health,
Education, and Welfare published a report and model statute dealing with child
abuse issues.[3] Many mandatory reporting statutes were enacted after the model
statute was published in 1963. The model statute required only physicians to report
suspected child abuse, and if they "knowingly and willfully" failed to report it, it
was a punishable misdemeanor.[4] By the end of 1967, all the states had adopted child
protection statutes with reporting requirements, but these earlier statutes limited
mandatory reporters to physicians and required reports only on physical abuse.[5]

In statutory revisions made during the late 1960s and early 1970s, legislatures
added more professionals to these mandatory reporting statutes. Definitions of
abuse were expanded as well to include sexual abuse and exploitation.[6] The Federal

2. Ashley Jackson, "The Collision of Mandatory Reporting Statutes and the
Priest-Penitent Privilege," 74 UMKC L. Rev. 1057, 1065 (2006).

3. Mitchell, supra, 723, 726; Cassidy, supra, 1627, 1666–67. "The Department of Health,
Education, and Welfare drafted the first model reporting statute in 1963. By 1967, every
state had passed a mandated reporting law."

4. Danny R. Veilleux, "Validity, Construction, and Application of State Statute
Requiring Doctor or Other Person to Report Child Abuse," 73 A.L.R. 4th 782, § 2(a)
(1989); Mitchell, supra, 723, 726–27. The model statute required physicians to report
suspected cases of abuse and designated as a misdemeanor a physician's knowing and
willful failure to report; Jackson, supra, 1057, 1065. "In 1963, the Department of Health,
Education, and Welfare published a model statute aimed at addressing the evolving problem of child abuse. Under the first model reporting statute, physicians were required to
report any suspected cases of child abuse and were guilty of a misdemeanor for failure
to do so. Due to the close proximity and relationship physicians exhibited with children,
the sentiment was that they would be the first to encounter child abuse, and therefore,
they were designated as mandatory reporters."

5. Mitchell, supra, 723, 727; Christopher R. Pudelski, "The Constitutional Fate of
Mandatory Reporting Statutes and the Clergy—Communicant Privilege in a Post-*Smith*
World," 98 Nw. U. L. Rev. 703 (2003–2004). "During the last forty years, all states adopted
mandatory reporting statutes requiring anyone exposed to information that a child has
been or will be abused to report this to law enforcement authorities."; Jackson, supra,
1057, 1065–66. "By 1967, all fifty states adopted some form of a reporting statute aimed
at protecting children. However, since 1967 most statutes have been amended at least one
time."; Julie M. Arnold, "'Divine' Justice and the Lack of Secular Intervention: Abrogating
the Clergy-Communicant Privilege in Mandatory Reporting Statutes to Combat Child
Sexual Abuse," 42 Val. U. L. Rev. 849 (2008). "The call for reporting statutes began in the
early 1960s and included disclosure primarily by physicians and other medical practitioners. By 1967, all fifty states had adopted some form of a statute mandating reports of
known or suspected instances of abuse to law enforcement officials."

6. Kalichman, supra, 15; Mitchell, supra, 723, 727. Since the 1960s, most states have
amended their statutes, enlarging the reportable circumstances and persons mandated
to report; Jackson, supra, 1057, 1065. "Statutes were quickly expanded to include as
mandatory reporters those likely to encounter child abuse—teachers, law enforcement
and social workers. The expansion process transformed the statutes into the modern
mandatory child abuse statutes."

Child Abuse Prevention and Treatment Act of 1974 required states to have mandatory reporting laws for child abuse in order to receive federal funding for prevention and treatment services.[7] After the passage of the Act, all states now have mandatory reporting laws based on a reasonable suspicion of child abuse or neglect.[8]

The federal Child Abuse Prevention and Treatment Act helped set the standard for state mandatory reporting laws, alleviating early problems and differences surrounding the definition of child abuse and child neglect.[9] The development of mandated reporting statutes has progressed in a few stages. Most states have amended their statutes at least once since 1967.[10] The first mandated reporting statutes had listed "medical personnel, who were likely to encounter evidence of child abuse in a treatment context, and law enforcement personnel, who were likely to encounter such evidence in responding to domestic disturbance."[11] The federal Act and a revised model reporting statute issued by the American Medical Association in 1975 led most states to amend their statutes to require reports from a larger class of professionals with access to or responsibility for children, "including teachers, social workers, and in some instances, attorneys and members of the clergy."[12]

From the 1960s to the 1980s the growth in case reporting was 14 times higher that the pre-statute rate of reporting for child abuse, an increase that has been attributed to the proliferation of abuse-reporting statutes and the increase in media attention to child abuse cases.[13] From 1980 to 1986 alone, reports of sexual abuse in particular tripled.[14] During this time period in the early 1980s, sexual

7. Inger J. Sagatun & Leonard P. Edwards, Child Abuse in the Legal System 36 (Dorothy J. Anderson ed., 1995); Veilleux, supra, § 2(a). "To qualify for federal grants under the Child Abuse Prevention and Treatment Act, 42 U.S.C.A., passed in 1974, states must provide for the reporting of known and suspected child abuse and neglect, and demonstrate that a number of necessary procedures and programs are in effect."; Pudelski, supra, 703, 706. "CAPTA provides federal funding to states in support of prevention, assessment, investigation, prosecution, and treatment activities and also provides grants to public agencies and nonprofit organizations for demonstration programs and projects."

8. Virginia C. Weisz, Children and Adolescents in Need: A Legal Primer for the Helping Professional 26 (Yvonne Konneker ed., 1995).

9. Pudelski, supra, 703.

10. R. Michael Cassidy, "Sharing Sacred Secrets: Is It (Past) Time for a Dangerous Person Exception to the Clergy-Penitent Privilege?," 44 Wm. & Mary L. Rev. 1627, 1667 (2003).

11. Id.

12. Id.; Julie M. Arnold, "'Divine' Justice and the Lack of Secular Intervention: Abrogating the Clergy-Communicant Privilege in Mandatory Reporting Statutes to Combat Child Sexual Abuse," 42 Val. U. L. Rev. 849, 887 (2008). "Over the years, the statutes expanded so as to include more professionals likely to encounter child abuse."

13. Kalichman, supra, 17–18.

14. Weisz, supra, 53; David T. Fenton, "Texas' Clergyman-Penitent Privilege and the Duty to Report Suspected Child Abuse," 38 Baylor L. Rev. 231, 237 (1986). "Since the enactment of reporting statutes, the number of reports of child abuse has increased substantially."

abuse of children was widely publicized.[15] In 1986 it was estimated that instances of child abuse ranged from 76,000 to 4.1 million cases per year.[16]

10:3 OPERATING PRINCIPLES OF THE ABUSE REPORTING LAWS

The reporting laws are based on three principles:

(1) expediting the identification of abused children;
(2) designating appropriate agencies to receive, investigate, and manage child abuse cases; and
(3) mobilizing protective services to protect children from further abuse.[17]

The effect of the statutes is to aid the states' social welfare agencies in identifying and assisting abused and neglected children. The design of the reporting requirements helps the agencies in prevention and prosecution of child abuse cases.[18] If there is child abuse, then the states are empowered by the statutes to remove the child from the home, administer social services, terminate parental rights in the child, and bring a criminal action against the child's abuser.[19] Each state's mandatory reporting statutes clarify professional duties to report suspected child abuse.[20]

The reporting laws share certain components. They all:

(1) define abusive situations;
(2) specify reportable circumstances and the degree of certainty reporters must attain, the age of reportable children, and details on who is a mandatory reporter;

---

15. Weisz, supra, 53.

16. David T. Fenton, "Texas' Clergyman-Penitent Privilege and the Duty to Report Suspected Child Abuse," 38 Baylor L. Rev. 231, 237 (1986). "Child abuse is a significant problem in American society. While the actual number of instances of abuse is unknown, estimates range from 76,000 to 4.1 million cases annually."

17. Kalichman, supra, 17; Mary Harter Mitchell, "Must Clergy Tell? Child Abuse Reporting Requirements versus the Clergy Privilege and Free Exercise of Religion," 71 Minn. L. Rev. 723, 727–28 (1987). Child protection statutes are meant to protect children by having those with reporting requirements be the finders of the child abuse and call official intention to it, leading to an investigation; Cassidy, supra, 1627, 1667. "Modern mandated reporting statutes generally require professionals with frequent contact with children to file a report with the state Department of Social Services, or an equivalent child protection agency, whenever they have reasonable cause to believe that a child has suffered abuse."; Arnold, supra, 849, 876–78. "Because government intervention and prosecution of child sexual abuse crimes is made possible only by first discovering the need to act, states fashioned mandatory reporting statutes 'for the purpose of detecting and eradicating child abuse.'"

18. Fenton, supra, 231, 237.

19. Mitchell, supra, 723, 728.

20. Weisz, supra, 26.

(3) impose penalties for failure to report; and

(4) grant immunity from civil or criminal liability for reporters who file reports in good faith.[21]

10:4 ADDITION OF CLERGY TO MANDATORY REPORTERS

Reporting statutes are a type of investigative tool that the states utilize to assist in the difficult task of "prosecuting sexual abuse."[22] Public awareness of clergy sexual misconduct has been increasing, in the Catholic Church and elsewhere. For example, from 1987 to 1997 "the Episcopal Church has seen the incidence of clergy sexual misconduct almost double."[23] As the trend to expand the list of professionals required to report has increased, some states have included "religious healers."[24] The addition of clergy to mandatory reporting statutes' list of professionals was an attempt to make the statutes more effective.[25]

Adding clergy to the list of mandatory reporters has created criticism and concern for violations of religious freedom under the First Amendment. Although some states require clergy to report, reporting might violate many clergy members' religious tenets not to disclose confidences.[26] For example, Massachusetts revised its statutes to include all clergy members to report reasonable suspicions of child abuse. However, information gained purely through confessional or similar communications in other religions remains confidential.[27]

Note the effect of the time of past events upon these statutes. Although adding clergy to the list of mandated reporters will help to address present and future cases of clergy sexual abuse of minors, new statutes cannot always help rectify past cases of child sexual abuse by clergy, where the past mandatory reporting statute did not cover clergy members. For instance, a Connecticut statute requiring members

---

21. Kalichman, supra, 18; Mitchell, supra, 723, 728. Statutory child abuse reporting requirements tend to share common characteristics. The statutes typically address who must report, reportable conditions, reporters' immunity, penalties for the failure to report, and the abrogation or application of certain privileges.

22. Arnold, supra, 849, 876.

23. Arthur Gross Schafera & Darren Levinea, "No Sanctuary from the Law: Legal Issues Facing Clergy," 30 Loy. L.A. L. Rev. 177, 205 (1996).

24. Kalichman, supra, 19.

25. Arnold, supra, 849, 878.

26. Martin R. Gardner, Understanding Juvenile Law 62 (LexisNexis ed., 2d ed. 2003). "While many states require clergy to report instances of abuse, revealing confidences transmitted during religious rituals would violate many clerics' religious tenets, thus raising constitutional questions under the Free Exercise Clause of the First Amendment."

27. Gardner, supra, 62 "In light of revelations regarding child abuse by clergy in the Catholic Church, some states, such as Massachusetts, have revised child abuse statutes to include all clergy. The Massachusetts statute, while requiring that clergy report reasonable suspicions of abuse, does exempt information "solely gained in a confession or similarly confidential communication in other religious faith." Discussing Mass. Gen. Laws Ann. Ch. 119, § 51A (West 2002).

of clergy who suspect abuse of minors to report it was not retroactively applicable without a clear showing of legislative intent.[28]

10:5 THE CONNECTICUT CASE EXAMPLE

In *Martinelli v. Bridgeport Roman Catholic Diocesan Corp.*,[29] plaintiff sued a priest, Father Brett, and his diocese for three instances of sexual abuse between 1961 and 1963, when plaintiff was between 13 and 15 years old. Plaintiff asserted that his memories of the abuse had been repressed, but were recovered through psychotherapy in 1991.[30] The claims brought against the defendants included: (1) intentional infliction of emotional distress by both defendants, (2) assault and battery against Father Brett only, (3) breach of fiduciary duty by both defendants for failure to disclose the sexual abuse, (4) negligent infliction of emotional distress by both defendants, (5) negligent retention of Father Brett by the Bridgeport diocese, (6) vicarious liability of the Bridgeport diocese for Father Brett's misconduct, and (7) negligent training and supervision by the Bridgeport diocese.[31] The diocese's summary judgment motion was granted in part, and denied in part.[32] The priest had induced the boys into sexual conduct with him. A 19-year-old complained to the church that Brett sexually abused him in 1964, which Brett confirmed was true. In 1966 another sexual misconduct incident was brought to the attention of the church, which incident had occurred in 1963. However, the church apparently did not refer that complaint to diocesan authorities.

Over the next few years, Father Brett worked in California, New Mexico, Maryland, and Connecticut, in a variety of ecclesiastical and nonecclesiastical positions. In 1992 and 1993, new allegations of sexual abuse arose regarding his work in New Mexico and California.[33] The court stated that there "is little dispute that the Diocese intended to conceal Father Brett's misconduct."[34] Martinelli contended that there was a legal duty by virtue of a fiduciary relationship between himself and his parents on the one hand, and the diocese on the other, for the diocese to investigate and warn him and his parents about Brett's sexual misconduct.[35]

Plaintiff relied on Conn. Gen. Stat. § 17-38a, which imposes reporting requirements on members of the clergy who suspect abuse of a minor. However, the reporting statute had only been amended to include clergy 8 to 10 years after the sexual abuse occurred.[36] Because plaintiff could not identify any legislative intent for the

---

28. C.G.S.A. § 17-38a (1989). Martinelli v. Bridgeport Roman Catholic Diocesan Corp., 989 F. Supp. 110 (D. Conn. 1997).
29. 989 F. Supp. 110 (D. Conn. 1997).
30. Id. at 112.
31. Id.
32. Id.
33. Id. at 113.
34. Id. at 115.
35. Id. at 116.
36. Id. at 120.

addition of clergy members to the reporting statute to be applied retroactively, the court would not rely on the statute to establish that a fiduciary duty to warn existed. Ultimately, because no common law duty existed for the church to warn children and parents of the sexually predatory nature of its priests, the summary judgment was granted in favor of the diocese on the issue of breach of fiduciary duty.[37] The 1971 mandatory reporting statute was not cited by Martinelli to support any of his other claims against Brett and the diocese.

10:6 THE KANSAS CITY CONVICTION

The bishop of Kansas City, Missouri, received information that one of his diocesan priests was found in possession of extensive quantities of child pornography, including young female genitalia and "upskirt" photos of young girls. He was indicted and convicted for failing to report the information for five months.[38] Observers believe that some of the photos are of local children, though the evidence of the priest's activities was developed at his 2012 conviction. Unlike the Canadian bishop who is in prison for a long sentence relating to his own laptop's collection of 588 graphic images of children, 33 videos and the texts of stories featuring the enslavement of children,[39] there was no evidence that Bishop Robert Finn engaged in sexual misconduct. The failure to report violated Missouri law that requires reporting when child abuse is discovered by a church.

37. Id.
38. Judy Thomas, "Bishop Finn and Diocese Are Indicted," Kansas City Star (Oct. 14, 2011).
39. Ian Austen, "Canada: Bishop Pleads Guilty in Child Pornography Case," N.Y. Times (May 4, 2011).

CHAPTER 11

๛

Evidence Privileges and Clergy Abuse Issues

11:1 CONFLICTS WITH THE STATE LAW CLERGY-COMMUNICANT EVIDENCE PRIVILEGE[1]

Most states have curtailed professional privileges obligating certain job holders to remain silent in the face of child abuse. Around 30 years ago, states began to change the scope of their clergy-communicant privilege statutes. Simultaneously, every state had enacted a statutory duty to report child abuse. While there are some differences in the scope of the clergy privilege described, there is increased variability among the state child abuse reporting statutes regarding whether clergy are mandatory reporters, and if so, whether clergy must report communications covered by the clergy-communicant privilege.[2]

Some courts have held, for example, that "in cases involving the physician-patient, clergy-penitent, and social worker-client privileges...the defense of privileged communications was unavailable to persons having a statutory duty to report child abuse."[3]

For instance, the Arizona Appellate Court found that the legislature re-established the clergy/penitent privilege to the extent of permitting members of the clergy to withhold consent on the penitent's behalf to examination concerning the penitent's confidential communications, During the course of child-related

---

1. Seth C. Kalichman, Mandated Reporting of Suspected Child Abuse: Ethics, Law, & Policy 19 (American Psychological Association ed., 2d ed. 1999).

2. Norman Abrams, "Addressing the Tension between the Clergy-Communicant Privilege and the Duty to Report Child Abuse in State Statutes," 44 B.C. L. Rev. 1127, 1128 (2003).

3. Danny R. Veilleux, "Validity, Construction, and Application of State Statute Requiring Doctor or Other Person to Report Child Abuse," 73 A.L.R. 4th 782, § 2 (a) (1989).

litigation, the court in a 1988 case[4] recognized that the privilege was not available as a ground for the clergy's failure to report under the child abuse reporting statute. The court addressed the extent of the privilege after a child's mother sought to discover information to support her claim that the Church negligently exposed children to abuse when it earlier undertook to counsel and treat a child molester, did so carelessly, and violated its affirmative duty to report his conduct to appropriate authorities.[5]

Most reporting statutes contain some provision to abrogate or reaffirm some privileges. Many of these provisions abrogate privileges only for "proceedings" or "judicial proceedings" flowing or resulting from a report. These statutes do not directly address whether a person may claim a privilege to avoid reporting in the first place. However, other statutes explicitly state that certain privileges shall not excuse mandatory reporting.[6] Regarding the clergy, "[m]ost of these statutes abrogate the privilege for any 'proceeding' regarding child abuse, failing to indicate whether the privilege is still available to justify a cleric's failure to report abuse in the first place."[7]

---

4. Church of Jesus Christ of Latter-Day Saints v. Superior Court, 764 P.2d 759, 13 Rep 59 (Ariz. App. 1988).

5. Veilleux, supra, 782, §13 (b).

6. Mary Harter Mitchell, "Must Clergy Tell? Child Abuse Reporting Requirements versus the Clergy Privilege and Free Exercise of Religion," 71 Minn. L. Rev. 723, 791 (1987);

Ashley Jackson, "The Collision of Mandatory Reporting Statutes and the Priest-Penitent Privilege," 74 UMKC L. Rev. 1057, 1066 (2006). "Mandatory child abuse reporting statutes as they relate to the priest-penitent privilege tend to fall within one of three categories: (1) statutes that specifically abrogate the priest-penitent privilege in cases dealing with suspected child abuse; (2) statutes that include clergy in a catch-all provision requiring 'any person' to report; and finally, (3) statutes that maintain the clergy privilege by affirmatively exempting members of the clergy from reporting."

Abrams, supra, 1127, 1128–1129. "Among the states that do impose a duty to report, some expressly abrogate the application of the clergy privilege in the reporting context, that is, they require reporting despite the otherwise privileged nature of the communication. At the same time, a significant number of states take the opposite tack and exempt from the reporting requirement communications that fall within the clergy privilege." See also abrogated clergy privilege statutes: The Abrams article lists these as: N.H. REV. STAT. ANN. § 169-C:32 (2002); N.C. GEN. STAT. § 7B-301 (2003); OKLA. STAT. tit. 10, § 7103(A)(3) (2002); R.I. GEN. LAWS § 40-11-11 (2002); TEX. FAM. CODE ANN. § 261.101(c) (Vernon 2003); W. VA. CODE § 49-6A-7 (2003).)" See also statutes with clergy exemptions; the Abrams article lists these as: ARIZ. REV. STAT. § 13-3620 (2003); CAL. PENAL CODE § 11166(c)(1) (West 2003); COLO. REV. STAT. § 19-3-304(2)(aa)(II) (2003); DEL. CODE ANN. tit. 16, § 909 (2003); FLA. STAT. ch. 39.204 (2003); IDAHO CODE § 16-1619(c) (Michie 2003); 325 ILL. COMP. STAT. 5/4 (2003); KY. REV. STAT. ANN. § 620.050(3) (Michie 2002); LA. CHILD. CODE ANN. art. 603(13)(b) (West 2003); MD. CODE ANN., FAM. LAW § 5-705; ME. REV. STAT. ANN. tit. 22, § 4011-A(1)(A)(27) (West 2003); MASS. GEN. LAWS ch. 119, § 51A (2003); MICH. COMP. LAWS § 722.631 (2003); MINN. STAT. § 626.556 subd. 3(a)(2) (2002); MO. REV. STAT. § 352.400 (2003); MONT. CODE ANN. § 41-3-201(4)(b) (2003); NEV. REV. STAT. 202.888 (2002); N.M. STAT. ANN. § 32A-4-3 (Michie 2003); N.D. CENT. CODE § 50-25.1-03(1) (2003); OR. REV. STAT. § 419B.010(1) (2001); 23 PA. CONS. STAT. § 6311(a) (2002); UTAH CODE ANN. § 62A-4a-403(2)."

7. Mitchell, supra, 723, 791.

The issue of whether there is a conflict between the reporting statute for child abuse and the clergy penitent privilege is not an issue for nearly one-third of the states, as they do not include clergy in their list of mandatory reporters.[8] However, there is an instance where a clergyman reported child sexual abuse by a youth counselor, even though the information was privileged under the clergy-communant privilege.[9] In that case, the minister was not required to report as a clergy member, but he was as a psychologist.

The Supreme Court of Illinois ruled that the prosecution resulting from the report would not be quashed, and that an evidentiary exception applied in cases where communications between clergy and penitent were not secretive and could have been reported by someone else.[10] Notably, clergy are now included among mandatory reporters in Illinois.[11]

There are typically three different categories into which mandatory reporting statutes dealing with the clergy-communant privilege fall: "(1) those that specifically abrogate the clergy-communant privilege in cases pertaining to suspected child abuse; (2) those that include clergy in a catch-all provision requiring 'any person' to report; and (3) those that preserve the clergy-communant privilege by affirmatively exempting members of the clergy from reporting."[12]

As of a 2003 survey, 35 states that imposed a reporting requirement on clergy either through a specific listing or by using a catchall "any person" approach were further grouped into three categories. The largest number of states (22), provided an express exception from their reporting requirement for clergy-privileged information.[13]

---

8. Abrams, supra, 1127, 1139 (2003). These statutes include the following cited in the Abrams article: "ALA. CODE § 26-14-3 (2003); ALASKA STAT. § 47.17.020 (Michie 2003); ARK. CODE ANN. § 12-12-507 (Michie 2003); GA. CODE ANN. § 19-7-5 (2003); HAW. REV. STAT. § 350-1.1 (2002);IOWA CODE § 232.69 (2002); KAN. STAT. ANN. § 38-1522 (2002); N.Y. SOC. SERV. LAW § 413 (Consol. 2003); OHIO REV. CODE ANN. § 2151.421 (Anderson 2003); S.C. CODE ANN. § 20-7-510 (Law. Co-op. 2002); S.D. CODIFIED LAWS § 26-8A-3 (Michie 2003); VT. STAT. ANN. tit. 33, § 4913(2002); VA. CODE ANN. § 63.2-1509 (Michie 2003); WASH. REV. CODE § 26-44.030 (2003); WIS. STAT. § 48.981 (2003)."

9. People v. Burnidge, 178 Ill. 2d 429 (1997).

10. Id.

11. 325 Ill. C.S. 5/4 (1994)

12. Julie M. Arnold, "'Divine' Justice and the Lack of Secular Intervention: Abrogating the Clergy-Communant Privilege in Mandatory Reporting Statutes to Combat Child Sexual Abuse," 42 Val. U. L. Rev. 849, 878–879 (2008). Moreover, the following is a list of the states in their respective categories: "States maintaining the clergy-communant privilege in full include: Alaska, Arkansas; Florida, Georgia, Hawaii, Idaho, Iowa, Kansas, Maine, Maryland, Minnesota, Montana, New Mexico, New York, Ohio, Oregon, South Dakota, Utah, Virginia, and Vermont. States that simply include clergy members among the other listed professionals with a duty to report are: Arizona, California, Colorado, Connecticut, Illinois, Massachusetts, Michigan, Mississippi, Montana, North Dakota, Pennsylvania, South Carolina, and Texas. Finally, states that utilize a catchall phrase, such as 'any person[,]' to include clergy members are: Delaware, Indiana, Kentucky, Nebraska, Nevada, New Jersey, Oklahoma, Tennessee, Wisconsin, and Wyoming"

13. Abrams, supra, 1127, 1139. The statutes listed in the Abrams study include the following: ARIZ. REV. STAT. § 13-3620 (2003); CAL. PENAL CODE § 11166(c)(1) (West 2003); COLO. REV. STAT. § 19-3-304(2)(aa)(II) (2003); DEL. CODE ANN. Tit. 16, § 909

In 2003, only six states abrogated the application of the clergy-communicant privilege to the abuse reporting requirement (that is, the privilege did not operate to protect the confidentiality of the relevant communications).[14]

Abrogating the clergy-communicant privilege could accomplish two different outcomes in regards to mandatory reporting statutes. The statutory change might mean that the clergy member is required to report suspected child abuse even if he learns of it in a privileged setting. The other outcome is that it could mean that "the clergy member is required to testify about the child abuse if he is later called as a witness in a judicial proceeding."[15] Using the 2003 study as a baseline:

- In Wyoming, clergy appear to have a duty to report child abuse even if it is learned in a privileged setting, but have no duty subsequently to testify in judicial proceedings.
- In Delaware, Mississippi, New Hampshire, North Carolina, Oklahoma, Rhode Island, Texas, and West Virginia, clergy have a duty to report child abuse even if learned in a privileged context, and must later testify about the privileged communication in judicial proceedings arising out of the child abuse or neglect.
- In Idaho, a clergy member has no duty to report child abuse if the abuse was learned of in a privileged context, but does have a duty to testify about the same privileged communication if later called as a witness in a judicial proceeding.[16]

And so, as of 2003 there were only seven remaining states where the issue of exception for, or abrogation of, the clergy privilege is not dealt with by statute.[17]

(2003); FLA. STAT. Ch. 39.204 (2003); IDAHO CODE § 16-1619(c) (Michie 2003); 325 ILL. COMP. STAT. 5/4 (2003); KY. REV. STAT. ANN. § 620.050(3) (Michie 2002); LA. CHILD. CODE ANN. Art. 603(13)(b) (West 2003);MD. CODE ANN., FAM. LAW § 5-705; ME. REV. STAT. ANN. Tit. 22, § 4011-A(1)(A)(27) (West 2003);MASS. GEN. LAWS ch. 119, § 51A (2003); MICH. COMP. LAWS § 722.631 (2003); MINN. STAT. § 626.556 subd. 3(a)(2) (2002); MO. REV. STAT. § 352.400 (2003); MONT. CODE ANN. § 41-3-201(4)(b) (2003); NEV. REV. STAT. 202.888 (2002); N.M. STAT. ANN. § 32A-4-3 (Michie 2003); N.D. CENT. CODE § 50-25.1-03(1) (2003); OR. REV. STAT. § 419B.010(1) (2001); 23 PA. CONS. STAT. § 6311(a) (2002); UTAH CODE ANN. § 62A-4a-403(2)."

14. Abrams, supra, 1127, 1139. The statutes listed by Abrams included: "N.H. REV. STAT. ANN. § 169-C:32 (2002); N.C. GEN. STAT. § 7B-301 (2003); OKLA. ST. Tit. 10, § 7103(A)(3) (2002); R.I. GEN. LAWS § 40-11-11 (2002); TEX. FAM. CODE ANN. § 261.101(c) (Vernon 2003); W. VA. CODE § 49-6A-7 (2003)". And see also Mitchell, supra, 723, 791. "About half of the reporting statutes seem to include the clergy privilege in their general abrogation of all professional privileges, or all except the attorney-client privilege."

R. Michael Cassidy, "Sharing Sacred Secrets: Is It (Past) Time for a Dangerous Person Exception to the Clergy-Penitent Privilege?," 44 Wm. & Mary L. Rev. 1627, 1669 (2003). "Fifteen of the thirty-two states that apply their mandated reporter statutes to clergy provide that the clergy-penitent privilege survives the duty to report; that is, that the clergy member is exempt from the statutory duty to report suspected child abuse if the information was obtained in a privileged setting, and will have a duty to report only that information received outside of the confidential spiritual counseling context."

15. Cassidy, supra, 1627, 1670.

16. Id. at 1671.

17. Abrams, supra, 1127, 1140. The statutes quoted by Abrams include the following: "CONN. GEN. STAT. § 17a-101 (2003); IND. CODE § 31-33-5-1 (2002); MISS.

Courts are left to make the decisions about reports of privileged information, when a statute imposes a reporting requirement on clergy members without an express exception for communications covered by the clergy-communicant privilege or express abrogation of that privilege.[18] When the statute includes an express exception for clergy-communicant privileged information, this exception comes in a variety of forms. "In some statutes, the exception is framed in broad terms, such as in the Maine statute, which states: 'except for information received in confidential communications [under the cleric privilege].' In some instances, the exemption is formulated in the same terms as the terms of the privilege, such as 'information received in the capacity of a spiritual adviser.'"[19]

None of the states that include only confession to count as protected by the clergy-communicant privilege have abrogated the privilege in favor of the reporting requirement. Instead, most of the confession-only states create an exception to the reporting requirement for confessional communications.[20]

The only states in which the clergy-communicant privilege has been abrogated are those that include spiritual advice within their clergy-communicant privilege, or have an even broader clergy privilege.[21]

11:2 CROSS-REFERENCE OF DISCLOSURE STATUTES TO PENITENT PRIVILEGES ⸱

Many of the mandated reporter statutes for child abuse cross-reference their state's clergy-communicant privilege statutes. Other statutes exempt from the duty to disclose some "otherwise privileged" communications. And others define precisely the

CODE ANN. § 43-21-353 (2003); NEB. REV. STAT. § 28-707(2) (2002); N.J. STAT. ANN. § 9:6-8.10 (West 2003); TENN. CODE ANN. § 37-1-411 (2003); WYO. STAT. ANN. § 14-3-205 (Michie 2002)."

   Cassidy, supra, 1627, 1669–1670. "In seven states, it is unclear whether and how the legislature intended to preserve the clergy-penitent privilege... North Dakota, for example, abrogates testimonial privileges between 'any professional person and the person's patient or client, except between attorney and client...' in cases involving child abuse and neglect. N.D. Cent. Code § 50-25-1-10 (1999). No court has yet construed whether a minister engaged in counseling represents a "client" for purposes of this statute. "Moreover, when a state enacts a statute that requires certain professionals to report, and does not address specifically the effect of a preexisting statutory privilege on this reporting obligation, a difficult statutory interpretation question arises as to whether the later-enacted reporting requirement was intended to abrogate the otherwise general rule of privilege."

18. Abrams, supra, 1127, 1140; 38 Am. Jur. *Trials* 1 § 39 (1989). "The problem arises where the cleric's sole source of information, like that of a psychotherapist, comes from a revelation made in confidence by the abusive parent or caretaker (or the abused child) during a professional relationship. In other words, the question is whether the disclosure is covered by the clergy-penitent privilege."

19. Abrams, supra, 1127, 1140.

20. Id.

21. Id. at 1127, 1141.

types of confidential communications that are exempt from disclosure in instances of child abuse.[22]

A 2006 commentator observed: "Many state legislatures have specifically reaffirmed the priest-penitent privilege by not subjecting clergy to mandatory reporting statutes. While protecting the clergy in some situations, many legislatures have unknowingly placed the holder of the privilege in a difficult position. States that have not placed an affirmative duty upon any specific professions but instead have a general 'any person' requirement are not as worrisome, because they specifically exempt the clergy from reporting and do not place an affirmative duty on any other profession. The problem is more cumbersome when a legislature enumerates a list of people who have an affirmative duty to report, because an affirmative duty is placed upon the person in his or her profession, even though the information may have come from an otherwise privileged communication."[23]

11:3 DISCLOSURE AND PRIVILEGE AS A CRIMINAL DEFENSE ARGUMENT

Criminal cases pose an interesting twist on this issue: Can the defendant argue that the statute protects the abuser? An Illinois case involved a church youth worker who was convicted by a jury trial on two counts of aggravated criminal sexual abuse and sentenced to 36 months of probation together with nine months imprisonment, along with $1,500 in restitution fines to the victim. The trial court's decision was affirmed by the appellate court.[24] The appellate court rejected the defendant's argument that the prosecution should have been dismissed because the church's minister had improperly disclosed the confidential information received from the defendant.[25]

The minister testified that he reported the information to the Department of Children and Family Services (DCFS) because, as a pastor and psychologist, he believed he was required to report the child sexual abuse to comply with section 4 of the Illinois Abused and Neglected Child Reporting Act.[26] He had called and conferred with DCFS, and was told that he was not required to report as a clergy member, but he was as a psychologist. DCFS then relayed the report to the Lake County sheriff's office, and that office reported the information to the State Attorney. The trial judge had suppressed the conversations between the abuser and the minister, but he allowed

---

22. Cassidy, supra, 1627, 1669.

Christopher R. Pudelski, "The Constitutional Fate of Mandatory Reporting Statutes and the Clergy—Communicant Privilege in a Post-*Smith* World," 98 Nw. U. L. Rev. 703, 715 (2003–2004). "Generally speaking, these statutes can be divided into those that clearly state their intended effect, if any, on evidentiary privileges, and those that are unclear or neutral about their effect on evidentiary privileges."

23. Jackson, supra, 1057, 1066.

24. People v. Burnidge, 178 Ill. 2d 429, 430–431 (1997).

25. *Id.* at 433.

26. 325 ILCS 5/4 (West 1994).

the information from the report to come in as evidence.[27] The defendant youth worker asserted that his communications with the minister were privileged, and because the minister was not mandated as a clergyman to report the sexual abuse of a minor, that the report that flowed from the minister, and led to the defendant's prosecution, should be quashed, and his conviction reversed.[28] The court reasoned that even if the reports were suppressed, the communications would still not be secretive because of admissions that the abuser, the victim, and the victim's family made. The court was persuaded by the facts that the victim had provided the prosecutor with the information needed for the conviction, and the minister did not name the defendant in his report.[29] The court rejected the abuser's contention that but for the report, the victim and her family would have been content with allowing the Church to settle the issue.[30] The court recognized the "inevitable discovery" exception[31] to the rule requiring the exclusion of evidence obtained as a result of a violation of a defendant's constitutional rights.[32] The court continued, "the rationale for the "inevitable discovery" exception is that, while 'the prosecution is not to be put in a better position than it would have been in if no illegality had transpired', the prosecution should not be put "in a *worse* position simply because of some earlier police error or misconduct."[33] The court was further persuaded by the impact statement from the victim and her family, which suggested that they would have reported the incident to authorities had it not already been reported.[34]

11:4 WHAT ARE THE PENALTIES FOR NOT REPORTING? ₒ

The diocese of Kansas City and its bishop were convicted for failing to make a timely report of child sexual abuse.[35] The archdiocese of Cincinnati pleaded in 2003 to the criminal charge of failure to report child abuse.[36] Relatively few other cases have reached the media or appellate reports as virtually all are settled. Mandatory reporters are often required to report when there is a reasonable suspicion that child abuse is occurring. Typically, phrases such as "reason to believe" or "having reasonable cause to suspect" are used to describe conditions required for reporting, and are followed by a time frame for reporting.[37] Such criminal penalties impose

27. Id. at 434.
28. Id. at 435.
29. Id. at 436.
30. Id.
31. Nix v. Williams, 467 U.S. 431 (1984).
32. Id. at 436–437.
33. Id. at 437.
34. Id. at 438–439.
35. Judy Thomas, "Bishop Finn, Diocese Indicted in Abuse Case" Kansas City Star (Oct. 14, 2011).
36. "Archdiocese of Cincinnati Fined in Sex Abuse Scandal," N.Y. Times (Nov. 21, 2003), on Web at http://www.nytimes.com/2003/11/21/us/archdiocese-of-cincinnati-fined-in-sex-abuse-scandal.html?src=pm.
37. Kalichman, supra, 26.

a misdemeanor and a fine.[38] In some states, failure to immediately report via telephone or as soon as possible can lead to the mandatory reporter being punished with a misdemeanor, subject to confinement in a county jail and/or a fine of up to $1,000.[39]

The purpose of criminal penalties is deterrence, to ensure that all mandatory reporters who suspect child abuse will report it to a protective agency.[40] In all 32 states that include clergy as mandated reporters, a clergy member who learns of abuse of a child from a victim, a victim's relative, or another clergy member in most instances would be subject to criminal prosecution and penalty for failure to notify authorities of these allegations. However, in the few states that have swept within the reach of their clergy-penitent privilege statute any confidential communication with a minister in his "professional capacity," regardless of the spiritual counseling nature of the conversation, a court can consider such employment-related discussions privileged if intended to be kept confidential, and therefore no prosecution could be pursued.[41]

Despite the fact that there are criminal penalties for a failure to report child sexual abuse, few clergy members have been prosecuted for their failures. As of 2004, no church officials had been prosecuted criminally for "aiding or abetting or failure to report as mandatory reporters."[42] The 2012 Philadelphia trial and jury conviction of a priest-administrator who knew of abuse by several priests, but failed to report them, has set new precedents in 2012 and beyond.

Clergy sexual misconduct is not often reported and when it is, it is rarely prosecuted because of the influence of church leaders within the political system. Often, church officials will approach the investigating law enforcement agency about the allegations, emphasize that the sex crime was an isolated incident, and urge that the public interest will be best served by removing the offender from the parish and sending the person to treatment. "Even more often, when faced with a trusted cleric accused of this heinous crime, the temptation has been to disbelieve the victim

---

38. Stein, Child Welfare and the Law 107–108 (Child Welfare League of America, Inc. ed., 3d ed. 2006).

Cassidy, supra, 1627, 1667. "These statutes generally provide the mandated reporter with immunity from civil liability for filing a report and set forth misdemeanor criminal penalties, usually a fine, for failure to report when required to do so."

Arnold, supra, 849, 878. "The statutes typically provide immunity from suit for reporting as well as threaten both civil and criminal liability for failing to do so."

39. Inger J. Sagatun & Leonard P. Edwards, Child Abuse in the Legal System 37 (Dorothy J. Anderson ed., 1995). Mitchell, supra, 723, 732 (1987). "There are criminal penalties in most jurisdictions and additional civil liability in some. Failure to report is usually a misdemeanor requiring a willful or knowing failure to report and is usually accompanied by the criminal penalties of a fine or a few days to a year in jail."

Stein, supra, 107–108. Some state laws provide for criminal and civil penalties when mandated reporters fail to report suspected child abuse.

40. Sagatun, supra, 38.

41. Cassidy, supra, 1627, 1669.

42. 91 Am. Jur. *Trials* 151 § 8 (2004).

because of the passage of time, the age or fragility of the victim and to prematurely conclude its not worthy of investigation or prosecution."[43]

11:5 IMMUNITY FOR CLERGY MEMBERS WHO REPORT CHILD ABUSE

When clergy members report suspected child abuse, as required by law, they are given civil and criminal immunity from liability. Immunity is still given even if a report of suspected child abuse is never proven. However, if it is determined that a clergy member knowingly made a false report of child abuse, then no immunity is afforded.[44] Although all states mandate reporting of child abuse, because clergy are often exempt from these laws, they thereby become immune from prosecution for a failure to report.[45] Moreover, immunity is usually given in later judicial proceedings that deal with the same legal matter.[46]

Most state reporting statutes do not require absolute proof that abuse has taken place, only that the reporting person suspects abuse has taken place. Often, the "reasonable cause" standard is utilized. However, delineating what constitutes that amount of cause can be difficult.[47] The intent of legislators in providing immunity is to encourage reporters to come forward, by eliminating any hesitation that abuse might not have occurred, even though it is suspected.[48]

In order to qualify for federal assistance under the Child Abuse Prevention and Treatment Act,[49] states must grant immunity from prosecution to those people who report instances of abuse and neglect. While a few statutes grant absolute, unqualified immunity, more frequently statutes provide for limited immunity for "good faith" reports. Further, immunity may be expressly limited to reporters having "reasonable cause" to suspect abuse or neglect. Other statutes provide a presumption of good faith for reporters.[50]

43. Id.
44. Sagatun, supra, 37. "These mandated reporters are provided immunity from civil and criminal liability as a result of making required and authorized reports of suspected child abuse when, in fact, no abuse can be proven. However, persons who report are not liable either civilly or criminally unless it can be proven that a false report was made and that the person knew the report was false."
Mitchell, supra, 723, 732. "Every state specifically provides immunity for the reporter from criminal and civil liability resulting from the report."
Kalichman, supra, 19. Some states presume that all reports are made in good faith, even if they are unsubstantiated.
45. 91 Am. Jur. *Trials* 151 § 12 (2004).
46. Mitchell, supra, 723, 732.
47. Sagatun, supra, 38.
48. Kalichman, supra, 20.
49. 42 U.S.C. §§ 5101–5106 (2010).
50. Veilleux, supra, 782, §2(a).

11:6 INSTANCES OF CONVICTION FOR
FAILURE TO REPORT

The Kansas City bishop's conviction in 2012 was a historic milestone in elevating the risk of church leaders' involvement with secrecy of priest abuse.[51] There are cases in which mandatory reporters are convicted for a failure to report. The professional category into which reporters are slotted makes an incredible difference in the outcome of a case. A 1992 case set a precedent and also triggered legislative change.[52] Since the time of this case, clergy are now listed as mandatory reporters for child abuse in California.

The appellants, Nobbs and Hodges, were a pastor and assistant pastor of the South Bay United Pentecostal Church, as well as the president and principal of South Bay Christian Academy, respectively. They appealed from a conviction for violating the Child Abuse and Neglect Reporting Act, Cal. Penal Code § 11166 (a), which provides that any child care custodian who has knowledge or observes a child in his or her professional capacity or within the scope of his or her employment "whom he or she knows or reasonably suspects has been the victim of child abuse shall report the known or suspected instance of child abuse to a child protective agency immediately or as soon as practically possible....".[53] An abuse victim told a teacher, who in turn reported to Hodges, that her stepfather, who was also a minister at the church, had been sexually abusing her for many years. Nobbs then gave Christine permission to go home for the rest of the school day. Hodges learned of the sexual abuse that the victim endured from her stepfather.[54] Hodges met with her stepfather and sent him on a retreat. The victim ran away from home, and Hodges told her that if she did not return home with her stepfather, she would not be allowed to attend school any more. He never reported the abuse to any authority or child protective agency.[55] A detective investigated the case after a call from the victim alleging molestation. The defendants were charged with violating the mandatory reporting statute, and were found guilty.[56]

The issues raised on appeal were: (1) the sufficiency of evidence to find that they were child care custodians within the meaning of the statute, (2) whether Cal. Penal Code § 11166 violates due process for failure to give adequate notice to pastors involved in church schools, (3) impingement of the appellants' free exercise of religion and freedom of speech in the federal and state constitutions, and (4) whether the reporting statute violates the First Amendment of the United States Constitution.[57]

---

51. Thomas, supra.
52. People v. Hodges, 10 Cal. App. 4th Supp. 20 (1992).
53. Id. at 23–24.
54. Id. at 24.
55. Id. at 25.
56. Id. at 26–27.
57. Id. at 24.

Regarding the first issue, as to whether there was substantial evidence to support the convictions, appellants argued that they were not acting as "child care custodians" within the meaning of Cal. Penal Code 11166. They argued that they were counseling the victim, a church member with a spiritual problem, as a pastor of the church. The defendants also noted that most of their meetings were not during school hours, and that Mr. Nobbs was not acting as a child care custodian. The jury instruction on the definition of a child care custodian under to section 11165.7 was as follows: "'[C]hild care custodian' means a teacher; . . . administrative officer, supervisor of child welfare and attendance . . . of any public or private school." Neither Hodges nor Nobbs objected to this definition.[58] Factors the court considered persuasive in finding that the appellants were acting in the capacity of child care custodians instead of spiritual counselors included: the church and school were part of the same building; the school taught both religious and academic courses; appellants were administrators of the school, which included daily management by Nobbs and immense decision-making responsibilities for Hodges.[59] The court found that there was ample evidence that the appellants were acting as child care custodians. Convictions against both appellants were affirmed.[60] (The other constitutional issues and issue on notice are not discussed as they are outside the scope of this chapter).

11:7 CIVIL TORT CONSEQUENCES FROM NOT REPORTING

The negligent actions of the diocese in responding to clergy sexual abuse are the centerpiece of the plaintiff's tort case, and the reporting issue aids the plaintiff in a settlement negotiation. Because the criminal justice system has fielded few prosecutions against clergy members accused of child sexual abuse, most of the suits pursued by victims are in the civil courts. Typically, a survivor of child sexual abuse will file a civil lawsuit against the offending clergy member and the church responsible for supervising clergy.[61]

In some states, there could also be civil penalties for a failure to report child abuse.[62] A few states expressly provide a civil cause of action for a child who is injured by abuse against the person who failed to make a required report that might have led to prevention of that abuse.[63] Tort liability is a possible sanction resulting from a professional's failure to report child abuse.[64] The civil penalties create liability for damages to the abused child.[65] As charitable immunity from tort liability has

58. Id. at 27.
59. Id. at 28.
60. Id.
61. 91 Am. Jur. *Trials* 151 § 9 (2004).
62. Sagatun, supra, 37.
63. Mitchell, supra, 723, 732.
64. Virginia C. Weisz, Children and Adolescents in Need: A Legal Primer for the Helping Professional 27 (Yvonne Konneker ed., 1995).
65. Stein, supra, 108.

begun to disappear for religious organizations, more tort actions against churches and other religious organizations have proliferated.

Where sexual misconduct of the clergy is involved, the recovery has been sought most frequently on theories of negligent hiring, ordination, retention, training, or supervision of the offending clergy member.[66] Other theories based on clergy sexual misconduct include interference with a marital relationship, if the congregant is married, and intentional infliction of emotional harm.[67] A clergy member may be liable for inflicting emotional distress if the victim proves that the clergy member intentionally or recklessly caused severe distress and anguish.[68]

However, sometimes clergy members have a cause of action for intentional infliction of emotional distress when they experience retaliation from other church members for reporting child abuse. For instance, in California, a clergy member's causes of action against his archbishop for intentional infliction of emotional distress and defamation, based on a claim that the archbishop violated the Child Abuse and Neglect Reporting Act by retaliating against the clergy member for reporting possible child abuse by a pastor, were subject to judicial review. These claims were not directed to any decision by the archbishop to discipline or terminate the clergy member but to the clergy member's exercise of his duty as a mandatory reporter under the Act.[69]

Moreover, religious institutions might become defendants under the doctrine of respondeat superior. Employers could be responsible for the torts of their clergy employees if the tort was committed within the time, space, and scope of employment and the act is the kind of which the employee is hired to perform.[70]

Evidence of a failure to report sexual abuse of children can be used to support a negligent hiring, retention, or supervision claim. Additionally, evidence of a "pedophilic behavior" within a church or religious organization by the offending clergy member or on the part of other clergy members within the church can be utilized as support.[71] A Pennsylvania court has held that evidence of "a bishop's and diocese's knowledge of improper conduct in a male minor's negligent supervision action against the bishop and diocese arising from the alleged molestation of the minor by the priest" was relevant. The court found that the prejudicial nature of relevant evidence of the failure of the diocese to report incidents of sexual abuse to the appropriate authorities did not outweigh its probative value, where the trial court correctly instructed the jury on two occasions on the limited purpose for which the

66. Marjorie A. Shields, "Liability of Church or Religious Organization for Negligent Hiring, Retention, or Supervision of Priest, Minister, or Other Clergy Based on Sexual Misconduct" 101 A.L.R. 5th 1, 2b (2002).

Arthur Gross Schafera & Darren Levinea, "No Sanctuary from the Law: Legal Issues Facing Clergy," 30 Loy. L.A. L. Rev. 177, 205–206 (1996). "The particular clergyperson may also be liable for the negligent hiring, supervising, and training of those who commit sexual transgressions."

67. Schafera, supra, 177, 205

68. Id. at 177, 205.

69. Conley v. Roman Catholic Archbishop of San Francisco, 85 Cal. App. 4th 1126, 102 Cal. Rptr. 2d 679 (1st Dist. 2000).

70. Schafera, supra, 177, 206.

71. Shields, supra.

EVIDENCE PRIVILEGES AND CLERGY ABUSE ISSUES (133)

evidence was received, and the jury was also specifically told that the diocesan parties did not have a duty to make any such reports.[72]

The California *Conley* case tested whether the court could enforce the legislative mandate that clergy members are not sanctioned for reporting suspected child abuse pursuant to Cal. Penal Code § 11166.0, which is the statute governing mandatory reporting. The court concluded that it did have the authority to enforce Cal. Penal Code § 11166.0, because to determine otherwise would relieve the Church of any responsibility for violating the statute,[73] and that in turn would eviscerate the legislative intent behind the statute.[74]

The court in the *Conley* case highlighted the development of the child abuse reporting laws in California. California's first reporting statute was conceived in 1980, as the Child Abuse Reporting Law (Cal. Penal Code § 11165), which imposed mandatory reporting requirements designed to increase identifying cases of child abuse. In 1987, the statute took a new form as the Child Abuse and Reporting Act (Cal. Penal Code § 11164). The statutes were clearly meant to protect children and linearly increased the state's list of mandated reporters. In 1996 Cal. Penal Code 11166 named clergy members as mandated reporters. Clergy were required to file a report to child protective agencies when they knew or suspected child abuse. The court surmised that the legislative intent for the inclusion of the clergy was to address the reluctance of religious institutions to report child abuse, to help train clergy in recognizing child abuse, and to provide immunity for those clergy members who reported child abuse.[75]

The mandatory reporting statute not only required "any clergy member" to report suspected child abuse when such suspicions arose in the course of his or her professional capacity, but it also afforded reporters immunity from suffering any sanction once they complied with the statutory provisions.[76] The statute reads "reporting duties under this section are individual, and no supervisor or administrator may impede or inhibit the reporting duties, and no person making a report shall be subject to any sanction for making the report."[77]

The court agreed that there was merit to Conley's allegations that Conley was being sanctioned by the Church, and moreover, it agreed that the Church's behavior constituted an outrageous act, violating subdivision (h) of the statute that forbid an "outrageous act sufficient to support a cause of action for intentional infliction of emotional distress."[78] Ultimately, the court reversed the trial court's judgment and overruled the demurrer, so that Conley would have the opportunity to try his case.[79]

In the Pennsylvania case, a minor male with limited mental capacities alleged that a Catholic priest had sexually molested him from around age 10 or 11 until

72. See Hutchison ex rel. Hutchison v. Luddy, 2000 763 A.2d 826 (Pa. Super. Ct. 2000), reargument denied (Jan. 4, 2001).
73. *Conley*, 85 Cal. App. 4th 1126.
74. Id. at 1131.
75. Id.
76. Id.
77. Id. at 1132 and see Cal. Penal Code 11166 (3)(e) (2007).
78. Id.
79. Id.

he 17. His mother brought a civil action to recover damages for the harm alleged to her son.[80] Two different causes of action formed the legal suit: (1) that under section 317 of the Restatement (Second) of Torts (1965), the church organization negligently hired, supervised, and retained the priest; and (2) that pedophilic behavior of priests was deliberately ignored and/or not remediated by the church organization. Plaintiff won both compensatory and punitive damages in excess of $1,500,000.[81] Eventually, the trial court reduced the punitive damages to $50,000 against the priest and $1 million against the diocesan parties.[82]

The diocesan parties appealed, raising 10 issues, one of which was whether "evidence of the failure of the Diocesan Parties to report incidents of child molestation by priests to the police or other civil authorities was admissible."[83]

Regarding that issue, the court held that evidence of a failure to report sexual abuse was relevant to, and probative of, the diocesan parties' knowledge of improper conduct in the plaintiff's negligent supervision action. The court found that the prejudicial nature of relevant evidence of the failure of the diocese to report incidents of sexual abuse to the appropriate authorities did not outweigh its probative value.[84]

The *Hutchinson* court acknowledged that such evidence could be seen as inflammatory and emotionally charged, but the fact that the evidence was unfavorable to the diocesan parties did not render it more prejudicial than probative, even though clergy were not mandated reporters of child abuse at the time of the offenses.[85] There were later developments in this case.[86]

11:8 IMMUNITY AS AN INCENTIVE ☙

For the protection of the reporters, all states allow for anonymous reporting.[87] As with immunity for criminal liability, reports made in good faith provide the reporter with immunity from civil and criminal liability.[88] Again, immunity is meant to encourage mandatory reporters to come forward and file reports of suspected child abuse by eliminating looming fears of potential lawsuits.[89]

---

80. Hutchison ex rel. Hutchison v. Luddy, 763 A.2d 826, 830 (Pa. Super. Ct. 2000).
81. Id. at 830.
82. Id. at 831.
83. Id.
84. Id. at 847.
85. Id.
86. One of the holdings of this case, that negligent supervision cannot give rise to punitive claims, was vacated in *Hutchison ex rel. Hutchison v. Luddy,* 582 Pa. 114, 870 A.2d 766 (2005).
87. Mitchell, supra, 723, 732.
88. Stein, supra, 108.
89. Veilleux, supra, 782, §2(a). "To encourage reporting by eliminating the fear of potential lawsuits, the statutes generally grant immunity from civil or criminal liability to the person submitting the report."

CHAPTER 12

⌒⌀⌒

Repressed Memory Inducement Cases

12:1 WHAT IS REPRESSED MEMORY?

Memories of our younger years form the basis of our adult personalities, according to psychologists, and some of the memories are not happy ones. Psychologists debate the impact that unhappy memories of events can have on the child as he or she grows older. This book explores clergy sexual abuse of young people. One of the key phenomena that crosses legal and psychological lines is the incident of adult recollection of a child or teen sexual encounter, which leads to a lawsuit asserting that the long-delayed suit should be permitted in court because the bad memory had been "repressed."[1]

Some psychologists believe that memories of childhood sexual assault are likely to be repressed, as being painful memories, and that when the recollections arise in that individual's adult years, they are recalled to mind by the adult. Other psychologists firmly disagree with the repressed memory claims and their diagnosis, "dissociative amnesia."[2] The American Psychological Association explains the doubts about the validity of this theory and the absence of a substantial base of valid studies.[3]

The debate forms a part of the complex social science basis for the legal dispute concerning whether courts should hear claims of child sexual abuse that are years or decades old.[4] These incidents may have occurred, but delay in filing suit means that they will be dismissed when the claims are beyond the state statutes

---

1. A useful legal background is found in John Daly Cooney, "Determining When to Start the Clock: The 'Capable of Ascertainment' Standard and Repressed Memory Sexual Abuse Cases," 72 Mo. L. Rev. 633 (2007).

2. Susan Roth & Matthew Friedman, "Childhood Trauma Remembered: A Report on the Current Scientific Knowledge Base and Its Application," 7(1) J. Child Sexual Abuse 83 (1998).

3. www.apa.org/topics/trauma/memories/aspx.

4. Elizabeth Kuniholm & Kim Church, "Repressed and Recovered Memory," in 4 West's Litigating Tort Cases 54:13 (2013).

of limitations,[5] as discussed in Chapter 5. There are exceptions in the statutes of limitation that allow for belated "discovery"[6] and some that allow "tolling," or suspension of the time to prosecute, and plaintiffs argue for expansion of that period to include time when the childhood memory had been "repressed."[7]

This chapter deals with plaintiffs who seek to file late claims for damages and who assert as a basis for delay that they had repressed painful memories of the acts of abuse.[8] These are difficult cases for plaintiffs to win,[9] leading a plaintiff's advocate to refer to the "clerical iron curtain" that shielded abusers from liability.[10]

If we look back on the most active years of recent debate, the issue of repressed memory as a rationale for belated reporting has been one of the most controversial innovations attempted by adult plaintiffs. An accusation of sexual contact with a seminarian, and a later tearful retraction, in the case of Cardinal Joseph Bernardin,[11] focused attention on the debates over the validity of "inducing" a set of "repressed" memories of bad events in one's past. Advocates for plaintiffs praised the use of these memory-recovery tools for allowing compensation,[12] while opponents derided their use.

Courts generally did not accept the claims of repressed memory.[13] This chapter examines the current knowledge on this controversial aspect of the cases.

12:2 HOW DOES THIS THEORY RELATE TO STATUTES OF LIMITATIONS?

The courts ask whether the plaintiff has filed the lawsuit within the time permitted by the state's statute of limitations. If not, the claim is barred, unless a specific exemption applies, such as proof of a conspiracy to conceal a fact. The plaintiff must demonstrate that each element of the exemption is satisfied.[14]

This is a difficult burden for the plaintiff, because most adult litigants admit that they knew of the sexual abuse as of a certain date, but that they repressed or

5. See e.g., E.W. v D.C.H., 754 P.2d 817 (Mont. 1988) and Annotation, "Running of Limitations against Action for Civil Damages for Sexual Abuse of Child," 9 A.L.R. 5th 321 (1993).

6. Doe v Roe, 191 Ariz. 313, 955 P.2d 951, 959 (1998).

7. See e.g., Annotation, "Emotional or Psychological 'Blocking' or Repression as Tolling Running of Statute of Limitation," 11 A.L.R. 5th 588 (1993)]; Sheila Taub, "The Legal Treatment of Recovered Memories of Child Sexual Abuse," 17 J. Legal Med. 183 (1996).

8. A useful model for analyzing these facts of repressed memory is Dalrymple v. Brown, 701 A.2d 164 (Pa. 1997).

9. See e.g., Demeyer v. Archdiocese of Detroit, 593 N.W.2d 560 (Mich. App. 1999).

10. Susan Heylman, "As States Suspend Time Limits on Sex Abuse Suits, Clergy Cases Proceed, 43 Trial 72 (Oct. 2007).

11. Edward Walsh, "Man Who Accused Cardinal Bernardin of Sexual Abuse Drops Lawsuit," Wash. Post (Mar. 1, 1994).

12. Heylman, supra.

13. One of the best descriptive analyses on this issue is found in the case of John BBB Doe v. Archdiocese of Milwaukee, 565 N.W.2d 94 (Wisc. 1997).

14. See e.g., Roe 58 v. Doe 1, 120 Cal. Rptr. 3d 311 (Cal. App. 2 Dist., 2011).

downplayed the significance of that emotionally damaging event. For example, in a Connecticut case, the molestation occurred in 1961 but the plaintiff asserted the memory was repressed until 1991.[15]

The concept of notice and "inquiry notice" is applied. Inquiry notice means the date on which a reasonable person would have asked questions. In Missouri and other states, an objective test is applied to what he or she knew and when he or she knew it: "when a reasonable person would have been put on notice that an injury and substantial damages may have occurred."[16] In Alabama, an older statute suspended the running of the statute of limitations for persons with temporary insanity; this was held not to apply to claims of repressed memory of past abuses.[17] In Indiana, the plaintiff must present expert opinion to aid the court in determining reliability of the memory evidence,[18] but in Arizona and New Jersey such testimony is not required.[19]

Early in the sequence of events that became the clergy abuse crisis, there were numerous efforts to drill an exception through the barrier of limitations on belated filings, asserting that the statute of limitations should not apply, because the abusive priest had allegedly induced the child not to disclose the sexual encounter, and so the child had repressed the memory of the event.[20] Fear of the abuser and embarrassment about sexual matters were said to have caused the repression.[21] That scenario was used to justify a lawsuit long after the abuser was dead, or the records or recollections of others had been discarded or lost.

Psychologists' opinions are divided. Disagreements within the community of psychology professionals have led most of the courts to decline the invitation to give full credit to a case based upon recovery from repressed memory.[22]

Some courts have criticized the repressed-memory concept as well as its application in these cases.[23] Other courts have accepted its use, in some cases.[24] If the

---

15. Martinelli v. Bridgeport Roman Catholic Diocesan Corp., 989 F. Supp. 110, 112 (D. Conn. 1997). (His memories of the abuse had been repressed but were recovered through psychotherapy in 1991).

16. Powel v Chaminade College Preparatory Inc., 197 S.W.3d 576, 584 (Mo. 2006); accord, State ex rel. Marianist Province v. Ross, 258 S.W.3d 809 (Mo. 2008); Demsey v. Johnston, 299 S.W.3d 704 (Mo. App. 2009).

17. Travis v. Ziter, 681 So. 2d 1348 (Ala. 1996).

18. LaCava v. LaCava, 907 N.E.2d 154 (Ind. App. 2009).

19. Confidential Claimant 87/204 v. Roman Catholic Church, 319 Fed. Appx. 566 (9th Cir. 2009); Phillips v. Gelpke, 921 A.2d 1067 (N.J. 2007).

20. These are dealt with by courts and advocates; see e.g., Taub, supra.

21. Ayon v. Gourley, 47 F. Supp. 2d 1246 (D. Colo. 1998), aff'd, 185 F.3d 873 (10th Cir. 1999).

22. S.V. v. R.V., 933 S.W.2d 1 (Tex. 1996).

23. Albright v. White, 503 S.E.2d 860 (W.Va. 1998).`

24. See e.g., Hearndon v. Graham, 767 So. 2d 1179 (Fla. 2000); Doe v. Schults-Lewis, 718 N.E.2d 738 (Ind. 1999); Bertram v. Poole, 597 N.W.2d 309 (Minn. App. 1999); McCollum v. D'Arcy, 638 A.2d 797 (N.H. 1994); Moriarty v. Garden Sanctuary Church of God, 534 So.2d 672 (S.C. 2000).

defense counsel missed the opportunity to object to the repressed memory claims, then the jury could accept it or not.[25]

12:3 EFFECTS OF THE *DAUBERT* STANDARD

The federal courts and many state courts have chosen to pre-screen the admissibility of proffered expert testimony, seeking to exclude witnesses who are not "relevant and reliable." The so-called *Daubert*[26] hearing occurs before the jury will hear the expert witness. The plaintiff puts forward the expert witness and the defendant cross-examines, or vice versa. The expert should explain the methodology and the degree of peer-reviewed scientific literature in support of the claims. If the court applies the "*Daubert* test" and does not accept the witness, the plaintiff must produce alternate credible support for his or her case or the claim will be dismissed. In some federal courts, clergy abuse claims have been dismissed because the key expert who was to testify about the plaintiff's "repressed memory" is excluded.[27]

12:4 FUTURE OF THE REPRESSED MEMORY CASES

Any history of clergy sexual abuse can track the incidence of lawsuits within a state by the state appeals court's acceptance of repressed memory claims. Some courts have allowed the plaintiff to belatedly "discover" that a childhood incident of oral sex with a clergyman had occurred, and the discovered memory causes emotional trauma as an adult.[28] But two decades of news publicity about these kinds of misconduct events has made most Americans aware that wrongful conduct may have occurred to them, so it is less likely that an adult in his 40s or 50s would today "discover" a memory of sexual encounters at age 8. A firm rejection of the theory by state courts would discourage attorneys from accepting the potential plaintiff's case. Those states that were more receptive to belated "discovery" claims have experienced more of these lawsuits.

Trends in the law of evidence have tended toward requiring firm scientific support before a jury can hear expert testimony about highly technical matters. Repressed memories discovered after decades are an exception to well-established statutes of limitations. Some states accepted these theories in previous years.[29] As the psychology community has trended away from acceptance of the theory, it is less likely that a court in the 2010s would accept a claim that would have been well received in the 1990s.

25. Martinelli v. Bridgeport Roman Catholic Diocesan Corp., 10 F. Supp. 2d 138, 157, 158 (D. Conn. 1998), aff'd in part, vacated in part, 196 F.3d 409 (2d Cir. 1999).

26. Daubert v. Merrell Dow Pharms., 509 U.S. 579 (1973).

27. Confidential Claimant 87/204 v. Roman Catholic Church, 319 Fed. Appx. 566 (9th Cir. 2009).

28. Doe v. Roe, 191 Ariz. 313, 955 P.2d 951, 959 (1998).

29. Id.

CHAPTER 13

⌀

Fraud and Nondisclosure in the Assignment of Clergy

13:1 LAWSUITS CHALLENGING TRANSFERS OF ABUSERS TO CONTACT WITH CHILDREN

This chapter asks:

- Is the diocese negligent for assigning this priest, against whom allegations of sexual misconduct had been made, to a new post having contact with children?
- If so, is the diocese liable for fraud in keeping silent about the background of this abuser?
- Does the priest have rights that would be violated if the bishop made public an allegation of sexual misconduct before it has been adjudicated?

In the Roman Catholic Church, priests in diocesan service are sent to assigned parishes by the bishop or his personnel director, typically titled "Vicar for Clergy." Priests in religious order communities such as the Jesuits are sent to assignments for the needs of the order. After an assertion of sexual misconduct arises, the natural question is: Why was this priest in contact with this child or teen in this place?

Proximity of the defendant abuser to the victim was typically the result of an assignment of that priest to this particular role working with young people. Negligence law applies a "but-for" principle: but for the assignment to this parish or school, Father X would never have met plaintiff Y. The Boston archdiocese continued to assign Father John Geoghan to parish work despite an auxiliary bishop's 1984 memo that he had a "history of homosexual involvement with young boys."[1] Geoghan continued being counseled and then reassigned, and as a result, he molested dozens

---

1. Nicholas Cafardi, Before Dallas: The U.S. Bishops' Response to Clergy Sexual Abuse of Children 13 (2008).

of boys.[2] He died in prison and the archdiocese of Boston endured years of scandals and settlements of lawsuits.

The legal issue is whether the assignment of a priest into contact with children, despite such a dangerous record of past alleged abuse, was an act of diocesan negligence for which damages can be awarded. Is it fraudulent for a bishop not to disclose to parents at the new parish the set of known claims and the pending allegations of criminal sexual predation by this incoming priest, to whom parents will entrust their vulnerable children? Apart from legal causes of action, is it morally prudent for a bishop to reassign a priest to school and parish work after a credible allegation of child sexual abuse has been made?

There is no officially recognized tort of "willful blindness allowing child molestation," but such a claim might be referred to as "negligence in assigning this priest after allegations or credible evidence of his sexual attraction to young people." The choices made by Catholic diocesan and religious order leaders in the reassignment of priests who are accused of sexual misconduct have been a significant issue in numerous civil tort trials. Juries are not sympathetic to dioceses when a pattern of such assignments emerges in the facts, and these are the cases that are most likely to be settled by the diocese, before there can be a jury verdict.

In 2004, the National Review Board selected by the U.S. Conference of Catholic Bishops said that "it is clear in hindsight that the Church could have prevented numerous acts of sexual abuse, had its leaders reported all allegations of sexual abuse by priests to the civil authorities."[3] Is that hindsight a basis for tort verdicts against bishops?

The problems were nationwide and pervasive. A serial child molester who was a priest of one Indiana diocese was known to have that problem with boys; he was given permission to work in a Florida diocese, where that diocese knew of his proclivities, and he molested more boys. Neither diocese acted, and neither disclosed the "deviant sexual tendencies," so both were sued by victims for their negligence.[4] The Boston sexual abuse turmoil and huge financial settlement reflected a set of practices that *Boston Globe* reporters described in chilling terms in 2002. A predator priest was "shuttled from parish to parish to avoid public scandal" while details of his patterns of abuse "were a closely held secret to be kept from the parishioners who welcomed him into their homes."[5] The Philadelphia archdiocesan Vicar for Priests was convicted of the crime of assigning certain accused predator priests to several parishes despite his knowledge of their past accusations of abuse.[6] Chicago's archbishop wrote to all parishes apologizing for having assigned to St. Odilo's parish a priest who had a prior lawsuit for sexual abuse 10 years before.[7] California abuser priests had easy access

2. The Boston Globe Investigative Unit, Betrayal: The Crisis in the Catholic Church (2002).

3. National Review Board for the Protection of Children & Young People, A Report on the Crisis in the Catholic Church in the United States 110 (2004).

4. Doe v. Emerson, 2006 Westlaw 2971314 (Fla. Cir. Ct. 2006).

5. The Boston Globe Investigative Unit, supra, 23.

6. "U.S. Bishops Renew Vow to Oust Predator Priests, Following Grand Jury Rebuke of Philly Diocese," Associated Press (Mar. 24, 2011).

7. Cafardi, supra, 82.

to families and schools in new parishes, according to several accounts. What did the bishop know and when did he know it?

The decision of the individual diocese or religious order is evaluated in retrospect: Was it negligent or willful to send this alleged abuser to this new venue, where children were present and where abuse might (and did) recur? Should the diocese compensate the later abuse victims for the diocese not having stopped the priest after learning of his earlier pattern of child abuse allegations?

A particular priest may have had a pattern of multiple past allegations from multiple venues, for example, a high school and then a parish, a parish and then a hospital, etc. The priest had been moved from one post to another, always accepting the move under the Church's solemn vow of obedience to the bishop. But this transfer occurs in silence, without the diocese giving notice about these past allegations to the people of the parish or other post that is receiving him.[8] Is that a compensable action when a later-abused child sues the diocese? Did the bishop reasonably believe the priest would not abuse other teens, before sending him to new areas where his prior reputation was not known?

During these decades of 1960–2000, American bishops had a common problem: the number of priests available was less than the number of posts that required their ministry. What set of parents, if told of abuse allegations, would have accepted the reassigned priest into their parish? Given the shortage of priests (and the occasional reliance on the psychologists who ran treatment programs for abusers among the clergy), was it a "reasonable bishop" who put a priest with a past of child sexual abuse into another school or parish role?

In 1983, in the first widely publicized priest sexual abuse case, a Louisiana bishop sent the predator priest on six different parish assignments after learning of his molestations.[9] In one of the Dallas cases, the diocese actively urged authorities not to prosecute after clear evidence of child sexual abuse arose, and the priest was sent to a parish where school children would be in his care.[10] He then abused other children.

13:2 THE ROLE OF DIOCESAN CONCEALMENT

The 2004 National Review Board report to the U.S. Conference of Catholic Bishops concluded that the lack of candor by bishops "avoided scandal in the short term while sowing seeds for greater upheaval in the long term."[11] The pattern of "normal" secrecy about allegations of past abuse reflects the reality that a priest whose prior sexual conduct had been publicly disclosed would never have been accepted by the parish or school families at the new venue. When claims of abuse were made,

8. *Emerson*, 2006 Westlaw 2971314.

9. Mary Gail Frawley-O'Dea, Perversion of Power:Sexual Abuse in the Catholic Church (2007).

10. Brooks Egerton, "Judge in Kos Case Lets Emotions Out", Dallas Morning News (July 22, 1997).

11. National Review Board, supra, 108.

dioceses such as Boston and Camden would pay a settlement quickly, before the lawsuit occurred or the family went public, and their payments carried a promise of the victim's nondisclosure.[12]

Silence and reassignment were the key negligent acts that are charged in the plaintiff's negligence claim. As three experts wrote in their text on this topic, "It remains a mystery why the histories of scores of abusing priests record promotions within the system after they have been reported for abusive behavior."[13]

Defense of a negligence claim turns upon the knowledge and foreseeability factors. What were the bishops thinking? They kept abuse allegation information away from the affected parishioners, and even kept information away from therapists who tried to deal with the misbehaving priests. "Some also pressured victims not to inform the authorities or the public of the abuse."[14] These bishops' decisions to keep secret a fact about the priest who is assigned to minister to children is likely to infuriate the parents when that fact becomes known. When a Kansas City priest was arrested for child pornography offenses and attempted suicide in 2011, his bishop faced very angry parishioners and said, "I deeply regret that we didn't ask the police earlier to conduct a full investigation."[15] That bishop was criminally convicted for the failure to make a timely report of the priest-abuser's apparent offenses.[16] An estimated 24 priests with serious abuse allegations in their past have moved back to Mexico, where they are still in ministry.[17] Others have committed suicide when child abuse charges were made against them.

Any observer would acknowledge that considerations of individual privacy rights and the aspects of "innocent until proven guilty" are at stake when a bishop considers public dissemination of information about a priest's past difficulties. As later chapters demonstrate, adjudication of abuse cases against priests in the internal Church tribunals takes years.

The shortage of priests is severe in many dioceses, serving as a disincentive for a bishop to "sideline" any priest out of parish or school assignments. We also acknowledge that some accusations were false and malicious. Cardinal Joseph Bernardin was wrongly accused of sexual misconduct with a former seminarian, before that lie was retracted with an apology,[18] and in some of the thousands of allegations of sexual misconduct against priests, some of the priests were and are innocent. But the U.S. Conference of Catholic Bishops' independent National Review

12. The Boston Globe Investigative Unit, supra, 47.

13. Thomas Doyle, A.W.R. Sipe & Patrick Wall, Sex, Priests and Secret Codes: The Catholic Church's 2,000 Year Paper Trail of Sexual Abuse 193, 196–198 (2006).

14. National Review Board, supra, 108.

15. Joshua McElwee, "Warnings Ignored in Year before Priest's Arrest," Nat'l Cath. Rptr. (June 10, 2011).

16. Judy Thomas, "Bishop Finn, Diocese Indicted in Abuse Case." Kansas City Star (Oct. 14, 2011).

17. N.C. Aizenman, "Alleged Abuse Victim Continues Fight against Clergyman in Mexico," Wash. Post (Apr. 20, 2010), at 4.

18. Cafardi, supra, 101.

Board properly found in 2004 that the insistence of Church leaders on secrecy ran counter to a need to find the facts; disclosure "might have given additional victims the courage to come forward and would have helped the diocese determine the validity of complaints."[19]

13:3 WHAT THE DATA SHOWS

The 2011 study by John Jay College about priests who committed sexual abuse has excellent data for statisticians, but a tragic story to tell for families of the victims. For priests who were subject to an accusation of sexual misconduct, prior to 1985, 35 percent were sent back to a parish after a reprimand. "From the 1980s forward, the likelihood of a reprimand and quick return to duty decreases, and the likelihood of being put on administrative leave or suspended increases. . . . When specifically considering post-1985 treatment, the most common type of treatment for accused priests was specialized sex offender treatment programs. . . . The likelihood of a priest being reprimanded and returned to the parish or reinstated after an accusation changes . . . to 18 percent for reinstatement and 5 percent for reprimand-and-return for those first accused after 1985. If only priests accused after 2000 are considered, 8.5 percent were reinstated. For priest abusers sent to treatment before 1990, their average number of victims is six, and three out of four had four or more victims. In comparison, if all priests who were *accused* of sexual abuse before 1990 are considered, their average number of victims is three, and a majority (60 percent) had one or two victims."[20]

Said another way, two of three abusers were sent back to the parish or another parish prior to 1985 (when most of the U.S. reported abuse cases occurred), and the molested child is likely to have been only one of multiple victims for that priest. Another study observed that the average number of victims per priest offender was six.

Step back from that number of six or more victims and one can understand why a plaintiff's lawyer would focus on suing regarding negligent assignment decisions by the bishop, and why the lawyer would argue that the bishop took too great a chance that sexual misconduct would be repeated. The defense lawyers for a bishop would advise settlement in most of these cases, facing the recidivist abuser statistics and the retrospective jury considerations of the choices made by the defendant bishop. The defense has even a harder time with belated claims of long-past abuse, as the bishop may no longer be alive or, in the case of Philadelphia, may have retired with memory deficits, making him unavailable for the defense.

19. National Review Board, supra, 108.
20. John Jay College, The Causes and Context of Sexual Abuse of Minors by Catholic Priests in the United States, 1950–2010, at 80 (2011) (hereinafter "John Jay College Report").

13:4 HOW PRIEST TRANSFERS WERE MANAGED

Non-Catholic readers may be surprised to learn that in the Catholic Church, the lay members of the parish or school community have no role in selecting the pastor or priest assigned to them. There is virtually no role for parish members or school parents to validate or scrutinize the individual priest, once they have been assigned to the parish or school by the bishop. Likewise, a council of laity can request that the Vatican appoint a particular bishop or characteristic of bishop, but their wishes often count for very little.[21]

The potential existed in the 1960–1985 period that a priest who was a high-risk candidate for a recurring episode of sexual abuse risk would be reassigned after a report of past abuse,[22] but the receiving parish community had, and has today, no way to learn of these past experiences or to protect itself, if the priest repeats his prior bad conduct in the new location. Theoretically, a diocese could be sued for fraudulent concealment of a known risk of injury, if a plaintiff shows the consistent pattern of diocesan failure to disclose the material fact of sexual abuse behaviors, where a legal or equitable duty to disclose exists. (Imposing a civil law duty to communicate within a church by its leaders may be an infringement by "entanglement" in First Amendment freedoms of the church, as Chapter 8 relates.) In these reassignments of abusers, the plaintiff's counsel will argue that silence about the transferee's past was indicative of negligence, or worse, of misrepresentation, if the silence led parents to trust this priest to be alone with their children. A plaintiff could assert that a diocese implicitly intended to induce parishioners to assume the safety of their child, in reliance on the nondisclosure, and parish families in fact relied upon this silence about past abuse, to the actual detriment of the parishioners and their children.[23] Again, laypersons have no vote in Catholic priest assignments, and they cannot vet the candidate, as Protestant churches routinely do. Priests coming to the end of their period of typical assignment can request a particular new parish assignment, but canon law provides that the bishop makes the sole decision. This absence of any explanation in normal times in some ways helps the bishop, who would argue that his silence about this incoming priest is no different than his silence about all others.

Bishops may have been hesitant to "jump to conclusions" about allegations, because of the harm to the reputation of the priest that is being moved. Later chapters discuss the length of time needed for internal Church discipline of priests who abuse children or teens. The reasons for suddenly reassigning a priest may be varied (e.g., a sudden need to fill a vacancy, or to cover for a priest who is ill or injured). But

---

21. In his one-time role as president of an archdiocesan pastoral council, the author Prof. O'Reilly drafted and the council transmitted a request for appointment of an archbishop to fill a vacancy in his archdiocese; if the nuncio ever read the letter, it apparently had no impact on the selection process, as the new leader was the opposite of the laity council's recommendations.

22. This was the Chicago experience; see Cafardi, supra, 82.

23. Picher v. Roman Catholic Bishop of Portland, 974 A.2d 286, 295 (2009).

in some cases, the reason was that his prior relationship with male or female abuse victims was becoming known, and could cause a scandal in the parish or school community if it persisted. In the past before the adoption of national standards, at this critical decision point—when the bishop thinks the accusation is credible and the priest must be moved away from his victim– the bishop had most often chosen not to inform civil authorities such as the police, and not to disclose the basis for removal. Prior to the Dallas 2002 meeting that adopted the "Essential Norms" for bishops, credible allegations of misconduct would be unknown to those families that may have teens or children at risk. That failure to notify is the crux of the liability cases against the diocese.

13:5 PRIEST ABUSE CONTRASTED TO LIABILITY UNDER TRADITIONAL EMPLOYMENT LAW

Ordinary concepts of the manager's responsibility for the worker's bad conduct, largely grouped under the concept *respondeat superior*, may hold a trucking company liable for the tort of misconduct of its employee driver in a collision. But priests are not in an ordinary occupation, and their sexual abuse cases are obviously not normal acts of an employee in furtherance of the Church's mission. The First Amendment has a role to play in diminishing the entanglement of civil courts with inner workings of the Church.

Statistically, most courts have refused to hold the diocese or bishop liable for the tort of sexual abuse by priests. These fact patterns of concealed sexual acts with vulnerable young persons are not only "outside the scope" of the priest's duties, they are contrary to the whole mission of the "employer" diocese.[24] But the diocese at some point may have been "on notice" of misconduct. It may have sent the priest for counseling, may have paid for therapy, may have temporarily suspended him, etc., but in hindsight the measures taken failed. It is the claim of negligent or intentional reassignment of this priest that facilitated his further contacts with youth, after an allegation of sexual abuse, which is the focal point of many plaintiffs' claims. In the national policy established by the 2002 Dallas "Essential Norms," one proven case of sexually abusing a minor is enough to preclude that priest from active ministry in the future. Therefore, the plaintiff who was molested before 2002 argues an implicit duty was breached by the bishop at the time the priest was again assigned to a role in contact with young people; the plaintiff after 2002 asserts an explicit willful failure to follow the national standard of care that other bishops had routinely followed. Faced with the catastrophic bankruptcy consequences that other dioceses encountered, as Chapter 9 relates in detail, the prudent bishop will

24. Doe v. Catholic Bishop, 306 S.W.3d 712 (Tenn. App. 2008) citing Note, "A Higher Authority: The Viability of Third Party Tort Actions against a Religious Institution Grounded on Sexual Misconduct by a Member of the Clergy," 30 Fla. St. U. L. Rev. 957 (2003).

enforce the "one strike and you're out" rule[25] as soon as the credible allegation of abuse is proven in an investigation by the diocesan review board or the police.

Consider the plaintiff's posture. The conventional truck driver accident results in a claim that the truck company intended the truck to be driven and the company is accountable for mistakes in that driving. Sexual abuse is not in the job description of the priest. Without access to the easier route of *respondeat superior* obligations for the diocese, a plaintiff's effort to pin liability upon a diocese requires some effective pleading of persuasive facts. Fraudulent concealment, misrepresentation, and conspiracy claims have been offered, but the claims are often dismissed for lack of basic documentary support for the allegations.[26]

This situation of a bishop making decisions about transfers of priests who have vowed their obedience to that bishop does not fit very neatly into labor and employment law concepts in civil or common law. Ordinarily, an individual is an employee at will, who can quit or be fired at any time. There is no legal obligation for a former employer to make any further disclosure to subsequent employers of the ex-employee's problems in previous jobs. Many private sector employers decline as a policy matter to discuss aberrant aspects of any former employee's performance. But the policy of transferring clerics without notifying the parish of his problems is a double concealment, keeping the pending accusations of criminal activities from the police, and keeping news of the accusations from the parish community to which he is being assigned. Thus, dioceses should be distinguished from other private sector employees, and because of its special position of trust and care for young people, the diocese should have a duty to report credible misconduct allegations to civil authorities. With accusations totaling 4,392 priests and 10,667 victims before 2003,[27] the case for a victim to argue that dioceses did too little or notified too few vulnerable families is bolstered by the statistical data.

The plaintiff in an ordinary civil case involving employee misconduct is likely to argue that negligent hiring of that worker by the current employer had contributed to the harm. The plaintiff will say that if a full background evaluation had been performed, the individual would not have been accepted in the new role, and the tort would not have occurred. The lack of attention to background checks or other verification of prior conduct leaves the receiving employer vulnerable to negligence liability for any new cases of abuse. Schools, nursing homes, hospitals, and other sites with vulnerable populations will try to prevent such predatory persons from transferring in, by examining a state or national "registry" of past offenders. No such list is ever published by the U.S. Conference of Catholic Bishops or the decentralized entities that collectively constitute the institutional "Catholic Church." The closest is the privately maintained and somewhat hostile listings on

25. Unless there is a compelling reason to believe the priest no longer presents a threat to children.
26. See e.g., Jane Doe 43C v. Diocese of New Ulm, 2009 Westlaw 605749 (Minn. App. 2009).
27. John Jay College Report, supra, 8.

the website bishopaccountability.org.[28] But the Church does not place the names of convicted abuser priests on any searchable database. If the priest is from a diocese that follows the 2002 Essential Norms, the "one strike and you're out of ministry" policy makes it less likely that the transfer of a convicted priest into another parish will occur.

13:6 CONCEALMENT OF DIOCESAN KNOWLEDGE OF THE PRIOR ACCUSATIONS

This problem of "stealth abuser" assignment, after a bishop's recognition of a priest's past abusive tendencies, is troubling, especially because assignment by the bishop is totally out of the control of the parish or school receiving that priest. In later liability lawsuits against the hierarchy of the diocese or the superior official of a religious order of priests, plaintiffs can assert that the bishop or superior had knowledge of an accusation that gave rise to a duty to stop the abuse, and that the failure to stop the abuse at the time of movement of the person was an egregiously negligent or intentional and willful action. This may give rise to a plaintiff asserting the longer statute of limitations under state fraud laws, as intentional concealment and fraud claims are involved.[29]

It may be argued by plaintiffs that, but for the individual diocese or religious order having failed to disclose, the injury would not have occurred at the new location. The classical case of this pattern was the Boston archdiocese defense of its several transfers during the criminal sexual abuse exploits of Father Paul Shanley. Shanley and Fathers John Geoghan and James Porter were allegedly shuffled from abuse site to abuse site without any substantial warnings given, actions restricted, or oversight mandated from the archdiocesan offices.[30]

The response most bishops would assert from the 1960–1990 period is that the bishop had acted within the available advice that sexual misconduct patterns could be "cured"; that the priest who was known to have problems had been sent to inpatient therapy centers,[31] and that he was returned to parish work after being released by the therapists.[32] "I thought he was cured, before he reoffended" is their defense. Even the efficacy of post-abuse treatment centers was controversial.[33] Today's psychological knowledge about errant sexual behavior is quite different,

---

28. Author Prof. O'Reilly was startled to find his seventh grade religion teacher, a Franciscan brother, had been listed on www.bishopaccountability.org for his alleged misconduct with boys in a subsequent parish assignment.

29. Jane Doe 43C v. Diocese of New Ulm, 2009 Westlaw 605749 (Minn. App. 2009).

30. The Boston Globe Investigative Unit, supra.

31. These centers were very controversial and remain so today. New Life Center, Inc. v. Fessio, 229 F.3d 1143 (4th Cir. 2000) (includes a useful recap of the literature and case law of these disputed centers).

32. John Jay College Report, 75–80.

33. Servants of the Paraclete, Inc. v. Great Am. Ins. Co., 866 F. Supp. 1560, 1563–1564 (D.N.M. 1994).

and the juries today might seem to be harsh in judging the past practices of the bishops from prior decades.

13:7 HOW JURY DECISIONS WOULD BE MADE

When a credible allegation is made in a parish regarding a priest and sexual misconduct, its public disclosure is likely to cause scandal, and will produce the priest's temporary removal from the parish, during the re-examination of that priest's fitness for his assignment in contact with young people.[34] Years later, after a civil lawsuit by persons who were abused by that priest at his new assignment, the jury in the damages trial will examine the decisions of the bishop, the Vicar for Clergy of the diocese. or the equivalent for the religious order. These decisions made by jurors in a civil court trial, about decisions of a religious entity to forgive and offer a second chance, will involve the jury making decisions about the self-governance of that church entity. There will be legal issues involved with the liability claim; the plaintiff is asserting error in the diocesan governance decision to move or not move that particular priest after receiving the allegation. The legal issues of knowledge, timing of knowledge, and extent of knowledge will be very fact-specific decisions in each case.

The potential defense of the diocese is that when sexual abuse events became known, the response was appropriate according to the norms of that time period. The pattern for abusers in the 1980s appears to have been that the accused priest was taken out of the parish; the diocese then paid many thousands of dollars to place him in a rehabilitation setting; the psychological opinion of that time period was supportive of a "cure" being achieved[35]; when the psychologists "released" the abusive priest he was returned to duty with some supervision.[36] Although a significant percent of the "treated" priests then reoffended, the diocese would assert that reoffending was not foreseeable, so the diocese would argue that the diocese should not be found to have been negligent, according to the therapeutic mode of that time. It's a hard sell to a modern jury, and many defense counsel have encouraged settlements.

The acceptance of this defense assertion regarding past practices for diversion of accused priests has a flaw: it requires the jury member to ignore the subsequent event's horror for the later victims, and instead focus on the treatment center supervisor, on whom that bishop had relied as of the time of reinstatement of the "treated" priest for active parish duties.[37] In studying these cases, we examined the court decisions and read the views of therapists. We found the great majority of the cases were settled, and that those that went to a jury usually penalized the diocese for its negligence in assignment of the priest, even after the attempts at his

---

34. See e.g., Janon Fisher & Jose Martinez, "Retired Brooklyn Monsignor, 78, Arrested for Alleged Criminal Sex Acts with Two Teen Boys," N.Y. Daily News (Oct. 15, 2011).
35. *New Life Center,* 229 F.3d 1143 (useful recap of the controversial treatments).
36. John Jay College Report, supra, 75–80
37. New Life Center, Inc. v. Fessio, 229 F.3d 1143 (4th Cir. 2000).

rehabilitation. Jurors are average people of average experience, and the abstraction of "what might have been the result of what should have been a successful rehabilitation" has not been a successful defense with average jurors.

In the discovery phase of the civil case asserting negligent assignment of this priest to that parish or school, the clergy personnel records will be reviewed and the reasons for the accused priest's pattern of sudden departures and reassignments will inevitably be questioned. Prudent plaintiffs will seek to reconstruct some apparent indicators of awareness by the diocese of the priest's prior sexual misconduct. The jury will be told that for most diocesan priests in the United States, the regular assignment length is two years for associates, or six years for pastors, depending upon the particular context. The plaintiff will then say that the sudden, premature reassignment of the priest must have reflected knowledge by the diocese or religious institution that misconduct had occurred; discovery of the documents will aid this claim, unless key documents were destroyed. And assignment of the priest to an expensive therapy center until "cured" is a step that is used when the diocese has notice that the priest is a serious violator of clergy standards of moral behavior.[38] We note that therapy for alcohol or emotional problems is used in some cases, so the mere fact that the priest was sent to therapy does not imply a sexual abuse problem existed.

The best evidence for a plaintiff would be a paper trail of explanations of this priest's bad conduct, if the personnel files and the bishop's secret files were to be examined. Boston files were full of damning statements about its predator priests.[39] If no records are available, because no records were written down or files had been purged, then inferences must be drawn. The record shows that this priest was hastily reassigned to a posting without contact with children, such as a prison ministry. That will send a message to the jury that the assignment was made for purposes of isolating the priest, in an implicit recognition of the awareness of his prior bad actions toward children. If the priest was sent to one of the special rehabilitation centers for troubled clergy members, that could be claimed to infer that the sexual abuse issues were known and the bishop had accepted the risk that the predator tendencies may return during the next in-parish assignment. Dioceses will respond that many of the therapy centers dealt with mental and substance abuse issues in addition to sexual issues,[40] so it is not correct to infer sexual misconduct was being treated.

13:8 TRANSFERS AMONG DIOCESES

The bishop of a diocese has control over priests who are incardinated to his diocese. Church law does not provide for involuntary transfers from diocese to diocese. Instead, the move is "voluntary" and the underlying facts are usually downplayed

38. New Life, id.
39. The Boston Globe Investigative Unit, supra.
40. *New Life Center*, 229 F.3d 1143.

in the transfer paperwork; files often demonstrated concealment of past sexual abuse when the transfer was being facilitated; the priest "wants a change of place" and the receiving diocese agrees. In a future claim, the sending diocese would be charged with negligence and concealment of the known past sexual misconduct of the priest. So, for example, a Connecticut diocese whose priest was sent to New Mexico for therapy could be sued by victims assaulted in New Mexico. The New Mexico treatment center's failures were controversial[41] and the archdiocese that contained the treatment center almost had to declare bankruptcy because of the number of abuse claims.[42]

When a priest is voluntarily moved from one diocese to another, absent some very clear rationale for the movement, the plaintiff may argue that the diocese that sent the priest was "dumping" him there, as a result of his prior misconduct, and that the receiving diocese had a duty to perform due diligence about the behavior and character of the priest. In practice, priests are transferred on the basis of their request, if that meets the needs of the diocese. Paperwork usually includes a letter of introduction and decree of excardination from the sending bishop to the receiving bishop. The receiving bishop must consent in writing to incardinate the priest. The church doctrine of priest "incardination" means that the priest comes under the authority of the bishop in his diocese. For the one-third of U.S. priests who are members of religious orders such as the Dominicans, the transfers are routine and do not involve these incardination formalities. In some instances, when a priest from a large diocese sought to be reassigned to a small diocese, there usually has been a letter stating some rationale for his departure from the home diocese to a distant post. When such a letter had concealed sexual misconduct charges, the sending diocese can expect to be sued by a future victim "downstream."

13:9 THE FREEDOM OF RELIGION FACTOR AND THE JUDGE'S ROLE

Can the jury be told about these diocesan transfers, and allowed to draw an adverse inference of escape or flight, subsequent to the news that an abuse had occurred? The U.S. Constitution's protection for religious freedom[43] forms the backdrop for arguments of the defenders in the civil tort case against the diocese. Churches are free to decide who their ministers will be, and where, and for what length of time. The civil plaintiff asserts that the diocese fraudulently moved a "predator priest" after notice of his problems. That priest was reassigned to another position, or even to another diocese, after the date when an allegation of sexual misconduct was known or should have been known by the diocese in which the priest had served.

---

41. Servants of the Paraclete, Inc. v. Great Am. Ins. Co., 866 F. Supp. 1560, 1563–1564 (D.N.M. 1994).
42. Paul Logan, "Archdiocesan Audit Called a Beginning," Albuquerque J. (Jan. 7, 2004).
43. U.S. Const. amend. 1.

The jury will be told by the plaintiff that the diocesan removal of that priest must have responded to some knowledge of the allegation, especially when the sending diocese had spent thousands of dollars on rehabilitation and counseling. The jury will be told further that the movement breached a duty of disclosure of that priest's abuse risks to the receiving parish or school. This is a risk-avoidance notice that the plaintiff believes should have been given to the parents of vulnerable young people at the receiving school, parish, or diocese.

Note the distinction: the juror is being invited to draw a separation between (1) the shield for the church's merciful forgiveness in its self-governance methods, as a subset of the church's protection under the First Amendment; and (2) the very practical consequence of the decision to conceal reasons for the movement of the accused predator priest. If the priest violated standards of church morality, that is a religious discipline matter. If the priest sexually abused one or more young people in the new assignment, after having had allegations of sexual misconduct made against him in the earlier assignment, then there will likely be civil liability problems for the sending diocese, which had control of his records, his ability to move, and assignment.

That inference-drawing may be unnecessary where the diocese had spent many thousands of dollars on an inpatient therapy facility for abusers,[44] and then had sent the priest to another parish assignment, at which place he abused the plaintiff. Knowledge of the priest's high risk of sexual abuse was inherent in the spending needed to "rehabilitate" him. The treatment center released him, and the bishop argues in retrospect that it was reasonable for him to presume the treatment had worked. Most of these cases settled so the case law is silent on what could have occurred in an appellate court: Was there a real breach of duty?

The best defense for a Catholic diocese as defendant may be to show a letter from the therapy center "clearing for duty" that priest, the way a doctor's note will permit a food plant worker to return to cutting fruit. The diocese could be challenged for the rapid reassignment of that priest. It would reply, from the calendar of routine reassignments, that those prior allegations were of no real significance in the "normal rotations and routine shifts" that occurred. If a pattern of movement of pastors or associate priests occurred across the diocese every two years, or six years for pastors, then the routine movement would not appear to be related in any way to allegations of prior misconduct.

On the other hand, a sudden midterm removal listed in the church bulletin as a transfer would appear in retrospect to jurors as a reflection of the bishop's urgent choice to detach the priest from the scene of the accusation, in response to allegations about misconduct. The defense will argue that the old position had been filled during the therapy period and that a new assignment was routine when the priest returned from the inpatient treatment. If the individual priest commits a second offense at his new location, plaintiffs will certainly argue that the action of the

---

44. Such as the New Mexico center in *Servants of the Paraclete*, 866 F. Supp. at 1563–1564 or the center in *New Life Center*. 229 F.3d 1143.

diocese went beyond mere suspicion, to the extent of covering up the known propensity for sexual misconduct. And that is likely to stoke the later call for punitive damages against the diocese.

13:10 CHARGES OF A CONSPIRACY OF SILENCE

In some cases the plaintiff, an adult, recalls the sexual abuse years or decades later, and sues the diocese for a "conspiracy" that concealed the abuse. Conspirators would be the priest, the bishop, and the Vicar for Clergy or other administrator of priest personnel records. Federal RICO or state conspiracy claims might be asserted. The existence of the conspiracy is then asserted to have been manifest by secrecy, so as to override the barrier of the statute of limitations.[45] These are very fact-specific claims. This is not likely to succeed.

13:11 VERDICTS AND CONSEQUENCES

The unique power of ordination and incardination over the individual priest's life and work choices cannot be underestimated. In the Catholic Church, unlike the workers in the civilian world, the candidates for priesthood prepare for years for the moment that they lie prostrate on the floor of the cathedral altar and swear a vow of obedience to the bishop or their religious order's superior. It is a powerful and traditional ceremony, full of sacramental rituals of permanent commitment. After ordination, the priests' assignments are made entirely from above (absent resignation or retirement), so legal accountability and liability flows upward in many cases. The punishment of the individual priest (often penniless and judgment-proof) and punishment of the transferring diocese are likely to be sought by the injured plaintiff. There will be major fiscal consequences to such a civil damages punishment, as Chapter 15 demonstrates.

Of course, the jury will expect that their verdicts have consequences to protect later victims. If the civil courts punish the bishop for nondisclosure in this case, this would be setting a high standard of care for the Church's subsequent behavior. The impact would lead to the defensive response of this and other dioceses making public disclosure of credible allegations of abuse violations. These "one strike and you're out" provisions of the Essential Norms have produced significant changes in the operation of the current systems in many dioceses.

The end of this process is a lose/lose decision for the diocese whose movement of priests could be suspect, unless the bishop can demonstrate an obvious need for that priest to be transferred, for example, the sudden death of another priest. Prior to the 2002 policy change, transfers occurred and reoffending occurred; if

---

45. See e.g., Doe v. Roman Catholic Archbishop, 692 N.W.2d 398 (Mich. App. 2004), accord, Hassett v. Archdiocese of Detroit, 2005 Westlaw 3018432 (Mich. App. 2005).

the parishioners had been told that a priest who was a "rehabilitated" former child molester is being sent among them, many would balk and many would walk (away). Since 2002, when the U.S. Conference of Catholic Bishops "Essential Norms" standards relating to past abuse allegations were instituted, there would be no further assignment once the act of child sexual abuse was proven. The norm terminates the ability of the diocese to use the services of those individual priests who had proven abuse allegations against them.[46] The priests who face "credible allegations" that are not yet proven are stuck in a very uncomfortable condition during the period of time until their alleged misconduct can be proven or disproven. They can be barred from receiving any diocesan salary, pension, or sustenance payments.[47] What level of disclosure is needed, and the consequences of making the disclosure, will have a significant consequence for the diocese.

Currently, a priest who has had an allegation made public is "untouchable" for reassignment until he is found guilty, not guilty, or "charges not proven." The Essential Norms require suspension pending resolution. It is possible—although no data is public—that hundreds of priests are in this state of suspension. This status is especially challenging when the abuse claims have pushed the diocese into bankruptcy court.[48] The bishop will be concerned about his own liability if he had failed to act and is personally prosecuted.[49] The cleric who faces a "credible allegation" will need to await exoneration and then leave the priesthood, or leave the diocese to "start over anew." Even with the bishop's canonical power to select the cleric's next assignment, he will not be sent. The public disclosure of the allegation would color the reception he would receive. The likelihood of hostility and anger in the receiving parish means that he would not be accepted by parishioners, at least not until after the acquittal or dismissal of all charges. The receiving parish, school, or entity, which has children among its members, will certainly not want to take the risk that the allegation made at a priest's prior venue was correct and that he could offend again.

Most bishops will wish to make it clear to the receiving parish, where it is accurate, that the allegations were retracted, the charges were dismissed, or the evidence was found to not support the allegations. Even then, suspicions linger and reputations are almost impossible to repair, certainly not in the climate of opinion in recent times about clergy abuses.

46. Presumably a member of a religious order could continue inside the order to provide limited services under close supervision without contact with young persons.

47. In re Roman Catholic Archbishop of Portland, 661 F.3d 417 (9th Cir. 2011).

48. Id.

49. Thomas, supra.

CHAPTER 14

⌁

Defenses and Claims of Immunity

14:1 OVERVIEW

The plaintiff who reveals that he was sexually molested by a priest has begun a legal process that may ultimately result in payments of damages in compensation for what he has suffered. These are difficult cases to win. A few vestiges of older common law defenses still affect the availability of damage claims to the plaintiff in a clergy abuse lawsuit. This chapter explores these defense options.

Fairness arguments can be expected from both sides. The diocese will argue that it is unfair to bankrupt the diocese, and thereby to punish the many recipients of charitable and educational efforts of the diocese, for rogue acts of criminals that violated the laws and moral standards of the Church. "We did all that we could with Father Doe at the time and his acts were beyond the scope of his employment," was a common response by dioceses and bishops before the 2002 U.S. Conference of Catholic Bishops "Essential Norms" were adopted.[1] The 2011 John Jay College report to the U.S. bishops observed that: "Prior to 1984, the common assumption of those who the bishops consulted was that clergy sexual misbehavior was both psychologically curable and could be spiritually remedied by recourse to prayer."[2] Much has since been revealed about the "treatment" centers that tried to deal with abusers.[3]

Age of the claims is a significant defense argument, invoking state limitations on lawsuits regarding older offenses or injuries. The abuse victim will argue that it is unfair to have the abuser and his "employer," the church, avoid any tort liability by asserting that the claims are too old for the state's statute of limitations on

1. Jennifer Weinhold, "Beyond the Traditional Scope of Employment Analysis in the Clergy Sexual Abuse Context," 47 U. Louisville L. Rev. 531 (2009).
2. John Jay College, Report to U.S. Conference of Catholic Bishops, The Causes and Context of Sexual Abuse of Minors by Catholic Priests in the United States, 1950–2010, at 77 (2011).
3. New Life Center, Inc. v. Fessio, 229 F.3d 1143 (Table), 2000 WL 1157800 (4th Cir. 2000).

tort claims. There is a compelling argument of unfairness against a law allowing a serial "predator pedophile" to walk free because of his young victim's coerced silence, while the victim sustained long-term trauma as a consequence of abuse. Some judges could feel torn between the two opposing arguments, but would be likely to follow the stricter statute, because limitation statutes have a jurisdictional constraint on judicial authority that moral reprehensibility alone does not have.

14:2 STATUTES OF LIMITATIONS

These clergy sexual abuse cases are unusual crimes, and unusual defenses are applied. Any discourse on defenses in the ordinary robbery or fraud case would not begin with the statutes of limitations defense, but these cases are quite different. As Chapter 10 describes, the victims in many of the clergy sexual abuse cases suppress and keep secret for years—often at the direction of the priest—the facts of an event that left the victim feeling ashamed and embarrassed. The manipulation of the young victim results in a frightened refusal to share the facts of the abuse with parents, teachers, or other adults. Immediately reported cases are rare.[4]

So a primary benefit to the defendant priest is the expected delay in the victim's reporting of the past abuse. This has been called by plaintiffs a "clerical iron curtain" against liability.[5] Assume that an incident of oral sex by a priest with a 10-year-old boy ends with a demand that the victim not tell anyone. Assault on a child may carry a two-year statute of limitations, from either the date of the event or the date when the child reaches the age of 18. The two-year or even eight-year statute of limitations is likely to pass before the abused victim tells others about the abuse that has happened to him. Even with liberal pleading norms and limitation laws favoring minors, allowing the child to sue after reaching 18, the plaintiff's complaint that opens the litigation must state when, where, and by whom he or she has been abused, and a prudently drafted tort complaint will explain why the action was not brought during the days immediately after the sexual incident.

If the statute of limitations applies, and the date of abuse is older than the statute would allow, then the limitation bars the court's jurisdiction over the lawsuit, unless an exemption applies. As the issue is jurisdictional, the judge must rule on it early in the proceedings, before the case proceeds to trial. The odds against a remedy rise rapidly as the victim ages.

States adopt their statutes of limitations for certain crimes as a means to provide fairness and due process, preventing long-lost memories from being used as a

---

4. But see e.g., Janon Fisher & Jose Martinez, "Retired Brooklyn Monsignor, 78, Arrested for Alleged Criminal Sex Acts with Two Teen Boys," N.Y. Daily News (Oct. 14, 2011).

5. Susan Heylman, "As States Suspend Time Limits on Sex Abuse Suits, Clergy Cases Proceed," 43 Trial 72 (Oct. 2007).

basis for liability, when the defendant lacks the ability to reconstruct all the facts needed to rebut the plaintiff's assertions. California has an interesting statutory exception; if the abuser is knowingly kept on the payroll of the church, the statute of limitations is tolled (suspended from ending the ability to prosecute or sue).[6] Chapter 5 discusses these exceptions in detail.

14:3 DIOCESAN RESPONSES

Because many of these cases are older, the priest involved may be dead or retired or, as with the Philadelphia grand jury report, the mental condition of a bishop who is a potential target may make him unable to fully participate in defense of a trial. So the age and capacity of the defendant is a factor at the outset of these cases.

If the abuse claim is made while the plaintiff is still a child, the diocese must decide how to respond to the claim. The Essential Norms policy directs the bishop toward a pastoral response when evidence indicates that the claim is true. In the period before 2002 when the Norms were adopted, the USCCB recommendations from the early 1990s were not universally adopted or practiced.

One response from some of the dioceses before 2002 was to turn the file over to civil lawyers who would do their routine zealous defense of their client. One such response by the white-collar-crime attorneys for the diocese was to aggressively attack the credibility of the child and the parent. And some dioceses allowed their attorneys to do so; but many found that attacking the parent could and did backfire. That kind of a defense often provoked a publicity backlash against the bishop, resulting in claims that the diocesan tactics were not what the public should expect of a church. In one of the first such damage suits, diocesan lawyers told the jury: "The actions of going public and subjecting this young man to the embarrassment and, if you will, possible ridicule among his friends and others in the community has greatly increased the damages that this young man has sustained." This tactic was less than effective; the jury deliberated just two hours and awarded $1,250,000 to the victim.[7] Donald Cozzens commented: "Church officials appear to think they are justified in using hardball tactics in response to what they consider to be the hardball tactics of victims and their attorneys. The effects of such assumptions on the part of the church have compounded the pain and suffering of victims."[8]

Of course, if there are specific claims of a date or place that can be rebutted by records such as a camp or hotel attendance register, these are valid tools for the rebuttal and cross-examination. The investigator retained to gather the facts will certainly seek out the documentation and witnesses as the case is assembled.

---

6. Karol Jackowski, The Silence We Keep: A Nun's View of the Catholic Priest Scandal 182 (2004).

7. Elinor Burkett & Frank Bruni, A Gospel of Shame 125 (1993).

8. Cozzens, quoted in Mary Gail Frawley O'Dea, Perversion of Power: Sexual Abuse in the Catholic Church 6 (2007) at 136.

Sometimes the hardball defense tactics cause surprise and hostility in the larger community, In a 2013 revelation of Milwaukee archdiocesan documents, the news media detailed its lawyers' response to the claims of more than five hundred abuse claimants that the Church committed fraud: "The archdiocese denies the fraud allegations. But if it had defrauded victims, its lawyers have argued, the six-year statute of limitations expired because the archdiocese posted the list of 43 abusive priests on its website in 2004. Under Wisconsin law, the clock on the statute of limitations begins ticking when a victim has reason to suspect that he has been defrauded. And church lawyers suggest that the posting should have alerted the priests' victims that they may have been defrauded."[9]

14:4 PRESENTATION AND REBUTTAL OF EVIDENCE

Contemporaneous evidence of the child's complaint to a responsible adult, or some documentation such as a motel register, or some witness such as another priest who lived in the same rectory, would be helpful to lay the foundation for the abuse claim. If the same resources can be used to rebut the claim, they will undercut the allegation. Absence of video or DNA makes it easier to defend the allegations.

Few cases will be as well documented as a 2010 lawsuit alleging that the family of a teenaged girl had secretly videotaped a Pennsylvania priest having sex with the female student in the basement of their home. The lawsuit was filed after the priest's baby was born; he had left the Church-paid assignment as an inpatient at a treatment center and had no diocesan assignment, when reporters found the couple and their baby living in a suburban apartment.[10] This is the rare exception; darkness and concealment are the environments within which most of the sexual abuse situations arise.

As one author observed: "All the adversarial tactics employed by the Church were legal, and most were standard boilerplate defenses marshaled in personal injury lawsuits. Spokespeople for bishops cited the legality of their defense strategies and justified them as necessary to protect the assets of the Church in order to keep dioceses running."[11]

14:5 ELEMENTS OF THE DAMAGES

Unlike the case of the videotaped intercourse and later pregnancy, direct proof of the connection between acts by the defendant priest and the harm to the mental

---

9. Annysa Johnson & Ellen Gabler, "Milwaukee Archdiocese Releases Thousands of Pages from Priest Sex Abuse Files," Milwaukee J. Sentinel (July 2, 2013).

10. Michael Rubinkam, "Suit: Priest Impregnates Pennsylania Teenager," Associated Press (Aug. 27, 2010).

11. Mary Gail Frawley-O'Dea, Perversion of Power: Sexual Abuse in the Catholic Church 135 (2007).

or physical condition of the victim is hard to identify. Most plaintiffs will bring on psychologists as their expert witnesses. The defense in turn will use pretrial *Daubert* hearings, discussed in Chapter 12, as a screening out of dubious expert opinions. The defense also will file motions *in limine* to exclude evidence of the connection between the sexual assault and the present state of the victim.

The complaint in an abuse lawsuit would typically explain that the plaintiff adult believes his or her depression, suicidal behavior, job troubles, absence of intimacy, or other psychological conditions arose out of the past incidents of clergy abuse that he or she experienced as a child. The burden of showing the causal connection to emotional problems becomes much more difficult over the years, as there is no baseline from which to draw a particular connection. Jurors are likely to be skeptical of the diocesan attorney who asserts that no emotional damage was caused by a child's sexual encounter with a priest. However, jurors are just as likely to be skeptical of plaintiff's assertion that his problems at age 30 match those of the child who had been molested; the many other complications of decades of life, and other experiences of trauma, might diminish the ability of the plaintiff to convince jurors that the sexual episode in the rectory at age 10, even if traumatic at the time, was the primary reason for his subsequent life problems. In the rare event of an immediate report of child abuse by anal intercourse, that can be documented by health professionals through then records of a rape examination at the hospital, accompanied by some acute medical treatment costs, would aid the victim. The rare instance of an immediately reported case with medical evidence would induce the diocese and/or priest to pay compensation and pay for both medical and psychological follow-up to the victim, without litigation.

14:6 EMOTIONAL INJURY NOT ACCOMPANIED BY PHYSICAL HARM

If the tort claim is one for emotional distress, the plaintiff faces a problem of proof. State tort law often requires the claim of emotional distress to be linked with a particular physical injury to which the emotional harm is connected. In this scenario, a physical injury to the child would have to be shown to have occurred at the time of abuse, if an accompanying mental distress is claimed to have been caused by the abuse.

A person burned in a movie theater fire would, for example, have suffered burns as well as adverse emotional effects from that fire. In a car wreck, the slightly bruised mother of a child who witnessed the death of her child will be terribly upset. In the case in which the teenage boy's anal bleeding was observed on bed linens by a parent, there might be a claim for the accompanying mental distress. But most of the abuse cases have involved transitory physical contact such as oral copulation that were never externally manifested as an injury. So the defense will seek to eliminate claims that did not involve some physical manifestation. Each state's tort law has its own variations upon these themes.

14:7 PRIVILEGE FOR PRIEST-PENITENT DISCLOSURES

The law in most states does not compel the religious minister, to whom a confession is made in confidence, to disclose that communication.[12] This evidentiary privilege does not apply to excuse the abuser's physical acts, but there is a public policy shielding the priest's verbal admissions of misconduct, but only if they were freely made in the religious context.[13]

Admissions outside of the religious counseling context are not confessional and not likely to be treated as privileged. State laws on this exception vary, but will typically cover statements made in religious counseling settings.[14] When a pretrial deposition of the bishop is noticed for a particular day, there could be a motion for a protective order in which the diocese attorney asserts that the bishop need not testify, as it is asserted that the bishop had learned the details of the abuse in a confession to him by the abuser priest. These are tricky situations for the trial judge, Constitutional norms do not allow the state legislature to define what is included within a sacrament, such as the Catholic sacrament of reconciliation, but a secular decision can be made concerning the whole circumstances of the disclosure as a context that is or is not a religious confession.[15]

The debate would then be: Can the state compel disclosure of an operative fact that was disclosed by a defendant religious minister, to another religious minister, in the latter's role of administrative oversight? A bishop can hear confessions and provide absolution as part of the Catholic sacrament. But not all statements made to a bishop are within the sacrament. One would ordinarily differentiate the roles of counselor from the role as "boss," but in this context of religious sacramental assertions, the First Amendment entanglement problem arises when the prosecutor or civil plaintiff tries to force disclosure, upon the argument that the disclosure was not a confession, but was an administrative matter affecting the employee's performance of his church responsibilities.

The evidentiary privilege has some exceptions for disclosure of admissions made in non-counseling settings.[16] Not all are shielded.[17] Some have argued that the availability of the privilege unfairly assists the criminal abuse defendant in clergy cases.[18] This is a controversial argument for the accused abuser to assert against prosecutors in states with mandatory abuse reporting.[19]

---

12. Mockaitis v. Harcleroad, 104 F.3d 1522, 1534 (9th Cir. 1997).

13. Julie Sippel, "Priest-Penitent Privilege Statutes," 43 Cath. U. L. Rev. 1127 (1994).

14. See e.g., Michigan Compiled Laws 600.2156.

15. State of Utah v. Patterson, 294 P.3d 662 (Utah App. 2013).

16. See e.g., Magar v. State, 826 S.W.2d 221 (Ark. 1992); Church of Jesus Christ LDS v. Superior Court, 764 P.2d 759 (Ariz. App. 1988).

17. *Patterson*, 294 P.3d 662.

18. Julie M. Arnold, Note, "'Divine' Justice and the Lack of Secular Intervention: Abrogating the Clergy-Communicant Privilege in Mandatory Reporting Statutes to Combat Child Sexual Abuse," 42 Val. U. L. Rev. 849, 851 (2008).

19. Christopher Pudelski, "Constitutional Fate of Mandatory Reporting Statutes," 98 Nw. U. L. Rev. 703 (2004); Note, "Confession and Mandatory Child Abuse Reporting," 24 BYU J. Pub. L. 117 (2009); Arnold, supra; Andrew Beerworth, "Treating Spiritual and Legal Counselors Differently," 10 Roger Williams U. L. Rev. 73 (2004).

14:8 CHARITABLE IMMUNITY FROM LARGER DAMAGES

Charitable entities were at one time held immune from damages lawsuits, but gradually that immunity was reconsidered and removed, and the Restatement of Torts further eliminated that defense.[20] Scholars have considered this phenomenon in detail elsewhere.[21] The great majority of states have removed charitable immunity by statute or abrogated the doctrine by appellate decisions.[22] States moved at different speeds to eliminate this defense.[23] The clergy sexual abuse issues spurred some legislative attention.[24] Bishops have been quite concerned about the implications of these trends in light of the abuse scandals.[25] Intentional torts such as the known risk of a bishop's moving a priest who is an abuser to another parish have been ruled to be outside of the statutory immunities.[26]

Several states such as Massachusetts and New Jersey[27] have capped the amount of damages that a nonprofit entity can be forced to pay in a tort case.[28] This has been raised as a defense bargaining chip opposing large settlement demands by the Boston plaintiffs, before that class of claimants accepted the settlement.[29] Because of the $20,000 cap, lawyers for victims often settled for modest sums without a lawsuit.[30] New Jersey law prevented the award of civil damages against facilities that had charitable immunity, and this held down some of the awards available in sexual abuse claims against dioceses.[31] But settlements by the Camden diocese for $700,000 in a 13-year-old boy's sexual assault claim suggested that the Church did not want to have the immunity law put to the test in the context of clergy abuse.[32]

Maine's Supreme Court rejected charitable immunity for intentional torts such as fraudulent concealment of a priest's abuse risks to children, but upheld an older immunity statute for negligent conduct that limited liability to the maximum amount of the entity's liability insurance.[33]

---

20. Restatement of Torts 2d § 895E (1979).
21. Victor Schwartz & Leah Lorber, "Defining the Duty of Religious Institutions to Protect Others," 74 U. Cin. L. Rev. 11 (2005).
22. Matthew Cobb, "A Strange Distinction: Charitable Immunity and Clergy Sexual Abuse," 62 Maine L. Rev. 703 (2010).
23. Carl Tobias, "Reassessing Charitable Immunity in Virginia," 41 U. Rich. L. Rev. 9 (2006).
24. Samantha LaBarbera, "Secrecy and Settlements," 50 Vill. L. Rev. 261 (2005).
25. Bishop Thomas Paprocki, "As the Pendulum Swings from Charitable Immunity to Bankruptcy, Bringing it to Rest with Charitable Viability," 48 J. Cath. Legal Stud. 1 (2009).
26. Picher v. Roman Catholic Bishop of Portland, 974 A.2d 286 (2009).
27. LaBarbera, supra.
28. Mass. Gen. Laws ch 231 §85K (2012), N.J. Stat. Ann. §2A:53A-7 (1995).
29. Douglas McLeod, "Church's Coverage at Risk," 36 Bus. Ins. 1 (June 24, 2002).
30. The Boston Globe Investigative Staff, Betrayal: The Crisis in the Catholic Church 48 (2003).
31. Jason Berry & Gerald Renner, Vows of Silence 107 (2004).
32. Id.
33. Picher v. Roman Catholic Bishop, 974 A.2d 286 (Maine 2009); Cobb, supra; Peter Swisher & Richard Mason, Liability Insurance Coverage for Clergy Sexual Abuse Claims, 17 Conn. Ins. L.J. 355 (2011).

14:9 CONSTITUTIONAL DEFENSES

The Constitution's First Amendment prevents a state or federal court from "considering claims requiring the interpretation of religious doctrine."[34] In the sexual abuse cases, the authority of the bishop is sometimes an element of the decision of how to attribute liability to a defendant other than the impoverished, retired, or deceased abuser. The defense argues that the case involves too close an entanglement of torts with church doctrine.[35] But the courts that have written more sophisticated analyses of these issues have not accepted that defense.[36] The jury could accept or not accept the claims about the role of the priest or bishop for sacramental purposes. But the jury "can objectively examine those church characteristics in disputes over property" and likewise can examine the civil law aspects of the claimant's allegations.[37]

14:10 LACK OF THE BISHOP'S KNOWLEDGE

In the cases that involve "negligent supervision" or "failure in duty to protect children," the defense probably won't get far with a claim that the diocese had no powers of oversight of its priests. If the claim in the civil action is one of inadequate supervision, plaintiff's expert for the standard of care will need to be rebutted by equally competent defense experts. The consequence of this conflict will be a high cost for the defendant; the newer plaintiff's counsel will benefit from coordinating with the four or five plaintiffs' counsel who have done multiple claimant cases and who have forced large settlements on several diocesan defendants.

To what extent is the bishop to be held responsible for his priests? Yes, under canon law, he should provide for their reasonable care. But must he be responsible for any priest's violations of church law, state law, and moral codes? No. The relationship between the bishop and the priest of his diocese is complex, not easily characterized by modern norms of employment law.

The defense by a diocese may begin its argument with the tax status of the priest. Chapter 2 cites the Internal Revenue Service treatment of the priest as an "independent contractor." But the canon law and tradition, as well as the records of the diocese, will indicate that bishops control the assignments of the diocesan priest and keep records on him. The files of personnel records and complaints may be scattered in the diocesan offices, requiring extra efforts by the plaintiff's discovery team and perhaps a special master to oversee discovery; but in some cases the records cumulatively will have value to plaintiffs, as facts to be cited against the bishop or other diocesan officials who may have known of the priest's criminal

34. Softcheck v. Imesch, 855 N.E.2d 941 (Ill. App. 2006).

35. State of Utah v. Patterson, 294 P.3d 662 (Utah App. 2013).

36. Kelly Clark et al., Of Compelling Interest: The Intersection of Religious Freedom and Civil Liability in the Portland Priest Sex Abuse Cases, 85 Or. L. Rev. 481 (2006).

37. *Softcheck*, 855 N.E.2d at 949.

behavior. The records revealed in the Boston cases are remarkable.[38] The Milwaukee archive release in 2013 was a major revelation of timing and awareness of priest misconduct.[39]

The charitable immunity that still lingers on some states' statutes is aimed at negligent conduct, not intentional acts. So a claim that the bishop had known of the record of abusive behaviors, before transferring the priest to another assignment that involved contact with children, would be an intentional tort that statutory immunity was never intended to cover.[40]

14:11 SOVEREIGN IMMUNITY OF VATICAN OFFICIALS AND THE POPE

The hierarchy of the Roman Catholic Church is much more complex than the plaintiff's lawyers may realize. American litigants will likely be vexed in their efforts to connect up the actions or negligence of one priest with his diocese, and with the Vatican.[41] Those unfamiliar with the internal workings may see the heavily centralized theology of common belief, but may not see the very decentralized administrative operations of the dioceses around the world.

Efforts to assert a form of tort "enterprise liability" for the entire international Roman Catholic Church have been postulated, but proving these by analogy to RICO or other enterprise cases will carry serious problems for the litigant in a state court tort action.[42] Plaintiffs have attempted to utilize the internal instructions issued by a Vatican official on reporting abuse cases to local police, as an example of a cover-up extending to the Vatican.[43]

Seeking testimony, depositions, or documents from the Vatican is an effort that several lawyers have attempted, but without success.[44] Creative plaintiffs were trying a variety of arguments to win jurisdictional footholds against the central authorities around the pope.[45] As the Vatican is recognized as a sovereign nation,[46] the immunity of that nation from U.S. civil lawsuits (except through specific

38. Boston Globe, supra.

39. Johnson & Gabler, supra.

40. Picher v. Roman Catholic Bishop of Portland, 974 A.2d 286 (2009); and see Cobb, supra.

41. See e.g., Roman Catholic Archbishop v. Superior Court, 93 Cal. Rptr. 338 (Cal App. 1971).

42. Stephen Bainbridge & Aaron Cole, "The Bishop's Alter Ego: Enterprise Liability and the Catholic Priest Sex Abuse Scandal," 46 J. Cath. Legal Stud. 65 (2007).

43. Laurie Goodstein, "Vatican Warned Bishops Not to Report Child Abuse," N.Y. Times (Jan. 18, 2011).

44. Patrick Condon, Lawyer for Priest Accuser Says Vatican Rejected Lawsuit Alleging Abuse at Wis. School for Deaf," Associated Press (Jan. 31, 2011).

45. Complaint in Mother Doe 100 v. Holy See, 2011 Westlaw 1791587 (pleading pending in N.D. Ill. 2011).

46. Note, "The Atypical International Status of the Holy See," 34 Vand. J. Transnat'l L. 597 (2001).

international law processes) under the Foreign Sovereign Immunities Act[47] has been sufficient to defeat the efforts of U.S. plaintiff lawyers. Those attorneys seeking to reach the deep pocket defendant, the Vatican, have attacked these immunity claims,[48] while more conservative Catholic media have defended the immunity arguments.[49]

In 2011, the Supreme Court declined to hear a claim for review of an Oregon decision in the U.S. Ninth Circuit Court of Appeals. There, the plaintiff argued that sovereign immunity had an exception, as the Vatican had allegedly promoted the Code of Canon Law in 1983 as a set of updated standards of conduct for the clergy, including the abuser.[50] The Ninth Circuit case is instructive. A plaintiff would need to demonstrate a solid basis for Vatican liability, alleging that a tort had occurred by the actions of the Vatican, which directly impacted upon the abuse, for example a deliberate decision to endorse or accept the abuser's assignment to a school, parish ministry, or child welfare position despite his past incidents of abuse. Discovery may be allowed regarding the priest's relationship to the Vatican as supervisor of his activities.[51]

In most cases, the Vatican has no role in daily operations of the 3,000 dioceses worldwide. However, particularly difficult for the defense would be cases in which the Vatican offices, the Congregation for Clergy or the Congregation for the Doctrine of the Faith, had ordered reinstatement of a suspended abuser, and the abuser then had further contact with children, and thereafter an incident of abuse had occurred. Delays in removal of a priest's canonical status have been a factor in some news media coverage of the abuse cases,[52] No specific statistical data is released by the Vatican or by dioceses on how many such reinstatements have been made.

Defense counsel sometimes are "creative" with disposition of past records. A bishop who was also a civil lawyer reportedly referred in a speech to canon lawyers in favor of the sending of papers relating to abuse cases to the Apostolic Delegate, the pope's ambassador, as having "immunity to protect something that is potentially dangerous, or that you consider to be dangerous." He later denied that this signaled his support for a cover-up plan.[53] After the debacle in the Boston archdiocese, more prudent leaders have discounted this step as being a counterproductive obstruction of civil justice.

---

47. 28 U.S.C. §1602 et seq. (2010).

48. Stephen Rubino, "A Response to Timothy Lytton," 39 Conn. L. Rev. 913 (2006) ("...all significant attempts at true reform have been blocked by the Vatican, whose primary concern is maintaining the power of the clerical hierarchy"). The Americans United for Separation of Church & State's journal has covered this issue from their viewpoint; see Rob Boston, "Unholy Immunity," Church & State Magazine 7 (May 2010).

49. See e.g., "Lawsuit Tests Relations between Bishops, Rome," 20 Cath. World Report 15 (July 2010).

50. Doe v. Holy See, 557 F.3d 1066 (9th Cir., 2009), cert. den. __ U.S. __ (2010).

51. Doe v. Holy See, CV-02-430-MO (D. Or. 2011) ("The Holy See refuses to acknowledge or deny whether it knew of Ronan's abuse, or whether it played any role in his training, education, transfers or removal.")

52. Johnson & Gabler, supra.

53. Jason Berry & Globe Staff, Betrayal: The Crisis in the Catholic Church 40–41 (2002); Burkett & Bruni, supra, 161.

14:12 ABSENCE OF DIOCESAN ACCOUNTABILITY FOR THE "ROGUE" PRIEST

Chapter 4 addresses the status of the priest in legal relationship to his bishop. If the plaintiff's counsel aimed the entire case for damages at the employer and employee status, he would lose. In the Sacramento case in 1994, the jury sided with the diocesan arguments that no damages against the diocese should be awarded, on grounds that sexual misconduct by a priest was not reasonably foreseeable because of his vow of chastity, that the molestation was not authorized, and that sex with a child was outside the scope of employment of the priest; but because of news media coverage for the past two decades, a different jury today would probably make a different judgment.[54]

Reasonable foreseeability among church supervisory officials about clergy sexual abuse is a standard that moves, along with the advance of defendant and juror experience with other cases, and years after that 1994 verdict there has been so much public awareness of the issue that the defense would face a much more difficult time convincing a jury of these arguments. The head of the church insurance pool observed that few of the older claims are likely to arise in the future because so much publicity has pervaded society that most of the possible claims of past misconduct have already surfaced.

14.13 IS A COUNTERSUIT POSSIBLE?

In this litigious society, defendants often counter-sue the plaintiff for libel or trade defamation when the basis of a well-publicized lawsuit is doubtful. After an extensive review, your authors were unable to find court decisions awarding libel damages to a priest who had been accused. One 1992 Arizona threat of a defamation suit by lawyers for a priest who pleaded guilty and accepted a 10-year sentence for child abuse did not produce a published outcome.[55] A 2011 case pending in Ireland alleged libel of a priest for rape of an underage girl; after the television broadcast about the priest he was suspended from his ministry.[56]

14:14 DEFAULT

A default verdict can award damages if no answer is filed after service of the plaintiff's complaint. A defrocked former Franciscan, age 70, conceded that he had abused children, and served prison time for the abuse. But he said he had no money

---

54. Joanne Wojcik, "Church Scandals Prompt Action," Bus. Ins. (Jan. 3, 1994).
55. Burkett & Bruni, supra, 123.
56. Tim Healy, "Priest's Libel Case to Proceed Normally," Irish Independent (July 9, 2011).

for an attorney, and the court awarded $3 million in damages against him.[57] The plaintiff may have the personal satisfaction of winning, but there may be no actual dollars behind the newspaper headline. As the Portland archdiocesan bankruptcy showed, many of the older priests, whether dismissed or not, have few assets that can be taken by the plaintiff's collection efforts.[58]

57. "Mass. Judge Awards $3M in Abuse Case," Boston Globe (Oct. 21, 2011).
58. In re Roman Catholic Archbishop of Portland, 661 F.3d 417 (9th Cir. 2011).

CHAPTER 15

༜

Damages Issues

15:1 OVERVIEW

This chapter deals with civil tort claims that result in an award of damages to the persons affected by the clergy sexual abuse, or a settlement prior to judgment. Most victims have accepted individual payment settlements with confidentiality stipulations; some have opted to accept a share of publicized "global" or group settlements with other sexual abuse claimants. A smaller number have gone through civil trials and received a jury award of compensation; within that group, a small number have had their awards reduced because of state laws dealing with caps on damages.

The three types of damages relevant in this book's cases are compensatory damages for the cost of medical and psychiatric care, non-economic damages for pain and suffering, and punitive damages to punish the persons who acted in a manner causing egregious harm.

Dollar amounts of verdicts and settlements in these sexual abuse cases appear quite large, but the actual amount received after costs and attorneys' fees is relatively small in most cases. This chapter looks at the various awards of damages, and seeks to draw lessons about whether and how the facts of particular outcomes have impacted the amounts of damages awarded.

15:2 PREREQUISITES TO DAMAGE AWARDS

The U.S. legal system for compensation arising out of civil liability is centered upon the concept of negligence by an institution (diocese) or person (bishop and priest) in their actions toward the plaintiff (victim). Some of the abuse acts were also litigated as intentional torts such as assault and battery, but they are a minority of the cases.

The four elements of negligence are:

- the existence of a duty toward the victim by the Church;
- the breach of that duty by the clergy predator and by the diocesan managers who failed to adequately oversee the actions of the priest;
- the proximate causation of the victim's harm from the breach of duty; and
- damages incurred by the child or teen who was molested.

In most of the clergy sexual abuse cases, the victim was a student, a counseling recipient, a youth sports team member, an altar boy, or a parishioner. Duties of care toward such persons are easily inferred under the state's case law of negligence decisions or under state statutes. Protection of children from harm is well recognized as a societal need, reflected in statutes and court decisions.

Breach of the duty by the clergy person is the sexual act with a minor. The sexual act and the accompanying shame and secrecy aspects are the proximate causes of the emotional or psychological harms experienced by the victim. Breach of the duty by the diocese is the failure to reasonably protect the persons who could be harmed by foreseeable misconduct by the priest, once there was reason to believe misconduct was occurring.[1] The diocese had made a decision not to act, or acted inadequately.[2] Having placed an individual clergy member into an assignment that involves children, the duty of the institution was to oversee his performance in a manner that avoids harm.

The proof of the causation of harm that is required to be presented by the injured person in a civil damage case must be by a "preponderance of the evidence." For the immediately reported events of sexual abuse, the contemporaneous physical evidence such as semen on clothing or anal bruising would routinely be obtained at the time of the hospital examination of the victim. The police would photograph the scene, examine the clothing, obtain the medical report, take the abuser into custody, and begin questioning him. Relatively few clergy abuse cases fall into this category of urgent response.

Months or years after the event has occurred, a claim of sexual abuse would be much harder to prove. Recollections fade with time. Dates of contact may be incorrectly remembered; places will have changed over the years; records may be incomplete or discarded. In a Los Angeles case, the young teen accurately described the unusual artwork on the wall of the priest's bedroom in the rectory. In future cases, there may be text message or email correspondence. The typical cases become "he said/he said" tests of credibility, memory, and witnesses' "stage presence" in front of the jury.

---

1. Roman Catholic Diocese of Jackson v. Morrison, 905 So. 2d 1213 (Miss. 2005) (parent confronted diocesan officials, was assured abuse would stop, but abuse continued by that priest for several years).

2. Id. ("The Diocese may ordain whomever it concludes is worthy, and it may engage in whatever religious speech it desires. But if it has specific knowledge that children within its care are in danger of sexual molestation, and if it has the authority, power and ability to protect those children from that known danger of abuse and molestation, it is for a jury to determine whether it took reasonable steps to protect the children.")

The plaintiff will show economic damages by producing medical bills, psychologist counseling costs, medications for treatments of psychological harm remediation, bills for hospitalization, loss of work (if any), and other quantifiable numbers of injury. In some states, this economic damage amount is crucial because the non-economic damages, sometimes called "pain and suffering," are capped in liability cases at a figure selected arbitrarily by the legislature for all tort claims. Minnesota courts have found that sexual abuse of a teen was an injury, as a matter of law. But a Connecticut plaintiff asserted "spiritual damage" as a Catholic from the sexual abuse incident that had involved a priest; this element of harm could not be adjudicated in secular courts without infringing on the First Amendment rights of the Catholic Church.[3]

15:3 PREREQUISITES TO PUNITIVE DAMAGES

Once a jury decides that compensation should be awarded for the medical and psychological expenses and lost wages (if any) of the victim, and for the pain and suffering, which are not quantifiable as specific expenses, the state law and state court rules may allow the plaintiff to receive additional damage compensation that is intended to punish the defendant. These "punitive damages" are not a government fine or criminal penalty but a jury decision. This form of jury award means the action of the defendant was egregiously bad and deserves to be punished. Society is protected from future bad conduct by the economic punishment of the defendant.

The amount of punitive damages cannot constitutionally be greater than a 9:1 ratio of compensatory damages, except in very unusual situations.[4] These damages cannot be awarded without some showing of bad conduct for which the jury has awarded compensatory damages. Statistically, punitive damages are awarded in a very small number of cases, perhaps 2 percent of all civil tort cases that go to trial. But the priest sexual misconduct cases tend to stimulate jurors to punish the diocese, and these feelings are likely to be upheld on appeal.[5]

Cases in which egregiously bad conduct has been shown would involve testimony that actions of the diocese in overseeing this abuser were reckless, not merely negligent. A 2011 Illinois priest sexual abuse case upheld an award of $2,400,000 in compensatory damages and $2,600,000 in punitive damages.[6] The record of one priest's causing injury to others may be helpful, but cannot be used as a basis for specific punitive awards in another case.[7] States vary in their use of restraints and caps on punitive damage awards. These caps and constraints in legislation are usually related to the lobbying strength of the manufacturing and insurance industries in the state. For example, Ohio's cap came as a result of intense political lobbying by the companies that were likely to be sued for tobacco and asbestos harms, and their insurers.[8]

3. Givens v. St. Adalbert Church, 2013 WL 4420776 (Conn. Super. 2013).
4. BMW of North America v. Gore, 517 U.S. 559 (1996).
5. Diocese of Covington v. Secter, 966 S.W.2d 286 (Ky App. 1998).
6. Wisniewski v. Diocese of Belleville, 943 N.E.2d 43 (Ill. App. 2011).
7. Philip Morris USA v. Williams, 549 U.S. 346 (2007).
8. James O'Reilly, Ohio Tort Reform Legislation (2005).

In some of the Catholic Church cases, jury awards have included punitive damages showing the jury's anger, such as the $3.6 million award of compensatory and punitive damages in a 1990 Minnesota case; the judge later reduced the award to around $1 million.[9]

15:4 EFFECTS OF CAPS ON DAMAGE AWARDS

State laws may cap the amount of non-economic damages at a dollar ceiling, or at a particular multiple of actual economic damages. The laws also may cap punitive damages at a dollar ceiling or at a particular multiple of the economic and non-economic damages. For example, Massachusetts caps the damages that can be awarded in cases against nonprofit charities with a dollar amount. Lobbyists for manufacturers and insurance companies have successfully argued in several states for these "tort reform" limitations.[10]

Caps deter attorneys from taking contingent fee cases. Pursuing compensation through the courts for sexual abuse is expensive, as it is for product design tort liability claims. Few abuse victims can afford a first-class hourly rate law firm effort. These lawsuits are less viable for a lawyer to accept on contingency, from an economic viewpoint, if the state caps hold the potential recovery for the plaintiff so low that they deter lawyers from accepting the plaintiff's representation request. Outraged and angered by the facts, the lawyer may wish to accept the case, but if the potential income from a successful verdict is artificially low because of damage caps, the suit will not be pursued.

The result will be harsh for some plaintiffs whose abuse was not recent and not well documented. Wage loss and hospital bills are typical aspects of the economic damage that an accident victim, such as a car-collision plaintiff, has endured. A clergy sexual abuse report 15 years after the abuse probably has retained neither form of proof, as the child was not working and the shame of being molested led him or her to conceal the abuse.

The state laws might be so protective of defendants that the once-abused adult plaintiff would be so tightly limited in the amount of damages that an experienced plaintiff's lawyer would decline to take the individual case on a contingent fee. (The great majority of modern tort cases are contingent fee, rather than hourly payment cases, because the majority of victims do not have the economic ability to prepay a large retainer and then to sustain the costs of expert witnesses and the hourly cost of very competent plaintiff's counsel.)

A class of similarly situated plaintiffs could file a coordinated action under state procedures or a class action under federal rules.[11] But the cases are not easily

9. The Boston Globe Investigative Staff, Betrayal: The Crisis in the Catholic Church 41 (2003).

10. Id.

11. Fed. R. Civ. P. 23.

aggregated because of their different sets of facts, so they would lack the "commonality" needed in federal class actions. Litigating each would go on for years. Settling all the cases against a diocese for a moderate amount per case, including those that would not be winnable by conventional measurements, might be attractive to the diocese as a "global settlement" to resolve the disputed cases. Milwaukee in 2013 was dealing with 575 claimants.[12]

If each case were fought to a verdict, the diocese might win some, perhaps half, and might pay relatively affordable amounts (after caps and limits are imposed by the trial judge to reduce the jury award). But that would mean the diocese deals with years of news headlines, depositions of the bishop, disruptive demands for records disclosure, and an outcome that is hostile to the public perception of the Church as a beneficent, charitable institution. "Molested altar boys suing rogue priest lose after 5 years in court" undercuts the diocese's religious mission. No bishop wants that outcome; several of the nine diocesan bankruptcies discussed in Chapter 9 were forced when efforts for a global settlement failed at the last moment.[13]

15:5 AWARDS OF PLAINTIFF'S LEGAL FEES

How much of a fee should the lawyer for the abuse victim receive? The contract in which the victim is retaining the lawyer should explain the contingent fee arrangement carefully, to comply with ethical rules and statutes. Typically the lawyer charges the costs of the suit to the plaintiff's account and then takes 40 percent of the first $100,000 and one-third of the amount over that figure.

In the case of a class settlement of multiple cases, the percentage that the lawyer receives is negotiable, subject to possible challenges if ethically improper or excessive by standards of that field or that state. In a windfall award, the judge may be interested in the rate at which the plaintiff pays for the contingent legal fees out of the award or settlement. Some attorneys have faced ethics charges arising out of the fees charged for clergy abuse settlements.[14]

Meanwhile, on the other side of the conflict, dioceses are paying very large legal fees, investigator fees, and witness costs, so a victory at trial might cost the diocese more than $100,000 in assorted expenses, before considering the costs of the appeal(s) that will follow.

12. Annysa Johnson & Ellen Gabler, "Milwaukee Archdiocese Teleases Thousands of Pages from Priest Sex Abuse Files," Milwaukee J. Sentinel (July 2, 2013).

13. David Gregory, "Some Reflections on Labor and Employment Ramifications of Diocesan Bankruptcy Filings," 47 J. Cath. Legal Stud. 97 (2008).

14. Jon Newberry, "Chesley Fights Diocese Settlement Allegations," Cin. Bus. Courier (May 24, 2011).

15:6 CHURCH-PAID COUNSELING AND THERAPY AS A DAMAGE ELEMENT

Though headlines have concentrated on the cash value of jury awards and settlements, an additional cost element should not be overlooked. The diocese may also pay for the counseling and therapy needed for the abuse victim to recover from the trauma. This is especially relevant to cases in which the long-delayed therapy was preceded by years of emotional problems. For example, the Charlotte, North Carolina, diocese paid $1 million in settlement and funded $47,500 in therapy expenses for an abuse victim.[15]

15. Associated Press, "Charlotte Diocese Settles Abuse Lawsuit for $1 million" (May 7, 2010).

CHAPTER 16

⌒⌒

Fiscal Impacts of Abuse Cases on the U.S. Catholic Church

16:1 OVERVIEW OF U.S. ROMAN CATHOLIC CHURCH FINANCES

This text is about the legal effects, and not the accounting consequences, of the clergy abuse scandal. However, we must cover the financial aspects of courts imposing the remedy of civil damages compensation. These judgments, settlements, and defense costs for the diocese are an integral part of the defense strategies to be employed by attorneys representing the diocese. Should this claim be paid? Should this litigation be settled? Will insurance pay some or all of the damages?

Settlement strategy decisions have a direct impact on the viability of the diocese's other programs. One large verdict in a class action could consume the annual income of the whole diocese. The litigated cases also have an indirect impact, as the adverse publicity might trigger a reduction in donors' willingness to give funds to the church.

No definitive accounting of total church payments relating to clergy sexual abuse has been found in public sources. A few estimates of $106 million to $1 billion were cited in 2002, but much more has been distributed in settlements and spent in preventive programs since that time.[1] A *Washington Post* story in 2011 quoted a scholar who estimated that abuse related costs 1950–2010 surpassed $2 billion.[2] When one considers the settlements, verdicts, criminal case payments, defense attorney costs, witness costs, prevention training programs, and other related costs, we believe the total exceeds $3 billion.

Some might assume the Vatican would pay for all these costs, but that is not the flow of funds that actually occurs. It is not publicly known how much each of

---

1. Douglas McLeod, "Church's Coverage at Risk," 36 Bus. Ins. 1 (June 24, 2002).
2. Maryclaire Dale, "Suit: Pa. Catholic Leaders Failed to Protect Kids," Wash. Post (Feb. 14, 2011).

the 3,000 dioceses around the world, or the 196 in the United States, send to the Vatican in each year. One particular Sunday collection is designated for the world-wide charities of the pope, called the "Peter's Pence" collection. A 2011 lawsuit against the Vatican asserted that $100,000,000 was raised from U.S. donations for the annual Peter's Pence collection in 2008.[3] The specific figures are not publicly known.

16:2 UNINSURED LOSSES FROM SEXUAL ABUSE CASES

Church liability insurance is not a complete response to the financial crisis. As Chapter 7 has demonstrated, the diminished availability of diocesan liability insurance coverage for the sexual abuse incidents has been a source of great anxiety to bishops for decades. Prior to the mid-1980s, the generic liability coverage wording in diocesan insurance policies would have permitted a diocese to claim coverage for some sexual misconduct claims.[4] But this was only under some insurance contract language, and was always subject to the insurance carrier's ability to sustain a denial of coverage in litigation for the "intentional" act of assault rather than the accidental "occurrence" of sexual misconduct harms.

Other contracts of insurance would not have required coverage, and the 1987 ISO standard "abuse or molestation" language on the exclusion of sexual misconduct claims[5] soon became the norm. In doing so, the ISO language swept away most of the arguments that could have been made for coverage in the post-1987 insurance policies. Special coverage was sold by some carriers as a "risk pool," charging a high premium on a per-priest or per-employee basis, but this coverage was not universally available and was not always selected by the dioceses that could have opted for the coverage. There are now over 60 dioceses and church entities that entered the Catholic Mutual risk pool program,[6] which was known as the Bishops' Program.[7] The dioceses can buy insurance for sexual misconduct liability from the Catholic Mutual group.[8] Its cost is significantly greater than the diocese had paid in years prior to 1980.

The size of the non-insured losses for sexual abuse claims, when cumulated along with other claims that were contingent but not yet ripened, posed a real risk of diocesan bankruptcy, as Chapter 9 explains. The 1987 exclusion of sexual

3. Complaint posted on Westlaw in Mother Doe v. Holy See, 2011 Westlaw 1791587 (N.D. Ill., pending 2011).
4. Elinor Burkett & Frank Bruni, A Gospel of Shame: Children, Sexual Abuse, and the Catholic Church 206 (1993).
5. ISO CG 21-46-07-98.
6. Risk pool terms are described in http://www.catholicmutual.org/Coverages/CUPII.aspx.
7. Matt Kelly, "The Costs of Penance Becoming Clearer," 159(12) TIME 53 (March 25, 2002).
8. Coverage is discussed at http://www.catholicmutual.org/Coverages/Property Casualty.aspx.

misconduct claims was little notice and rarely commented upon until the 1990s, and that exclusion has been important in recent years to shape decisions of the dioceses regarding settlements.

16:3 IMPACT OF SETTLEMENTS AND VERDICTS

The first publicized verdict in a child sexual abuse case came in Minnesota in 1990, with $3,600,000 awarded in compensatory and punitive damages.[9] San Francisco archdiocesan verdicts for $5,950,000 for four victims of a priest were widely reported in 2005.[10] San Diego and San Bernardino settled 144 claims for $200,000,000.[11]

In 1998, the archdiocese of Dallas lost a $119,600,000 verdict to 11 plaintiffs who had been abused as young people; the diocese settled on appeal for $31 million.[12]

Huge settlements created an incentive for further litigation demands; $660 million was paid to 508 claimants, in addition to an earlier $114 million payout, by the Los Angeles archdiocese,[13] and $100,000,000 was paid by the church in Orange County, California, to resolve 87 claims.[14] Seattle church settlements paid $7,870,000 in 2003.[15] Santa Rosa diocese in California settled for $3,315,000.[16] The Oakland, California, diocese settled for $1,930,000.[17] Separate settlements have been reached by non-diocesan entities including Jesuits, Franciscans, and Carmelites.[18]

Later on in the cycle of abuse cases, the numbers became less extreme. Indianapolis archdiocesan officials used self-insurance funds to pay $199,000 to a man who had been victimized 34 years before; this was one of 14 claims brought against the diocese involving a predatory priest who was removed from ministry in 1984, but whose acts led to court cases after the criminal and civil statutes of limitations had expired.[19]

9. Boston Globe Investigative Staff, Betrayal: The Crisis in the Catholic Church 41 (2002).

10. Bob Egelko, "Church, Insurers Dispute Molest Payouts," S.F. Chron. B1 (Apr. 23, 2005).

11. Bishop Thomas Paprocki, "As the Pendulum Swings from Charitable Immunity to Bankruptcy, Bringing It to Rest with Charitable Viability," 48 J. Cath. Legal Stud. 1 (2009).

12. Boston Globe Investigative Staff, supra, 43.

13. "$660 Million," 134(14) Commonweal 5 (Aug. 17, 2007).

14. Egelko, supra.

15. Dan Gilgoff, "A Settlement in Boston," 135(9) US News & World Report 28 (Sept. 22, 2003).

16. Egelko, supra.

17. Id.

18. Gillian Flaccus, "L.A. Archdiocese Agrees to $600 Million Abuse Settlement," Wash. Post A14 (July 15, 2007).

19. "Archdiocese Reaches Settlement in Abuse Case," Indianapolis Criterion (May 14, 2010).

The Cincinnati archdiocese spent more than $11 million on clergy abuse issues 2003–2009 and paid $589,000 for legal fees, victim counseling costs, and salaries and housing for suspended priests. It experienced 159 allegations up to 2009, and in 2003 set up a $3 million fund to hear claims from victims, as part of a plea bargain with local prosecutors.[20]

16:4 IMPACTS OF ABUSE CASES ON REVENUES

American Catholic donations through parish collections totaled about six billion dollars a year according to a 2005 study, but all the estimates are subject to variation and none are officially published.[21] Bishops have apologized in some dioceses regarding their clergy sexual abuse settlements and cases, with the comment that: "Some (donors) have chosen to express their displeasure by withholding financial contributions."[22] A pithy comment from an experienced priest-journalist was: "People in the pews are not willing to pony up for this. They're willing to give money to their parish and Catholic education, but they don't want to pay to settle these suits, not with their hard-earned money."[23] An insurance expert speculated in 2008 that a church that has a publicized case of sexual abuse may lose 10 percent of its church members, and the parish school will lose perhaps 15 percent of students, and they may never be regained.[24]

Loss of donor allegiance could be devastating to a diocese; as the media covers this aspect of the story, "shaken Catholics may have to decide whether they want to spend much more money to bring the church out of moral bankruptcy."[25] Effects of the abuse scandal on donations has been measured by an economist's 2005 study in which Mass-attending Catholic donors were asked about the effect of sexual abuse issues on their likelihood to donate to the Church.[26] When acceptable options for dioceses to pay for the clergy abuse financial settlements were sought, a diocesan-wide collection was supported by 44 percent of the sample. "Other options also received some significant support, including: 38% favored the sale of church property; 33% favored a reduction in diocesan program offerings; 32% favored declaring bankruptcy; and 32% favored closing parishes in order to save

20. "Cincinnati Archdiocese Says Clergy Abuse Cost $11 Million," Associated Press (Jan. 23, 2009).

21. Foundations and Donors Interested in Catholic Activities, Inc., 2005 Donor Attitude Survey (hereinafter "FADICA"), conducted by Prof. Charles Zech, Villanova University et al.

22. Cincinnati Archbishop Daniel Pilarczyk, quoted in Dennis Coday, "Costs of Abuse Scandal Becoming Clearer," Nat'l Cath. Rptr. 5 (Oct. 3, 2003).

23. Larry Stammer, "Oregon Diocese First to File Bankruptcy," L.A. Times A1 (July 7, 2004).

24. Robert Velasco, "Protecting Kids Not Child's Play for RMs," National Underwriter Magazine 22, 23 (Dec. 8, 2008).

25. Kelly, supra.

26. FADICA, supra.

money." If cash from parish collections were taken by a bankruptcy court to pay off the creditors and abuse claimants, 26 percent of the survey group said that they would contribute less to the Church. The percentage of regular, Mass-attending Catholics, who were concerned that the financial impact of the settlements would affect the ability of the Church to meet its mission, was 62 percent in 2005.[27] The survey report concluded:

> In the 2005 survey, 9% of the respondents indicated that they had decreased their contributions to their parish in the last year; 14% had decreased their contributions to the diocese; and 12% had decreased their contributions to the national collections that are supported by the United States Conference of Catholic Bishops. In each case, the number one reason given for the decline was anger over the clergy abuse scandal.[28]

Other studies also showed that the abuse cases made a big impression; most Catholics in a phone survey, and especially younger Catholics criticized the cover-up of sexual abuse by the bishops. In that 2004 survey, 85 percent called clergy sexual abuse a "serious" problem, and 77 percent said it was a serious problem that bishops had not done enough to prevent the abuse. Even among regular Catholics who are active in their parishes, a majority of laypersons in the survey "suspect the bishops are not telling the whole truth about the scandal."[29]

A Philadelphia auxiliary bishop, responding to questions about the grand jury report in 2011, said it was not clear what effect the indictments of priests would have on donations. He urged donors to continue to give to the capital campaign; "it cannot go toward the defense of priests or legal fees, he said, and so only the poor, the sick and the needy would suffer if those donations dried up."[30]

16:5   EFFECTS OF LIQUIDATING ASSETS

Catholic dioceses have been described as "land rich but cash poor," but situations vary among the 195 dioceses. For example, bankruptcy court filings for the Spokane, Washington, diocese showed contingent liabilities for sexual abuse claims, and other liabilities of $81.3 million against assets of $11.1 million.[31] The funds available to settle claims for sexual abuse are taken first from insurance, and if none, from the cash accounts of the diocese, then from investment accounts, then from unrestricted but designated funds, and then from other assets. The parish funds can legally be reached for these expenditures, if the diocese is a corporation sole,

27. Id.
28. Id.
29. "Catholics Suspect Bishops of Covering Up Pacts," 191(3) America Magazine 4 (Aug. 2, 2004).
30. Katherine Seelye, "New Cases Loom in Priest Scandal," N.Y. Times (Mar. 4, 2011).
31. Egelko, supra.

for reasons discussed in Chapter 3. The complexity of ownership of church property has been described by Father Thomas Doyle, a canon lawyer, as the "Ecclesiastical Shell Game."[32]

Assets can be mortgaged or sold to pay the legal costs. In 2006 news reports about its $660 million abuse settlement said the Los Angeles archdiocese owned $4 billion in real estate and a portfolio of about $300 million in investments.[33] That archdiocese sold its administrative building and was considering sales of 50 "nonessential" church properties.[34] Milwaukee reported legal fees of $500,000 in 2002–2003 for defense, and Tucson sold its archdiocesan headquarters building to raise funds for settlement of nine pending lawsuits.[35] The news media reported that Boston liquidated its reserve bonds and stocks during "the same period during which the diocese was making hefty secret payments to abuse victims."[36] Sale of diocesan property was the most frequent means by which funds were made available to pay settlements for years subsequent to the insurers' exclusion of abuse.[37]

16:6 COSTS APART FROM SETTLEMENTS

There is no reliable figure available for the costs of the legal defense, lobbying, public affairs, and related support services used by the dioceses and the U.S. Conference of Catholic Bishops on sexual abuse matters. Costs have increased for the conventional liability policy, which excludes abuse and molestation (as described in Chapter 7), and of insurance "pool" costs for those dioceses that wanted sexual abuse liability coverage available only from a pool of other dioceses. "Child sexual abuse cases are prime examples of losses that can result in catastrophic lawsuits. Besides the staggering dollar amount of the lawsuits, a painfully ugly situation exists at the center of the case."[38]

A cost in virtually every settlement has been the psychological counseling assistance for victims.[39] These therapy costs have been a part of the settlement offers from dioceses for years. No figure for their cost is published, but it was speculated by a Boston archdiocesan official that the 552 plaintiffs who received a settlement could receive $1 million per year in treatment and counseling, beyond the $85 million that the victims received.[40]

32. Thomas Doyle, A.W.R. Sipe & Patrick Wall, Sex, Priests and Secret Codes: The Catholic Church's 2,000 Year Paper Trail of Sexual Abuse 257 (2006).
33. Bill Frogameni, "Where's the Money, Cardinal?," 18 Ms. Magazine 14 (Winter 2008).
34. Flaccus, supra.
35. Coday, supra.
36. Kelly, supra.
37. Burkett & Bruni, supra.
38. Velasco, supra.
39. Sam Dillon & Leslie Wayne, "Sex Abuse Scandal Takes Toll on Catholic Church's Finances," Hous. Chron. 13 (June 13, 2002).
40. Mark Miller, "The Wages of Sin," Newsweek 34 (Sept. 22, 2003).

16:7 LOST OPPORTUNITIES FOR CHARITABLE ACTIONS BY THE CATHOLIC CHURCH

We can only postulate in retrospect that the misconduct of individuals within the institution reduced the institution's ability to excel in its public mission. The 2004–2005 FADICA study showed serious concern that the sexual abuse payments and settlements had drained the Church's "financial ability to fulfill its mission because of the costs related to the crisis of sexual abuse of minors by clergy."[41] Before the Portland bankruptcy, that Oregon diocese had laid off 20 workers and cut budgets 30–50 percent to have the cash for these settlements.[42] A Chicago bishop reported that their 90-year-old foster care program was ended because it could no longer get insurance.[43] After listing the many large settlements and verdicts, he said: "The amounts are staggering; the ramifications of these payouts will continue to unfold for some time."[44]

Catholics who are journalists and commentators have noted the lost social spending, with one observing of the American Church hierarchy that the "cover-up has cost a fortune and been a betrayal worthy of Judas. The money spent came from social programs, Catholic schools and the poor. This should be a sin that cries to heaven for vengeance."[45] Not all the critics have been so harsh, but the opportunity cost of the legal fees and settlements has apparently been a diminution of social ministry spending. No definitive figures are available.

41. "Catholics Fear Abuse Costs Curtail Church Work," 192(3) America Magazine 5 (Jan. 31, 2005).

42. Larry Stammer, "Oregon Diocese First to File Bankruptcy," L.A. Times A1 (July 7, 2004).

43. Paprocki, supra.

44. Id. at 4.

45. Maureen Dowd, "The Church's Judas Moment," N.Y. Times (April 7, 2010).

CHAPTER 17

༺❀༻

Impact of Abuse Cases on External Relations of the Catholic Church

17:1 WHY WOULD THE CATHOLIC CHURCH BE CONCERNED ABOUT ITS EXTERNAL RELATIONS?

The Roman Catholic Church in the United States is not isolated and is never alone. In the 1800s it experienced discrimination, violent antipathy, and extremes such as lynching and the burning of churches and convents by anti-immigrant nativists. The late 1800s and early 1900s placed the Church into a controversial role of providing social services to the underclass and minorities whom the government chose to ignore.

Today's American Catholic Church has built its strengths upon a complex interweaving of its messages about moral responsibility for the poor, with usually favorable public opinion surveys, political leaders' general (but selective) support, donor cooperation, and government co-funding of social service efforts to aid the poor. The external relations of the Church with these external entities determines its temporal success in its charitable mission; the moral success of its religious mission is helped, but would survive even the hostility of the governing body and the majority of residents, as its mission does in fervently Islamic nations.

A negative mood or malaise over the Church's moral mandate has been cast by the shadow of bad choices by some bishops. More than 80 percent of a national survey sample of 1,442 active Catholics told *National Catholic Reporter* in October 2011 that the "political credibility" of Church leaders had been damaged by the handling of the scandal.[1] The clergy sexual abuse issues have dampened the enthusiasm for cooperation with the Church among certain public entities. Criminal conviction of the bishop of Kansas City[2] for failing to report a priest's sexual conduct with children

---

1. "Catholic Reactions to the Sex Abuse Scandal," Nat'l Cath. Rptr. 17a (Oct. 28, 2011).
2. Judy Thomas, "Bishop Finn, Diocese Indicted in Abuse Case," Kan. City Star (Oct. 14, 2011).

may chill the moral preaching of the diocese about Catholic social action priorities in the public sphere.

Critics have often denounced "hypocritical" behavior and patterns of secrecy by bishops. Very reputable Catholic commentators have observed that the bad reputational consequences of exposing the long-concealed abuse cases have tainted the institutional mood of respect or allegiance to which the American Church had aspired for more than a century. As editorialists for the *National Catholic Reporter* opined in July 2011, "The bishops have little credibility in the wider culture and diminished authority within the church, because in the case of sexual violence against young people by members of their clerical culture, they responded in ways that any reasonable and healthy segment of society would have considered disdainful."[3]

17:2 HOW WERE CHURCH DEFENSES IN ABUSE CASES PERCEIVED?

The popular press in America has never been a devout follower of the policies espoused by the conservative leaders of the Church hierarchy. Before there was Fox News, there were archconservatives in the press corps who represented the moral viewpoint of the Church on social issues and civic matters. So when the secular news media looked carefully at the several responses by the institutional Church to sexual abuse reports, the coverage was shocking. Led by journalists from the *Boston Globe*[4] and elsewhere, the facts spilled out an ugly picture of Cardinal Bernard Law and his peers who were knowingly concealing tragic patterns of misconduct by certain priests. Pressure mounted, and a grand jury was empaneled; Cardinal Law resigned from Boston, left immediately for Rome, and was reassigned to a quiet corner of the Vatican. His exit made way for a reconciling healer, Cardinal Seán O'Malley, who had earlier handled the unraveling of abuse reports in a smaller diocese. That new archbishop then settled the Boston abuse claims and cases, and worked toward positive internal change within his new archdiocese.

Journalists follow the herd. The consensus among media observers has been uniformly harsh toward bishops, whether the newspeople were previously deemed friends or enemies of the Church. Certain truths seem to be universal: scandal sells, exposure wins promotion and prizes, and reporters who study institutional hypocrisy highlight the institutions' weaknesses for their viewers or readers. What the *Washington Post* did to Watergate, the *Boston Globe* did to the Church's sexual abuse scandal. There has been a very highly negative response in the news media to the details of repeated sexual abuse, compelled concealment, and "paid silence" that has shrouded the Church sexual misconduct cases. Even the moderates in Catholic journalism have expressed regret and dismay at the actions of the bishops in the decades that were the height of the scandal.[5] Surveys show serious negative results from the

---

3. Editorial, "Gay Marriage, Bishops and the Crisis of Leadership," Nat'l Cath. Rptr. 24 (July 8, 2011).

4. Boston Globe Investigative Unit, Betrayal: The Crisis in the Catholic Church (2003).

5. See e.g., Editorial, "Gay Marriage, Bishops and the Crisis of Leadership," supra.

scandal among active Catholic adults, so it is not likely that the news media alone has caused the dissatisfaction that is so widely seen among older adult Catholics.[6]

The bishops who were perceived to show extreme "defensive deafness" damaged the image of the Church as a credible institution. That image needs repair, and incremental improvements have been made among some parts of the clerical leadership. In speaking with bishops on this sensitive issue, the younger bishops "get it" and want to get past the cloud of suspicion by enforcing the 2002 "Essential Norms" described in Chapter 2. It is also noteworthy that perceptions motivate civil juries, and that civil jury awards against the Church offer a form of oblique insight into the damage that has been done to credibility of the dioceses and the Church in general.

The perception problems of the U.S. Catholic Church have an impact on civil juries. Leaving aside the facts of the specific cases, the jury pool members in a clergy sexual abuse case that actually gets to trial are likely to be a randomized collection of average citizens whose opinions of the Church at the start of their respective trials mirror general public views. These jurors' reactions to the clergy abuse cases at the end of the trials offer an insight into the way the Church has been perceived. Tens of millions of dollars have been awarded in jury trials. Persons with or without personal contact with the U.S. Catholic Church have heard of the sexual abuse scandals. After reading the two devastating grand jury reports from Philadelphia, there would be wide agreement that the Church's image among non-Catholics has been severely damaged.[7]

The best study of the scandal was the 2011 report prepared by scholars from John Jay College on clergy sexual abuse. When this highly critical report was issued, the response among media observers was skeptical and curious, probably as a result of mistrust and hesitation about the institutional patronage of the research by the U.S. Conference of Catholic Bishops.

17:3 WHAT AUDIENCES HAVE MATTERED?

Among the audiences that make for a powerful ally or a powerful opponent of the Church are several:

- Legislators,
- Business leaders,
- Large past donors to the church,
- Social service agency managers,
- Foundation gift-selection committee members,
- Editors of the news media,
- Leaders among other churches,

6. "Catholic Reactions to the Sex Abuse Scandal," supra.
7. Id.

- Leaders among lay Catholic organizations,
- Once-abused persons alienated from the Church,
- Former priests who have left the institution,
- Faithful Mass-attending Catholic laypersons, and
- Average residents of the community who are called for jury duty.

17:4 LEGAL RESPONSES BY THE CHURCH THAT FAILED OR BACKFIRED

Sometimes, an aggressive litigation strategy that works in a commercial dispute can make things worse in a very different context. Lawyers for some dioceses harmed their clients by their bad advice. Among the tactical choices made by many bishops in the period 1980–2011 to respond to the clergy sexual abuse problems, several of the church responses to news media inquiries included:

- Refusal to comment at all,
- Denial that a priest could have done these terrible acts,
- Strong denial of knowledge or suspicion of such abuse by the diocese,
- Attacks on the credibility of the victim and parent,
- Insistence that statutes of limitations had passed so nothing could be done about the abuse even if it had occurred,
- Denials that the priest was under the supervision of the diocese, or
- Assertions that the past sexual contact was being exaggerated to maximize damage awards.

Parts of each of these responses might have been a prudent short-term holding action while facts were gathered. But the stone wall was erected so high that when the factual releases undermined the wall during pretrial discovery, the credibility of the bishop was damaged. Depending on the facts of each specific case, one could analyze the response of the bishop who dealt with exposure of clergy sexual abuse in his diocese, and ask in hindsight whether that bishop should have followed steps listed in the 2002 "Essential Norms" in his response to allegations. Cardinal John Cody of Chicago wrote in a 1970 letter that an abuse accusation "should be forgotten by (the alleged abuser) as it has been forgotten by me. No good can come of trying to prove or disprove the allegations, and I think you will understand this." His letter was front page news in the local newspaper when it was revealed in 2014.[8] Had the Norms been in place at the time of abuse, and had they been followed, much of the damage could have been mitigated rather than litigated.

8. Manya Brachear Pashman, "Papers Detail Decades of Sex Abuse by Priests," Chic. Trib. (June 22, 2014).

17:5 SUCCESSFUL RESPONSES THAT AID THE DEFENSE

By contrast to the majority, the tactical choices made by a few bishops in the same period 1980–2011, which tended to preserve the positive external relations of the Church in their area, have included:

- Listening empathetically and letting victims "vent,"
- Apologizing in private and in public to those victimized,
- Acknowledging the wrongfulness of the conduct,
- Expressing sincere empathy with the family,
- Suspending the priest from contact with youth, and
- Offering payment for counseling and therapy to aid the victim.

These are the elements that should have been "best practices" within diocesan offices during the critical years of the height of the clergy abuse scandal. There would still have been some significant problems, but the choices made by the more progressive bishops would have lessened the national attention and isolated the harm to the "rogue" priest rather than to the institution of the Church and that diocese in particular.

17:6 "FALLOUT" FROM CLERGY SEXUAL ABUSE

Loss of external support for the policies of the Roman Catholic Church has consequences on other issues about which the Church is seeking to form a collective consensus, especially as to sexual morality issues impacting the region and nation, for example abortion-related legislative debates, gay marriage versus traditional marriage, death penalty; public education in-school birth control services, public funding of auxiliary services aid for Catholic school students, etc.

To the extent that hypocrisy is charged or complicity/secrecy is alleged to have existed, the ability of the hierarchy of the Church to deliver its message with secular audiences is undercut. A bishop who calls on the state senator for support about one policy issue is likely to be asked about what his diocese is doing for the widely publicized case of child abuse victims in that district. To the extent that the Essential Norms for bishops are understood outside the Church, even in broad strokes, the failures of the diocese to work within those norms will be reported in the press and magnified when the bishop seeks to garner support from major donors: Why are we out of step with these national standards? What is the reason that Nebraska is the exception to rules that apply in every other state?

Would the scandal of the attempted suicide by an arrested child pornography distributor, who happened to be a priest, be worse because the bishop was indicted,[9] as the bishop had not disclosed these known problems when that priest was

---

9. Thomas, *supra*.

transferred into a post having contact with children? Was the community reaction to Milwaukee archdiocesan statements affected by the record of a local priest who "was facing 42 counts of child abuse in Wisconsin and California when he jumped to his death from a Mexico hotel room in 2003"?[10]

In a complex budget environment, allocating public funds to charitable purposes with Church institutions is already a challenge. External relations damage done to the diocese by the bishop's choices in sexual abuse cases cannot be overlooked when one considers the fallout from the scandal. Can the Catholic Church clean up its internal issues and sustain public and nonprofit agency support for its charitable works?

10. Annysa Johnson & Ellen Gabler, "Milwaukee Archdiocese Releases Thousands of Pages from Priest Sex Abuse Files," Milwaukee J. Sentinel (July 2, 2013).

CHAPTER 18

ᴄᴠᴏ

Responses Vary Inside and Outside
the United States

18:1 OVERVIEW

This chapter hopes to dispel a common misconception. Viewed through the lens of the U.S. national media, the Catholic Church is regarded as a monolithic mega-institution with a history of uniformity and an image of central Vatican control and power.

Yet behind this perception is the reality that makes the solution to clergy sexual abuse more difficult. Under the Church's canon law, each bishop is autonomous, able to operate different systems or operations than those that are common among their national peers. The U.S. Conference of Catholic Bishops does not control all diocesan bishops, although most have concurred and conform to the nationally recommended "Essential Norms for Diocesan/Eparchial Policies Dealing with Allegations of Sexual Abuse of Minors by Priests or Deacons." A bishop is otherwise free to operate outside of the USCCB's Essential Norms.

If a bishop fails to comply with essential church doctrine, or expressly rejects direct orders from the Vatican offices, then the central management "Curia" that administers the Church can recommend that the pope fire that bishop, which was an action taken in Australia in 2010. But with 3,000 dioceses worldwide, the autonomous actions, missteps, or non-actions by a U.S. bishop are his own mistakes and rarely, almost never, can be attributed to decisions of the pope himself.

The great majority of bishops voluntarily comply with the USCCB's recommended set of Essential Norms for handling abuse-related claims, promulgated in 2002 and later updated. (One bishop in Nebraska has refused to comply, and asserts his autonomous power to do so.) The great majority are attuned to the results of studies such as the 2011 John Jay College[1] and the 2004 National Review Board ones. As

---

1. John Jay College, Report to U.S. Conference of Catholic Bishops, The Causes and Context of Sexual Abuse of Minors by Catholic Priests in the United States, 1950–2010, at 76 (2011).

stated above, a bishop's errant policies can only be fixed with papal intervention. When the pope sacked an Australian bishop for suggesting that women might be ordained to the priesthood someday, it was an expression of the pope's doctrinal authority. In contrast, the pope and his central officials have accepted that there will be variable attitudes on the clergy responses to sexual abuse allegations, both across and within nations. The Vatican has required each national conference of bishops to adopt guidelines toward responding to clergy sexual abuse allegations,[2] and those may soon be in place globally.

18:2 CENTRAL VATICAN AUTHORITY OVER BISHOPS

This chapter focuses on civil law issues, while later chapters address the canon law implications over control of bishops by congregations and the duty of each bishop to make his required visit with the pope every five years. Some Americans have the image that the Vatican is directing the decisions regarding sexual abuse cases; as one digs into the specific record of actions taken by several Vatican entities concerned the situation does look more confusing. The previous pope, Benedict XVI, was initially involved while he served as a senior administrator at the Vatican, but his exact role is hard to discern from the conflicting signals one could draw from the limited information made public by the Vatican bureaucracy. Benedict upheld some punishments[3] but his staff department also delayed some discipline cases.

   Within the Catholic Church, the pope has the final say on religious doctrine and on all major policies that apply to all dioceses, but the pope does not see or approve every communication from the Vatican offices. The Congregation for Bishops and other Vatican organizations provide policy direction that must be followed. Later Chapter 19 explains that the autonomy of the individual bishop is very broad, but that discretion ends where the Vatican makes a binding edict to be followed in every diocese.[4]

   For the limited purpose of defending civil litigation regarding child sexual abuse, the Vatican has important needs for distancing itself from decisions of the bishops at each individual diocese.[5] The Vatican has internal operating procedures, and in theory could make specific choices for or against local actions, but it is a perplexing administrative structure. Some sexual abuse plaintiffs believe that the Vatican had a duty to do more than it did, and its acceptance of a passive role should expose it to awards of damages for the victims whom it failed to protect. The legal barrier to such accountability and liability is insurmountable under current U.S. treaty obligations. The Vatican, known to diplomats as "The Holy See," is recognized by the

---

   2. Vatican Circular Letter, "To Assist Episcopal Conferences in Developing Guidelines for Dealing with Cases of Sexual Abuse of Minors Perpetrated by Clerics" (May 16, 2011).
   3. John Heilprin, "Pope Defrocked 400 Priests in 2 Years," Associated Press (Jan. 20, 2014)
   4. See infra Chapter 19.
   5. Doe v. Holy See, 557 F.3d 1066 (9th Cir 2009), cert. denied 130 S. Ct. 3497 (2010).

U.S. government as a sovereign nation, and so the Foreign Sovereign Immunities Act bars the imposition of U.S. state or federal court liability against the Vatican. The rare efforts to ascribe liability to the Vatican have so far failed, but they continue as this book goes to press.

18:3 ROLE OF U.S. CONFERENCE OF CATHOLIC BISHOPS.

The U.S. Conference of Catholic Bishops is not a formal part of the Roman Catholic Church's hierarchy of power. Episcopal conferences are created to coordinate and not to pontificate. So the USCCB has not been able to impose uniform responses on every U.S. diocese, because it lacks the internal legal authority under church law to do so. An audit reported that more than 50 dioceses were not complying with all of the policies required under the 2002 Norms, though many of these were in partial compliance. Immediate suspension of accused priests was controversial; reporting abusers to police was controversial. Some observers wished that the messy variations and deviations from the Essential Norms from Nebraska to California and elsewhere could be replaced with a "czar" who could set U.S. policies for all dioceses nationwide,[6] and who could establish an alternate dispute resolution tribunal in an attempt to keep abuse cases out of the U.S. civil and criminal court systems.[7]

18:4 DIPLOMACY AND VATICAN LITIGATION: EFFECTS ON THE UNIVERSAL CHURCH

Many lay Catholics are unaware that the Vatican has an extensive army of ambassadors in virtually every national capital, reporting to Rome on the political developments in those nations. In rare cases, as happened in Dublin, a Vatican-trusted bishop from the diplomatic service comes home and attempts to remedy the scrambled local mess of the sexual abuse scandal, thereby drawing fire from inside the local church for disrupting its normal means of dealing with abuse cases,[8] Sometimes the diplomats who carry Vatican credentials are called back to the diocese of their origin to answer for past sexual abuse complaints.[9] The point is that, just as with the U.S. external relations crisis of sexual abuse cases, the Vatican's ability to credibly interact with kings, presidents, and prime ministers will be impacted by the international news coverage of church concealment of sexual abuse cases. In the

6. Patrick Schiltz, "The Future of Sexual Abuse Litigation," America Magazine (July 7, 2003).

7. Id.

8. Archbishop Diarmuid Martin of Dublin, speaking at Marquette Law School, Milwaukee WI (April 4, 2011), available on Web at Marquette.edu/cgi-bin/site. pl?2216&deEvent_eventID=3256&date+04-04-2011.

9. In 2009, the Cincinnati archdiocese called back a priest who was at the Vatican embassy in India, as a result of his prior accusations of sexual misconduct.

2009 Oregon abuse case involving a priest's asserted relationship to the Vatican, the Ninth Circuit held that the abuse victim "failed to state a vicarious liability claim against the Holy See based upon the conduct of the Archdioceses and other defendants because Plaintiff failed to allege that the Holy See exerted day-to-day, routine control over those parties."[10]

The broader lessons of the abuse cases for the American Church are being studied in other nations. Belgium experienced a crisis of doubt about its clergy;[11] the nation recorded 507 reports of child sexual abuse and 13 suicides related to clergy abuse.[12] The Archbishop of Dublin, Ireland, told his people that many Catholics had lost confidence in the Church as a result of revelations of sexual abuse scandals: "The reality of the abuse of children that took place in Ireland and the manner in which it was dealt with has been a source of immense hurt for those who were the victims and survivors, but also for the members of the church, lay people and priests."[13]

18:5 FISCAL RESPONSIBILITY OF CATHOLIC CHURCHES IN OTHER NATIONS

The status of the Roman Catholic Church varies in the legal systems of other nations, so we make no effort to account for all of these arrangements. Other sources do so quite well, as shown in the bibliography. In some cases, the U.S Catholic Church had hired foreign contract priests, who departed after abuse allegations; the Memphis diocese paid $2 million for an abuse claim against a Bolivian priest after he departed the United States and could not be arrested.[14]

The common element of interest is whether sales of church real estate and other church assets will be compelled, as the funds to pay compensation for clergy abuse settlements or verdicts are collected. These liquidations of investments and forced asset sales are likely to necessitate force a diversion of what had been funds for charitable works, so as to compensate victims and their attorneys.

In some nations such as Australia,[15] Canada, and Ireland, the complex set of shared responsibilities of Church entities and governmental entities for social services at sites such as native population schools might shift the costs of abuse cases onto the government, but situations will vary greatly. In Austria, where persons

10. Doe v. Holy See, 557 F.3d 1066, 1080 (9th Cir. 2009), cert. denied 130 S. Ct. 3497 (2010).

11. Steven Erlanger, "Belgian Catholics Remain Anguished by Abuse," N.Y. Times (Sept. 19, 2010).

12. "Belgian Catholic Church 'in Crisis'," Irish Independent (Sept. 13, 2010).

13. John Cooney, "Exclusion from Abuse Conference Not a Snub for Martin," Irish Independent (June 27, 2011).

14. Lawrence Buser, "Church Secrets: Abusive Memphis Priest Reassigned rather than Reined In," Memphis TN Commercial-Appeal (April 8, 2010).

15. Mark Coleridge, "Roots of Scandal Go Deep and Wide," Nat'l Cath. Rptr. 7 (Aug. 20, 2010).

register their religion as a form of per-person tax or subsidy, thousands quit the church when credible allegations of abuse were made against the most senior cardinal in the country.[16] The church in Belgium receives 86 percent of the nation's $417 million annual subsidy for religions, but hundreds of Catholics have officially resigned as Catholics from the system of per-capita payments based on religion, many citing the abuse scandal surrounding a bishop who molested his nephew for 13 years.[17]

16. Katrinn Bennhold, "Future Pope Tried to Get Fuller Inquiry in Abuse Case," N.Y. Times (April 26, 2010).
17. Erlanger, supra.

CHAPTER 19

✧

The Church's Internal Big Picture— Governance and Law

"Propter scandalum evitandum veritas non est omitenda,"[1]

19:1 INTRODUCTION

Earlier chapters of this book examined the civil law's evolving role in response to clergy sexual abuse in the United States. But that examination only informs how the civil law is responding to the problem. In order to understand what got the Catholic Church to this crisis, and how it is attempting to clean it up, one must go beyond state civil or criminal laws and look within the mindset, governance, and legal structure of the Catholic Church.

The Church has been dealing quietly with the crime of child sexual abuse almost since its inception. It has had laws both forbidding the crime, as well as canons for punishing the offender since the third century. Canon law is the universal law of the Church, and it has been binding on members of the Church and on whole societies for centuries. But because canon law in modern times is generally not a legal system that is enforced in civil jurisdictions, it is a system that not only runs in parallel to the civil legal system, but often has conflicts with it.

The following chapters deal with the various internal aspects of the sexual abuse crisis. They are intended to provide a window or lens into the ways in which the national and international Catholic Church thinks, legislates, and operates. It is an attempt to explain the Church's public reaction to the initial scandal, how it found itself in this situation, and how the Church internally is attempting to resolve the myriad of related issues.

The canonical section of the book tries to give the overall picture of the history of the problem. It explains the canonical issues and difficulties involved, how the

---

1. "Truth should not be omitted in order to avoid scandal." *Liber Extra*, D. 41, 3, 25.

processes for dealing with clergy sexual abuse have evolved, and the actual procedures and processes currently in use internally to investigate and adjudicate cases of the sexual abuse of a minor by a Catholic cleric.

While this book often discusses the internal canonical options available under church law to deal with this issue, it also discusses the past noncompliance in some dioceses where these remedies were either applied only sporadically, or not applied at all. Recent history indicates that some dioceses are still deficient in their responses, though inadequate responses have decreased significantly since 2002. If we look back at the history of this crisis within American dioceses, in many cases the canonical principles and remedies were simply ignored.

It is not the purpose of this book to defend particular church actions in the United States or elsewhere, but to try to give insight into reasons for some of these responses and why so many dioceses responded by ignoring their own rules. This book further explains in detail the current internal processes[2] the Church is using to remedy this problem, as well as continuing issues and concerns regarding the implementation of these various canonical requirements.

There were clearly significant problems in administrative oversight of sexually abusive priests that have had civil legal and criminal legal consequences. However, in the past the Church's response, or seeming lack of response to this crisis, has oftentimes made a bad situation worse. While there have been numerous verified cases of the Church's inability to respond in an appropriate or timely fashion, some of the confusion regarding the Catholic Church's hierarchical response to this scandal came from a lack of an awareness of the Church's internal law coupled with a particular mindset and outlook of the institution at large. Indeed, the popular view of the Church and its organization often sets expectations that the institutional Church cannot meet.

In this chapter, we will first look at the cultural and institutional mindset of the international Church, and the specific ways that mindset contributed to the escalation of the sexual abuse scandal in the United States. Then we will quickly look at the role Cardinal Ratzinger/Pope Benedict played in this crisis, as well as postulating what we might expect from Pope Francis. Finally, canon law itself will be defined, particularly in contrast to the common law system that those in the United States are familiar with.

19:2 ROLE OF THE CANON LAW PROFESSIONAL COMMUNITY

There is one important group to note that is rarely mentioned positively: those people working within the Church's internal legal system as part of their ministry. There has been much attention given (and deservedly so) about the sometimes callous disregard on the part of some bishops, some canonists, and other diocesan

---

2. It should be noted that Pope Francis and his advisors are discussing a complete reorganization of the Vatican bureaucracy, or Curia. It is possible that the processes discussed here could change if Vatican structures are changed in the overhaul.

officials to the plight of the victims of clerical abuse. Rarely mentioned are the cadre of priests, religious, and lay men and women, most of them canonists and their staff but others as well, who are working faithfully within the Church legal system, to help clean up this problem and to ensure that it does not happen again.

These people have been working behind the scenes, some for more than 20 years, listening to victims, and trying to deal fairly and justly with the accused by the methods provided within the Church's own laws. Some of these persons are acting on review boards, and others are acting in other various capacities, including conducting internal diocesan penal trials.

Regardless of the role, this is heart-wrenching and grueling work, with very little personal reward and no positive recognition. Certainly for most priests working in this area, though it is now a part of their ministry to the Church to have to adjudicate these cases or act as canonical lawyers for accusers or the accused, handling sexual abuse cases is not something they would have entered ministry to do, or would likely be doing if they had a choice. Most feel angry for the criminal actions that have necessitated this work, and they feel sickened by colleagues who have so profoundly betrayed those entrusted to their care. It is emotionally draining to be prosecuting cases of priests who in the past were colleagues and possibly friends, and to have to deal with the enormity of these crimes. Undoubtedly, most of the staff member priests would prefer ministering in their parishes and performing the ministries that they anticipated doing when they were ordained. This work is hard and demoralizing, but it must be done, and done with compassion, fortitude, and skill.

This book will explain the processes that govern the efforts of canonists and their staff. Many mistakes were made in dealing with clergy sexual abuse that have had profound effects on the lives of the victims and their communities. However, it is also important to acknowledge the generations of people who are spending years of their lives and ministries trying to fix these past mistakes and establish the means to prevent them from ever being made again. For their benefit, we hope that this work is of assistance and contributes to the positive work of those who continue to assist the Church to clean up this problem and prevent its reoccurrence.

19:3 ORGANIZATIONAL NORMS AND CHURCH MINDSET

To understand the way the Vatican initially dealt with clergy sexual abuse, one must first understand the mindset and controlling norms of the Church as an organization. The Catholic Church has been in existence for almost two thousand years, and it is an institution that is very mindful of its age and its history. In its past, and in more limited ways in the present,[3] it has been a sovereign state and had the ability to wield temporal power both inside and outside its borders.

---

3. For example, for Catholics in Lebanon ecclesiastical courts adjudicate marriage annulments (not divorces) and are the courts that assign child support and alimony to the parties. Italy grants civil recognition to Church-granted annulments as part of Italy's Accord with the Holy See. These court decisions are civilly binding and enforceable.

In other words, this is a Church whose laws have governed temporal states for centuries. The Church continues to have universal laws that bind all Catholics everywhere. Some of these laws were once the official law of the land in various countries (and continue to be, in limited circumstances). In some nations, church law has been, and continues to be deferred to by their civil legal systems. These laws are part of the fundamental governance of the Church and are meant to regulate all aspects of its inward and outward life.

Because of this reality, it is critical to understand that the Church thinks of itself as a sovereign state, not as a nonprofit corporation (though as discussed in previous chapters, its presence in the United States is manifested through multiple separate civilly incorporated entities). In many ways, the internal and external handling of the sexual abuse cases in the United States has been a continual tension in comparative international law and conflict of laws, rather than simply an international nonprofit corporation trying to address a critical problem in corporate governance and discipline. Thus its methods of dealing with this crisis more closely resemble that of a nation rather than a corporate or business model.

Furthermore, the Catholic Church is keenly aware that it is primarily a *European-influenced* national state (Vatican City) as well as a Church, with its own Code-based laws, its own ambassadors, and its own expectations and legal traditions of how things are done. Its modus operandi follows the European model, and is not necessarily similar to the way in which a nation governed by the common law would respond. Thus attempting to intuit legal responses that would be expected in common law countries from an entity whose governance is a European Code-based legal system will quickly lead one astray.

19:4 VATICAN INITIAL PERCEPTIONS OF THE CRISIS

An important factor that must be taken into account when assessing the Church's international response to the crisis is the actual makeup of the Vatican itself. One often hears of people speaking of "the Vatican" as a monolithic entity run by the pope. This is partially true. The Vatican is a centralized bureaucracy that oversees the various aspects of the international Church related to people, theology, education, law, missions, and ecumenism. However in some ways the Vatican is less monolithic than one might assume.

The Vatican is run by dicasteries (departments) called "congregations" and "councils." With rare exceptions, each of these is headed by a cardinal or an archbishop, and these cardinals and archbishops are from countries all over the world. Likewise, the staffs of the congregations are priests, members of religious communities, and laypersons who are also from various countries. Each brings his or her own priorities, sensibilities, and cultural conditioning.

It is difficult for people in the United States to realize the effect that an international curia (the central bureaucracy of the Church in Rome) has on the way the Vatican responds to local problems. While local problems are seen by the locals as having great import and in need of immediate attention, that sense of priority is not always understood or shared in the much more international halls of the Vatican. Thus when local problems arise, it is sometimes difficult to fully explain the scope and seriousness of that problem to the various curial officials because issues get lost in the translation or the person has no context for the problem. This can take considerable time to sort out, particularly if those who are affected must travel to Rome to do the translating.

Furthermore, though canon law may designate a particular behavior as criminal, it does not mean that those running the Vatican personally see it as a serious problem, much less think it needs the kind of immediate attention that people in a single country or jurisdiction such as the United States believe it deserves. The United States had slowly been educated civilly over the course of 40 years or so about the crime of sexual abuse and its ramifications on the lives of its victims. The majority of those running the Vatican did not have that same education or exposure.

It is also well known that these congregations inside the Vatican do not communicate well with each other, and oftentimes do not work well with each other, if they work together at all.[4] It is possible for two dicasteries to be working on the same issue and not know that the other is dealing with the same problem. This internal lack of communication can make responding efficiently and consistently to an urgent problem rather difficult.

There has been much written about the Vatican's slow, and to some its incomprehensible, response to this crisis, particularly in the beginning.[5] Part of the difficulty was the necessity of convincing key international Vatican bureaucrats that it was in fact a serious problem, and one that was likely going to spread beyond the English-speaking world. It was a widely held belief among many churchmen internationally that the sexual abuse scandal was first an American issue, then an English-speaking nations' problem, but one that would never affect their own home countries.[6] Ironically, they held this belief despite the fact that even back to 1962 the problem worldwide was serious enough for the Congregation for the Doctrine of the Faith (CDF) to update universal legislation on the subject in the form of the document *Crimen Sollicitationis*.

The sex abuse scandal was often seen internationally as a crisis brought on by greedy American lawyers looking to tarnish the good name of the Church. Once the scope of the problem in the United States became evident, it took considerable

4. This is one reason that Pope Francis has called eight cardinals from all over the world together to form an advisory council to help him reform the Curia. One of the factors in his election was an expectation that he would reorganize the Curia to make it more efficient, coordinated, and streamlined. It remains to be seen how successful he will be.

5. John Jay College, Report to U.S. Conference of Catholic Bishops, The Causes and Context of Sexual Abuse of Minors by Catholic Priests in the United States, 1950–2010, at 85 (May 2011) (hereinafter "John Jay College Report"). "Commentary by church insiders has documented the delay and resistance shown by Vatican authorities to the problem of clergy sexual abuse and that this lack of response was considered by many bishops to be a major obstacle."

6. Francis G. Morrisey, "Addressing the Issue of Clergy Sexual Abuse," 35 Studia Canonica 404 (2001).

personal convincing by high-placed U.S. cardinals that this problem was not simply an American aberration. It did not help that the pontiff at that time was elderly and in failing health. It took the intervention of those influential cardinals personally going to Rome to speak personally with the pope and other Vatican officials in the spring of 2002 before the gravity of the situation was taken seriously.

It was only in May 2011 that norms similar to the ones promulgated by the USCCB in 2004 were distributed to other international bishops' conferences for use in their home countries. The document was issued by CDF, and is entitled "Circular Letter to Assist Episcopal Conferences in Developing Guidelines for Dealing with Cases of Sexual Abuses of Minors Perpetuated by Clerics."[7] Bishop Daniel Conlon mused that "a reasonable inference may be drawn from the issuance of the circular letter a year and a half ago: in Rome a narrow, localized view of the child abuse problem no longer holds sway." As the bishop continued, "That is good news for children and young people everywhere."[8]

As this text went to press in mid-2014, Pope Francis named the members of the special commission and it will convene to study these issues in fall 2014.

19:5 INTERNATIONAL CHURCH/STATE INTERACTION

Another important factor to consider is the Church's history of interactions with other state jurisdictions. Throughout its history, the Catholic Church has had a decidedly mixed experience in its dealings with other civil states. Some countries have had positive relationships with the Church, or at least have left it alone. However, it is not uncommon for there to be open hostility toward the Church, particularly in non-Christian countries, but even in countries with historically Catholic populations. The assassination in El Salvador of Archbishop Oscar Romero was a well-known example of a disastrous interaction by clergy with a state that lacked tolerance for the Church and its social teachings. The Catholic Church has a long institutional memory as an international entity. So in response to what it sees as possible state interference in internal matters, the Church tries to maintain as much independence from civil authority as possible.[9]

Avoidance and prevention of national government interference has long been an ideal sought by Church leaders. One way that the Church accomplishes this is by instilling the necessity for a sense of reserve among its clergy, and especially among its hierarchy, regarding making public its inner workings and its internal problems.

7. Congregation for the Doctrine of the Faith, Circular Letter to Assist Episcopal Conferences In Developing Guidelines for Dealing with Cases of Sexual Abuses of Minors Perpetrated by Clerics, Online (May 3, 2011, http://www.vatican.va/roman_curia/congregations/cfaith/documents/rc_con_cfaith_doc_20110503_abuso-minori_en.html.

8. Conlon, R. Daniel. "Going Global with the Charter and Essential Norms, Proceedings, 74 (2012) 62-76.", 63).

9. John Allen, "Pope's Reluctance to Impose American Way Not a Shocker," Nat'l Cath. Rptr. Online (July 16, 2010), http://ncronline.org/blogs/all-things-catholic/popes-reluctance-impose-american-way-not-shocker.

This goal also is accomplished by encouraging its leaders and members to resolve internal difficulties via internal means, without resorting to the involvement of external government officials and processes.

This institutional desire for autonomy and secrecy might not make sense to people living in stable societies with dependable and trusted judicial systems and impartial police. However, in countries where Christians and Catholics are a persecuted minority, or in places that have experienced years of civil unrest, this reticence in trusting local and national governments to deal fairly with accusations against its own people is not necessarily misplaced. For example, Cardinal Darío Castrillón Hoyos from Colombia was severely criticized for issuing a number of letters congratulating bishops for not releasing information about the sexual abuse of a minor to civil authorities. While not defending his statements, such statements from the Vatican curia reflect an attitude that might be more understandable if one factors in the person's experiences with his or her own local and national government. A person's distrust of civil government makes more sense if that person's experience includes such factors as corrupt police forces, political instability and guerrilla warfare, and local governments controlled or influenced by drug cartels. Although a cleric accused of a crime in the United States, Ireland, or Australia will have his case professionally investigated, and will likely get a fair trial, one may not be able to say this about clergy in countries such as Iraq, Syria, China, Egypt, and other places where Christians are persecuted or where governments are unstable or compromised.

There may be no excuse in Western democratic countries for the Church not to comply fully with the demands for transparency made by state prosecutors and investigators, but it is also understandable why the Catholic Church would balk at issuing a universal policy requiring full international cooperation with all civil authorities and state and local police. Providing such direct disclosure in some countries could be tantamount to a death sentence for the person accused (perhaps falsely accused)—a situation of which the Vatican is painfully aware.

The difficulty with having an international organization such as the Catholic Church is that the policies and practices necessary for dealing with particular circumstances in one country do not necessarily translate well when applied to a different place. Secrecy and internal discipline has a positive benefit in oppressive dictatorships and/or in countries hostile toward religion or Christianity, but is seen very differently in countries that are functional, tolerant, and/or democratic. The Church needs to be aware of such differences, and to adjust its practices accordingly. However, it is also important for such a global institution to make very clear to its people in a particular place and circumstance that when problems arise, there are reasons such blanket pro-disclosure policies are not always beneficial or appropriate in a global context.

19:6 MANAGERIAL ACCOUNTABILITY CONFLICTS

Another important factor that influenced the Vatican's response to the sexual abuse crisis is how the institution views administrators, particularly those that are bishops. In the United States and in most other countries, bishops are assigned to a particular diocese by the pope. A bishop is expected to remain the bishop of the diocese to which he is assigned until he dies, retires, or is transferred to another diocese by the pope (cc. 401, 418). Bishops are not accountable to their metropolitans, dioceses, priests, or councils for their behavior; rather they are answerable only to the pope. A bishop is asked to submit a letter of resignation that goes into effect on his seventy-fifth birthday. This may or may not be accepted by the pope. If the pope needs him to remain in his diocese for a few years longer, the pope can choose not to accept the bishop's resignation at that time. If a bishop wants to resign before age seventy-five, he must have a good reason for doing so (e.g. for ill health), and his resignation must be accepted by the pope.

As one can see, the pope directly controls the tenure of bishops in their dioceses. Furthermore, if a bishop commits a canonical crime, it is either adjudicated by the pope personally, or in particular cases the pope has delegated this authority to specific Vatican offices. For example, CDF's document *Sacramentum sanctitatis tutela* gives these offices the explicit task of adjudicating cases for cardinals, archbishops, and bishops.[10] There is no local forum within the Church to hold a bishop accountable for his actions.

A theological value that has resulted in considerable consternation among Catholics and non-Catholics alike is how the Vatican should respond to claims of a bishop's personal mismanagement of clergy sexual abuse. In other words, what is the proper and expected response upon the discovery that a bishop is found to have caused or gravely mishandled a problem within his diocese? In the civic and business culture within the United States, when it has been discovered that an executive has grossly mishandled a problem in his or her political or administrative office or corporation, it is expected that the person will immediately resign from his or her post. American society considers this to be the proper and appropriate response as well as a type of punishment for the person's behavior. Failure to do so fuels public outrage, because it is perceived as failing to acknowledge the seriousness of the person's mismanagement and that person's responsibility for it.

The Catholic Church has had a different view when it comes to mismanagement by bishops. There is a long-standing theological understanding that a bishop has a spiritual relationship with his diocese, and that in fact he is "married" to his church.[11] Much like spouses are expected to remain in a relationship even when there are serious problems, a bishop was expected to stay in his diocese and work though those problems unless he was physically or mentally unable to do so. As stated above, bishops are allowed to retire only when the pope accepts their

---

10. SST/10 art. 1.

11. Historically, bishops were rarely transferred from their dioceses once they became a bishop. In recent times bishops are often transferred between dioceses, which somewhat weakens this analogy, but it has been the traditional theological understanding of the relationship between a bishop and his diocese. It will be interesting to see what Pope Francis's policy on the transfer of bishops is, given that he is trying to reduce a notion of careerism within the Church. Pope Francis may choose for the most part to keep bishops where they are initially assigned rather than transferring them to another diocese.

resignation, so even if a bishop petitions for resignation it is not automatic that it will be granted. In the past, the Vatican was quite willing to let the offending bishop "stew in his own juices" until he cleaned up the mess he had made.[12]

The sexual abuse scandal highlighted the conflict of these values, when Catholics of the various affected countries called for the resignation of their bishops, and were frustrated and infuriated when those calls were not heeded. In the United States, this practice gained international attention in Boston in 2002—a situation that may have been the catalyst for a fundamental change in Vatican practice. Both Pope Benedict and Pope Francis have been much more willing to accept the resignation of a bishop or to retire a bishop prematurely if it is shown that the bishop has misused his office, or his action or inaction has caused scandal in his diocese.

19:7 THE CHURCH'S DISTASTE FOR HASTE

Historically and with few exceptions, the Catholic Church does not act in haste. The Church has a rather particular and somewhat peculiar understanding of time. There is a standing joke among those familiar with the inner workings of the Church that there is regular time and there is Church time, with Church time having no correlation to regular time. Church time moves very slowly. The Catholic Church in its governance thinks in millennia. If a project is not completed this year, there is always next year, or the next, or even ten, fifty, or a hundred years from now. This is not an exaggeration.

For example, Pope John XXIII called for a revision of the code of canon law in the early 1960s during Vatican II. The Code under which the Church was functioning at that time was codified over 40 years before in 1917. The new code of canon law was not promulgated until 1983, more than 20 years after a pope declared it was needed, and more than 60 years after it was first promulgated. Although this thinking might stand it in good stead for predictability, stability, and consistency, it does not make for an institution that is able to quickly respond to a legal or disciplinary crisis. In this specific case, the difficulty its internal structures had in being able to respond quickly made the Church seem both reluctant and ill-equipped to deal with the growing crisis.

This understanding of time is strongly connected with the value of tradition. The Catholic Church does not like to be seen as deviating from its own history and tradition. Rather it places more value on the appearance of continuity and timelessness. The John Jay College Report of 2011 noted that "Over time, Roman Catholicism has been more likely to focus publically [sic] on tradition than on innovation, and when innovation occurs, leaders present it as completely continuous with what preceded it. Some structural characteristics of Catholicism impede innovation, especially

---

12. John Allen, "Why Rome Scorns Resignations, and a Great Week for Wonks," Nat'l Cath. Rptr. Online (Aug. 10, 2010), http://ncronline.org/blogs/all-things-catholic/why-rome-scorns-resignations-and-great-week-wonks.

when they appear to clash with key dimensions of its identity..."[13] In other words, even when innovation is necessary, it generally is presented in such a way that it seems consistent with previous practice, even when that is not necessarily accurate.

Knowing these fundamental values, laws, priorities, and underlying assumptions are useful to remember when thinking about this crisis, because in one way or another they affect almost every internal decision, particularly on the international level, that has been made regarding the scandal. While these principles do not account for faulty, negligent, or criminal use of judgment, or failure to use the resources that canon law provided them, they do help to explain certain seemingly baffling responses coming from Catholic bishops and the Vatican hierarchy.

19:8 THE ROLE OF CARDINAL RATZINGER IN CLEANING UP THE MESS

There has been much discussion and debate about the role of Cardinal Ratzinger, now Pope Emeritus Benedict, in the Church's international response to the sexual abuse of minors. During the 1990s and until he became Pope Benedict in 2005, then Cardinal Ratzinger was the head of the Congregation for the Doctrine of the Faith, the congregation that was eventually tasked with handling all international sexual abuse of minors cases.

Clearly, being an international organization with an international staff greatly influenced the Vatican's timing and ability to "get it." Many did not. However, the one Curial official who did get the requisite education regarding the scope and severity of the clergy sexual abuse issue was Joseph Cardinal Ratzinger, now Pope Emeritus Benedict. During his pontificate, some called for Pope Benedict's resignation due to his early handling of this scandal, or for cases that occurred prior to his tenure at the Vatican. However, what must be taken into account is that awareness of the severity of this issue and its inability to be cured did not happen all at once. Furthermore, though awareness of the sexual abuse of children may have been raised through front page news in the United States, one cannot extrapolate from that that it was happening in the rest of the world, much less within the Vatican Curia. It takes time and awareness to "get it," and that is exactly what happened to Cardinal Ratzinger as prefect of CDF.

Cardinal Ratzinger's time as prefect of CDF had a profound effect on his understanding of the horrors of the sexual abuse crisis, its worldwide implications, and the Church's desperate need to get it cleaned up. Based on that experience, he was the only member of the senior hierarchy in the Vatican who had a sufficient overview and grasp on the situation to have a reasonable chance of getting it resolved. No other cardinal associated with the Vatican Curia had that same perspective of the gravity of the worldwide problem.

13. John Jay College Report, supra, 84.

In an article written in 2010 for the National Catholic Reporter, Vatican reporter John Allen traced the evolution of Cardinal Ratzinger/Pope Benedict's response to the worldwide sexual abuse scandal, as it has developed over the past 12 years. His insights are so apropos that the passage is reproduced in its entirety. He states:

> Though it didn't look like it at the time, the turning point in Ratzinger's attitude came in May 2001, with a legal document from John Paul II titled *Sacramentum sanctitatis tutela*. Technically known as a *motu proprio*,[14] the document assigned juridical responsibility for certain grave crimes under canon law, including sexual abuse of a minor, to Ratzinger's congregation. It also compelled diocesan bishops all over the world to forward their case files to Rome, where the congregation would make a decision about the appropriate course of action.
>
> In the wake of the *motu proprio*, Ratzinger dispatched a letter to the bishops of the world, subjecting accusations of sexual abuse against priests to the authority of his office and insisting upon "confidentiality," which critics typically regard as a code-word for secrecy. Whatever the merits of the 2001 letter, it set the stage for a dramatic change in Ratzinger's approach.
>
> Msgr. Charles Scicluna, a Maltese priest who serves as the Promoter of Justice in the Congregation for the Doctrine of the Faith—in effect, its lead prosecutor—said in a recent interview with the Italian Catholic paper *L'Avvenire* that the *motu proprio* triggered an "avalanche" of files in Rome, most of which arrived in 2003 and 2004. Eventually, Scicluna said, more than 3,000 cases worked their way through the congregation.
>
> By all accounts, Ratzinger was punctilious about studying the files, making him one of the few churchmen anywhere in the world to have read the documentation on virtually every Catholic priest ever credibly accused of sexual abuse. As a result, he acquired a familiarity with the contours of the problem that virtually no other figure in the Catholic Church can claim.
>
> Driven by that encounter with what he would later refer to as "filth" in the church, Ratzinger seems to have undergone something of a "conversion experience" throughout 2003–04. From that point forward, he and his staff seemed driven by a convert's zeal to clean up the mess.
>
> Of the 500-plus cases that the Congregation for the Doctrine of the Faith dealt with prior to Benedict's election to the papacy, the substantial majority were returned to the local bishop authorizing immediate action against the accused priest—no canonical trial, no lengthy process, just swift removal from ministry and, often, expulsion from the priesthood. In a more limited number of cases, the congregation asked for a canonical trial, and in a few cases the congregation ordered the priest reinstated.
>
> That marked a stark reversal from the initial insistence of Vatican officials, Ratzinger included, that in almost every instance the accused priest deserved

---

14. A "motu proprio" is a term used for a document when it is issued on the legislator's own initiative and not at the request of another. It literally means, "on his own initiative." John M. Huels, The Pastoral Companion (1995).

the right to canonical trial. Having sifted through the evidence, Ratzinger and Scicluna apparently drew the conclusion that in many instances the proof was so overwhelming that immediate action was required.

Among insiders, the change of climate was dramatic. In the complex world of court politics at the Vatican, the Congregation for the Doctrine of the Faith became the beachhead for an aggressive response to the sexual abuse crisis. Ratzinger and his deputies sometimes squared off against other departments which regarded the "zero tolerance" policy as an over-reaction, not to mention a distortion of the church's centuries-long canonical tradition, in which punishments are supposed to fit the crime, and in which tremendous discretion is usually left in the hands of bishops and other superiors to mete out discipline.

Behind the scenes, some Vatican personnel actually began to grumble that the Congregation for the Doctrine of the Faith had "drunk the Kool-aid," in the sense of accepting the case for sweeping changes in the way priests are supervised and disciplined.[15]

Clearly, Cardinal Ratzinger had a change of perspective after personally review-ing the thousands of cases being submitted to CDF, and seeing the scope and sever-ity of the problem. No other high-ranking cleric had that experience. Though it may have taken him time over the course of a few years to come to this realization, it is apparent that Pope Benedict eventually "got it" and was motivated to fix the problem. When Cardinal Ratzinger became Pope Benedict, he spent his pontificate working to clean up the problem and to punish the perpetrators because he had seen firsthand the damage it had inflicted. It was his perseverance that forced the international Church to come to terms with this issue within their individual con-texts, and to realize that this was and is not simply an American problem.

19:9 MOVING FORWARD AND POPE FRANCIS

Fortunately, it seems that Pope Francis also sees the problem of the sexual abuse of minors in the same light and with the same urgency as Pope Benedict, and that he has the same commitment to its eradication. He has certainly surrounded him-self with close advisors who have a keen sense of the scope of this problem, most notably Cardinal Seán O'Malley. Cardinal O'Malley became archbishop of Boston in July of 2003 after having been responsible for cleaning up sexual abuse scandals during his two previous assignments in the dioceses of Fall River, Massachusetts, and Palm Beach, Florida. It is likely that no other prelate in the United States has had such vast experience of the effects that the sexual abuse of children by clerics can have on the victims, a diocese, and its people.

---

15. John Allen, "Will Ratzinger's Past Trump Benedict's Present?," Nat'l Cath. Rptr. Online (Mar. 17, 2010), http://ncronline.org/news/accountability/will-ratzingers-past-trump-benedicts-present.

It was announced on December 5, 2013, that the pope intends to form an international commission for the protection of minors—a commission suggested by his council of eight cardinals who are helping him craft a general reform of the Vatican Curia. According to Cardinal O'Malley, the commission's aim will be "advising Pope Francis on the Holy See's commitment to the protection of children and in pastoral care for victims of abuse."[16] More specifically, Cardinal O'Malley said that the commission will "'study current programs' in place for the protection of children and 'formulate suggestions for new initiatives' on the part of the Curia, in collaboration with bishops, bishops' conferences, religious superiors and conferences of religious superiors. He also said it would identify those best suited to the 'systematic implementation of these new initiatives.'" Finally, the cardinal suggested that those implementing the system "could include laypersons, religious and priests with responsibilities for the safety of children, in dialogue with the victims, in mental health and in law enforcement."[17] It remains to be seen how effective such a commission will be, but an international commission may be good in formulating additional universal practices and policies to aid those places that have yet to deal with this problem.

Pope Francis has in another way demonstrated a concrete commitment to punishing those who have been found guilty of the sexual abuse of minors. There has been a fascinating development in regard to the Vatican's policy in dealing with the sexual abuse of minors and other crimes from within its own ranks at the Vatican. When the Vatican City State was created in 1929, it adopted the Italian legal system to adjudicate crimes committed within the Vatican.[18] The Vatican has an agreement with the Italian government that in the event that the Vatican court convicts someone of a crime, the Vatican will pay the Italians to keep that person incarcerated.[19] This system operates in addition to the canonical courts that prosecute canonical crimes, but its reach was limited. In the summer of 2013, Pope Francis changed the rule so that those with Vatican citizenship and even high-ranking Vatican public officials could be prosecuted by the Vatican City State for crimes they commit,[20] While the document mentions crimes such as organized crime and terrorism, it also extends to such crimes as the sexual abuse of a minor. On July 11, 2013, Pope Francis issued the motu proprio "On the Jurisdiction of Judicial Authorities

---

16. Edward Pentin, "Pope Francis Creates Commission on Sexual Abuse," Nat'l Cath. Register (Dec. 6, 2013), available on Web at http://www.ncregister.com/daily-news/pope-francis-creates-commission-on-sexual-abuse/#ixzz2pp28cMyk.

17. Id.

18. Catholic News Service, "Unique Vatican Court System Tackles Petty to Serious Crimes" (May, 30, 2012) This court is in addition to the Vatican canonical courts set up to adjudicate canonical crimes.

19. Brian Palmer, "How Does Vatican City Deal With Criminals?," Slate (May 30, 2012), available on Web at http://www.slate.com/articles/news_and_politics/explainer/2012/05/paolo_gabriele_case_how_does_the_vatican_deal_with_criminals_.html.

20. Prior Vatican crimes have been as minor as pickpocketing or shoplifting, and as serious as a double-murder/suicide that occurred in 1998, and the Vatileaks scandal where the pope's butler was arrested for possessing documents stolen from the pope.

of Vatican City State in Criminal Matters." It extends Vatican City jurisdiction to Vatican public officials, which includes:

1. Members, officials, and personnel of the various organs of the Roman Curia and of the Institutions connected with it.
2. Papal legates and diplomatic personnel of the Holy See.
3. Representatives, managers or directors, as well as persons who even de facto manage or exercise control over the entities directly dependent on the Holy See and listed in the registry of canonical juridical persons kept by the Governorate of Vatican City State.
4. Any other person holding an administrative or judicial mandate in the Holy See, permanent or temporary, paid or unpaid, irrespective of that person's seniority.

This is relevant to this discussion because in August 2013 a Polish archbishop who was the nuncio (papal ambassador) to the Dominican Republic was recalled because he was accused of the sexual abuse of children in his territory.[21] There are also allegations that he abused children in his native Poland.[22] Because of his ambassador status, he possessed diplomatic immunity in the Dominican Republic, so he could not be tried there unless his immunity was waived. However, by being a Vatican nuncio he is also a Vatican citizen.

According to the Vatican spokesman, Archbishop Jozef Wesolowski is currently under investigation in not one but two Vatican courts: by CDF for canonical crimes and by the Vatican City State for violating its laws criminalizing the sexual abuse of minors.[23] Before, though papal diplomats could be ecclesiastically sanctioned and even laicized, they were not able to be prosecuted by the Vatican in a way that could land them in jail. However, with this change in the law, if the archbishop is convicted, not only could the Vatican defrock him but it could have him incarcerated in an Italian prison. If he is found guilty and he is incarcerated, it may go a long way to demonstrate that the Vatican has had a true conversion regarding its response to the sexual abuse of minors, and that it is committed to its eradication within its own ranks, even if it is committed by particularly high-ranking clergy.

As this text goes to print it is still very early in Pope Francis's pontificate, so it remains to be seen how his priorities and goals will affect addressing this issue worldwide. Pope Francis has certainly made it clear that he expects that clergy and bishops will get more involved in the daily lives of their people, which might reduce the problems of clerical isolation and lack of perspective. Like Pope Benedict, Pope Francis also has the authority to completely change the current way cases of sexual abuse are adjudicated, or even create regional or national canonical courts to hear these cases,

21. Catholic News Service, "Dominican Official to Investigate Claims of Sexual Abuse Against Nuncio" (Sept. 6, 2013).
22. Catholic World News, "Vatican Reveals Investigation of Former Nuncio; Denies Refusing Extradition" (Jan. 13, 2013), http://www.catholicculture.org/news/headlines/index.cfm?storyid=20174.
23. Id.

if he wants to do so. Currently, Western countries have been dealing with these problems for many years, and with better screening, attention, and awareness, new cases of abuse are becoming increasingly rare. This is not the case in other parts of the world, where there has been less of an awareness of the problem and no significant pressure to do something about it. It is likely that the challenge facing Pope Francis on the issue of the sexual abuse of minors may not stem from the Western world at all, but will be the result of a growing awareness of this problem in other parts of the world.

19:10 CANON LAW

Knowing how the institutional Church thinks of itself, how it functions in Rome, and how it interacts with the societies around it is an important factor in understanding how these conditions shaped the international response to the scandal. The other factor that originates from the Vatican and affects the way the Church functions is its system of internal laws, known as canon law.

One of the little understood factors in the sex abuse scandal affecting the Catholic Church has been the role of the Church's internal canon law in determining whether and how those accused of sexual abuse are dealt with. The law of the Catholic Church, known as canon law, has been in existence for well over a thousand years. It is an ancient field of study (there were faculties of canon law at the medieval universities of Bologna, Paris, and Oxford), with modern master's degrees granted after the completion of a three-year program. Students can also continue in the field and earn a doctorate. It has only been during the twentieth century that all of the various documents that made up canon law were compiled into one manageable text that was "modeled after the Napoleonic codes which at the beginning of the 20th century were quite common in Europe."[24] The first Code of Canon Law was promulgated in 1917.

The second Code of Canon Law,[25] which was promulgated in 1983, is the current governing structure for most of the Catholic Church worldwide.[26] This is the law that controls and limits all aspects of the inner workings of its national and international dioceses and churches. It is a code that contains not only church laws, but also "theological canons" that provide a theological rationale and interpretation for those laws. In other words, canon law is not strictly legal in that it contains both

24. Kevin McKenna, "Canon Law and Civil Law: Working Together for the Common Good," Canon Law Seminar for Media 3, United States Conference of Catholic Bishops (2010).

25. *Codex iuris canonici, auctoritate Ioannis Pauli PP. II promulgatus*, Vatican City, Libreria editrice Vaticana (1983). Most American canonists use the American commentary on the Code (John P. Beal, James A. Coriden, and Thomas J. Green, New Commentary on the Code of Canon Law (2000).

26. There is also a Code of Canons for the Eastern Churches (CCEO) that was promulgated in 1993. This Code binds the 21 Eastern Catholic Churches (e.g., the Melkites, Maronites, Ukranians, Ruthenians, etc.) that are in union with Rome.

the legal norms as well as some of the theological rationale behind these norms within its text.

Furthermore, the current Code of Canon Law (hereinafter "CIC/83" or "the Code") is a legal codification of laws, similar to the "civil law" that governs the State of Louisiana in the United States and the province of Quebec in Canada, and is like the governing legal codes of many European countries. It is not based on the common law, English, American, or otherwise. For example, unlike the common law, judicial precedent does not influence the interpretation of the Code, because in canon law there is no concept of binding precedent. Rather, each case, regardless of how similar the facts or circumstances, is judged on its own merits—much to the chagrin of many civil lawyers in common law jurisdictions.

This is a critical difference in the Church's approach to the law, which often runs counter to the thinking of those whose primary experience of law is the common law. However, as any law student knows, there is a reason that legal textbooks repeatedly must state in effect that "this legal principle is applicable to every state in the United States except Louisiana," and why attorneys who wants to practice law in Louisiana must take the state's unique civil law bar exam. The civil law is simply different, and different rules and different processes apply.

19:11 GOVERNING STRUCTURES

In canon law there is no separation of powers (canon 331, hereinafter "c. 331"). The pope is the supreme executive, and he is also the primary legislator for the Church. Although an ecumenical council (c. 338) or a national bishop's conference (c. 455) can draft laws, they must be approved by the pope to have legal force.[27] There is also a papal judiciary that has both primary level (in canonical parlance called first instance courts) and appeals level courts (called second and third instance courts) called the Roman Rota (c. 1443) and the Apostolic Signatura (c. 1445), but there can always be an appeal directly to the pope (c. 1442). Furthermore, some particular cases, such as the trial of a bishop, can be adjudicated only by the pope himself (c. 1405) or by a congregation that has been delegated to act on his behalf.

This model also holds true locally (c. 391). The bishop has the same relationship to his diocese as the pope does to the Church. The bishop is the supreme executive in his diocese. He is also the supreme legislator within the diocese and is able to promulgate local laws as long as they do not conflict with the Code or moral or theological teachings of the international Church. While the bishop has a judicial vicar to administer his local judiciary (c. 1420), ultimately the bishop is the primary judge in his judiciary. It is rare that a bishop ever gets personally involved in the running of his diocesan tribunal (court). He almost always leaves that to his judicial vicar and canon lawyers. Nevertheless, if he wanted to act as a judge for a particular case in his diocese, he has that right.

---

27. For an ecumenical council, the approval is called an "*approbatio.*" For a bishop's conference, it is a "*recognitio.*"

To sum up, while the laws of the church distinguish between executive, legislative, and judicial authority, that authority resides internationally in either the person of the pope, or locally in the person of the bishop.

19:12 OVERVIEW OF THE CODE

The Code of Canon Law regulates all the different facets of church governance. It has its own norms on how the law is to be interpreted, which govern the rest of the Code. It has sections regarding the rights and obligations of laypersons as well as its deacons, priests, bishops, and those in religious communities. It has sections governing Catholic education at all levels. It has a section regarding property and its sale, acquisition, and transfer. And finally, it has sections specifying crimes according to its law, and procedures for how internal disputes and criminal trials are to be conducted, as well as administrative disciplinary processes. Both processes can be used to impose penalties and sometimes dismissals (colloquially known as laicizations) in certain cases.

19:13 PENAL ASPECTS OF CANON LAW

Regardless of whether a civil or criminal trial has been conducted in civil courts, for a priest to be disciplined or dismissed in the Catholic Church, the Church is required to follow its own internal law. Due to the current problems facing the Church internationally regarding child sexual abuse, this entire section (Book 6) of penal law is in the process of being revised.[28]

Though the section on penal law is due to be revised, what has not changed is the procedure for the actual penal trial. The canons governing the running of trials, and penal trials in particular, are rather general. In the older Code of Canon Law that was promulgated in 1917 (CIC/17), there were 500 canons (cc. 1552–1999 and 2142–2194) governing its procedures for conducting a trial. In the CIC/83, that number was reduced to 292 canons (cc.1399–1691).

While the common law has very specific requirements regarding how criminal trials should be conducted, as well as having the rights of the accused clearly specified, canon law is much more vague on the subject. As more canonical penal trials are being conducted both nationally and internationally, some of these questions are being answered in subsequently published norms. But the lack of specificity in canon law regarding aspects of conducting these trials has been problematic.

Despite having canons on how canonical trials were to be conducted, prior to 2002 penal law was an area of canon law that few canonists had any experience with, other than in the context of a marriage tribunal. Dioceses in the United States

---

28. Francis Morrisey "The Preliminary Investigation in Penal Cases: Some of The Better Practices," 2(2) The Canonist 185 (2011). However, it is not certain if or when these new norms will be promulgated.

rarely used the canons regarding penal trials, though they did more frequently use administrative processes in the law that allowed for administrative laicizations under particular circumstances. These processes will be discussed in later chapters.

Prior to 2002, many canon law schools offered only a one-credit class on the penal law, with professors occasionally informing their students that "they were likely never going to need this material." Unfortunately they were very wrong. The lack of experience among canon lawyers in dealing with such cases was made worse by the fact that cases at the Vatican involving clerical sexual abuse were not published, so there was little shared information or direction about how to conduct such cases or trials.

In 2001, bishops and then the general public were made aware in the document *Sacramentorum Sanctitatis Tutela*[29] (SST/01) that in 1962 the Congregation for the Doctrine of the Faith had issued guidelines in a document called *Crimen solicationis*.[30] These were based on an earlier Instruction by the same name issued in 1922, but the guidelines were issued only to a limited number of bishops and had never been generally published. The 1922 version of the instruction detailed the circumstances under which grave crimes such as child sexual abuse should be referred to the Holy Office (the prior name of CDF) to resolve, and it provided instructions on how to resolve the issue administratively. However, due to its limited distribution, few bishops and canonists knew of this document's existence, until it was revealed in SST/01 in 2001.

19:14 CONFLICTS IN LEGAL VALUES

Besides having a different legal structure, many of the canonical laws reflect different societal and theological values than those found in the common law. One difference between the common law of the United States and the canon law of the Catholic Church is how both bodies resolve the tension between the community versus the individual.

The Catholic Church in its outlook, and more specifically enshrined in its law, is fundamentally communitarian. In a showdown between an individual's rights and the good of the community, it will be the perceived good of the community that will usually win—though it must be noted that what constitutes "the good of the community" is determined by the bishop or his vicars. At the end of the section of the CIC/83's section listing the general rights and obligations of Christ's faithful is canon 223. It states:

> Canon 223 - §1 In exercising their rights, Christ's faithful, both individually and in associations, must take account of the common good of the Church, as well as the rights of others and their own duties to others.

29. Congregation for the Doctrine of the Faith, "Sacramentorum Sanctitatis Tutela," 93 Acta Apostolicae Sedis 785–788 (May 18, 2001).
30. Suprema Sacra Congregatio Sancti Officii, "Crimen Sollicitationis," (Mar. 1962).

§2. **Ecclesiastical authority is entitled to regulate, in view of the common good, the exercise of rights which are proper to Christ's faithful**. (emphasis added)

Clearly, the Church shares a European view and theological position that the good of the community trumps the exercise of an individual's rights. Professor Jim Provost explained this well when he stated:

[T]he difference in perception can be stated in terms of differing views of social order. The European experience has developed a special sense of the social unit, whether under traditional monarchies or in various forms of democratic states, East and West. The social order assures the welfare of the individual. In the American mindset, a strong sense of local autonomy has been prized, even if not always carried out in practice. The theory has been that the welfare of the individual assures the social order. These differences lead to differing sensitivities with regard to rights. From a European perspective, the focus is on the social order; rights result from respect for the social order. From an American perspective, the focus is on the person; social order results from respect for personal rights.[31]

Though one can see the validity of both approaches to how one's society is ordered, both can also have serious drawbacks. A drawback of the canonical viewpoint is that the "good of the community" is defined as what those in the hierarchy perceive is the greatest good for the community. Thus, in most of the cases regarding sexual abuse, the good was defined to prevent scandal and protect the Church's good reputation. Obviously this attitude regarding the need to protect the community at the expense of the individual can and was taken too far, particularly when the situation becomes so outrageous that it results in neither the society nor the individual being protected. Furthermore, this viewpoint of many bishops, coupled with a strong sense of the need to protect the clergy and to "protect" the faithful from scandal, created an internal ethos in which clergy sexual abusers oftentimes had the opportunity to abuse children with few consequences for their misdeeds.

19:15 CURRENT CANON LAW REGARDING SEXUAL ABUSE

After examining some of the overarching influences that have governed the Catholic Church's response to the clergy sexual abuse problem, and defined what canon law is, one must then consider the specific law that governs this canonical crime. There has been recognition that the sexual abuse of a minor is a crime in canon law well before the codes of the twentieth century were promulgated. As far back as the Council of Elvira in early 300 A.D., the church was legislating against

---

31. J.H. Provost, "Promoting and Protecting the Rights of Christians: Some Implications for Church Structure," 46 The Jurist 298–299 (1986).

the sexual abuse of young boys. A canon on the subject was included in the Code of 1917 (CIC/17), and then included again in the CIC/83. In the current code, there is only one canon in the CIC/83 that addresses sexual abuse directly. The canon is at the end of the Code's section on Penalties and Other Punishments. The second part of canon 1395 states:

> 1395 §2. A cleric who has offended in other ways against the sixth commandment of the Decalogue, if the crime was committed by force, or by threats, or in public, or with a minor under the age of sixteen years, is to be punished with just penalties, not excluding dismissal from the clerical state if the case so warrants.

For non-canonists, the language of the canon is curious. Unless one is able to understand canon law "code-speak," it would not be immediately evident that this canon is the applicable one to the sexual abuse of a minor. This is because in traditional terms, an offense against the "sixth commandment of the Decalogue" is the biblical Old Testament commandment forbidding adultery, which is sexual intercourse between a married person and a person who is not his or her spouse.

A plain-text reading would seem to prevent a cleric from committing adultery with a minor under the age of 16.[32] However, section 2336 of the Catechism of the Catholic Church explains that this commandment has traditionally been used as a theological catch-all for any offense against the "whole of human sexuality," including the sexual abuse of minors. So it is, in fact, the quoted canon 1395 above, now coupled with a recently updated *Sacramentorum Sanctitatis Tutela* (SST/10), that provides the legal basis that enables the Church to prosecute and punish a cleric with penalties up to and including dismissal from the clerical state.

Tragically, neither this problem nor this remedy is new. A similar canon was found in the prior Code that was promulgated in 1917. In it, canon 2359 § 2 states:

> 2359 §2 If they [clerics] engage in a delict (canonical crime) against the sixth precept of the Decalogue with a minor below the age of 16, or engage in adultery, debauchery, bestiality, sodomy, pandering, incest with blood-relatives or affines in the first degree, they are suspended, declared infamous, and are deprived of any office, benefice, dignity, responsibility, if they have such, whatsoever, and in more serious cases, they are to be deposed.[33]

Clearly, the drafters of the 1917 Code anticipated the various sexual crimes that clerics could engage in, and they legislated penalties ranging from suspension to deposition or dismissal. It is interesting to note that in the CIC/17, adultery and sodomy are also listed as a specific crime for clerics, with equally stringent penalties.

The fact that the sexual abuse of minors has been an issue that has been legislated as a crime warranting dismissal since the very beginnings of the Church

---

32. This is technically impossible as presumably neither the priest nor the minor is married, and one party must be married for it to be adultery in the technical sense.
33. The 1917 Pio-Benedictine Code of Canon Law (Edward N. Peters ed., 2001).

would seem to indicate that not only has there been a historical awareness of the problem, but one that was grave enough to incur the most serious penalties. In the canonical realm, that penalty is the dismissal from the clerical state.

Although the canon refers to violations of the sixth commandment of the Decalogue, because of the intentional vagueness of the language, there are many questions that this legal formulation did not answer. It also has made the prosecution of clerics for violations of this crime difficult because of its lack of specificity. For example, traditionally, the sexual abuse of a minor required some sort of physical interaction or physical contact. However, technology has been advancing at such a rate that new questions are arising as a result. Technology is making it possible to have a sort of sexual encounter without the parties even being physically in the same place.

For example, can a priest be penalized for a criminal violation of c. 1395 where the cleric never physically touched a minor? Is Internet pornography included under this canon, and is there a difference between surfing and downloading? What about a virtual reality sexual encounter with a computer-generated minor? What about explicit conversations with a minor in an Internet chat room? What if there is credible evidence that the minor intentionally lied about his or her age, so that the cleric had a legitimate reason to believe that the minor was an adult?

To answer some of these questions, CDF and the U.S. bishops have promulgated (legislatively pass) additional norms, some specifically for the United States, and some that bind the entire Church. The Preamble to the Essential Norms promulgated by the bishops in 2002 attempted to define sexual abuse of a minor when it stated:

> Sexual abuse of a minor includes sexual molestation or sexual exploitation of a minor and other behavior by which an adult uses a minor as an object of sexual gratification....A canonical offence against the sixth commandment of the Decalogue (CIC, c. 1395 §2; CCEO, c. 1453 §1) need not be a complete act of intercourse. Nor, to be objectively grave, does an act need to involve force, physical contact, or a discernible harmful outcome.[34]

Interestingly, this definition was removed when the Norms were revised in 2006, though the CDF added possession of child pornography and abuse of vulnerable adults back to the list in 2010. Even with a somewhat more specific definition, questions concerning what constitutes the sexual abuse of a minor remain. Some of these questions are addressed in later chapters, and others remain for the Vatican to decide.

The following chapters will hopefully help to answer such questions, as well as other such questions regarding what has influenced bishops to act as they have, what has been the history of this crisis, what are the current processes used, and what have been the shortcomings and drawbacks of the Church's response.

34. United States Conference of Catholic Bishops, "Essential Norms for Diocesan/ Eparchial Policies Dealing with Allegations of Sexual Abuse of Minors by Priests or Deacons," 32 Origins 415–418 (June 2004).

CHAPTER 20

❧

How Episcopal Culture Contributed to Administrative Failure

20:1 UNDERSTANDING THE CULTURE

Having discussed generally some of the international Catholic Church's worldview, assumptions, legal system, and law, next we turn to examining the episcopal culture that influenced Catholic bishops within the United States, and how these influences affected their administrative response to clergy sexual abuse.

20:2 TWO SEPARATE ISSUES

There are two separate problems to examine when looking at the issue of clergy sexual abuse. First there is the issue of dealing with the allegations of the actual abuse perpetrated on minors by Catholic clerics. There is also a second and equally important issue—the issue of a failure of the Church's administrators, with the ultimate responsibility resting on individual bishops, to appropriately and effectively deal with the problem and act in such a way as to protect additional minors from being abused.

Bishops in the United States are part of a particular ecclesiastical culture that has its own influences, attitudes, and beliefs. This culture significantly influenced their decisions regarding clergy sexual abuse. To fully understand the issues, we must delve into the broad underlying beliefs and mindset of that ecclesiastical culture. Some of these influences are directly canonical, while others reflect a greater attitude that affected whether and how internal canon law was applied in these cases.

It is important to note that these are broad generalizations regarding episcopal culture, and obviously there are bishops who do not or did not fit these descriptions. One cannot paint every bishop with the same brush, nor does every factor apply to every bishop. It should also be noted that most of the bishops in office at the time when the abuse took place are no longer in office. There has been a sea change regarding the vast majority of bishops' current understanding of the problem and their responses to it.[1] Nevertheless, individually or taken together these influences within the episcopal culture were prevalent, and shaped how many U.S. bishops historically approached this crisis.[2]

20:3 DIOCESAN INDEPENDENCE .

A Catholic diocese can be defined as the people in a specific territory that is governed by a bishop. Canon 369 defines a diocese as "a portion of the people of God which is entrusted to a bishop." In canon law, the bishop is given responsibility for governing his own diocese, which includes full administrative, legislative, and judicial functions.[3] A bishop regulates Catholic teaching in his diocese. A bishop is also responsible for regulating Catholic worship in his diocese.[4] While bishops are in union with the pope, they have considerable autonomy and discretion to administer their dioceses the way they want to, as long as it is not contrary to the universal beliefs and teachings of the Church.

The bishop's right to govern gives a bishop both the power and authority to govern his diocese and to impose particular legislation on his own diocese without much external interference or oversight. Many bishops carefully guard their own autonomy. Although there are national organizations of bishops, including the United States Conference of Catholic Bishops (USCCB), these entities are much like a trade organization in that they do not have coercive power or the power of governance to force diocesan bishops to act.[5] In some of the early debates regarding imposing national sexual abuse norms on the country, some bishops resisted because they did believe it was appropriate to tell other bishops how to run their own dioceses.[6] Though bishops are bound to follow canon law, there is no real way for the Vatican to monitor enforcement, particularly when there are over three thousand diocesan bishops worldwide.

1. John Jay College, Report to U.S. Conference of Catholic Bishops, The Causes and Context of Sexual Abuse of Minors by Catholic Priests in the United States, 1950–2010, at 4 (May 2011) (hereinafter "John Jay College Report").

2. Id. at 76. "Bishops who were not in position in the late 1990s were far more likely to acknowledge that the earlier diocesan protective focus on the priest-abuser eclipsed the most serious dimension of clergy abuse: harm done to the victim. The failure to recognize the harm of physical or sexual abuse was not atypical in American society generally in the late 1970s and 1980s; this was a time when the understanding of the rights of women and children was just developing."

3. Canon 391 (hereinafter "c. 391").

4. C. 376.

5. It will be interesting over the next few years to see if this is going to change. Pope Francis seems to be indicating that he would like national bishops' conferences to exercise more local control and decision-making. If this desire becomes policy, there may be a local option for bishops to collectively exercise authority over another bishop's diocese.

6. Peter Steinfels, "The Church's Sexual Abuse Crisis," Commonweal 15 (Apr. 2002).

A bishop ultimately is answerable to the pope for his actions. However, a bishop is only summoned to Rome once every five years to make a personal report to the pope regarding the state of his diocese.[7] With very few exceptions, individual bishops have no other oversight concerning what happens within their own dioceses.[8]

It is a common but erroneous belief that in the Catholic hierarchy, a bishop works for an archbishop or cardinal. Thus it is often thought that an archbishop has some level of control over the bishops and their dioceses (known as suffragan[9] dioceses) that fall within his region. While a metropolitan archbishop has very specific circumstances under which he can exercise some authority over his suffragan dioceses[10] (for example, a suffragan bishop starts acting erratically or teaching false doctrine, or is engaging in behavior that is significantly out of the ordinary or causing scandal), these circumstances are very rare. As a result, bishops wield an extraordinary amount of both power and discretion, which can lead to serious problems if that power and discretion is misused.

20:4 BISHOP ACCOUNTABILITY

One of the frustrations most commonly voiced by laypersons involved in dealing with this scandal is the issue of bishop accountability.[11] They point out that while the Church is making considerable strides in dealing with clergy sexual abuse cases, the one issue not addressed is holding bishops accountable for their response to this crisis. The Church is dedicated to cleaning up the problem of priests and deacons sexually abusing minors. However, in the years since their meeting in Dallas in 2002, in the United States the Holy See has not imposed any other means of accountability on bishops outside of specific Vatican hierarchical oversight.[12]

While some in the United States question why there is not a more localized way to hold bishops accountable, the Holy See has both historical and theological reasons to explain this decision. There has been well over a thousand years of history where bishops have resisted the imposition of any control or accountability from outside Church structures.[13] The Church historically has constantly had to struggle

---

7. C. 399. This is called a quinquennial report.

8. John Jay College Report, supra, 85. Because of this structure, the JJR/11 posited that in the 1990s, there was not widespread adoption of the suggested norms published by the NCCB because "In a distributed authority structure of dioceses where bishops are autonomous and answer only to the Pope, no assigned resonant authority was in place to articulate an innovation decision that would conclusively resolve the questions of response to sexual abuse by priests."

9. "Suffragan" is as opposed to a "metropolitan." A suffragan diocese is a diocese that is not an archdiocese. The archbishop is referred to as the metropolitan bishop, and those other bishops in his territory are known as suffragan bishops.

10. Cc. 435–436.

11. Symbolic of these views is www.bishopaccountability.org.

12. See *Sacramentorum sanctitatis tutela* Art. 2 § 2.

13. The conflict between the archbishop of Canterbury, Thomas Becket, and Henry II of England that resulted in Becket's death in Canterbury Cathedral in 1170 is a good illustration of this tension.

to maintain its independence in the face of outside pressure. These historical struggles, and the global struggles to maintain autonomy in an international context, are realities that are likely not going to be sacrificed for any one particular cause, regardless of how just that cause may be. For the Church writ large, it is believed that the greater good is for it to retain as much autonomy to independently function as possible, and to resist any sort of oversight by either civil authorities or an internal, non-episcopal body.

Even in the wake of the abuse scandal, given this long history of trying to guard and protect its autonomy, it is unlikely that the Holy See would create a circumstance where a bishop was forced to be canonically accountable to anyone other than another bishop. There is certainly no evidence that there will be a shift in that direction in the future, despite the numerous calls from various laypersons and groups for more accountability and transparency. In dealing with this scandal, it is evident that bishops, clergy, and laypersons are going to need to find creative ways to address these issues given that it is unlikely for there to be a formal change in the institutional structure.

20:5 AN ALTERNATE APPROACH TO LAW

The status of a Catholic bishop has been and continues to be extraordinary. The theology and law of the Church supports some of this deference, given that bishops are held to be the successors of the apostles.[14] As apostolic successors, bishops have a privileged place within Catholic society and often in the greater civil society as well.[15] Because of this privilege, Catholic bishops in the United States have been able to wield considerable amounts of power and influence both temporally and within the Church. Many bishops traditionally have expected and received extraordinary amounts of deference in both civil and Church realms, particularly in cities with large Catholic populations. Traditionally many Catholic priests have also experienced a considerable level of public deference, though to a lesser extent than bishops.[16] This deference, coupled with a lack of desire to prosecute clerics or to embarrass the Church, often motivated civil authorities to look the other way when bishops and priests violated the civil law.

It has not been uncommon in some communities for priests to be warned instead of ticketed for traffic infractions, and for priests who were intoxicated to be escorted home rather than arrested. More serious legal violations were often treated by civil officials as internal Church problems that were reported to the local bishop, not to local law enforcement.[17] Few prosecutors wanted to prosecute Catholic clergy. This unofficial civil legal protection given to clergy over the years

---

14. C. 375
15. John Jay College Report, supra, 92.
16. Francis G. Morrisey, "Addressing the Issue of Clergy Sexual Abuse," 35 Studia Canonica 406 (2001).
17. Boston Globe, Betrayal: The Crisis in the Catholic Church 8 (2002)/

cultivated in many bishops and priests a general ignorance or disregard for the civil law, as well as the belief that they themselves were not bound to comply with certain parts of it.[18]

This selective enforcement of legal precepts and norms also extended into the canonical realm. Though there are exceptions, some bishops and priests have a long-standing tradition of ignoring canon law if it proves troublesome or inconvenient, often to the chagrin of their canonists. Particularly after the Second Vatican Council, canon law often was viewed as being too rigid, too legalistic, and not pastoral in its application. Many of the changes to the 1983 Code of Canon Law reflected the view that the law needed to be less punitive and coercive. Violations of the law were seen as being sins that needed to be forgiven rather than canonical crimes that deserved punishment. This was in keeping with what was seen as new and more pastoral developments in response to Vatican II.

Rather than using the legal tools provided in the Code for canonical precepts[19] (official warnings that threaten more serious punishment if violated), or for conducting canonical trials, bishops often chose to follow less legalistic options when it came to disciplining wayward priests. Even serious transgressions of legal and moral norms were dealt with in an internal forum within the sacrament of penance rather than externally with warnings, trials, and penalties. Again, this was in response to a belief that the law previously had been overly punitive. Although this approach may have been suitable for dealing with less harmful offenses,[20] in hindsight it was not the appropriate way to handle allegations of the sexual abuse of minors, particularly when there was a pattern of evidence that the cleric would likely reoffend.

20:6 AMBIVALENCE REGARDING LAY PEOPLE

There is among some bishops, as well as among some clergy, a real ambivalence when it comes to laypersons. Bishops and clergy encounter laypersons all the time in various roles and capacities. But there is a sense among much of the Catholic clergy that only clerics can understand the lives and struggles of clerics. When this sensibility is coupled with the theologically, canonically, and liturgically enshrined distinctions between the clergy and the laity, this can lead to a very real sense

18. National Review Board for the Protection of Children and Young People, A Report on the Crisis in the Catholic Church in the United States 46. (United States Conference of Catholic Bishops 2004).

19. C. 1319. A canonical precept is an "individual decree by which a direct and legitimate injunction is placed upon a determined person to do or to omit something, especially concerning the urging of the observance of a law." A penal precept is "a precept that threatens to impose a penalty." John M. Huels, The Pastoral Companion 406–407 (1995).

20. For example, c. 1392 prevents a cleric from engaging in trade or business. A penitential solution for a priest engaging in a side business might be more appropriate than penalties, depending on the type of commerce.

that the clergy belong to a special group that does not admit outsiders into its closed ranks. It is this sense, along with a historical and theological foundation for clerical authority that keeps the exercise of authority in the Catholic Church clergy-centered.

Much has been written on clericalism and its effect on the governance of the Catholic Church.[21] The causes for it are theological, cultural, and to some extent, practical. Historically, the role of laypersons in the Church became mostly limited to "praying, paying, and obeying." While Vatican II and its subsequent reforms have allowed laypersons much greater access and influence, these reforms still have not fully been worked out on the practical level. Particularly when it comes to Church governance, most bishops are exceedingly reluctant to cede any control or authority to laypersons, or to be accountable to laypersons for their actions.[22] Catholic theology and canon law that defines the role of the bishop supports this reluctance, and provides only very limited instances where non-bishops can check the power of a bishop.[23]

Prior to Vatican II, laypersons were often treated as children within Church structures, with the clergy taking the role of spiritual parents. This role was oftentimes appropriate, given that the general population lacked access to theological, scriptural, and canonical educations. However, the reforms of Vatican II have allowed for a maturing process among laypersons in the Church. More than ever before laypersons are getting trained in the areas of theology, scripture, pastoral work, and canon law. The maturing process is a result of a move within the Catholic Church for greater lay participation and engagement, though this move has often been fueled by an acute need for personnel, which is created by a shortage of clerics and women religious,[24] to fill parish and other Church positions.

Yet, given the time it takes for any new idea in the Church to be fully embraced and implemented, laypersons in the Church are at a point where they are regarded by clerics in a manner somewhat like inconvenient adolescents. Adolescents are oftentimes mouthy, opinionated, demanding, awkward, unpredictable, and notoriously hard to control. The Church leadership is profoundly ambivalent on embracing an expanded and more "adult" role for the laity, because it is concerned that these expanded roles infringe on those roles and responsibilities traditionally exercised by clergy. Like parents of adolescents, Church leaders seem not quite sure which would be preferable: regarding laypersons as those who should not be given too much responsibility or independence, or encouraging them to "grow up," though this often results in all the associated growing pains. This is an ongoing tension that has manifested in a number of ways throughout this scandal, particularly when it comes

21. See e.g., George Wilson, Clericalism: The Death of Priesthood (2008).

22. Though there are certain parish and diocesan committees that have laypersons on them, except in very prescribed circumstances these roles are advisory only.

23. E.g., c. 1292 regarding the sale of property is one of the few times where a diocesan bishop needs the consent of his diocesan finance council (with laypersons on the council) and his college of consultors (which consists of priests) before he can sell property.

24. Women religious are sisters or nuns, for example the Dominicans, Franciscans, Benedictines, etc.

to putting laypersons in roles (e.g., canonical judges, review boards) that have the potential to monitor, discipline, or control bishops and clergy.

Along the same lines, there is also the issue that, practically speaking, bishops cannot exercise the same control over laypersons as they can over their clergy. This is increasingly evident among laypersons who are well educated and well-informed in theology and other Church matters. A priest makes a promise of obedience to his bishop when he is ordained. If a priest of the diocese speaks out of turn, or he acts out, or he publishes something the bishop disapproves of, the bishop has considerable power to act. The bishop has the power to move him to another location, to silence him under obedience, and ultimately to remove him from the priesthood altogether. Bishops, as a practical matter, do not have this power over the laity. With the Internet and social media flourishing, it is increasingly difficult for a bishop to wield any coercive authority over laypersons, with the possible exception of a lay teacher or theologian teaching in a Catholic educational institution.

It is practically impossible for a layperson to be silenced. This has been seen repeatedly in the publication of various critical articles written and public opinions voiced by lay members of review boards and victims' coordinators, and by lay Catholics involved in the civil aspects of this process.[25] This lack of coercive power can make bishops a bit wary when dealing with laypersons because it is not an interaction they can control.

20:7 RESULTING FRUSTRATIONS

The lack of general education regarding the laws of the Church is a manifestation of this ambivalence. While bishops increasingly are sending laypersons to school to become canonists for the Church, there does not seem to be much widespread effort on the part of bishops and priests to educate untrained laypersons in the various aspects of Church law. While many parishes offer series of classes on the Catechism, relatively little time is spent on helping laypersons to understand the laws of the Church and how the law broadly affects decisions that are made by their priests and bishops. This may be somewhat shortsighted because it affects the way the Church's internal processes are perceived.

In published grand jury reports and various articles written by well-educated laypersons involved in this process, there is a common frustration voiced when a perceived roadblock to justice is thrown up by various Church authorities, and justified by the rationale "that's a requirement of canon law."[26] It is evident in

25. For example, see the article written by the chairperson of Philadelphia's Diocesan Review Board. (Ana Maria Catanzano, "The Fog of Scandal: The Chair of the Philadelphia Review Board Speaks," Commonwealmagazine.org. (May 12, 2011), http://commonweal magazine.org/fog-scandal-1.

26. An example of this is in the Grand Jury Report in the First Judicial District of Pennsylvania, released January 21, 2011. There was a dialogue between the Philadelphia district attorney and the diocese's victim's assistance coordinator, where the coordinator explains why she seemed to change her mind about a recommendation she had given

these reports and articles that there has been few attempts at an explanation, few attempts to educate, and no serious attempt on a large scale to bring the uninitiated into a fuller knowledge of the Church's legal system.[27]

This leaves those same laypersons, who are also district attorneys, judges, victim assistance coordinators, review board members, etc., wondering how the Church and its law can be so unfair and unjust.[28] If the Church through its bishops, administrators, and priests was more educative about how the internal processes work, and what rights the various people have in those processes, much confusion and despair could be avoided.

Even if canon law is being strictly followed, it is not enough that justice is being done. It is important for all involved—the victims, the accused, those outside the process but somehow affected by it, and the general public—to see and believe that justice is being done. So far this is not a widespread perception, and each new revelation of a diocese's recalcitrance makes that public perception of injustice worse.

20:8 ISOLATION AT THE TOP

Although being a bishop carries with it some prestige, it can also be a very isolating experience for the individual.[29] Bishops no longer have parishes with which they are closely connected on a day-to-day basis. Though they technically have charge of their cathedral, in reality it is run by the cathedral's rector because a bishop is constantly governing and traveling around his diocese. It is hard for a bishop to maintain close friendships with his priests because he wants to avoid favoritism. The bishop may not know anyone in his diocese if he is not originally from the diocese.[30] His close contacts may be with family or friends from outside his diocese, or with those he works closest with within the chancery.

As with anyone in a position of authority, this can lead to the bishop having few reliable outside sources of information. Bishops do not get "word on the street"

previously to the diocese. She states, "When I got to the Archdiocese, what I found was there's this whole canon law thing that I knew nothing about. ... I mean there has to be a process." With no further attempt to explain the process or what it entailed, the district attorney concludes, "Ms. Achilles did not explain how the existence of canonical procedures justified her acquiescence to a process that harms victims and obscures the truth." Report of the Grand Jury, MISC. NO. 0009901-2008 (Court of Common Pleas, First Judicial District of Pennsylvania, Philadelphia January 21, 2011), at 86.

27. There have been some noted exceptions to this. For example, the archdiocese of Milwaukee produced a number of very good pamphlets that explain the whole process in language meant for non-canonists to understand.

28. Report of the Grand Jury, supra, 26.

29. John Jay College Report, supra, 93. Though the section in the report is about the isolation experienced by priests, it is not a stretch to also apply these same conditions to bishops, who are oftentimes even more personally isolated than their priests.

30. Sometimes a bishop is transferred to an entirely different part of the country, for example, Archbishop Charles Chaput, whose ministry as a bishop first was exercised in the diocese of Rapid City, North Dakota, and then in the archdiocese of Denver, before he was transferred to be archbishop of Philadelphia.

information from a wife or child because the bishops are unmarried. Priests are oftentimes reticent about conveying bad or troubling news to the bishop because he is their superior. And as clergy-culture in general can be isolating and self-referent, relying on other priests for the "word on the street" is at best unreliable. Traditionally there are oftentimes few lay members of the diocese who are comfortable being friends with the bishop, particularly in dioceses with high levels of clerical deference. This lack of regular friendships with laypersons within the diocese narrows the possibilities for a bishop to "hear it like it is" from outside his normal clerical sources, or in fact to find trusted laypersons to whom he is willing to listen.

It is very important to note that this isolation is usually not self-imposed. The overwhelming number of bishops want to know about the problems and issues in their dioceses. The difficulty is finding trustworthy people who will tell the bishop what he needs to know rather than what they think he wants to hear. If bishops are then somewhat limited to getting their information primarily from other bishops, diocesan lawyers, or people with particular agendas, this isolation can have disastrous consequences.

This isolationism is manifested clearly in the incongruity between the laity's reaction to accusations of sexual abuse and bishops' response. While the laity's reaction has been one of horror, grief, and outrage, it was clear that many bishops did not react with that same passion about these crimes. In many ways, it appeared that the bishops simply did not know how to respond.[31] Their response in some cases seemed remarkably distant, clinical, and detached, which seemed all the more disconcerting because the victims were children.

The National Review Board made it quite clear in their report that for many bishops, it was only after they actually talked to the victims of sexual abuse that they were able to understand its horrors and effects.[32] The bishops were often so removed from the experience of regularly being around children and families that they treated the problem as another administrative personnel difficulty to be dealt with. In seeing many of the bishops' initial reactions, it was not apparent to the general public that bishops realized that these were real victims, real children involved.

20:9 ANTI-CATHOLICISM?

There have always been some elements of anti-Catholicism within the greater American society, as well as in other countries. Bishops are keenly aware of the presence of these sentiments. Because they are real, they often start to look for it in the face of any public criticism of the Church. There is a sense among some in the Catholic hierarchy that there are people and institutions "out to get us" by trying to embarrass, discredit, or harm the Church. The secular press is often viewed with

31. John Jay College Report, supra, 76.
32. National Review Board for the Protection of Children and Young People, supra, sec. IV B 2.

skepticism, if not outright suspicion and hostility. The initial reaction to criticism of the Church is for some bishops to cry foul, to claim anti-Catholic bias, and to blame a host of other motivations for any bad publicity the Church receives.

Unfortunately, in rigorously defending the Church against all criticism, many bishops have sometimes failed to consider whether the criticism might be true, or have some elements of truth to it. Furthermore, because of their isolation they may not have any other source to corroborate that there is in fact a serious problem that needs immediate attention. Much of the publicity regarding the Church's most egregious sexual abuse cases had initially been called "false" and "anti-Catholic," only later to be discovered that the reports were in fact true.[33] The extent of the problem in many major dioceses would not have come to light without the efforts of the secular press and the civil justice system soldiering on in the face of claims that this was all a result of anti-Catholic bias and persecution.[34] Ironically, many of those who were investigating the most vigorously are themselves Roman Catholics. Both the isolation of bishops and the tendency to discount accusations against the Church as "anti-Catholic bias" has led to some bishops not giving real problems, such as sexual abuse, appropriate attention.

20:10 SECRECY AND THE AVOIDANCE OF SCANDAL

Avoidance of scandal is an important value in the Code of Canon Law. The avoidance of scandal or the causing of scandal is mentioned in 24 different canons of the Code. Undoubtedly, this is something that the Catholic Church takes very seriously. However, though there is a colloquial definition of scandal, it is important to note that in this context, the Code is referring to a canonical/theological definition of scandal, which according to section 2284 of the Catechism of the Catholic Church is:

> An attitude or behavior which leads another to do evil. The person who gives scandal becomes his neighbor's tempter. He damages virtue and integrity; he may even draw his brother into spiritual death. Scandal is a grave offense if by deed or omission another is deliberately led into a grave offense.

This definition is quite different than simply trying to avoid an action or event that creates moral outrage to the community. It also highlights one of the supreme ironies in this situation. By actively attempting to suppress the community's knowledge about abuser priests, these decisions actually led directly to the creation of true scandal: engaging in a behavior that allowed abuser priests free rein to do evil. Its direct result clearly damaged virtue and innocence as well as the integrity of the entire institution, and was a source of spiritual death to those children who were victims of the abuse and their families. It is a classic case of scandal.

33. Morrisey, supra, 404.
34. Boston Globe, supra.

Clearly, secrecy and confidentiality in institutions, and institutions such as the Church, has its place. For example, it is well known that within the Catholic sacrament of penance, what is said under the seal of confession is inviolate. A priest will go to jail rather than reveal the highly confidential content of a confession. Another example is that each diocese is required to have a secret archive, which is a locked file cabinet or room that contains sensitive materials.[35] The bishop directly controls who has access to those files so that they are not able to be accessed by unauthorized office staff. Canonical trials, including marriage nullity cases, are subject to secrecy lest a person's reputation be unnecessarily tarnished, confidential information be revealed, or witness testimony tainted. In addition, part of avoiding scandal can legitimately be preventing those things that could cause scandal from being known to the greater community. But in preventing scandal one must ensure that things that are kept confidential are being kept confidential for the right reasons, and that one does not actually cause greater scandal by keeping information confidential.

In the context of the sexual abuse of minors, the desire for secrecy and confidentiality was heavily weighted toward the protection of the priest's good name. In the most egregious cases, bishops risked the safety of children so as to not tarnish the priest's reputation. In some cases, priests who had abused multiple times were quietly sent to treatment centers, then repeatedly transferred to new parishes or schools without any warning to the parishioners. Parishioners were not fully informed of the reason if their priest was suspended and/or sent to treatment. Priests were transferred to other dioceses without telling the receiving bishop about the priest's known and documented proclivities. In these cases, the desire to protect the reputation of the priest and give him a "fresh start" was given priority over protecting children from priests who the diocese knew were repeat offenders.[36] Though these actions obviously are not representative of every bishop or every diocese, those bishops that did act in this fashion helped create a profound crisis of trust in the Church's hierarchy and actually caused the scandal that they had attempted to prevent.

20:11 CONSEQUENCES FOR ABUSE VICTIMS

Victims were necessarily involved in the Church's attempts to prevent scandal, though their participation was not always voluntary. When it was voluntary, victims oftentimes requested confidentiality because they did not want the publicity and embarrassment associated with a public accusation of abuse.[37] Although this was often the case, it was just as often that victims were coerced into silence. Victims frequently were forced to sign confidentiality agreements if they settled a

---

35. Canons 489–490. Calling it the "secret archive" (based on its Latin translation) in American culture sounds like one needs the secret codes and password to have access. In the United States it would be more accurate and less inflammatory to call it the diocesan confidential files.

36. John Jay College Report, supra, 89.

37. Id. at 76.

case out of court. They were often told not to tell anyone, including the civil authorities, about their accusations. There was at least one instance of a victim reporting his abuse directly to a cardinal, only to find himself unexpectedly "bound by the power of the confessional never to speak about this again to anyone else" by this same cardinal.[38] Rather than being encouraged to report to civil authorities, victims were often told there would be repercussions if they did report. Even other priests who reported to bishops that their colleagues were engaging in unlawful behavior were sometimes reprimanded.[39]

There is no question that protecting a person's reputation is important. And certainly priests accused of the sexual abuse of minors should have their reputations protected as much as possible until it can be ascertained that the accusation has a semblance of truth to it. This is especially true given that in today's climate even the accusation of sexual abuse can end a priest's career, even if the claim is later proven to be false. However, what many laypersons find hard to understand is how in the name of preventing scandal some bishops who knew a particular priest was a repeat offender allowed that person multiple "second chances," particularly when these second chances clearly put innocent and vulnerable children at risk.

20:12 THE ROLE OF THE DIOCESAN CIVIL LAWYER

One development that has occurred over the past 30 years has been bishops' increasing dependence on diocesan civil lawyers' advice regarding how they should respond to allegations that one of their priests has committed sexual abuse. This advice has been geared to protect the Church and its assets, while avoiding any admission of guilt that could lead to possible civil and criminal lawsuits.[40] Diocesan lawyers are often consulted as soon as the diocese receives an accusation, and remain a part of the diocese's response team as long as the accusation is being civilly investigated and/or adjudicated.

It can certainly be assumed that the diocesan lawyers are only trying to do their job to protect what they perceive as their client's best interests. However, to state the obvious, the lawyers' priorities should not necessarily be those of the bishop. Civil law business clients have interests that may lead them to act independently of the advice of their counsel, for example in recalling a product that proves to have been poorly designed and is known to cause harm to people. In reviewing diocesan responses to claims of abuse, it appears that bishops have not often deviated from utilizing rigid legal defensive approaches.[41] More often than not they have chosen this route over a

---

38. John Allen, "Will Ratzinger's Past Trump Benedict's Present?," Nat'l Cath. Rptr. Online (Mar. 17, 2010), http://ncronline.org/news/accountability/will-ratzingers-past-trump-benedicts-present.

39. John Jay College Report, supra, 90.

40. See Chapter 4, sec. 4:11 for earlier treatment of the role of the diocesan civil defense lawyer.

41. John Jay College Report, supra, 89.

more paternal or fraternal concern for the victims and their aggrieved families once an abuse incident was verified. As the NRB Report points out, "It appears that many dioceses and [religious] orders made disastrous pastoral decisions relying on attorneys who failed to adapt their tactics to account for the unique role and responsibilities of the Church."[42]

As previously noted, Catholics believe that bishops are the successors to the apostles.[43] They are the spiritual leaders of their communities, and are expected to be examples of Christian behavior.[44] They are certainly understood to be the spiritual shepherds and caretakers of all of the people of their diocese. At the very least, they are bound to follow the laws governing the Church.

Canon 128 of the Code binds all Catholics. It states that "Whoever illegitimately inflicts damage upon someone by a juridic act, or by any other act placed intentionally or negligently, is obliged to repair the damage inflicted." Canon law requires that one is bound by the law to repair any harm inflicted on another person by one's illegitimate action. Certainly in cases where a person's victimization has been documented, one would expect that a bishop's response would be in keeping with scriptural mandates and canon law, and that he would not by his subsequent actions contribute to further that infliction of harm.

But this has not always been the response. This scandal has put bishops in the position of oftentimes feeling that they must choose between responses that can either be pastoral or financial but not both. Unfortunately, these positions generally are mutually exclusive.

Pastorally, a bishop could get personally involved, have contact with victims, apologize for his actions or those of the guilty cleric, or make some other personal response or gesture indicating remorse or contrition on the part of the Church for the pain that the person has suffered. For an analogy to another culture, recall photos of the management of a Japanese power company as they bowed deeply to apologize to the families harmed by escaping power plant radiation.

Yet financially, for fear of harsher financial consequences in future possible jury trials, bishops are often advised by their defense lawyers to not meet with victims. Bishops have been told not to personally apologize because this can be construed as a legal admission of guilt and may become the basis for liability in a civil court. Furthermore, they have been advised to detach themselves from the entire abuse investigation process as much as possible, and to leave interaction with victims to others. For different reasons, this ironically was likely the advice of the canon lawyers as well. As head of the diocesan judiciary, meeting with victims might affect the bishop's objectivity if he was required to judge the accused priest in a canonical process.[45]

42. National Review Board for the Protection of Children and Young People, supra, sec. IV B 6.

43. C. 375.

44. C. 387.

45. It will be dealt with in a more in-depth fashion in subsequent chapters, but this is certainly one of the incongruous outcomes of following canon law that clearly indicates that the law was not set up to judge these kinds of complicated cases. There is no good

One can see the inherent conflict between these responses. While there have been some bishops that have ignored their civil lawyers' advice, the response of most bishops in the United States reflects more reliance on the advice of their civil lawyers. The John Jay Report confirms that part of what has exacerbated this issue is that "Diocesan leaders failed to understand the importance of direct contact with victims, thereby giving the impression that they felt no personal responsibility for the harm sustained by victims."[46] By choosing not to meet with victims, they gave the impression that they did not care about them or the trauma that they suffered.

Time after time, victims and their families have come forward, saying to the news media that all they want from the diocese is an apology and an assurance that the priest will no longer be in a position to hurt children.[47] A formal and sincere apology on the part of the diocesan bishop may have lessened some of the victims' anger, and helped in their process of healing. But at least in the past, this did not seem to be the method used, based on the advice of the lawyers.

This begs the question: Had bishops from the start risked financial exposure and reacted to abuse victims in a more pastoral fashion, might they have actually achieved both goals? Had bishops reacted by apologizing to victims and using the canonical means at hand to remove offenders from ministry, would this ultimately have resulted in fewer civil lawsuits? Should the protection of diocesan assets outweigh a response more in keeping with gospel values? Though most bishops in the United States will never know the answer, for other countries just beginning to deal with this problem, it is certainly worth considering.

Instead, those who have felt their allegations dismissed or ignored by the diocese often feel forced into filing lawsuits as a last resort. Victims frequently have stated that the only way to get the bishop and the diocese's attention was via a civil lawsuit with the potential for large damage awards. Over the course of the late 1980s through the 1990s, the John Jay Report stated that "Victims were frustrated and confused by the delays and lack of response on the part of the diocese. Civil litigation by victims became more common after the mid-1980s, and such legal action further complicated the diocesan response to victims."[48] Many victims hoped that these cases would create a deterrence effect of prior bad conduct and perhaps corrective measures inside the diocese.

20:13 A CHANGING CULTURE

There are certainly aspects of episcopal culture that is changing or has changed in response to this problem. Bishops are much more aware of the effects of the sexual abuse of minors and of the profound harm caused when the perpetrator is a

---

way for a bishop to avoid a conflict of interest in the case because his role as shepherd conflicts with his role as judge.

46. John Jay College Report, supra, 89.
47. Boston Globe, supra, 81.
48. John Jay College Report, supra, 89.

cleric. The USCCB has resources, offices, and personnel dedicated to raising awareness and prevention. Dioceses have seminars for the ongoing education of clergy. Most dioceses have instituted policies requiring everyone—priests, employees, even parent-volunteers who work with children and young people—to go through awareness training through a nationally recognized program. Almost all dioceses have information about sexual abuse on their diocesan websites. There are hotlines on diocesan websites to report such crimes, and people are encouraged to report suspected crimes to the authorities. These are certainly all changes for the better.

Unfortunately, in many cases the damage is done and it will take a very long time to undo it. Bishops used to be given the benefit of the doubt; now it is much more likely for one to assume bad intentions. Priests were trusted to be around children; now they are often viewed with suspicion. There is certainly a general lack of trust of the Church's leadership that has been building over the past 30 years, and a cynicism about whether the institution can change or has changed. It has also resulted in a climate that when a priest is accused it is assumed that he is certainly guilty, even before the facts are known. And the reputation of the Church at large has taken an incalculable blow—all one must do is to read the "comments" following online stories about the Church to see what this scandal has done to the Church's reputation and credibility. It is going to take a very long time and a lot of work before the harm caused not only to specific victims, but to the Church at large, can be remedied and trust can be restored.

CHAPTER 21

༄

The Development of the Problem: 1950 to 2002

21:1 INTRODUCTION

The crisis of clergy sexual abuse in the United States did not develop overnight. Rather, it developed over a number of decades during the latter part of the twentieth century. Though abuse cases started to gain notoriety in the early 1980s, the numbers of reported abuse cases first began to rise in the 1950s. The subsequent decades coincided with a number of civil and ecclesiastical upheavals, and not surprisingly, the incidences of abuse spiked during that time.

The 30-year era where the most abuse occurred was from 1950 to 1980. Ironically, in the 1980s at the start of a measurable drop in actual incidents of clergy sexual abuse, public recognition of the problem and public outcry regarding the handling of those cases began. So in the United States, while the 1950–1980s was characterized by the vast majority of actual abuse cases occurring, 1980-present has been a 30-year process of cleaning up the mess, attempting to learn from past mistakes, creating processes to address those cases that are pending, and implementing programs to prevent further abuse.

According to the John Jay College Report of 2011 (JJR/11), part of the difficulty in addressing the problem has been the time lag between most of the incidents of abuse and these being reported many years later.[1] It was common for victims, particularly the adults, to have great difficulty in obtaining a satisfactory diocesan response to their allegations. Some of the reasons for the inadequate responses were because (1) the majority of the reports of abuse were not current, (2) many of the victims were no longer children at the time of the reporting, (3) the long-term

---

1. John Jay College, Report to U.S. Conference of Catholic Bishops, The Causes and Context of Sexual Abuse of Minors by Catholic Priests in the United States, 1950–2010, at 4 (May 2011) (hereinafter "John Jay College Report").

effects of this crime were not well understood, and, (4) during the early years, dioceses did not have policies about what, if anything, to do to help victims.

By the mid-1990s, however, the National Conference of Catholic Bishops (NCCB) and individual bishops were well aware of the problem of clergy sexual abuse of minors. By the late 1990s, many bishops believed that the problem had been adequately dealt with, that their awareness had been sufficiently raised, and that they had done what was needed to remedy the problem. They were obviously mistaken.

This chapter gives an overview of the timeline between the 1950s when the numbers of documented abuse cases began to grow, and the watershed year of 2002 when this issue became the subject of national and international news and scrutiny.

21:2 THE LEARNING CURVE AND THE STANDARD OF JUDGMENT

One of most difficult aspects to remember when discussing responses to the sexual abuse of minors by clerics is that in looking at this timeline, one must evaluate administrative responses to accusations of sexual abuse by the standards and knowledge of the time. It is important to know what was known, and when it was known—not only about the abuse itself but also what was considered the appropriate way to deal with it within the greater society. Responses to accusations of child sexual abuse have been steadily evolving over the past 40 years. Clearly there were responses to accusations of child sexual abuse that, even taking the norms of that day into account, were egregious and woefully inadequate, and seemed to defy common sense. Some responses were likely criminal.

Nevertheless there were many bishops who tried in good faith to remedy the problems in their dioceses based on what they knew about sexual abuse and abusers, on how society viewed the problem, and on the recommendations of psychiatric and psychological experts on how to remedy or even cure the problem. It is for this reason that some dioceses seem to have emerged from this crisis relatively unscathed, while others have suffered not only financial bankruptcy, but a moral crisis of confidence and diminished faith in the institution.

21:3 THE YEARS PRIOR TO THE 1960S

In the decades prior to 1980, the sexual abuse of children was not an issue that was commonly or publicly discussed, either in the Church or in the greater society. Children were not encouraged to report abuse, and even if they did report they were often not believed. Catholics were taught that under no circumstances was a person to bring scandal to the Church, and certainly accusing a priest of sexual abuse was considered to bring scandal. In general, American civil society did not see sexual abuse as being a pressing issue. Furthermore, it was not an issue that either the police or prosecutors wanted to deal with, particularly as this issue was generally considered a family matter, or in the case of the Church, a matter to be handled internally.

Administrators within the Church certainly knew that sexual abuse of minors was an ongoing problem. This crime has been addressed in Church law since the earliest days, and was a specific crime in the Code of Canon Law (1917) governing the Church at the time. Bishops knew that the problem of priests who sexually abused children existed. However, they did not know the extent of the problem, and would not have known its prevalence beyond the confines of their own diocese. Sexual abuse of minors was not a subject that was discussed formally by the bishops and there was very little published about the subject before 1985.

In the 1950s, there was little or no discussion regarding the sexual abuse of minors. The National Review Board in its Report (NRB Report) indicated in its findings that "In the 1950s and early 1960s, many Church leaders viewed sexual abuse as a moral lapse only and did not understand the psychological causes and consequences of such conduct."[2] If the bishop did not believe that the priest's conduct warranted canonical dismissal, oftentimes abusive priests were sent on spiritual retreats in an attempt to rehabilitate them. Many bishops simply did not know what to do with their repeat offenders, despite the fact that the behavior was criminalized within the law at the time. The lack of understanding did not begin to change until the early 1980s.

It was during the late 1950s that within the Church a new model began to emerge about what to do with problematic clergy. It was thought among Church circles that there needed to be places where clergy and religious with problems such as alcohol abuse, drug addiction, depression, and other mental illnesses could go to be treated where the professional mental health doctors and their staff would understand the special situations of priests and members of religious institutes.[3] In the 1950s, both individuals and religious orders started to open these specialized facilities.[4]

21:4 WHAT HAPPENED IN THE 1960S?

At the end of the 1950s, Pope John XXIII called for a council of the Church. What resulted was the Second Vatican Council, known as Vatican II, which lasted from 1962 to 1965. The Council changed and modernized the Catholic Church. It was also at this time that the pope called for a revision of the Code of Canon Law that was in keeping with the values elucidated in Vatican II. That revision of the Code was not promulgated until 1983. As the new Code was in its draft stages, in the 1960s and 1970s American bishops began moving away from a rigid enforcement of canon law. For many, the laws found in the Code of 1917 were seen as being contrary to "the spirit of Vatican II," and too harsh, rigid, and legalistic.

2. Thomas Doyle, A.W.R. Sipe & Patrick Wall, Sex, Priests and Secret Codes: The Catholic Church's 2,000 Year Paper Trail of Sexual Abuse 70–71 (2006).

3. Members of religious institutes are dealt with in Chapter 24. These are groups such as the Benedictines, the Franciscans, the Jesuits, and the Dominicans.

4. John Jay College Report, supra, 76.

Like any significant change, for good or for ill it took many years for the Council's effects to be assimilated. For about two decades after Vatican II the Church was in a time of great change. For all the good that Vatican II did, many of the legal changes it enacted did not assist the bishops in addressing the sexual abuse of minors within the Church. Ironically, in some ways the Council and the subsequently drafted 1983 Code of Canon Law actually limited their options and hindered bishops' ability to adjudicate these cases in a timely fashion. Fundamentally, neither the Council nor the Code envisioned such a crisis, particularly one that would need a rapid, particular, and definitive canonical remedy.

Over the course of the 1960s bishops' handling of the sexual abuse of minors moved from a punitive process to almost exclusively a "pastoral approach"—at least in dealing with accused priests. Because of these new understandings, though the sexual abuse of minors remained a canonical crime, it was increasingly seen as a moral and psychological issue to be treated rather than a delict[5] or canonical crime to be punished. During the 1960s treatment centers whose sole purpose was dealing with priests' and religious' psychological issues, substance abuse issues, and psycho-sexual issues including attraction to minors became more common. It became increasingly the practice for bishops to send priests accused of sexually abusing minors to these centers for evaluation and treatment, often for many months at a time.[6] Historically there has been a connection that often priests accused of clergy sexual abuse also abused alcohol or other substances.[7] At these treatment centers, it was thought that both problems could be addressed and treated. As treatment centers became the norm for dealing with these issues, bishops continued to move further away from using canonical penal law in dealing with sexual abuse crimes.

Unfortunately, as with the general society, there was very little understanding of the kind of psychological and spiritual damage that this behavior inflicted on the victims, so victims were not given or provided pastoral access to counseling or other assistance by the Church.[8]

At the same time as the convening of Vatican II, the Supreme Sacred Congregation of the Holy Office[9] reissued the Instruction entitled *Crimen Sollicitationis* on March 16, 1962. It was an updated version of a similar Instruction of the same name issued in the 1920s, and it had the force of law. Though it dealt specifically with the crime of solicitation within the confessional, it also dealt with other sexual types of clerical crimes such as homosexual sex and pederasty.[10] The document gave competence for the Holy Office to deal with such crimes either administratively or judicially,

5. A delict is a crime, an offense for which a canonical punishment has been established in the law.

6. Doyle et al., supra, 72.

7. John Jay College Report, supra, 45.

8. National Review Board for the Protection of Children and Young People, A Report on the Crisis in the Catholic Church in the United States (sec. IV B 2) (United States Conference of Catholic Bishops 2004).

9. The precursor to the Congregation for the Doctrine of the Faith (CDF).

10. Nicholas Cafardi, Before Dallas: The U.S. Bishops' Response to Clergy Sexual Abuse of Children 7 (2008).

and there was no prescription or statute of limitations for the prosecution of these types of crimes.

Oddly the document was never promulgated in the Vatican's newspaper *Acta Apostolicae Sedis,* the place where canonical legislation primarily is published. Though there were enough copies produced to send one to every diocesan bishop worldwide, they were never distributed unless a bishop specifically asked advice for what to do in a particular case. For those that were distributed, the document instructed that it be placed in the secret archives. In dioceses in the United States, those dioceses with copies filed them in the archive files and most were promptly forgotten. This became increasingly true as dioceses had bishops retiring and new ones being appointed. The new bishops simply were not aware of the document's existence.

In the civil realm, the 1960s was also a time of profound change. It was at that time when state governments started giving attention to the rights and protections of women and children, and this began to be reflected in state legislation. Civil reporting laws started coming into effect at the beginning of the decade, and by 1968 almost every state had such a law. However, this legislation made an exception for clergy as mandatory reporters of abuse.[11]

In 1966 the U.S. bishops formed the National Conference of Catholic Bishops (NCCB) to deal with internal issues, and the United States Catholic Conference (USCC) to deal with external issues within society. These two groups were merged in 2001 to form the United States Conference of Catholic Bishops (USCCB). These organizations gave bishops on the national level the ability to meet as a body and discuss issues important to the Church in the United States. These organizations became increasingly important as bishops corporately determined how to address clergy sexual abuse.

21:5 THE 1970S—THE PEAK OF ABUSE

The 1970s was a time of turmoil within the United States. Civilly the country was coping with Vietnam and the antiwar movement, the implementation of civil rights, the women's movement, and Watergate. Within the Church it was also a time of great change. The Church continued to implement the changes of Vatican II. Many priests were being ordained with the understanding that they would soon be allowed to marry. The NRB Report states that over twenty thousand priests left the priesthood when those changes that they thought were imminent never materialized.

It was during the 1970s that awareness of the issue of child sexual abuse began to be discussed in civic conversations in the United States. State governments had started dealing with the issue in the 1960s, and in 1974, the federal government followed the states and passed a federal reporting law for child sexual abuse. However, like most state laws it exempted clergy as mandatory reporters.[12]

11. Doyle et al., supra, 69.
12. Id.

It was also during the 1970s that the instances of actual abuse of children by priests in the Church were most frequent. The National Review Board reports that:

> The majority of the victims were males between the ages of eleven and seventeen. The number of reported male victims in this age group increased from 353 in the 1950s, to 1,264 in the 1960s, to a peak of 2,129 in the 1970s. The number then decreased to 1,403 in the 1980s and 363 in the 1990s. The number of girls who have been the victims of sexual abuse by priests has varied much less over time. The total number of female victims between eleven and seventeen when the abuse began peaked in the 1960s at 305 and has decreased every decade since then.[13]

During this time, the NCCB commissioned a study known as the Kennedy-Heckler study.[14] It was published in 1972, and it indicated that more than half the priests in the United States were considered psychologically and emotionally "underdeveloped," and 8 percent were "mal-developed." This did not bode well for the mental and psychological health of much of the Catholic clergy of the time. When trouble arose, bishops increasingly began relying on treatment and treatment centers to deal with their abusive, immature, psychologically damaged, or substance-abusing clerics. As the NRB Report stated, "Won over by the promise of therapeutic cures, some bishops failed to recognize the typically compulsive and habitual nature of sexual abuse. This was understandable in the 1960s and 1970s, when even psychologists lacked a genuine understanding of the nature of sexual disorders."[15] Bishops truly believed that these treatment centers could "cure" their clergy, and the treatment centers often gave them clinical support for that belief.

In 1971, the Congregation for the Doctrine of the Faith (CDF) promulgated a new administrative process for the laicization (permanent removal) of priests. The process was to be less of a formal juridical process and more of a "pastoral investigation" to see whether there were sufficient grounds for laicization. In certain cases, the norms allowed for the diocesan bishop rather than the priest himself to petition for laicization in cases where the priest was living a "depraved life" or because of "doctrinal errors," or for other serious reasons. This was particularly useful in cases where the priest refused to petition for laicization voluntarily. In these cases the bishop could compile the case, send it to CDF, and the Congregation could laicize the priest whether he wanted it or not.[16]

It is somewhat ironic that in the midst of this spike in child sexual abuse, it was at the end of that decade that the newly elected Pope John Paul II became concerned about the ease with which priests had been laicized during the 1970s.

---

13. National Review Board for the Protection of Children and Young People, supra, sec. III C 3.

14. Eugene Kennedy & Victor Heckler. The Catholic Priest in the United States: Psychological Investigations (1972).

15. National Review Board for the Protection of Children and Young People 2004, supra, sec. IV B 5.

16. O'Connor, James I., ed. Canon Law Digest. Vol. VII., at 117 (1975).

He was also concerned about the sheer number of priests leaving the priesthood. In 1980, CDF revised the canonical norms for administrative laicization that they had promulgated just nine years before. Instead of making the process easier, this time they made the process much harder, if not impossible. Bishops once again were unable to request an administrative laicization without the cooperation of the priest. This meant that the easiest way to get rid of the priest was to convince or cajole him to file the case himself—though as a practical matter this meant that the diocese often needed to "sweeten the deal" to persuade the priest to consent. Though this change was meant to stem the tide of easy-to-receive laicizations, for the United States this unfortunate change came just when bishops needed these options to laicize sexually abusive clergy.

Why had these cases spiked between the 1950s and the 1970s? Both the JJR/11 and the NRB report indicate that a significant part of the problem was in the lack of screening of perspective seminarians, and their lack of training for their life and work while they were in seminary.

21:6 FAILURE TO SCREEN AND TRAIN SEMINARIANS

During the 1950s–1970s there were a large number of men accepted to seminary and later ordained for ministry who were fundamentally unsuited for priesthood. Many of these immature and unstable priests went on to abuse children. Sadly, this cycle continued until Church leadership began working to solve the problem by identifying and eliminating problematic candidates while they were still in seminary, and well before ordination.

Though the JJR/11 spends considerable time on the failures and shortcomings of seminary training during the latter half of the twentieth century,[17] the NRB Report breaks the issue down into two major problems. First, in choosing candidates to send to seminary training, local dioceses did not screen them properly to weed out those who were either profoundly immature or sexually dysfunctional. Second, while in seminary, seminarians were not adequately prepared for the rigors of priestly life, particularly in preparing for the celibate life of a parish priest.[18]

According to the JJR/11, most of the priest-abusers were ordained between 1950 and 1980. The NRB Report indicates that in the 1950s and 1960s, men were allowed to attend seminary and were being ordained when it was evident to those in the seminary that they were insecure, immature, and sometimes even psychologically disturbed. Despite concerns and even objections being voiced during their seminary years, those men more often than not were subsequently ordained.[19]

17. John Jay College Report, supra, 40–46.
18. National Review Board for the Protection of Children and Young People 2004, supra, sec. IV A 1–2).
19. This was clearly the case with John Geoghan, who had numerous reports in seminary of having problems, but was ordained despite the multiple reports raising concerns.

Why were these men admitted to the seminary in the first place? There are many reasons. The NRB Report posits that bishops presumed that a person who "heard God's call" to priesthood would not be someone with such serious psychological flaws. There was no notion that someone might intentionally subvert the process and try to "play the system," so there were no careful or systematic inquiries about the person's background or fitness for ministry.[20] At that time, candidates for ministry were not given the battery of psychological tests and background checks that are mandatory for today's candidates.

Because virtually every applicant was accepted, there was a large influx of applicants into seminaries in the 1950s.[21] These applicants included ones who applied due to family pressure or other reasons, and not from a sense of vocation. Twenty years later as applications dropped off significantly in the 1970s, there developed the reverse pressure to ordain candidates regardless of their qualifications because there were not enough priests.

Once a man was admitted to seminary, both the JJR/11 and the NRB Report indicate that there was a fundamental lack of preparation of candidates for the life and ministry they were about to adopt. Although there were classes on Spiritual Formation, it was only in the mid-1990s that seminaries began to include in the curriculum courses on "personal formation," to require consultation with formation advisors that were different from spiritual directors,[22] and specifically to deal with the issue of celibacy.[23] Formally dealing with these issues was not a part of seminary curriculum in the 1950s–1970s.

Furthermore, many diocesan priests have said of their own seminary experiences that while their ministry was going to be an active one in a diocese, their seminary training seemed to be in preparation for living a monastic life within a monastic community. Seminarians lived, prayed, and studied in community.[24] This training gave them little preparation or formation for the problems and stresses they would face once in their actual ministerial situation, or for often living alone in a diocesan rectory in towns far distant from other clergy and support systems.[25]

Preparation for priesthood has changed dramatically between the years 1950 and 2000 in response to these problems. Over 70 percent of priests who were accused of abusing children between the years of 1890 to 2002 were ordained between 1950 and 1980.[26] However, after 1985 the numbers of ordained abusers dropped

20. National Review Board for the Protection of Children and Young People, supra, sec. IV A 1.

21. Id.

22. This was a very important change. A spiritual director can also be a confessor, and therefore there is an understanding that the sessions between the seminarian and the spiritual director are private and not discussed with the rector of the seminary. A formation advisor is a member of the seminary staff whose conversations with the seminarian are not private, and therefore if the advisor becomes aware of problems, it is his job to make the rector aware of the problems he's observed.

23. John Jay College Report, supra, 44.

24. Id. at 70.

25. Id. at 115.

26. Id. at 39.

sharply.[27] Besides a much more prominent public awareness of the problem, this drop can be attributed to better and more effective screening of applicants to the priesthood, and positive and practical changes in seminary curriculum.

21:7 THE 1980S

It was during the 1980s that the issue of clerical sexual abuse of minors began to be publicly addressed and confronted both in civil society and within the Church. Though this decade showed a significant drop in the actual number of incidences of abuse, it was also the time that the Church began having to address the public outcry about these crimes and the way diocesan officials handled these cases. The year 1985 was one of two defining ones (the other being 1993) prior to 2002 where considerable public and Church attention was given to the issue.

In 1983, the new Code of Canon Law was promulgated. While it continued to recognize "offenses against the sixth commandment of the Decalogue" as being a canonical crime, it also had the effect of further limiting what bishops were able to do under canon law to punish, remove, or laicize abusive priests. Bishops were finding their options for getting rid of priests rapidly shrinking. First, as discussed above, CDF removed the administrative option for a bishop to laicize a priest without the priest's participation. Now, the new Code added additional limitations on a bishop's ability to penalize and laicize a problem priest in a canonical criminal procedure. This was unfortunate, because soon after the Code's promulgation, the need for bishops in the United States to have an efficient way to laicize priests became acute.

In 1984 the first stories began breaking about clergy sexual abuse and the handling of these cases in Lafayette, Louisiana. The criminal prosecution of Father Gilbert Gauthe was the first high-profile case of a priest accused and convicted of sexually abusing children. He was indicted on 34 separate counts of abuse and ultimately sentenced to 20 years in prison. In prosecuting this case, which was one with multiple victims, the lawyers discovered that the diocese had known about Gauthe's proclivities since the early 1970s, and had sent him to treatment before putting him back into a different parish.[28] Not only did this story make national news, but the father of one of the victims refused to settle quietly and instead sued the diocese. It was this case that effectively gave the general public an awareness of this issue. Suddenly, an issue that had previously been quietly dealt with behind the closed doors of diocesan chanceries became a national front page news story. Bishops across the nation started to worry what the ramifications would be for their own dioceses, particularly after seeing the amount of monetary damages awarded to plaintiffs in these cases.

By 1985, bishops in the United States had all heard about the problem of sexual abuse because of the publicity surrounding the case in Lafayette.[29] In 1985 there

27. National Review Board for the Protection of Children and Young People, supra, sec. III C 6.
28. Cafardi, supra, 10.
29. John Jay College Report, supra, 75.

were three experts, a canonist named Father Thomas Doyle; the lawyer who represented Gilbert Gauthe in the Lafayette case, Ray Mouton; and a psychiatrist, Reverend Dr. Michael Peterson, who drafted a manual regarding suggested methods of handling cases of the sexual abuse of minors.[30] The manual was not commissioned by the NCCB. Limited numbers of copies of this report were distributed at a NCCB meeting in 1985 but were not generally distributed to the membership. It was at that NCCB meeting that the issue of the sexual abuse of minors officially was discussed for the first time in executive session.[31] However, the manual was not on the agenda at the NCCB meeting, there was no formal discussion of it, and the NCCB did not adopt its recommendations. It is after 1985 when Father Peterson mailed a copy of the manual to each bishop in the United States that many in the Catholic community consider that the bishops were put on notice about the breadth and potential severity of the problem.

After 1985, individual bishop's responses to this issue varied wildly. From this time until 2002, there also seemed to be a growing disconnect between the actions and pronouncements of the NCCB as a whole, and the continued actions or inactions taken by some individual bishops.

In some dioceses bishops either ignored the allegations against their priests, or the offending priests were sent to treatment, then quietly reassigned to another parish without the parish being given any sort of warning of the danger.[32] In some dioceses, accused priests were removed from ministering in places with children, but were allowed to continue in such capacities as prison or hospital chaplains, chancery office workers, or chaplains to various religious communities.[33] Bishops believed that it was safe for them to minister as long as they had no ministerial access to children. Some priests were retired; others were voluntarily laicized.

There were bishops who expressed valid concern about permanently laicizing these priests because as a priest of the diocese, the bishop had some control over the priest and an ability to monitor his actions. Once the cleric was laicized, the bishop no longer had any control over him and he was simply let loose in the general population with no oversight.[34] It was the thought of some bishops that as the bishop had responsibility for the priest, that the bishop was responsible for monitoring the priest so that he did not reoffend. Laicization seemed to them like an abdication of their responsibility, both to society and to the offending priest.

As early as 1986 some forward-thinking bishops began crafting diocesan policies for allegations of clergy sexual abuse.[35] However, most dioceses did not start drafting such policies until the 1990s. Other bishops continued their previous practices, which usually consisted of treatment, then reassignment. Many bishops believed that offenders could be cured and rehabilitated, and they based their belief on the professional

---

30. Doyle et al., supra, 99–174.
31. Cafardi, Before Dallas, 49–50.
32. John Jay College Report, supra, 89.
33. Cafardi, supra, 138–139.
34. National Review Board for the Protection of Children and Young People, supra, sec. III G 2.
35. Cafardi, supra, 80.

opinion of psychological experts.[36] It was still not generally understood that pedophilia might be treatable but was not permanently curable.[37] Sometimes these "rehabilitated" priests were sent to parishes with schools. To protect his reputation, parishioners frequently were not told about the previous allegations against the priest.

As the JJR/11 states, while some bishops took proactive, innovative approaches to dealing with the problem, "Other Bishops, often in dioceses where the Catholic Church was highly influential, were slow to recognize the importance of the problem of sexual abuse by priests or to respond to victims. The media often focused on these 'laggards,' further perpetuating the image that the bishops as a group were not responding to the problem of sexual abuse of minors."[38]

In 1987, the National Conference of Catholic Bishops drafted five recommendations for bishops to follow in dealing with clergy sexual abuse. These recommendations were not made public until a NCCB meeting held in June of 1992. At that meeting, the bishops had a day-long executive session meeting on the subject of clergy sexual abuse.[39] In his concluding statement to the NCCB, then president Archbishop Daniel Pilarczyk of Cincinnati reminded the bishops of the uniform recommendations that had been suggested in 1987. The recommendations from 1987, known as *The Five Steps*, were:

1) Respond promptly to all allegations of abuse where there is reasonable belief that abuse has occurred.
2) If such an allegation is supported by sufficient evidence, relieve the alleged offender promptly of his ministerial duties and refer him for appropriate medical evaluation and intervention.
3) Comply with the obligations of civil law as regards reporting of the incident and cooperating with the investigation.
4) Reach out to the victims and their families and communicate sincere commitment to their spiritual and emotional well-being.
5) Within the confines of respect for privacy of the individuals involved, deal as openly as possible with the members of the community.[40]

Though these recommendations were made in a memorandum drafted in 1987 and sent to the bishops, they were not made public. Also in 1987, the general secretary of the United States Catholic Conference (USCC) named their civil general counsel as the spokesperson on this issue. The following year the general counsel produced the first published statement about clergy sexual abuse.[41]

36. Id. at 131.
37. Id. at 132–133.
38. John Jay College Report, supra, 4.
39. Id at. 86.
40. Daniel Pilarczyk, "Statement of Archbishop Pilarczyk, President of the National Conference of Catholic Bishops on the Sexual Abuse of Children." Statements of National Conference of Catholic Bishops and the United States Catholic Conference on the Subject of Sexual Abuse of Children by Priests 1988–1992 (1992).
41. Cafardi, supra, 76.

According to the John Jay College Report, 80 percent of dioceses responded in some way to the five principles.[42] Some bishops went home from the NCCB meeting and did their best to enact these principles within their diocese. Others went back to their home dioceses and "'decided that their colleagues were wrong, that they could proceed with business as usual.' As a result, according to one bishop, 'There were just very bad decisions. I just have to say that it is very clear not every bishop got it.' This foot-dragging was inexcusable and, as we know now, had disastrous consequences."[43]

By the end of the 1980s, bishops were getting increasingly frustrated with their inability to laicize sexually abusive priests. Bishops were choosing not to use the canonical processes available, for reasons that will be discussed in the next chapter. Though individual bishops had been asking the Holy See for a more efficient laicization process, it was in 1989 that the NCCB/USCC began discussing formal ways to come up with canonical legal alternatives for processing penal abuse cases.[44]

21:8 WHAT WAS HAPPENING WITH VICTIMS

While the focus on abusive priests was shifting from a punishment model to a treatment model, often there was very little concomitant attention given to assessing the psychological and material needs of victims. Further, the Church's way of dealing with victims varied diocese to diocese. This was certainly true prior to the NCCB addressing the issue in the early 1990s.

According to the JJR/11, more than 80 percent of all accusations made prior to 1985 were made within a year of the abuse, and overwhelmingly they were made by family members of the young victim. In most cases the victim and/or their families did not want publicity nor did they want to go public about their allegations. Rather, according to the report, the request most commonly made was for the priest to "get help."[45]

Overall, up until the late 1980s or 1990s, victims in general were not treated well by their dioceses. Oftentimes their reports were dismissed or marginalized. Victims were rarely able to meet in person with the bishop, but were usually met by another diocesan official or officials and occasionally the diocesan lawyer.[46] Victims, or their parents if the victim was still a child, often were given a variety of responses, including: that the Church was handling their problem, that the cleric would be appropriately dealt with, that Father was "sick" and needed help, or that he would no longer be in contact with children. Oftentimes the victim or his or her family was pressured not to report this behavior to civil authorities. Some

---

42. John Jay College Report, supra, 86.

43. National Review Board for the Protection of Children and Young People, supra, sec. III D.

44. Cafardi, supra, 64.

45. John Jay College Report, supra, 76.

46. National Review Board for the Protection of Children and Young People, supra, sec. IV B 2.

did not receive any response at all, and the allegation or allegations were ignored completely.[47]

If the person had a civil lawyer, often a financial settlement was reached quietly, though most victims had to agree to a confidentiality clause. Most of the early victims consulted civil lawyers only after their dioceses failed to take care of the problem, or failed even to acknowledge that there was a problem that needed resolving.

Despite assurances to the contrary, after the offending priest completed treatment the priest was often placed in a new parish if the treatment center gave the bishop the go-ahead to return the priest to ministry.[48] Sometimes the bishop actually tried to influence the diagnosis of the therapist based on the bishop's need for a priest, any priest, in a parish.[49] Often the treatment centers gave recommendations regarding monitoring or a recommendation that allowed limited ministry, conditioned upon the cleric having no access to children. Civil court documents indicate that these recommendations were sometimes followed, but in many cases they were not.[50]

In later decades, there would be innovations such as victims' coordinators, diocesan protocols, and reporting hotlines for victims. However, these remedies were generally not available until the 1990s. Because of the difficulties that victims had in dealing with various dioceses, it was at the end of the 1980s, in 1989, that one of the most well-known victims' advocacy groups was formed. SNAP, or the Survivors Network of those Abused by Priests was formed to connect victims and to provide advocacy and support for them. SNAP continues to be active both nationally and internationally.

21:9 THE 1990S

The 1990s, and the early 1990s in particular, was a very active period in the bishop's individual and collective attempts to deal with the sexual abuse crisis. An increasing number of bishops during the early 1990s began drafting diocesan policies regarding allegations of clergy sexual abuse. Cardinal Bernardin of Chicago created a wide-ranging diocesan policy regarding allegations of abuse in response to the revelation that a pastor who had repeated accusations against him had been reassigned to a parish where he continued his pattern of child abuse.[51] The diocesan policy included the first lay review board that was empowered to examine the archdiocese's clergy files.[52] It also enacted as policy that no sexually abusive priest

47. Boston Globe, Betrayal: The Crisis in the Catholic Church 41 (2002).
48. John Jay College Report, supra, 89.
49. Cafardi, supra, 137–138.
50. National Review Board for the Protection of Children and Young People, supra.
51. Chicago Archdiocese, "Chicago Policy regarding Clerical Sexual Misconduct with Minors," 22(16) Origins 273–278 (Oct. 1992).
52. Cafardi, supra, 83.

would be returned to ministry. Cardinal Bernardin sent copies of Chicago's policy to all the U.S. diocesan bishops with the hope that it might be useful within their own diocesan context.[53]

21:10 NCCB-VATICAN DISCUSSIONS

During this time, bishops individually and collectively intensified their efforts to find less cumbersome ways to permanently laicize their abuser priests. During the early 1990s, bishops and dioceses were facing an increasing number of large sexual abuse lawsuits. For example, in 1991 the Servants of the Paraclete's treatment center in Jemez Springs, New Mexico, had the first of 187 lawsuits filed against it because the center had allowed priests admitted to their treatment program to minister in local parishes on weekends. Many of those priests in treatment then sexually abused children in those local parishes.[54] The center was closed in 1994.

This case was closely followed in 1992 with a criminal case in Fall River, Massachusetts, against a former priest, James Porter, who had abused between 50 and 100 children.[55] He had been treated at the same treatment center in Jemez Springs, and committed sexual abuse while he was there.[56] That priest, who had left the priesthood in 1973, was eventually sentenced to 18–20 years in prison.

Bishops became increasingly determined to get the Vatican to change the canonical rules regarding involuntary laicization. In the late 1980s bishops began formally requesting that Rome provide them with a less cumbersome and preferably administrative way to permanently remove priests. Having heard repeatedly about the problems that U.S. bishops were having with clergy sexual abuse, in 1993 Pope John Paul II wrote a letter to the U.S. bishops that recognized this difficulty and informed the bishops of how he believed the issue could be resolved.[57]

The pope called for the creation of a joint commission made up of representatives from the Holy See and the NCCB. It was created in May 1993 to discuss the recommendations made by the NCCB.[58] The non-published 13-page report produced by this committee was given to the NCCB's Canonical Affairs Committee for further study and recommendations.

Some but not all of the Committee's recommendations were approved on April 25, 1994, by the Holy See for the United States.[59] Overall, the changes were helpful, but not retroactive. First, the Holy See changed the definition of a minor for the

53. Id. at 83.
54. National Review Board for the Protection of Children and Young People, supra, sec III C 6.
55. Cafardi, supra, 10–11.
56. National Review Board for the Protection of Children and Young People, supra, sec. III D.
57. Pope John Paul II, "Vatican-US Bishops' Committee to Study Applying Canonical Norms," 23(7) Origins 102–103 (July 1993).
58. Cafardi, supra, 70.
59. In 1996, this change was also extended to Ireland.

purposes of prosecuting sexual abuse. A minor was now a person under the age of 18 rather than being a person under age 16. This change was made part of universal canon law in May 2001.[60] However, this change was not retroactive, so it applied only to new victims who were victimized after April 1994.

Second, the Holy See allowed for a broadening of the prescriptive period (the canonical statute of limitations) so that a case could be initiated up until the victim's 28th birthday, as long as it was initiated within a year of the victim's report of the abuse. The prior rule had been that the victim only had five years from the last sexually abusive act to report.[61] However, this change was also not retroactive, so it also applied only to new allegations.

These changes, while being somewhat helpful, did not actually change the canonical landscape all that much. They were very useful for new cases that arose after 1994. However, the changes did not fix the bishops' most pressing problem because the new changes were not retroactive. What bishops really needed were processes that could take care of "old" cases, particularly as the research provided by the JJR/11 documents that the vast majority of abuse cases that were surfacing had been committed many years before. That was not what they were given.

21:11 THE NCCB RESPONSE

On the national front, the Five Steps that had been enumerated in 1987 were officially endorsed by the NCCB in June 1992. There were some objections voiced to the creation of a uniform policy by some bishops, because of their reluctance to tell other bishops how they should run their diocese.[62] Nevertheless, the endorsement passed without objection.

Although this was a step in the right direction, the endorsement of these steps had no binding canonical effect. Canonist Sister Sharon Euart explained that the reason that these new rules were not binding was "Because the episcopal conference is not a governing body with the power to enact regulations binding its members except in those matters where universal law (i.e., the Code of Canon Law) requires it...or where a special mandate of the Holy See has permitted it *motu proprio* (at its own initiative) or at the request of the episcopal conference (canon 455)."[63] Thus these suggestions were not legislation because the bishops had not asked for a mandate to make it so from the Holy See.[64] Bishops within their own dioceses could choose to follow these steps, or they could choose to ignore them. If they were ignored, the only pressure that could be brought to bear was moral pressure from

60. Congregation for the Doctrine of the Faith, "Sacramentorum Sanctitatis Tutela," 93 Acta Apostolicae Sedis 785–788 (May 18, 2001).

61. Canon 1362 (hereinafter c. 1362).

62. National Review Board for the Protection of Children and Young People, supra, sec. IV B 1 d.

63. Sharon Euart, "Canon Law and Clergy Sexual Abuse Crisis: An Overview of the US Experience," USCCB/CLSA Seminar; USCCB (May 25, 2010), at 4.

64. C. 455.

other bishops. At the time that the Five Steps was officially adopted, only about half of U.S. dioceses had created formal sexual abuse policies, and of those that did, not all of those policies were being consistently followed.[65]

It was at this same bishops' meeting that the NCCB's Priestly Life and Ministry Committee formed an ad hoc subcommittee on sexual abuse, headed by the president of the St. Luke Institute.[66] The St. Luke Institute is one of the nation's major treatment centers for clergy. They held a "Think Tank" in February 1993 where a panel was convened to "offer these experts the chance to reflect honestly and off the record about various dimensions of the problem, especially pastoral care of the victims, reassignment after treatment, and research and education."[67] The chair of the subcommittee presented the findings and recommendations from the Think Tank to the bishops in a report at the June 1993 NCCB meeting. These recommendations were meant to flesh out the five steps that had been endorsed by the NCCB in 1992. However, even in these recommendations there were no proposals for penal actions or punishment for the offender. Rather, it firmly recommended treatment and monitoring of priest-offenders.

Though the NCCB declined to specifically adopt the Think Tank's recommendations, they decided at their meeting in June 1993 to establish an Ad Hoc Committee on Sexual Abuse and named Bishop John Kinney of Bismarck, North Dakota, as its chair.[68] The committee was given six tasks. They were to:

- To look at assisting the membership in effectively dealing with priests who sexually abuse minors and others;
- To examine what the NCCB can do pastorally nationwide to assist in the healing of victims and their families;
- To address the issue of morale of bishops and priests burdened with the terrible offenses of a few;
- To assist bishops in screening candidates for ministry and assessing the possibility of reassignment of clergy found guilty of the sexual abuse of minors;
- To recommend steps to safeguard against sexual abuse of minors by employees or volunteers of the Church; and
- To address the national problem of sexual abuse of children, coming from many directions, including families.[69]

In fulfilling his duties as chair, Bishop Kinney began meeting with victims' groups. This apparently made a considerable impression on him. After he was

65. National Review Board for the Protection of Children and Young People, supra, sec III D.

66. Cafardi, supra, 91.

67. Ad Hoc Committee on Sexual Abuse. "Brief History: Handling Child Sexual Abuse Cases." *Origins* 23, no. 38 (March 1994): 666–670.

68. Cafardi, supra, 95.

69. United States Conference of Catholic Bishops Ad Hoc Committee on Sexual Abuse, "Efforts to Combat Clergy Sexual Abuse against Minors—Chronology," Restoring Trust: A Pastoral Response to Sexual Abuse 3 (2002).

appointed in 1993, Bishop Kinney had a compelling point to make in his speech to his committee. He said:

> If someone says of us, even today, "The bishops just don't understand the prob-
> lem"; if they don't agree that "we bishops get it," then our goal as your committee
> is to help all of us understand and "get it" both intellectually and in our hearts for
> the sake of the victims, for our priests, our people, and even ourselves.[70]

The Ad Hoc Committee between 1993 and 1996 was very active and put much effort into helping bishops to "get it," though through hindsight, one must question whether the committee was ultimately effective. The NRB Report indicated that one bishop reported that this commission's effectiveness was lessened because though it had the power to recommend, it "had no teeth." He also posited that it also lacked support by "influential bishops" because it directly interfered with a bish-op's authority within his own diocese. Finally, there was some concern expressed that the efforts of this committee might actually increase the amount of litigation against the Church.[71]

This Committee produced some important work. By November 1994 it had published the report *Restoring Trust, A Pastoral Response to Sexual Abuse*, which was presented to the bishops at their fall meeting. The report was useful in that it reviewed 157 diocesan abuse policies, reported on clergy treatment facilities, and provided further resources on the subject of sexual abuse.[72] The report also gave various guidelines regarding diocesan policies, prevention, dealings with the civil law, insurance issues, dealing with both victims and the accused, and media inter-action. However, in this report is the recommendation from a doctor working at St. Luke's Institute, Dr. Frank Valcour, that priests who have successfully completed their treatment should be reintegrated into ministry.[73]

In 1995, the committee published *Restoring Trust: A Pastoral Response to Sexual Abuse vol. II*. This volume dealt with care of victims and contained more treatment center reviews. During the time the second volume was being drafted, the committee attempted to get the conference's Administrative Committee to commission a study to collect data from the various dioceses regarding their abuse statistics, much like the National Review Board did after 2002. However, that proposal was rejected. The NRB Report states that it was rejected because "diocesan attorneys advised that the results would be subject to subpoena and could be used in future litigation."[74]

70. Bishop John F. Kinney, "NCCB Establishes Committee on Sexual Abuse," 23(7) Origins 104–105 (July 1993).

71. National Review Board for the Protection of Children and Young People, supra, sec III D.

72. (Ad Hoc Committee on Sexual Abuse, *Restoring Trust: A Pastoral Response to Sexual Abuse*. Vol. 1. Washington, DC: National Conference of Catholic Bishops, 1994.)

73. Ad Hoc Committee on Sexual Abuse 1994, 9 **Id. at 9**.

74. National Review Board for the Protection of Children and Young People, supra, sec III D.

The Ad Hoc Committee produced one more volume of *Restoring Trust* in 1996, which was a summary of the efforts of the committee thus far. It was the committee's last publication.

During this time, for dioceses that chose to act on the Ad Hoc Committee's recommendations, the reports they produced were helpful. However, because of the lack of enforceable "teeth" and the documents' nonbinding nature, a great disparity was created between those dioceses that chose to draft and implement sexual abuse policies, and those that chose to ignore the issue and hope it would go away. As the JJR/11 summarizes about this time, "Despite the unanimous affirmation of these guidelines for action, their development in the *Restoring Trust* documents, and the establishment of written policies that encoded them, the promise of these principles were not uniformly fulfilled."[75]

At the beginning of the 1990s most American bishops seemed to be responding in some official way to deal with the issue of sexual abuse. Yet 10 years later, the scandal in Boston and its effect on the rest of the country was a sobering reality check that the way dioceses dealt with the issue of clergy sexual abuse was far from uniform. In fact, something had happened during this time to one of the bishop's own, which significantly lessened their enthusiasm for dealing with the issue.

21:12 THE EFFECTS OF AN ACCUSATION AGAINST CARDINAL BERNARDIN

The archdiocese of Chicago in the 1990s had been in the vanguard in attempting to deal with the sexual abuse scandal. The archdiocese had implemented a lay review board that looked at the cases of any priest with a credible allegation against him and permanently removed priests who had offenses against children.[76] The cardinal had personally tried to encourage other bishops to implement similar sexual abuse policies by distributing Chicago's policy possibly to use as a template, and had been very active in his advocacy on this issue.

Yet just three days before the bishop's meeting in November 1993, Joseph Cardinal Bernardin was himself accused by a former seminarian of sexually abusing him, based on the seminarian's "recovered memories." Obviously the accusation garnered considerable and sustained media attention, and caused great embarrassment to the Church and to the cardinal. Cardinal Bernardin immediately and categorically denied having ever abused the seminarian.

In February 1994, four months after making the accusation, the former seminarian recanted and withdrew his accusations and his lawsuit. Given that the accusation was false, the media was embarrassed about their coverage and backed off the issue for a number of years.[77] Although it was obviously a very positive thing that Cardinal

75. John Jay College Report, supra, 84.
76. Cafardi, supra, 100.
77. Cafardi, supra.

Bernardin was exonerated, on the national stage this entire situation effectively put the brakes on many of the efforts underway to address the issue of clergy sexual abuse of minors. The problem was that the accusation against the cardinal and subsequent recantation gave the erroneous impression that many of the accusations being made were actually false. This gave bishops a false sense of security that came back to haunt many of them in 2002.[78]

21:13 POST-1994

In the years after the Bernardin accusation, ecclesiastical focus on the issue had died down somewhat but was not entirely quiet. There were some large judgments awarded in well-publicized civil lawsuits during the latter half of the 1990s. The most publicized was in 1997, when the diocese of Dallas was hit with a huge judgment in civil court. The jury awarded $119 million to the plaintiffs, though that figure was later reduced to the still-considerable sum of $31 million. The jury found the diocese negligent because the bishop ordained a man despite the fact that the diocese had marriage annulment files in its offices that claimed that the marriage was null because the man was a pedophile. After ordination, he continued to abuse children from 1981 to 1992, despite numerous attempts at therapy.[79] The former priest was later convicted and sentenced to life in prison. Although this case garnered attention, it did not cause a national outcry. From then on, there was very little national attention given to the issue until Boston in 2002.

In the late 1990s, American bishops remained frustrated that there was no easy way to unilaterally laicize problem priests, even ones who had been criminally convicted and were serving time in prison. Responding to this frustration, in 1998, the Congregation for Clergy issued a private reply where they confirmed that their Congregation had developed procedures to assist bishops in administratively laicizing priests whose cases were public but who refused to request voluntary laicization.[80]

This response was following a report in the secular press that in three cases, including the Dallas one and two from Boston where the priests had admitted to sexually abusing minors, the Holy Father administratively had dismissed these men from the clerical state. There was no formal judicial penal process. Interestingly, the rescript/decree from Rome was issued on the letterhead from the Congregation for Divine Worship and the Discipline of the Sacraments, and not the Congregation for the Clergy.[81] It included that the decision was "supreme and unappealable and

78. John Jay College Report, supra, 89.

79. Cafardi, supra, 12.

80. Congregation for the Clergy, "Private Reply" (Nov. 11, 1998), prot. No. 2169/98.

81. Congregation for Divine Worship and the Discipline of the Sacraments, "Rescript" (June 26, 1998), prot. No. 1770/97/S.

liable to no recourse."[82] However, there was no formal document issued by the Congregation for the Clergy about these procedures.[83]

By 2001 this development became unimportant, because both Congregations that had been dealing with this issue were told that they were no longer competent for hearing these cases. The Vatican's Congregation for the Doctrine of the Faith under Joseph Cardinal Ratzinger issued the document *Sacramentorum sanctitatis tutela*, which took all of the abuse cases to itself, and formulated its own procedures for dealing with these cases.

21:14 SUMMARY

After 1993, many people believed and fervently hoped that the Church administratively had this issue under control. There was certainly a national awareness of the problem. At least on the surface, it appeared that the NCCB on the national level and individual dioceses on the local level had properly dealt with abusive priests and had been educated about appropriate interaction with victims. The NCCB had given bishops considerable education and resources to deal with the issue. It had been discussed and debated during numerous NCCB meetings. Most dioceses had sexual abuse policies in place. Big lawsuits had clearly alerted bishops to the financial hazards of not properly handling these cases. The thought was that though there might be further lawsuits in furtherance of cleaning up prior mistakes, the bulk of the problem had been addressed. As was discovered in 2002, this was far from the truth.

After the false accusation of Cardinal Bernardin, the Church had a bit of a respite from public attention. As Nicholas Cafardi describes it, "It was almost as if American public opinion was saying, 'Okay bishops, you have made some serious mistakes, but you have promised to change. You are on probation. Don't let it happen again.'"[84] And yet, when the scandal in Boston broke, it was evident that in many places the efforts and strides made by the NCCB in the 1990s had been ignored, and ignored by some of the largest and most prestigious dioceses in the country. It was not that the Catholic Church in the United States had not made considerable progress in dealing with the issue, because it had. By the end of the 1990s the overwhelming majority of dioceses in the country had policies to address clerical sexual abuse of minors. The problem was that there was no national consistency or uniformity imposed by law on all bishops. Bishops were reluctant to impose norms on other fellow bishops, many of whom were quite influential. And because of this reluctance, the fallout from the scandal in 2002 has been immeasurable.

82. John P. Beal, "At the Crossroads of Two Laws: Some Reflections on the Influences of Secular Law on the Church's Response to Clergy Sexual Abuse in the United States," 25 Louvain Stud. 115 (2000).

83. Francis G. Morrisey, "Addressing the Issue of Clergy Sexual Abuse," 35 Studia Canonica 412–413 (2001).

84. Cafardi, supra, 113.

One of the best analogies to describe the bishops' continuing response to the sexual abuse crisis was penned by John C. Gonsiorek. He described the bishops' response to this issue in the years preceding 2002 as "akin to watching a person falling down the same flight of stairs over and over again."[85] Not only is the fall painful for the one falling, but it is painful for all forced to watch the descent. One would have thought that after having fallen a few times, there would have been a collective recognition among bishops that they all needed to be very careful, watch their step, and proceed with extreme caution. Certainly the subsequent events of 2002 and beyond indicated that those stairs are still a hazard. And even over 10 years later, we are still witnessing the lessening but occasional "thunk, thunk, thunk, crash" of dioceses that apparently have not learned the lessons many thought had been learned in 1985, 1993, and 2002.

85. John C. Gonsiorek, "Barriers to Responding to the Clergy Sexual Abuse Crisis within the Roman Catholic Church," in Sins against the Innocents 52, edited by Thomas G. Plante (2004).

CHAPTER 22

⌒⋏⌒

The Perfect Storm in Canon Law: What Went Wrong?

22:1 OVERVIEW

So far we have looked at the broad influences that have shaped how the international Church and how ecclesiastical culture in general contributed to the Church's inadequate response to the issue of clergy sexual abuse of minors. Then we examined the timeline of the Church's attempts to remedy this problem up until the story in Boston broke in 2002. But this history and these factors do not adequately explain what brought the Catholic Church, and specifically the Church in the United States, to this point of crisis.[1]

What got the Church to this place? Given that the Church has had hundreds of years of both recognizing and combating this problem, has its own legal system in place to deal with such violations, and has had the sexual abuse of a minor specifically criminalized during the entire scandal, how could this have happened?

There is no sound bite or simple answer to these questions. These answers are rather multifaceted and certainly complex. It is possible to point to some specific factors that contributed to bringing this crisis to a head. However, those factors must be assessed in light of the influences and circumstances of the time, as well as the attitudes and outlook of those Church leaders who were in positions of authority both nationally and internationally.

It should also be noted that while some dioceses have been devastated by this crisis, many have come through completely or relatively unscathed. So while there have been bishops whose choices have made the sexual abuse crisis worse, there are

---

1. While we recognize that dioceses in other countries are dealing with the same problems, it is not as clear whether all of the same factors apply regarding the circumstances that created the problem. So while many of these factors may be applied to similar situations in other countries, it is likely that not all of them would apply to dioceses outside the United States.

many bishops that managed to deal with their problem priests in a consistent and effective manner, despite the problems discussed in this chapter.

The discussion that follows builds upon our experience in working with and speaking with others within the canon law system. To preserve confidentiality, portions of the next few chapters will include personal experiences that are not footnoted, but reflect the common experience of canon lawyers who have many years of experience working within the canonical system.

22:2 REMEDIES PREVIOUSLY AVAILABLE IN THE 1917 CODE

Prior to the promulgation of the 1983 Code, the Code of Canon Law that governed the Church was the 1917 Code of Canon Law.[2] In it, the Code gave bishops various ways of dealing with problematic, immoral, or criminal actions of clergy, and not just those problems involving sexual abuse. Most of these remedies allowed a bishop to suspend a cleric, though they did not result in the complete removal from the priesthood. Nevertheless, they were very useful in allowing bishops the ability to act decisively in cases where immediate action was warranted.

22:3 *SUSPENSIO EX INFORMATA CONSCIENTIA*

The 1917 Code recognized that there are times when a bishop has private, solid, and credible evidence regarding the conduct of one of his priests that required the priest's immediate suspension based on that information. Canon 2186 of the 1917 Code stated that "It is permitted that Ordinaries may, in virtue of an informed conscience, suspend their clerics from office, whether in part or in whole." This non-judicial suspension was known as *suspensio ex informata conscientia*, or suspension based on the informed conscience of the bishop. Canonist Edwin J. Murphy, in an article about this option, describes the process this way:

> Now in the decree *ex informata conscientia* all [the] formalities of procedure are omitted; there is no trial; witnesses need not necessarily be heard; the defendant need have no opportunity to defend himself; guided only by his own judgment the Bishop pronounces the decree *ex informata conscientia*.[3]

This procedure was envisioned for situations where the crime or behavior was not widely known, but that it was of such a serious or scandalous nature that it called for immediate action. In these cases, it was thought that there was not time

2. The 1917 Pio-Benedictine Code of Canon Law (Edward N. Peters ed., 2001).
3. (Murphy, Edwin J. Suspension Ex Informata Conscientia, Canon Law Studies, 1932, 2–3.)

to go through a full judicial hearing.[4] Canon 2186 stated that this suspension should not be done if the bishop could proceed according to the norms of law without "grave inconvenience." However, given the particularly delicate circumstances surrounding a cleric sexually abusing a minor, and the need for immediate action, those circumstances certainly meet the criteria for the imposition of this suspension. Though this suspension could not be imposed in perpetuity (c. 2188 2°), it could be imposed for "as long as exists the cause for which it was imposed."

Though this remedy was primarily envisioned to deal with behaviors that were not public, there were instances where even if the behavior was known publicly, it could still be imposed. In circumstances where (1) there were trustworthy witnesses willing to talk to the bishop but who were not willing to testify at a trial (c. 2191 §3 1°), or (2) the priest behaves in such a way to impede the formal process (c. 2191 §3 2°); or (3) if conducting a formal process either causes grave scandal or problems in civil law (c. 2191 §3 3°), a bishop could use this method to immediately suspend the priest.[5]

Although the bishop did not have to conduct any formal process, he did have to gather proofs of the priest's behavior (c. 2190) and issue the suspension in writing (c. 2188). The priest could appeal his suspension to the Holy See (c. 2194). In that case, the bishop was to send the proofs he had collected to support the suspension and the lack of a formal process (c. 2194). The priest remained suspended during the time of his appeal.

This remedy seems tailor-made for dealing with sexual abuse of minors. The bishop could act quickly and immediately suspend the cleric from office as soon as he was aware of a credible allegation of abuse. He did not have to give any sort of warning to the priest prior to his suspension. This process took into account that witnesses in these types of cases, particularly children, often will not testify in a formal process. It also took into account the desire of the diocese not to interfere if there is also a civil investigation being conducted. Although the suspension was not supposed to be permanent, it could be imposed for as long as the bishop believed there to be a danger.[6]

The one drawback to this process is that while a bishop could use this process for a long-term suspension, it was not a process that could result in the permanent removal from the priesthood. Nevertheless, it was a very useful process when a bishop had a priest accused of sexual abusing minors and needed immediate removal of that priest from his parish.

However, when the Code of 1983 was drafted, this process was not incorporated into the new Code. While at the time this decision was seen as being more in keeping with the sensibilities and teachings of Vatican II, it had the unfortunate effect of eliminating a very efficient method by which bishops could quickly and effectively remove an abusive priest.[7]

---

4. Nicholas Cafardi, Before Dallas: The U.S. Bishops' Response to Clergy Sexual Abuse of Children 59 (2008).

5. Id. at 59–60.

6. Id.

7. Id. at 60.

22:4 OTHER INSTANCES IN WHICH A BISHOP COULD ACT UNILATERALLY

A second remedy in the 1917 Code existed for cases where the bishop either (1) strongly suspected or had reason to believe that a cleric had committed a crime, or (2) was certain that a crime had been committed but canonical prescription (similar to a statute of limitations) precluded a formal judicial proceeding. In these circumstances, c. 2222 stated that the bishop had "not just the right but the duty" to prohibit that priest from exercising ministry, and even to remove him from office. Interestingly, the canon states that this removal was not a penalty. Instead, the bishop's action was an exercise of the executive power inherent in his office as bishop.[8] This canon allowed the diocesan bishop the ability to discipline a priest even if the canonical time limit had run—a power that unfortunately was not granted to bishops in the 1983 Code.

Like c. 2186 discussed above, c. 2222 was not included in the 1983 Code. This meant that with the new code, bishops were no longer able to suspend or remove a priest from office on the strong suspicion of malfeasance, or, more importantly, outside the prescriptive/statute of limitations time limit.[9] Again, just when bishops were in dire need of ways to canonically suspend and remove priests, the promulgation of the new Code of Canon Law of 1983 effectively wiped out two of their most useful methods of removal.

22:5 ADMINISTRATIVE LAICIZATION CREATED, THEN RESTRICTED

In the 1950s, Catholic seminaries were packed with seminarians. One reason for this was that the Church had low standards for both acceptance into seminary and for the seminarian's eventual ordination.[10] Another factor was that there was an increase in applications to seminaries in the years following World War II.[11] Not surprisingly, those times produced a lot of priests. Few questions were asked regarding the source of the seminarian's call, and there was little examination regarding

---

8. Id. at 61.

9. Id.

10. National Review Board for the Protection of Children and Young People, A Report on the Crisis in the Catholic Church in the United States 35 (United States Conference of Catholic Bishops 2004).

11. John Jay College, Report to U.S. Conference of Catholic Bishops, The Causes and Context of Sexual Abuse of Minors by Catholic Priests in the United States, 1950–2010, at 37 (May 2011), on Web at http://www.usccb.org/issues-and-action/child-and-youth-protection/upload/The-Causes-and-Context-of-Sexual-Abuse-of-Minors-by-Catholic-Priests-in-the-United-States-1950-2010.pdf (hereinafter "John Jay College Report").

whether that call was valid.[12] The Church hierarchy became used to having multiple priests residing in large parishes—this was seen as the norm.

After Vatican II, and partially in response to the volatility in the general society, the number of men applying to seminaries began dropping off. In addition, after Vatican II some dioceses began closing their minor seminaries.[13] These were generally all-male high school boarding schools run by dioceses or by religious orders that educated and trained boys who believed they could have a religious vocation, then directed them into the major seminaries if they wanted to go.[14] As they were all male and ostensibly intended to form future priests, many had restrictions on such things as dating or socialization with high school girls. As these schools closed, the Church lost one significant way of ensuring that there were a "sufficient" number of priests for later generations. Finally, many priests who were ordained in the years following Vatican II had what turned out to be unrealistic expectations about what practices the Church was going to change. Many were ordained believing that the Church was going to change its rules on celibacy and allow a married clergy.[15]

When this did not materialize, many priests, including ones who had only been ordained a short time, left the priesthood. The Catholic Church lost 3000 priests worldwide in 1975.[16] With vocations down, minor seminaries closing, and many priests leaving ministry, in the late 1970 some hierarchs at the Vatican started to believe that it was too easy for clergy, who had made a vow to God to be a cleric, to leave the priesthood.[17] So as the incidences of clergy sexual abuse were rising, Vatican officials who were unaware of the growing problem began looking for ways to rein in what they saw as the increasing abandonment of priesthood by the clergy.[18]

Prior to Vatican II, there had been priests who had left the priesthood to marry, and there were some quiet options that allowed them to formally return to the lay state. However, these petitions were infrequent, and mainly were envisioned for former priests who were over 50 and who had been civilly married a long time. Most were living in a place where few people knew that he had been a priest, and there was little chance of the priest returning to ministry.[19]

In 1971, the Congregation for the Doctrine of the Faith (CDF) promulgated new norms regarding the process of laicization. In cases where the priest desired laicization, it allowed for the bishop to compile a pastoral investigation and then send

12. National Review Board for the Protection of Children and Young People, supra, 35–36.

13. Id. at 36.

14. This was not mandatory, however, and many of the young men graduated and went on to secular schools and secular employment. Priests who attended minor seminary, graduated to a major seminary, and then went on to be ordained are affectionately known as "lifers."

15. National Review Board for the Protection of Children and Young People, supra, 39.

16. Michael O'Reilly, "Recent Developments in the Laicization of Priests," 52 The Jurist 687.

17. Cafardi, Before Dallas, supra, 62–63.

18. O'Reilly, supra, 687.

19. Id. at 686.

the case to CDF to determine whether the petition should be granted. However, in that same decree, in cases where the priest "because of a depraved life, or doctrinal errors, or other serious reason, after necessary investigation, must be reduced to the lay state,"[20] the bishop was permitted to petition for the priest's laicization. It did not require the participation or even consent of the priest in question. The sexual abuse of a minor by a priest certainly qualified as "living a depraved life." This allowed the bishop to petition to get rid of the priest even if he was recalcitrant and refused to petition for laicization himself.

At the end of 1978, Pope John Paul II was elected pontiff. The new pope soon became concerned about the large numbers of clergy being allowed to abandon their sacred vows and their ministry.[21] So, despite the fact that the rules had been changed less than 10 years previously, the new pope had CDF promulgate new norms making it more difficult if not impossible for a diocesan bishop to administratively laicize a priest who had not requested the laicization himself.[22] In addition, the priest had to be at least 40 years old and had to be out of active ministry for at least 10 years before Rome gave any consideration to his case.[23]

For former priests desiring marriage in the Church, the procedure became much more formal, and cases were heard by CDF. For priests not desiring to marry, both the Congregation for Clergy and the Congregation for the Discipline of the Sacraments had competence for cases that did not involve a dispensation from the obligation of celibacy. In 1989, the pope gave the full responsibility for handling dispensations from the obligations of priestly orders to the Congregation for Divine Worship and the Discipline of the Sacraments. In 2005, competence for laicization in non-criminal instances was given back to the Congregation for Clergy. Regardless of the congregation responsible for the process, it was exceedingly inefficient and cases could (and usually did) drag out over a number of years. The result of these changes was that the one way that a bishop could unilaterally laicize a priest who could not be convinced to make the request himself was discontinued.

The promulgation of the 1983 Code of Canon Law was the completion of the goals Pope John XXIII laid out in his call for Vatican II. These goals included a much greater emphasis on the protection of rights.[24] Its promulgation also eliminated three significant methods that bishops had previously in their arsenal for dealing with sexually abusive clergy. Professor Nicholas Cafardi explains that this is part of the reason that American canonists lacked any experience in using the

---

20. James L. O'Connor, ed., Canon Law Digest. Vol. VII, at 117 (1975).

21. Cafardi, Before Dallas, supra, 62–63.

22. Congregation for the Doctrine of the Faith, 72 Acta Apostolicae Sedis 1132–1137 (Oct. 14, 1980); O'Reilly, supra, 695.

23. O'Reilly, supra, 691. This laicization process was not used only for problem or abusive priests; rather this process was for priests who had "left" the priesthood, usually to marry.

24. Pontificia Commissio Codici Iuris Canonici Recognoscendo, Communicationes 1969, p. 83.

penal canons to remove abusive priests. He posits that prior to the 1983 Code and with these canonical means of removal:

> American bishops seldom called on their canonists to conduct penal trials of sexually abusive priests. There simply was no need to do so because prior to 1983 these other alternatives existed to deal with this problem. But a new code, a new emphasis on individual rights, and a de-emphasis on penal processes, changed all that.[25]

22:6 WHAT ADMINISTRATIVE PROCESSES WERE AVAILABLE

The Code of 1983 did not abolish all administrative processes. Administrative processes resulting in penalties were still available, but without exception it prohibited bishops from using this process within their dioceses to impose a perpetual penalty such as dismissal from the priesthood. Administrative penalties could be imposed, but there were restrictions. If the bishop was going to impose an administrative suspension as a medicinal penalty,[26] it was required that at least one official warning be issued prior to its imposition (c. 1347). The penalty had to be imposed for a determined period of time. Furthermore, the bishop had to set conditions under which that administrative penalty could be lifted. If a bishop tried to impose a penalty that seemed to circumvent the proper process or looked like it might be perpetual, the priest could appeal the bishop's decision to Rome. It was not uncommon for the bishop's decision to be overturned, and for the bishop to be told to reassign the priest.[27] This put bishops in an impossible position of having to either ignore a direct order from the Signatura, or having to put a patently unfit priest back in ministry. Some bishops just simply refused to comply with the order from Rome.[28]

Because of this limitation, and the concern that Rome would insist that the bishop return an abusive priest to ministry, oftentimes bishops were left with having to convince their abusive priests to voluntarily petition for laicization, and they had little recourse if the priest refused. Often these priests were offered what amounted to severance packages to induce them to voluntarily petition for

---

25. Cafardi, Before Dallas, supra, 63.

26. Medicinal penalties are suspension, excommunication, and interdict. These are called "medicinal" because they are supposed to inspire/coerce the person to change his ways. Or, as canonist John Beal colloquially put it, medicinal penalties "are meant to function like cast iron frying pans 'upside the head' to get the offender's attention and impress upon him the need for a change of heart and behavior." (J. Beal, "Crime and Punishment in the Catholic Church: An Overview of Possiblities and Problems." USCCB, 2010.). This is in contrast to expiatory penalties, which are intended to punish. These would include such things as limitations on ministry, specifying residence, loss of some powers or offices, certain penances, and dismissal from the clerical state.

27. Apostolic Signatura, Definitive Sentence, P.N. 22571/91 CA (Mar. 9, 1993).

28. Ann Rodgers-Melnick, "Vatican Clears Priest, Wuerl Rejects Verdict," Pittsburgh Post-Gazette, A-1+ (Mar. 21, 1993).

laicization. Bishops and canonists thought "Only voluntary laicization or dismissal from the clerical state free the diocese from all obligations in justice toward the cleric,"[29] and if they could not depend on Rome to dismiss the priest, they were stuck with cajoling them to voluntarily leave. Bishops remained unaware that it was possible to send such cases to CDF where the pope could impose an involuntary administrative laicization through a little-known process found in a little-known document published by CDF in the 1960s called *Crimen sollicitationis*.

Because of these limitations, some bishops looked for creative alternatives to "suspend without formally suspending" their priests. One option that some bishops tried was using c. 1044 to refuse to assign the priest, with the cited reason being that the priest suffered from a "psychic defect" that made him incapable of exercising ministry. Cafardi explained this strategy this way:

> In these situations, the bishop has refused an assignment, citing the instances of pedophilia or ephebophila as an impediment to the exercise of orders, and has informed the priest that he will be given an assignment as soon as a psychiatric or psychological expert gives the bishop an assurance that the psychic defect causing the impediment, i.e., the pedophiliac or ephebophiliac condition, no longer exists. Given the reluctance of the healing professions to promise or certify any cure, especially in circumstances where their certification, if relied on, proves to be in error and thus opens them to malpractice charges, such assurances are unlikely, a situation which means the priest, under c. 1044, could remain unassigned indefinitely.[30]

Although this did not get the priest permanently removed from the priesthood, it did result in the "removal of the priest from active ministry where he might be a source of injury to other children and to the Catholic community."[31] However, without the priest being permanently removed from ministry, the bishop was obligated to provide the priest with "decent support" according to c. 281. This forced maintenance of a legal relationship with the abuser priest also left the bishop and the diocese potentially open to civil lawsuits.

As late as the 1990s, bishops were not precisely sure which congregation at the Vatican was supposed to process cases of clerical recourse or removal. Sister Sharon Euart, who worked many years with the USCCB, stated, "At that time, there seemed to be a lack of clarity over which Roman congregations had final authority in these matters, a situation that left many bishops frustrated in their attempts to discipline priest offenders."[32] After many consultations with American bishops, eventually

---

29. Betram F. Griffin, "The Reassignment of a Cleric Who Has Been Professionally Evaluated and Treated for Sexual Misconduct with Minors: Canonical Considerations," The Jurist 326–339 (1991).

30. Nicholas P. Cafardi, "Stones Instead of Bread: Sexually Abusive Priests in Ministry," 27 Studia Canonica 154 (1993).

31. Id. at 154.

32. Sharon Euart, "Canon Law and Clergy Sexual Abuse Crisis: An Overview of the US Experience," USCCB/CLSA Seminar; USCCB (May 25, 2010), at 6.

the Congregation for Clergy developed a swift way to dismiss a priest in very particular and highly publicized cases. By 1998 the Congregation for Clergy issued a private reply confirming that there was an extraordinary administrative process to laicize priests who refused to petition themselves. The letter stated that "this Dicastery would like to confirm that there is the possibility of seeking, through these same offices, dismissal from the clerical state *ex officio* and *in poenam* from the Holy Father for priests who refuse to freely request the dispensation. The judgment of the exceptional nature of a particular case is based upon thorough examination of the merits of each one..."[33] However, it is doubtful that this process was widely known. It was only a few years later that CDF changed the entire landscape by taking to itself all of these cases having to do with clergy sexual abuse.[34]

It took until 2001 for the Vatican to get deeply involved in trying to help bishops solve their problem to permanently remove sexually abusive clergy. CDF promulgated the new laws dealing with clergy sexual abuse in the motu proprio *"Sacramentorum sanctitatis tutela"*(SST/01) on April 30, 2001. A letter signed by Cardinal Joseph Ratzinger and Archbishop Tarcisio Bertone, the Prefect and Secretary of the Congregation for the Doctrine of the Faith, was sent to all the Roman Catholic bishops on May 18, 2001, informing bishops that all cases regarding clergy sexual abuse were to be sent to CDF for evaluation if the allegation could not be dismissed for being frivolous or false.

This allowed not only for CDF to get an international overview of the extent of the problem, but also gave bishops the possibility that in some grave and notorious cases, the priest could be administratively dismissed through this process. It also lessened the confusion regarding which Vatican congregation (dicastery) was responsible for handling these cases. Although there was some initial grumbling by some canonists about CDF pulling a power grab over the other curial offices, the centralization and the expertise that CDF has developed has been of great benefit to the Church.

22:7 CANONICAL EMPHASIS ON PROTECTING PRIEST'S RIGHTS

The priority given by the 1983 Code to strengthen the rights of priests[35] and to move away from church sanctions had another unintended result in reference to sexual abuse cases. It practically ensured that any formal process took years to complete.

For a bishop to be able to permanently dismiss a priest, he had to go through the full penal process (particularly as he likely was unaware of the CDF document

33. Congregation for the Clergy, "Private Reply" (Nov. 11, 1998), prot. No. 2169/98.
34. Congregation for the Doctrine of the Faith, supra.
35. Francis G. Morrisey, "Addressing the Issue of Clergy Sexual Abuse," 35 Studia Canonica 405 (2001).

of 1962 that allowed such cases to be sent to CDF to be processed). At every step of the way, the accused priest was entitled to canonical counsel.[36] Like a civil lawyer, the canonical advocate can make objections to the way the case is being heard. The advocate can appeal the final judgment of the court, whether or not a penalty is imposed. And as the sentence cannot be executed until all appeals have been decided, the accused priest remains a priest of the diocese or of his religious order during the entire appeal process. Oftentimes this process literally took years to complete—particularly if the case was appealed to Rome. For bishops who were facing huge lawsuits and who needed to have these internal penal cases adjudicated quickly and efficiently, this scenario was a disaster.

When an appeal was filed, it went to one of the Vatican courts. The National Review Board reports that bishops knew that "the Vatican courts tended to err on the side of protecting a priest because of a concern that bishops could seek to use canon law to rid themselves of a priest whom they did not like or with whom they disagreed."[37] Neither the Vatican courts nor the various Congregations had an adequate understanding of the crisis brewing in the United States, nor did they understand the need for quick and efficient action. On the other hand, American bishops were very concerned that even if there was a "conviction" in an internal diocesan penal trial that the judgment would eventually get overturned by a Vatican appeals court on a technicality. Then the case would either be sent back to be done correctly, or dismissed completely. Bishops had heard of cases that were overturned by Rome on technicalities, with the appeal being sent back with an order to reinstate the priest—even after a criminal conviction in the local civil jurisdiction.[38] Given the realities of the crisis in the United States, that order was impossible for a bishop to fulfill. As the National Review Board summarized:

> Under canon law, some convictions could be reversed by tribunals in Rome years after the fact because of a failure to follow all technical procedural requirements, injecting the potential for inordinate delays into cases that did go forward. One bishop told us that his fellow bishops avoided recourse to canon law because they "weren't sure where Rome would come down," adding that, "it was extremely hard to press your case in Rome and be sure that you would be heard." Another [bishop] told the Board, "We were all very hesitant to do a canonical trial because if there's any procedural flaw in it you can easily be overturned on appeal to Rome."[39]

This worry that a case could be overturned on a procedural flaw was a real concern, particularly as no one in the United States knew how to properly conduct a penal trial.

36. C. 1481.
37. National Review Board for the Protection of Children and Young People, supra, sec. IV B 3 b.
38. Cafardi, Before Dallas supra, 37–38.
39. National Review Board for the Protection of Children and Young People 2004, supra, sec. VI B 3 b.

22:8 AMERICAN CANONISTS HAD NO EXPERIENCE CONDUCTING A PENAL TRIAL

Another big problem for American bishops and their canonists is that although there are canons in the Code that instruct how one conducts a canonical penal trial, it is not an exaggeration to say that no one had used them. American canonists had expertise in conducting trials only in the context of the marriage tribunal. Prior to the promulgation of the 1983 Code, penal trials were not strictly necessary. Penal trials required additional expertise, and additional degreed canonists.

The need for additional personnel was and is a serious problem. With the number of clergy shrinking as Catholic populations continued to grow, there was more pressure on bishops to keep their priests in parishes rather than having a priest work full-time in the diocesan chancery for the bishop. Offices that had traditionally been run and staffed by priests, such as the marriage tribunal or the office of canonical services, were hiring laypersons as "tribunal directors" or "tribunal coordinators" to do much of the administrative and judicial work. This meant that in many dioceses and particularly in the smaller ones, rather than a priest being a full-time canonist, he worked part-time in the chancery while also running a parish and sometimes a school as well. This need for priests to staff parishes also limited a bishop's ability to send priests to study canon law—they simply could not spare them for the two and now three years' worth of canonical studies. Furthermore, much like those who study civil law, not every person has the mind or the temperament to study canon law, which limited the pool of candidates a bishop could send to study. As a result, bishops were having difficulty finding qualified staff to do their internal canonical work, even though the 1983 Code allowed for laypersons to act as judges in some marriage cases.

In the context of conducting penal trials, these problems were magnified. If a bishop did not have the trained canonical personnel to staff his marriage tribunal, he certainly lacked the personnel to adjudicate a canonical penal trial. Prior to 2002, the trial of a priest required that the judges and the other members of the court must be clerics with doctorates in canon law.[40] Canon law requires at least three canonists per trial to act as judges (c. 1421). The promoter of justice (the canon law equivalent of the civil law prosecutor) had to be a priest with a canonical doctorate degree. The advocate (defense lawyer) for the accused priest had to be a trained priest. Furthermore, as there cannot be even the appearance of bias, the priest-judges should be from other dioceses so that they do not personally know the accused. This meant that the judges must travel to the accused's diocese to adjudicate various stages of the case, thus requiring that they schedule considerable amounts of time away from their parishes and their own diocesan canonical duties. There have been many conversations among canonists regarding how trials could ever be run in a reasonable amount of time, given how overloaded everyone was with the duties they had lready been assigned.

40. Congregation for the Doctrine of the Faith, supra, art. 10–15.

Even if there was sufficient qualified personnel in the near vicinity to conduct a canonical penal trial, American canonists had not been trained in how to do it. One of the authors clearly remembers in the first class of her one-credit penal law class being told that they were going over this material as it was in the Code, but it is likely that it would never be used. Other canonists have related the same experience of being told that although the subject matter would be taught it is likely that the material would never be used.[41] One canonist wrote in 1988, "Even though theoretically we can hold canonical trials, seldom would it seem advisable to do so."[42]

No American canonist knew how to prosecute such a case. No one had been trained to judge such a case. No one had been trained on how one writes a defense brief for a penal trial. Certainly no one trained canonists on how they should interview victims and their families. Even the most prominent and highly qualified American and Canadian canonists were publicly admitting that no one knew or had any experience in how to run such a trial.[43]

All of the nuances that civil lawyers learn both in law school and from watching other lawyers try cases was not part of canonists' canonical training. In fact, knowing how to judge, prosecute, or defend a client in a common law civil trial might actually prove more of a hindrance than help due to the considerable differences between the systems. While canon law had the basic outline of how a penal trial should be conducted, it has since been discovered in conducting such cases that there are large holes in the instructions for how one proceeds with the day-to-day, nitty-gritty aspects of running a criminal case.

For example, could the various canonical investigators or judges ask leading questions? If not, are there penalties if they do? Though there are no specific *Miranda*[44] rights for the accused in a penal trial, c. 1728 states that the accused does not have to admit his offense or be forced to take an oath. If the accused was not aware of this canon, that person have been made aware of it prior to talking to an

---

41. Daniel E. Hoye, "Reintegration and Restoration of Exonerated Priests," 73rd Annual Convention, Canon Law of Society, Jacksonville, Florida (Oct. 11, 2011).

42. Jerome E. Paulson, "The Clinical and Canonical Considerations in Cases of Pedophilia: The Bishop's Role," 22 Studia Canonica 107 (1988).

43. Cafardi, Before Dallas, supra 25–28; Elizabeth McDonough, "Sanctions in the 1983 Code: Purpose and Procedures; Progress and Problems," 52 CLSA Proceedings 213 (1990); Francis G. Morrisey, "The Pastoral and Juridical Dimensions of Dismissal from the Clerical State and of Other Penalties for Sexual Misconduct," 53 CLSA Proceedings 224 (1991); John P. Beal, "At the Crossroads of Two Laws: Some Reflections on the Influences of Secular Law on the Church's Response to Clergy Sexual Abuse in the United States," 25 Louvain Stud. 113 (2000); (John P. Beal, "Doing What One Can: Canon Law and Clerical Sexual Misconduct," 52 The Jurist 678 (1992): 642–683; Thomas P. Doyle, "The Canonical Rights of Priests Accused of Sexual Abuse," 24 Studia Canonica 346 (1990).

44. A *Miranda* warning is the civil criminal warning that law enforcement must give to the accused during an arrest as decided in a U.S. Supreme Court case, *Miranda v. Arizona* in 1966. It is this statement regarding self-incrimination: "You have the right to remain silent. Anything you say can and will be used against you in a court of law. You have the right to speak to an attorney. If you cannot afford one, one will be appointed for you. Do you understand these rights as they have been read to you?"

investigator? Should this affect the outcome of the case? How many witnesses are too many? How long should a defense brief be? Who submits the final briefs first? No one knew.

Finally, there are many who have said that only having clerics judging clerics is patently biased because clearly the notion of solidarity among the brotherhood of priests trumped finding a fellow priest guilty. Although that might be so in some cases, it is not that way across the board. It is important to point out that even before Boston many priests have been as angry, as frustrated, and as embarrassed about this problem as many of the laity.[45] Although the focus of their anger might be slightly different (many are furious that a small percentage of priests have betrayed their vows, and everything priesthood should stand for; and has made their already difficult ministry harder) it is no less present. Faithful priests have had to deal with the suspicion, the nasty comments, and the invasive questions regarding their lives and their fitness for ministry from both parishioners and complete strangers.[46] Priest-canonists have the added burden of being forced to canonically clean up the damage that their brethren have wrought. Even before 2002, for many clerical can-onists this problem had taken years of their life that they would have preferred to dedicate to some other ministry. So while on its face this requirement seems to favor the accused cleric, under scrutiny this assumption is not necessarily accurate.

22:9 DIFFICULTIES WITH INVESTIGATIONS AND PROOFS

There were also considerable concerns about conducting the actual internal inves-tigation needed to prosecute a canonical criminal penal trial. First, the question arises: Who should be conducting the inquiry? In c. 1717 the Code suggests that it could be the bishop, though this option certainly is problematic. The Code allows that it can be some other suitable person, but who? Should it be another priest? Should the Church hire a professional private investigator? Could it be the diocesan civil lawyer? Should it be?

Besides determining who should be the investigator, there was also the question of when to conduct the investigation. If there was a criminal case being built against an accused priest, the Church did not want to be seen as interfering with the crimi-nal investigation. The Church was concerned that its own internal investigations might conflict with civil ones, and the Church did not want to be seen as "meddling, raising contradictory evidence, or even obstructing the course of justice."[47] In fact, it was a well-known practice that if there were criminal charges pending against a cleric, there was no Church investigation until after the entire case was adjudicated.

45. Amy J. Strickland, "To Protect and Serve: The Relationship between the Victim Assistance Coordinator and Canonical Personnel," 71 CLSA Proceedings 241 (2009).

46. Cardinal Timothy Dolan blogged about such an encounter on March 18, 2011. Though this experience happened to a bishop, this type of confrontation is fairly repre-sentative, http://blog.archny.org/?p=1127.

47. Morrisey, Addressing the Issue of Clergy Abuse, supra, 411.

If the cleric was found guilty and sent to prison, oftentimes the procedure was put off until there was a possibility of his release.

Another question was what should and could be used as evidence. If the priest had already been prosecuted in a civil criminal trial, then it seems clear that the bishop could use the evidence already gathered for the criminal trial along with the public testimony from that case to conduct an internal proceeding. For the Church, the issue became much more difficult if (1) there had been an arrest but no trial yet; or (2) for whatever reason, there was no criminal prosecution contemplated, but there was a civil suit pending; or (3) there was only the canonical allegation with no civil proceedings contemplated. Without any way to compel the cooperation of the accuser and other witnesses, the thought was that it would be too difficult to find enough evidence to substantiate an allegation.

There was another reason that Church officials were hesitant to begin an internal canonical investigation, or at least to have the results of that report documented in writing. They were afraid of being sued by the alleged victims. As Cafardi stated, "Not only did this litigious characteristic spill over, there are those who would say that it was allowed to hijack the canonical process."[48] Diocesan civil lawyers were advising bishops against conducting a thorough investigation because they were worried that anything produced by the diocese was civilly discoverable by plaintiff's attorneys trying to put together a case against the diocese.[49] They were also worried that the bishop, his investigator, or other diocesan officials could be subpoenaed to testify in civil court.[50] The more prevalent civil lawsuits against dioceses became, the more hesitant bishops and their lawyers were to commit to writing anything that could be used as evidence in the civil realm.

This fear increased when considering what evidence needed to be compiled to internally prosecute a full judicial trial. Regardless of the actual outcome of the penal trial, it was feared that all of the witness testimonies, defense statements, briefs filed by the canonical advocates, and other evidence produced in the case would immediately be civilly subpoenaed as discovery in a civil lawsuit.[51] The civil diocesan lawyers desperately did not want to be forced to hand over what amounted to a completed case with sworn evidence to lawyers who were suing them.[52]

22:10 THE NEED FOR VICTIM COOPERATION IN A PENAL TRIAL

In pursuing the permanent removal of a priest, there was a real concern that to find the accused priest guilty and dismiss him from the priesthood, the court must be

48. Cafardi, Before Dallas, supra 44.
49. National Review Board for the Protection of Children and Young People, supra, sec. III F.
50. Cafardi, Before Dallas, supra, 45.
51. National Review Board for the Protection of Children and Young People, supra, sec. III F.
52. Cafardi, Before Dallas, supra, 44–45.

presented with clear evidence of his offense. And the best and sometimes the only evidence of the commission of that offense is the testimony of the alleged victim and the victim's family. This was and continues to be a serious problem, particularly in cases where it is a single allegation from many years ago. It is an even more serious problem if the victim is still a child.[53]

Those responsible for conducting a penal trial often find themselves in an uncomfortable and no-win position. After the 1983 Code eliminated a bishop's ability to suspend a priest *ex informata conscientia*, there was no way for a bishop to act on an accusation and suspend a priest outside a formal process. Under the 1983 Code, although the bishop may have desired to spare the victim and their families any further pain or suffering, nevertheless, the victim's accusation had to be dealt with in a formal canonical process if the bishop wanted to permanently remove the priest. As the National Review Board noted, "A number of bishops, concerned in part that victims would find it traumatizing to address their abuse in a formal proceeding, were reluctant to ask them for assistance."[54]

The Church has repeatedly been criticized for its mishandling of victims and their allegations, and in many cases this criticism is well-deserved. But lacking the ability to suspend and dismiss a priest without a process, the bishop was forced to proceed formally to remove a priest from ministry. For a canonical trial to proceed, the promoter of justice had to obtain evidence to prove that the accused was guilty of the act alleged.[55] If the promoter did not meet his burden of proof, the priest could not be convicted and dismissed.

This was not a problem if there had already been a civil or a criminal case containing the depositions of witnesses or trial transcripts of testimony. However, in many of these cases the statute of limitations had run so no criminal prosecution was possible, or the district attorney had declined to prosecute for lack of evidence, or there had not been a prior civil trial where the victim has testified. In these circumstances it meant that someone from the canonical court needed to formally depose/interview the accuser.[56] Furthermore, canon law requires that the accused priest be given the opportunity to mount a defense or the process is null (c. 1620). In order to do so, the testimony of the accuser must be provided to the canonical advocate (lawyer) for the accused priest so he can defend himself. Furthermore, that advocate has the right to be at the canonical trial during the accuser's testimony.[57]

This is problematic on a number of fronts. Church officials and lawyers were concerned about having to ask victims to submit a signed formal statement regarding the circumstances surrounding the allegations, and also to ask them to testify further in front of a panel of priest/judges.[58] Given the effort it often takes just to make an allegation, it can be rather insensitive to ask them for further participation.

---

53. Id. at 44.
54. National Review Board for the Protection of Children and Young People, supra, sec. III F.
55. C. 1526, c. 1721.
56. C. 1547.
57. C. 1559. See Chapters 25 and 27. Chapters 22 and 24.
58. C. 1558.

In canon law only judges or auditors are allowed to ask questions so there is no cross-examination.[59] Even then, being questioned by a panel of three priests/judges in a formal hearing is likely problematic for many accuser/victims.[60] In the event that there is civil litigation pending between the victim and the diocese, the Church cannot expect any cooperation with the internal canonical process. In most of those cases, the civil attorney will not let his or her client ever speak to a diocesan official, much less take the accuser's testimony.

The necessity of taking the testimony of a child is also profoundly problematic, and not surprisingly most parents refuse to allow it.[61] The civil courts have considerable experience and expertise in how to allow a child to testify. Canonical courts have no such experience. If the victim is a child or adolescent, canon law actually prohibits the testimony of children under the age of 14.[62] Although there is an exception, it is clear that canon law discourages having children testify in canonical court. In canon law it is possible under c. 1558 that the child's testimony could be taken somewhere else, with the questions being asked by a delegated person with this kind of expertise.[63] However, the process could still be traumatic and most parents simply forbid it.

For the same reasons, it is likely that to support the testimony of the victim, other people such as friends and/or family members must testify.[64] Given the nature of the allegation and the volatility naturally surrounding these cases, this can be an almost impossible request for a diocese to make.[65] The grand jury report about the archdiocese of Philadelphia made it a point to object to having the testimony of victims and witnesses taken, only to be given to the advocate for the accused to try to rebut the accusations in canonical court. They describe it as being almost a re-victimization.[66] So the Church is in a Catch-22 situation of needing to have the cooperation of victims and their witnesses to prosecute these cases, while being profoundly hesitant of doing so for fear of further damaging victims.[67]

Furthermore, various people may be actively discouraging the victim from talking to church officials. Many parents are reluctant to have even the police or the district attorney talk to their child. The parents of a victim understandably may be even more wary of having another priest, much less lots of priests talking to their child.[68] The civil attorneys for the victim may not want their client or their client's family to have anything to do with diocesan officials. But without some direct testimony from the victim, it is very difficult to determine the accused priest's guilt.

59. C. 1561.
60. Cafardi, Before Dallas, supra, 41–42.
61. Id. at 42.
62. C. 1550.
63. Beal, Doing What One Can, supra, 654.
64. Id. at 655.
65. Cafardi, Before Dallas, supra, 43.
66. Report of the Grand Jury, MISC. NO. 0009901-2008 (Court of Common Pleas, First Judicial District of Pennsylvania, Philadelphia, January 21, 2011) at 86–87.
67. Cafardi, Before Dallas, supra, 42.
68. Id. at 42.

Because of fear of interfering in civil investigations, fear of providing evidence for civil lawsuits against themselves, and fear of further antagonizing victims and their families, bishops often chose not to even begin the canonical judicial penal processes required to permanently laicize their priests.

22:11 THE CANONICAL PENAL PROCESS IS CLUNKY, VAGUE, AND INEFFICIENT

Clearly there were many reasons bishops chose not to conduct a canonical trial. However, even if one had, there are serious issues with the efficiency and effectiveness of the actual process. In other words, even if American canonists had been trained in how to conduct a canonical penal trial, they were still bound to use a legal system that is not adequate for the job.

The Church has been dealing with what to do with clergy who commit canonical crimes, including the crime of the sexual abuse of a minor, for many years. Therefore it is not surprising that there is a canonical process in existence to deal with such clergy that includes the ability to permanently remove them from priesthood.

However, when the 1983 Code was being drafted, there was a sense that the penal procedures in the 1917 Code were outdated. This new Code instead focused on respecting rights, while diminishing the canonical sections on trials and punishments. Eliminating suspensions at the bishop's discretion was seen as a step forward to protect priests from bishops' arbitrary exercise of power. The issue of clergy sexual abuse was not yet on the national or international radar.[69] Furthermore, there was no awareness when the Code was drafted that a functional penal process might be necessary for more than just a handful of extraordinary cases.

What was not anticipated was the "perfect storm" of factors that came together when bishops began dealing with cases of the crime of clergy sexual abuse. Voluntary laicization processes became long and drawn out, even if the priest admitted to the allegation and was a willing petitioner. The John Jay Report recognized that in cases where the accused priest denied the allegation and refused voluntary laicization, "the canonical process of determination of guilt was lengthy and cumbersome."[70]

When the rubber met the canonical road, what canonists and bishops alike discovered is that the canonical processes available to them could not adequately address all of the competing interests and special circumstances of these cases. As a noted canonist and professor of canon law Father Francis Morrisey stated, "the laws of the Church had not been written in the perspective of such cases, especially given the serious financial and public relations consequences arising from criminal and civil proceedings against the offending priest as well as against the diocese or religious institute to which he belonged."[71]

69. Id. at 23,
70. John Jay College Report, supra, 86.
71. Morrisey, Addressing the Issue of Clergy Abuse, supra, 404.

For it to be fair and impartial, the judges empaneled to try a penal case against a priest needed to come from somewhere outside the local diocese. Although this might not be such an issue for urban northeastern dioceses in close geographic proximity to each other, it can be a serious challenge for dioceses in parts of the country where dioceses encompass large geographic areas. During the various stages of the trial, the panel of three judges needs to meet to discuss how to proceed, needs to interview witnesses, and needs to deliberate to reach a verdict. This is very difficult to organize and coordinate, it is time-consuming and inefficient, and is expensive.

Further, as the process itself is vague and unspecific regarding many of the particulars of conducting the trial, there are many questions and specifics that all the various parties must figure out as they go along. Given the serious nature of the proceedings, it is not the most appropriate time for the entire court, including the judges, the promoter of justice (prosecutor), and the advocate (defense attorney) to be learning while "on the job." Canonists take their jobs very seriously, and most would find their own lack of expertise troubling. It is even more troubling when the most respected names in one's field are equally inexperienced in how this process ought to be conducted. This is not a recipe for justice or fairness.

It was made worse by the fact that if the case was not tried correctly, there was always the risk that the accused priest would appeal to Rome where the conviction could be overturned on a technicality.[72] Thus a process that had already lasted for years would have been drawn out even longer. The bishop either had to retry the case or figure out some other way of dealing with the priest. Given that American canonists admittedly did not know how to adjudicate these cases, that was a very real risk and one that most dioceses were unwilling to take.

22:12 ISSUES WITH PARTICULAR CANONICAL REQUIREMENTS

Besides having general reservations about initiating a canonical penal process, there were some particular elements in the law itself that caused bishops and their canonists to look for other options. Many of these requirements precluded bishops from acting, or, while allowing them to act, required that any penalty imposed stop short of full dismissal.

22:13 THE LAW ITSELF DISCOURAGES PENAL TRIALS

Within the law itself, canon law actively discourages the use of the penal process unless all other avenues of dealing with the problem are exhausted. Canon 1341 states that an administrative or judicial proceeding should not be used unless

---

72. National Review Board for the Protection of Children and Young People, *supra*, sec. IV B 3 b.

"neither by fraternal correction or reproof, nor by any methods of pastoral care, can the scandal be sufficiently repaired, justice restored, and the offender reformed." Clearly, the law encouraged the bishop to attempt to exhaust all other possibilities for reform, coercion, correction, or treatment, because the penal process was seen as a last resort. Bishops and canonists were aware of this requirement, particularly the part about first utilizing "pastoral care" prior to a penal trial.[73] Respected canonists such as Bertram Griffin were making statements such as, "The penal procedure is secondary to the reform of the offender, the restoration of justice, and the reparation of scandal (c. 1341)," and writing articles about the reintegration of priests back into ministry after treatment.[74] They figured that rather than the problem be handled as a crime requiring punishment, it was more appropriate for it to be handled as a psychological illness requiring treatment. Given the proliferation of treatment centers and the belief that with treatment the priest could be cured and returned to ministry, this was most often the route chosen.

22:14 THE DEFINITION OF A MINOR

In some of the cases that could have potentially been prosecuted, there was a problem in defining who counted as a minor. Canon 1395, the one that deals with violations of the sixth commandment of the Decalogue, defined a minor as someone who was 16 or younger. However, many of these crimes were being committed with adolescents who were 17 or 18. Under the Code, if the adolescent was over 16, it was not a violation of this canon. Though the age ceiling of who was considered a minor was raised in 1994 by CDF from 16 to 18, that change was not retroactive and applied only to new allegations. This precluded a canonical trial being heard under the original canons on the basis of an allegation by an older adolescent.

22:15 PRESCRIPTION—THE CANONICAL STATUTE OF LIMITATIONS

Like the civil law, canon law also has rules concerning how long a person had to bring an action against a person accused of a canonical crime. In the civil law, this time limit is called the statute of limitations. In canon law, a similar time limit for prosecuting cases is called prescription.[75] The rationale for prescription in canon law is the same as that for having a statute of limitations: as time passes witnesses die, memories fade, the precise details of what happened gets fuzzy, and it is hard to remember exactly who said what. However, the crime of the sexual abuse of a

73. Cafardi, Before Dallas, supra, 2008.
74. Griffin, supra, 334.
75. Gregory Ingels, "Dismissal from the Clerical State: An Examination of the Penal Process," 33(182–183) Studia Canonica 169–212 (1999).

minor poses some unique challenges that make enforcing prescription in these cases problematic.

The CIC/83 specifically stated in c. 1362 that for the crimes covered by c. 1395 (which includes the sexual abuse of a minor), the accused had to be prosecuted within five years from the last time a violation occurred. So if a child was abused at age 8, the child and/or his parents had until he was 14 to report it, and for the bishop to act on that report. Obviously, this legal limitation was not drafted with the current understanding of the psychology of reporting sexual abuse. Given that many of these incidents were only reported many years after the incident occurred, in most of these cases canonists presumed that the prescriptive period had run and canonical prosecution was no longer possible.[76] This was a serious limitation to the canonical prosecution of this crime.[77]

Many bishops chose to send their abusive priests to various treatment centers once the abuse was discovered. This also posed a problem because bishops normally tried this option first before trying to permanently remove the priest. If the report of the abuse came after a few years and the priest was at a resident treatment center for months at a time, it was more likely that prescription had run for that crime by the time it became evident that the priest's problem was unfixable and that he likely still posed a threat. Prescription also prevented the initiation of a formal action where allegations were brought to the bishop's attention only after prescription had run, but the bishop believed that the priest continued to pose a risk for reoffending. The 1917 Code allowed for the bishop to take action in that circumstance, but that option was removed in the 1983 Code.

Upon the request of the American bishops, in 1994 CDF raised the definition of a minor from 16 to 18 for cases in the United States.[78] They also extended the period of prescription from five years from the last offense to the time of the victim's 28th birthday for offenses committed after the promulgation of the document. For crimes that had already been committed, the period of prescription was raised until the victim turned 23—five years after the victim turned 18. In 2001, the document SST declared for the entire Church that the crime of sexual abuse of a minor is actionable until the victim's 28th birthday.[79] Even canonists find this confusing—particularly as the rules change depending on when the abuse took place.

Currently, CDF often waives the requirements of prescription completely, though these decisions are made on a case-by-case basis.[80] Given the level of scandal and notoriety these cases are garnering internationally, it is unlikely that a process will be prohibited by CDF just because the allegation is made outside the time of prescription.

76. Beal, Doing What One Can, supra 678.
77. Cafardi, Before Dallas, supra, 28–29.
78. National Review Board for the Protection of Children and Young People, supra, sec. III F.
79. Congregation for the Doctrine of the Faith, supra.
80. *Ex audientia Summi Pontificis*, 7 Nov. 2002, confirmed May 6, 2005.

This problem could have been circumvented had American bishops and canon-ists known about the existence of CDF's Instruction from 1963, *Crimen sollicitatio-nis*. In that Instruction, not only did CDF have the competence to deal with cases of the sexual abuse of minors, but the limitations of prescription were not applicable to these cases. Unfortunately, when the document was issued it was not publicly promulgated. Those bishops who possessed a copy were told to put the document in their secret archives where it was promptly forgotten.[81]

By the time the sexual abuse problem surfaced nationally, most of the bishops who received the document were either retired or had died.[82] No bishop or canonist dealing with this issue remembered that this instruction existed, and until 2002 no one from CDF "reminded" bishops that the instruction was valid for dealing with these sorts of crimes. We will never know why this was the case; however, in hind-sight it does seem as though much pain and frustration could have been prevented had this option been more widely publicized.

22:16 CULPABILITY

Another significant problem with using the canonical norms for sexual abuse cases was how culpability was determined. If in a penal trial the person is found guilty of abusing a minor, next the judges determine what is the appropriate punishment to impose for the crime. Much like the civil law, canon law determines various levels of culpability of the person who committed the crime. In civil law, there are legal defenses that lawyers will claim to mitigate the punishment imposed by the judge. In civil court, if the person is mentally ill or if he or she acted in the heat of passion, oftentimes judges will not punish as harshly as they might if the person had full control of his or her faculties. Canon law has a similar practice.

For a person to be considered fully culpable for his or her behavior, the person needs to have acted in full knowledge that the behavior was a crime, and there can be no mitigating factors involved. Canon 1321 states that a person's imputability or responsibility for the crime is presumed whenever there has been an external viola-tion of the law. However, if the advocate for the defense can prove that the person was somehow impaired, then a judge must take that into account and impose a lesser penalty.

This legal requirement strongly influenced bishops' and canonists' decision not to use the penal process because bishops and canonists believed that in cases of child sexual abuse, a judge could never impose the penalty of dismissal from the clerical state.[83] This is because they believed that pedophilia was a diagnosable mental illness that was usually accompanied by either another diagnosable men-tal illness or substance abuse (either chronic or at the time the abuse occurred).[84]

81. Beal, Doing What One Can, supra, 655.
82. Cafardi, Before Dallas, supra, 31.
83. National Review Board for the Protection of Children and Young People 2004, supra, sec. IV B 3 b.
84. Cafardi, Before Dallas, supra, 33.

Both psychological factors as well as diminished capacity due to substance abuse are grounds for the mitigation of a penalty under c. 1324.

If the advocate for the accused admitted the behavior but argued that the abuser was mentally disturbed and thus was not fully responsible for his actions, then the judge was bound to impose a lesser penalty. If drugs or alcohol were involved, and they often were, it was argued that this also diminished the cleric's imputability (c. 1324). This conundrum was explained well by canonist and professor John Beal, who wrote that while canonical penalties are imposed only in cases where the offense is "seriously imputable," that:

> [T]his presumption of imputability may be rather easily rebutted in clerical sexual misconduct cases. Sexual disorders are often characterized by a high degree of compulsivity that may diminish or extinguish an offender's freedom. Moreover, sexual misconduct is often associated with drug or alcohol abuse or addiction. In fact, the more treatment an offender has received, for sexual misconduct, the more evidence there is likely to be that he acted with diminished capacity. If an offender's imputability is wholly extinguished, he is not liable to any penalty (c.1323).

Ironically, this leads to the counterintuitive results that the more egregious the priest's behavior, the less likely it was that he could be permanently removed.[85] Because he was presumed to be psychologically ill and in need of treatment, the law called for a lesser punishment. It is for this reason that many bishops and canonists chose to avoid penal sanctions altogether and instead chose treatment. They figured that internally if this was going to be the likely outcome of the trial, it would be easier to bypass the trial and go directly to the treatment option.

22:17 TREATMENT RATHER THAN PUNISHMENT

Throughout this scandal it has been evident that bishops were almost uniformly choosing to send their priests to treatment rather than holding them criminally accountable for their actions. This was even recognized by CDF, who included in their 2001 document dealing with the crime of clergy sexual abuse that:

> A "pastoral attitude" to misconduct was preferred and canonical processes were thought by some to be anachronistic. A "therapeutic model" often prevailed in dealing with clerical misconduct. The bishop was expected to "heal" rather than "punish." An over-optimistic idea of the benefits of psychological therapy guided many decisions concerning diocesan or religious personnel, sometimes without adequate regard for the possibility of recidivism.[86]

---

85. National Review Board for the Protection of Children and Young People, supra, sec. IV B 3 b.

86. Congregation for the Doctrine of the Faith, supra.

Given the limitations previously discussed regarding conducting canonical penal trials, and following the changes made in the 1983 Code, bishops and canonists tried to find other ways to deal with and possibly rehabilitate problem priests. During the 1970s, centers specializing in treating abusive clergy became an increasingly popular method of "doing something" with abusive clergy. After the 1983 Code came into effect, bishops no longer had more efficient canonical ways of suspending and removing clergy guilty of sexually abusing minors. As an alternative, bishops began embracing the "treatment option" as their primary method of dealing with sexually abusive clergy.

When an allegation was made, the course of action was usually that the priest was put on "administrative leave."[87] Administrative leave is not a concept found in the Code, so many canonists saw this as being an extrajudicial penalty.[88] After the allegation was investigated, if there was some basis to it, the cleric was sent for an evaluation. If the evaluation revealed a problem, then the priest remained for a course of treatment.[89] Of course, one serious limitation to the treatment solution was that the priest had to voluntarily consent to go to treatment.[90] Bishops could not compel a priest to get treatment, though they induced "voluntary" treatment by continuing to put limitations on the priest such as removing him from his parish, removing his faculties, and even removing his financial support until he "chose" to go.[91] Despite the fact that the Congregation for Clergy strongly disapproved of bishops ensuring "voluntary cooperation" through what was effectively coercive measures, bishops continued to use this method to get their priests out of their parishes and into treatment.

At least up until the mid-to-late 1980s, it was thought that those who sexually abused minors could be cured with intensive treatment.[92] Treatment centers offered inpatient programs, most of them lasting 6–12 months, which specialized in treating clergy.[93] Treatment centers then released the priest back to the diocese, often with the assurance that it was "safe" to reassign him. Oftentimes there were recommendations for supervision or follow-up therapy, though frequently these recommendations were not followed. Certainly from the early 1990s on, it was known in the psychiatric community that although pedophiles could be treated, they could not truly be cured.[94]

Bishops were oftentimes overly optimistic and trusting of the opinions and treatment given by these treatment centers. They also sometimes tried to influence

---

87. Beal, Doing What One Can, supra, 662.

88. Cafardi, Before Dallas, supra, 118.

89. Id. at 121.

90. Morrisey, Addressing the Issue of Clergy Abuse, supra, 412.

91. Peter Steinfels, "Giving Healing and Hope to Priests Who Molested," N.Y. Times A1+ (Oct. 12, 1992).

92. Canice Connors, "Clerical Sexual Abuse Priests and Their Victims Find Healing," Ligourian 23–27 (Nov. 1994).

93. John Jay College Report, 80.

94. National Review Board for the Protection of Children and Young People, supra, sec. IV B 5.

the treatment by not giving the treatment centers all of the information on their client.[95] With ordinations down and with an aging clerical population, bishops did not want to lose priests if they could somehow be salvaged. If the bishop felt as if there was no legal option to permanently remove the priest, then the bishop at least wanted the man to do some work to earn his remuneration. Because of the bishop's obligation of decent support (c. 1350), even if the priest was suspended the bishop was canonically required to ensure that he had enough resources to live on. Bishops sometimes sent a priest to a different treatment center for a second opinion if the priest was not given the green light to be released back for ministry.[96] Bishops also liked the idea of therapy rather than punishment because bishops have a duty to care for their clergy, and this seemed like a good way to fulfill that duty and to not appear overly punitive.

Treatment centers knew that bishops were depending on them to "fix" their clients. As almost all of these treatment centers were Church affiliated, they not only understood the pressures that the bishops were facing, but they also had a vested interest in keeping bishops and religious superiors happy.[97] The happier the bishop, the more likely it was that he would continue to utilize their facility.[98] So often facilities released the priest after his course of therapy and gave abusive priests the green light to return to ministry. Unfortunately, sending recidivist priests to multiple treatment centers often taught these abuser priests how to "play the system." Priests such as John Geoghan, who were already consummate manipulators, learned how to give the "right" answers and say the right things to ensure that they were "cured" enough to get put back in ministry, where many of them proceeded to reoffend.[99]

For many bishops, treatment seemed like the only viable option. However, it had its obvious flaws, including not actually fixing the problem. It also seemed to give bishops a false security that they were, in fact, doing all that could be done to cure or curb the deviant behavior of abusive priests—a behavior that they did not understand they did not otherwise know how to handle.[100] Common sense indicates that if a second round of treatment became necessary, that a reasonable person would not risk the possible, if not likely, risk/harm to children.[101] Yet there were priests who were sent repeatedly to treatment centers, then reassigned.[102] This begs the question: How many times must an abusive priest be sent to treatment before someone in authority realized that he posed a perpetual risk? At what point should common sense and the reasonable person standard operate in these cases?

95. Cafardi, Before Dallas supra, 136.
96. National Review Board for the Protection of Children and Young People, supra, sec. IV B 5.
97. Cafardi, Before Dallas, supra, 133.
98. National Review Board for the Protection of Children and Young People, supra, sec. IV B 5.
99. Cafardi, Before Dallas, supra, 128–129.
100. Id. at 144.
101. Id. at 128–129.
102. Id. at 131.

22:18 THE UNWILLINGNESS OF BISHOPS TO INTERACT WITH SECULAR ENFORCEMENT AUTHORITIES

Another critical piece of what went wrong is that in all of the various options that the bishops considered, cooperating with or turning the accusations over to the civil authorities was never considered a viable option.[103] There are many reasons for this. Bringing scandal to the Church and feeling the need to protect the Church was certainly a factor. Avoiding entanglement with or interference by the civil authorities was another.

The relationship between bishops and their priests is such that many bishops would consider turning a priest over to the civil authorities as similar to having a family member turn in another family member. Generally speaking, that is a rare occurrence. There is certainly a very strong notion that internal problems should be kept and dealt with in-house.[104] Finally, on the part of many Catholics there was a serious difficulty with the thought of having a priest in prison—in much the same way that people have had difficulty believing that a priest would ever behave in such a manner to deserve going to prison. For many people, this was a difficult notion to process. For some bishops it is still a foreign concept. They are still trying to somehow "help" the priest and protect him rather than following diocesan policy, their own norms, and occasionally the civil law.

Because of the hierarchical nature of the Church, a bishop is not answerable to anyone for the decisions that he makes, except possibly the pope. This includes having no one to hold a bishop accountable if he does not report abuse to the local authorities. As Ladislas Orsy notes, "In each diocese, the bishop enjoyed virtually unlimited discretionary power without serious checks and balances. The life and employment of every priest depended on him, every complaint converged on him, and all decisions originated from him. He was immune from any control from within his jurisdiction; no outside person or agency (apart from the pope or a Vatican office) could ever enter into a diocese, assess its administration, and provide help if needed."[105] Thus not only were bishops unwilling to report, there was no oversight from anyone who would call the bishop to account if he did not report abuse, or if he failed to discipline or remove known abusers.[106]

Unfortunately, this continued reluctance to report has repeatedly demonstrated to laypersons that they cannot necessarily trust their bishops to follow the law and protect their children from predatory priests. This has caused a profound crisis of confidence within the laity and with many priests as well in the bishops of the

---

103. National Review Board for the Protection of Children and Young People, supra, sec. IV B 4.

104. Id.

105. Ladislas Orsy, S.J., "Bishops' Norms: Commentary and Evaluation," 44 B.C. L. Rev. 999, 1025 (2003).

106. National Review Board for the Protection of Children and Young People, supra, sec. IV B 8.

Church. It is certain that it will likely take many years before prior levels of faith and trust in local bishops will be restored.

22:19 THE CUMULATIVE EFFECT

A final factor in assessing what went wrong is some bishops' lack of imagination and vision coupled with an overoptimistic sense of complacency. This resulted in a sense that despite what was going on elsewhere, the lawsuits, bad publicity, and public furor would never and could never happen to them. This was not true with all bishops. There were many bishops, particularly after 1994, who went through their clergy files and responded to the various allegations by removing accused priests. They laicized those that they could convince to petition for it, and they found ways to suspend, retire, or otherwise sideline others who were uncooperative. For this reason, many dioceses had largely dealt with the problem well before 2002, and have subsequently not had to deal with large lawsuits.

However, in other dioceses it has become almost commonplace to hear about a large jury award or settlement in a civil case involving clergy sexual abuse. We have seen dioceses selling assets and some declaring bankruptcy to pay victims millions of dollars in damages. Back in his 1985 report, Father Thomas Doyle predicted that if this problem was not addressed adequately that the personal and financial costs could be staggering. However, it seems as though many bishops lacked the imagination to envision what the result might look like for their own diocese if they did not deal with their problem clergy. This lack of imagination literally has cost the Church millions of dollars, thousands of souls, and much of its credibility.

An analogy here might be helpful. The movie *The Queen* gave a fictionalized account of the aftermath of Princess Diana's death. The royal family is vacationing in Scotland away from public media at the time of her accident. They are completely isolated from the sentiment of their people, who as the days pass, are increasingly horrified that their monarch is not responding to this event. The movie depicts the prime minister pleading with the queen that she needed to come back, because she was so out of touch with her people that it could put the future of the monarchy in jeopardy. When she does return, she is shocked at the depth of feeling about Diana's death, as well as the depth of sentiment directed against her personally. She has been so out of touch that she could not see what the problem was, or have a context for why her people were so upset.

This is very much the way some bishops reacted to this issue. The sexual abuse of children is a crime that is obviously of great concern to parents. When it is committed by someone in the guise of a trusted person who represents God, it can be both personally devastating and soul-killing. As a parent, even the thought of anyone harming your child in that way can evoke a rather substantial level of passion and outrage. Yet as public awareness and fury over this issue was growing steadily during the 1990s, there were bishops who remained convinced that, for whatever reason, the predicted dire consequences would never happen to them or their diocese. Maybe they simply could not fathom the depth of concern, awareness, and anger that the laity developed over the course of the late 1980s and 1990s on this issue.[107]

Moreover, the effect on parents and other laity in hearing about priests sexually abusing children is cumulative. Generation X has been hearing about the issue of clergy sexual abuse and its effects regularly since they were in middle school or high school. In 2002, the issue already had been making the front page of national media for 18 years. Millennials have spent their entire lives hearing about this problem. This generation has now come into adulthood and they are starting their own families. As they have been exposed to this issue continuously since their teenage years, every new criminal conviction and every newly discovered diocesan misstep is one more indication that their Church cannot be trusted with their children. Furthermore, with this generation's exposure to this problem and the Church's seeming inability to respond, they are considerably less likely to ever give a bishop or the Church the benefit of the doubt. Rather, if they believe there is a problem, they are likely to bypass reporting to the Church at all and take their complaint straight to a district attorney or a civil lawyer.

Certainly the unquestioned trust that prior generations had in their Church, their clergy, and their hierarchy was both unrealistic and naïve. Yet one wonders about the effect of having generations with 20-plus years of media and court re-enforcement that their church has a problem that it cannot seem to remedy.

22:20 SUMMARY

There was a psychic disconnect among the bishops in the United States regarding priests who abuse children. On the one hand, almost every bishop has had the problem in his own diocese, and with most it has been more than one case. Whole treatment centers in various parts of the country opened to address this specific problem. Finally, civil cases with large verdicts continued to spring up all over the nation. Yet until 2002, the size and depth of this problem did not seem to be fully realized.

It is evident that there were many problems with the canonical processes available to bishops. In some cases the treatment option was easier, and in others treatment and/or some sort of perpetual suspension was seen as the only option. Recourse to Rome was risky and took years. Yet, it is telling that out of the dioceses in the entire United States, there were almost no penal trials initiated, even when cases could have been pursued.

We will never know, given the difficulties faced in the United States, why more bishops were not informed that CDF had competence for these cases with no prescription requirements. We will also never know if the national outcomes would have been different had bishops and their canonists chosen to proceed with penal trials to permanently remove priests from the very beginning, or at least to use

---

107. Id. at sec. IV B 2.

the administrative penal procedures available more robustly. What we do know is that all of these factors came together and resulted in what for many bishops was a powder keg primed and ready to blow. All it took was for the Boston archdiocesan scandal in 2002 to light the fuse, and the reverberations from the resulting explosion are still being felt more than a decade later.

CHAPTER 23

༄

2002 and Beyond

23:1 UNDERSTANDING THE EVENTS

The annus horribilis[1] of 2002 was a watershed year for changes to the Catholic Church's internal dealings with the issue of clergy sexual abuse in the United States. Between 1994 and 2002 there was little sustained coverage of this issue in the national media. Although there had been some large abuse cases being tried in the civil arena, the national furor that had occurred during the early 1990s had died down.

Many dioceses in the United States had learned from their prior mistakes, and many were removing accused priests from ministry using whatever processes they had. Perpetual "administrative leave" became the unofficial and non-canonical way that many bishops dealt with the problem of abusive priests, sometimes in defiance of directions from Rome to return the priest to ministry. In 2001, the Congregation for the Doctrine of the Faith (CDF) issued a document that gave the congregation sole competence to act in cases of certain serious canonical crimes. It was intended to aid bishops in dealing with these issues, including the issue of child sexual abuse. The new rules were meant to streamline the process, and to clarify which Vatican congregation had competence to deal with clergy sexual abuse. The document was called *Sacramentorum Sanctitatis Tutela*.

23:2 *SACRAMENTORUM SANCTITATIS TUTELA, 2001*

During 2001, the Vatican's Congregation for the Doctrine of the Faith promulgated the document *Sacramentorum Sanctitatis Tutela* (hereafter "SST/01" and "SST/10" for the revised edition in 2010) for the entire Church. This meant that the document

---

1. The translation of a "horrible year" was used in a speech by Queen Elizabeth II to Parliament in 1992. It described the various losses and tragedies suffered by the royal family during the preceding year.

had the force of law and was complementary law to the 1983 Code of Canon Law. SST/01 was meant to deal with only those canonical delicts[2] that were considered to be similar to "capital crimes" in the civil law. These were not just "grave delicts," but the Latin phrase used to describe these crimes is *"graviora delicta"* or *"more* grave delicts."

Although SST/01 dealt with a number of canonical crimes, for our purposes the most important act it dealt with was the sexual abuse of a minor. SST/01 provided directions to all diocesan bishops concerning the procedures for handling allegations of clergy sexual abuse. The document spelled out the process for adjudicating these accusations, including the fact that after an initial investigation, all cases alleging clergy sexual abuse must be sent to CDF to determine how the case should be handled (art. 13). SST/01 universally raised the canonical age of a minor from reaching one's 16th birthday to reaching one's 18th birthday (art. 4). It also extended the period within which claims could be prosecuted in canonical trials to 10 years after the victim reached the age of 18 (art. 5). This document along with the Code provided the foundation on which the subsequent particular canon law for the United States would be based.

23:3 BOSTON AND 2002

The stage for the 2002 crisis was set in the civil arena in 2001. That year there were a number of hostile disputes in various dioceses over court orders for disclosure of internal diocesan records to be used in civil litigation. One of the most visible dioceses to be involved in such a fight was the archdiocese of Boston headed by Cardinal Bernard Law. During the winter of 2001–2002, the *Boston Globe* began a series of investigative reports on the situation in the archdiocese of Boston.[3] The paper published articles that were based on information found in the diocesan files obtained by civil lawyers for civil lawsuits. The stories detailed the way the archdiocese had a track record of ignoring victims and reassigning priests who had extensive files that documented their repeated abuse of children. Some of these priests had been sent for treatment a number of times, and some literally had over one hundred victims. The most notorious of these cases were John Geoghan, James Porter, and Paul Shanley.

Over the course of that winter, increasing numbers of victims began coming forward publicly with their stories. The more the *Boston Globe* investigated, the worse a picture it painted of an extensive Church cover-up of the problem, coupled with a pattern of repeated treatment-then-reassignment of abusive priests. Other media outlets, including the National Catholic Reporter, began covering the story, and began uncovering problems and practices in dioceses across the country that many in the Church believed had been dealt with almost 10 years before.

2. A canonical crime.
3. The *Boston Globe* published a narrative of its findings in the book *Betrayal: The Crisis in the Catholic Church* (2002).

The revelations about the archdiocese of Boston started the national avalanche. What became apparent is that while there were many smaller dioceses that had effectively taken care of their sexual abuse issues, there were many more dioceses, and many of the largest and most prominent dioceses in the country, such as Boston, New York, Los Angeles, and Philadelphia, who had not learned their lesson from the early 1990s. Within the first four months of 2002, 176 priests from across the United States were put on administrative leave pending further investigations.[4]

What would have been unimaginable in such a traditional Catholic diocese as Boston became probable, when local, national, and international pressure began to build to have the cardinal of Boston resign. By mid-April of 2002, 65 percent of Catholic Bostonians believed their cardinal should resign. Bishops in other countries such as France, Wales, Ireland, and Poland were forced to resign for various reasons, all having to do with sexual abuse. In April 2002, the American cardinals were called to Rome to meet with the pope and other officials to discuss the growing problem.

The Vatican's general policy for bishops was that you are "married" to your diocese and like a marriage, if times are bad you stay and clean up your mess. However this policy became progressively more difficult to maintain in Boston, where it became increasingly evident that Cardinal Law needed to resign for the good of the Church. On December 2, 2002, Cardinal Law submitted and the pope accepted his resignation from the archdiocese of Boston. This would have previously been unthinkable.

Furthermore, the civil authorities began investigating whether there was criminal complicity or other laws that had been broken on the part of the cardinal and/or other diocesan officials. There was an investigation by the Massachusetts attorney general in 2003. Although the report ultimately concluded that neither the cardinal nor diocesan officials had broken any laws, the attorney general noted that the investigation (1) "produce[d] evidence that the widespread abuse of children was due to an institutional acceptance of abuse and a massive and pervasive failure of leadership"; and (2) revealed that "Cardinal Law personally participated in decisions concerning the final disposition of clergy sexual abuse cases, including decisions whether to permit accused priests to return to ministry duties."[5]

23:4 THE USCCB MEETING IN DALLAS, TEXAS

Due to the unrelenting national attention the story continued to receive, the United States Conference of Catholic Bishops (USCCB) decided to dedicate its entire June 2002 meeting in Dallas, Texas, to dealing with the issue of clergy sexual abuse. More than any other event, the public relations and financial debacle suffered by

4. Boston Globe supra, 4.
5. National Review Board for the Protection of Children and Young People, A Report on the Crisis in the Catholic Church in the United States (sec. III E) (United States Conference of Catholic Bishops 2004).

the Boston archdiocese and the continued ripple effect for dioceses across the country sharply focused the attention of bishops on the urgency of the need for collective, decisive, and binding action.

The result of this meeting in Dallas were two draft documents creating a national policy and national norms that were binding on all of the dioceses in the United States. Interestingly, they were also intended to be binding on those in religious orders as well, though the bishops did not have the authority to make canonical legislation for them.[6] *The Charter for the Protection of Children and Young People* (hereinafter "Charter") set out the overall policy and direction for dealing with these cases. *The Essential Norms for Diocesan/Eparchial Policies Dealing with Allegations of Sexual Abuse of Minors by Priests or Deacons* (referred to as the "Essential Norms" or the "Dallas Norms") is the law promulgated by the USCCB and approved by the Vatican as supplementary law to be used in conjunction with SST and the Code of Canon Law to adjudicate these cases.

23:5 THE CHARTER AND NORMS

The Charter and Essential Norms were drafted and adopted over the course of six months. They were first put forward at the USCCB meeting in Dallas, Texas. After going through a revision process, they were adopted by the USCCB at their November 2002 meeting. Because of the legally binding nature of the Norms, to take effect they had to be approved (given a canonical "*recognitio*") by the Vatican. The Vatican made some changes, and granted its approval in December 2002. In January 2003, the USCCB issued the final version of the Norms.

The USCCB states in an explanatory booklet on its website[7] that:

> ...Catholic bishops of the United States adopted the *Charter for the Protection of Children and Young People* in June 2002. The *Charter* was revised and approved in June 2005. The *Essential Norms for Diocesan/Eparchial Policies Dealing with Allegations of Sexual Abuse of Minors by Priests or Deacons* was approved by the Apostolic See in December 2002 and a revision was approved January 2006. The two documents approved by the United States Conference of Catholic Bishops (USCCB), the *Charter for the Protection of Children and Young People* and *Essential Norms* together form a unity, but are different in nature.

The Charter and Essential Norms are different from prior diocesan and national efforts, because of (1) the Norms are binding law, not helpful but nonbinding suggestions such as the ones made by the bishops' conference in 1994; and (2) they are binding for every diocese in the United States. The distinction between the Charter and the Norms is important: the Charter declares the bishops' intention for future policies and provides a framework for the implementation of the Norms.

---

6. This will be discussed in further depth in Chapter 24.
7. www.usccb.org/ocyp.

The Norms, having received the required Vatican approval ("*recognitio*"), "constitute particular law for the dioceses/eparchies that belong to the United States Conference of Catholic Bishops. As such, the Essential Norms bind those subject to them."[8] While the bishops/eparchs freely agreed to follow the provisions of the Charter, the bishops/eparchs are legally bound by particular canon law to observe the Norms. The specific requirements of the Norms regarding the procedures to follow in abuse cases will be extensively examined in Chapters 25and 27.

Besides enumerating processes for dealing with child sexual abuse, both the Charter and the Norms created new entities to assist bishops in dealing with this issue. On a national level, the Charter created three new or reconstituted entities. First, the Charter mandated that the USCCB create the "Office for Child and Youth Protection." Second, the new office would be assisted and monitored by a National Review Board (arts. 8–9). The USCCB invested funds into an annual audit to ensure that the Norms were being followed, and empowered the Office for Children and Youth Protection to carry on with auditing and responding to issues as they arose. Third, the Charter mandated that the bishops' Ad Hoc Committee on Sexual Abuse be reconstituted, and that it have members from all of the episcopal regions of the country (art. 10). For individual dioceses, the Norms mandated that each diocese create its own diocesan review board. It is meant to function as a confidential, consultative body to the bishop on matters relating to the sexual abuse of minors by priests and deacons. These diocesan review boards will be discussed in further depth in Chapter 25.

There is one glaring issue that has been repeatedly mentioned in both civil and canonical circles regarding the Norms. While the Norms detail the procedures for disciplining clerics, this only includes priests and deacons. It does not include disciplining bishops. As stated in c. 1405 and reiterated in SST/10 art. 1, bishops and cardinals can only be judged by either the pope himself or by the Congregation for the Doctrine of the Faith. There is no other mechanism in place canonically for judging the actions of bishops and cardinals. Though this has been the cause for much discussion, the law and the Catholic understanding of the nature of bishops makes it unlikely if not impossible for this to change. Within the Church, it is highly unlikely that the Vatican would ever let a bishop be judged by anyone other than by other bishops, and would certainly never cede this authority to either priests or laypersons.[9]

8. Id.
9. Pope Francis has indicated that he would like there to be more local autonomy and authority given to local bishops' conferences. In 2013 when a German bishop was suspended for gross overspending, Pope Francis indicated that he wanted the German bishop's Conference to deal with their brother bishop instead of doing the disciplining through CDF or personally through the pope. It could be in cases of bishop misconduct or malfeasance that Pope Francis will formally designate local bishops' conferences to adjudicate such cases and discipline the offender, though he has not officially done so at this time.

The Norms were certainly not perfect; these were laws created quickly and by an ad hoc committee in just six months.[10] As with any quickly drafted legislation, errors were soon discovered. Furthermore, many canonists argued that the canons in the Code would have been sufficient—that there was no need for new norms, and that the Norms further complicated an already complicated process, though these objections were never acted upon.

By January 2006, it was apparent that modifications to the Norms were needed. The revised *Essential Norms for Diocesan/Eparchial Policies Dealing with Allegations of Sexual Abuse of Minors by Priests or Deacons* was developed by the Ad Hoc Committee on Sexual Abuse of the USCCB and by the Vatican-U.S. Bishops' Mixed Commission on Sex Abuse Norms.[11] Upon the recommendations of the ad hoc committee, the USCCB reissued the Norms with several changes. A second revision was approved at the June 2011 general meeting of the USCCB.

23:6 THE NATIONAL REVIEW BOARD

It is fair to say that the Dallas meeting of the U.S. Conference of Catholic Bishops in 2002 was perceived as a huge news media event, coming so soon after the *Boston Globe* and National Catholic Reporter's investigative reports. Eager to have a "civilian" face on the remedy to the problem of a hierarchy under attack and lacking credibility, the bishops adopted one of the innovations made by Cardinal Bernardin in Chicago,[12] but adapted it to encompass the entire Bishops' Conference. They created a National Review Board. They then recruited several prominent Catholic lay leaders to participate in the national effort to clean up the mess.

The Review Board was tasked to undertake certain activities to implement the objectives set by the Norms, and in particular:

- directing the John Jay College research project for a comprehensive scientific study;[13]
- performing ongoing audits of diocesan compliance using investigators from outside the church;
- undertaking a periodic review of the wisdom of applying the "one strike and out" penalty to priests who had no subsequent abuse allegations;
- overseeing the stronger scrutiny of the seminary student intake, to preclude the priesthood from readily accepting persons with psychological problems;

10. Ladislas Orsy, S.J., "Bishops' Norms: Commentary and Evaluation," 44 B.C. L. Rev. 999, 1006 (2003).
11. http://www.usccb.org/issues-and-action/child-and-youth-protection/reports-and-research.cfm
12. Nicholas Cafardi, Before Dallas: The U.S. Bishops' Response to Clergy Sexual Abuse of Children 83 (2008).
13. United States Conference of Catholic Bishops. "Charter for the Protection of Children and Young People" (art. 10) (2006).

- permitting meaningful lay consultation regarding selection of new bishops by the Nuncio and Vatican; and
- reporting all discovered allegations of sexual abuse to civil law enforcement.

Members of the National Review Board were recruited, given staff and funding, and set about to study the causes and the context of the crisis. They provided some credibility that the bishops were rapidly losing, but with that credibility came the Board's public criticism of the past hierarchical responses to the abuse cases. The Board's committees funded John Jay College to perform research, and Board members interviewed 85 persons within and outside the Church to learn their views on clergy sexual abuse issues.[14] Then in 2004, the Board produced its own report documenting its findings.

The National Review Board's February 2004 *Report on the Crisis in the Catholic Church in the United States* (hereinafter "Report") delivered some very significant criticisms of U.S. bishops. The Report concluded that too many bishops had failed to deal appropriately with these issues. Failure to respond properly included "(i) inadequately dealing with victims of clergy sexual abuse, both pastorally and legally; (ii) allowing offending priests to remain in positions of risk; (iii) transferring offending priests to new parishes or other dioceses without informing others of their histories; (iv) failing to report instances of criminal conduct by priests to secular law enforcement authorities, whether such a report was required by law or not; and (v) declining to take steps to laicize priests who clearly have violated canon law."[15]

One of the Review Board's most significant critiques spoke of the connection between church and state, and the state's reaction to the Church's response to the crisis. It noted the impact this scandal was having on the state and national legal landscape, when the Report stated, "(F)ailure of some bishops to exercise proper governance, choosing instead to minimize or rationalize or forgive or just ignore misconduct, or else to pass along problems to other unsuspecting dioceses, has led to governmental intervention that could threaten the independence of the Church in the United States."[16]

This quote makes a direct connection between the bishop's inaction and the civil state more closely regulating the Church's internal affairs. The quote certainly implies that while those who have sexually abused children have in the short term harmed the Church's reputation and credibility, the harm caused by the bishops' cover-up may ultimately cause the institution far greater and more long-term harm. In other words, bishops are the ones responsible for the changes in state mandatory reporting laws, the receptivity of judges to punitive damages, the unwillingness to shield diocesan records from disclosure, the statute of limitations windows, and other forms of the "governmental intervention" that were not in place prior to this

14. National Review Board for the Protection of Children and Young People, supra, sec. I.
15. Id. at sec. IV B.
16. Id.

scandal. The Report infers that absent the many bishop errors, these legal changes would not have been required or needed.

In the Board's Report are recommendations for moving forward and dealing with the issue. Among their recommendations were:

- To require greater screening and oversight of seminary students.
- Showing greater sensitivity and effective responses towards victims.
- An improvement of accountability of church leaders.
- Improving interactions between diocesan leaders and law enforcement.
- Requiring less secrecy and more transparency by the dioceses in dealing with sexual abuse issues.[17]

In December 2007, five years after the creation of the first National Review Board, the Board issued a three-page report addressed to "The Catholic Faithful of the United States."[18] It documents the successes that the Board has accomplished, lays out what work it sees is yet to be done, and describes challenges that it sees ahead. The Board lists its successes as its audits and research projects, as well as some of its oversight initiatives. Most of the "work to be done" in the way of implementing "best practices" programs, independent audits, and outside reports had been completed by 2011.

In the category of challenges with which the Board continues to struggle, the Report lists a number of issues described as being "extremely complex" to solve. These include:

- One of the most significant issues is the need for a greater understanding of victimization and its consequences. Discussions with victims provide evidence of serious needs that still must be addressed in order for the victims and their families to find the healing that they need. The Board is hopeful the results of the *Causes and Context Study* will provide needed insights and recommendations.
- Another set of issues relates to the relationship of the Church to its priests, the vast majority of whom are not involved in the scandal, but many of whom feel alienated from both the bishops and the laity.
- There is a particular need to provide appropriate protection and restoration for those accused but later found innocent.
- Other issues include the need for greater speed in the process of determining credibility of allegations and consequent responses, as well as determination of an appropriate role for the Church in the supervision of offenders.
- During the past few years, it has become apparent to members of the NRB that parishes also become victims of sexual abuse. Members of parishes experience both a sense of betrayal or outrage over accusations that lead to the removal of a pastor or associate. Often parishioners do not know how to respond to victims

17. Id. at sec. V.
18. National Review Board. Report of the National Review Board, December 2007 (2007).

and their families and agonize over the lengthy process of determining appropriate responses. This is an area that needs much more attention.
- Finally, the Board is seeking ways to communicate more effectively to the laity so that members of the Church are both better informed on the positive responses the Bishops have made and more active observers of the programs and processes in their parishes and dioceses. Such communication is vitally important since the work of the National Review Board is strengthened by vigilant parents and parishioners who investigate the presence and quality of the programs in their parishes and dioceses. The obligation to provide safe environments that prevent damage to children, young people, families, parishes, dioceses, and the Church rests with all Catholics.[19]

23:7 THE USCCB OFFICE OF CHILDREN AND YOUTH PROTECTION

Another entity that the Charter created is the *Secretariat of Child and Youth Protection*. Upon its creation, this office was assigned three central tasks as enumerated in art. 8 of the Charter:

- To assist each diocese and eparchy (eastern Rite Churches) in implementing "Safe Environment" programs designed to ensure necessary safety and security for all children as they participate in church and religious activities.
- To develop an appropriate compliance audit mechanism to assist the Bishops and Eparchs in adhering to the responsibilities set forth in the *Charter*.
- To prepare a public, annual report describing the compliance of each diocese and eparchy to the Charter's provisions.[20]

Article 8 of the Charter mandated that this office would be located at the USCCB national headquarters in Washington, D.C., and that it will "have staffing sufficient to fulfill its basic purpose."

The office's website describes its purpose this way:

The Secretariat for Child and Youth Protection is a resource for dioceses/eparchies for implementing safe environment programs and for suggesting training and development of diocesan personnel responsible for child and youth protection programs; taking into account the financial and other resources, as well as the population, and demographics of the diocese/eparchy. The Secretariat produces an annual public report on the progress made in implementing and maintaining the standards in the *Charter for the Protection of Children and Young People* following an annual audit process. The report is public and includes the names of dioceses/

19. Id. at 2–3.
20. http://www.usccb.org/about/child-and-youth-protection/who-we-are.cfm.

eparchies that the audit shows are not in compliance with the provisions and expectations of the *Charter.*[21]

It is interesting to note that one of the specific duties of this office is the obligation to list those dioceses that are not in compliance—in effect, to call them out and make it known that they are not cooperating.[22] It is a small but important way to attempt to keep bishops and dioceses accountable.

23:8   THE USCCB'S COMMITTEE FOR THE PROTECTION OF CHILDREN AND YOUNG PEOPLE

The charter mandated that the former USCCB Ad Hoc Committee on Sexual Abuse be reconstituted. The USCCB renewed the mandate of the former committee, and reconstituted it as the Committee for the Protection of Children and Young People. The USCCB also changed and upgraded the committee's status from being an ad hoc committee to becoming a standing committee of the Bishops' Conference. In accord with art. 8 of the Charter, the membership of the new committee must have bishop representatives from all the episcopal regions of the country. Appointments on the committee have been staggered to help retain continuity and institutional memory.[23]

The Committee's mandate is "to advise the USCCB on all matters related to child and youth protection and is to oversee the development of the plans, programs, and budget of the Secretariat of Child and Youth Protection. It is to provide the USCCB with comprehensive planning and recommendations concerning child and youth protection by coordinating the efforts of the Office and the National Review Board."[24]

23:9   THE JOHN JAY COLLEGE STUDIES

To further understand the sources and extent of this problem, the National Review Board commissioned a very large and detailed retrospective study by researchers at John Jay College in New York of the causes of the sexual abuse phenomenon, entitled *The Nature and Scope of the Problem of Sexual Abuse of Minors by Catholic Priests and Deacons in the United States* (JJR/04). Data in the report came from "seven unique sources—a fact overlooked in most media reports. The data were derived from bishops and priests, victim assistance coordinators, victim advocates,

21. Id.

22. Robert J. Kaslyn, "Accountability of Diocesan Bishops: A Significant Aspect of Ecclesial Communion," 67 The Jurist 109–152, 129 (2007).

23. http://www.usccb.org/about/child-and-youth-protection/committee-for-the-protection-of-children-and-young-people.cfm.

24. http://www.usccb.org/about/child-and-youth-protection/committee-for-the-protection-of-children-and-young-people.cfm.

survivors, clinicians, seminaries, historical and court documents."[25] The initial results were published in 2004 with the final report issued in 2011. The principal academic investigator, a non-Catholic, remarked that the benefit of the study has been a "strong and broadly based commitment to address the gaps in current policies of prevention and oversight that allowed these unhealthy patterns of abuse to continue for so long in the U.S. and elsewhere."[26]

The JJR/04 was published as a book and is available online.[27] The report covered the period that began in 1950 and ended in 2002. The report showed that the number of alleged incidents of abuse increased in the 1960s, peaked in the 1970s, declined in the 1980s, and by the 1990s had returned to the levels of the 1950s. Some 11,000 allegations had been reported by bishops to the researchers, and of these 3,300 were not investigated because the allegations were made after the accused priest had died; 6,700 allegations were substantiated; and about one thousand could not be substantiated. Constant press attention to the issue in 2002 encouraged victims to come forward with accusations, so one-third of the accusations were made in the years 2002 and 2003.

In the John Jay Report's review of sexual abuse allegations, slightly more than 27 percent of the allegations involved a cleric performing oral sex and 25 percent involved penile penetration or attempted penile penetration. The majority involved touching over or under clothing.

Factors identified with the sexual abuse allegations included several common themes: failure by the hierarchy to grasp the seriousness of the problem, overemphasis on the need to avoid a scandal, use of unqualified treatment centers for clergy removed for rehabilitation, a sort of misguided willingness by bishops to forgive sexual misconduct as a moral failing and not treat it a crime, allowance of recidivism upon reassignment of the priest, and insufficient accountability of the hierarchy for inaction.

The supplemental report issued in 2006[28] showed a significant variation among dioceses regarding their handling of allegations of clergy sexual abuse. The detailed survey results analyzed in the 2006 Report were more specific than those that had been published in JJR/04. The 2006 Report observed: "The percentage of diocesan priests accused of sexual abuse ranges between 3% and 6% when the information is arranged by region and also when the information is arranged or sorted by the size of the diocese. Similarly, the percentage of religious priests with allegations ranged from 1% to 3% across all sizes of religious communities, when those with 10 or fewer members are excluded. From the consistency in the prevalence of allegations of sexual abuse in dioceses, the John Jay College researchers concluded that the problem was a general problem, not one that could be linked to dioceses in a

25. Catholic News Service, "John Jay Investigator Criticizes Bad Reporting about Abuse Report" (June 23, 2011).

26. Id.

27. http://www.bishop-accountability.org/reports/2004_02_27_JohnJay/index.html.

28. http://www.usccb.org/issues-and-action/child-and-youth-protection/upload/Nature-and-Scope-supplemental-data-2006.pdf.

particular area of the country, or to those with density of population or number of parishes."[29]

The later, more comprehensive retrospective John Jay Report was issued in 2011 (JJR/11), as the 60-year retrospective of the clergy sexual abuse problems and causes from 1950 to 2010. This report also is available on the Web.[30] It found that accusations were consistent across regions, with roughly 3–6 percent of accusations per region. There were 4,392 priests accused between 1950 and 2002, about 4 percent of active priests during that period, but remarkably 3 percent of the alleged abusers had 27 percent of the allegations. Of those accused and disciplined, 40 percent went to a treatment program, about a hundred served time in prison, and 20 percent were deceased, retired, or inactive. In 143 cases, priests who were transferred between or among dioceses abused in both places. There were a total of 10,667 allegations, some not substantiated; of these, 81 percent of the victims were male. The allegations were present in the 1950s, grew in the 1960s, peaked in 1970s, and then decreased dramatically in the 1980s and 1990s.[31]

The JJR/11 concluded that the data indicated a historical problem, with the vast majority of cases occurring from the mid 1960s to the mid 1980s.[32] Some 94 percent of all cases occurred before 1990, and 70 percent of clergy cited in the allegations had been ordained as priests before 1970. In the report, there are parallels to other studies of large youth organizations such as schools, Boy Scouts, etc. involving male leaders of children. The researchers concluded that the vast majority of clergy sex offenders are not technically pedophiles, but are "situational generalists violating whoever they had access to. Pedophiles, by definition, seek sexual gratification from pre-pubescent children of one gender and target this age and gender group (especially while under stress). Clergy sexual offenders in the Church were more likely to be targeting whoever was around them (and they had unsupervised access to) regardless of age and gender."[33]

The researchers concluded that there was no causative relationship between either celibacy or homosexuality and the sexual victimization of children in the Church. They found that being celibate or being homosexual did not increase the risk of violating children.[34]

These reports, while comprehensive, are not perfect. However, Dr. Thomas Plante, an academic psychologist who has studied the issue in his many books and articles, concluded in 2011 that "The Catholic Church, as well as society in general,

29. Id. at 4.

30. http://www.usccb.org/issues-and-action/child-and-youth-protection/reports-and-research.cfm.

31. John Jay College, Report to U.S. Conference of Catholic Bishops, The Causes and Context of Sexual Abuse of Minors by Catholic Priests in the United States, 1950–2010 (May 2011) (hereinafter "John Jay College Report").

32. Id.

33. Thomas Plante, blog posting at http://www.psychologytoday.com/blog/do-the-right-thing/201105/the-new-john-jay-report-clergy-abuse-in-the-catholic-church (posted May 18, 2011).

34. Id.

certainly must use the very best available research data, such as that provided in this new John Jay report, and the very best practices in clinical treatment, evaluation, prevention, clinical science, and law enforcement to guide our thoughts and actions. Sadly, hysteria often has ruled the day during the past decade regarding this tragic topic. The responsible use of quality research science, education, and best practices will keep children safe, not strong opinions and emotional hysteria."[35]

There is a limitation on the accuracy of the clergy sexual abuse data that is peculiar to the power structure of the Catholic Church, in that any one bishop in one diocese can refuse to cooperate with the John Jay investigation and/or with the yearly reporting that is called for in the Charter. The surveys, audits, and instructional materials were accepted and used by 97 percent of U.S. dioceses. But some bishops adamantly refused to participate. As the requirement is found in the Charter and not the Norms, their refusal to participate is not a violation of canon law, and no coercion is possible to force the issue because inter-diocesan cooperation is voluntary and the relationship among the bishops is limited to "fraternal correction."

There was one somewhat hopeful factor that the 2011 Report revealed. Instead of indicating that this problem was getting worse, the 2011 Report[36] observed: "In 2002, the public response was focused on the leaders of individual dioceses. and then on the collective hierarchy of the Catholic Church. What this outpouring of pain and indignation failed to accommodate was the temporal disjunction between the historical occurrence of these incidents of abuse and the emerging knowledge by Catholic leaders of the extent of the abuse." A clearer translation of this rather confusing statement would be: what people fail to understand is that most of the cases that are coming to the fore are "historic" meaning they are old, and the bishops who are currently in office are generally not the ones who made these decisions to move and protect abusive priests. This is not to say that there are not current cases of abuse and bishops mishandling the problem. The indictment of the bishop of Kansas City in 2011 and the revelations of possible diocesan administrative malfeasance in St. Paul, Minnesota, attests to the fact that cases are still being mishandled. However, the frequency with which new cases are being discovered has dropped precipitously.

23:10 *SACRAMENTORUM SANCTITATIS TUTELA*, 2010

Much occurred in the years between 2001 and 2010. It became increasingly evident that this is an emerging scandal of global proportions, and is not one simply limited to the United States or to English-speaking countries. Germany, Belgium, Malta, France, and other countries have increasingly had to cope with revelations about the sexual abuse of minors by clerics within their borders.

In recognition of the sexual abuse of minors being a global problem, and to address issues that had been raised during the intervening years, in May 21, 2010,

35. Id.
36. John Jay College Report, supra, 75.

CDF announced that they were promulgating updates and revisions to the document *Sacramentorum Sanctitatis Tutela* that they first promulgated in 2001. These additions were for the entire Church, not just for the United States. Some of the changes reflected the particular laws that were included in the U.S. Essential Norms.

Some of the significant changes to SST/10 were:

- Prescription (the canonical statute of limitations) rules for the crimes specified in the document were extended to 20 years, with CDF reserving the right to derogate or make an exception to that rule on a case-by-case basis (art. 7).
- Now included as a "more grave delict" is making the abuse of a developmentally disabled person or someone "who habitually lacks the use of reason" the equivalent to the abuse of a minor (art. 6).
- Now included as a "more grave delict" is a cleric's "acquisition, possession, or distribution ... of pornographic images of minors under the age of fourteen, for purposes of sexual gratification, by whatever means or using whatever technology" (art. 6).

23:11 2011 CDF CIRCULAR LETTER

The Essential Norms were promulgated by the USCCB for the United States. Thus they are only binding on bishops and dioceses within their territory. There are other countries that have been dealing with the issues of the sexual abuse of minors, and for them, they had only had the Code and SST/10 to guide them in investigating and adjudicating these crimes.

Recognizing that other bishops' conferences may want to create particular binding norms of their own, on May 16, 2011, CDF issued a circular letter addressed to all of the Episcopal Conferences of the world. The circular letter states that it was written "To assist Episcopal Conferences in developing Guidelines for dealing with cases of sexual abuse of minors perpetrated by clerics."

The Circular Letter is not law. Rather it is a document issued by CDF to give national bishops' conferences guidelines on those things that they should consider when drafting their own national norms. The letter covers such issues as appropriate interaction with and treatment of victims, the proper formation of priests and religious, cooperation with the civil authorities, and the procedures governing the preliminary investigation and the referral of the case to CDF. The recommendations are further explanations of the requirements in the Code and SST/10, as well as for the most part mirroring the requirements of the Essential Norms.

23:12 ANTICIPATED CANONICAL LEGISLATION

In 2011, canonists became aware that the Vatican intends to revise the entire section in the 1983 Code of Canon Law on Sanctions in the Church (Book 6). At the time this book is going to print, there have been multiple drafts of the new Book 6 being sent to various academics and other interested canonists for them to make suggestions, comments, and changes.

There is no way to know when or if the final revisions might be promulgated. It may go through other consultations and revisions, or it could be dropped completely. However, it is thought that the changes will simply reflect those additions to the law that are already found in SST/10 and the other local particular laws rather than there being a complete overhaul of the penal law. Given Pope Francis's desire to overhaul and simplify, there is also the possibility that the whole project could be scrapped and the drafters be told to start over.

23:13 CONCLUSION

The reaction of the Church in the United States to the events beginning in 2002 has been profound. For the good, there is new canonical legislation that governs the investigation and adjudication of these cases with possibly more legislation pending. There are now offices in the USCCB that are dedicated to child protection. There have been many studies detailing the causes of this crisis and making recommendations to go forward. There is greater lay participation in parts of the process. And there is a recognition worldwide that the problems that started in the United States are not ones that are limited to the English-speaking world.

Unfortunately, this crisis is not over yet. As events in Kansas City and Minneapolis/St. Paul indicate, even the best legislation cannot force diocesan officials to follow the rules. Members of diocesan review boards continue to try to understand their role, while bishops and other diocesan officials are trying to figure out how best to use them. Across the country there are canonical trials pending, as all of this new legislation and procedures are being implemented. This has not been either an easy transition or learning curve, and the canonical legislation and procedures continue to evolve.

In all of this, there are religious communities such as the Dominicans or the Jesuits, who had this legislation effectively imposed upon them by the diocesan bishops. They are trying to figure out how it all relates to them, to their lives, and to their ministry. Chapter 24 deals specifically with religious communities, and how all of these new laws can be and must be applied to circumstances that are often very different from clerics in a diocesan context.

CHAPTER 24

๛

The Particular Issues of Religious Communities.

24:1 OVERVIEW

So far these chapters have discussed the issue of clergy sexual abuse of minors primarily in the context of diocesan priests and diocesan bishops. However, as Chapter 4 notes, diocesan clerics are not the only types of priests and deacons who must deal with this issue. In the Catholic Church, there are also clerics who belong to religious communities such as the Benedictines, the Jesuits, the Franciscans, etc. The priests and deacons in these communities are not diocesan clergy, but are called "religious" because they belong to religious communities, institutes, and associations.

Like dioceses, religious communities are being forced to deal with the issue of their members being accused of committing sexual abuse with a minor. There are a number of religious communities that have been civilly sued in these cases, and large judgments have been returned. So far, communities such as the Dominicans, the Franciscans, the Benedictines, the Jesuits, the Christian Brothers, and others have faced both accusations and civil lawsuits about members in their communities.[1]

While religious clerics and their superiors are bound to follow the canonical Norms, they have unique issues that must be addressed separately from the diocesan model. Unfortunately, there has been very little canonical scholarship on this subject. Although references are used when possible, much of the research for this chapter's material has been gathered directly from canonists and religious who work in this area.

1. Barbara Bradley Hagerty, "Sex Abuse Scandal Catches Up with Religious Orders," Nat'l Public Radio (Dec. 31, 2007), http://www.npr.org/templates/story/story.php?storyId=17728112.

24:2 BACKGROUND ON RELIGIOUS ORDERS

Some background about religious orders will help in this discussion, because for those who do not belong to these communities, their structures, jurisdictions, and terminology can be very confusing. However, one must understand their structures to understand where their issues differ from the diocesan model. The next few sections will give a very brief overview of how religious orders are organized before delving into how these differences affect their dealing with the sexual abuse issue.

24:3 TYPES OF RELIGIOUS LIFE

There are two categories of religious orders that this book addresses. There are the institutes of consecrated life, whose members are monastically based and who take solemn vows of poverty, chastity, and obedience. They generally live in community, though they can do work that requires them to live and work apart from their monastery, house, or friary. Their members who are priests or deacons are incardinated within their order, not the diocese where they reside (c. 266). These are such groups as the Benedictines, Cistercians, and Trappists, as well as the mendicant orders of the Franciscans and the Dominicans.

There are also societies of apostolic life. Their members may live in community but are not required to do so. Their members may make a promise or vow (sometimes on a yearly basis, and sometimes they vow poverty, chastity, and obedience, but not always) but do not make solemn vows. They usually work doing such apostolates as education, healthcare, or missionary work. Like the institutes, their priests are incardinated into their order, and not into their local diocese unless their constitutions specify otherwise (c. 266). For example, these are groups such as the Maryknolls, the Paulists, and the Sulpicians.

Although both groups can potentially work in apostolates (ministries) where they are in contact with children, the Societies of Apostolic Life are exclusively active within the greater community. Institutes of Consecrated Life often own and run schools and colleges, and even can be given responsibility for diocesan parishes, but there are also communities that are cloistered, which means that they live within their monastery and have only limited contact with the outside world. The Roman congregation responsible for the administration of these communities is the Congregation for Institutes of Consecrated Life and Societies of Apostolic Life (CICLSAL).

24:4 CANONICAL STATUS

These groups, once independently established, have two possible canonical classifications. Some groups, and particularly newer ones, can be diocesan institutes (c. 589). Though these institutes are independently governed by their own internal superior, the diocesan bishop has special oversight for the community (c. 594). There are usually only a few houses or even a single house of the order, and they are generally located within the diocese that created them. It is possible for members of a diocesan order to work in another diocese, and it is possible for there to be one group that exists in two or more dioceses as diocesan institutes. Priests ordained for a diocesan institute are incardinated in the institute, not into the diocese.

These groups also can be created as a pontifical institute (c. 589). These can be a single local autonomous monastery or they may have multiple houses. Depending on the size of the order, they can be regional, national, or international. Pontifical institutes answer directly to the pope for their governance and discipline (cc. 590, 593) through CICLSAL. Members who are ordained are incardinated into their institute, not their local diocese.

These pontifical groups do not answer to a local diocesan bishop, though the bishop has oversight over a member or members who formally work for him as pastors of his parishes, or teachers or administrators in his schools, or have some other apostolate (public religious or charitable ministry such as a food bank, a hospital, a nursing home, etc.) within his diocesan boundaries. Even if through their employment they answer to a diocesan bishop, ultimately the person with authority over these clerics is the superior of their community (c. 596). However, because of the scope of the diocesan bishop's authority within his own diocese, even for pontifical institutes the bishop has oversight over an institute's apostolate (public mission or outreach), public worship (church services that are not solely for the members of the institute), and "care of souls."

Knowing the status of the particular religious order is very important in determining who ultimately has the authority over the institute, and over the member who has been accused or convicted of abuse. For diocesan institutes, the diocesan bishop has considerably more oversight over the workings of the institute than he does if the order is pontifical.

24:5 CONFLICT BETWEEN ORDERS AND BISHOPS

Given that religious are often hired by bishops to work in various capacities in his diocese, there are bound to be some conflicts in jurisdiction between the bishop and the superior of the community. The National Review Board actually noted that one of the factors that contributed to the creation of the clergy sexual abuse problem was "a lack of communication between the religious orders and the dioceses.... There often has been an uneasy relationship between the religious order clergy and the diocesan clergy."[2]

2. National Review Board for the Protection of Children and Young People, A Report on the Crisis in the Catholic Church in the United States (sec. IV B 7) (United States Conference of Catholic Bishops 2004).

In cases where there has been an accusation, the diocesan bishop has the authority to remove the priestly faculties[3] granted by the diocese for a religious priest. But, that only affects the priest being able to function publicly within the diocese. The religious priest retains his ability to function elsewhere and internally within his community unless the faculties granted to him by his superiors are also removed. This can cause tensions between bishops and religious superiors.

Another issue that has arisen is if a religious cleric who has been working in a diocesan parish or other diocesan entity is accused, which entity investigates the accusation? It should be the member's religious superior, though the superior could agree to have the diocese conduct the process if they are better equipped to do so, or if the accusation is made within the context of the cleric's work for the diocese. However, it sometimes has been the case that the diocesan processes get started, but it is only later that the religious's superior is notified or consulted. Good communication between the diocese and the religious order is necessary in these cases to avoid both misunderstandings and duplicated efforts of investigation.

The bishop has the right to have a voice concerning which religious are allowed to live and work in his diocese (c. 679). A bishop may not want residing within his diocese a religious who has been civilly or canonically accused or convicted of the sexual abuse of a minor. However, if the religious community does not have alternate houses where the religious can live, and many consist of only one house, this can cause significant conflict between the diocese and the religious community.

A further issue that can cause conflict is if the religious has had an accusation made against him, but his superior in consultation with his review board has determined that the allegation is not credible and there is no civil or criminal investigation of the case. Must this information be shared with the bishop? What if the diocesan bishop wants to, in effect, rehear/review the allegation before allowing the religious in his diocese? There is no prohibition against double jeopardy in this case, and nothing preventing the diocesan bishop from conducting his own investigation. If the cleric is going to be working directly for the bishop, that seems to be a stronger argument than if the religious is simply going to reside and work within his community, but it is still problematic from the perspective of the religious community.

Many of these issues do not have clear-cut answers, and must be worked out on a case-by-case basis between the bishop of the diocese and the superior of the religious community.

---

3. Faculties are the permissions necessary for a priest to function as a priest in a particular place or for a particular group. It is customary for a bishop to grant faculties to religious priests who work in his diocese, even though the religious priest would already be granted faculties to function for and on behalf of his religious order.

24:6 MEMBERSHIP .

Religious communities are made up of members, many of whom have made permanent vows to belong to the community.[4] Once a religious has taken permanent vows, leaving the community or being dismissed from the community requires permission from CICLSAL if the institute is pontifical, and requires permission from the diocesan bishop if it is a diocesan community.

There are also other forms of membership or association with the order. There are those who have taken temporary vows but have not made their final profession of solemn vows (c. 655). These members can choose to leave the institute, or the community can choose to ask them to leave prior to making solemn vows. There are novices, who are new members of the community, usually within their first or second year (c. 646). They are learning about the community and are in a process of formation, called the novitiate. Then there are postulants, who are not formally attached to the community but who live with the community and are discerning whether they want to join that community. The process lasts a number of years, and those in the process can leave or can be asked to leave up until the profession of solemn vows.

Most male communities have both members who are priests and those who are brothers but not priests. If they are a clerical institute (meaning they have member-priests), male religious communities must by law be governed by a priest (c. 588). Communities are governed by a leader known as a superior (cc. 617–620), though to assist him in governance the Code requires him to have a council (c. 627). If there is more than one level of authority, each level has a superior, though for those at lower levels the superior can be either elected to that position or appointed (c. 625). The Supreme Moderator is required to be elected (c. 625).

Religious communities often cross diocesan boundaries. Some communities are governed independently, but are loosely associated in federations. Some communities are regional or provincial,[5] some are national, and some are international. If the institute is national or international, there can be levels of authority on each of the local, regional/provincial, national, and international levels. While there are usually local superiors, the ultimate superior of a religious order could be in a different state or even a different country.[6]

All of these communities are governed internally by their own laws (known as their Rule), their constitutions, their statutes, and their directives. In fact, canon

---

4. Although this is the norm, there are other types of communities who only take simple vows that must be renewed once a year. There are some communities that take the vows of poverty, chastity, and obedience, while other communities, such as the Jesuits, may add a fourth vow. There are usually exceptions to the general rules.

5. "Provincial" can have two meanings. The first is a territory made up of provinces. The second is the shorthand term for the superior of a province. So one can have a provincial territory governed by the community's provincial.

6. A well-known example of an international superior was Mother Theresa. She was the Superior General of the Missionaries of Charity, a community that has local religious houses all over the world.

law requires that communities have their own constitutions (c. 587). These internal laws of the community are implemented and enforced by their superiors, and violations of these laws are handled within the community or by CICLSAL, according to their laws, as well as according to the laws of the universal Church found in the Code of Canon Law.

24:7 ORDERS AND DIFFICULTIES WITH CANONICAL PROCESS

Religious orders oftentimes have problems with the canonical processes and requirements that are unique to their situation. It has been commented upon by those who have worked closely as canonical advocates for accused religious that overall they have found that the leadership in religious communities are often less familiar with canon law than their diocesan counterparts. While religious leadership is very aware of their own governing laws, they are often not versed in canon law. Unlike a diocesan bishop, who is required to have a judicial vicar who has expertise in canon law, religious communities are not required to have a community canonist (though many do). Oftentimes this has made it difficult for religious provincials to get good canonical advice, as well as for an accused religious to find an advocate to represent him. It is common that an accused religious has never had any contact with a canon lawyer, and has no idea where to start to look for canonical representation following an accusation.

Besides having difficulty with finding a canonical advocate (which for a penal case is required by canon law), the accused religious has sometimes had difficulty in being able to pay for an independent advocate to represent him. Most religious takes a vow or promise of poverty, and have no property or financial resources of their own. As a result they have no funds independent of the order to use to pay an advocate. If the religious community refuses to pay for the religious's advocate, the religious must resort to asking his or her family or a benefactor, or find an advocate who will do the case pro bono. There have been cases where the community will only pay for the services of a certain advocate, or have put a cap on the amount that they will compensate the advocate.

Frequently advocates have discovered that superiors have little tolerance for the conflicts and tensions that these cases bring and want these problems resolved as quickly as possible. Unlike many bishops, who have worked as diocesan administrators, many provincials prior to their service in their community's leadership have been working in ministries that do not give them much experience in dealing with these issues. They know very little about formal canonical processes and, oftentimes are not particularly interested in learning more about them. As a result, it has been some canonists' experience that this results in unnecessary delay in addressing the problem, and when the problem must be addressed it has often not been handled appropriately. Fortunately, this situation is improving.

24:8 RELIGIOUS AND THE NORMS

In the months following the 2002 news reports from Boston, the USCCB began working on the Norms to regulate and standardize the handling of the cases of accused priests and deacons in the United States. In the frenzy after the Boston scandal broke, those bishops in the USCCB who were working on drafting the new Norms failed to recall that diocesan clergy were not the only type of Catholic clergy to be dealing with this issue.

The male religious equivalent of the USCCB is the Conference of Major Superiors of Men (CMSM). Because of the bishops' oversight, when the Charter and Norms were drafted in 2002 by the USCCB, initially there was no consultation with CMSM and no mention in the original drafts of religious priests or deacons. The Norms that the bishops initially passed in November 2002 made no mention of religious priests. The Norms then had to be confirmed by CDF to be promulgated. It was only then that the oversight was noticed. As a result, religious clergy were added by CDF, though only in limited parts of the body of the document. They were included by footnote in footnote 1 of the Norms.

When the document was promulgated religious priests and deacons were surprised to discover that they were included, albeit primarily in a footnote, because they were included without any consultation or collaboration with the CMSM. In fact, neither the CMSM nor the CICLSAL were consulted or informed that religious clerics would be included in the Norms. Given the intense spotlight on the problem and the haste with which the Norms were drafted and promulgated, the oversight is not surprising, but it was certainly a rather impressive breach of protocol. In fact, one bishop noted that in compelling the religious to adopt legislation that was effectively the creation of the USCCB, "If I were a Religious Superior...I would feel that our independence has been trampled to some extent, and it has been."[7]

The original footnote was obviously a last-minute addition, and simply stated, "In applying these Norms to religious priests and deacons, the term 'religious ordinary' shall be substituted for the term 'bishop/eparch' *mutatis mutandis*."[8] The question was that the footnote in the Norms did not specify "who is applying the *Norms* to 'religious priests and deacons,' who is substituting 'religious ordinary' for 'bishop/eparch,' or whether the term 'religious' includes secular institutes and societies of apostolic life."[9] Thus there was a broader canonical legal question regarding whether a notation in a footnote constituted law that was binding on religious.[10]

---

7. National Review Board for the Protection of Children and Young People 2004, *supra*, sec. IV B. 7.

8. United States Conference of Catholic Bishops, "Essential Norms for Diocesan/ Eparchial Policies Dealing with Allegations of Sexual Abuse of Minors by Priests or Deacons," 32 Origins fn. 1 (June 2004). "Mutatis mutandis" means "the necessary changes having been made."

9. Ladislas Orsy, S.J., "Bishops' Norms: Commentary and Evaluation," 44 B.C. L. Rev. 999, 1004 (2003).

10. Id.

Certainly there was no question that the law was applicable to a religious priest or deacon who was working in some capacity for the local bishop in the local diocese. What was not clear was whether the Norms bound a religious who was not under the authority of his local bishop. It was certainly a legal anomaly as diocesan bishops cannot legislate for religious communities. Given that diocesan bishops have no authority over the religious and thus cannot bind them, this was an interesting predicament. It resulted in at least some canonists concluding that the Norms had no binding force on any religious institute of pontifical right, because the USCCB had no power of governance over such institutes. However, institutes of diocesan right would likely be bound because of the amount of oversight over these institutes that the Code gives the diocesan bishop.[11]

After the Norms were promulgated, it became evident that there were a number of problems with them that needed to be fixed. The text of the 2002 Norms required that they be evaluated after two years. In those years, there was considerable consultation between the USCCB and the CMSM, who were now invited to give their suggestions. CICLSAL was also asked to make recommendations regarding how the Norms should be applied to religious communities. It is important to note that it was not that religious communities objected to being included in the Norms in principle: it was that that Norms needed to be clarified regarding how to apply them specifically within the special context of a religious community.

The result was that when the Norms were reviewed and revised in 2005, the initial footnote that included religious was considerably changed. It was amended to state:

> These Norms constitute particular law for the dioceses, eparchies, clerical religious institutes, and societies of apostolic life of the United States with respect to all priests and deacons in the ecclesiastical ministry of the Church in the United States. When a major superior of a clerical religious institute or society of apostolic life applies and interprets them for the internal life and governance of the institute or society, he has the obligation to do so according to the universal law of the Church and the proper law of the institute or society.

The footnote applies the Norms to priests and deacons in both religious institutes and religious societies.[12]

It is clear from a simple reading of the Norms that even the revised ones are drafted primarily for diocesan clergy under the authority of a bishop, and not for religious. When applied to religious, the Norms are not an exact fit for their situation. This footnote recognizes this when it states that the interpretation and

11. Id. at 1005.
12. In 2012, Pope Benedict created a new structure in the Church called Ordinariates. They are like a diocese but are not a diocese, and they are headed by an Ordinary who can be, but is not necessarily, a bishop. Currently, all three Ordinaries are married Monsignors, not bishops. Technically, the Ordinariates do not fall under any of these headings either, but at least for the Ordinariate in North America, they have voluntarily bound themselves to the Charter and Norms.

application of these Norms may differ institute to institute. It also leaves the precise interpretation and application of norms to leadership of institutes and societies, who have a better understanding of how these must be adjusted for religious life. This way the Norms can be appropriately tailored to the laws, circumstances, nature, and resources of the particular religious community.

The revised Norms also include some other references that specifically apply to religious, particularly with the notification requirements between diocesan bishops and religious superiors regarding religious priests and deacons being transferred. This often occurs when the religious order has multiple houses, and the accused cleric is being moved between houses.[13]

24:9 THE NORMS AFFECTING RELIGIOUS

We will be dealing in Chapters 25 and 27 with the process that must be observed when a cleric is accused of sexually abusing a minor. But there are permutations of the Norms that specifically relate when a member of a male religious order is accused that would not be applicable to a diocesan priest.

Like dioceses, when there is a credible accusation against a cleric, religious communities are required to have the accusation reviewed by a review board. The review boards of religious institutes are quite similar to those of dioceses except they are generally smaller (5 members instead of 10–12). These review boards try to have members with expertise in psychology, law enforcement, civil law, and canon law. Autonomous larger monasteries usually establish their own boards, but the smaller monasteries can share a board with another monastery in the same federation. Generally, local houses of religious communities that have other communities within the region or country do not have local boards. Rather, the review board is usually created at the provincial level. If the religious institute does not have provinces, the institute will have one board for the entire institute.[14]

How an allegation in handled within religious communities is different from the diocesan process. Diocesan priests have one level of local authority that handles an accusation, and that is the diocesan bishop. Religious priests have the potential for more than one level of authority, and the question becomes: Who handles the allegation and the subsequent case if the allegation is deemed credible?

The general procedure has been that if there is a provincial superior, the provincial is the one who judges that a member of his province has a credible allegation. Then the provincial superior sends the case to his superior general for review with his council. Much like a diocesan bishop, it is the superior general who then drafts his *votum*, or official opinion of the case, and sends the case to CDF to make the final decision concerning how it should be handled. If the community is local, then it is handled by

---

13. United States Conference of Catholic Bishops, supra, art. 12.
14. Paul Golden, private communication, Aug. 2011.

the local superior, unless for a good reason the superior has delegated the case to the diocesan bishop.[15]

24:10 TRANSFERS BETWEEN RELIGIOUS HOUSES

The national and international nature of religious orders also presents some specific challenges regarding the transfer of its members. Religious communities cross diocesan and even national boundaries. It is common for religious priests to be transferred to different ministries in different dioceses on a fairly regular basis. Though not included in the 2002 Norms, the 2005 updated Norms now specifically address how superiors and bishops should work together regarding transfers—particularly the transfer of a known offender. Although known offenders cannot be transferred to work in the new diocese, oftentimes that person for various reasons will be ordered to live in the new diocese.[16] When transferring a religious into a new diocese, Norm 12 states:

> ... the major superior shall inform the diocesan/eparchial bishop and share with him in a manner respecting the limitations of confidentiality found in canon and civil law all information concerning any act of sexual abuse of a minor and any other information indicating that he has been or may be a danger to children or young people so that the bishop/eparch can make an informed judgment that suitable safeguards are in place for the protection of children or young people. This will be done with due recognition of the legitimate authority of the bishop/eparch ...

It is still being worked out what specific information the superior should or must share with the diocesan bishop. Certainly any safety plan for the cleric should be shared with the diocesan bishop, along with a brief description of the facts of the case against that religious. Such documents as psychological reports and material that is attorney/client-privileged are likely not sharable because of their confidential and privileged nature.

It should always be clear that although the diocesan bishop is being informed, he is not asking for a level of information that gives the appearance that he is the one responsible for making the final determination. The religious remains the responsibility of his religious community. Too much involvement by the diocesan bishop exposes him to potential civil liability if it appears that the bishop is assuming oversight for that religious.[17]

---

15. Id.

16. Sometimes these transfers are necessary because there is a more substantial religious house that has a better ability to monitor the offender than his former residence did, or the order wants to have all of their accused offenders living in one facility/residence. These are typical reasons for such a transfer.

17. Daniel J. Ward, OSB, "Sexual Abuse and Exploitation: Canon and Civil Law Issues Concerning Religious," 67 CLSA Proceedings 236 (2005).

Norm 12 forbids a known offender from being transferred elsewhere to another ministerial assignment. However, there have been times when a member of an international community has long since been transferred to another country. When the member is already overseas and the allegation is made many years after the alleged incident occurred in the United States, many religious communities are handling this by putting the accused on a leave of absence from ministry in the country where he is currently residing. He oftentimes is brought back to the United States for investigation and judgment, though this is not required by the Norms. It is less clear if the norms apply if a member of an American province is assigned overseas and the allegation is for abuse in the other country.[18] Now that CDF is legislating procedures for how cases are handled in other countries, it is likely that the norms of the country where the religious is currently residing will govern what process is required.

24:11 WHAT ABOUT NON-CLERICAL MEMBERS?

One issue that religious communities have that is unique to their way of life is that they had to address what to do if one of their brothers who is not a priest is accused of sexually abusing a minor. The Norms bind only religious and diocesan clerics, which include only priests and deacons. They do not apply to the communities' non-clerical members.[19] What was decided was that in cases where a brother has been accused of sexual abuse of a minor, instead of being reviewed by CDF, the case is reviewed by CICLSAL. Reports indicate that this is an exceedingly inefficient and time-consuming process because they lack the expertise that CDF has gained in having to process so many of these cases.

24:12 PENALTIES

One of the biggest differences between religious clergy and diocesan clergy are the different limits regarding penalties that can be inflicted on the cleric. If a diocesan priest is found guilty in a penal trial, the normal result is that he is dismissed from the clerical state. He can no longer function or present himself as a priest. Although this penalty can be inflicted on a religious priest such that he cannot publicly present himself as or function as a priest, it does not have the effect of removing him from his religious order.[20] To have a member removed from the order requires a second process, because CICLSAL is the only congregation with the jurisdiction to dismiss a member from their order.

18. Golden, supra.
19. This means that these norms are also not applicable to the women's communities because women are not clerics. Although there have been allegations of physical and psychological abuse by women religious, the incidence of sexual abuse of a minor by a woman religious is exceedingly small. Ward, supra, 232.
20. Id. at 234.

Although many dioceses are conducting penal trials for cases where there has been no admission of guilt, so far this has not been the case for religious. As religious orders generally are not equipped to conduct a penal trial,[21] it is possible that an accused religious priest could be tried by CDF itself, or CDF could assign a penal trial to a local or nearby tribunal. For diocesan priests, the penalty of dismissal is final, and the priest is dismissed. In contrast, because as a religious the man remains a member of the order, even if the cleric is dismissed from the clerical state the order remains responsible for caring for and monitoring their offending member. This is particularly true because a religious has taken a vow of poverty, and has no outside personal financial resources to draw upon.

Total dismissal of a religious requires two separate processes, one for the clerical laicization and one for the dismissal from the community, presuming that the member does not want to leave voluntarily. Very few institutes desire to dismiss their offending members or to seek their involuntary laicization.[22] Due to the seriousness with which communities view the vows,[23] many communities have adopted the mantra "we carry our wounded." Furthermore, unlike dioceses, religious communities often have the resources to keep their religious as members because the communities have the ability to both house and closely monitor them. Thus in general, religious communities believe that they have a responsibility to remain in a relationship with the offending cleric despite a civil or canonical conviction, or a confession to the crime.[24]

Instead of conducting a penal trial, the route that religious communities are taking is that after consultation with CDF (or CICLSAL in cases for nonclerics), superiors are proceeding extrajudicially using a process found in canon 1720 of the Code. This process can be used to determine guilt, and also impose penalties up to the penalty of dismissal.[25] Canon 1720 states:

> If the ordinary thinks that the matter must proceed by way of extrajudicial decree:
> 1° he is to inform the accused of the accusation and the proofs, giving an opportunity for self-defense, unless the accused neglected to appear after being properly summoned;
> 2° he is to weigh carefully all the proofs and arguments with two assessors;
> 3° if the delict is certainly established and a criminal action is not extinguished, he is to issue a decree according to the norm of cc. 1342–1350, setting forth the reasons in law and in fact at least briefly.

21. Besides the fact that many communities do not have the canonists to conduct such a trial, and unlike dioceses they do not have judicial vicars, there might also be some conflict of interest issues raised.

22. Sam Dillon "Catholic Religious Orders Let Abusive Priests Stay," N.Y. Times (Aug. 8, 2002), http://www.nytimes.com/2002/08/10/national/10PRIE.html?todaysheadlines.

23. In canon law and tradition, there is a difference between a vow and a promise. Religious view vows as being objectively more binding and less able to be broken or dispensed from than the promises made to diocesan bishops by diocesan clergy.

24. Golden, supra.

25. See c. 1342.

Once guilt is determined, communities draw up comprehensive "safety plans" requiring close supervision for their members, and the member under his vow of obedience is bound to comply. If the member fails to comply under obedience to his safety plan, the community has the ability to petition to CICLSAL for his permanent dismissal from the community.[26] The safety plan should be reviewed on a regular basis to ensure that it continues to be adequate, appropriate, and up to date, as well as to ensure compliance. Circumstances change, and safety plans should reflect those changes.[27] Other penalties could also be imposed by the religious superior. These need to be spelled out in the decree that imposes the penalties.

One lesser penalty envisioned in the Norms is imposing a life of "prayer and penance" on the offending cleric (Norm 8). This penalty has often been used in cases of diocesan priests who, because of age or infirmity or for some other reason, have not been dismissed from the clerical state. The penalty of leading a life of "prayer and penance" instead of being dismissed from the clerical state seems even more appropriate for members of a religious community. Norm 8 continues that when this penalty is applied, the priest is further restricted from celebrating Mass publicly or administering the sacraments. Although a diocesan priest is instructed not to wear clerical garb or to present himself publicly as a priest, these requirements could be modified, if necessary, for religious who wear habits and who exclusively are working internally within the community.

After an accusation is received, the Norms require the restriction of the "ecclesiastical ministry" of an accused or convicted cleric. However it is not clear what this means for members of a religious community who may be functioning as a cleric both publicly within a diocese and privately within his community. In the context of religious clerics, at least one canonist believes that this norm:

> [R]efers to ministry within organizations under the control of the bishop. Therefore, work or ministry within an institute or society or its works is not considered subject to the restriction of the Norms . . . The priest or deacon continues as a member and he needs to continue to live a productive life and contribute to the overall mission of the institute or the society.[28]

Of course, the superior assigning the cleric to this internal work or ministry must always take into account the potential risk to children to ensure that these clerics are not a continued threat. The superior should also take into account the recommendations of the review board, and the requirements of the cleric's safety plan.

---

26. See cc. 696, 1371.

27. For example, the religious is barred from residing within 1000 feet of a school. If the religious has health issues, is elderly and no longer mobile, and is confined to a care-facility that is close to a school, the safety plan needs to reflect that change in circumstances.

28. Ward, supra, 235.

24:13 PROACTIVE EFFORTS

To help religious communities with these cases and to prevent further cases from occurring, most male religious communities in the United States have hired a risk-management firm called Praesidium.[29] This firm provides assistance to religious communities to help them deal with the various aspects of these issues. They provide an accreditation program and review for religious communities, provide workshops and voluntary standards to follow, and can provide background checks for communities. They also help religious communities draft safety plans for their accused or convicted members.

To be accredited with Praesidium, the institute or society "has to establish policies and procedures regarding sexual abuse of minors, to have regular oversight of members, and have a procedure for developing and implementing safety plans for members who have abused."[30] Praesidium follows up with reviews of these institutions to ensure that the measures "on the books" are actually being put into place.

There are those who have considerable doubts about Praesidium's use and effectiveness. However, at this time they are the most commonly used way for religious communities to set proactive policies, to get accredited, to provide continuing education, and to monitor those religious who have been accused or convicted of these crimes.

24:14 SUMMARY

The Norms are not a perfect fit for religious communities. They were not initially drafted with them in mind, and even with revisions the Norms still require considerable tweaking to encompass the various situations of religious clergy and their communities. It is an ongoing process that requires coordination not only within the community, but with the local diocesan bishop as well. Though it is clear that religious communities must be in conversation and consultation with the diocesan bishop, how these religious leaders determine that these processes are handled between them is an ongoing issue. There is a fine line between assistance and overreaching, and with such a volatile issue it is often hard to find that delicate balance. This can get even more difficult when diocesan bishops and religious superiors are pursuing divergent goals.

Religious communities have not been immune to the problem of clergy sexual abuse of minors, and they like dioceses are paying a heavy price. However, on a positive note, there have been comparatively fewer allegations made against religious priests (2.7 percent) than there were against diocesan clergy during the same period (4.3 percent).[31] The advantage that communities have over their diocesan

29. http://www.praesidiuminc.com/.
30. Ward, supra, 232.
31. National Review Board for the Protection of Children and Young People, supra, art. III C 2.

counterparts is that their members have a community to support them. Many times the abuse of a minor has taken place because the priest-abuser is isolated, lonely, and lacks healthy and mature relationships with others. Living within a religious community can prevent those types of abuse cases by avoiding creating these conditions of isolation and lack of accountability.

There are likely people who say that any religious cleric accused or convicted of abuse should immediately be dismissed from his community. However, if religious communities are able to ensure that their offending members follow safety plans, and they are able to monitor these members, then there is certainly a valid argument to be made that this is potentially a safer situation for children than dismissing these men into the general public where no one is keeping an eye on them. Furthermore, religious communities because of their communal nature are in a much better position to monitor their members and keep them from reoffending than are their diocesan counterparts.

CHAPTER 25

cᐯɔ

The Investigation and Pretrial Canonical Process

25:1 CANONICAL SOURCES FOR PROCEDURE

Now that we have discussed various factors that got the Church to this point, and the history of actual events, it is time to deal with the process that occurs when an accusation is made against a Catholic cleric.

This chapter and the chapters following reflect the best available information concerning the publicly available and the unpublished aspects of the practices in place as of 2013 for disciplinary proceedings associated with the charge of clerical sexual abuse within the Roman Catholic Church in the United States. As this text went to press, though there are broad Essential Norms and canons from the Code of Canon Law that generally govern this process, there is not a single comprehensive and uniform practice manual or model to be cited that governs the process. Rather, the process must be compiled using the Code of Canon Law, *Sacramentorum Sanctitatis Tutela* (hereinafter "SST/10"),[1] the Essential Norms, unpublished resources from the Congregation for the Doctrine of the Faith (hereinafter "CDF") and other canonists, and practical experiences in conducting trials.

Unlike the civil law, in canonical penal law the legal "gloss" does not come from precedential case law because there is no binding precedent in canon law. Rather it is derived from (1) official published opinions and recommendations from the pope or Vatican congregations; (2) unofficial, non-published opinions and recommendations from sources in the Vatican who work in this area, particularly the Congregation for the Doctrine of the Faith (hereinafter "CDF"); or (3) from judicious use of c. 19. This canon, in the case of a non-defined area or "hole"[2] in the law,

---

1. SST/10 is a document published originally in 2001 and revised in 2010 by the Congregation for the Doctrine of the Faith that governs how cases involving "more grave delicts" should be handled.
2. In canon law, a legal "hole" is called a lacuna. A lacuna is a subject that canon law does not address, or a gap in the procedural law.

gives the bishop to right to "fill" the hole by using "laws issued in similar matters, general principles of law applied with canonical equity, the jurisprudence and practice of the Roman Curia, and the common and constant opinion of learned persons."

Practically, this means that the practice of conducting trials in canon law is often being created by those canon law practitioners who have argued that their way of filling in or glossing the law is most in keeping with justice, equity, and canonical legal tradition. Thus, many of the procedural statements here are derived from informal interviews with experienced canon law practitioners or Vatican officials, and so these are believed to be current best practices. The authors recognize that some readers will be uncomfortable without citations to conventional law resources such as Federal Reporters and highly detailed procedural statutes. For the most part, in canon law these either do not exist, or are published at such lengthy intervals that they are of little current value. Furthermore, decisions in diocesan penal cases are unpublished, and are unable to be published due to their being internally confidential (c. 1455) and to protect the privacy of the parties and witnesses. Thus the inclusion of anecdotal material is the best available alternative resource for a reliable treatise.

There is no question that the sexual abuse of minors is a serious crime, both in the civil and canonical realms. In both legal realms, the commission of this crime against children warrants punishment. It also must be noted that in the past, and less frequently in the present, there have been many instances within the Church in which the victims of these crimes have been egregiously treated and offenders have not been appropriately punished. Furthermore, diocesan authorities have not always acted in ways that have inspired either trust or confidence in their handling of these cases, which has exacerbated the overall problem. This has created a climate in which it is very difficult for justice within the canonical system to be done.

25:2 WHY SHOULD THE CHURCH CONDUCT AN INVESTIGATION?

There are two groups affected by this issue who often feel that the Church has "thrown them under the bus." The first group is those children and their families who have accused a cleric of sexual abuse. It is well documented that the Church's response to victims has oftentimes been inadequate, insensitive, and not in keeping with behavior that one would expect from a Church.[3] These issues have been widely discussed in other publications and in the media. The accuser's part in this canonical process will be detailed in Chapter 26.

---

3. The treatment of victims has been documented in many sources. National Review Board for the Protection of Children and Young People, A Report on the Crisis in the Catholic Church in the United States, United States Conference of Catholic Bishops (Feb. 27, 2004), on Web at http://old.usccb.org/nrb/nrbstudy/nrbreport.htm; Boston Globe, Betrayal: The Crisis the Catholic Church 2002).

However, there is another group[4] that also feels that they are being unfairly and unjustly treated, and they are priests who have been accused but who either (1) categorically deny the accusation, or (2) admit that something happened, but hold that the behavior was not such that it rose to the level of requiring a penalty of dismissal.[5] These priests often have expressed that they are treated like they are "guilty until proven innocent," that they have their lives turned upside down, their privacy and good name tarnished, and their careers and livelihoods ruined without any appropriate due process. Furthermore, they claim that any attempt to advocate for a balanced, fair, and rigorous examination of the accusations against them results in accusations from the accuser that the Church is privileging the priest over his accuser. This is particularly true in cases where the civil authorities are unable to pursue the case or have dismissed the accusations altogether, and the only process underway is the internal canonical one. As an accusation of abuse that goes public often effectively ends the career and reputation of the accused priest, the stakes for the cleric are incredibly high.[6]

Although not diminishing the horror that victims of sexual abuse have suffered, it should be noted that there are accusations made against clergy that after investigation are determined to be unsubstantiated or false.[7] Chapter 12 talked about the unreliability of "recovered memories." Particularly in cases that happened many years ago, there is the possibility of error. There are some people who have come forward with wildly implausible stories, or they recount stories that can be disproved easily because known facts contradict the accuser's[8] story or timeline (e.g., the priest was not yet ordained, or was assigned elsewhere, or was demonstratively elsewhere at the time the crime was alleged).[9] In addition, because of the substantial amounts of money that dioceses have been paying to victims, coupled with the high visibility of these cases, there are some unscrupulous people who are making false claims simply for financial gain.[10]

---

4. This group generally does not include cases where the cleric has admitted his guilt or where there has been a criminal conviction, unless the criminal conviction was somehow flawed and is being appealed in the civil realm.

5. For example, a cleric who was a principal of a school in the 1970s admits that he paddled a fully clothed student on his buttocks for a disciplinary offense (a common punishment at that time, both in secular and Catholic schools), but denies any sexual context for that action.

6. An exonerated priest's ministry and reputation can be rehabilitated, but it is incredibly difficult.

7. John Jay College, The Nature and Scope of Sexual Abuse of Minors by Catholic Priests and Deacons in the United States. (Study, Washington, DC: United States Conference of Catholic Bishops, 2004).

8. Because the next few chapters deal with canonical legal processes, we are going to use juridic terms for the parties involved. The person bringing the accusation will be called "the accuser" rather than victim or survivor, and the accused priest will be referred to as "the accused" or "the defendant" unless his guilt has been established in a civil or canonical process.

9. Robinson, Walter V. "Reinstated Priest: Yes, I'm Angry." Boston Globe (November 24, 2002).

10. Rabinowitz, Dorothy. "The Trials of Father MacRae," The Wall Street Journal, May 10, 2013.

In more recent years there has been another category of accusations that are quite disturbing. In almost every diocese, due to the publicity given this issue it is well known that a public accusation has immediate and dire consequences for the priest. There have been some cases where reports have been made against a priest where the adult accuser has a grudge against the priest and makes an accusation out of a sense of spite, or revenge, or to get him out of the accuser's parish. Although this is uncommon, it is also not unheard of. Therefore it is very important in all cases that while the accusers deserve respect, sensitivity, and help, as in the civil realm these stories must be examined to determine that the allegation is true.

Unfortunately, the Church's finding that an allegation is groundless is often perceived as suspect due to the frequent past practice of diocesan officials to deny or minimize allegations, regardless of their veracity. The Church has brought this suspicion on itself, and deserves much of the skepticism. Nevertheless, it does not change the fact that there have been numerous false accusations, and when they occur they are tragic. False accusations minimize the trauma and the suffering of those who truly suffered this abuse, and pursuit of the false story takes time and resources away from dealing with the real cases.

When an accusation is made, the Church has its own internal process, which, in accord with canon law, it is bound to follow. The process, or at least parts of the process, can run concurrently with potential civil court processes. The Church's internal legal process is little known and much misunderstood outside of canonical circles.

25:3 CANONICAL VERSUS OTHER ORGANIZATIONAL PROCESSES

When people think of an organizational process to determine whether to discipline an employee, they likely think of an internal administrative process. It is possible also in the civil realm that an employee accused of misbehavior might simply be an "at will" employee, where an employer can fire the employee with or without cause with no formal process involved. These are the employment models many people in the United States know. If recourse is available, oftentimes it must be made outside the institution through the civil courts.

In contrast, the Church is governed by canon law, a legal system that had once been used to govern nations, but one that is often unfamiliar to those from common law jurisdictions. To understand the Church's process, one must always keep in mind that the institution does not view itself as some sort of religious corporation;[11] its self-understanding and judicial model is akin to being a state. Thus its disciplinary processes are more akin to the law of a government or state

---

11. Though the institution's sense of itself may be state-like, as discussed in our earlier chapters, in the United States the Church exists with each diocese being its own corporation or corporations headed by a bishop. There is no overarching "Vatican corporation" that controls local dioceses.

rather than a corporate disciplinary model. This outlook is important to under-standing the way in which the Church handles allegations against its priests.

In canon law, someone who is accused of a crime has defined rights: the right to a good name (c. 220), the right to privacy (c. 220), the right to vindicate and defend one's rights, to be judged according to the law applied with equity, and the right not to be punished with penalties except according to the norm of law (c. 221), a right to canonical representation (c. 1481 § 2), a right not to be forced to incriminate him-self (cc. 1531–1532), and a host of procedural rights that arise as various processes unfold. There are also very specific administrative and judicial procedures that are meant to determine the veracity of the accuser's claim, and a range of appropriate punishments to inflict if the cleric is found guilty.

When an accusation is made, the diocese acts like a civil jurisdiction, in that it is responsible for investigating the allegation and determining if it is credible. If a trial is necessary, it is conducted as a criminal trial. The case against the accused priest is not handled as a case of the accuser versus accused, with the accuser as a party to the case. Rather canonical cases resemble a state's criminal prosecution. In canon law it is the Church versus the accused, with separate, trained members of the Church's judiciary acting as the canonical equivalent to a prosecutor, defense attorney, and judges (much like a civil court's local prosecutor and civil court judges both work for the state, but each has his or her own role).[12] The accuser is the prime witness in the case, but he or she is just the prime witness, not the plaintiff.[13]

As discussed in an earlier chapter, although this canonical judicial process is similar to one conducted by a court in the United States, the process is not exactly the same. Canon law is based on European and specifically Italian code law, which means that judicial rules (e.g., procedure and evidence) are different than those in the common law. For example, there is no jury in canonical cases. Witnesses and the accused are not questioned by a prosecutor ("promoter of justice") and/or the defense advocate but rather by the judges themselves or an auditor who has been delegated by the judge (c. 1561). As canonists say, the process is investigational rather than confrontational. There is no binding rule of precedent in canon law, nor are cases compiled and publicly recorded as cases are in the civil law. While advo-cates are bound to represent their clients zealously, they also have a higher duty to the court, to the Church, and to God to help uncover the truth of the matter. Such differences and distinctions must be taken into account to understand the canoni-cal process.

These canonical processes are wholly separate from their civil equivalents. A canonical process can take place after a civil process (criminal or civil) has begun or has been completed. It could be conducted concurrently with a civil/criminal case. A canonical process can also take place in cases where civil or criminal pros-ecution is impossible or unlikely due to the expiration of the civil statute of limita-tions or the prosecutor's refusal to prosecute for lack of evidence. If evidence has

---

12. Ronny E. Jenkins, "Jurisprudence in Penal Cases: Select Themes from the Judicial Doctrine of the Tribunal of the Roman Rota," 67 CLSA Proceedings 109.
13. Like the civil law, there are no plaintiffs in canonical criminal cases.

been collected for a civil trial, that evidence can be introduced into the canonical procedure. Therefore, although there can be some overlaps, the civil and canonical procedures are wholly separate processes, and in fact "the civil and canonical determinations should be made separate from one another and based on the particular legal provisions applicable to each legal system."[14]

25:4 THE ROLES OF THE BISHOP

The bishop has three distinct roles within this process, many of which present him with conflicting priorities. First, as spiritual leader and chief pastor of the diocese, he has pastoral responsibility for the accusers and their families, as well as for the safety and well-being of his diocese (c. 383). It is his responsibility to ensure that victims' needs and concerns are met and that the people entrusted to his oversight are physically and spiritually kept safe.

Second, as father to his priests, a bishop is responsible for their maintenance, well-being, and morale, and for their spiritual and material welfare (c. 384). This relationship between a bishop and his priests extends well beyond a normal or standard employment-type relationship because of the extent to which the bishop is directly responsible for the priest's welfare.

Third, as the possessor of judicial power in the diocese, the bishop is responsible for ensuring that all canonical laws and procedures are followed, that cases are fully investigated, that his court behaves in a fair and impartial manner to discover the truth in any case before it, and that the rights of the accused and the witnesses are respected (c. 1419). The old saying is that "you cannot be all things to all people" and this certainly applies to bishops in these circumstances. It can be very difficult to balance all of these roles simultaneously. Often in fulfilling the responsibilities of one, it means that one or both of the others may be compromised. It can truly be a "no win" proposition.

25:5 THE COMPLAINT

The first step of the canonical process is the reporting of an accusation or complaint. This is similar to the civil law, where an alleged crime is reported to the authorities, or a complaint in a civil suit is filed that enumerates the harm that is alleged to have been committed. There are a number of sources from which the diocese could receive a complaint or allegation. The complaint can come from the alleged victim. It can come from a third party (e.g., a parent), it can be made anonymously, or it can be made by someone in the public sphere such as a reporter, or some other media outlet.[15] The complaint information can also come indirectly, for example, when the

---

14. Bishops' Committee on Canonical Affairs Task Force, A Resource for Canonical Processes for the Resolution of Complaints of Clerical Sexual Abuse of Minors 7 (2003).
  15. Id. at 6.

accuser bypasses the diocese completely and reports to the civil authorities, or goes to a civil lawyer who may hold a press conference, or is reported to a victim's group who then holds a press conference.[16] Finally, it can also come from the discovery of clergy criminal behavior because of his use of social networking such as a Facebook page or a web page. For example, a complaint against a Missouri priest resulted when his pornography collection was publicly reported in the news; he went on to stand trial in the criminal case while his bishop was indicted for a long-time failure to report the potential abuser.[17]

All complaints, regardless of their source, and regardless of whether they are directly or indirectly reported, should be treated seriously and given appropriate attention and investigation. In these cases there does not necessarily need to be a formal accuser, as c. 1717 refers only to a bishop "receiving knowledge of an alleged offense."

If the complaint is made anonymously, the matter should be investigated even if the identity of the person making the complaint is not known. Sometimes the accuser will make an allegation, but will ask that the accused not be told the identity of the person accusing him. In these cases the complainant should be made aware that eventually the accuser must be told the identity of the accuser, if the accusation is to be internally acted upon. If the diocese becomes aware of a complaint through the news media but without the accuser officially contacting the diocese, the allegations still should be investigated.[18]

When a complaint is received by a diocese, the diocese should inform the accuser that the accuser should notify the civil authorities of his or her accusation, and inquire whether the accuser needs any assistance. The person receiving the intake information, (who according to the Charter art. 2 should be a "competent person or persons to coordinate assistance") records as much information as the accuser is comfortable providing. It is important, however to record basic facts. Specifically, (1) who is being accused; (2) who is the alleged victim, if the person reporting the crime is not the victim; (3) if the accuser is not the same person as the victim, what is their relationship; (4) what is the alleged action of the accused; (5) when did it happen; (6) where did it happen; (7) was this a single incident or were there multiple incidents; and (8) the age of the victim at the time the event occurred. Such information provides the diocese with sufficient information to begin the process of determining the credibility of the allegation.

Obtaining this information is often more difficult than it might seem. This is particularly the case when trying to get precise information regarding an allegation

---

16. In cases where the diocese learns of the allegation indirectly, it is often difficult for the diocese to get further information regarding the facts of the allegation. If the allegation is made to the civil authorities, getting the facts can be very difficult due to the privacy laws. If the allegation comes from the client of a civil lawyer, the lawyer often advises his or client not to speak to the diocese so as to not prejudice a civil suit. Lagges, personal communication, October 24, 2011.

17. Judy Thomas, "Bishop Finn, Diocese Indicted in Abuse Case," Kansas City Star (Oct. 14, 2011).

18. Bishops' Committee on Canonical Affairs Task Force, supra, 7.

that occurred decades ago. As canonist Father Patrick Lagges explains, many times the person making the allegation cannot be very precise regarding the timeframe of the alleged abuse because it happened so long ago. He states that "Accusers often have a sense that something happened, but they can't quite pinpoint it in time. Or they mix up time frames...If a person says that something happened in the 7th grade, and later changes it to 8th or 9th grade, the advocate is going to point out the inconsistency."[19] Because these inconsistencies are going to later be highlighted by the advocate for the accused, it is very important that the person taking the initial information try to get accurate information from the outset, if possible.

25:6 THE PRELIMINARY INVESTIGATION

Once the accusation is made, the procedures for the preliminary investigation found in SST, the Code of Canon Law, and the Essential Norms begin.[20] The preliminary investigation is not a trial, or even a mini-trial. Rather it is an administrative action that "is meant to give the ordinary/hierarch a sense of probability that a delict [crime] did or did not occur."[21] This preliminary investigation establishes whether the accusation is one that triggers an appropriate action in the law and whether the allegation, after an initial assessment of the known facts and circumstances, has at least the semblance of truth. It does not mean that the allegation has been proved with moral certainty, only that the allegation cannot be summarily dismissed.[22]

25:7 IS THE ALLEGED ACT A "MORE GRAVE DELICT"?

Initially, it must be determined whether the nature of the accusation falls under the scope of SST and the Essential Norms. The first determination is whether the action for which the cleric is accused qualifies as a "grave delict" (a canonical crime) that does not fall under the Essential Norms, or a "more grave delict" (one of the more serious canonical crimes) as defined by SST.

19. Lagges, personal communication, supra.

20. For other articles on this topic, see J.J. Foley, "Preliminary Investigation: Consideration and Options," in Patricia M. Dugan, ed., Towards Future Developments in Penal Law: U.S. Theory and Practice 33–54 (2010); Patrick Lagges, "Elements in the Preliminary Investigation, " in Advocacy Vademecum 153–168, Patricia M. Dugan ed. (2006); Patrick R. Lagges, "The Penal Process: The Preliminary Investigation in Light of the Essential Norms of the United States," 38 Studia Canonica 394 (2004); Francis Morrisey, "The Preliminary Investigation in Penal Cases: Some of the Better Practices," 2(2) The Canonist 185 (2011).

21. Bishops' Committee on Canonical Affairs Task Force, supra, 9. The Ordinary or hierarch is usually the bishop.

22. Canon Law Society of America, Revised Guide to the Implementation of the U.S. Bishop's Essential Norms for Diocesan/Eparchial Policies Dealing with Allegations of Sexual Abuse of Minors by Priests or Deacons 21 (2004).

A "grave delict" would be any canonical crime for which one can be punished with the imposition of a canonical penalty. An example of this would be a cleric who is having a sexual relationship with or cohabiting with another adult in violation of c. 1395 § 1. Even if the canonical crime is not a violation specifically mentioned in the canons, c. 1399 allows violations of "divine or canon law" to be punished with a "just penalty." However, c. 1318 establishes a subcategory of crimes, which in the Code is referred to as "certain singularly malicious delicts which either can result in grave scandal or cannot be punished effectively by *Ferendae sententiae*[23] penalties." SST refers to these canonical crimes as "*Graviora delicta*" or "more grave delicts." These canonical crimes are akin to "capital crimes" in the civil law. They can be punished with the most serious punishments available in canon law, and are considered to be "*infamia*" or infamous in their nature. Because of the seriousness of the alleged offense, it is required by SST that the case be referred to the CDF.[24] There are a number of canonical delicts that fall into this category, but we are concerned only with the "more grave delict" of the sexual abuse of a minor. SST/10 defines the "more grave delict" of the sexual abuse of minor as:

Art. 6 §1 1° the delict against the sixth commandment of the Decalogue committed by a cleric with a minor below the age of eighteen years; in this case, a person who habitually lacks the use of reason is to be considered equivalent to a minor.

2° the acquisition, possession, or distribution by a cleric of pornographic images of minors under the age of fourteen, for purposes of sexual gratification, by whatever means or using whatever technology;

As SST/10 does not specifically define what a violation of the sixth commandment of the Decalogue might be, CDF has given bishops guidance that this delict may be sexual contact with a minor that includes open-mouth kissing, handling or fondling, oral sex, frottage, production of pornography, intercourse, bondage, anal sex, and/or bestiality. It can also include the non-contact behaviors of using pornography, exhibitionism, voyeurism, and/or sexual comments made in person, by phone, or over some form of electronic communication.[25] If the allegation involves behavior other than what has been listed above, it may be considered a grave delict. However, it is not necessarily a "more grave delict" that is subject to being judged under the SST or the Essential Norms.

23. A *ferendae sententiae* penalty is one that must be imposed through some sort of canonical process. This is as opposed to a *latae sententiae* penalty, which is incurred at the time when the crime is committed. It does not require a process for it to be imposed.

24. This means that in all cases where one of these crimes is alleged, unless the accusation is patently false the case is governed by SST. After the investigation is complete, the bishop must send the results to CDF for the congregation to make a determination how the bishop should proceed.

25. Congregation for the Doctrine of the Faith, Handout, unpublished, 2003.

25:8 IS THE PERSON A CANONICAL MINOR?

After it has been established that the alleged action could be considered a "more grave delict," the next step is to determine if the person making the allegation was a minor at the time of the alleged action. This is an important step in the process because the definition of a minor in the law has changed twice since 1990.

According to the Code of Canon Law, c. 97 defines a minor as anyone who has not yet completed his or her 18th year of age. However, c. 1395 defined the sexual abuse of a minor as sexual acts with a person below the age of 16 years. In response to the request from U.S. bishops, on April 25, 1994, the pope granted the United States derogation from the law, which raised the age of a minor to 18 for these crimes. The derogation stated, "With regard to canon 1395, §2 2°: this norm is to be applied to delicts committed with any minor as defined in c. 97 §1 and not only with a minor under sixteen years of age."[26] This exception to the law was initially granted for five years. On December 4, 1998, it was extended for another 10 years.[27] In 2001 this derogation was made permanent and extended to the Universal Church.[28]

This determination may be further complicated because though these changes were made, they were not retroactive—meaning they apply only to cases according to the date of the actual behavior. This non-retroactivity of the law was kept because within canon law, c. 9 declares that as a rule, new laws are not retroactive. In canon law, as in the civil law, one can only be punished for committing an act that was considered a crime at the time the act was completed, using the range of penalties available at that time for that crime. It is understood under both canon and civil law that it is unjust to punish someone for an act that was either not illegal or was not penalized as severely until the law was changed. Consequently the determination of whether SST and the Essential Norms apply depends on the year in which the delict was alleged to have been committed. Thus:

- Under the 1917 Code (abuse occurring prior to 1983), a minor is below the age of 16.
- Under the 1983 Code, for abuse occurring between 1983 and 1994, a minor is below the age of 16.
- For abuse occurring in the United States (but not elsewhere) after April 25, 1994, a minor is below the age of 18.
- For abuse occurring after 2001, universally a minor is below the age of 18.

This means that if the incident occurred prior to April 25, 1994, allegations by a young person between the ages of 16 and 18 are not governed under the Norms and legally are not considered a "more grave delict."

---

26. Rescript of the Secretariat of State, April 25, 1994, Prot. N. 346.053.
27. Letter of the Secretariat of State, December 4, 1998, Prot. N. 445.119/G.N.
28. Congregatio pro Doctrina Fidei, *De delictis gravioribus eidem Congregationi pro Doctrina Fidei reservatis* (Dei 18 mensis maii anno 2001), 93 AAS 785, 786–787 (2001).

25:9 PRESCRIPTION

As discussed in Chapter 22, prescription is similar to the civil court's statute of limitations, though it is not an exact equivalent.[29] Prior to 1994, many older allegations were unable to be adjudicated because the prescriptive time had run. After 1994, the prescriptive period has been extended. Currently, the rules are that:

- For acts alleged to have occurred prior to November 27, 1983 and reported before that date; the crime is no longer actionable five (5) years from the date of the act.
- For acts alleged to have occurred on or after November 27, 1983, and reported prior to April 25, 1994; the crime is no longer actionable five (5) years from the date of the act.
- For acts alleged to have occurred before April 25, 1994 but reported to the bishop or another ordinary after that date; the crime is no longer actionable five (5) years from his eighteenth birthday—until the minor reaches his twenty-fourth birthday.
- For acts alleged to have occurred on or after April 25, 1994, and reported on or after this date; the crime is no longer actionable (10) years after the victim's nineteenth birthday, unless less than one year has passed from the denunciation, as long as the report was made before the accuser had completed his twenty-eighth year.
- For acts committed or reported following the promulgation of SST on April 30, 2001, prescription of ten (10) years begins to run from the day on which a minor reaches the eighteenth year of age.[30]

It appears that even the most expansive reading of the law requires that an allegation of the sexual abuse of a minor must be made prior to the accuser's 29th birthday. However, it is common in these cases that the incident or incidents are not reported until long after the abuse occurs. Thus many reported cases of alleged abuse fall well outside the prescriptive time period.

In these cases, CDF may extend the prescriptive period for a particular case if the bishop requests it.[31] This power to derogate (to make an exception) from the

29. Prescription has classically meant that after the time period runs, one's ability to act on the crime has not just expired but is extinguished. In other words, it permanently vanishes. Interestingly, in dealing with these cases of the sexual abuse of a minor, CDF has been treating canonical statutory time limits as if they were statutes of limitations rather than using the traditional understanding of prescription. This is because statutes of limitations can be waived, whereas an action barred by prescription technically cannot be waived because it no longer exists. Charles G. Renati, Prescription and Derogation from Prescription in Sexual Abuse of Minor Cases (2007).

30. Canon Law Society of America, Guide to the Implementation of the U.S. Bishop's Essential Norms for Diocesan/Eparchial Policies Dealing with Allegations of Sexual Abuse of Minors by Priests or Deacons 21–25 (2003).

31. *Ex audientia Summi Pontificis*, 7 Nov. 2002. This is another difference between canon law and common law. In canon law, there are ways that the law of prescription can be dispensed with. This means that, for a good reason CDF can decide that for the greater

prescriptive limits was reiterated in SST/10 art. 7 § 1, which states that "A criminal action for delicts reserved to the Congregation for the Doctrine of the Faith is extinguished by prescription after twenty years, with due regard to the right of the Congregation for the Doctrine of the Faith to derogate from prescription in individual cases." Currently, though prescription is still a factor in a bishop's ability to adjudicate a case, it is no longer the absolute bar that it once was in bringing older cases.[32]

25:10 THE INVESTIGATION

Once it has been determined (1) that the alleged abuse is governed by SST and the Norms, (2) that the accuser was canonically a minor at the time of the alleged incident, (3) that it is within the prescriptive time period, (4) that the allegation is plausible and not able to be immediately dismissed, and (5) that the accused was a cleric at the time of the alleged offense,[33] the canonical process begins. According to c. 1719, the canonical investigation should be initiated with a formal decree to begin the inquiry.

There are three different canonical statutes that govern what should be done when an allegation is received by the diocese. The first is c. 1717 of the Code of Canon Law. This preliminary process is often referred to as the 1717 investigation or preliminary investigation. Canon 1717 states:

> Can. 1717 §1. Whenever an ordinary has knowledge, which at least seems true (saltem veri similem), of a delict, he is carefully to inquire personally or through another suitable person about the facts, circumstances, and imputability, unless such an inquiry seems entirely superfluous.
>
> §2 Care must be taken so that the good name of anyone is not endangered from this investigation.

good, the law barring the canonical action does not apply in a particular case. In the common law, there is no concept of a "dispensation" from the civil statute of limitations.

32. Lawrence A. DiNardo, Canonical Penal Procedures 4 (Canon Law Society of America, 2010).

33. Particularly for older accusations, if the accused was not yet ordained a priest, there can be some question regarding whether he was a cleric at the time of the alleged offense. "While at the present time a man enters the clerical state at the time of ordination to the diaconate, up until the *motu proprio Ministeria quaedam* in 1972, a man entered the clerical state once he had been tonsured. Moreover, in the time immediately after the promulgation of *Ministeria quaedam,* there were certain other hybrid liturgical practices in which a person was tonsured, but did not receive any of the other 'minor orders,' instead receiving the ministries prescribed in the *motu proprio.* Therefore, it is necessary in each and every case to examine whether the person had entered the clerical state at the time the alleged action occurred. If he was not a cleric at the time, his case cannot be heard under *SST* or the *Essential Norms* for the United States." (Lagges, The Penal Process, supra, 386.

§3. The person who conducts the investigation has the same powers and obligations as an auditor in the process; the same person cannot act as a judge in the matter if a judicial process is initiated later.

The requirements of this canon were included and elaborated upon in Norm 6 of the Essential Norms.

Norm 6—When an allegation of sexual abuse of a minor by a priest or deacon is received, a preliminary investigation in accordance with canon law will be initiated and conducted promptly and objectively (CIC, c. 1717; CCEO, c. 1468). During the investigation the accused enjoys the presumption of innocence, and all appropriate steps shall be taken to protect his reputation. The accused will be encouraged to retain the assistance of civil and canonical counsel and will be promptly notified of the results of the investigation. When there is sufficient evidence that sexual abuse of a minor has occurred, the Congregation of the Doctrine of the Faith shall be notified. The bishop/eparch shall then apply the precautionary measures mentioned in CIC, c. 1722, or CCEO, c. 1473—i.e., withdraw the accused from exercising the sacred ministry or any ecclesiastical office or function, impose or prohibit residence in a given place or territory, and prohibit public participation in the Most Holy Eucharist pending the outcome of the process.

Finally, SST also governs the process, and it mandates:

SST—Art. 16: Whenever the Ordinary or Hierarch receives a report of a more grave delict, which has at least the semblance of truth (*notitiam saltem verisimilem*), once the preliminary investigation has been completed, he is to communicate the matter to the Congregation for the Doctrine of the Faith which, unless it calls the case to itself due to particular circumstances, will direct the Ordinary or Hierarch how to proceed further, with due regard, however, for the right to appeal, if the case warrants, against a sentence of the first instance only to the Supreme Tribunal of this same Congregation.

After the initial facts are ascertained, the bishop or his delegate, according to the canon, must establish if the allegation "seems true" or has some semblance of truth. The USCCB clarified that their understanding of when an allegation "seems true" is "any allegation that is not manifestly false or frivolous is subject to a canonical preliminary investigation."[34] It is strongly suggested that the person responsible for taking the initial reports be someone such as a victims' assistance coordinator who has expertise in making the initial determination of credibility, as well as someone trained in knowing what questions to ask.[35] As was the case in Kansas City in 2011, having one priest as the sole intake person was not the best choice.

---

34. United States Conference of Catholic Bishops, Diocesan Review Board Resource Booklet 6 (2008).
35. Lagges, The Penal Process, supra, 392.

The preliminary investigation is to be done quietly and discreetly, to protect the reputation of the accused priest until it can be determined whether the allegation has the semblance of truth.[36] The purpose of the investigation is twofold: (1) is there a semblance of truth that sexual abuse actually occurred, and (2) is the cleric accused of the crime the one who committed it?

The preliminary investigation is not a mini-trial. Rather, it is a process to gather both inculpatory and exculpatory evidence to determine whether there is enough evidence to proceed with a canonical process.

25:11 WHO CONDUCTS THE INVESTIGATION? .

Canon 1717 states that the person who conducts the initial investigation cannot be a judge if there is a canonical trial. Because the bishop is the judicial authority of the diocese, to preserve his impartiality it is strongly suggested that someone else, for example, another priest or "another suitable person," investigate the allegation.[37] Some dioceses use the Vicar for Clergy, the Vicar General, or another priest or deacon to do the investigation.

Many dioceses prefer to have an outside investigator, a private investigator, or a civil law attorney conduct the investigation so as to preserve impartiality. They are able to gather evidence and testimony without bias.[38] There has been considerable criticism that when a priest or someone "in house" conducts the investigation, the investigative findings have oftentimes been biased, downplayed, or dismissed. Most recently in Kansas City,[39] an independent report was produced after a priest was arrested and, among other things, found to have child pornography on his computer. The report documents that the internal investigator, the diocesan Vicar General, dismissed multiple credible prior reports of the priest's misconduct. Because he was the only person determining whether the report was credible enough to be sent to the review board, cases and evidence that should have been submitted to the diocesan review board were instead summarily dismissed.[40] The report's conclusion was that the internal investigator was given too much discretion and too little oversight in making such decisions.[41] This problem can be avoided if the investigator is someone who investigates professionally, rather than

---

36. DiNardo, supra, 5.

37. Morrisey, supra, 190.

38. People often presume that the bias would be favorable to the priest in question. What is not taken into account is that in the course of various interactions over the years it is just as likely that a priest-investigator might actually be biased against the accused. Like all human beings, priests are not immune to having strong feelings of dislike or antipathy toward others, including fellow priests.

39. In October 2011, the bishop of Kansas City and the diocese were criminally indicted for their failure to report potential abuse. Thomas, supra.

40. Todd P. Graves, The Report of the Independent Investigation of the Catholic Diocese of Kansas City-Saint Joseph 115, Kansas City: Diocese of Kansas City (2011).

41. Id. at 115–117.

a priest who is not trained in this work, and if there is more than just a single person deciding whether the review board should review the accusation.

In talking to witnesses, including the accuser, it is important that they be allowed to tell their story without being influenced or led by the investigator.[42] Many investigators can "lead" their witnesses, and may ask inappropriate questions because they are not trained to know any better. The investigator has the canonical status of an auditor,[43] but there is nothing in the Code, SST, or the Norms that gives requirements to ensure the training, competence, or fitness of the investigator. Therefore it is better for the diocese to err on the part of finding a person or persons who are trained in investigating and who know how to ask proper questions. There are also professionals who are trained in dealing with alleged victims of sexual abuse, given the particular difficulties and sensibilities involved. Using such a professional is often a good idea, and is strongly suggested if the victim is still a minor. Further, some additional training in proper canonical questioning techniques and requirements should be given. It should be stressed to the investigator that his job is to "confine the inquiry to the facts, circumstances, and imputability *concerning the specific action.*"[44] The investigation is not a "fishing expedition" but is meant to be geared toward proving or disproving the specifically alleged crime.

The law does not require that the investigator take the witnesses' testimony verbatim. It allows that the testimony can be summarized and the investigator sign his summary.[45] However, when this occurs, it means that the testimony of the witness is necessarily filtered through the investigator. Though it is not required, it is fairer that during both the initial investigation and when the accuser and witnesses are deposed that the testimony is recorded and transcribed.[46] This way the accused can know precisely of what he is being accused and what questions were asked of the accuser and the witnesses, and he can then mount an appropriate defense.

The evidence gathered can be in the form of testimony or other physical evidence. It can be direct or circumstantial evidence. The evidence should be gathered objectively, and should include evidence that could prove the cleric's innocence as well as evidence that could indicate his guilt.[47] The accuser often suggests witnesses to be interviewed. Oftentimes the evidence consists of interviews with other people

---

42. Oftentimes, any contact with the accuser will be controlled by his or her civil lawyer. Frequently the civil lawyer for the accuser does not allow the accuser to give testimony to an investigator or to the diocese. In other cases, the lawyer wants to tightly control access to the accuser. This makes it difficult for the investigator or for the judges in the process to obtain testimony in the case. Lagges, personal communication, supra.

43. Auditors are discussed more fully in Chapter 24. In brief, a canonical auditor is named by the canonical judge to act on behalf of the judges to question witnesses and to run the day-to-day aspects of a canonical trial. An auditor can be one of the judges on the case, or can be someone else named by the judge.

44. Lagges, The Penal Process, supra, 399.

45. This opinion was verbally conveyed to leaders of the Canon Law Society of America when they went on their biannual visit in 2010.

46. Morrisey, supra, 192.

47. Renati, supra, 178–179.

who might have knowledge of either the incident or of the parties involved.[48] This process can be waived if there is evidence from a civil trial or from other sources that the allegation is true. It is also important that the internal process not interfere with any ongoing civil or criminal investigations or procedures.

25:12 WHEN IS THE ACCUSED NOTIFIED? ⌁

There are many "holes" or absences of direction in the canonical processes that are not addressed in any of the procedural laws. One glaring hole is a definitive determination of when is the proper time to notify a cleric that an accusation has been made against him. Notification is not mentioned at all in SST.

It is not clear in the law at what point the accused cleric is to be notified about the accusation against him. Norm 6 of the Essential Norms implies that the accused is told soon after the accusation is made, because it states that he is to be informed of the outcome of the inquiry, and that in the meantime, he should be encouraged to retain the assistance of civil and canonical counsel. However, it is not specified whether that notification would come (1) within a set number of days after the allegation is made, (2) after the bishop has established that the allegation cannot be immediately dismissed, (3) after the investigator has completed his investigation, (4) when the review board reviews the allegation, or (5) at the outcome of the review board's decision that the allegation is credible. Furthermore, some dioceses are known to wait to inform the cleric of the accusation until after CDF[49] responds with its direction on how the case should be handled.

When the accused priest is notified, in the past it has often not been handled very well, though some dioceses are trying to improve the handling of this situation. Many dioceses do not alert the cleric that he should engage a civil/canon lawyer before the cleric is summoned to the bishop's office to be told about the allegation. The cleric often has no idea what the meeting with the bishop is about. When told of the allegation, the accused cleric often panics and in his terror may say things to the diocese that he might later regret. Canon law has no equivalent of the familiar "*Miranda* warnings" found in the civil system. Nevertheless, the accused has a right to representation and he should be made aware of this fact before the formal accusation is presented. Also some dioceses use that first meeting to get the priest to resign his pastoral office and to agree to go away for therapy. Thinking he is "being cooperative," the accused signs all that is presented to him without understanding the implications or his rights.

48. Internally, these witnesses could be priests who were assigned to the same parish and who lived in the same rectory, housekeepers, secretaries, school principals, or parishioners (particularly parents with children the same age) who would have worked closely with the accused.

49. SST requires that CDF review all cases that are not patently false, and it is CDF that makes the final determination how the case will be handled.

This causes much consternation among canonists who represent accused clerics. They believe that a cleric should know if a case is being put together against him so that, in justice, he has the opportunity to defend himself. No mention is made in the Norms whether the accused cleric is permitted to submit exculpatory evidence to either the bishop or the review board during their review of the allegation. Although this practice is not forbidden, neither is it explicitly permitted.[50]

Interestingly, the Code of Canons for the Eastern Churches (CCEO)[51] includes in its initial canons on the preliminary investigation that "Before making any decision in the matter, the hierarch is to hear the accused and the promoter of justice regarding the delict...(c. 1469)." Consequently, canonists argue this is seen as a progressive development that was lacking in the 1983 Code, it should be incorporated into the praxis of all prior investigations. Furthermore, the Circular Letter issued by CDF on May 16, 2011, to assist Episcopal Conferences to develop their own national guidelines, states in section III-e that "unless there are serious contrary indications, even in the course of the preliminary investigation, the accused cleric should be informed of the accusation, and given the opportunity to respond to it."

Many canonists who represent canonical defendants believe that the inability of the accused to present exculpatory evidence cements the presumption of guilt of the accused in the minds of the bishop and the review board. They would hold that in justice, as soon as a case is being investigated and built against a cleric, he should have the right to be informed of the accusation, and to be able to present his side of the story, as so much is at stake.[52]

There are other canonists who argue that the review board acts like a civil grand jury. Grand juries are given information provided by the civil prosecutor to determine whether there is enough evidence to bring an indictment. Therefore, the argument is that because this body functions like a grand jury, the accused's right to present a defense attaches only after the review board has made a determination that the allegation has enough merit that the case be sent to CDF to review. In some of these cases, the accused cleric has actually been forbidden by his bishop from hiring his own private investigator or from doing any independent investigating to attempt to establish his own innocence.

The fact of the matter is that there is no constant practice or norm among dioceses when it comes to this issue. Everyone agrees that the accused must be informed of the accusation so that he can defend himself, but when that right becomes actionable, and the limits on his investigation and self-defense, will depend on the policy of each individual diocese.

50. Some dioceses invite the accused priest to come before the review board and make a presentation. Some clerics decline to do so on the advice of their civil attorney, but others come to the review board along with their civil or canonical counsel and make a presentation. Lagges, personal communication, supra.

51. The CCEO is the code of canon law that binds the Eastern Churches in union with Rome and that was promulgated in 1990, years after the Code of Canon Law of 1983.

52. Daniel E. Hoye, "Reintegration and Restoration of Exonerated Priests," Proceedings, 73 (Oct. 2011) 118–129.

Whenever the accused is notified, much like a civil *Miranda* warning, the cleric should be told "of his right to remain silent and warned that anything he says could be used against him, not only in an ecclesiastical penal process, but possibly also in a criminal or civil action."[53] The accused cleric is often in shock at this point, and this should be taken into account. Furthermore, the person informing the cleric of the allegation "should not induce an accused to unwittingly waive his natural, canonical or civil rights."[54] Finally, if the accused cleric chooses to give the investigator a formal statement, it should be put in writing, and it should be signed and then notarized.

25:13 DIOCESAN REVIEW BOARD

Once the investigators complete the bulk of their investigation, the information that they have collected is given to the bishop. At this point, the bishop is to make use of his diocesan review board. A review board was mandated by both the Dallas Charter for the Protection of Youth and the Essential Norms that were approved by the USCCB in 2002. This requirement for a review board has also been renewed at several intervals since 2002. It is meant to be a vehicle for laypersons with expertise in the area of child sexual abuse to assist the bishop in assessing allegations against clergy.[55] As a canonist in CDF pithily describes it, the review board has one job: to sniff the case put together by the investigator and see if it smells, and if it does, then notify the bishop of their opinion.

The requirement for diocesan review boards was created in the Essential Norms, nn. 4–5. Norm 4 gives the parameters for the review board regarding its formal task. It states:

4. To assist diocesan/eparchial bishops, each diocese/eparchy will also have a review board which will function as a confidential consultative body to the bishop/eparch in discharging his responsibilities. The functions of this board may include:
   a. advising the diocesan bishop/eparch in his assessment of allegations of sexual abuse of minors and in his determination of suitability for ministry;
   b. reviewing diocesan/eparchial policies for dealing with sexual abuse of minors; and
   c. offering advice on all aspects of these cases, whether retrospectively or prospectively.

There are important details in this description. First, the review board is a consultative canonical body for the bishop. It does not have binding authority, but is to provide the bishop with a range of external, expert opinions on the subjects and

53. Canon Law Society of America, Revised Guide, supra, 2004.
54. Id. at 20.
55. DiNardo, supra, 4.

cases presented to it. This board is effectively a canonical entity governed by canon law. Although the bishop has the freedom to grant various functions to the board, the Norms state that the bishop "may" do so, not that he "must" do so. Norm 5 gives further specifics about the makeup of this board. It states:

> **5.** The review board, established by the diocesan/eparchial bishop, will be composed of at least five persons of outstanding integrity and good judgment in full communion with the Church. The majority of the review board members will be lay persons who are not in the employ of the diocese/eparchy; but at least one member should be a priest who is an experienced and respected pastor of the diocese/eparchy in question, and at least one member should have particular expertise in the treatment of the sexual abuse of minors. The members will be appointed for a term of five years, which can be renewed. It is desirable that the Promoter of Justice participate in the meetings of the review board.

Again, some interesting points to note. The review board is to have at least five persons with the majority being laypersons who are not employed by the diocese. The Norms require at least one member with special expertise in the treatment of sexual abuse. As the board is debating fitness for clerical ministry, the Norms require the board's membership include at least one veteran priest.

The actual number of board members and the particular makeup of the board are ultimately up to the bishop. Many bishops include professionals who either directly or tangentially work with victims of child sexual abuse. These would often include social workers or psychologists, police officers or other law enforcement officials, civil lawyers, judges, teachers, and healthcare professionals who deal on a regular basis with abuse issues. Sometimes, boards include persons who have been child abuse victims or parents of victims. Though the majority of the review board should be Catholic, the board may include non-Catholics as well. Oftentimes a diocesan canon lawyer is on the board to help answer the canonical issues raised.

The review board is not an investigative body.[56] Rather, it is a body whose purpose is to conduct an assessment of the results of the investigation to determine two things.[57] First, it is to assess the allegation made against the cleric. Canon 1717 gives the standard of proof for this determination as an accusation that is *"saltem veri similem"* or "at least seems true." This is a much lower standard than a final determination of guilt, for which the standard of proof is "moral certitude." Second, it is to make a determination regarding the accused cleric's suitability for ministry. The review board is not to hold a trial, nor is it asked to determine if the allegation is fully substantiated. Rather, it is to "assess whether the proofs which are gathered are sufficient to support the probable nature of the allegation."[58]

As many dioceses treat the review board as being similar to a grand jury, the accused and his advocate in these dioceses do not appear before it and do not

56. United States Conference of Catholic Bishops, supra.
57. Canon Law Society of America, Revised Guide, supra, 20.
58. Id. at 21.

submit some form of defense. However, many review boards invite the accused to submit evidence and/or appear before them. Given that it is usually after the review board's intervention and after the bishop makes his decision that the accusation is made public, it is fairer to ask the accused cleric to present some defense to the review board.[59] In some cases this would prevent cases being made public where the cleric can prove his innocence, or from forcing him to submit to all of the restrictions that come after the bishop concludes that the accusation is credible.

As part of the review board's mandate in the Norms is to advise the bishop to help him make a determination regarding the accused cleric's fitness for ministry, it can be argued that its mandate could be broadened if the bishop desires it. Questions have been raised about whether in determining suitability, what if the cleric's actions do not technically fall under the Norms but indicate that the cleric is not suitable for ministry? For example, the accused misconduct involves multiple 18-year-olds, or the action was civilly illegal (e.g., the inappropriate touching of a 17-year-old in 1973) but not a canonical crime at the time? It is the decision of the diocesan bishop whether he would want to broaden the scope of the review board's purview to include acts that are not Norm violations but would be relevant to the cleric's overall suitability for ministry in accord with Norm 4a. If the bishop chooses to broaden the scope of review in such a fashion, as a canonically created entity, the board still must follow the directives of the Norms and principles of universal canon law.[60]

Ultimately, the review board reviews all of the evidence submitted to it, both exculpatory and evidence that supports the accusation. There is no legal standard put forth in the Essential Norms defining what is the threshold for a credible allegation. According to the USCCB Task Force, different review boards have used such standards as "believable and plausible, reasonable and probable, or preponderance of the evidence."[61] This base threshold should be set by the bishop prior to the review board beginning its work.[62]

The review board then submits its opinion to the bishop as to whether or not the members believe that the accusation made against the accused cleric is credible. It is not clear from the Norms whether this opinion should be in writing or verbally voiced to the bishop.[63] However, it seems logical that if the review board finds the allegation credible, its report giving the reasons for its findings should be in writing and should be included in the case evidence submitted to CDF.[64] It is also not clear that, if the members of the review board are in disagreement, how the report should be presented—should both opinions be given to the bishop, or only the majority

---

59. Hoye, supra, 121.
60. Canon Law Society of America, Revised Guide, supra, 22.
61. United States Conference of Catholic Bishops, supra, at 6.
62. Morrisey, supra, 197.
63. Thomas J. Green, "Clerical Sexual Abuse of Minors: Some Canonical Reflections," 63 The Jurist 63 398 (2003).
64. There are review boards that do not keep minutes, or if they do, they are minimal. This is to prevent these written records from being subpoenaed for a civil or criminal trial. Lagges, personal communication, supra.

opinion? Last, it is unclear whether the accuser should at this point be notified of the opinion of the review board.

If the review board does not believe that the allegation is credible, it advises the bishop of its opinion. If the bishop agrees with the board's assessment, then he issues a decree closing the investigation and the matter ends (c. 1719).

However, if the review board's assessment is that there is sufficient reason to find the accusation credible, and the bishop agrees, then the investigation enters a new, more public phase.[65] The accused is notified of the results of the bishop's investigation. If he has not yet been told to obtain both civil and canonical counsel, he is then informed that he should do so.

It is at this point that the cleric's ministerial activity is curtailed in accord with c. 1722. Canon 1722 states:

> To prevent scandals, to protect the freedom of witnesses, and to guard the course of justice, the ordinary, after having heard the promoter of justice and cited the accused, at any stage of the process can exclude the accused from the sacred ministry or from some office and ecclesiastical function, can impose or forbid residence in some place or territory, or even can prohibit public participation in the Most Holy Eucharist. Once the cause ceases, all these measures must be revoked; they also end by the law itself when the penal process ceases.

Likewise, Norm 6 of the Essential Norms states that the bishop should "withdraw the accused from exercising the sacred ministry." The accused cleric is suspended from his ministerial office; he can be told where to live, and can be prohibited from public participation in Eucharist or other Church functions.[66] In accord with Norm 7, the diocese can request that the cleric "seek, and may be urged voluntarily to comply with, an appropriate medical and psychological evaluation at a facility mutually acceptable to the diocese/eparchy and to the accused." However, the cleric can refuse such an evaluation, or could "give qualified permission for psychological evaluation."[67] In other words, the cleric can choose to submit to some specific types of evaluation or he can choose to be evaluated having first agreed on who will be allowed to have access to the results.[68]

Between the time that the priest is suspended and prior to a final judgment or determination made in his case, he is entitled to diocesan financial support.[69] It has

65. Morrisey, supra, 194.
66. Id. at 195–196.
67. Canon Law Society of America, Revised Guide, supra, 24.
68. HIPAA governs the disclosure of mental health evaluations of the priest in a clinical setting. The cleric must sign a HIPAA release for the professional evaluation to be disclosed to the bishop by the treatment center or therapist. However, the information could be subpoenaed by the police. There are some constraints on the disclosure of the police file to the bishop, under local practice, and especially of the police copies of the HIPAA-protected mental health records.
69. Father Patrick Lagges wrote an insightful article regarding the necessity for the financial support of the priest both during a canonical proceeding and after the

unfortunately been the case that when a priest has been suspended, some dioceses have reacted further by suspending the cleric's insurance, his stipend, and other parish or diocesan financial supports. At times even his pension is suspended. If the priest is told to vacate the parish rectory, he is sometimes not given an alternative place to live.

When a man becomes a priest, with few exceptions he generally gives up the potential for a large salary and the ability to accumulate wealth. For suspended priests, the cleric is not allowed to work because of the restrictions placed upon him, and he likely has only limited or no means to support himself. The situation can be even more serious if the cleric is retired and has no alternative means of support. For these reasons, it is important that for the duration of the investigation and canonical processes that the diocese should continue to financially support the cleric.[70]

25:14 WHAT ARE THE ACCUSED CLERIC'S CANONICAL RIGHTS?

Once the accused cleric has been notified of the accusation against him, his canonical rights come into play.[71] The accused has the right not to incriminate himself, the right not to be coerced to confess, and the right not to be put under oath (cc. 1531–1532). He has the right to a canonical advocate, and the diocese must provide him one if he cannot afford to hire one himself (cc. 1481 § 2, 1723). Interestingly, while there is an obligation for the diocese to provide the accused with an advocate, there no obligation in canon law that the diocese must pay for a specific advocate that is independently hired. According to c. 1490, the diocese is supposed to have canonical advocates on salary, and the diocese can provide the services of one of its advocates to the accused—much like the state pays for the services of particular defense attorneys for indigent defendants.

Once the cleric has retained a canonical advocate, the advocate has the right to know the charge against his client (cc. 1507–1508, 1720), and to see what evidence has been gathered and presented against his client. The advocate should be given access to any of the testimony, witness testimony, and other evidence presented by the promoter of justice so that the defense has the opportunity to refute it (cc. 1598, 1603).

Like the civil law, the accused has the right to know what the accusation is against him, and who made it. He also has the right to refute that allegation, though the

proceeding is concluded. The article may be found in "Canonical Issues of Renumeration and Sustenance for Priests Accused of Sexual Misconduct," 71 Proceedings 150–167 (2009).

70. Ronny E. Jenkins, "The Charter and Norms Two Years Later: Towards a Resolution of Recent Canonical Dilemmas," 66 CLSA Proceedings 131–132 (2004); James I. Donlon "Remuneration, Decent Support, and Clerics Removed from the Ministry of the Church." 66 CLSA Proceedings 106–107 (2004).

71. Morrisey, supra, 186–187.

1983 Code of Canon Law (as opposed to the Eastern Code) does not have an explicit provision that the bishop must hear the cleric's side of the story prior to sending the bishop's case recommendation to CDF.[72] If CDF mandates a trial, the accused has the right to refute the witness testimony and any evidence the witness formally presents, and to present his own exculpatory testimony, witnesses, and evidence. He also has the right to be informed that he is innocent until proven guilty, and that the burden of proof is on the diocese to prove his guilt. He is not compelled to prove his innocence.

At this time, the cleric should also be informed that if he so desires, he can voluntarily petition CDF to be returned to the lay state and be dispensed from all clerical obligations. This option in particular should be offered to those clerics who have confessed, or in cases where there is little dispute that the allegation is true. If the cleric chooses this option, the petition will be voluntary rather than forced, and the process is somewhat abbreviated. However, if the cleric denies the charges against him and the evidence in the case as it stands is inconclusive, this is certainly not an option.

25:15 THE CASE PROCEEDS TO CDF

If the bishop agrees with the review board that based on the investigation there is enough evidence to indicate that the allegation is *"saltem veri similem"* or "at least seems true," then according to art. 16 of SST/10 the case must be submitted to CDF. Article 16 states:

> Art. 16 Whenever the Ordinary or Hierarch receives a report of a more grave delict, which has at least the semblance of truth, once the preliminary investigation has been completed, he is to communicate the matter to the Congregation for the Doctrine of the Faith which, unless it calls the case to itself due to particular circumstances, will direct the Ordinary or Hierarch how to proceed further, with due regard, however, for the right to appeal, if the case warrants, against a sentence of the first instance only to the Supreme Tribunal of this same Congregation.

In cases where the cleric's guilt has already been established either by his confession or through a civil criminal process, and the bishop or Ordinary did not deem it necessary to conduct an investigation, SST article 17 allows CDF to carry out any preliminary steps that would normally have been done locally.

---

72. However, there are those canonists who argue that there is an indirect requirement because c. 50 requires that before a canonical authority can issue a decree, he must seek out the proofs and hear those whose rights can be injured. Thus the bishop would need to hear the accused before he could make a decision that affects or harms the accused's rights.

25:16 THE BISHOP'S *VOTUM* OR OPINION

Before sending the case to CDF, the diocesan bishop must write his canonical opinion, or *votum*, regarding how he believes the case ought to be handled. The bishop's opinion should be a comprehensive overview of the case, and should answer (1) whether in his opinion the cleric's conduct gives a basis for initiating a penal process, (2) whether there is sufficient evidence to proceed with a judicial trial or other process, (3) whether to request a dispensation from prescription, and (4) whether it is practical (due to such circumstances as the cleric's age, health, or other extenuating circumstance) to proceed with a judicial trial, or to handle the case in a different manner. Other information should include the bishop's recommendation for how the case should proceed, and should give his reasoning for why he is making that suggestion.[73]

In the *votum* the bishop gives his own opinion concerning the accusation, and whether he believes the cleric's actions to be fully imputable to the cleric. The bishop must give an overview of the cleric's age, health, and any other circumstance about the cleric that CDF might find illustrative—including other issues or problems in ministry that the priest may have had. The bishop should inform CDF whether there has been any civil or criminal litigation, and the status or outcome of those cases. Finally, if the bishop does recommend that the cleric be dismissed, he should inform CDF that he offered the cleric the option of being voluntarily laicized, and he should recount what the accused cleric's response was to that offer.

The accused cleric does not have the right to see the bishop's *votum*. The *votum* is not a legal document because it is the bishop's personal opinion of the case. It is based on the investigation and his personal knowledge of the cleric, and meant to provide guidance to CDF. It is not a formal decree or judgment, and there is no recourse for the opinions stated within it.

25:17 WHAT ARE THE CONGREGATION'S OPTIONS?

Once the case is sent to CDF, the Congregation has a number of options from which to choose. Any of these options can be requested by the diocesan bishop in his *votum*, but the Congregation makes the final decision. It is important to keep in mind once again that canon law does not recognize legal precedent as being binding. So it is entirely possible that CDF could assign different processes to two seemingly identical cases, based on who is making the decision in CDF, on what the cleric's bishop recommended, or on other factors known to CDF. The disposition of one case has absolutely no influence on the way a subsequent case will be handled.

---

73. CDF is competent to derogate in particular cases (*ex audientia Summi Pontificis* 7 November 2002) and SST/10 article 7.

25:18 VOLUNTARY RETURN TO THE LAY STATE

CDF's first option is that if the cleric petitions for it, they can return the cleric voluntarily to the lay state and dispense him from his clerical obligations. The cleric files his petition with CDF along with the *votum* of support from the diocesan bishop. If the cleric asks for further dispensation from celibacy, that request should be included in the petition. That dispensation is not always and not automatically granted, though it is more likely to be granted if the cleric petitions for the dispensation.

25:19 CDF TAKES THE CASE ITSELF

Article 16 of SST/10 reserves the right of CDF to "call the case to itself due to particular circumstances." Although the authors are unaware of any instances where CDF has actually exercised this option, the option exists if CDF ever desires to do so.

25:20 AUTOMATIC *"EX OFFICIO"* DISMISSAL

In particular cases the bishop can request and the Holy Father can grant that the cleric be dismissed automatically, or ex officio. Article 21 of SST/10 allows CDF in the most serious cases to:

> Art. 21 §2 2° [However, the Congregation for the Doctrine of the Faith may:] present the most grave cases to the decision of the Roman Pontiff with regard to dismissal from the clerical state or deposition, together with dispensation from the law of celibacy, when it is manifestly evident that the delict was committed and after having given the guilty party the possibility of defending himself.

The case is decided by CDF and the decision is confirmed by the pope on a case-by-case basis. In these cases no canonical trial is necessary, though the accused cleric is usually given the right to respond and defend himself if he chooses prior to the decision being made. There are times, however, when this process has been completed and the cleric has been dismissed without either the priest or his advocate knowing that the bishop requested this option. This process is generally reserved for the most serious, the most egregious cases of abuse. These are usually the ones that are notorious and have caused great scandal, and there is no doubt of the guilt of the cleric involved. The USCCB task force envisions that this option is appropriate for cases where:

- The accused has admitted his crimes, especially if his admission occurred in a civil judicial forum;
- The accused is already incarcerated following a civil penal process;

- Public notoriety surrounds the accused's actions (and subsequent civil processes which addressed them);
- The public good of the Church demands immediate action to resolve the issue.[74]

There is no appeal of this decision. As with the voluntary process, the cleric can either be dismissed from the clerical state without dispensing the cleric from celibacy (*dimissio e statu clericali*) or they can dismiss while also dispensing the cleric from celibacy (*depositio, una cum dispensatione a lege caelibatus*).

25:21 JUDICIAL TRIAL

The usual canonical process used for cases where the cleric denies the allegation is the canonical judicial trial. SST Art. 21 §1 states that "the more grave delicts reserved to the Congregation for the Doctrine of the Faith are to be tried in a judicial process." This process will be described in great detail in Chapter 27.

Unlike the civil law, there are three possible outcomes for a judicial trial. When CDF authorizes such a trial, its decree includes a tripartite distinction regarding one of three kinds of verdicts: *sententia condemnatoria* (guilty), *sententia absolutoria* (innocent), or *sententia dimissioria* (guilt not proven). Furthermore, the court can impose the penalty of dismissal (which according to Norm 8 is the standard penalty for a cleric who is guilty of sexually abusing a child), or impose a lesser penalty such as a life of prayer and penance that allows the cleric to remain a priest, but with limited or no faculties[75] to act as a priest for a guilty verdict.[76] In either case, a guilty verdict prevents the cleric from ever publicly functioning in ministry again. If a guilty verdict is returned, the cleric has the right to appeal that decision to CDF as the appellate court. If the priest is exonerated, then the dictates of Norm 13 state that "When an accusation has been shown to be unfounded, every step possible will be taken to restore the good name of the person falsely accused."

25:22 ADMINISTRATIVE PROCESS

CDF also has the option to authorize the diocesan bishop to conduct an administrative penal process in accord with c. 1720 instead of a judicial trial. This process would generally be preferred if it is likely that there is not sufficient evidence in the case for a judicial trial, or if there is an ongoing civil or criminal investigation that

---

74. Bishops' Committee on Canonical Affairs Task Force, supra, 20.

75. A priest's "faculties" are granted to him by a diocese. It is the formal permission to act as a priest in the diocese, and they specify what sorts of actions the priest is allowed to perform while in that territory.

76. "A Life of Prayer and Penance" is supposed to be imposed as a penalty only if there is some good reason not to dismiss completely, for example, the cleric's advanced age or health are such that the diocese cannot dismiss him.

precludes the Church from being able to gather evidence.[77] It is also appropriately used when the case is clear-cut, the testimony against the accused cleric is clear and substantial, all the proofs effectively have been gathered, and there is no contradictory evidence. Some bishops believe that an administrative process is faster than a judicial trial. In cases where the evidence is clear, this may be true. However, in cases where the evidence is not clear-cut, the process can take just as long as a judicial trial, even sometimes years to complete.

There is an inherent dilemma with this process. The same bishop who makes the final determination in this case is also the one: (1) who made the initial judgment that the allegation is credible, (2) who has publicly removed the cleric from ministry, (3) who may have informed the alleged victim and the family that he would never return the cleric to ministry, (4) who may have paid thousands of dollars to send the cleric for inpatient treatment, and (5) who is negotiating through his lawyer and insurance company on settlement of claims from that priest's misconduct. This certainly raises the question about whether the bishop can be objective and non-prejudicial in this new process. However, it is presumed by the Code that he can be impartial. Canon 1720 gives the outline for the process. It states:

> Can. 1720 If the ordinary thinks that the matter must proceed by way of extrajudicial decree:
>
> §1 he is to inform the accused of the accusation and the proofs, giving an opportunity for self-defense, unless the accused neglected to appear after being properly summoned;
>
> §2 he is to weigh carefully all the proofs and arguments with two assessors;
>
> §3 if the delict is certainly established and a criminal action is not extinguished, he is to issue a decree according to the norm of cc. 1342–1350, setting forth the reasons in law and in fact at least briefly.

Once CDF has authorized an administrative process, the bishop should open the process with a new decree,[78] and the investigation resumes.[79] If any further evidence comes to light, it should be added to the case. The accused cleric has the right to not only be informed of the accusation and proofs against him, but he has the right to self-defense. This includes giving testimony, suggesting witnesses, and presenting exculpatory evidence. In some cases, the accused will hire his own investigator to assist in proving he did not commit the crime.

77. Canon Law Society of America, Revised Guide, supra, 27–28.
78. Morrisey, supra, 196–197.
79. There is some debate about this. Some canonists argue that the administrative penal process presumes that all the proofs have been gathered. Thus if there are more proofs to be gathered, one cannot use the administrative process and a trial is needed. These canonists claim that if more proofs are being gathered, then what seems like an administrative action actually is a trial without the full protection of the law on trials, which is problematic. Other canonists maintain that it is perfectly acceptable to gather more proofs in an administrative penal process. Father Lagges, personal communication, supra.

After the accused has been heard and any further evidence has been submitted, the accused's advocate is given the right to present a defense brief to the bishop. The testimony, evidence, and the advocate's defense brief are then weighed by the diocesan bishop and two assessors, which are people who are qualified to advise the bishop on the matter before him (cc. 1720, 1424). It is a good practice to use assessors who are not from the diocese so as to ensure that they are able to be unbiased in their evaluation of the evidence. Using local assessors to advise their own bishop about a fellow diocesan priest is not a good or fair practice. Furthermore, though the law does not require it, assessors should be canonists who are familiar with the law. The USCCB suggests that assessors be "canonists of proven ability and with some years of experience."[80] This is over and above the requirement in the Code that the assessors need only to live an "upright life." Given the stakes of the decisions being made, it is important to ensure that there is an element of impartiality to the process.

It is clear from the text that the expectation is that all three (the bishop and two assessors) will be in the same room discussing and deliberating, though most of the time the assessors evaluate the case, draft an opinion, and then give that opinion to the bishop. Then the bishop makes the final decision. If the bishop finds with moral certitude that there is sufficient evidence that the accused committed the crime, he issues a penal decree to impose punishment. If the penalty is dismissal or any other permanent penalty, it must be imposed by CDF before it takes effect (SST art. 21, 27).

Like the judicial trial, while the penalty is usually dismissal from the priesthood, on a case-by-case basis SST/10 Art. 21 §2 1° permits in certain circumstances that the penalty be less severe. It is also possible that after further investigation and upon hearing the evidence provided by the accused, the bishop and his assessors are not able to reach moral certitude[81] that a violation occurred. However, this lack of moral certitude does not necessarily mean that the cleric will go back to work, or that he is completely exonerated. This is certainly true if the determination is that while the conduct was not a technical violation of the Essential Norms or SST/10, it was still serious enough that it calls into question the cleric's suitability for ministry.[82] Unlike the Eastern Code of Canon Law, in the Latin Code of Canon Law, clerics do not have an explicit right to ministry; thus it is possible that a bishop can decide that the priest's actions "have so betrayed the trust of the bishop and the people that he just cannot be trusted again" in a ministerial position.[83]

80. Bishops' Committee on Canonical Affairs Task Force, supra, 20.

81. "Moral certitude is a practical judgment on the part of the judge based on the available proofs, considered as a whole and not a collection of isolated factors. Moral certitude is not absolute certainty where there is no possibility of the opposite being true. It is characterized by exclusion of reasonable doubt and it does admit of the possibility of the contrary. In a sense it is the human certainty that a person is guilty of a crime." DiNardo, supra, 5.

82. Canon Law Society of America, Revised Guide, supra, 29.

83. Lagges, personal communication, supra.

There is a canonical argument that has been put forward by a number of canonists (though not all canonists agree) that c. 223 § 2 allows the bishop *"pro bono ecclesia"* or "for the good of the Church" to continue to restrict a cleric from engaging in active ministry. This restriction could be imposed in the event (1) that in older cases the law was such that the victim was not considered a canonical minor or the man was not yet a cleric at the time of the abuse; or (2) that the bishop believes that the cleric might constitute a risk to minors; or (3) that it would be a cause of scandal to the faithful if he were returned to ministry. As this restriction would be administrative in nature, the cleric could appeal this decision to CDF.[84]

There are a number of other canonical penalties or restrictions that the bishop could impose short of dismissal. The bishop could request that the accused cleric resign on his own accord from any ecclesiastical office (e.g., pastor of a parish) he holds (cc. 187–189). If the cleric refuses to resign, and if the bishop considers the cleric unsuitable to remain in that office (c. 149 § 1), the bishop can follow the procedures to remove the cleric from office (cc. 192–195, 1740–1747). The bishop can remove or restrict the faculties (the ability to function as a priest) of a cleric who does not hold an ecclesiastical office (cc. 391, 142, 764). The bishop can restrict a priest's ability to publicly celebrate the Eucharist or administer sacraments (c. 906). Finally, the bishop can decide that for the good of both the cleric and the Church, that the cleric is dispensed from the obligation of wearing clerical attire (c. 284). If the bishop chooses to impose one of these lesser penalties, it should be done in a written decree (cc. 45–58). The accused cleric has a right to lodge an appeal to the CDF against any decree imposing on him a canonical penalty.[85]

25:23 LIFE OF PRAYER AND PENANCE

There are some cases where the cleric has admitted to, has been canonically convicted of, or has been civilly convicted of committing the crimes for which he is accused. However, because of advanced age, or disability, or for some other compelling reason, the court or the bishop believe that he should not be totally dismissed from the clerical state. The Essential Norms Number 8 states:

> If the penalty of dismissal from the clerical state has not been applied (e.g., for reasons of advanced age or infirmity), the offender ought to lead a life of prayer and penance. He will not be permitted to celebrate Mass publicly or to administer the

84. If the cleric desires to appeal this decision, there is some debate regarding whether the appropriate place of appeal is CDF or the Congregation for Clergy if the case is an old one and the victim was not considered a canonical minor at the time. CDF claims competence by virtue of the matter (which is now a crime, but was not one at the time). The Congregation for Clergy claims competence because at the time it was not a crime and therefore CDF does not have jurisdiction. It remains to be seen how this will resolve itself. Lagges, personal communication, supra.

85. Canon Law Society of America, Revised Guide, supra, 28–29.

sacraments. He is to be instructed not to wear clerical garb, or to present himself publicly as a priest.

In these cases, CDF can authorize the local bishop to issue a decree prohibiting or restricting the public ministry of the priest without fully dismissing him from the priesthood. In these cases, the priest can take recourse to the CDF against the decision.

What some dioceses have done is to give the cleric specific instructions regarding what prayer and penance means within the context of a penal precept.[86] For example, the bishop could mandate such things as attending a support group or counseling, spiritual direction, specific time for prayer for victims of sexual abuse, a specific time for other types of prayer, etc. These acts can and should be closely monitored by the diocese to ensure that the cleric is following the bishop's requirements. If he does not, the penalty of dismissal can be revisited.[87]

In these cases, and presuming that the cleric is healthy enough to do so, the priest should be dispensed from c. 286 that prohibits the cleric from secular employment, and the diocese should consider providing the cleric with some employment counseling or job training so that he could find secular employment if possible.[88]

25:24 CONCLUSION

With many cases, at this point, the process ceases. Either the cleric has been exonerated, or he has been found guilty and dismissed, or he has incurred some sort of administrative penalty that restricts his ability to minister publicly. Most cases are handled in this fashion, and although few would describe these processes as expeditious, they can be handled reasonably swiftly.

However, there have been many cases where the evidence is not clear. The cleric disputes the accusation, and there is no way to make a determination of his guilt or innocence without further inquiry. These are the cases where CDF generally requires that the diocese conduct a full, formal canonical penal trial. That process will be discussed in depth in Chapter 27. However, before discussing how a canonical trial is run, we must first examine the formal role of the accuser in the canonical process, particularly in the context of a canonical trial.

86. A penal precept (c. 49) is a decree from the bishop that obliges a person to do particular acts or things. It acts as a warning, because if the precept is violated, then the bishop can act to impose further canonical penalties, including dismissal.

87. Lagges, personal communication, supra.

88. Lagges, "Canonicle Issues of Renumeration," supra, 165.

CHAPTER 26

⌀⌀

The Accuser and the Canonical Process

26:1 CANONICAL ROLE OF THE ACCUSER

Earlier in this text, we reminded the reader of our central principle, that healing for the child or teen who has reported an assault is an essential response, even before the various legal systems interact with that person's legal interests. This chapter deals once again with that individual, and how the canon law system interacts with that person in his or her canonical role as the prime witness in a canonical trial. In that legal role, the person is always the accuser. As we are talking about a specific legal process, this chapter will refer to that individual as the accuser rather than the victim as the process is intended to determine the veracity of that person's claim. Similarly, the alleged perpetrator is referred to as the accused until that person is convicted of the offense or has admitted his or her guilt.

In Chapter 25, we briefly touched on the official role that the accuser plays in the canonical system. It is a role that is similar to the person's civil role if the case is criminally prosecuted in the civil system. Specifically, the accuser is the prime witness against the accused. The accuser is not a party to the case; therefore the case is not the accuser versus the accused, but the Church versus the accused. This means that in the canonical legal system (like the civil legal system), there are legal rights and protections afforded a defendant that are not mirrored for the accuser.

Though the canonical penal process is currently being used most often to hear cases of clergy sexual abuse, it could also be used to prosecute other canonical delicts or crimes, for example, a cleric, religious, or layperson misappropriating funds from his or her local parish. Those same rights of the defendant attach in those cases as well, and the accuser in such a case is again only a witness, and not a party, to the criminal case. In other words, the Church did not create penal norms that provide defendants in sexual abuse cases any more or less protection than they would have been given if they had been accused of canonical embezzlement.[1]

---

1. If anything, CDFs ability to laicize immediately with no recourse available to the defendant is actually a limitation of the rights of the accused for those particular crimes. That limitation is not present if the priest were accused of embezzlement.

With that having been said, accusers have both options and rights that they can exercise within the canonical system. One of the most fundamental of these is to be informed from the outset what their role is within the canonical system and what their choices are in fulfilling that role.

26:2 IMPORTANT DISCLOSURES

One of the harshest criticisms of the canonical process came in the Philadelphia Grand Jury Report. It goes into great detail regarding how in cases in the archdiocese, accusers were misled regarding their role and the use of their personal information.[2] In those instances, the reasons for the canonical procedures and investigation were not explained to those making the accusations. The results reflected the grand jury's outrage at the process and the Church's lack of transparency.[3] In fact, because of the archdiocese's unwillingness or inability to articulate canonical reasons for its actions, the grand jury concluded that the only explanation for the Church's actions was that "It is only rational as a strategy for avoiding civil and criminal liability."[4]

A canonist reading the report knows that there are specific canonical legal reasons for the archdiocese's actions and requests. It was trying to gather evidence to use to prove the canonical case against the accused cleric. But at the same time, that canonist can easily see how such actions would be viewed as cruelly violating and re-traumatizing the accuser, because there was no effort made by the archdiocese to inform accusers of what it was doing, why it was doing it, and who would ultimately have access to that information. As a result, accusers were not given the opportunity to decide what, if anything, they wanted to disclose, or to have control over how their personal information was used.

26:3 FULL PROCEDURAL TRANSPARENCY

To avoid such future criticism, it is therefore critical that a diocese make full disclosure to the accuser of the possible canonical processes from the beginning, with continued transparency for the duration of the process.[5] A pamphlet or other written material that details the process and the accuser's role is very helpful in explaining what will happen and what is involved. One really good example is the archdiocese of Milwaukee's booklet that describes the process in terms that are understandable to the public. This is a useful method by which Church officials can

---

2. Report of the Grand Jury, MISC. NO. 0009901-2008 (Court of Common Pleas, First Judicial District of Pennsylvania, Philadelphia January 21, 2011), at 92.

3. Id. at 86–88.

4. Id. at 89.

5. Amy J. Strickland, "To Protect and Serve: The Relationship between the Victim Assistance Coordinator and Canonical Personnel," 71 CLSA Proceedings 234–235 (2009).

interact with those making inquiries or accusations about clergy sexual abuse. Such a pamphlet is designed specifically to answer the questions of accusers and their witnesses about their role, about the procedure, and about what to expect.[6] It can also be kept and referenced as the canonical process goes forward. That way, accusers and their witnesses are not accidently or purposefully misled by requests for information or disclosures from the diocese.

This information should be conveyed by the diocesan victim's assistance coordinator, or whoever is responsible for diocesan interaction with accusers. It should be done in a gentle, respectful, and compassionate manner. This information need not be conveyed to the accuser in the initial conversation, particularly if the accuser is not in an emotional condition to process the information. However, it is wise for dioceses to have written materials to give to the accusers that explain their role and their rights so that the accuser can process that information at a better and less emotionally charged time. It is also helpful as a follow-up by the victim's coordinator to discuss these issues with the accuser in a sensitive manner so that the diocese is sure that the accuser understands his or her role and rights. This should be done prior to the accuser being asked for any information that is more detailed than the initial intake conversation, so that the accuser can make an informed choice about what he or she is willing to disclose.

26:4 IS THE ACCUSATION COVERED BY THE NORMS?

As discussed in our last chapter, there is a very specific universe of cases that are defined as "more grave delicts" by *Sacramentorum sanctitatis tutela* and are governed by the Essential Norms.[7] Therefore, if the accusation is made by someone who was 19 at the time of the incident, or by someone who was between 16 and 18 but it occurred before the age was raised initially in 1994, or the crime in question is not one covered by the Norms, then the Norms do not apply. If the Norms are not applicable, the accuser needs to be gently informed that while what he or she is reporting will be investigated as improper and possibly canonically criminal[8] behavior, it will not be handled in the same way as a "more grave delict"[9] would under the Norms. The accuser needs to know what laws will apply from the beginning, and what the range of outcomes might be.[10]

---

6. Archdiocesan Tribunal of Milwaukee, "Trials According to the Canon Law of the Roman Catholic Church: Important Questions for Victim/Surviors or other Witnesses," Milwaukee, Wisconsin, at 1–16. This booklet can also be found on the Archdiocesan website at: www.archmil.org/Resources/TrialsAccordingtotheCanonLawoftheRomanCatholicChurch.

7. United States Conference of Catholic Bishops, "Essential Norms for Diocesan/Eparchial Policies Dealing with Allegations of Sexual Abuse of Minors by Priests or Deacons," 32 Origins fn. 1 (June 2004).

8. Canonically criminal behavior would be behavior that is considered a crime, or delict, under canon law. It can be prosecuted in the canonical system by a canonical court, and can result in canonical penalties being imposed.

9. See Chapter 25 for an explanation on what constitutes a "more grave delict."

10. Strickland, supra, 234–235.

26:5 THE ACCUSATION TRIGGERS A FORMAL CANONICAL INVESTIGATION

At the outset, accusers should be told that along with any civil ramifications that might ensue from their accusation, an accusation against a priest triggers a formal canonical investigation. They should be told that the Church will conduct its own internal investigation. This will likely include requests to get additional information from the accuser, and possibly from other witnesses. Accusers should be informed that they have the right to suggest witnesses who can corroborate their claim, and they can submit any other evidence in their possession to the canonical court to substantiate their claim.

The accuser should also be informed that if the accusation passes an initial assessment, the accusation will be further investigated. The investigative findings will be passed to the review board, which reviews the evidence to determine if and what further action is warranted. Further, the accuser should be told that besides the review board, the diocesan bishop and the Congregation for the Doctrine of the Faith at the Vatican in Rome are responsible for determining how a particular case is going to be handled. However, the diocese will not know definitively how the case will be processed until CDF has advised the bishop how the bishop is to proceed.

As discussed in the prior chapter, there are five possible canonical processes that could be applied to the accusation, depending on the circumstances of the case. Ultimately it is the decision of CDF on how to proceed, based on the recommendations of the local bishop. However, it is important for the accuser to not only be aware of the different processes, but to understand why a particular process was assigned to hir or her case.

26:6 WHAT ARE THE ACCUSED CLERIC'S RIGHTS?

The accuser should also know what will happen with the accused cleric after the accusation is received by the diocese, and what rights the accused cleric is afforded. This way, the process and his or her possible role will be known, and there will be no unpleasant or unexpected surprises. Though the practice varies diocese to diocese, at some point the accused will learn of the accusation against him. At that time he will be encouraged to seek civil and canonical counsel (c. 1723), and a canonist will be provided to him if he cannot afford one. He may be asked to submit exculpatory evidence to the bishop and/or the review board. If the review board determines that there is enough evidence to go forward, then the cleric will be notified, will generally be put on leave, and the case will be sent to CDF for its evaluation. Like the civil law, the cleric has the canonical right (cc. 1531–1532) not to incriminate himself by being asked directly, or by being forced to answer under oath whether he is guilty.

In the canonical system, the advocate for the accused priest has the right to see what evidence has been gathered and presented against his client. This means that he will have access to any of the accuser's testimony, witness testimony, and other evidence presented by the promoter of justice. As in the civil law, the accused has the right to know what the accusation is against him, and to refute that allegation by refuting the witness testimony and evidence, and by presenting his own exculpatory testimony, witnesses, and evidence. This is very important for the accuser to know—that the accused will have access to any evidence the accuser produces, and that he will have the opportunity to refute it.

26:7 DOES THE ACCUSER GET AN ADVOCATE?

Because the accuser is a witness and not a party to the case, the witness does not have a canonical advocate provided for him or her by the Church. The "prosecutor" or promoter of justice is not the accuser's attorney, but instead functions like a district attorney.[11] Accusers are free to hire their own canonical advocate if they so desire, but they do not have to. Some dioceses have a local policy of providing their accusers with canon lawyers. Because they are witnesses and not parties, accusers do not have a legal right to have an advocate provided to them.[12]

26:8 WHAT IS DONE WITH THE ACCUSER'S INFORMATION.

The accuser needs to know who will have access to the information provided to the diocese, including any testimony, records, or other evidence. This is very important, because once the internal process begins, there will be a number of people who will have access to this information. This will necessarily include the bishop, the victim's assistance coordinator, the review board members, and most important, the accused and his canonical advocate. Given the formality of the process and the dire consequences for the priest if he is found to be guilty, he is entitled to know who is accusing him and of what he is accused. As this knowledge may affect what the accuser is willing to disclose, he or she should be informed of this at the very beginning of the process.

It is critical that accusers be informed that it is their choice what they disclose to the Church court. They should be informed that it is possible that the Church promoter of justice (the canonical prosecutor) might ask them to release various materials, sometimes including confidential records (medical, psychological, etc.) about themselves. They have the right to refuse such a request, and the right not to be badgered by anyone to release their records. They should, however, be informed

11. Another harsh criticism in the Philadelphia Grand Jury report is that one of the accusers was told that the canonists (presumably the judicial vicar and/or the promoter of justice) who were working with him were "his advocates." (Grand Jury, supra, 92, 104). This is misleading and incorrect. Canonists need to be very careful that all roles are properly and clearly explained.

12. Grand Jury, supra, 104–105. This practice is the same in the civil courts. Defendants are by law provided with a defense attorney, and the state provides one if they cannot afford an attorney. The alleged victim is not provided an attorney by the state in criminal cases.

that to remove a cleric requires that the Church prove his guilt, so that anything the accuser chooses to disclose will aid the tribunal in discovering the truth of the matter. The burden of proof is on the promoter of justice to prove his case; the priest, as in the civil law, does not have the burden to prove his innocence.

If the priest denies the accusation, and/or the available evidence is not incontrovertible, and CDF mandates a canonical trial, then the diocese is obligated to conduct a full canonical penal trial. The people associated with running the trial, for example, the judges, the promoter of justice, the notary, and other tribunal staff working on the case, will have access to the information provided by the accuser and all the other witnesses. Although all are bound to secrecy regarding the case, the universe of people with access to this information is comparatively sizable.

For the court to have enough evidence to make a determination, witnesses including the accuser will be asked to testify or to submit testimony. This testimony will become the evidence on which the case is heard. If the witness is willing to give testimony, the person needs to be clearly informed that a copy will be given to the accused and his advocate, and the witness especially needs to understand the legal reasons for this disclosure.

26:9 THE ACCUSER'S RIGHTS

In addition to those things that the accuser should know about the process, the accuser should also be clearly informed of his or her own canonical rights within the system. Accusers should be given any additional information and given access to the resources needed for them to adequately exercise these rights.

26:10 THE RIGHT TO BE HEARD

First and foremost, the accuser has the right for his or her accusation to be heard, both externally and internally.

Externally, the accuser has the right to report his or her allegations to the civil authorities, and to comply with whatever is required for a civil investigation. Furthermore, this should be exercised free from any coercion or interference from the Church. This is supported by article 4 of the Charter for the Protection of Children and Young People, which states that "In every instance, dioceses/eparchies are to advise victims of their right to make a report to public authorities and support this right."[13]

Internally, the accuser has the right to present his or her allegation to someone within the Church, to have that allegation heard, and to present any personal needs that stem from the alleged abuse. In article 1 of the Charter, the bishops stated that "The first obligation of the Church with regard to the victims is for healing and

---

13. Archdiocesan Tribunal of Milwaukee, supra, 5.

reconciliation,"[14] so it is the obligation of the Church to facilitate whatever is necessary to promote and further that healing. Canon 212 § 2 states that "the Christian faithful are free to make known to the pastors of the Church their needs, especially spiritual ones, and their desires..." Canon 212 § 3 continues that the person has "the duty to manifest to the sacred pastors their opinion on matters which pertain to the good of the Church." Canon 213 specifies that the Christian faithful have the right "to receive assistance from the sacred pastors out of the spiritual goods of the Church" if the need arises. After their needs are known, the Charter states that the Church must provide outreach to accusers, which "will include provision of counseling, spiritual assistance, support groups, and other social services agreed upon by the victim and the diocese/eparchy."[15]

If the allegation is such that the Church as a mandatory reporter must report the allegation to the civil authorities, this report should be made only after the victim or the victim's guardians have been advised and consulted with that such a report is being made.[16]

26:11 RIGHT TO REPUTATION AND PRIVACY

In canonical matters, both the accusers and the accused are entitled to their reputation and their privacy. The accused is entitled to such protection at least until the accusation must be publicly acted upon. Then he is entitled to as much protection as can be provided, until there has been a definitive guilty determination in his case, in the tradition of one being innocent until proven guilty.

The accuser is also entitled to have his or her reputation and privacy protected. Accusers have the right:

- To expect that their names will not be made public to the greater Church community, whether their allegation leads to a canonical trial or not. This includes any reference by the accused to his friends or colleagues. The accused, who himself enjoys the same right and expectation of privacy, must clearly understand that he is required to respect the victim/survivor's right in this regard and must limit any communication of information regarding the victim/survivor only to those who might be assisting him with a particular canonical process.[17]
- Any persons involved with the canonical investigation are expected to refrain from speaking to any unauthorized persons about the case, to protect the reputation and privacy of all the parties involved (c. 1455).[18]

14. United States Conference of Catholic Bishops, "Charter for the Protection of Children and Young People" (2006).

15. Id.

16. Canon Law Society of America, Revised Guide to the Implementation of the U.S. Bishop's Essential Norms for Diocesan/Eparchial Policies Dealing with Allegations of Sexual Abuse of Minors by Priests or Deacons 5 (2004).

17. Archdiocesan Tribunal of Milwaukee, supra, 5.

18. Canon Law Society of America, supra, 5.

- The information compiled for a canonical case should be accessible only to those who must have access to that information.
- If the Church provides counseling or other assistance to the accuser, these arrangements should be done in as confidential a manner as possible, with all diocesan personnel expected to adhere to this standard.[19]
- Accusers cannot be compelled to undergo any sort of psychological evaluation—it is an unwarranted invasion of their privacy.
- Any psychological records voluntarily submitted to the tribunal by the accuser can only be given to those to whom the accuser has given permission.
- The person has a right to a copy of any assessment that the person voluntarily undergoes, and it is unethical to withhold it from him or her.
- All documents or records generated from an accuser's participation in a Church process are to be kept private, unless the accuser has been informed otherwise from the outset of the process (c. 1455).[20]
- If the accuser's reputation has been injured or his or her privacy violated, the person has the right to have that injury to his or her reputation repaired (c. 128) in the canonical forum, though it may mean that a separate judicial trial is necessary.[21]

26:12 THE RIGHT TO ASSISTANCE

Once abuse has been proven, the diocese has a responsibility to help the victim. This responsibility to assist the victim attaches even if the identity of the perpetrator cannot be established. This responsibility can be assumed by the diocese or such assistance could come as a result of a cleric's guilty verdict. If a cleric is found guilty, a canonical court can require the cleric to pay damages to the victim. Canon 1718 also allows the bishop to "resolve equitably the question of damages" to be paid by the guilty cleric without a canonical trial, if it is expedient for him to do so.[22] Unfortunately, there are serious difficulties with the Church being able to enforce a judgment that includes damages, particularly if the punishment given is dismissal from the priesthood. In those cases, damages would likely have to be in the form of an equitable remedy (e.g., the Church pays for the victim's counseling), as the dismissal of the cleric ends any ability of the Church to coerce the perpetrator to comply with a canonical judgment against him.

   If the victim believes that the damages assigned by the bishop are inadequate, he or she has the right to challenge the resolution of the case through hierarchical recourse, in accord with cc. 1732–1739. If a canonical trial is running, the accuser can initiate a concurrent contentious action to be heard, with its specific purpose being the reparation of the damages suffered by the accuser (c. 1729). This action

19. Id.
20. Id. at 6.
21. Id.
22. Id.

can be brought against the cleric concurrent with his or her penal trial, or separately if there is no penal trial or if the trial is unduly delayed. It is also possible for the accuser to bring a canonical contentious action against the juridic person of the diocese, or a cleric or layperson in the diocese, who the accuser alleges abused a position of trust and responsibility (c. 1389).[23] The plaintiff in such a case would have to prove (1) that the alleged offender "abused a position of trust and responsibility by sexually abusing a minor in the course of his or her work," and that the pastor of the parish or bishop of the diocese was made aware of the situation but "failed to address the matter properly."[24]

26:13 CONFLICTING PROCESSES

What we have been discussing is, in the absence of other factors, the interactions between the diocese and the accuser. However, the fact that for a canonical prosecution to be successful the cooperation and testimony of the alleged victim is highly desirable, if not absolutely necessary, is actually a serious difficulty with this process. This is because in the years following 2002, accusers have often approached the diocese and made an accusation after having retained a civil lawyer. In making the accusation, the accuser oftentimes is either contemplating or fully intends to sue civilly the diocese, the bishop, and/or the accused.

Because the accuser and the diocese are adversaries in the civil process, civil lawyers are generally hesitant if not hostile to allow their clients to provide any sort of information or assistance to the diocese beyond the basic facts of the allegation. This is, of course, presuming that the accuser otherwise would have been willing to assist the diocese, which oftentimes he or she is not. This is particularly true if the victim is still a minor at the time of the investigation. Civil lawyers do not want the diocese to have access to information from their client that would prejudice their civil case. They certainly do not want to hand confidential information about their client over to the opposing side.

This puts the diocese in a bit of a quandary. In cases where CDF has mandated a penal trial, the promoter of justice (the canonical district attorney) must prove his case with moral certitude based on the evidence, and the most compelling evidence (and sometimes the only evidence) comes from the testimony of the accuser and his or her witnesses. Without any cooperation of the accuser outside the basic allegation, the diocese must either wait to prosecute the case and hope that more information will emerge in civil discovery that it can import into the canonical trial, or the diocese must try the case based on the limited and incomplete evidence that its own internal investigation reveals.

This situation also creates an internal conflict for the diocese between its internal judiciary and its civil lawyers. If the diocese is aware that a civil suit is pending, it may not want to be gathering information that might have a bearing on the civil

23. Id. at 7.
24. Id.

process or might limit what the diocesan bishop is willing to disclose to the judges of the canonical trial. However, this will delay any judicial process because of the potential lack of evidence, and keeps the cleric in juridic limbo. The bishop as a canonical judge may be hesitant to assign damages because it will be interpreted civilly as an admission of guilt on the part of the diocese rather than an attempt by the bishop to "make whole" the accuser by repairing the harm inflicted upon him or her.

Finally, it has been the experience of some diocesan officials that some civil plaintiff's attorneys are advising their clients to not cooperate with diocesan processes as a very specific strategy. If the diocese does not have enough evidence to convict in a canonical process, it is left with the options of either returning a not guilty or a not proven verdict. As soon as one of those verdicts are returned, the attorney then comes back with the claim that the diocese did not remove the abusive priest; thus the client who refused to participate in the canonical process becomes entitled to damages for the Church's failure to permanently remove the accused cleric.

26:14 CONCLUSION

There is no good or easy fix to be found for these conflicts. On the one hand, the diocese needs to treat the accusers compassionately and sensitively, and needs to ensure that if they have sustained an injury that their immediate and long-term needs in dealing with this trauma are met. The Church has this as a moral obligation.

On the other hand, by making a formal accusation that will likely permanently affect the life and livelihood of the accused cleric, the accuser assumes a particular formal role in the canonical process. His or her accusation begins a series of formal inquiries, investigations, and penal procedures that require a high level of proof to substantiate the allegations. As a witness in a canonical action, accusers will necessarily be asked to fulfill that role by giving evidence. To support them in this role, the diocese needs to be absolutely transparent and forthright about what this role entails, what information may be requested from them and their witnesses, and what will be done with it if and when it is received. The accuser needs to be informed of his or her full range of canonical options and rights, so that there will be no undue trauma inflicted through the canonical processes. Some dioceses have figured out how to do this well, and others have not been so successful. Historically, the Church has not been open about its internal processes, and this is now coming back to haunt it through an increased resistance to cooperate with those processes.

Finally, in all these cases there is the overarching likelihood of civil action or process that will make a healing interaction with the Church difficult or impossible. The Church has brought this situation on itself by its prior, and unfortunately continued, inability to communicate about the rights, expectations, and role of the accuser. This has resulted in widening the conflict between the two legal systems and made it even more difficult for the Church to follow its own rules and processes.

CHAPTER 27

⌀⌀⌀

Canonical Penal Trials and Outcomes

27:1 THE TRIAL

The Canonical Penal Trial is the ordinary way that a contested accusation against a cleric is resolved. The penal trial in many ways resembles criminal trials conducted in civil law, with notable exceptions. As the procedure for a canonical trial is similar to the procedural law of code-governed countries (or states, as in the case of Louisiana), there are certain procedural norms that vary significantly from the procedures found in common law jurisdictions.

Canonist Father Larry DiNardo, from the archdiocese of Pittsburgh, describes some of the significant differences this way:

> Unlike criminal proceedings in the United States, which are primarily an adversarial contest between the prosecutor and the defense attorney, the penal procedure of the Church is primarily inquisitional in that the purpose of the trial is to arrive at truth. While our American criminal system places the responsibility on the jury to be the finder of fact, the canonical penal process places this responsibility on the Judges of the tribunal. While the traditional criminal procedure in the United States may take a matter of days, the canonical process can take a lengthy period of time as the Judges gather testimony, documents and other evidence so that they may be able to arrive at moral certitude in the case.[1]

Furthermore, common law jurisdictions take very seriously the notion that due process must be followed for the outcome of a trial to be just. This is not the case

---

1. Lawrence A. DiNardo, Canonical Penal Procedures 8 (Canon Law Society of America, 2010).

in canonical penal law. Rather, canon law has a different understanding, which is explained by canonist and civil law professor Father Ladislas Orsy:

> "Due process" is not a standard term with a recognized content in canon law. Canonists tend to interpret it as "a process according to our procedural law"—no more. Lawyers in the English common law tradition go further and insist on some substantive elements that the process must include in order to be fair and due, such as the right to the presumption of innocence, to confront witnesses, to trial by an independent court, and so forth. Not all such "rights" are protected by the canonical procedures.[2]

It is important to keep these differences in mind as the canonical process is outlined. Assuming that either the trial ethos or the actual trial procedures are identical in canon law and civil law will rapidly lead a person into error.

27:2 WHO CONSTITUTES THE COURT

A canonical penal trial has a similar array of court personnel as does a civil criminal trial. Like a civil court system where judges and prosecutors work for the same civil jurisdiction, though all of the various positions are filled by Church canonists or experts, each position has its own independent function.

For all of the major canonical roles (e.g., Judge, Promoter of Justice, Notary, and Procurator and Advocate), the standard requirement is that the person acting in that role will be a priest. Further, traditionally the law has required that the priest have a doctorate in canon law. Because there are few priests with doctorates in canon law, and because even fewer of those with doctorates are working on penal trials, SST/10 art. 15 allows that the requirements of priesthood and having a doctorate can be dispensed with (an exception can be made) for all of these offices, if the exception is approved by the Congregation for the Doctrine of the Faith (CDF). CDF has been very willing to dispense those able to act in these various roles from having a doctorate as long as one has a master's degree[3] (licentiate) in canon law and has actually worked in a diocesan tribunal. However, for some offices CDF is less likely to dispense (though they are still able to do so) from the requirement of priesthood, because "CDF has been given the authority to dispense from this requirement for the office of Promoter of Justice, Notary and Advocate but not for those who act in the capacity of Judges."[4]

It is important that in each case there be no conflicts of interest with any of the court's officials or personnel. In fact, c. 1448 states that the person is supposed to recuse himself if there is "[R]eason of consanguinity or affinity in any degree of the

---

2. Ladislas Orsy, S.J., "Bishops' Norms: Commentary and Evaluation," 44 B.C. L. Rev. 999, 1016 (2003).

3. A master's degree in canon law (JCL) is currently a three-year course of study—the same length of time it takes to get a civil law degree (JD) in the United States.

4. DiNardo, supra, 7.

direct line and up to the fourth degree of the collateral line or by reason of trustee-ship, guardianship, close acquaintance, great animosity, the making of a profit, or the avoidance of a loss."

Not only does the necessity to recuse oneself in the case of a conflict of interest bind the officers mentioned above, but also assessors and auditors of the case. If a party believes that a conflict of interest exists with any of these people, c. 1449 allows the party to formally object to that person's participation. The judge hears the objection for all of the offices except his own. If he is not the judicial vicar, then the judicial vicar makes the decision. If the judge is also the judicial vicar, then the bishop makes the decision regarding the objection.

27:3 THE JUDGES

As stated above, the canons required that judges for canonical penal trials be priests who have a doctorate in canon law. However, SST/10 art. 15 allows CDF to dispense from the requirements of being a priest and having a doctorate so that a deacon or layperson could function as a judge, and he or she could have a master's degree (a canonical licentiate), not a doctorate in canon law. Despite the fact that an exception can be made to allow a layperson to function as a judge, to our knowledge this has never happened. If it ever does happen, there can be no more than one layperson on the panel (c. 1421). The bishop could also be a judge if he so desired (c. 1419), but given his various roles this practice is strongly discouraged.

The judges' panel, or *turnus*, consists of at least three judges. SST/10 Art. 22 states that there should be 3–5 judges, with there being a presiding judge and at least two other collegiate judges. The judges could be local priests, though they would have to meet the necessary requirements. The current praxis has been to name judges from outside the diocese, and even outside the province, to ensure impartiality. Using local judges can give the impression of bias, even if the local judge believes that he can be impartial.

If a judge believes that he cannot be impartial for any reason, or he is related to any of the parties or witnesses, he is required to recuse himself from the case (c. 1448). Furthermore, if one of the parties has an objection to the judge's participation in the case, the party can formally object to his being on the *turnus* (c. 1449). If the judge is not the bishop, then the objection is reviewed by the judicial vicar. If the objection is against the bishop, he is simply to recuse himself (c. 1449)

27:4 THE PROMOTER OF JUSTICE

The promoter of justice in a canonical trial is the canonical equivalent of the civil district attorney. The promoter of justice is the officer of the court that is charged with "providing for the public good. (c. 1430)" It is his ot her job to compile and present the arguments and evidence against the accused in an attempt to prove that the allegation of sexual abuse is true. The promoter of justice presents documentary evidence, calls witnesses, makes objections, and crafts the case against the accused.[5] CDF has granted many dispensations to allow diocesan promoters of justice to be deacons or laypersons with master's degrees in canon law. Many have functioned in these roles.

27:5 THE CANONICAL NOTARY

The notary in canon law acts the same as a notary in the civil law. It is the notary's job to ensure the authenticity of documents, to authenticate the various decrees and other judicial acts in the penal trial, and to sign and seal any procedural documents (cc. 484, 1437). The various acts of the case are invalid if they have not been properly notarized by a canonical notary.

27:6 THE AUDITOR

Auditors are used to assist the judges in the day-to-day running of the canonical trial. The auditor can be one of the judges, or it can be someone that the bishop has approved for this function (c. 1428). As judges are usually from different cities or states from the location of the trial, auditors serve as a local contact and resource. They are responsible for keeping track of the evidence as it comes in, and gathering the testimonies and evidence to give to the judges. The auditor can also decide what further proofs or evidence are needed, and how they are to be collected (c. 1428). Canon law specifically allows auditors to be laypersons, though if there is a lay auditor for the case that person is probably not acting as a judge on the panel.

27:7 THE PROCURATOR/ADVOCATE

Although canonists usually refer to a procurator/advocate, these are actually two separate positions that resemble the difference in the British legal roles of barrister and solicitor. Canon law requires that the accused have an advocate to represent him (c. 1481). The advocate's job is to be the canonical defense lawyer, and to make arguments on his client's behalf. The advocate gathers and organizes evidence, and advises and assists his client in preparing his defense. He can be present when his client, other witnesses, and case experts are questioned (c. 1561). The advocate can submit questions for the judge to ask witnesses and can file objections if necessary. The advocate writes the various briefs and rebuttals putting forward his or her client's arguments for innocence.[6]

The procurator is a legal proxy or alter ego for the accused. The procurator can be designated to receive court documents, and act on behalf of the accused if

---

5. Id.

6. Ward, Daniel J. "Canonical Advocacy: Practical Representation of a Party." CLSA Proceedings, 55, (1993): 98–107 (D. J. Ward 1993).

necessary. Although there may be many advocates appointed, there is usually only one canonical procurator (c. 1482). Procurators may be used in the case where the defendant is currently incarcerated, or for whatever reason cannot be present for the canonical trial (c. 1508).

27:8 EXPERTS

An expert in canon law is "one whose knowledge, experience or art, makes him an authoritative specialist on a particular field."[7] Experts are often used in sexual abuse cases. They can be experts on the abuse itself or its effects, they can be psychological experts, computer or handwriting experts, experts on a particular culture, or experts to help the judge interpret other kinds of evidence. Admission of this testimony is up to the discretion of the judge.

Though they are technically not a part of the formal court personnel, experts play a very important role in canonical trials. Not only is the defendant allowed to suggest experts, but the judges can choose to appoint experts of their own if they need their opinion or expertise to help understand aspects of the case (cc. 1574–1575).

If the court decides to admit expert reports or testimony, the judge has the authority to decide in a formal decree what issues or questions he wants the expert to address (c. 1577). He also can exclude the testimony or report of an expert (c. 1576), and both the defendant and the promoter of justice are allowed to object to a particular expert.

27:9 BALANCE RE-TRAUMATIZING OF VICTIMS WITH RIGHTS OF THOSE ACCUSED

As discussed in the last chapter, there are those who claim that the internal church process is an unnecessary and cruel trauma that the church inflicts on the accuser. The expectation is that once an accusation is made, actions should be taken permanently to remove the accused from ministry without further examination into the allegations or without a formal process to adjudicate the claims.[8]

---

7. E. Caparros, M. Theriault & J. Thorn, Code of Canon Law Annotated 997 (1993).
8. The Philadelphia Grand Jury Report specifically asks "[W]hy Archdiocese officials would disregard the additional pain that this canonical process has caused a victim and his family. If church practices, inscrutable or not, fail to reflect an overriding interest in justice for predator priests and compassion for their victims, then we worry that the perils to which the Archdiocese has exposed minors for decades are more likely to persist." *Report of the Grand Jury.* MISC. NO. 0009901-2008 (Court of Common Pleas, First Judicial District of Pennsylvania, Philadelphia January 21, 2011). The problem is that in this case the diocese failed to adequately explain why there is an overriding interest in justice in these cases for having the victim testify. The legal intention is neither inscrutable nor unjust. However, the canonical reasons that the tribunal needed the accuser's

However, there are oftentimes legitimate and disputed questions regarding the guilt of the accused. Particularly if the civil courts have not adjudicated the claims of the accuser and/or there is no definitive verdict of a civil court, (e.g., where statutes of limitations or lack of evidence led prosecutors to decline indictment, and/ or barriers to tort lawsuits led potential plaintiffs to decline or withdraw a civil damage case), it is not unjust to expect that the allegations against the priest be subjected to examination prior to being permanently acted upon. Although there are cases in which the guilt of the accused is strongly supported, there are also cases in which there is little evidence to support the claim.

A claim of sexual abuse against a cleric irreparably alters his life. Although this is certainly necessary if the allegation is true, if it is false, it is a heavy burden to carry. Vindication in the canonical penal trial may be the only opportunity he has to "clear his name." In going forward with the trial, an attempt must be made to balance these competing interests so that everyone's rights and the good of all can be protected.

27:10 GETTING STARTED—PROCEDURAL DELAYS

There is a legal maxim that "justice delayed is justice denied." This maxim is enshrined in c. 1453, which establishes that trial cases are not to be prolonged beyond a year, with an additional six months allotted for an appeal. Canon law requires that two courts, a diocesan court (court of first instance) and an appeals court (court of second instance), return a verdict for the case to be final. The code indicates that one year should be sufficient to complete the initial trial (trial at first instance) and it should take no more than six months for the automatic appeal (trial at second instance). Once CDF has mandated a canonical trial, the trial should get underway in a reasonable amount of time and should be concluded within the canonical time limits.

Unfortunately, despite CDF's mandate that there be a trial, many trials are not initiated until years later. This leaves the accused in canonical limbo, with no method to defend or exonerate himself, and as he is suspended from the active priesthood, he has no way to work or support himself in the interim. Though there are some understandable reasons for the delay (e.g., there are only a limited number of judges to hear these trials and they are currently overloaded, or there is a civil/criminal case pending), many delays are inexplicable. Advocates tell of cases where it has taken two to four years to constitute the *turnus* of judges. Others tell of instances where the defendant has been notified that a trial will take place and that a *turnus* will soon be constituted, but subsequently was not notified that this had occurred for another two years.

testimony were obviously never explained in a way that made sense to those who were asking the questions. It is imperative that Church officials improve their explanations of what they are doing, and why they are doing it. If they do not, canonical processes will continue to be described as being "inscrutable" at best and traumatic and cruel at worst.

This kind of delay is harmful to all involved. It draws out a very painful process for both the accused, who must somehow continue to live in this unresolved limbo, and for the accuser, for whom the delay makes it very difficult to put the process and the experience behind him or her. For example, a boy of 10 who alleges an assault may be 17 or older by the time the canonical penal trial seeks to call on him as a witness. He may have testified in a criminal trial at age 12 or in a civil trial for damages at age 13; the later request for testimony in the canonical trial may be resisted as the youth has grown and wants to move on with his life.

27:11 THE TRIAL BEGINS

If CDF notifies the bishop that he is to conduct a penal trial, then the bishop must initiate the trial in a timely fashion. A list of priests who are qualified to be judges is drawn up with preliminary inquiries about availability.[9] Given how stretched most canonists who are doing this work are, it can be very difficult to find judges who are willing to take on another case. The USCCB Task Force recommends that "In the interest of assuring an unbiased court, however, it is strongly recommended that the diocesan/eparchial bishop consider appointing judges from outside the diocese/eparchy."[10]

The bishop begins by constituting the court, and naming judges, a notary, and the promoter of justice to the case in a formal decree (cc. 483, 1421, 1430). After the court has been constituted, the bishop is obliged to give all of the information, testimony, and evidence that has previously been collected to the promoter of justice (c. 1721). At that point, the promoter of justice drafts a *libellus* or a petition of the accusation to the judges (c. 1502, 1721). It should be directed to a particular tribunal, and specifically spell out the accusation of the precise delict (crime), what law has been violated, a summary of the evidence, and what penalty is being sought and why. It should be signed and dated by the promoter of justice (c. 1504). If at any point the promoter of justice discovers that the allegations against the defendant are unfounded, he can renounce the trial if the accused consents (c. 1724). The accused may not choose to consent to renounce the trial, because if he is innocent he may want to vindicate his good name in a formal trial.

The proceedings of the court, according to SST/10 art. 30, are bound to be kept secret. Canonist Father Kevin McKenna explains that the legal requirement for secrecy has a legitimate purpose. This is because:

> In the canonical system it is the role of the judges (or those delegated by the judges) rather than the representatives (or lawyers) of the parties, to gather oral and written evidence. The process for finding facts and testimony takes place in a series of hearings that are normally conducted over a long stretch of time rather

9. The USCCB can assist dioceses in finding judges for penal cases.
10. Bishops' Committee on Canonical Affairs Task Force, A Resource for Canonical Processes for the Resolution of Complaints of Clerical Sexual Abuse of Minors 17 (2003).

than in a single trial as in a civil case. Because in the canonical system of law evidence is normally to be accumulated and assembled over time, judges typically impose "confidentiality" restrictions upon witnesses and their testimony to prevent the possible contamination of other witnesses who may appear later before the court. This is in contrast to the common law system and its trial procedures which would utilize cross-examination before its trial procedures which would utilize cross-examination before juries. While both systems have a valid system for identifying the truth, the two systems operate differently from one another and, in particular, have different but valid ways of ensuring the integrity of evidence and a just outcome.[11]

Canon law mandates that once the *libellus* is submitted the accused must have an advocate.[12] He has the option of either hiring one himself, or having one appointed for him (c. 1723). While some clerics may have their own sufficient resources to pay for the expense of a qualified canonical advocate, many if not most clerics do not have such financial resources. Ironically, oftentimes an accused cleric no longer has the resources to pay for the services of his canonical advocate because of the reductions in his support imposed by the diocese after the accusation is made public. Therefore, as is the case for religious clerics who are accused, it is important that if the cleric cannot afford an advocate that his diocese help him pay for an advocate's services.

Although it is clear in the law that at this point the accused must have an advocate, what is not clear is whether he may or must have one prior to the submission of the *libellus*. As discussed in Chapter 25, some canonists argue that the penal process and thus the right of defense does not begin until the initial investigation is completed and the *libellus* is submitted. Other canonists argue that the penal process begins at the time of the accusation, when the accused's rights are first in jeopardy.[13] Canonists might also make the distinction between the judicial penal process (which according to c. 1507 begins no later than the citation), and the administrative penal process (which according to c. 1720 begins when the Ordinary informs the accused of the accusation and the proofs) in making a determination as to when the right of defense attaches, stating that they attach at different times for the different processes.[14]

However, c. 1718 states that as soon as an Ordinary has determined that there is a semblance of truth to an allegation of wrongdoing, the Ordinary is to make a decision to initiate a process that will have significant consequences for the accused cleric's life and freedom. In justice, many canonists argue that the right to defense

11. Kevin McKenna, "Canon Law and Civil Law: Working Together for the Common Good," Canon Law Seminar for Media 7, United States Conference of Catholic Bishops (2010).

12. Though arguably the accused should have gotten an advocate well before this time during the preliminary investigation and before the case is sent to CDF for review.

13. DiNardo, supra, 7.

14. Patrick R. Lagges, "The Penal Process: The Preliminary Investigation in Light of the Essential Norms of the United States," 38 Studia Canonica 394 (2004).

arises whenever an authority is to make a decision that could harm the rights of another.[15] Furthermore, the right of defense includes the right to a canonical advocate who can advise the accused in protecting those rights (c. 221).

As soon as the *libellus* is presented, the judge has 30 days to accept it. The accused, his advocate, and the promoter of justice must receive a decree of citation, with a copy of the *libellus* included, which informs the accused of the formal grounds or charges against him (c. 1508). This notification can be made by mail or in some other secure fashion (c. 1509). Once properly notified, the defendant is canonically considered to be cited, even if he refuses to accept the citation (c. 1510).

Once the defendant has been legitimately cited, the accusation in now considered subject to judgment, the case becomes part of the competence and jurisdiction of that particular tribunal, prescription (the canonical equivalent of the civil statute of limitations) is interrupted, and the matter is considered to be formally pending (c. 1512).

27:12 JOINDER OF THE ISSUES

After the defendant receives the *libellus*, he and his advocate have 10 days to respond to the accusation and to present any objections they might have. After hearing the responses from both sides either in person or in writing, the court is to decree the joinder of the issue (*contestatio litis*). The purpose of the decree of joinder is to focus the scope of the trial, and declare what specifically is to be proved, which in canon law is known as the *contradictorio*. Canon 1513 states that "the joinder of the issue occurs when the terms of the controversy, derived from the petitions and responses of the parties, are defined through a decree of the judge." Thus the judge is to issue a decree framing the issue(s) that ultimately the judge's sentence, which he issues at the end of the proceedings, must answer. The judge needs to be precise regarding what is the specific charge or allegations against the accused, instead of using verbatim the allegations made by the promoter of justice. Further, the judge should take into account any evidence submitted by the accused in making this determination.

The parties are given a copy of the decree of joinder, or at least informed of the specific contents of the decree. The parties are then given 10 days to petition the judge if they disagree with the defined grounds and want them changed. If the grounds are contested, then the judge is bound to make the determination regarding whether to change the grounds expeditiously (c. 1513).

Once the *contradictorio* has been decreed, the promoter and the accused's advocate must address the specific question(s) enumerated in the *contridictorio*. The

---

15. As with many issues regarding procedural canon law, these opinions are expressed by canonists who are involved in penal trials but who are not writing journal articles expressing their opinions. Thus there is no academic citation, despite the fact that this is a commonly held belief. Father Pat Lagges's argument that the right to an advocate attaches at the time of the accusation is a variation of this argument.

focus of the trial then becomes proving or disproving only those things that are specified in the decree—anything outside the scope of the decree is also outside the scope of the trial. Oftentimes at this point the accused's advocate will file an initial petition to exclude various materials found in the diocesan files that have no relevance to the facts or circumstances of the current case.[16] For example, the cleric's file may contain a letter of complaint about the priest from a parishioner regarding an aspect of his ministry or the content of a sermon. Such a letter would have no bearing on whether the cleric committed the crime of the sexual abuse of a minor, and thus should be excluded from the formal proofs of the trial.

In canon law, the burden of proof is on the promoter of justice to prove with moral certitude the allegations against the accused. Interestingly, there is no explicit doctrine in the Code of Canon Law that the priest is presumed innocent until proven guilty.[17] However, the opposite is also true: there is no explicit presumption of guilt either. Article 5 of the Charter for the Protection of Young People issued by the USCCB in conjunction with the Essential Norms states: "A priest or deacon who is accused of sexual abuse of a minor is to be accorded the presumption of innocence during the investigation of the allegation and all appropriate steps are to be taken to protect his reputation." However, unlike the Norms, the Charter is not law.[18]

With the burden of proof resting on the person who brings the allegation, that is, the promoter of justice, and the responsibility in canon law not to unlawfully impugn a person's good name, one can certainly extrapolate that though the doctrine is not explicit, "as a defendant in a criminal action [the accused has] no burden to meet regarding what the accuser asserts. This is at least because the law does not presume [that the accuser is] guilty of the charge [he] faces. Consequently, if the promoter of justice is unable to meet the burden he faces, the court is bound to acquit."[19]

27:13 DISCOVERY

There are actually two phases in the canonical process that can loosely be called "discovery," though canon law does not use that terminology. The first occurs during the preliminary process. Though there is no promoter of justice at that time, the

16. Patrick R. Lagges, private communication, Nov. 10, 2011.

17. Although the Code does not have an explicit presumption of innocence until proven guilty, in CDF's circular letter published in May 2011, it states that "The accused cleric is presumed innocent until the contrary is proven." Congregation for the Doctrine of the Faith, 72 Acta Apostolicae Sedis 1132–1137 (Oct. 14, 1980).

18. The bishops published two documents concurrently, the Charter for the Protection of Young People, and the Essential Norms. The Vatican approved the Essential Norms as particular law for the United States, which means that the Norms carry the force of binding canon law for the United States. The Charter acts as a framework for the Norms and declares the bishops' intent for their future actions, but the Charter is not and is not intended to be canon law.

19. Ronny E. Jenkins, "The Charter and Norms Two Years Later: Towards a Resolution of Recent Canonical Dilemmas," 66 CLSA Proceedings 117–118 (2004).

investigator for the bishop is putting together his case. If the accused has been notified to retain an advocate, the advocate starts building a defense case at that time. The second is during the actual canonical trial. If the advocate is not brought into the process until after the preliminary investigation is over, then the advocate only has the time prior to and during the trial to build the defense's case. Although there are canonical rules that govern the discovery process, the rules regarding discovery during the investigative phase are not clear—at least not regarding as to what the various figures in the case specifically are entitled to.

During the preliminary investigation and/or the time prior to the beginning of the trial, there is no direction regarding who gets access to what. Does the accused get the same access to the discovery materials as his advocate? Does the review board get more information than the advocate? Does the accuser get any access to the information in the case, and if so, access to what? What standard should be used to determine who has access to what information? The answers to these questions are not clear.[20]

As a practical matter, the diocesan response to evidentiary requests from the advocate vary widely from diocese to diocese, and there is no consistency of praxis. Unlike the civil law, there is no way for the defense advocate or the promoter to compel the diocese to produce discovery materials. Some bishops believe that it is best to give the advocate access to everything in the diocesan files. Given that the purpose of a canonical trial is to uncover the truth, this would seem to be a practice that would be most in keeping with that goal. It is logical that the diocese would want the accused to know the evidence against him, because if it is strong enough it might convince the accused to admit his guilt and voluntarily petition for laicization.[21]

However, in many dioceses bishops restrict what access the advocate has to the materials they have collected. Though many bishops and representatives from CDF hold that the advocate is not entitled to obtain a copy of the bishop's opinion or *votum*, some will give it to the advocate as part of their policy that the advocate gets everything. Furthermore, some canonists make a similar argument that the advocate is not legally entitled to the findings of the review board, because their purpose is simply to provide counsel and their opinion to the bishop. It would be considered as similar to an expert report commissioned by the prosecution, and would be considered similar to "work product." Thus the argument is that the review board's report is not discoverable, though there is nothing barring the bishop from sharing the report if he so desires. Sometimes the various files are "scrubbed" of what diocesan officials feel may be embarrassing or not relevant material. Much of the time, even if the advocate gets access to the files, they are not given actual copies of the file's contents. Rather, they have to take handwritten or typed notes of what

---

20. Daniel Smilinac, "Clergy Personnel Files and the Instruction of an Allegation," 69 CLSA Proceedings 197 (2007).
21. Petitioning voluntarily is a much easier and quicker process if the accused admits his guilt and agrees to petition.

is contained in the files. This can be very time-consuming, particularly if there is much material in the files.

Some dioceses have required advocates to sign a non-canonical civil legal waiver[22] before giving them access to the files. These dioceses are very concerned that the information from the case will be given to the press or used against the diocese in civil litigation, and it sees limiting the advocate's access to the information in the case as a way to protect itself.[23] Advocates also have been informed in some cases that despite the advocate's request for the documents, the diocese does not believe that the advocate in fact needs those documents; thus the diocese will not provide them. For defense advocates, the lack of clear and consistent guidelines regarding the treatment of discovery and what must be provided to the advocate is very frustrating. While it might be equally frustrating for an advocate to have to wade through files containing irrelevant materials, it is likely better from the advocate's perspective to be able to make the determination personally that certain materials are not relevant rather than have the diocese make that determination for the advocate.

Obviously, the advocate for the defendant wants access to as much information and evidence as he or she can get. The advocate will want copies of the records, testimony, documents, etc. from any civil proceeding involving the client. These are not always available even if there is a civil suit, because many suits settle before there is a trial. Furthermore, most settled cases do not contain an admission of guilt. The advocate will likely request copies of all of the priest's personnel files, including any psychological reports (including those from seminary) that may be contained in the file. Unfortunately, many dioceses have a rather haphazard and decentralized method of keeping records, which means that depending on the nature of the file and the problem or complaint, relevant files could be in many different offices.[24] For example, it is possible that the bishop, the chancellor, the Vicar General, the Vicar for Clergy, the office for human resources, and the vocations office could each have its own file on the priest. It is possible that some of the information in the files could be duplicative, but it is also just as likely that each file is unique to that area. It is also likely that much of the information in the various files is irrelevant to the case under adjudication. However, allowing the advocate access to the files also allows the advocate to petition to exclude those files whose contents have nothing to do with the current case and thus help focus the trial on the relevant evidence.

After the trial begins, canon law is much clearer on what evidence the accused, the advocate, and the promoter are supposed to have available for their review. Ultimately, the accused, his advocate, and the promoter of justice must be given access to view whatever evidence the judges have collected from the parties and

---

22. Some waivers have included such language as requiring the advocate to personally indemnify the diocese if anything that the advocate has been privy to in the file is publicly disclosed, or prohibiting the advocate from showing his or her client or giving the client a copy of the written definitive decisions made by the court.

23. Paul Golden, "Advocacy for Clerics Accused of Sexual Abuse of Minors." 68 CLSA Proceedings 137 (2006).

24. Id.

from other sources, and they must be able to know on what evidence the judges intend to base their sentence.

After the joinder of issues, the advocate and the promoter of justice continue to compile evidence to submit to the judges to support their arguments. Furthermore, the judges and/or auditor continue to collect evidence themselves. For the trial, the advocate wants to make sure that he or she has the material that was collected for the preliminary investigation, including both physical evidence and testimony, and any additional evidence that has been added to the file since the case was sent to CDF. The advocate should get copies of any decrees from the diocese, all the materials that were sent with the bishop's *votum* to CDF, and what was returned to the bishop by CDF, particularly if CDF gave the bishop any directives in regard to the trial.

What has sometimes been discovered in receiving this information is that if there is exculpatory evidence presented prior to the bishop's initial determination, that evidence was not sent to CDF in the case sent with the bishop's *votum* (the canonical and pastoral opinion of the case that is submitted to CDF). The reasons this omission occurs will vary; but the canonical trial phase has not yet begun, so under canon law there is no pretrial disclosure rule. CDF's review is not like a U.S. grand jury evaluation of competing evidence. Unlike the U.S. criminal courts, in which a violation of the mandatory pretrial evidence disclosure "*Brady*" rules earns a new trial for the accused, canon law does not make a pretrial failure to disclose into a sufficient reason for reversal of the outcome in the first instance trial. However, if the final sentence contains evidence that has not been made available to the parties during the course of the trial, under c. 1598 the entire decision could be declared null (cc. 1620, 1622).

It is important to remember that at this point, there are really four distinct entities that are now involved in "discovery" efforts: (1) the judges who are conducting the trial, (2) the promoter of justice, (3) the defense advocate, and (4) the diocesan bishop/diocese that ultimately is in possession of most of the documentary evidence. For the promoter, the canons direct the bishop to give all of the investigative evidence to him prior to the submission of the *libellus*.

Though it is likely the bishop has given the promoter access to all of the investigatory evidence and the full contents of the cleric's various personnel files, it is not always the case. There have been times when the diocese does not want certain documents or records in the acts of the trial, and dioceses have been known to withhold documents from their own promoters, and even from the request of the judges in the trial.[25] Ultimately, there is no way to compel a bishop to release evidence in his possession if he does not want it released. However, if there is evidence that is

---

25. The bishop may believe that the document is irrelevant to the case, or believe that the defense advocate might make the document public by publishing it in the media or using it as the basis for a lawsuit against the diocese, or it might contain other confidential information that has nothing to do with the present case, which the bishop wants to keep confidential. There are also times where federal privacy laws prevent certain documents from being included in a file. These materials are usually withheld on the advice of the diocesan civil attorneys. Patrick Lagges, private communication, November 2011.

obviously used in a judicial sentence but is evidence that was not made known to the accused and his advocate, that is grounds for a defense to appeal and claim that the entire process is null (*restitutio in integrum*, cc. 1645–1648). It is also possible that the promoter of justice has access to the contents of the bishop's *votum*. Again, that is not always the case, and there is no way for the advocate to know unless the *votum* is quoted by the promoter. If the promoter submits records, testimony, or documents to the formal acts of the case, the advocate is entitled by law to have access to those documents.

27:14 PSYCHOLOGICAL RECORDS .

The use of psychological treatment records in penal trials is an area that has been very contentious. In cases where a cleric has psychological or other problems, he will often be sent for treatment, usually at an inpatient facility. Sometimes the treatment is for a problem such as drug or alcohol addiction, depression, or even engaging in sexual relationships with consenting adults. However, in past cases where there was an allegation of sexual abuse, the cleric was immediately placed on administrative leave, and then if he consented, he was sent to an in-house treatment center for evaluation. This was the common practice for dioceses until 2002.

Psychological evaluation continues to be a possibility in current penal cases. In the Essential Norms Norm 7, it suggests that the accused be offered the opportunity to voluntarily be evaluated by a "mutually acceptable" facility. In these cases, the priest's consent to this must be voluntary—it cannot be coerced.

Many times the cleric will consent to being evaluated because he wants to demonstrate that he is being cooperative with the process.[26] This is not always the best option from the defense's perspective. The accused is expected to sign a release form so that the results of his evaluation can be given to the bishop. Oftentimes the accused is not aware of the extent to which those records are released. In some ways, for the accused this is a perfect "Catch-22" situation. If the accused consents to being evaluated, he is usually subjected to various testing instruments that could reveal information about issues that have nothing to do with the allegation of sexual abuse.[27] Although this might be useful information for the bishop to know, evaluations in these cases are not supposed to be "fishing expeditions," but are only to provide information regarding the facts, the circumstances, and the imputability of the cleric concerning the current allegation of the sexual abuse of a child (c. 1717).

Furthermore, many of the therapy centers used to evaluate clerics do not operate on a therapeutic model. A therapeutic model evaluates the cleric simply to see if there is a diagnosable problem (asking "how can I help you?") and then treating the cleric for that problem.

26. Golden, supra, 139.
27. Id.

However, many therapy centers operate on a forensic model (asking the cleric to "tell me what you did") in anticipation of the treatment records being used in a trial to support the accused's guilt or innocence. This leads to situations where instead of trying to determine if there is a problem, the in-house psychologists assume that there is a problem that the cleric is not revealing. They might say such things as "I can't help you because you won't admit to abusing the child." If the cleric then continues to protest his innocence, rather than considering whether he may actually be innocent, he is considered guilty and uncooperative. In other words, if the cleric is innocent, he is put in a "no win" situation.[28]

Clearly in the therapeutic model, if the cleric is cooperative, the openness with which the cleric might be able to discuss any problems he is having would be significantly greater than if the cleric knows that this evaluation is going to end up before a judge or jury. Also, psychological evaluations and records are considered to be manifestations of one's conscience, and are supposed to be protected by the cleric's right to privacy in accord with c. 220. Thus it has been the Vatican's stance that it is improper to use psychological reports that were created as part of the cleric's treatment to be used against him, unless (1) he knew that the evaluation was being done in preparation for litigation, and (2) he freely consented to the evaluation and to giving the bishop access to the results.

Certainly, a bishop often will ask for access to the psychological records or at least to a formal evaluation in these cases because if there is not clear evidence of the cleric's guilt, the bishop wants to evaluate whether the priest is fit to return to ministry. This request could occur regardless of the reason that the priest was sent for treatment. And if the cleric refuses to release at least part of those records to the bishop to demonstrate his fitness, then the bishop can restrict the cleric's ministry to protect the Church or refuse to pay for the treatment.[29] However, if the cleric is sent or has been sent to a treatment center to be evaluated and treated, and that treatment was not in anticipation of litigation, then the records are not supposed to be used in a trial where a possible outcome is dismissal from the priesthood, unless the cleric freely consents to their admission.

27:15 WITNESSES, DEPOSITIONS, AND HEARINGS

During the time that the prosecution and the defense are gathering evidence, the judges are also supposed to be evaluating the case and determining what further evidence they may need. Canons 1428–1429 and 1530–1534 direct the judges (not the advocates) to gather information. Many canonical commentaries posit that having the judges responsible for gathering evidence allows the judge to direct the trial and evaluate the case more thoroughly than leaving discovery solely in hands of the other actors in the trial. As a practical matter, this can become a problem when, to preserve impartiality, judges are brought in from outside the diocese.

28. Paul Golden, private correspondence, August 2011.
29. Golden, supra, 139.

Some dioceses are able to bring in all three judges to interview the accused and the major witnesses in the trial. Even if the local auditor who is not a judge does the actual questioning of the witnesses, the judges are able to hear the testimony in person and see the demeanor of the witnesses.

However, in some of these instances it is difficult for all three judges to be present when witnesses are being deposed, particularly if the depositions cannot all be scheduled at the same time. In these cases a canonical auditor is often used to question witnesses and gather evidence. Some use one local judge and two judges from outside the diocese, which allows the local judge to question witnesses even if the other judges cannot be present. However, it still means that only one of the three judges has the ability to judge the demeanor and credibility of the witnesses, the way they present their story, and the overall trustworthiness of their statements. It also means that it is difficult for judges to go see evidence for themselves in cases where the scene of the alleged crime is relevant.[30]

Both the defense advocate and the promoter of justice are allowed to suggest witnesses to be deposed. However, in trying to determine whether the person could be a witness, there are no canonical guidelines regarding what can and cannot be asked prior to a witness's formal testimony, or how much the potential witness can be told about the process and what he or she should expect. Canon 1565 prohibits the witnesses from being given the questions before giving testimony so as to avoid collusion or coaching. This creates a difficult balance because the advocate or promoter must discover if the witness has pertinent information to divulge, without these initial inquiries crossing over into a violation of c. 1565. As there is no civil enforcement or penalty if these norms are violated, the only possibility of disciplining the advocate or promoter if that person transgresses is through the judge in the case.

Interestingly though, c. 1565 allows the judge to inform a witness before his or her testimony what the nature of the questions are going to be if "the matters about which testimony must be given are so remote to memory that they cannot be affirmed with certainty unless previously recalled." In other words, if the court recognizes that the subject matter of the testimony happened so long ago that the witness is going to need some time to think about his or her answer, then the judge has the right to inform the witness of the general line of the judge's questions.

Judges (or auditors), not the advocates, are responsible for deposing the witnesses in canon law, though both the advocate and the promoter can be present during the judges' questioning (c. 1559). Though the defendant or his advocate, the promoter, or any other advocate present can submit particular questions to the judge to be asked to the witness, they cannot question the witness directly.

---

30. The need to see the scene does not happen very frequently, but it does happen. For example, seeing the layout of a rectory can make a real difference in determining whether the crime alleged actually fits the description of the place where it was alleged to have occurred. For example, a priest is accused of abusing a minor behind a stairwell in a specific rectory. A visit to the scene reveals that the rectory's staircase is enclosed, and there is no way to actually be behind it.

The judge can also decide not to pose that particular question to the witness. The Code requires that questions should be brief, direct, clear, non-leading, not offensive, and suited to the age and intelligence of the person being interviewed (c. 1564).

Canon law (c. 1549) permits anyone to be a witness,[31] unless the person is under the age of 14 or is "of limited mental capability." However, under special circumstances the judge can make an exception and allow the testimony of a minor or a person who is mentally limited (c. 1550). As auditors can be used to question witnesses (c. 1428), it is strongly suggested that in cases where the witness is a child, and the child is allowed to testify, that the diocese use as an auditor someone who has professional expertise in questioning children about this issue. Canon 1555 allows the defendant to request the exclusion of a witness if he can show a just cause why he is making this request; for example, the person does not have any special knowledge relating to the alleged crime.

In sexual abuse cases, there is no way to avoid the fact that the subject matter of the questions is going to be unpleasant, personal, and likely painful. Unfortunately, these types of questions that are difficult both to ask and answer are sometimes not asked or followed up upon because judges do not want to cause accusers or their witnesses further pain. Canon 1530 allows a judge to "question the parties to draw out the truth more effectively." Without diminishing the pain of a person who may have been victimized, one must also remember that these hearings are deciding the vocational and occupational fate of the accused, which is also a big responsibility. Therefore the judges must balance these factors to get to the truth of whether or not the act was committed and whether the person on trial is the one who committed the act. This may mean that they must address and follow up on such issues as factual discrepancies in the testimony or statements that can be shown to be untrue or contradictory.[32]

This is also not the place for the judge or the auditor who is questioning the witness to be apologizing for the actions of the accused or the Church. There are many other times and places where apologies can, and in proven cases should, be made by the bishop or the diocese. However, it is not appropriate during canonical depositions for the judge or auditor to be publicly acknowledging in the record that the accused is guilty before a decision has been reached.

The accused may be deposed, but he has the right to refuse to answer. Canon 1728 states that the accused is not bound to admit his crime, and it waives the

---

31. Interestingly, canon law has some of the same privileges regarding disclosing information that was obtained in a professional relationship as the civil law does. Canon law excludes from testifying "clerics regarding what has been made known to them by reason of sacred ministry, civil officials, physicians, midwives, advocates, notaries, and others bound by professional secrecy even by reason of having given advice, regarding those matters subject to secrecy." (c. 1548). These exclusions are similar to physician-patient, attorney-client, and priest-penitent privileges found in the civil law.

32. An example of this would be that the accuser claims that the abuse occurred in the basement of a particular church rectory. Blueprints of the rectory demonstrate that there is no basement in that rectory, or in the church attached to that rectory.

requirement that he submit to being put under oath. All other witnesses must take an oath to tell the truth (c. 1532). The judge has the right to question the accused (c. 1530), but the accused has the right to refuse to answer in the same way that defendants in civil criminal court can "take the Fifth" and refuse to incriminate themselves. The accused may also choose to confess, though the confession cannot be "extorted by force or grave fear" (c. 1538). If the accused refuses to answer, the Code gives the judge the right to "decide what can be inferred from that refusal concerning the proof of the facts" (c. 1531).

As discussed above, the fact that judges interview witnesses can pose a bit of a logistical problem when the judges come from different parts of the country. Trying to schedule times when judges can all be present to question the often numerous witnesses can cause significant delays in the process. Because of this, judges will often delegate an auditor (who may or may not be a judge on the *turnus* or panel) to conduct the witness interviews (cc. 1428, 1561).

Although it is permissible to use an auditor and the Code places no restrictions on their use, in justice this method should be used only when necessary, particularly in a penal case, due to the seriousness of the allegations and the severity of the penalties. There are certainly times when an auditor can be helpful, for example, when unexpected scheduling conflicts arise such that none of the judges can attend the hearing, or when the judges do not speak the language of a witness and they need to conduct the interview in a language in which the judges are not fluent, or when the witness is a minor and the judges want someone trained in questioning children to ask the questions. But for most cases, as the law envisions the judges acting as the finders of fact as well as judging the case, it should be the judges and not the auditors who fulfill this role.

Unlike the civil law, most witness interviews in canon law are not videotaped as a matter of course. Canon 1567 states that "the notary is to write down the response immediately and must report the exact words of the testimony given, at least in what pertains to those points which touch directly upon the material of the trial." After being transcribed, the testimony is presented to the witness so that he or she can sign the deposition. The deposition can be electronically recorded (the 1983 Code is a bit dated on electronic recording; c. 1567 permits a "tape recorder" to be used). This means that if the judges are not present during the questioning of the witnesses, and the testimony is transcribed for them, the judges may miss out on being able to glean information from nonverbal cues such as voice intonation, emphasis, body movements, gestures, and emotional outbursts. As anyone who has conducted such an interview knows, such nonverbal communication can provide a fuller and more complete picture of a person's testimony. These nuances are lost if the judges have access only to the written testimony, though the notary is authorized in addition to recording the testimony to make mention "of everything worth remembering which may have occurred while the witnesses were being examined" (c. 1568). Although notations by the notary may be helpful, they are no substitute for the presence and participation of the judges.

It is up to the judges to evaluate the credibility of each party or witness. The judge, according to c. 1572, is supposed to take into account:

- what the condition or reputation of the person is;
- whether the testimony derives from personal knowledge, especially from what has been seen or heard personally, or whether from opinion, rumor, or hearsay;
- whether the witness is reliable and firmly consistent or inconsistent, uncertain, or vacillating;
- whether the witness has co-witnesses to the testimony or is supported or not by other elements of proof.

Sometimes in such cases, the accuser is the only person to testify regarding his or her allegation. In most canonical trials, the court is bound to follow canon 1573, which states: "The testimony of one witness cannot produce full proof unless it concerns a qualified witness making a deposition concerning matters done *ex officio*, or unless the circumstances of things and persons suggest otherwise." This means that in some trials, the testimony of one witness is often not enough for a judge to convict. However, while at CDF, Bishop Scicluna of CDF was clear that in these cases regarding the sexual abuse of minors, c. 1573 allows the judge to reach a canonical conviction on the testimony of a single witness if other evidence, circumstances, or proofs support a conviction.

27:16 PUBLICATION OF THE ACTS

Once all of the witnesses have been deposed and proofs have been collected, the judge issues a decree (the publication of the acts) giving the defendant and his advocate, and the promoter of justice, the opportunity to come in and review the acts of the case. The acts of the case are all of the witness testimony and evidence collected for the trial. The civil equivalent of the "acts of the case" would be the "trial record." In canon law, it is presumed that the defendant is going to take an active role in his defense, which includes permitting the defendant to review the evidence along with his advocate.

The defendant, the advocate for the defendant, and the promoter of justice have the right to go to the tribunal and inspect what has been submitted (c. 1598). Furthermore, the advocate has a right to receive a copy of the acts[33] of the case (c. 1598). If there is a good reason for the court to not show the advocate one of the pieces of evidence, they can do this by decree. However, if the advocate is not able to see that particular piece of evidence, then it cannot be used by the judges in adjudicating the verdict. In this context, publication of the acts means that the acts of

---

33. The acts of the case are all of the decrees, documents, evidence, witness testimony, and anything else contained in the case.

the case are "published" to the advocate and the promoter, not that they are given to the local paper for publication.

After reviewing the acts of the case, both the advocate and the promoter are able to propose additional proofs to be added to the evidence. However, if more evidence is added, then the acts are republished, and again both sides have the right to review the evidence. The entire case is null if the accused and his advocate are not given the right to inspect the acts of the case (c. 1598) each time the acts are published.

27:17   CONCLUDING THE EVIDENTIARY PART OF THE CASE

The evidentiary part of the case concludes when both sides have finished submitting additional evidence and the judge determines that the case has been sufficiently instructed (c. 1599). Both sides either declare that they have no more that they wish to add, or the time elapses for either side to submit new evidence. When this has occurred, the presiding judge is required to issue a formal decree, declaring that the case is formally concluded (c. 1599). The judges can choose after the case is concluded to admit new evidence that has come to light, though it must be of such import that "it is likely that the sentence will be unjust...unless the new proof is allowed (c. 1600)." If important new evidence is submitted or comes to light, it must be published to both parties.

27:18   FINAL STATEMENTS

After the last of the testimony and evidence has been submitted to the court, the promoter of justice and the advocate for the accused are given the opportunity to make their final arguments. They do this by submitting written briefs to the court that outline the facts of the case, the applicable law, and the reasons the accused should or should not be found guilty of the specific delict or crime for which the accused cleric has been charged.[34]

The timing of the submission of the briefs is somewhat unclear, because c. 1602 does not specify the exact order or timing in which the briefs are to be submitted. In some trials, the promoter and the advocate are told to submit their initial briefs at the same time. Then the promoter submits his rejoinder (c. 1603). Then the advocate for the defense submits the final rejoinder.

In other cases, both sides submit their briefs, the briefs are mutually shared, and then both submit their rejoinders at the same time. As the defense always gets the right to speak last (c. 1725), they are entitled to then submit one more brief. This is different from the civil law, where the prosecution always has the last word.

Because many courts have the two sides submit their briefs simultaneously, it can cause a particular problem for the defense. Recall that the legal burden of proof

---

34. DiNardo, supra, 8.

is on the promoter of justice. However, if both briefs are submitted together, the defense advocate cannot initially rebut any of the specific arguments of the promoter, and must argue generally against what is found in the *libellus*. It would seem to make more sense that the promoter of justice should submit his brief first, with the advocate then allowed to specifically address the arguments of the promoter in his brief. If the promoter subsequently chooses to submit a second brief, then the advocate can exercise his canonical right to have the final word. Currently there is no uniform procedure, and because trials are subject to pontifical secrecy (meaning that one is bound to keep the proceedings confidential), there is no way to know how most courts operate.

The structure of the canonical brief consists of (1) a short summary of the facts, (2) a clearly stated *contradictorio* or doubt, (3) a brief law section, (4) the arguments, (5) a conclusion, and (6) any special pleas, such as a plea for a stricter penalty or a request for leniency.

Canon 1602 § 3 gives the judge the authority to limit the length of the briefs being submitted, and to set the time limits in which the briefs must be submitted. Each judge in each trial has the ability to make the determination for that particular case. One can understand that the judges often want to limit excessive commentary in the brief and to ensure that defense briefs say what they need to say in a succinct manner. However, the amount of discretion that judges can exercise means that the assigned length of a brief could be 5 pages or 40 pages. It may be difficult in a complicated case for the defense brief to cover all of the relevant issues of law and fact within the allotted page numbers, even when writing succinctly.

Furthermore, the lack of consistency trial to trial regarding the time limits for the submission of briefs makes keeping up with each diocese's timing requirements very difficult for both advocates and promoters of justice, particularly if they are involved in more than one trial.

After the final briefs are submitted, c. 1604 allows for the judge to permit a "moderate oral debate to be held before a session of the tribunal in order to explain certain questions." This is allowed, but not required, and is up to the discretion of the judges. This would be akin to closing arguments in the civil law.

27:19 RENDERING THE DECISION

The final part of the first instance trial (the initial trial as opposed to the appeal) is when the panel of judges meet to examine the evidence and testimony that has been gathered by the court. The judges submit to one another their individual written assessments and opinions on the merits of the case. During their meeting, each judge then explains why her has come to his conclusion. Judges can change their opinion after hearing from the other judges. The majority opinion wins, though if there is a minority opinion, he can mandate that his opinion be included in the case sent to the appeals court (c. 1609).

Once they have reached a conclusion, the judges issue a written sentence that the Code requires to be definitive, determinative, and reasoned. As canonist

Father Larry DiNardo explains, "The sentence must be definitive in that it resolves the question of the guilt or innocence of the accused priest or deacon. It must be determinative in that it renders the appropriate penalty for the commission of the crime and it must be reasoned in that it must be motivated both in law and in fact."[35]

To issue a sentence, the judges must have reached their decision based on moral certitude (c. 1608). This terminology is not familiar to most Americans, who are more accustomed to the standards of "beyond a reasonable doubt" and "clear and convincing evidence." Moral certitude was defined by Pope Pius XII in the early 1940s as being "certainty which excludes all prudent doubt, being based on positive reasons. Absolute certainty of nullity, such as would exclude not only all positive probability, but also the mere possibility of the contrary, cannot be required."[36] A more recent clarification of moral certainty is that "it is a practical judgment on the part of the judge based on the available proofs, considered as a whole and not a collection of isolated factors. Moral certitude is not absolute certainty where there is no possibility of the opposite being true. It is characterized by exclusion of reasonable doubt and it does admit of the possibility of the contrary. In a sense it is the human certainty that a person is guilty of a crime."[37] Another way of defining moral certainty is found in the Church's norms for adjudicating marital nullity cases. *Dignitas connubi* art. 247 defines moral certainty as "a preponderance of the proofs and indications is not sufficient, but it is required that any prudent positive doubt of making an error, in law or in fact, is excluded, even if the mere possibility of the contrary remains. The judge must derive this certainty from those things which have been carried out and proven in the process."[38]

27:20 TRIAL VERDICT AND SENTENCING

The sentence is then drafted by the *ponens*, or judge assigned to draft the sentence. After the sentence is drafted, by law (c. 1614) it must be published before it takes effect. Publication here is similar to the publication of the acts prior to the judgment, in that publication does not mean that the acts are given to the local newspaper. Rather, the sentence is published either by giving a copy to the party or his advocate/procurator, or by sending them a copy (c. 1615). The accused has the right to be informed that a decision has been made (c. 1614), the right to receive a copy of the sentence (c 1615), and the right to seek a remedy against the sentence and to make an appeal (cc. 1628, 1727, § 1).

Despite the canonical requirement, some dioceses are reluctant to give the defendant or his advocate a copy of the sentence, primarily because dioceses worry that the sentence will be published in the media, that a civil lawyer will post it on a public website, and/or the sentence will be used against the diocese in a civil trial.

---

35. Id.
36. William H. Woestman, Papal Allocutions to the Roman Rota 14 (1994).
37. DiNardo, supra, 5.
38. Pontifical Council for Legislative Texts, Dignitas Connubii 175 (2005).

Sometimes the diocese requires the advocate or the defendant to sign legal waivers and nondisclosure agreements before allowing them access to the sentence. This is problematic, particularly if the tribunal found the accused guilty, and he needs the sentence to be able to draft his appeal.

In canon law, there are three possible verdicts that can be rendered. First, there is the verdict that declares the accused to be innocent (*sententia absolutoria*). Second, there is the verdict that concludes that the accusations have not been proven (*sententia dimissoria*). Third, there is the verdict that definitively finds the accused guilty (*sententia condannatoria*).

27:21 EXONERATION

There are cases where the trial results in the priest being exonerated from the canonical charges made against him. If the priest is exonerated, then it is the duty of the bishop to try to rehabilitate the priest and his ministry as much as possible. Announcements in the local paper and in the diocesan paper can help to restore the priest's reputation. Having the bishop come and celebrate the priest's return to ministry can sometimes be helpful, but with all of these options the local circumstances must be taken into account.

Many priests who have gone through the process, even if they are exonerated, have a very difficult time getting back into ministry.[39] Though public media loudly touts charges made against accused clerics, it is rare that when a priest is cleared that the media gives that fact the same amount of publicity or attention.[40] As the process often takes years, sometimes the priest has been out of active ministry for some time. Some choose to retire early, or they are already retired and just wanted to have their name cleared. Some choose to go somewhere else where they are not known and the charges against them are not as public, or they go into some sort of limited ministry by their own choice.

Many accused then exonerated priests never quite recover from the accusation made against them, particularly if the accusation was very public and the process was long. Some who have been falsely accused suffer from a form of post-traumatic stress.[41] Sometimes, even if the accusation has been proven to be patently false, the priest is hounded by people who continue to believe that he is guilty—often protesting wherever the priest is assigned. The priest's name is usually put on publicly accessible websites as having been accused of misconduct, so that the accusation, regardless of its veracity, will be hard to ever fully dismiss. If the cleric is exonerated, it would be helpful for the diocese to offer him and his family access to therapy to deal with the trauma that they have experienced.

---

39. Daniel E. Hoye, "Reintegration and Restoration of Exonerated Priests," 119 CLSA Proceedings 73, (Oct. 11, 2011): 118-129.
40. Id. at 124.
41. Id. at 119.

27:22 VERDICT OF NOT PROVEN

There is a distinction made in canonical courts between a person being proven innocent and a verdict that declares that the promoter has not proven his case to a moral certainty. Canon law allows the court to issue a decision of "not proven" in cases where there is neither enough evidence to exonerate the cleric nor to prove guilt to a moral certitude. This can happen frequently in cases where the allegation has been made, but the accuser will not cooperate with the canonical investigation or provide witnesses to testify on his or her behalf. Without the cooperation of the accuser, it is often difficult for the court to reach a moral certitude that the accuser is guilty. It can also happen in cases of a single accusation that happened such a long time ago that any possible witnesses have either died or cannot be located, and there is simply no way to determine the truth of the matter.

This verdict leaves the bishop in a bit of a quandary. What should the bishop do if there is some evidence that indicates the cleric might be guilty, but it is not enough to convict him? One canonist posited that because one cannot necessarily infer that the cleric is innocent when the court returns a verdict of "not proven," then the code in c. 1348 allows "for lesser measures, warnings and penal remedies to be specific, to be applied against the defendant by ecclesiastical authority even though the crime alleged could not be proven to a moral certitude."[42] This allows the bishop to consider limiting the priest's ministry or applying other types of limitations administratively for the good of the Church. However, if this is the case, then the diocese remains responsible for caring for and providing for that priest,

Of course, from the priest's perspective this means that he continues in ministerial limbo, neither dismissed from the priesthood, nor being considered a priest in good standing with a ministerial assignment. This can be a very frustrating, depressing, and humiliating response to a verdict that is not a conviction.[43] A canonist reports this regarding a client who had to live in perpetual limbo after having his ministry restricted twice, but who was ultimately exonerated by the district attorney:

> [T]he priest was in limbo for another few months. The stress was too much and the priest was hospitalized for depression. While he eventually returned to the parish he said that he could no longer take the pressure of public preaching. While the people accepted him he did not do well and died a relatively short time after he was restored the second time.[44]

42. Jenkins, supra, 118.

43. This circumstance of ministerial limbo is a very contentious issue in canon law circles, with many canonists believing that it is unjust for a bishop to act as if the priest has been convicted if there is no verdict of guilty. Monsignor Ronny Jenkins has written a thought-provoking article about balancing the "common good" of the Church with the priest's right to an assignment. Jenkins, supra.

44. Hoye, supra, 125.

27:23 A GUILTY VERDICT

The last possible outcome is a sentence that declares the cleric guilty of the charge against him. A trial that results in a guilty verdict does not automatically mean the priest will be dismissed from priesthood, though that is the norm specified in the Charter and Norms. It is almost always the case, but it is not absolutely required if there are special circumstances.[45] Usually those special circumstances involve the priest either being of advanced age or infirm, and in these cases the priest is usually told to lead a life of prayer and penance at a particular facility where he no longer has access to children.[46] Once a verdict is issued by the second instance appeals court, the judgment is imposed by a decree, which is then confirmed by CDF.

Most often, the result of a guilty verdict is that the priest is dismissed from the priesthood. The decree that imposes the penalty will inform the priest that he can no longer hold himself out as a priest. He cannot celebrate the sacraments, he cannot wear clerical garb, and he loses any other rights and privileges associated with being a cleric in good standing.

The decree ends the priest's right to be supported by the diocese. In the United States, this loss of a claim to support usually entails the termination of the dismissed cleric's health insurance. As most diocesan priest pension plans are non-contributory, priests do not acquire vested rights to a pension. Rather, pensions are provided to those whom the diocesan bishop determines to be "in good standing," though this term has no canonical significance. As they are no longer "in good standing" after dismissal, most diocesan clerics lose their eligibility for retirement pensions by the penalty of dismissal. Nevertheless, a bishop or superior retains an obligation in charity to see that a dismissed cleric is not left indigent as a result of the penalty (c. 1350 § 2).[47]

27:24 THE APPEAL

In canon law, the law requires that two courts issue verdicts for the sentence to take effect. Thus all cases decided in the first instance are sent to CDF, who can ratify it themselves, or they can hear the case at CDF in Rome, or they can delegate a local tribunal to act on their behalf as second instance. Unlike the civil law, in canon law the promoter of justice is entitled to appeal if he or she believes that the case was decided incorrectly (c. 1628). If either the advocate or the promoter disagrees with

---

45. However, a guilty verdict does mean that the accused priest should be removed from ministry and should never be put in a position where he can harm children.

46. Thomas J. Green, "Clerical Sexual Abuse of Minors: Some Canonical Reflections," 63 The Jurist 417 (2003).

47. (J. Beal, "Crime and Punishment in the Catholic Church: An Overview of Possiblities and Problems." USCCB, 2010, 8).

the outcome of the case, the case is then appealed. The advocate or promoter has 15 days to notify the judges of the appeal (c. 1630).

Because the accuser is a witness in the case rather than a party, the accuser does not have standing to appeal the court's verdict if he or she disagrees with the outcome. However, the accuser can certainly contact the promoter of justice and relay any concerns.

Article 26 in SST states that as soon as a definitive sentence has been made by the first instance court, a copy of the entire acts of the case should be sent to CDF as soon as possible. In addition to the right of the promoter of justice at first instance, the Congregation's promoter of justice also has the right according to art. 26 to challenge the sentence from the time he receives a copy of the case. According to art. 28, the decision of the court becomes final (*res judicata*) as soon as:

1° if a sentence has been rendered in second instance;
2° if an appeal against a sentence has not been proposed within a month;
3° if, in the appellate grade, the instance is abated or is renounced;[48]
4° if the sentence has been rendered in second instance by CDF.

Once the sentence is final, it has the force of law, and cannot be appealed (c. 1642). The only way that the sentence could possibly be changed is if the convicted party can show that a clear injustice has been committed, usually because evidence that was not part of the first trial has been discovered that would unquestionably change the decision of the court.[49] This is called a *restitutio in integrum* (cc. 1645–1648).

27:25 THE AFTERMATH

Canon law mandates that canonical trials are to be kept confidential (c. 1455). Therefore, unlike the civil law, the sentences issued in canon law are not published or compiled. A copy is supposed to be given to the defendant, and it is likely that both the diocese and CDF retain copies. However, the contents are not made known to the public, and there is no compendium of sentences that is published. Likewise, copies of the sentence are not given to the accuser in the case. As the accuser functions only as a witness in the canonical penal trial, he or she is not entitled to be formally informed of the outcome of the case.

---

48. "Abated" means not acted upon, so if the appellate court starts conducting the appeal and the defendant and his advocate stop participating, after six months the appellate judge can declare the sentence ratified (cc. 1520–1522, 1641). A case is renounced when either the advocate or the promoter decides that he or she no longer wants to pursue the case (cc. 1524–1525, 1636) and the person formally withdraws the appeal.

49. Ingels, Gregory. "Dismissal from the Clerical State: An Examination of the Penal Process." Studia canonica 33 (1999): 169–212.

27:26 CONCLUSION

Canonical trials are difficult for all involved. They are long, they are painful, and they are an imperfect means of dealing with the problem. Yet this is the system that the Church has in place, and there are many people of integrity attempting to make this system work under very difficult circumstances. It is evident that this process is far from ideal, and that it needs some significant changes to make it functional in the Church's current circumstances. In Chapter 28, we will examine in depth some of the problems with this system, and what might be amended or changed to make the process more just, fair, and timely.

CHAPTER 28

ఇ\>ు

Limitations and Weaknesses in the Canonical Penal System

28:1 VIABILITY OF THE CURRENT CANONICAL SYSTEM

Chapter 22 discussed factors that, in prior years, made it difficult within the Church to deal with the problem of clergy sexual abuse of minors. Although some of these problems still exist, many have been resolved in the legislation and norms internally promulgated within the Church since 2001. The Church in the United States is now depending on its own judicial and administrative processes to adjudicate the hundreds of cases that are currently working their way through the canonical penal legal system. And as more cases are reaching the point of a canonical trial, more issues and difficulties are being discovered.

The canonical legal system has the potential to be viable and functional, and to produce just results, and in some cases it fulfills that potential. However, there is a very important caveat. For the canonical system to work consistently and to achieve just results, it must be able to function as intended within the Church and within the society in which it is being used, and the assumptions that canon law makes about its own functioning and the people functioning within it must be generally true. As a result, fundamental problems arise when the Church attempts to use its internal system while functioning within:

1) a society possessing a common law legal system,
2) a civil milieu that does not understand a canonical or code-based system,
3) a local hierarchy that does not necessarily understand its own system, and
4) a fundamental distrust that the Church wants justice and will act accordingly.

Currently, none of these factors support or bolster the use of an alternate, internal system of justice that does not "play nicely" with the external civil system, and that is not understood by society at large. There are a number of outside influences and conflicts that the canonical system must overcome in the United States. These issues, coupled with systemic problems within the process, sets up the canonical process to fail.

28:2 WHAT IS AT STAKE IN THIS PROCESS

One measure of this failure is the number of educated and knowledgeable Catholic laypersons who perceive the process to be Byzantine, inefficient, and patently unjust. This perception exists despite efforts of those in authority in the Church to assert that this is a just system. Until the Church can fix the obvious and well-known internal glitches in the system, can visibly demonstrate to its people that the system is just, and takes the time to explain in understandable language how the system works, the Church would be wasting its time making such assertions of justice.[1]

Church authorities might question whether it really matters if the internal system of law is generally perceived by Catholic laity as being just. For an institution such as the Catholic Church, it greatly matters. As the FADICA study in Chapter 16 indicates, it makes a difference that the Church is perceived to be operating a system that lacks essential aspects of justice. Not only is it important from a theological standpoint that the Church acts justly, but as a practical matter the Church runs on donations, on volunteers, and on the goodwill of its people. It is absolutely critical that the Church's processes not only are just but that they are perceived as just, or, as has happened repeatedly over the past few years, people will simply leave.

An entire generation of young adults needed for active support of parish life has grown up hearing about this scandal. It is today's better-informed Catholic parents who now are raising the next generation of Catholics and who may worry about their own children being victimized. The current generation of young parents is the first to have spent their entire lives as Catholics fully aware that the Church has this internal problem that it cannot seem to resolve. Ineptitude or hostility expressed by leaders of the Church risk further alienating the entire generation, and possibly the next one as well. Parents who are ambivalent about church leadership are not likely to pass on to their children a tradition of loyal support and engagement. Volunteers for altar servers, volunteers for youth activities, and participation by families in the life of the parish may become scarcer if parents are reluctant to push their children to volunteer or to get involved in their local parishes. That prospect

1. The Philadelphia Grand Jury Report is a good example of people within the general society who are unconvinced that the Church and its internal processes are just. They state, "A final word. In light of the Archdiocese's reaction to the last grand jury report, we expect that some may accuse us of anti-Catholic bias for speaking of these painful matters. We are not church-haters. Many of us are church-goers. We did not come looking for 'scandal,' but we cannot close our eyes to the powerful evidence we heard. We call the church to task, to fix what needs fixing." *Report of the Grand Jury.* MISC. NO. 0009901-2008 (Court of Common Pleas, First Judicial District of Pennsylvania, Philadelphia January 21, 2011) (hereinafter "Grand Jury Report").

should be a very sobering thought that gestures to the profound loss of trust by the general population.

28:3 INADEQUACIES OF THE SYSTEM

The canonical system has a workable framework, but there are a number of ways in which the system is inadequate. Sometimes this is because the procedural laws themselves are flawed or the processes are not sufficiently developed to deal with the sexual abuse of minors. Some inadequacies arise because dioceses do not have qualified personnel or the money to spend to hire adequate personnel. Sometimes the system is inadequate because there are simply not enough trained people to do the work. A human problem that also should be addressed is that some of those people who are tasked with cleaning up the clergy sexual abuse issues in a diocese are overworked; they are getting tired, burnt out, and cynical, and are looking ahead at many more years of doing this work. These problems also need to be recognized and addressed among diocesan responses to these problems.

It should be noted that the section in the Code of Canon Law on penal law is anticipated to be revised in the next few years.[2] Furthermore, Cardinal Raymond Burke, who is the Prefect of the Supreme Tribunal of the Apostolic Signatura, in March 2010 "asked for the preparation of a document giving local bishops and their tribunals a detailed procedure for conducting the initial investigation of accusations of sexual abuse."[3] It certainly is possible that there may be some changes in the law that will improve the canonical processes in this area. However, as of the end of 2013, canonists must still use the penal procedures found in the current Code of Canon Law, the Essential Norms, and *Sacramentorum Sanctitatis Tutela* (hereinafter "SST/10"). Moving forward, the Church needs to reevaluate the way it handles penal law cases. Hopefully the reevaluation will find ways to adjust its structure, procedures, and personnel to better be able to justly, fairly, and efficiently adjudicate cases of the sexual abuse of minors.

28:4 THE JUXTAPOSITION OF CANON AND CIVIL LAW

It is obvious to say, but canon law is not well known. Very few Catholics, and practically no one else in the United States know what the canonical system is or how it functions. Even many lifelong Catholics are not aware that the Church has an alternate and comprehensive system of law. Catholics may have encountered bits and pieces of canon law at various times, but many have no sense of the overall system. Thus when asked, they cannot explain to others why a priest cannot be summarily dismissed, why a copy of the testimony of the accuser needs to be given

---

2. Francis Morrisey, "The Preliminary Investigation in Penal Cases: Some of the Better Practices," 2(2) The Canonist 185 (2011).
3. Id.

to the accused, and why the processes take such a long time. Couple that with the erroneous assumption that the Church functions administratively like a regular civil nonprofit corporation when it comes to disciplining employees and it is no wonder that there is widespread public confusion.

Once one clears the hurdle of explaining the existence of an actual alternate legal system, part of the reason for the failure of the system can be attributed to the fact that outside of Louisiana, people in the United States have no societal framework to understand how a code system works. So when confronted with a situation where canon law is invoked, questions are inevitable, for example: Why doesn't the law have a system of precedent? Because they lack a context, some U.S. Catholics unfamiliar with a code system have concluded that the only explanation is that the canon law system is grossly unfair and biased.

American discomfort with the operation of the canon law penal system is understandable. We have stated several times in this book that the canonical system is not the common law system. A code system is not "our" system here in the United States. Code systems have their own logic, their own ways of ensuring justice, and their own rules. Code systems work, but the system operates very differently from the one most Americans are used to. Like learning a second language as an adult, it is possible to learn another legal system. But like learning another language, one will never be quite as comfortable, quite as expert, quite as polished, or quite as accurate as with one's native language or system.

To comprehend a legal system requires more than just attending law school to study specific laws, cases, or legal maxims. Observations about a legal system are naturally shaped by the legal system in which one was raised. Television, for all of its sensationalism and errors, has done much to educate non-lawyer Americans on some basic concepts of the common law legal criminal system. Many non-lawyers can tell you about American legal concepts: innocent until proven guilty, *Miranda* warnings, proof beyond a reasonable doubt, instructing a jury, and other such concepts, because they are such a part of our daily life that we learn them just by paying attention. However, these are not concepts that necessarily translate into the code system.

The way the code system works is foreign for those raised in common law countries. For those who are native to a code judiciary, one can imagine that the number of lacunae or "holes" in canon law may not be such a problem, because those native to a code simply import the way things are done from their civil system into the canonical system. That is a legitimate way to fill canonical legal holes, and it could work quite well in similar systems. But juxtaposing aspects of the common law system with the code system does not work well at all.

However, this has not prevented bishops and others from trying to mesh the two systems together. Much like new speakers of a language who use a word of their mother tongue when they do not know the correct local phrase, bishops and canonists from common law jurisdictions will pull something from the common law (or from their own sense of the law) when they need an answer to a question that is not expressed in canon law or that reflects a decision that is left up to their discretion. Because it originates from a very different system or from no system at all, it is often contrary to what would be a correct answer within a code system.

In addition, because many who work inside the Church do not have a good understanding in general of how the canonical system works, they cannot turn around and explain it coherently when civil lawyers, district attorneys, the press, members of review boards, or others want answers. Instead of an explanation, which cannot be given in a brief "sound bite," the person answers, "that's what is required by canon law," with no further explanation. And once again, canon law appears to an observer to be arbitrary, Byzantine, and biased, instead of being shown to have its own logic, and having an approach to the law that is different from that which is familiar to most Americans.

Canon law and common law do not naturally interrelate. This puts those in common law countries at a disadvantage because code law is not our native system of justice. Those in the Church must work harder not only to make the system fair, but also to explain why the canonical system works the way it does. Comments in public documents such as a grand jury investigation report, stating that "The canonical process does not make the internal investigations any less biased in favor of protecting the institution, or the people who conduct them any more competent at arriving at the truth, or the victims feel any less re-victimized,"[4] show that the Church has a very, very long way to go.

28:5 VOLUME OF CASES

At least in the United States, even with SST/10, the Charter, and the Norms, the canonical penal system currently in place sets up bishops and canonists to fail. Fundamentally, the system as it stands was never intended to deal with the volume of hundreds of penal trials or the sensitive sexual subject matter of these cases.

At the outset, it must be noted that there is no way to know how many abuse investigations are ongoing and being judicially adjudicated in the United States. These numbers are being reported to the Vatican, but they are not being published to the general public. Although the USCCB keeps track and publishes the total number of allegations, these are not broken down by diocese or by how a case in process is being handled. So much of what is known regarding how many cases are being heard is through talking to canonists who are actually involved in judicial penal trials.

When the Code of Canon Law was drafted in 1983, the number of procedural canons was reduced, because it was anticipated that canonical cases would be rare. Those who put the Code together did not anticipate the need to process numerous cases on a local diocesan level. No one in their wildest dreams thought that within 25 years these canons would be needed for the volume of penal cases that are currently in process. When the current crisis necessitated use of the canonical penal system, it soon became evident that the system itself is not well equipped to handle large volumes of cases. It is also quite evident that while SST/10 and the Charter/

4. Grand Jury Report, supra, 86–87.

Norms have tried to remedy this problem, these legal Band-Aids are not adequate to ensure that canonical trials are fair, just, timely, and conducted in a consistent fashion.

The Code does not give enough procedural specificity for either consistency or fairness, and canonists and lawyers trained in the common law often do not have a broad grounding in code law to fill in the blanks consistently. And as so much discretion is left up to bishops and judges to fill these holes, what results is that one can have similar cases in different dioceses whose procedural requirements are vastly different. This lack of consistency adds one more layer of complexity to an incredibly complex system.

In 2003 a number of canonists, including one of the authors of this book, were sitting around a table and speculating about how a Church with a diminishing cadre of degreed canonists was going to adjudicate the hundreds of new trials lining up when they were already overwhelmed with their current canonical responsibilities. It was not a positive conversation. Priests who were judicial vicars of the diocese, as well as pastors of large parishes with attached schools, were already unable to handle their current caseload of work in a timely fashion. Now very important, very technical, and very time-consuming cases were going to be added to their already full schedules, and no one knew how they were going to manage. More than 10 years later, the result has been that cases are lasting years, canonists are stretched to the limit and getting burnt out, and there is no end in sight.

28:6 OVERARCHING ASSUMPTIONS

The canonical system, and in particular the canonical penal system for the United States, is set up with certain assumptions inherent in its structure. For this system to work, the assumptions must be true, or the system starts breaking down. The discussion of the penal procedures for the United States in this chapter include the rules and procedures found in the Code, in SST, and in the Essential Norms.

28:7 BISHOPS

There are many assumptions made regarding the behavior of bishops in the canonical system. One of the most difficult things that the law assumes is that a bishop can fulfill all of the disparate roles that he is expected to play. By law (c. 383), the bishop is responsible for the pastoral care and spiritual health of all the Christian faithful entrusted to his care, including the victims and their families. He is their shepherd and pastor, and it is his legal responsibility to ensure that they are safe and protected. Second, bishops also have a somewhat paternal relationship with their priests, and are legally tasked with their spiritual and physical well-being (c. 384). Third, the bishop is the judicial and administrative authority of the diocese, which means that he is responsible for the fair and unbiased administration of justice, as well as for stewarding the temporal property and assets of the diocese (c. 1419). In cases where a minor is abused, it is impossible for a bishop to fulfill all of these roles at the same time.

This puts bishops in a terrible moral quandary. If a bishop shows special solicitude and makes immediate apologies and overtures to the victim, does it prejudice him as a judge against the priest and open up the diocese to catastrophic civil liability with an "admission" of guilt? If he shows special solicitude to his priest by engaging him in the bishop's role as the priest's spiritual father and advisor and trying to rehabilitate him, does it prejudice the canonical case against the priest and set the bishop up for lawsuits or charges against the diocese and/or bishop personally for negligent oversight? If the bishop remains aloof from the parties to preserve his administrative and judicial neutrality and objectivity, does this mean that he has failed in his moral and legal obligations to be a spiritual father and protector of both the accuser and the accused, and does his lack of engagement with the victim set him up for accusations of being cold, aloof, and uncaring? The answer to all of these questions is YES. Bishops are put in a position where almost every decision they make in these cases is going to violate another legal obligation, as well as hurt and anger someone. Under the current law, there is no good solution for this dilemma. This is certainly underscored when one of the best canonical minds in thinking about this issue states: "The bishop has a duty to protect children whenever there is a risk; he has also a duty to protect his priests from false accusations. No universally valid principle can be given as to how to balance these two duties—both are absolutely binding."[5]

Additionally, the law assumes that the bishop is going to know and follow the law, and the processes within it, in a timely fashion. It assumes that when an allegation is made, that the bishop is going to immediately follow the process and begin an investigation, and that the bishop and his office will conduct a thorough investigation without prejudging the case. It also assumes that in the bishop's dealings with the Congregation for the Doctrine of the Faith (CDF) that the bishop will, as a matter of course, pass on the information and directions from CDF to the accused's advocates. This is extremely important, as CDF will only communicate directly to bishops, so that any information that is meant for the advocate is filtered through the diocesan bishop.

Once the preliminary investigation has been completed, the system assumes that bishops will act in a timely fashion, and that they will send the complete case file to CDF. Once a trial has been mandated, the law assumes that, within a short time, judges will be named and the trial will get underway, so that the matter can be resolved within the one-year time limit. Despite the expectations, this is often not the case. There are few reasons to justify a bishop taking more than a year to constitute a *turnus* or panel of judges for a case.[6] There are few reasons to justify a case taking more than a year to get started after the judges are named. And there

---

5. Ladislas Orsy, S.J., "Bishops' Norms: Commentary and Evaluation," 44 B.C. L. Rev. 999, 1020 (2003).

6. One legitimate and common reason to delay is if there is an ongoing civil or criminal court investigation in process. It is better that the Church allow the civil courts to conclude their investigations so that the Church does not interfere with their efforts.

is no reason an appeal should take over three years to adjudicate. Yet oftentimes, this is exactly the situation of the accused, who remains in canonical limbo while nothing is being done.

The canonical system does not take into account that there might be influences outside the canonical system that affect the decisions of the bishop. Nevertheless, outside influences frequently play a profound role in how a case is handled. If the bishop is hearing from his civil lawyers that he needs to "get rid" of the accused priest, or there are civil and criminal charges filed against the accused, the diocese, or possibly the bishop personally; or there are protesters daily on his cathedral doorstep; or he is getting lambasted in the public press, the bishop may be motivated to circumvent the canonical requirements.

Outside influences are a reality that must be factored into dealing with this issue. There are civil forces that will greatly affect how these cases are handled. Sometimes these factors have resulted in spotlighting and remedying injustice when the initial reactions have been unfair, offensive, or inadequate. Other times, these forces have actually resulted in a bishop's actions being less fair, less balanced, less just. Whichever way the forces push, it is certain that they will not be subsiding anytime soon. Thus the canonical system must take these forces into account in its own attempts to respect rights and to reach just conclusions.

28:8 LACK OF EPISCOPAL ACCOUNTABILITY

One other issue that is continually raised by laypersons and clerics alike is the sense that the law is unjust because while the Norms, SST, and the parts of the Code that sanction clerics apply to deacons and priests, these same laws specifically exclude disciplining errant bishops. The perception is that priests are subjected to the "one strike you're out" rule, while bishops have been able to get away with administrative malfeasance without comparative penalties attached to their actions. The only times that it seems that bishops are held publicly accountable for their actions (in the context of the United States, this means that the bishop is removed) is when there are criminal charges against the bishop or the scandal is so great that the pope has no choice but to remove him. As noted canonist Ladislas Orsy explains, "The *Norms* focus on allegations of abuse by priests and deacons only because the USCCB has no judicial authority over bishops and cardinals, who are directly subject to the Holy See or to the pope himself. Providing a remedy for lack of episcopal supervision or for structural deficiencies in the common law of the Church is beyond the competence of a conference of bishops."[7]

This issue has generated enough internal and external controversy that, as the National Review Board stated, "There appears to have been a general lack of accountability for bishops for the reassignment of priests known to have engaged

7. Orsy, supra, 1003.

in the sexual abuse of minors. Perhaps this is because, as one priest put it, 'Bishops are not used to explaining their decisions.'"[8]

This is a serious point of contention between what civil society understands to be just, and (1) the Church's understanding that a bishop's authority (the bishop as a successor to the apostles) is not subject to override or contradiction by those who are subject to him, and 2) that bishops are wedded to their dioceses and should clean up their mess rather than being relieved of duty.[9] Thus canon law protects the bishop and his internal decisions from being changed, censured, overridden, or otherwise checked by laypersons because it assumes that he is exercising the God-given authority of his office to teach, preach, and govern.[10] A bishop certainly is a citizen of the state where he resides and is therefore subject to its civil laws. However, bishops do not voluntarily put themselves or their decisions in a position of being countermanded by anyone other than the pope himself, except in those rare instances where the Code calls for mandatory permission from other bodies before the bishop can act.[11]

28:9 JUDGES

The Code, as well as the Norms and SST, presume that there are an adequate number of qualified, capable, and available clerics to serve as judges in penal cases. The reality is that this is simply not true. There are judges who are qualified, there are ones who are capable, and there are ones who are available to be judges, but it can be difficult to find judges that fit all three of these requirements at the same time.

The law assumes that the judge knows how to conduct a penal trial. Up until 2002, the only need for a judge or court in a canonical trial was in Catholic marriage tribunals. Although judges were comfortable adjudicating marriage cases, there were very few circumstances that called for other kinds of canonical trials. Then the problems in Boston went public and suddenly there was a need for a sophisticated canonical judiciary who were able to conduct and adjudicate the penal trials that were gearing up in dioceses all over the United States. Each trial requires a panel of three judges. Not only was there a great need for trained judges, but also canonical courts needed people trained to be canonical defense lawyers (advocates), prosecutors (promoters of justice), and auditors. To complicate matters, the Code requires

---

8. National Review Board for the Protection of Children and Young People, A Report on the Crisis in the Catholic Church in the United States, United States Conference of Catholic Bishops (Feb. 27, 2004 (sec. IV B 8) on Web at http://old.usccb.org/nrb/nrb study/nrbreport.htm.

9. A non-bishop may challenge the decision of a bishop in limited cases, but the matter must be decided by either another tribunal (where the appeal would be in Rome) or the case is heard in Rome. Any canonical crime allegedly committed by a bishop can be adjudicated only in Rome.

10. Orsy, supra, 1026.

11. E.g., c. 1292 requires that a bishop have the consent of his finance committee and college of consultors before he can alienate (sell) certain property.

that judges in penal cases be priests with a doctorate in canon law. This considerably narrowed the pool of potential judges.

In 2003 one of the first things that was changed from the SST/01 requirements, and was made permanent in SST/10, was to allow the requirements of priesthood and having a doctorate in canon law to be dispensed with. The Vatican also allowed for one layperson with the appropriate canonical degree to act on the judicial panel, though this has not yet been permitted. This change was tacit recognition that in 2003 there were not enough qualified priests to judge these cases, and this was before these judicial abuse cases even began to be adjudicated in earnest. That same year, in 2003, the CDF held training seminars to teach a core group of canonists how to adjudicate these cases. Again, this was recognition that canonists had been inadequately trained in how to fulfill the various canonical roles necessary to assist in penal trials. Though these training seminars were certainly helpful, most judges have had to learn their roles on the job. Unlike the civil realm where less experienced judges could use more experienced judges as a resource or mentor, and where they often have an experienced support staff to assist judges in doing their job, this was a case of the entire canonical judiciary being trained at the same time. This was certainly less than ideal for cases of such importance.

The lack of a trained judiciary has been quite a problem. Judges have had to learn canonical penal procedure while on judicial panels. This is not a time when training should be on the job.[12] Additionally, to ensure that the judges are impartial, judges are being brought in from all over the country to adjudicate cases. While this assures judicial impartiality, it creates other problems.

Judge availability is the source of one of the biggest frustrations with the system because it makes it nearly impossible to conduct a trial in a timely fashion. Overall, there are very few clerics who have been trained to be judges in these cases, and they are spread unevenly across the country. This means that the same small group of clerics is judging all of the cases across the country, with many judges being on the panel of multiple cases. As none of these clerics are only full-time judges, they have to balance the work they do on trials with the balance of their other responsibilities. Most of those priests who are judges are judicial vicars or other types of officials in their dioceses. They may also be pastors of a parish, in charge of running a Catholic school, or have other parish duties.

Cases take considerable time to adjudicate because of the scheduling difficulties caused by judges being both physically distant from each other and from the accused's diocese. Most have only extremely limited time to travel the distances necessary to conduct the trial. As most dioceses only use judges from outside the diocese, this often means clerics must drive long distances or fly to get to the

---

12. As one prominent canonist recently noted about the need for competence in adjudicating cases, "Over the past ten years or so, we have been acquiring practical experience and greater comfort with the processes, but we still need a good dose of humility, since we can make mistakes; yet, slowly but surely, we can fine tune our procedures (just as we did with marriage cases in the period following 1983). It is important to recognize that we are dealing with a 'work in progress.'" Morrisey, supra, 184.

diocese where the trial is being held. This can get very expensive, particularly for smaller dioceses that "may not have the human resources and the financial means to install and run a well-organized and efficient judiciary."[13]

This time/availability problem grows exponentially if the judge is on multiple panels. Trying to coordinate travel availability for three overworked judges (and likely for the accused's advocate as well) from three separate areas of the country is very, very difficult. And as the canonical system has expanded roles for judges in questioning witnesses and parties, this means that they often can have great difficulty in finding the time to fulfill their roles. Oftentimes judges are not able to personally hear witnesses but must rely on auditors to take testimony because they cannot find a time when they all can get away from their own diocesan responsibilities. It also makes it very difficult during the course of the trial for judges to make joint decisions regarding canonical motions or on other issues that arise within the context of a trial.

The result of having judges with no time to adjudicate cases is obvious. Canonical cases are taking years to process. This is worsening as many judges have more cases than they can already handle, and are refusing to take any more until the ones that they have are adjudicated. This leaves bishops unable to find judges for current pending cases.

28:10 JUDICIAL DISCRETION

Another assumption in the Code is that giving judges great discretion to decide things for their own tribunals is a good and positive thing. The reality is that having so many issues left up to the judges' discretion is making it very difficult for advocates with multiple clients to navigate the various rules set up in each diocese for each particular case. Different panels assign different time limits for such things as brief submissions, different brief lengths or styles, and different standards regarding what discovery is available to the advocate, and make different decisions on how many witnesses are allowed to be put forward, what order final briefs are submitted, etc. Different panels of judges can have different requirements within the same diocese, as each panel can fill in the "holes" as it sees fit. This makes it very difficult and exceedingly frustrating for advocates who represent multiple clients to keep track of what procedures must be followed for their individual clients.

There is no system of legal precedent in canon law. Thus cases heard in one part of the country may have a different outcome than a similar case in another part of the country. Canonical judges do not have the resources available to civil judges, in that there is little shared wisdom in the form of published canonical decisions to draw upon in making decisions. Although judging a case independently and completely on its own merits is appealing, this is certainly one area where the common law notion of what is equitable (that similar infractions should be punished using

13. Orsy, supra, 1014–1015.

similar standards and in a similar fashion) clashes with the canonical notion of what is equitable (judges should not be bound to precedent, but should be able to judge each case on its own unique merits).

The solution to many of these issues would be for phe Pope or the Signatura to create national or regional penal law tribunals with a stable judiciary to adjudicate these cases. A number of judges and an appropriate staff could be dedicated to hearing penal and other such cases in a timely manner. This way there would be judges who have the time to conduct cases and develop considerable expertise in the procedural law. Also, this would mean that the standards for witnesses, briefs, and other aspects of the trial that in canon law are left to the judges' discretion would naturally become more standardized. Cases would presumably take less time, and the whole process would be more professionally handled. However, there may be bishops who would object to this solution because it takes away some of their discretion in how they operate their own dioceses. Nevertheless, Pope Francis and his council of eight are working on how to make the Vatican curia and its associated structures more just and efficient, and the possibility of national or regional courts certainly could be part of that discussion.

A further element that should be considered is for judges, promoters, and advocates to be required to undergo a process of accreditation or certification or qualification to adjudicate these cases or to practice before these courts. Like the required Continuing Legal Education (CLE) programs for civil lawyers, there should also be additional training and continuing education requirements for judges, promoters, and advocates to ensure their continued competence and knowledge of the most current law and canonical processes.

28:11 ADVOCATES/PROCURATORS •

There is an assumption in canon law that the person who is tasked with representing the accused is going to be competent, professional, and act in good faith. However, sadly, this is not always the case.

There is no licensing requirement to be a canonical advocate or procurator. As long as the canonist possesses the requisite degree, and if the canonist attends the required seminars, the canonist can hold himself or herself out as a canonical advocate capable of representing clients. Yet just holding the degree does not necessarily make a canonist competent to represent clients. There should also be (1) a mechanism to report an advocate or procurator in the event that it becomes evident that the person is not capable or qualified to serve in this capacity, (2) a way to evaluate these complaints, and (3) a place to have that list publicly accessible.[14]

---

14. In the United States there is a national association of canon lawyers known as the Canon Law Society of America. This group has a Committee for Professional Responsibility that evaluates complaints of unprofessionalism and malfeasance. However, it is not mandatory that canon lawyers in the United States belong to this group, and the Society has no authority over canonists who are not members.

There is also a real difficulty from the advocate's perspective regarding communication with the Vatican's Congregation for the Doctrine of the Faith about the penal cases on which they serve as advocate. The issue is that CDF has a policy that it only corresponds with bishops. It does not directly correspond with individual advocates. This means that instead of both sides being notified at the same time regarding the disposition of a case, the letter, decree, answer to a question, or other document goes only to the diocesan bishop. It is then up to the bishop's office to communicate that information and/or the congregation's specific directions regarding the case, to the accused and his advocate. This is very frustrating to advocates, who would prefer not to be dependent on bishops and their offices to get information. This practice presumes both the goodwill of the bishop and the efficiency of his office. Unfortunately, advocates cannot consistently rely on either.

Furthermore, the law provides that dioceses should have advocates who are to be made available to represent the accused. However, these advocates are considered a stable part of and directly employed by the diocesan tribunal. This creates the situation for the accused that the advocate representing him works directly for the bishop. Thus the argument is that there is no way to escape bias by the advocate because there is no way for that person to wholeheartedly represent the interests of his or her client while employed by the bishop. There is always the possibility that the advocate could be fired if he or she does something that damages the interests of the bishop or the diocese. This is another area where common law and code law practices and mentalities diverge.

This becomes a problem when the accused instead wants to hire his own outside advocate, because it means that the priest must pay for the advocate's services. If the accused has few financial resources and must rely on the diocese for his advocate, this presents a conflict of interest. Yet, oftentimes the diocese will not pay for the services of an outside advocate because of the ongoing expense. Many dioceses argue that although they have the obligation to provide the accused with an advocate, they are not obliged to pay for that particular advocate's services.

It used to be that canonists were almost exclusively employed working in universities, tribunals, or chanceries. Thus compensation for the work of an advocate could be seen as something extra or supplemental. In addition, advocacy was done almost exclusively by priests—as reflected in the requirements of the Code. Currently, many advocates are laypersonse who require professional compensation. Many advocates are doing this work full-time, and it requires far greater amounts of time investigating and representing the needs of accused clerics and exercising their right of defense. Because good and competent advocates may not live in the accused's region, although much can be done over the Internet by e-mail, much of the "legwork" of putting together a defense case must be done on-site and in person. This requires travel, and travel can be expensive. The canonist in private practice also bears the full expense of original and continuing education and training, as well as the burden of an office, equipment, and support staff.

The work of a professional advocate is no longer a supplement to the canonist's "day job." It is his or her day job. The law needs to reflect this change that while advocates certainly should be accredited by the diocese to be able to practice in their jurisdiction, advocates should be guaranteed a fair and just wage by the diocese in the penal cases where they represent the accused. Both the expertise and the expense necessary to defend a client can be considerable. Therefore, appropriate compensation is a matter of justice for advocates who are developing a high level of training and skill in this area. Dioceses certainly compensate their civil counsel at appropriate levels, and the same consideration should be given to those professional canonists acting as judges, procurators, and advocates.

Another issue is that the law assumes that there are enough competent advocates to represent the number of accused clerics. However, it is a fact that like judges, there is only a small cadre of highly experienced advocates, and they all have full caseloads. There are very few advocates who currently want to take on new clients. Advocates are reporting that they often have too many cases to handle and they are getting exhausted. They are tired of not having any consistency, tired of being denied basic access to evidence, tired of feeling like they never get direct answers from CDF or from bishops, tired of feeling like judges are making it up as they go along, and tired of feeling like they are trying to advocate against a foregone conclusion. One canonist/advocate compared his job to that of a hospice worker, where all they do is hold their hands and help their clients to come to grips with the end of their ministry—regardless of the outcome of whatever process they are in.

There is a fairly small cadre of canonists who represent a large number of the accused in these cases; thus it is increasingly difficult to find an experienced advocate who is not already overloaded. Although overworked advocates know they should not be taking on more clients, many will take them anyway because they are being told that no one else will take a new case. This is a terrible choice to have to make—overworked representation or leave the person with the potential for less-than-competent or biased representation by an assigned advocate.[15]

There is one other sensitive issue that arises for advocates that must be addressed. If one has followed this crisis, there are names such as Gauthe, Geoghan, Shanley, Kos, Porter, Hughes, etc. that are immediately recognizable. Like all priests accused, notorious abusers also need canonical representation. However, they are so notorious that many if not most canonists do not want to represent them. There is nothing that requires a canonist to represent someone if the canonist does not want to represent that person. However, if the Church believes that justice requires that representation should be available for all, this must necessarily include those with the most difficult or disturbing cases. This is something for canonists and the greater Church to ponder.

15. This is not to imply that diocesan advocates are incompetent or biased. However, most dioceses do not have many trained canonists to begin with, and most do not have canonists who are trained in defense advocacy. Much like a defense lawyer in the civil law, it takes a certain amount of training to become a competent defense advocate. Although an accused priest could be simply given an advocate from the diocese (presuming they have one to spare), the advocate may have no experience in this area.

28:12 THE ASSUMPTION THAT TIMELINESS IS BENEFICIAL

When the canons require that the initial case be completed within a year, it embodies the legal maxim that "justice delayed is justice denied." Most of the time, one hears canonists and the accused complain that cases are not completed in a timely fashion, and that trials last for years without resolution. However, in some cases, it is not the accused who is complaining about the years it takes for a case to be resolved but rather the accused who is ensuring that the case drags on for as long as possible.

There are cases that are being adjudicated where the accused knows that he is guilty of the crime, knows that the evidence is sufficient for a guilty verdict, and knows that the penalty that he will be given will almost certainly be dismissal. Until the final judgment is reached and he is formally dismissed, the diocese is responsible for his sustenance. After the final judgment, the likelihood is that he will lose his health insurance, his benefits, his monthly stipend, and any other means of financial support that he may be receiving from the diocese. Therefore, it is in his best interest to prolong the case for as long as he can, and to postpone, delay, or manipulate the process for as long as possible. This is deeply frustrating to the judges and to the promoter of justice, who may be doing their best to complete the case in a timely and efficient manner.

Although the judge can in some ways try to ensure that the process is not manipulated, the judge must also allow the accused to exercise the rights to which he is entitled. Sometimes it is a fine line between the exercise of rights and the abuse of the system. This is something that each judge and each tribunal must assess.

28:13 THE ASSUMPTION OF WITNESS COOPERATION AND GOOD FAITH

The procedures in the Code of Canon Law assume that the accuser will be an adult, and that the person will cooperate as a witness in the case in good faith. In the canonical system, like the civil system, the accuser's testimony and evidence are used as the primary proofs to convict the accused priest. Unfortunately, although the canonical process is capable of handling such problems as financial crimes, it has become evident that this process is particularly unsuited for dealing with accusations of child sexual abuse. The canonical process is not suited for accusers who are minors, and whose parents do not want to subject them to more trauma by having them be interviewed or have to testify. It does not make provision for accusers who make an accusation but who refuse to participate in the process. Finally, there are also ways in which the civil and canonical processes can be abused if the accusers are not making their accusations in good faith.

As a rule, minors are discouraged in the Code from testifying in a canonical trial. Although the Code makes an exception to allow minors to testify in certain instances (c. 1550), this process does not make many other accommodations for accusers who are children, or for traumatized people for whom a canonical trial before priests might add to their distress. It is certainly not the best system for this type of crime—particularly as the canonical trial runs separately from the civil proceedings, so the child potentially would have to testify in both systems rather than just once. As the canonical trial does not have civil effects, a parent may be hard-pressed to justify putting his or her child through the unnecessary trauma of testifying in a court with no civil legal jurisdiction, particularly if the child has already had to testify in a civil forum.

Canon law also does not take into account accusers who are acting on the advice of their civil attorney and refuse to cooperate with the canonical trial. Because of the problems that many accusers have had in past dealings with diocesan officials, many civil attorneys have been advising their clients to bypass any interaction with the diocese at all. Particularly in cases where the accuser has a civil case pending against the diocese, the civil attorney does not want his or her client to have any interaction with officials who in the view of the attorney are "the other side." Although this certainly makes sense from the civil law perspective, it makes conducting a canonical trial where the whole case rests on proving the allegation of the accuser and his or her witnesses very difficult.

The Code does not take into account the possibility that the accuser may attempt to play the canonical system against the civil system for the accuser's financial benefit. If an accusation is made by an accuser, but the accuser is counseled by his or her civil attorney not to cooperate with the Church's internal process, there may be insufficient evidence without the accuser's cooperation to convict the accused in a canonical trial. If the priest is exonerated canonically due to lack of evidence, this exoneration has sometimes been used in civil trials to "prove" that the diocese is unwilling to discipline its abusive priests. This proof is presented to the jury in hopes that they will return higher civil damages for pain and suffering, or punitive damages for the Church's negligence. However, it is because the accuser refuses to cooperate and give evidence of the abuse that the tribunal has no choice but to declare either that the accused priest innocent or that the accusation is "not proven."

Finally, canon law presumes that the accuser and his or her witnesses are acting in good faith in reporting abuse, and not with malicious motives or for financial gain.[16] Although this is a very infrequent occurrence, there have been times where false allegations have been made against a priest. Sometimes this is simply a means to try to take advantage of the large amounts of financial compensation being paid by dioceses to victims.[17] Other times it is more personal, and used as a means to quickly get rid of the priest, or take revenge on him. In the regular course of parish life, there are people who dislike their priests for issues having nothing to do with sexual abuse. This is for various reasons, ranging from personality conflicts to profound theological differences. These differences most often resolve themselves

16. Cullen, Kevin. "Phony Cases a Danger in Abuse Battle." The Boston Globe, (August 5, 2002): A1.

17. Cooper, Jonathan. "Authorities: Man Falsely Claims Abuse by Priests." Seattle Times, (January 29, 2013).

by the family or the individual moving to a different parish, or the priest being transferred to another church.

There have been times when the dislike of a priest or the instability of a person escalates and becomes toxic. It is well known in the general community, and certainly among Catholics, that dioceses around the country have been adopting a "no tolerance" policy regarding accusations of sexual abuse. In many dioceses, the mere suggestion of an accusation results in the priest being automatically removed from his parish and his file being sent to Rome for evaluation. There have been times when a person falsely accuses a priest because he or she knows that an accusation often ends the priest's career. These cases are tragic, because they often ruin the reputation of the priest if the allegation is made public; they also tend to make people discount the accounts of the true victims. It is also an insult to those same victims because it exploits the profound trauma of those who have experienced this very real and very personal crime. However, it is for this unfortunate reason that a full and thorough investigation must be done before allegations are made public in order to prevent the permanent tarnishing of the career and ministry of an innocent cleric.

Given the very public failures of the Church to listen to victims and to get rid of abusive priests, there is a tendency to want to move far in the other direction and assume that every accusation made against a priest is true and that every accuser is a legitimate victim. When inconsistencies appear in the evidence, there is the tendency to want to discount discrepancies in testimony or evidence that calls into question the guilt of the priest. As we have emphatically stated before, this is in no way to denigrate the experiences or the veracity of those who have truly been victimized. Nevertheless, the tendency to convict on faulty evidence must be resisted because, as the case against Cardinal Bernardin proves, there are those priests who are accused but are in fact innocent, and they deserve to be exonerated. This, too, is a moral obligation of justice.

28:14 THE POTENTIAL FOR THE LACK OF A DEFINITIVE OUTCOME

The goal for a canonical process is that cases get processed quickly and result in a definitive outcome. The Code mandates, and thus presumes, that a canonical trial will take a year to be initially heard, and it allows another six months for the appeal. Then the judge is to issue a definitive sentence declaring that the cleric is innocent or guilty, and the whole process is supposed to be complete in 18 months. It does not, however, give pastoral direction regarding what the cleric is to do while in canonical limbo. This limbo arises in cases where the allegation of sexual abuse is being investigated and/or tried, but (1) the processes being used are taking years to complete, or (2) the result of the process is that the allegation cannot be proven or disproven.

Not all allegations of sexual abuse are either true or provable, as illustrated by the allegation against Cardinal Bernardin, which was later publically retracted. In cases where a cleric has been civilly convicted of abusing a child, or in cases where the cleric has admitted to abusing a child, the cleric can be rather rapidly dismissed or laicized. However, in cases where the cleric denies the allegation, where the case is old, where there is little corroborating evidence, or where there is no civil or criminal court that can or has adjudicated the matter civilly, what to do with the cleric during the trial or after a non-definitive judgment becomes an immediate and pressing issue.

A priest is incardinated into a diocese. This means that the priest, in a sense, belongs to the diocese. The priest promises obedience to his bishop, and promises celibacy when he is ordained. In turn, it is understood that the priest becomes a stable part of the "family" of the diocese. As the priest will not marry or have children, the diocese takes on responsibility to care for the priest, to make sure that he has sufficient resources to live on and that he has proper insurance, that he is attended to when he is sick or injured; the diocese will also care for him in his retirement until his death. Though it is usually a specific parish that actually pays a priest his stipend and other benefits, the diocese has the broader responsibility for his long-term care. This is very important, because along with not having a family to care for him, most priests are not independently wealthy. They do not earn a salary that would provide much extra for savings or to add to a retirement fund. Thus priests are very dependent on the safety nets provided by the parish and diocese to pay for their lodging, insurance, healthcare, and retirement.

In 2013, the average age of a Catholic priest at ordination is 32. Though this is changing somewhat, many if not most go directly from college into seminary instead of working in the secular world first. Most major in such fields as theology or philosophy, and receive their Masters Degree in Divinity upon their graduation from seminary. The problem with this track is that other than being a priest, a chaplain, or teaching at a Catholic school or university, this educational track does not prepare them well for finding a job outside the confines of the Church or, ironically, a school.

These factors become very important in the context of an accusation leveled against a cleric, or in the event of an unproven verdict. Unlike most secular jobs, a cleric is almost wholly dependent on the Church's support. Oftentimes he is living in a rectory owned by the parish, and he is driving a car provided by the parish. When an accusation is leveled against a cleric, most of the time he is immediately removed from his parish and told to move out of the rectory. This means that the cleric is effectively homeless unless the bishop is willing to house him somewhere else. Oftentimes the parish will stop paying for his healthcare and insurance. If the parish provides him with a car, it is often no longer available for him to use. If the priest has no independent wealth, he is left with meager if any savings on which to live, with no real opportunity to do work in his chosen or a related field. This becomes an increasingly pressing problem with older and retired clergy when the alleged act occurred many years ago. Frequently they have health problems that require regular medical care and are on medications that can be very expensive. They also have nowhere to go if the diocese refuses to house them.

It is a bad situation in the short term. It becomes an even more severe predicament in the event that, regardless of the process, there is no way to prove definitively either that the priest is innocent, or that he is guilty. Many bishops believe that for the good of the Church, a verdict of "not proven" means that although the cleric is not permanently removed from priesthood, the bishop can continue to refuse to give him an assignment. As a priest and particularly as one with an unproven accusation against him, his opportunities to work are limited. The bishop likely will not allow him to work in the civil sphere, but often gives the cleric no position in the diocese. There have also been times when the priest has been civilly exonerated, but he remains restricted from ministry through the canonical process.

Given the special relationship between the bishop and his priest, what is the bishop's responsibility in these circumstances? For civil legal reasons, oftentimes the bishop would prefer to distance himself as much as possible from the accused cleric. However, he is bound to provide the cleric what the Code refers to as "decent support" according to c. 384. As one might imagine, the definition of what constitutes "decent support" varies widely from bishop to bishop and from diocese to diocese. Some bishops cut these clerics off completely, leaving them to rely on family or friends for their support. Other bishops will provide a basic stipend, as well as such things as health insurance and a pension. This is an area where the USCCB would do well to develop consistent guidelines to ensure that the rights of clerics in this situation are respected and that their basic needs continue to be met until a definitive resolution can be reached.

28:15 THE INHERENT PROBLEMS WITH DISMISSAL

When a cleric has been found guilty of sexually abusing a minor, most often the penalty imposed upon him is dismissal. That certainly is the penalty that civil society expects, and in fact oftentimes the lawsuits against the Church make claims for higher damages if the guilty cleric is not dismissed.

It is clear that a priest who has been found guilty of abuse should not be allowed to have any contact with children or even to hold himself out as a priest. However, it is unfortunate that in the vocal calls to dismiss abusive priests, there is no real consideration given for the rational argument to maintain the diocese's relationship with the priest but heavily restrict him.[18] If the priest is not dismissed, his promises to the bishop remain; thus the bishop still can exercise control over the priest's life and movements. However, as canonist John Beal points out, "dismissing a person from the clerical state also cuts him loose from whatever imperfect systems for monitoring and control the Church may have and leaves him free in society."[19] Does

18. Of course, a civil problem with this issue is that if the bishop retains the priest this way, it can be used in a civil lawsuit against the bishop to indicate his negligent oversight, and it becomes an even more serious legal liability if the priest reoffends.

19. J. Beal, "Crime and Punishment in the Catholic Church: An Overview of Possiblities and Problems." USCCB, 2010, 17.

society really benefit from having the former priest thrown back into the secular society, with no monitoring, no support system, and likely no job skills other than those used in ministry?

Beal concludes that rather than furthering the safety of children, the practice of dismissing clerics may actually be counterproductive. He states:

> Our understanding of the psychodynamics of sexual abusers is quite limited, much more limited than we once thought, but it does seem clear that those prone to compulsive or addictive behavior are most likely to "act out" when they are under stress, lonely, and cut off from a social support network—precisely the situation in which dismissed clerics are likely to find themselves. The Church might benefit society by removing abusive clerics from ministry but stopping short of dismissing them from the clerical state so that it can at least attempt to monitor their behavior.[20]

The Church's ability to monitor is not perfect, but there are certainly actions that a bishop could take to restrict the cleric's actions and whereabouts. If the former cleric has not had any civil convictions against him, the Church may be the only institution that has any authority to restrict the cleric's activities. This ultimately may be a better and safer solution than simply allowing the dismissed cleric to go back into the general society with no one being able to monitor or control his movements, and no one knowing that he is potentially a threat to children.

Furthermore, total dismissal of the cleric almost certainly ensures that the convicted priest will never be able to pay damages to the victim in the event that either a civil court or a canonical court awards them. In other words, it almost certainly ensures that the perpetrator is perpetually "judgment proof." If a person has been accused or convicted of sexually abusing a minor, it is nearly impossible for that person to find alternate civil employment. If the person is able to find a job, it will likely be low paying. If there is a civil criminal conviction, the person also is likely under the state's restrictions regarding contact with minors, which means that the person is even more constrained about where her or she might work or live.

If the cleric remains within the ambit of the Church, the Church is responsible for the priest's basic sustenance. Thus he will usually have some sort of basic pension or other income. If he can be employed in some nonministerial capacity (e.g., maintaining the diocesan archives) that allows him an income, that income could be civilly garnished or canonically garnished to pay damages to the victim. However, if the convicted priest is completely outside the Church's control, then the likelihood is that there is no way for the Church to ensure that the convicted priest is living up to his financial responsibilities toward compensating the victim.

20. Id.

28:16 AN UNCOMFORTABLE QUESTION

There is no doubt that the abuse of children is a heinous crime. And those who commit this crime must be punished, both in the civil system as well as in the canonical system. However, as has been stated repeatedly in this book, the canonical system is administered by the Church. The Church is called by Jesus Christ to reconcile sinners, to encourage them to repent and reform their lives, and to support them in this journey.

Much deserved attention has been given to the Church's need to minister appropriately to those who have been victimized by sexual abuse, as well as to their families. The Norms created the position of Victims' Assistance Coordinators, whose job it is to work with victims. Dioceses routinely pay for counseling and other services designed to help heal and support victims. All of these efforts are being made to try to minister to those people who have been hurt by a leader of their Church.

But, the Church is also bound to ask a significantly uncomfortable question: What is it called by its own belief and theology to do with those who have been dismissed from the clerical state for this crime? Is sexual abuse the "unforgivable crime"? Does the Church have an obligation to care for its dismissed clergy? What should a diocese or parish do when it knows that a dismissed priest is living in its territory? This question becomes more interesting when studies show that a child abuser is much less likely to offend if he has some sort of supportive community surrounding him. Are there ways that adults within a parish could formally reach out to a dismissed priest in this circumstance? It is a question that cannot be easily discounted, and it raises some very interesting questions about how a Church can go about "practicing what it preaches" in what can be both uncomfortable and challenging circumstances.

28:17 UNREASONABLE EXPECTATIONS

In discussing all of these issues regarding sexual abuse in the Catholic Church and its internal procedures for dealing with it, there is one question that may be whispered among canonists but is rarely discussed in any real or academic way. This is because it questions the nature of the viability of the canonical system itself.

The question that must be asked is this: If in the United States (a country that has a stable government, consistent utilities, access to reliable transportation, and stable and functional communication systems, and is financially well resourced) the tribunal penal system is unwieldy, inefficient, and almost impossible for many dioceses to maintain the personnel and processes as they are required in the Code, then where is it possible? Should the entire system be overhauled? Why does the Church maintain a system that generally cannot be run properly even in a country and Church that is reasonably functional and well resourced? How can it expect countries who may be facing this crisis in future years, and who have fewer resources and less functional systems than those in the United States, to fulfill the canonical requirements necessary to conduct a judicial trial?

There is a canonical maxim that "one is not bound to the impossible." Is the Church binding itself to processes that for most places, including the United States, are functionally impossible to fulfill given the real-life limitations on budget, staff, time, and availability of appropriately educated and trained court personnel? This is a question that in justice, the Church needs to ponder.

28:18 CONCLUSION

Understanding the problem of child sexual abuse within the Catholic Church and how it is being dealt with internally is important for those people who are working with and within the Church to clean up this problem. If the Catholic Church operated like a large multinational corporation, it is likely that this would have been a much shorter book. However, the fact that it neither thinks of itself that way, nor judicially functions that way, further complicates the complex interactions among the Church, its people, civil society, and civil government. For all intents and purposes, judicially the Church functions like a sovereign state though it must exist and conform itself to the civil systems within which it functions. This results inevitably in tension and conflicts. With this particular scandal, it has resulted in the Church's re-evaluation of how it handles these accusations, as well as a relationship between the Church and the civil state that is continually being renegotiated.

It is difficult to find a vantage point in this crisis where one can see all sides, much less attempt on some level to examine each perspective. The personal stories attached to these issues are often so compelling that it is easy to be swept away by emotion, and to fail to see the whole picture. Even in writing this book, it was easy for one's perspective and sympathies to be swayed depending on whose perspective is being presented.

It is hard not to be angry and indignant at the victimization of children, horrified at the mistreatment of some victims, and sympathetic for the difficulty in having to ask them to retell their story yet again for another court. Yet, also compelling is the story of the innocent priest who is fighting a single false accusation from 30 years ago, where the civil courts have declined to prosecute for lack of evidence, and the priest finds himself in an interminable internal process in which he may never be able to completely clear his name or ever work as a priest again. One can feel compassion for all of the good people who are giving decades of their lives and ministries to clean up the disaster that abusive priests have caused; hearing story after horrific story of their confrères' crimes and taking on work that they had never expected to do. It is also possible to feel sympathy for some bishops, particularly for those who have inherited a disaster from their predecessors that they had no part in creating. They have conflicting legal, moral, and theological expectations placed upon them that they cannot possibly meet, and they despite having cleaned up their own dioceses must deal with the fallout from those of their brother bishops who, over 30 years after Lafayette, cannot seem to "get it." All these sides have some valid claims for compassion, or at the very least for some basic understanding of the complexity of the problems they face.

It is possible for there to be a workable, functional canonical system that can professionally and efficiently handle penal cases. However, it is going to take formal changes in the law, as well as the cooperation and coordination of CDF, the USCCB, diocesan bishops, and canonists working in the field to make it happen. It will also take more education on the part of dioceses, bishops, and canonists in ways to educate their people about the Church's system of justice so that it is not immediately assumed that the Church is engaging in one massive cover-up. "That's just what canon law requires" is not an adequate answer to complex questions of justice, fairness, and transparency. The Church's future depends on better answers, and Catholics and other members of our society deserve better answers than this.

CHAPTER 29

☙

Clergy Abuse Issues in Non-Roman Catholic Denominations

29:1 OVERVIEW

This chapter covers the legal issues of clergy sexual abuse in religious denominations other than the Roman Catholic Church. We offer a survey rather than an in-depth analysis because the wide dispersal of authority to local and regional entities makes it far more difficult to assemble a comprehensive account of the phenomenon within these entities than with the U.S. Conference of Catholic Bishops hierarchical model discussed elsewhere in this text. Clergy sexual abuse is a problem in all religious entities, as a human failing, and is not exclusive to any one faith.[1] The Episcopal Bishop of Chicago said it succinctly in 2002: "We would be naïve and dishonest were we to say this is a Roman Catholic problem and has nothing to do with us because we have married and female priests in our church. Sin and abusive behavior know no ecclesial or other boundaries."[2]

29:2 HOW OTHER CONGREGATIONS HAVE RESPONDED

After a claim of clergy sexual abuse is presented to a non-Catholic religious congregation's governing body, there are a variety of ways in which the congregation can handle it. The most productive methods might involve some combination of honesty and openness with congregants,[3] standardized rules and consequences for

1. Anson Shupe, In the Name of All That's Holy: A Theory of Clergy Malfeasance 6, 12 (1995).
2. Rt. Rev. William Persell, Bishop of the Episcopal Diocese of Chicago, Good Friday Sermon, 2002.
3. John Dart, "Risk Management: Protestants Confront Sexual Abuse," Christian Century 119 (June 5, 2002).

misconduct, mandatory reporting to law enforcement, and offers to pay for counseling of the victim. The insurance carriers for churches offer educational programs and recommend screening techniques that may reduce the presence of pedophiles among volunteers.[4]

No denomination has a perfect process or perfect record of dealing with reported sexual abuse incidences. The Episcopal Church[5] and some Jewish[6] sects have created formal policies and protocols for handling reports. This action standardizes treatment across many local congregations, though there will be some variations in members' personal views or agendas.

The author and psychologist Philip Jenkins cites the Episcopal church as a prime example of a non-Catholic entity dealing with the reports of abuse. Although its population is about 4 percent of the size of the Roman Catholic Church, Episcopal churches' average annual insurance claims for sexual misconduct-related matters rose from 5 in the 1980s to 39 in 1992 alone.[7] The John Jay College inquiry done for the Catholic bishops found that insurers estimated an average of 260 sexual abuse reports per year.[8] In this same study, researchers discovered that two insurance companies who insure Protestant churches, GuideOne and Brotherhood Mutual, paid approximately $4 million between 2005 and 2010 and over $7.8 million from 1995 to 2010, respectively.[9] Jeff Hannah, the executive director of GuideOne insurance, stated that based on filed claims and news reports, "sexual misconduct occurs in a variety of relationships—between 'staff and staff, staff and members, adult and child . . . regardless of church size or theology,'" emphasizing the universal pervasiveness of sexual abuse among religious organizations.[10]

Philip Jenkins quoted The Church Mutual Insurance Company in 1993, stating, "it currently has open claims against four hundred non-Catholic clergy and has closed three hundred others since 1984. About half of them concern child sex abuse."[11] In 2007, Jehovah's Witnesses settled nine sexual misconduct lawsuits for undisclosed amounts of money.[12] The Jehovah's Witness organization, along with The Church of Jesus Christ of Latter-Day Saints (Mormons), are noted for their secrecy and intra-faith methods of handling claims against church authorities. This secrecy makes it difficult to accurately assess the scope of sexual abuse

4. Arthur Gross Schaefer, "Combating Clergy Sexual Misconduct," in 41(5) Risk Management 34 (1994).

5. John Jay College, Report to U.S. Conference of Catholic Bishops, The Causes and Context of Sexual Abuse of Minors by Catholic Priests in the United States, 1950–2010, at 20 (May 2011) (hereinafter "John Jay College Report").

6. Richard Greenberg, "Clergy Misconduct," Washington Jewish Week (Jan. 17, 2007).

7. Philip Jenkins, Pedophiles and Priests 51 (1996).

8. John Jay College Report, supra, 20.

9. Id. at 20.

10. John Dart, "Risk Management: Protestants Confront Sexual Abuse," Christian Century 119 (June 5, 2002).

11. Jenkins, supra, 51.

12. John Jay College Report, supra, 21; and see: John Dart, "Background Check: Churches Respond to Safety Concerns," 124 Christian Century 21 (June 26, 2007).

within the Jehovah's Witness and LDS communities. Secrecy also simultaneously gives elevated status/importance to those exceptional cases that are reported to law enforcement or that are pursued by plaintiffs in civil court.[13]

The website Reformation.com provides a tally and collection of reports (via newspaper links) for ministers of Protestant denominations who have been accused of sexual abuse. Claiming a total of 838 Protestant ministers, the website lists numbers for Baptist, Fundamental/Evangelical, Anglican/Episcopalian, Lutheran, Methodist, Presbyterian, and "Various Church Ministers."[14] Though some of the groups have staggering numbers and others have just a handful, these numbers are not meant to be comprehensively correct, but rather the numbers are good indicators that some sexual abuse by clergy is occurring across all Protestant faiths. Our earlier chapters dealing with a centralized Catholic hierarchy were able to produce more definite statistical data with the benefit of the U.S. Conference of Catholic Bishops' field audits of diocesan records, to assure accuracy to the extent possible.

29:3 OTHER DENOMINATIONS

Until recently, most Jewish sects operated under a notion of silence about misconduct, and many Orthodox sects continue to hold strong to the code of silence. Now a majority of Jewish denominations (Orthodox excluded) have adopted "formal codes on the books that outline unacceptable clergy behavior and mandate precisely how complaints of sexual impropriety are to be investigated and adjudicated by in-house panels."[15] After the Orthodox community in Brooklyn was criticized, the Kings County District Attorney's Office created the *Voice of Justice*, a radio program that encourages victims of abuse to come forward, offers outreach programs at local schools seeking to educate about sexual abuse, and provides a hotline for sex abuse reporting from the Brooklyn Orthodox community.[16]

29:4 CONSTITUTIONAL ISSUES AND CASES OF NON-CATHOLIC DEFENDANTS

The Episcopal church's religious doctrines need not be considered in a case of clergy abuse. "Application of a secular standard to secular conduct that is tortious is not prohibited by the Constitution."[17] "Civil actions against clergy members and their superiors that involve claims of a breach of fiduciary duty, negligent hiring and

13. John Jay College Report, supra, 21; and see Laurie Goodstein, "Ousted Members Say Jehovah's Witnesses' Policy on Abuse Hides Offense," N.Y. Times 26 (Aug. 11, 2002).

14. Front page, reformation.com website (last visited Aug. 3, 2011).

15. Richard Greenberg, "Clergy Misconduct", Washington Jewish Week (Jan. 17, 2007).

16. John Jay College Report, supra, 22.

17. Moses v. Diocese of Colorado, 863 P.2d 310, 320 (Colo. 1993).

supervision, and vicarious liability are actionable if they are supported by competent evidence in the record."[18] "(A)n organization, confronted with the misdeeds of one of its agents, assumed control of the matter and in the process of protecting itself injured a vulnerable individual. The defendants have not argued that Bishop Frey's decision to assume control and resolve the problems created by Father Robinson and Tenantry's relationship was a matter of purely ecclesiastical concern. Tenantry's claims in this case do not involve disputes within the church and are not based solely on ecclesiastical or disciplinary matters which would call into question the trial court's power to render a judgment against the defendants. Our decision does not require a reading of the Constitution and Canons of the Protestant Episcopal Church or any other documents of church governance. Because the facts of this case do not require interpreting or weighing church doctrine and neutral principles of law can be applied, the First Amendment is not a defense against Tenantry's claims."[19] Other Episcopal church cases have concurred in this approach.[20] And similarly, Nazarene church doctrine was not implicated in a negligent hiring claim.[21] Likewise, Methodist doctrine was not involved in a negligent supervision claim.[22]

But the situations and the outcomes have varied. Jehovah's Witness doctrine would be implicated in a case asserting insufficient discipline of a member sued for sexual misconduct.[23] Presbyterian pastors are "not analogous to a common law employee. He may not demit his charge nor be removed by the session, without the consent of the presbytery, functioning essentially as an ecclesiastical court. The traditional denominations each have their own intricate principles of governance, as to which the state has no rights of visitation. Church governance is founded in scripture, modified by reformers over almost two millenia."[24]

Malpractice as a cause of action is unlikely to succeed, as it has failed in the context of the Catholic defendants' extensive case law. Malpractice would involve entanglement: "It would be impossible for a court or jury to adjudicate a typical case of clergy malpractice, without first ascertaining whether the cleric, in this case a Presbyterian pastor, performed within the level of expertise expected of a similar professional (the hypothetical 'reasonably prudent Presbyterian pastor'), following his calling, or practicing his profession within the community."[25] The court held that it could not constitutionally examine a church's doctrinal expectations of proper behavior for a minister: "Any effort by this Court to instruct

18. Id. at 321.
19. Id. at 321.
20. See e.g., Doe v. Evans, 814 So. 2d 370 (Fla. 2002).
21. Rashedi v. Gen. Bd. of Church of Nazarene, 203 Ariz. 320, 325, 54 P.3d 349, 354 (Ariz. Ct. App. 2002) (claim requires application of neutral and generally applicable tort law principles in negligent hiring case).
22. Smith v. Privette, 128 N.C. App. 490, 495, 495 S.E.2d 395, 398 (N.C. Ct. App. 1998).
23. Bryan R. v Watchtower Bible & Tract Society, 738 A.2d 839, 848 (Maine 1999).
24. Schmidt v. Bishop, 779 F. Supp. 321, 332 (S.D.N.Y. 1991).
25. Id. at 327.

the trial jury as to the duty of care which a clergyman should exercise, would of necessity require the Court or jury to define and express the standard of care to be followed by other reasonable Presbyterian clergy of the community. This in turn would require the Court and the jury to consider the fundamental perspective and approach to counseling inherent in the beliefs and practices of that denomination. This is as unconstitutional as it is impossible. It fosters excessive entanglement with religion."[26]

26. Id. at 328.

CHRONOLOGY OF SOME ASPECTS OF THE SEXUAL ABUSE ISSUE IN THE U.S. ROMAN CATHOLIC CHURCH

Note: *This chronology integrates legal actions, statutes, comments, and Church documents as indicators of the then-current response of the Church to sexual abuse allegations involving minors. The listing or omission in this chronology does not present any value judgment concerning the relative accuracy of the claims presented by those who are quoted or cited.*

FOUNDATIONS OF PRESENT LAW

309   The Synod of Elvira condemns presbyters and bishops who abuse children.

1051   St. Peter Damien condemns clerical homosexual behaviors in his writings.

1140   The *Decretum Gratiani*, a compilation of canon law, is published, containing specific references against homosexual relations with boys (pederasty) that could merit the death penalty against the cleric responsible.

1234   The *Corpus Iuris Canonici*, another compendium of canon law, condemns clergy homosexual relations.

1570   A priest in Verona, Italy, who had sex with a choirboy was defrocked, tried, and then beheaded; the boy was whipped and exiled.[1]

1568   The *Horrendum illud* is issued by Pope Pius V, also condemning clergy sexual abuse.

1917   The Code of Canon Law condemns clergy sexual misconduct and the failure of responsible leaders to deal with such misconduct.

1922   Clerical crimes legislation is adopted by the Roman Catholic Church.

THE MODERN ERA

1949   A Catholic religious order, the Servants of the Paraclete, opens a rehabilitation center catering to priests with serious problems, including alcoholism and sexual misconduct. This New Mexico facility later became the place to which dioceses sent priests to be reformed from prior molestation patterns, and the order opened similar centers around the globe. The main facility in New Mexico and many others closed as a result of subsequent abuse of children and teens by some of its residents who provided service in parishes in surrounding towns.

---

1. Stephen Rossetti, A Tragic Grace: The Catholic Church and Child Sexual Abuse 104 (1996).

1950s Seminary students who studied during this decade developed, over their subsequent years, more of a predilection for child sexual abuse than did later decades of priests. This generation of priests led to the discussion of 1960s–1970s seminary lifestyle conditions in John Jay College's 2011 report to the U.S. Conference of Catholic Bishops.

1960s Seminarians who became priests during this decade also exhibited a heightened pattern of abuse behavior in their later years, according to the John Jay College reports.

1962 March 16: The Vatican issues policy document *De Modo Procedendi in Causis Sollicitationis* (Instruction on the Manner of Proceeding in Cases of Solicitation), and the document *Crimen Sollicitationis* (the Offense of Solicitation) is distributed but not made public or published by typical Vatican legal notices. The 1962 documents were ordered to be kept in "secret" nonpublic files under control of the bishop alone. The documents gave orders on how to proceed in the event of cases of clergy sexual abuse. Attention would later be focused on the command that these notices be kept only in secret files, so that virtually all of the U.S. bishops after 1962 were unaware of the instruction's existence in their files.

1965 Changes in the population of priests in the United States were noted. There were 58,600 priests in the United States in 1965, but that number shrank to only 45,200 priests in 1991.

1970s The "permissiveness" in the U.S. seminaries during this decade has been criticized by some observers as a source of negative "culture" issues that may have contributed to sexual abuse patterns; these opinions are not, however, universally supported among scholars.

1978 An Oakland, California, priest pleaded no contest to a criminal charge for lewd conduct with two boys. The diocese sought Vatican permission to laicize the priest, and the offender was finally removed from the priesthood in 1987. In 2004, the ex-priest was sentenced to six years in prison for molesting a young girl in 1995.

    The diocese of Tucson, Arizona, found that a priest had abused boys since 1978. Action was taken to remove him; the case went to the Vatican, and he was finally laicized in 2004.

1980s This decade produced the highest number of reported occurrences of clergy sexual abuse incidents within the U.S. Catholic Church,[2] although many instances were reported 10 to 30 years after the alleged sexual contact had occurred.

1982 Joseph Ratzinger, later Pope Benedict XVI, becomes prefect of the Congregation for the Defense of the Faith at the Vatican. The CDF is the principal entity that tracks and adopts policies concerning priests and sexual misconduct.

1983 A new Code of Canon Law is adopted, displacing the 1917 Code, and expressly identifies sex with a minor by the priest as a canonical crime;[3] the Code also continues to hold bishops in the hierarchy responsible for the failure to act against known sexual abusers.

---

2. John Jay College, Report to U.S. Conference of Catholic Bishops, The Causes and Context of Sexual Abuse of Minors by Catholic Priests in the United States, 1950–2010, at 8 (May 2011), on Web at http://www.usccb.org/issues-and-action/child-and-youth-protection/upload/The-Causes-and-Context-of-Sexual-Abuse-of-Minors-by-Catholic-Priests-in-the-United-States-1950-2010.pdf.

3. Code of Canon Law 1395, 2.

1984   January 31: Vatican Cardinal Oddi writes a letter to Tucson, Arizona, bishop Moreno that the disclosure of priest personnel records to police or civil authorities "would be an intolerable attack upon the free exercise of religion in the United States; and we have no doubt that both Federal courts and public opinion would sustain us in this position. Your Excellency should therefore make known immediately and with clarity that no priest's files will be sent to any lawyer or judge whatever."[4]

       Father Gilbert Gauthe of Lafayette, Louisiana, is prosecuted and sentenced to 20 years in prison for child sexual abuse. Also, the victims sue him and his diocese in civil court for child sexual abuse; the result is a widely publicized $1.2 million jury verdict and national publicity for the topic of clerical sexual abuse. In depositions, the bishop admitted to having known about multiple sexual abuse allegations regarding Gauthe since 1974.[5]

       In Boston, Massachusetts, A. Reverend Eugene O'Sullivan is sentenced to probation for sodomizing a 13-year-old altar boy. Later that year, O'Sullivan is transferred to a diocese in New Jersey.

1985   May: a priest in Idaho was sentenced to seven years for child molestation.

       June: the U.S. Conference of Catholic Bishops hold a meeting on Clergy Sexual Abuse.

       June 8–9: The U.S. Conference of Catholic Bishops finalizes their Report, *The Problem of Sexual Molestation by Roman Catholic Clergy*. This expert report on clergy sexual abuse was prepared for and disseminated to all bishops by three experienced observers of the problem (Thomas Doyle, F. Ray Mouton, and M. Peterson). Their report was disseminated widely and discussed; later, however, the leaders of the USCCB decided not to endorse its contents.

1986   Father A.C. Andersen was convicted of 26 felony counts for the molestation of boys. He was not imprisoned, but requested to be sent away for "treatment" while on probation. While staying at the Paraclete rehabiliatoin center in New Mexico, he then molested boys again and was eventually sentenced to a long prison term.

1987   A study on child abuse in the Cleveland Middleborough area in the United Kingdom led to reforms in the handling of reports of child sexual abuse cases.

       The Canadian Conference of Catholic Bishops adopts *Policies & Procedures for Complaints of Sexual Abuse*.

1988   February 9: The U.S. Conference of Catholic Bishops adopts a statement on child abuse.

       February 18: Mark Chopko, the general counsel of the U.S. Catholic Conference, publishes the USCC's "Statement on Sexual Abuse of Children."[6]

1989   Survivors Network of those Abused by Priests (SNAP) was founded in Toledo, Ohio, as a support and advocacy group for the persons most directly impacted by clergy sexual abuse.

       November 16: The USCCB Bishops' Committee issues its *Statement on Priests and Child Abuse*.[7]

---

4. Vatican Congregation for the Clergy, Letter of Jan. 31, 1984, http://www.bishop-accountability.org/Vatican/Documents/1984_01_31_Oddi_to_Moreno_Priest_Files_R.pdf
5. Boston Globe, Betrayal: The Crisis in the Catholic Church 37 (2002).
6. Published in 17(36) Origins (Feb. 18, 1988).
7. Published in 19(24) Origins 394 (1990).

1990 March: Reverend Robert Kelley of Worcester, MA is sentenced to five to seven years in state prison for the rape of a nine-year-old girl.

 June: In Canada, the report of the "Archdiocesan Commission of Enquiry into the Sexual Abuse by Members of the Clergy" is published, regarding abuse cases in Newfoundland; and Archbishop Alphonsus Penney, who convened the Commission of Enquiry, resigns during the investigation of an alleged cover-up. Then separately, 200 criminal charges against 30 Christian Brothers are filed by Ontario Provincial Police. Later, separate charges of abuse result in a $23 million settlement for 700 former students of the Christian Brothers schools.

 October: Bishop A.J. Quinn of Cleveland, in an address to the Midwest Canon Law Society on "NCCB Guidelines and Other Considerations in Pedophilia Cases," is quoted as saying in a recording concerning diocesan records: "If there's something there you really don't want people to see, you might send it off to the Apostolic Delegate [Vatican diplomat in Washington D.C.] because they have immunity to protect something that is potentially dangerous, or that you consider to be dangerous."[8] Quinn later disagreed with critics who believed the words to mean that a cover-up of abuse files was planned using Vatican direction for the concealment.

1992 The Canadian Conference of Catholic Bishops publishes *Breach of Trust, Breach of Faith: Child Sexual Abuse in the Church and Society.*

 In New York, the *Jones by Jones* decision is issued on sexual abuse.

 Jason Berry publishes the book *Lead Us Not into Temptation*, regarding the clergy sexual abuse issues and examples such as the Gauthe prosecution.

 James Porter, former Boston priest, is arrested in Minnesota for dozens of molestations, ultimately pleading guilty to 41 counts of sexual assault.

 The U.S.Conference of Catholic Bishops meets in South Bend, Indiana, to discuss assertions that some bishops had covered up sexual abuse claims. The USCCB considers a draft of special norms for administrative removal of a cleric from the clerical state.

 The September issue of *Today's Parish* magazine publishes a report by priest and psychotherapist Father Stephen Rossetti, who found significant negative impacts in parish attitudes from the clergy sexual abuse scandal.

 November 18: Archbishop Daniel Pilarczk, head of the USCCB, calls clergy sexual abuse "...a tragedy of immense proportion for all institutions in this society which are concerned with the welfare of children." (In a letter to Reverend Thomas Doyle OP).

 The Jesuits of Ontario apologizes, pays compensation for, and settles 97 claims against a former missionary Jesuit priest in the far north.

 Reverend Richard Lavigne of Boston is sentenced to 10 years probation after pleading guilty to molesting three boys.

1993 January 14: The Bishops Conference of England & Wales report, "The Sexual Abuse of Children," is published.

 The USCCB forms the Ad Hoc Committee on Sexual Abuse, which issues "Brief Overview of Conference Involvement in Assisting Dioceses with Child Molestation Claims."

 8. Boston Globe, supra, 40; the actual transcript is on the Web at www.bishopaccount ability.org.

May 14: The Kentucky Court of Appeals decides the *Regazio* case, regarding the tort of "outrage."

June 11: Pope John Paul II addresses U.S. bishops in letter, "Woe to the World because of Scandals," focusing on child sexual abuse by clergy.

October: Elinor Burkett and Frank Bruni publish their book, *A Gospel of Shame: Child Sexual Abuse and the Catholic Church.*

November: The Colorado Supreme Court decides the *Moses* case, involving an Episcopal bishop who was found to breach his fiduciary obligations.

Allegations of past sexual abuse are made against Chicago Cardinal Joseph Bernardin by a former seminarian. The accuser later recanted, withdrew the allegation, and reconciled with Bernardin.

Vermont courts are involved in several reported clergy abuse decisions.

1994   The USCCB's Ad Hoc Committee on Sexual Abuse issues *Twenty Eight Suggestions on Sexual Abuse Policies.*

The Boston Archdiocese settles claims by several of the victims of Father John Geoghan for $15 million.

A revised edition of *Catechism of the Catholic Church* is published, condemning child sexual abuse: "The offense is compounded by the scandalous harm done to the physical and moral integrity of the young, who will remain scarred by it all their lives…"

The Fifth Circuit Court of Appeals decides the *Gallagher* case, regarding an insurer's duty to cooperate.

The USCCB issues the report, *Restoring Trust.*

A law review article asserts that if a diocese and bishop had not actually known of a priest's abuse, the First Amendment should prevent tort liability attribution to the diocese for the later merciful action of the religious superior toward the disciplining of the errant priest.[9]

1995   February: The Michigan courts decide the *Isley* case, regarding choice of law and statute of limitations issues surrounding abuse allegations against priests in two states.

April: Sociologist Anson Shupe publishes a social science study of the abuse phenomenon, *In the Name of All That's Holy: A Theory of Clergy Malfeasance.*

June 27: Wisconsin Supreme Court decides the *Pritzlaff* case, limiting civil jury scrutiny of internal church discipline on First Amendment grounds

July: The USCCB publishes "Canonical Delicts Involving Sexual Misconduct and Dismissal from the Clerical State."

September: Cardinal Hans Groer, Archbishop of Vienna, resigns from his position on the basis of reports of his past sexual abuse incidents in Austria. A few years later, he was stripped of his title and privileges as a bishop.

1996   The Irish Catholic Bishops Advisory Committee on Child Sexual Abuse by Priests and Religious issues "Child Sexual Abuse: Framework for a Church Response."

July 29: The Maryland appeals court in the *Doe* case rejects statute of limitations defense.

9. James O'Reilly & Joanne Strasser, "Clergy Sexual Misconduct: Confronting the Difficult Constitutional and Institutional Liability Issues," 7 St. Thomas L. Rev. 1 (1994).

September: The Catholic Bishops' Conference of England & Wales issue a report on clergy sexual abuse, "Healing the Wound of Child Sexual Abuse, A Church Response."

December: The Australian Bishops publish "Towards Healing: Policies and Procedures in Responding to Complaints of Sexual Abuse Against Personnel of the Catholic Church in Australia."

1997   The Vatican's Apostolic Nuncio in the U.S. writes to a bishop, questioning the policy of suspension and removal of alleged abuser priests "through the application of certain policies and procedures employed by many dioceses... [which] could be canonically null."[10]

Jan. 31: The Vatican's Apostolic Nuncio to Ireland tells all Irish bishops that "the situation of 'mandatory reporting' gives rise to serious reservations of both a moral and a canonical nature"; he also warns that canon law "must be meticulously followed under pain of invalidity of the acts involved if the priest so punished were to make hierarchical recourse against his Bishop."[11]

Feb. 16: The *Indianapolis Star* runs a series exposing 16 cases of priests in Indiana accused of abuse.[12]

July: In the Reverend Rudy Kos civil case, the archdiocese of Dallas is found by a jury to be liable to 11 male victims for $119,600,000.

The Wisconsin Supreme Court decides *John BBB Doe* case regarding repressed memory claims against priest.

The Maine Supreme Court decides the *Swanson* case.

August: The Missouri courts decided the *Gibson* case, dismissing charges on the basis that the statute of limitations had expired.

Australian bishops publish "Integrity in Ministry, A Document of Ethical Standards for Catholic Clergy and Religious in Australia."

1998   In Derry, New Hampshire, Reverend Roger Fortier was sentenced to 20–40 years in prison for sexual abuse cases; the diocese had consented to settlements with the New Hampshire Attorney General including five years of annual audits of complaints and systems for reporting of actions concerning clergy sexual abuse.[13]

June 22—West Virginia court decides *Albright* case regarding limitations.

1999   January 19—Michigan court decides *Demeyer v. Archdiocese of Detroit* case regarding "repressed memories."

Former Boston priest John Geoghan is indicted for past sexual abuse cases; sentenced in 2002 to 10 years in prison, he was killed by a prison inmate in 2003.

Washington appellate courts decide the *CJC* case.

2000   January 21—The Illinois Supreme Court rules in the *Kuhl* case against clergy sexual abuse claimant under statute of limitations, and rejects fraudulent concealment claims.

March 28—Missouri appeals court decides *HRB* case regarding repressed memories.

10. Jason Berry & Gerald Renner, Vows of Silence: The Abuse of Power in the Papacy of John Paul II, at 232 (2010).
11. Luciano Storero to each Irish bishop (Jan. 31, 1997).
12. Linda Caleca, "Faith Betrayed," Indianapolis Star (Feb. 16, 1997).
13. N.H. Attorney General's office, www.doj.nh.gov/criminal/diocese-reports.

2001   April 30—The document "*Sacramentorum Sanctitatis Tutela*" states the policy issued by the Vatican's Congregation for the Defense of the Faith (CDF) for handling of grave crimes, including clergy sexual abuse.

May 18—The document "*De Delictis Gravioribus*" is issued by the Vatican's CDF,[14] dealing with sexual sins by a cleric with persons under age 18, and concerning the criminal penal trial process. The bishop conducts the investigation and then sends the case to the Vatican, where the CDF determines offenses and sanctions under Article 52 of the Apostolic Constitution. The period of "prescription," like a civil statute of limitations, expires 10 years after the person reaches the age of 18.[15]

UK: "A Programme for Action, Final Report of the Independent Review on Child Protection in the Catholic Church in England & Wales."

2002   January 6—After extensive delays and litigation, the *Boston Globe* begins to publish large amounts of its extensive reporting regarding the archdiocese of Boston cover-up of clergy sexual abuse cases. Hundreds of stories follow with international news media coverage of the documented cover-up of abusive priest allegations.

January—In Ireland, religious orders settle sexual abuse claims for $110 million.

February—Boston serial abuser Reverend John Geoghan sentenced to 10 years in prison after jury conviction of indecent assault on a 10-year-old boy.

March—A French criminal court imposes upon Bishop Pierre Pican a criminal sentence (three months suspended) for failure to report sexual abuse by a priest.

March 10—Bishop Anthony O'Connell becomes the second bishop of Palm Beach (Florida) to resign for past sexual misconduct, as his predecessor had resigned for a similar reason.

March 24—*Los Angeles Times* reports[16] on Jesuits convicted of sexual misconduct with mentally disabled men residing at a Jesuit facility in California; four Jesuits are convicted and registered as sex offenders.

March 29—Cardinal Law of Boston in his Good Friday sermon says: "Betrayal hangs like a heavy cloud over the Church today."[17]

April 2–5—Private symposium is held at the Vatican regarding scientific opinions from experts on the phenomena associated with pedophilia.

April 15—Pope John Paul II calls U.S. cardinals and a few bishops who are the leaders of the U.S. Conference of Catholic Bishops for a summit at the Vatican: "There is no place in the priesthood and religious life for those who would harm the young."

May 6—Special Grand Jury Report regarding diocese of Rockville Centre, Suffolk County (New York); grand jury is extensively critical of inactivity in response to the many sexual abuse allegations. The report finds the diocese was "incapable of properly handling issues relating to the sexual abuse of children by priests."

Florida appellate court decides the *Malicki* case.

---

14. 93 Acta Apostolica Sedis 785 (2001).
15. Available on Web at www.bishopaccountability.org.
16. Glenn Bunting, "Cloak of Silence Covered Abuse at Jesuit Retreat," L.A. Times (Mar. 24, 2002).
17. Boston Globe, supra, iii.

June—U.S.Conference of Catholic Bishops adopts *"Charter for the Protection of Children and Young People"* in meetings at Dallas, Texas, known as "Dallas Norms," or "Essential Norms," and creates an Office of Child and Youth Protection that is empowered to audit performance of dioceses under the Norms. Several dioceses refuse to participate. The Conference of Major Superiors of Men endorses the Norms.

U.S.C.C.B. commissioned scholars at John Jay College of the City University of New York to study the implementation of the Norms nationwide.

September 29—Louisville diocesan documents are disclosed in a series of articles by the *Courier-Journal* newspaper.

October 14—Letter from Vatican Cardinal Giovanni Re objects to Dallas Norms, calls for a "Mixed Committee" of four U.S. bishops and four Vatican officials, to revise the text to meet the Vatican objections.

November 13—USCCB issues "A Statement of Episcopal Commitment."

December—Vatican gives official status to U.S.C.C.B. *"Essential Norms for Diocesan/Eparchial Policies Dealing with Allegations of Sexual Abuse of Minors by Priests or Deacons."*

December 13—Boston Cardinal Bernard Law's resignation is accepted and he departs for a new posting in Rome

2003   June 26—*Stogner v. California* is decided by U.S. Supreme Court. Though it involved extensive intrafamily sexual abuse by a father, the case has tremendous impact for clergy abuse reporting; the Court held 5-4 that it would be an unconstitutional ex post facto law for a state to extend an expired criminal (not civil) statute of limitations so as to allow belated prosecution. Only the civil liability could be expanded by state legislatures in older abuse claims against priests; the priests could not be prosecuted once the criminal limitation period in their state had closed.

National Review Board chairman, former Governor Frank Keating, resigns from the Board, asserting lack of cooperation by certain bishops.

Conviction of Father John Geoghan, sentenced to 10 years in prison for multiple acts of abuse, chronicled later by *Boston Globe*.

July 23—Report of the Massachusetts Attorney General, *The Sexual Abuse of Children in the Roman Catholic Archdiocese of Boston*.

August 18—Covington (Kentucky) diocese reports that 30 of its total of 372 priests over its past 50 years have had sexual abuse allegations for which there was "reason to believe" the claims.[18]

Reverend A.W. Richard Sipe publishes his social science study, *Celibacy in Crisis: A Secret World Revisited*.

2004   Statistics: 1092 new allegations against 756 priests reported in 2004 under the Dallas Norms. Psychologist Thomas Plante writes that "if the two to six percent figure of sex offending clergy is accurate, then we can expect to have between 1,000 and 3,000 sex offending priests currently (or until recently) working in ministry. This number swells to between 3,000 and 100,000 if we consider all of the priests working in ministry in the United States during the past half century.... (W)e could expect up to 100,000 victims of priest sexual abuse during the past 40 to 50 years."[19].

---

18. www.catholicweb.com/covington.
19. Thomas Plante, Sin against the Innocents 186 (2004).

February 25—Bishop William Franklin issues a report on sexual abuse in his clergy of the Davenport (Iowa) diocese.

Feb. 27—National Review Board report to the U.S. Conference of Catholic Bishops is issued, titled "A Report on the Crisis in the Catholic Church in the United States."

Feb. 27—John Jay College published "The Nature and Scope of Sexual Abuse of Minors by Catholic Priests and Deacons 1950–2002."

Father Andrew Greeley's book Priests: A Calling in Crisis, discussed sexual orientation among priests.

Mary Gail Frawley-O'Dea: "By the end of 2004, over seven hundred priests had been removed from ministry."[20]

July 6—first diocesan bankruptcy filed in Portland, Oregon, over abuse claims; the dioceses of Tucson and Spokane also entered bankruptcy in 2004 over abuse claims.

July 30—Wisconsin appeals court decides John Doe 67C case regarding limitations

2005   Conviction of Father Paul Shanley of the Boston archdiocese for multiple sexual abuse charges. Boston Globe reveals that Boston Bishop Robert Banks told other dioceses that "I can assure you that Father Shanley has no problem that would be a concern to your diocese."[21]

May 27—Portland, Maine, diocese documents are released after court order as a result of settlement with state attorney general.

June 11—Diocese of Tucson pays claimants $22,200,000 to settle abuse charges, and the settlement is approved by the Bankruptcy Court.

September 15—First report of the Philadelphia County Investigating Grand Jury regarding the archdiocese of Philadelphia: "It is hard to think of a crime more heinous, or more deserving of strict penalties and an unlimited statute of limitations, than the sexual abuse of children. This is especially so when the perpetrators are priests—men who exploit explicit the clergy's authority and access to minors, as well as the trust of faithful families, to prey on children in order to gratify perverted urges."[22]

2006   John Jay College publishes supplementary report on its diocesan audits for sexual abuse reporting.

January 24—Federal court in Minnesota decides Eller case, denying diocesan employer relationship to the priest-abuser.

September. 1—Illinois Appeals Court in Softcheck case denies First Amendment defenses.

October 10—Diocese of Davenport, Iowa, enters bankruptcy over claims against past abuse allegations concerning its bishop. The bishop resigned and "credible" allegations of past fondling were found by a review board and sent on to CDF.[23]

20. Mary Gail Frawley-O'Dea, Perversion of Power 138 (2007).

21. Letter of Bishop R.J. Banks to Rev. Philip Behan, Jan. 16, 1990, on Web at www.bishopaccountability.org.

22. Philadelphia County Investigating Grand Jury re the Archdiocese of Philadelphia, at 11 (Sept. 15, 2005).

23. "Reired Bishop Abused Minors," Nat'l Cath. Rptr. (Nov. 14, 2009).

October 22—Release of diocesan documents by San Diego (California) as a result of bankruptcy settlement.

2007   February 27—Diocese of San Diego files for bankruptcy and later settles for $198 million with 144 claimants.

Archdiocese of Los Angeles offers $650,000,000 to settle more than 500 victims' claims

July 11—Wisconsin Appeals court decides *John Doe 1* case.

November 28—California Appeals Court decides *Dangler* case regarding limitations.

Sociologist Anson Shupe publishes an extensive study in *Spoils of the Kingdom: Clergy Misconduct & Religious Community.*

2008   March 7—Diocese of Fairbanks, Alaska files for bankruptcy after abuse claims are filed

October 18—Diocese of Wilmington, Delaware, files for bankruptcy, after Delaware passes statute allowing reopening of the claims period for sexual abuse allegations and the claims for compensation exceed assets of the diocese.

December 23—Louisiana Appeals Court decides *Diocese of Lafayette* case.

Russell Shaw publishes his insightful short book, *Nothing to Hide: Secrecy, Communication and Communion in the Catholic Church.*

2009   January 9—Illinois Court of Appeals decides *Holy Family Church* case regarding repressed memory of past sexual abuse.

March 10—Minnesota Appeals Court decides *Diocese of New Ulm* case, regarding fraud exception to statute of limitations.

April 7—Psychologist Thomas Plante, Ph.D., publishes "A Perspective on Clergy Sexual Abuse" in which he concludes that the estimate of 4 percent for Catholic priests engaged in sexual misconduct "is consistent with male clergy from other religious traditions and is significantly lower than the general adult male population, which may double these numbers.... While even one priest who abuses children is a major problem, we need to keep this issue in perspective and remember that the vast majority of priests do not abuse children."[24]

June—$1,745,000 settlement paid by diocese of London, Ontario, for a case of five years' sexual abuse of a girl "that ended in a botched abortion."[25]

Ninth Circuit finds potential for claim against Vatican in an exceptional case, *Doe v. Holy See.*[26]

Ninth Circuit federal appeals court decides *Confidential Claimant* case.

September—Italy news media report significant clergy sexual abuse claims.

October 27—Missouri appellate court decides *Dempsey* case on repressed memories.

2010   April 23—Belgium's longest-serving bishop resigns and acknowledges sexual abuse of a young family member.

Pope Benedict XV apologizes publicly for clergy abuse cases.

2011   January 4: Archdiocese of Milwaukee files for bankruptcy.

24. Thomas Plante, on Web at www.psychwww.com/psyrelig/Plante.html.
25. Norman MacInnes, "Sexual Abuse Victim Wins $1.75-million Settlement," The Lawyers Weekly (Canada) (June 26, 2009).
26. 557 F.3d 1066 (9th Cir., 2009).

February 10: The Philadelphia archdiocese's Vicar for Clergy is indicted for cover-up of sexual abuse.[27]

February 22: In the *Sheehan v. Oblates of St. Francis de Sales* decision, the Delaware Supreme Court upholds the extension of the statute of limitations period by the state legislature's Child Victims Act of 2007.

May: John Jay College produces its second and more comprehensive report based on audits and investigations, *The Causes and Context of Sexual Abuse of Minors by Catholic Priests in the United States, 1950–2010*

May 3: The Congregation of the Doctrine of the Faith issues a Circular Letter to assist Episcopal Conferences in cases of the sexual abuse of minors by members of the clergy. This is the Vatican's directive for national groups of Catholic bishops as they deal with these cases.

July 13: Irish report of sexual abuse in the diocese of Cloyne spurred a national controversy and sharp criticism of the Vatican's role in sexual abuse cases.

October 14: Kansas City bishop Robert Finn is indicted for the failure to comply with laws requiring reporting of child abuse. The alleged abuser priest remained in jail awaiting trial.

2012 February 1: Philadelphia County grand jury issues its second report on clergy sexual abuse and the responsibility of archdiocesan officials.

February 15: Wilmington, Delaware, diocese opens files on clergy abuse cases.

June 22: Monsignor Lynn, Philadelphia Archdiocesan Vicar for Clergy (chief priest personnel officer), is convicted and imprisoned for three to six years for failure to report known cases of child sexual abuse by priests; case is reversed on appeal and Lynn is released in January 2014 pending retrial.

August 2—Kansas City, Missouri, diocesan priest Shawn Ratigan pleads guilty to 5 of 13 pending charges in child pornography case, is sentenced to 50 years in prison.

September 1—Kansas City, Missouri, bishop Finn is found guilty at trial of failing to report child sexual abuse issues. Sentence is two years probation.

September 6—*National Catholic Reporter* reports that Kansas City diocese spent almost $4 million on clergy abuse cases, with $1.39 million on defense of Bishop Finn and $1.6 million on older claims and cases. Diocese advises parishes to expect an 11 percent increase in costs of insurance premiums.

2013 January 30: Philadelphia area jury convicts a Philadelphia archdiocesan priest of sex crimes; victim had been an altar boy, age 10, and abuse occurred in church sacristy and church supply closet.

January 31—Records on clergy abuse, more than 30,000 pages, are ordered to be disclosed by the archdiocese of Los Angeles.

February—Reverend Curtis Wehmeyer, Roman Catholic pastor in St. Paul, Minnesota, pleads guilty to all 20 counts of child abuse and child pornography, sentenced to five years in state prison

August 13—International Criminal Court denies petition to investigate Vatican for worldwide child abuse allegations; ICC declines to take jurisdiction.

---

27. In re County Investigating Grand Jury XXIII, First Judicial District, Philadelphia County (Jan. 21, 2011).

August 21: Pope relieves Archbishop Jozef Wesolowski, papal nuncio to the Dominican Republic, after allegations he paid for sex with minors in that nation.

September 2013: St. Louis archbishop criticized for his handling of case of abuse against Reverend Joseph Jiang, criminally charged in Missouri courts.

September 2013—Minneapolis archbishop criticized for not acting rapidly against Reverend Curtis Wehmeyer for multiple abuse allegations.

September 20—Glenmary Missioners Reverend Robert Poandl convicted in Cincinnati federal court trial of sexual abuse.

September 26, 2013: The Philadelphia District Attorney's Office charges the Reverend Robert L. Brennan with Rape, Involuntary Deviate Sexual Intercourse (IDSI), and Aggravated Indecent Assault.

October 12: California governor Jerry Brown vetoes Senate Bill 131 that would have extended the statute of limitations on certain child sexual abuse claims.

BIBLIOGRAPHY

ROMAN CATHOLIC CHURCH AND CONSULTANTS' DOCUMENTS

Ad Hoc Committee on Sexual Abuse. "Brief History: Handling Child Sexual Abuse Cases." *Origins* 23, no. 38 (March 1994): 666–670.

—— *Restoring Trust: A Pastoral Response to Sexual Abuse.* Vol. 1. (Washington, DC: National Conference of Catholic Bishops, 1994).

Archdiocesan Tribunal of Milwaukee. "Trials according to the Canon Law of the Roman Catholic Church: Important Questions for Victim/Surviors or Other Witnesses." Milwaukee, WI. 1–16.

Covington KY Diocese, "A Report on the History of Sexual Abuse of Minors in the Diocese of Covington" (Aug. 18, 2003), on Web at covingtondiocese.org.

U.S. Conference of Catholic Bishops, *Essential Norms for Diocesan/Eparchial Policies Dealing with Allegations of Sexual Abuse of Minors by Priests or Deacons, No. 11* (December 2002). "Crime and Punishment in the Catholic Church: An Overview of Possiblities and Problems." USCCB, 2010.

Bishops' Committee on Canonical Affairs Task Force. *A Resource for Canonical Processes for the Resolution of Complaints of Clerical Sexual Abuse of Minors* (Washington, DC: United States Conference of Catholic Bishops, 2003).

Chicago Archdiocese. "Chicago Policy regarding Clerical Sexual Misconduct with Minors." *Origins* 22, no. 16 (October 1992): 273–278.

Congregation for Divine Worship and the Discipline of the Sacraments. "Rescript." June 26, 1998. prot. No. 1770/97/S.

Congregation for the Clergy. "Private Reply." November 11, 1998. prot. No. 2169/98.

Congregation for the Doctrine of the Faith. *Acta Apostolicae Sedis.* Vol. 72. October 14, 1980. 1132–1137.

—— "Handout." unpublished, 2003.

—— "Sacramentorum Sanctitatis Tutela." *Acta Apostolicae Sedis.* Vol. 93. May 18, 2001. 785–788.

Definitive Sentence. P.N. 22571/91 CA (Apostolic Signatura, March 9, 1993).

Graves, Todd P. *The Report of the Independent Investigation of the Catholic Diocese of Kansas City-Saint Joseph.* Kansas City: Diocese of Kansas City, 2011.

John Jay College Research Team. *The Causes and Context of Sexual Abuse of Minors by Catholic Priests in the United States 1950–2010: A Report Presented to the United States Conference of Catholic Bishops.* (Washington, DC: United States Conference of Catholic Bishops, 2011).

John Jay College. *The Nature and Scope of Sexual Abuse of Minors by Catholic Priests and Deacons in the United States.* Study. (Washington, DC: United States Conference of Catholic Bishops, 2004).

National Review Board for the Protection of Children and Young People. *A Report on the Crisis in the Catholic Church in the United States*. (Washington, DC: United States Conference of Catholic Bishops, 2004).

National Review Board. *Report of the National Review Board, December 2007*. (Washington, DC: United States Conference of Catholic Bishops, 2007).

Pilarczyk, Daniel. "Statement of Archbishop Pilarczyk, President of the National Conference of Catholic Bishops on the Sexual Abuse of Children." *Statements of National Conference of Catholic Bishops and the United States Catholic Conference on the Subject of Sexual Abuse of Children by Priests 1988–1992*. (Washington, DC: United States Catholic Conference, 1992).

Pontifical Council for Legislative Texts. *Dignitas Connubii*. (Vatican City: Libreria Editrice Vaticana, 2005).

Pope John Paul II. "Vatican-US Bishops' Committee to Study Applying Canonical Norms." *Origins* 23, no. 7 (July 1993): 102–103.

Suprema Sacra Congregatio Sancti Officii. "Crimen Sollicitationis." March 1962.

The 1917 Pio-Benedictine Code of Canon Law. Edited by Edward N. Peters. (San Francisco, CA: Ignatius Press, 2001).

United States Conference of Catholic Bishops Ad Hoc Committee on Sexual Abuse. "Efforts to Combat Clergy Sexual Abuse against Minors—Chronology." *Restoring Trust: A Pastoral Response to Sexual Abuse*. (Washington, DC: National Conference of Catholic Bishops, 2002).

United States Conference of Catholic Bishops. *Charter for the Protection of Children and Young People*. (2006).

—— *Diocesan Review Board Resource Booklet*. (Washington, DC: United States Conference of Catholic Bishops, 2008).

United States Conference of Catholic Bishops. "Essential Norms for Diocesan/Eparchial Policies Dealing with Allegations of Sexual Abuse of Minors by Priests or Deacons." *Origins* 32 (June 2004): 415–418.

JOURNALISTS' ACCOUNTS [MANY CONTAINING PERSONAL NARRATIVES]

Morris-Young, Dan, "Do Lawsuit Allegations Touch Diocese's Noncompliance Issues?," *National Catholic Reporter* (April 29, 2011).

Allen, John. "Pope's Reluctance to Impose American Way Not a Shocker." *National Catholic Reporter Online*. July 16, 2010. http://ncronline.org/blogs/all-things-catholic/popes-reluctance-impose-american-way-not-a-shocker (accessed May 5, 2011).

—— "Why Rome Scorns Resignations, and a Great Week for Wonks." *National Catholic Reporter Online*. August 10, 2010. http://ncronline.org/blogs/all-things-catholic/why-rome-scorns-resignations-and-great-week-wonks.

—— "Will Ratzinger's Past Trump Benedict's Present?" *National Catholic Reporter Online*. March 17, 2010. http://ncronline.org/news/accountability/will-ratzingers-past-trump-benedicts-present.

Carvajal, Doreen & Stephen Castle, "Abuse Took Years to Ignite Belgian Clergy Inquiry," *N.Y. Times* (July 12, 2010).

CANON LAWYER COMMENTARIES

Barr, Diane. "Trial Advocacy." *CLSA Proceedings* 69 (2007): 81–91.

Beal, John. "Administrative Leave: Canon 1722 Revisited." *Studia Canonica* 27 (1993): 293–320.

Beal, John P. "Hiding in the Thickets of Law, Canonical Reflections on Some Disturbing Aspects of the Dallas Charter." *America Magazine* (October 7, 2002): 15–19.

Beal, John P. "At the Crossroads of Two Laws: Some Reflections on the Influences of Secular Law on the Church's Response to Clergy Sexual Abuse in the United States." *Louvain Studies* 25 (2000): 99–121.

Beal, John P. "Doing What One Can: Canon Law and Clerical Sexual Misconduct." *The Jurist* 52 (1992): 642–683.

Beal, John P., James A. Coriden & Thomas J. Green. *New Commentary on the Code of Canon Law.* (Washington, DC: Paulist Press, 2000).

Canon Law Society of America. *Revised Guide to the Implementation of the U.S. Bishop's Essential Norms for Diocesan/Eparchial Policies Dealing with Allegations of Sexual Abuse of Minors by Priests or Deacons.* (Washington, DC: Canon Law Society of America, 2004).

Caparros, E., M. Theriault & J. Thorn. *Code of Canon Law Annotated.* (Montreal: Wilson & Lafleur Limitée, 1993).

DiNardo, Lawrence A. *Canonical Penal Procedures.* (Washington, DC: Canon Law Society of America, 2010).

Donlon, James I. "Remuneration, Decent Support, and Clerics Removed from the Ministry of the Church." *CLSA Proceedings* 66 (2004): 93–113.

Doyle, Thomas P. "The Canonical Rights of Priests Accused of Sexual Abuse." *Studia Canonica* 24 (1990): 335–356.

Dugan, Patricia M (ed.). *Towards Future Developments in Penal Law: U.S. Theory and Practice.* (Montreal: Wilson & Lefleur, 2010).

Euart, Sharon. "Canon Law and Clergy Sexual Abuse Crisis: An Overview of the US Experience." *USCCB/CLSA Seminar.* USCCB, May 25, 2010.

Foley, J.J. "Preliminary Investigation: Consideration and Options." Edited by Patricia M. Dugan. *Towards Future Developments in Penal Law: U.S. Theory and Practice* (Montreal: Wilson & Lafleur, 2010): 33–54.

Golden, Paul. "Advocacy for Clerics Accused of Sexual Abuse of Minors." *CLSA Proceedings* 68 (2006): 129–148.

EXPERT COMMENTARIES

Cafardi, Nicholas P. *Before Dallas: The U.S. Bishops' Response to Clergy Sexual Abuse of Children.* (Mahwah, NJ: Paulist Press, 2008).

Cafardi, Nicholas P. "Stones instead of Bread: Sexually Abusive Priests in Ministry." *Studia Canonica* 27 (1993): 145–172.

Doyle, Thomas P., A.W.R. Sipe, & Patrick J. Wall. *Sex, Priests, and Secret Codes.* (Los Angeles: Volt Press, 2006).

Gonsiorek, John C. "Barriers to Responding to the Clergy Sexual Abuse Crisis within the Roman Catholic Church." In *Sins against the Innocents,* edited by Thomas G. Plante, 139–153. (Westport: Praeger, 2004).

Lagges, Patrick R. "The Penal Process: The Preliminary Investigation in Light of the Essential Norms of the United States." *Studia Canonica* 38 (2004): 369–410.

McDonough, Elizabeth. "Sanctions in the 1983 Code: Purpose and Procedures; Progress and Problems." *CLSA Proceedings* 52 (1990): 206–221.

McKenna, Kevin. "Canon Law and Civil Law: Working Together for the Common Good." *Canon Law Seminar for Media.* United States Conference of Catholic Bishops, 2010.

Morrisey, Francis G. "Addressing the Issue of Clergy Sexual Abuse." *Studia Canonica* 35 (2001): 403–420.

Morrisey, Francis G. "The Pastoral and Juridical Dimensions of Dismissal from the Clerical State and of Other Penalties for Sexual Misconduct." *CLSA Proceedings* 53 (1991): 221–239.

Morrisey, Francis. "The Preliminary Investigation in Penal Cases: Some of the Better Practices." *The Canonist* 2, no. 2 (2011): 184–198.

O'Connor, James I., ed. *Canon Law Digest.* Vol. VII. Chicago: Chicago Province, S.J., 1975.

Paulson, Jerome E. "The Clinical and Canonical Considerations in Cases of Pedophilia: The Bishop's Role." *Studia Canonica* 22 (1988): 77–124.

Plante, Thomas, *Sin against the Innocents: Sexual Abuse by Priests and the Role of the Catholic Church* 186 (Westport CT: Praeger, 2004).

Strickland, Amy J. "To Protect and Serve: The Relationship between the Victim Assistance Coordinator and Canonical Personnel." *CLSA Proceedings*, 2009: 232–242.

Ward, Daniel J., OSB. "Sexual Abuse and Exploitation: Canon and Civil Law Issues Concerning Religous." *CLSA Proceedings* 67 (2005).

Wilson, George S.J. *Clericalism: The Death of Priesthood* (Collegeville, MN: Liturgical Press 2008).

Woestman, William H. *Papal Allocutions to the Roman Rota.* (Ottawa: Saint Paul University, 1994).

USEFUL RESOURCES

Allen, John, *All the Pope's Men* (New York: Random House, 2004)

Berry, Jason & Gerald Renner, *Vows of Silence* (New York: Free Press, 2004).

Boston Globe. *Betrayal: The Crisis in the Catholic Church.* (Boston: Little, Brown and Company, 2002).

Burkett. Elinor & Frank Bruni, *A Gospel of Shame: Children, Sexual Abuse, and the Catholic Church* 125 (New York: Penguin Putnam 1993).

Cozzens, Donald, *Sacred Silence: Denial and the Crisis in the Church* (Collegeville, MN: Liturgical Press, 2002).

Dillon, Sam. "Catholic Religious Orders Let Abusive Priests Stay." *New York Times*, August 8, 2002: http://www.nytimes.com/2002/08/10/national/10PRIE. html?todaysheadlines.

Frawley-O'Dea, Mary Gail, *Perversion of Power: Sexual Abuse in the Catholic Church* (Nashville, TN: Vanderbilt University Press, 2007).

Green, Thomas J. "Clerical Sexual Abuse of Minors: Some Canonical Reflections." *The Jurist* 63 (2003): 366–425.

Gregory, David, "Some Reflections on Labor and Employment Ramifications of Diocesan Bankruptcy Filings," 47 *J. Catholic Legal Studies* 97 (2008).

Hagerty, Barbara Bradley. "Sex Abuse Scandal Catches Up with Religious Orders." *National Public Radio*, December 31, 2007: http://www.npr.org/templates/story/story.php?storyId=17728112.

Hamilton, Marci, "The Rules against Scandal and What They Mean for the First Amendment's Religion Clauses." 69 *Maryland L. Rev.* 115 (2009).

Hamilton, Marci, "The 'Licentiousness'in Religious Organizations and Why It Is Not Protected under Religious Liberty Constitutional Provisions." 18 *William & Mary Bill of Rights J.* 953 (2010).

Hoyano, Laura, "Ecclesiastical Responsibility for Clerical Wrongdoing." 18 *Tort Law Review* 154 (2010).

Hoye, Daniel E. "Reintegration and Restoration of Exonerated Priests." Jacksonville, Florida, October 11, 2011.

Huels, John M. *The Pastoral Companion.* (Quincy, Ill.: Franciscan Press, 1995).

Jackowski, Karol, *The Silence We Keep: A Nun's View of the Catholic Priest Scandal* (New York: Harmony, 2004).

Jenkins, Ronny E. "Jurisprudence in Penal Cases: Select Themes from the Judicial Doctrine of the Tribunal of the Roman Rota." *CLSA Proceedings* 67 (2005): 95–122.

Jenkins, Ronny E. "The Charter and Norms Two Years Later: Towards a Resolution of Recent Canonical Dilemmas." *CLSA Proceedings* 66 (2004): 115–136.

Kalichman, Seth C. *Mandated Reporting of Suspected Child Abuse: Ethics, Law, & Policy* 13 (Washington, DC: American Psychological Association ed., 2d ed. 1999).

Kennedy, Eugene & Victor Heckler. *The Catholic Priest in the United States: Psychological Investigations*. (Washington DC: United States Catholic Conference, 1972).

Kinney, Bishop John F. "NCCB Establishes Committee on Sexual Abuse." *Origins* 23, no. 7 (July 1993): 104–105.

Lagges, Patrick. "Elements in the Preliminary Investigation." Edited by Patricia M. Dugan. *Advocacy Vademecum* (Montreal: Wilson & Lefleur, 2006): 153–168.

Lagges, Patrick R. "Canonical Issues of Renumeration and Sustenance for Priests Accused of Sexual Misconduct." *Proceedings* 71 (2009): 150–167.

O'Reilly, James & Joanne Strasser, "Clergy Sexual Misconduct: Confronting the Difficult Constitutional and Institutional Liability Issues" 7 *St. Thomas L. Rev.* 1, (1994).

O'Reilly, Michael. "Recent Developments in the Laicization of Priests." *The Jurist* 52 (1992): 684–696.

Orsy, Ladislas. "Bishop's Norms: Commentary and Evaluation." *Boston College Law Review* 44 (2003): 999–1029.

Provost, J.H. "Promoting and Protecting the Rights of Christians: Some Implications for Church Structure." *The Jurist* 46 (1986).

Pudelski, Christopher R. "The Constitutional Fate of Mandatory Reporting Statutes and the Clergy—Communicant Privilege in a Post-Smith World." 98 *Nw. U. L. Rev.* 703 (2003–2004).

Renati, Charles G. "Conducting Canonical Investigations and Interviews." *CLSA Proceedings* 67 (2005): 177–196.

Report of the Grand Jury. MISC. NO. 0009901-2008 (Court of Common Pleas, First Judicial District of Pennsylvania, Philadelphia January 21, 2011).

Rossetti, Stephen, *A Tragic Grace: The Catholic Church and Child Sexual Abuse* (Collegeville MN: Interfaith Sexual Trauma Institute, 1996).

Schwartz, Victor & Leah Lorber, "Defining the Duty of Religious Institutions to Protect Others." 74 *U. Cin. L. Rev.* 11 (2005).

Smilinac, Daniel. "Clergy Personnel Files and the Instruction of an Allegation." *CLSA Proceedings*, 2007: 193–202.

Steinfels, Peter. "The Church's Sexual Abuse Crisis." *Commonweal*, April 2002: 13–19.

OTHER LAW-RELATED MATERIALS

Arnold, Julie, Note, "'Divine' Justice and the Lack of Secular Intervention: Abrogating the Clergy-Communicant Privilege in Mandatory Reporting Statutes to Combat Child Sexual Abuse," 42 *Val. U. L. Rev.* 849, 851 (2008).

Bainbridge, Stephen, and Aaron Cole, "The Bishop's Alter Ego: Enterprise Liability and the Catholic Priest Sex Abuse Scandal," 46 *J. Cath.olic Legal Studies* 65 (2007).

Beerworth, Andrew,"Treating Spiritual and Legal Counselors Differently," 10 *Roger Williams U. L. Rev.* 73 (2004).

Cassidy, R.Michael, "Sharing Sacred Secrets: Is It (Past) Time for a Dangerous Person Exception to the Clergy-Penitent Privilege?," 44 *Wm. & Mary L. Rev.* 1627, 1667 (2003).

Catanzano, Ana Maria. "The Fog of Scandal: The Chair of the Philadelphia Review Board Speaks." *Commonwealmagazine.org*. (May 12, 2011).

Clark, Kelly, et al., "Of Compelling Interest: The Intersection of Religious Freedom and Civil Liability in the Portland Priest Sex Abuse Cases," 85 *Or. L. Rev.* 481 (2006) http://commonwealmagazine.org/fog-scandal-1.

Cobb, Matthew, "A Strange Distinction: Charitable Immunity and Clergy Sexual Abuse," 62 *Maine L. Rev.* 703 (2010).

Comment, "Separation of Church and Estate: On Excluding Parish Assets from the Bankruptcy Estate of a Diocese Organized as a Corporation Sole," 55 *Cath. U. L. Rev.* 583 (2006).

Fenton, David, "Texas' Clergyman-Penitent Privilege and the Duty to Report Suspected Child Abuse," 38 *Baylor L. Rev.* 231, 237 (1986).

Gardner, Martin R. Understanding Juvenile Law 62 (New York:LexisNexis ed., 2d 2003).

Heylman, Susan, "As States Suspend Time Limits on Sex Abuse Suits, Clergy Cases Proceed," 43 Trial 72 (Oct. 2007).

Jackson, Ashley, "The Collision of Mandatory Reporting Statutes and the Priest-Penitent Privilege," 74 *UMKC L. Rev.* 1057, 1065 (2006).

LaBarbera, Samantha,"Secrecy and Settlements," 50 *Villanova L. Rev.* 261 (2005).

Mitchell, Mary Harter, "Must Clergy Tell? Child Abuse Reporting Requirements vVersus the Clergy Privilege and Free Exercise of Religion.," 71 *Minnesota L. Rev.* 723, 726–727 (1987).

Note, "The Atypical International Status of the Holy See," 34 *Vand. J. Transnat'l. L.* 597 (2001).

Philadelphia County Grand Jury, *Report on Archdiocese of Philadelphia* 105 (2011).

Pudelski, Christopher, "The Constitutional Fate of Mandatory Reporting Statutes and the Clergy—Communicant Privilege in a Post-Smith World, " 98 *Nw. U. L. Rev.* 703 (2003--2004).

Rubino, Stephen, "A Response to Timothy Lytton," 39 *Conn. L. Rev.* 913 (2006).

Sagatun Inger J., & Leonard P. Edwards, *Child Abuse in the Legal System* 36. Edited by Dorothy J. Anderson. (_Belmont, Mass.,_:Wadsworth, 1995).

Schwartz, Victor and Leah Lorber, "Defining the Duty of Religious Institutions to Protect Others," 74 *U. Cin. L. Rev.* 11 (2005).

Sippel, Julie, "Priest-Penitent Privilege Statutes," 43 *Cath.olic U. L. Rev.* 1127 (1994).

Swisher, Peter, & Richard Mason, Liability Insurance Coverage for Clergy Sexual Abuse Claims, 17 *Conn. Ins. L. J.* 355 (2011).

Tobias, Carl, "Reassessing Charitable Immunity in Virginia," 41 *U. Rich.mond L. Rev.* 9 (2006).

Samantha LaBarbera, "Secrecy and Settlements," 50 *Vill.lanova L. Rev.* 261 (2005).

Stein, Theodore J. *Child Welfare and the Law* 104 New York, NY, Child Welfare League of America, Inc. ed., 3d ed. 2006).

Weinhold, Jennifer, "Beyond the Traditional Scope of Employment Analysis in the Clergy Sexual Abuse Context," 47 *U. Louisville L. Rev.* 531 (2009).

ADDITIONAL ARTICLES & RESOURCE MATERIALS

Ad Hoc Committee on Sexual Abuse. "Brief History: Handling Child Sexual Abuse Cases." *Origins* 23, no. 38 (March 1994): 666–670.

—— *Restoring Trust: A Pastoral Response to Sexual Abuse.* Vol. 1. (Washington, DC: National Conference of Catholic Bishops, 1994).

Allen, John. "Pope's Reluctance to Impose American Way Not a Shocker." *National Catholic Reporter Online.* July 16, 2010. http://ncronline.org/blogs/all-things-catholic/popes-reluctance-impose-american-way-not-shocker (accessed May 5, 2011).

—— "Why Rome Scorns Resignations, and a Great Week for Wonks." *National Catholic Reporter Online.* August 10, 2010. http://ncronline.org/blogs/all-things-catholic/why-rome-scorns-resignations-and-great-week-wonks.

—— "Will Ratzinger's Past Trump Benedict's Present?" *National Catholic Reporter Online.* March 17, 2010. http://ncronline.org/news/accountability/will-ratzingers-past-trump-benedicts-present.

Archdiocesan Tribunal of Milwaukee. "Trials according to the Canon Law of the Roman Catholic Church: Important Questions for Victim/Surviors or Other Witnesses." Milwaukee, WI. 1–16.

Barr, Diane. "Trial Advocacy." *CLSA Proceedings* 69 (2007): 81–91.

Beal, John. "Administrative Leave: Canon 1722 Revisited." *Studia Canonica* 27 (1993): 293–320.

Crime and Punishment in the Catholic Church: An Overview of Possiblities and Problems." USCCB, 2010.

Beal, John P. "Hiding in the Thickets of Law, Canonical Reflections on Some Disturbing Aspects of the Dallas Charter." *America Magazine* (October 7, 2002): 15–19.

Beal, John P. "At the Crossroads of Two Laws: Some Reflections on the Influences of Secular Law on the Church's Response to Clergy Sexual Abuse in the United States." *Louvain Studies* 25 (2000): 99–121.

Beal, John P. "Doing What One Can: Canon Law and Clerical Sexual Misconduct." *The Jurist* 52 (1992): 642–683.

Beal, John P., James A. Coriden & Thomas J. Green. *New Commentary on the Code of Canon Law.* (Washington, DC: Paulist Press, 2000)

Bishops' Committee on Canonical Affairs Task Force. *A Resource for Canonical Processes for the Resolution of Complaints of Clerical Sexual Abuse of Minors* (Washington, DC: United States Conference of Catholic Bishops, 2003).

Cafardi, Nicholas P. *Before Dallas: The U.S. Bishops' Response to Clergy Sexual Abuse of Children.* (Mahwah, NJ: Paulist Press, 2008).

Cafardi, Nicholas P. "Stones instead of Bread: Sexually Abusive Priests in Ministry." *Studia Canonica* 27 (1993): 145–172.

Canon Law Society of America. *Revised Guide to the Implementation of the U.S. Bishop's Essential Norms for Diocesan/Eparchial Policies Dealing with Allegations of Sexual Abuse of Minors by Priests or Deacons.* (Washington, DC: Canon Law Society of America, 2004).

Caparros, E., M. Theriault & J. Thorn. *Code of Canon Law Annotated.* (Montreal: Wilson & Lafleur Limitée, 1993).

Catanzano, Ana Maria. "The Fog of Scandal: The Chair of the Philadelphia Review Board Speaks." *Commonwealmagazine.org.* (May 12, 2011). http://commonwealmagazine. org/fog-scandal-1.

Chicago Archdiocese. "Chicago Policy regarding Clerical Sexual Misconduct with Minors." *Origins* 22, no. 16 (October 1992): 273–278.

John Jay College. *The Nature and Scope of Sexual Abuse of Minors by Catholic Priests and Deacons in the United States.* Study. (Washington, DC: United States Conference of Catholic Bishops, 2004).

Congregation for Divine Worship and the Discipline of the Sacraments. "Rescript." June 26, 1998. prot. No. 1770/97/S.

Congregation for the Clergy. "Private Reply." November 11, 1998. prot. No. 2169/98.

Congregation for the Doctrine of the Faith. *Acta Apostolicae Sedis.* Vol. 72. October 14, 1980. 1132–1137.

Congregation for the Doctrine of the Faith. Circular Letter to Assist Episcopal Conferences in Developing Guidelines for Dealing with Cases of Sexual Abuses of Minors Perpetuated by Clerics. Vatican City, May 3, 2011.

—— "Handout." unpublished, 2003.

—— "Sacramentorum Sanctitatis Tutela." *Acta Apostolicae Sedis.* Vol. 93. May 18, 2001. 785–788.

Conlon, R. Daniel. "Going Global with The Charter and Essential Norms." *Proceedings* 74 (2012): 62–76.

Connors, Canice. "Clerical Sexual Abuse Priests and Their Victims Find Healing." *Ligourian*, (November. 1994): 23–27.

Cooper, Jonathan. "Authorities: Man Falsely Claims Abuse by Priests." *Seattle Times*, (January 29, 2013).

Cullen, Kevin. "Phony Cases a Danger in Abuse Battle," *The Boston Globe*, (August 5, 2002): A1.

Dart, John. "Risk Management: Protestants Confront Sexual Abuse," 119 *Christian Century* at 8 (June 5, 2002).

Dart, John "Background Check: Churches Respond to Safety Concerns," 124 *Christian Century* 21 (June 26, 2007).

Definitive Sentence. P.N. 22571/91 CA (Apostolic Signatura, March 9, 1993).

Dillon, Sam. "Catholic Religious Orders Let Abusive Priests Stay." *New York Times*, August 8, 2002: http://www.nytimes.com/2002/08/10/national/10PRIE. html?todaysheadlines.

DiNardo, Lawrence A. "*Canonical Penal Procedures.*" (Washington, DC: Canon Law Society of America, 2010): 10

Donlon, James I. "Remuneration, Decent Support, and Clerics Removed from the Ministry of the Church." *CLSA Proceedings* 66 (2004): 93–113.

Doyle, Thomas P. "The Canonical Rights of Priests Accused of Sexual Abuse." *Studia Canonica* 24 (1990): 335–356.

Doyle, Thomas P., A.W.R. Sipe, & Patrick J. Wall. *Sex, Priests, and Secret Codes.* (Los Angeles: Volt Press, 2006).

Euart, Sharon. "Canon Law and Clergy Sexual Abuse Crisis: An Overview of the US Experience." *USCCB/CLSA Seminar.* USCCB, May 25, 2010.

Foley, J.J. "Preliminary Investigation: Consideration and Options." Edited by Patricia M. Dugan. *Towards Future Developments in Penal Law: U.S. Theory and Practice* (Montreal: Wilson & Lafleur, 2010): 33–54.

Golden, Paul. "Advocacy for Clerics Accused of Sexual Abuse of Minors." *CLSA Proceedings* 68 (2006): 129–148.

Gonsiorek, John C. "Barriers to Responding to the Clergy Sexual Abuse Crisis within the Roman Catholic Church." In *Sins against the Innocents*, edited by Thomas G. Plante, 139–153. (Westport: Praeger, 2004).

Graves, Todd P. *The Report of the Independent Investigation of the Catholic Diocese of Kansas City-Saint Joseph.* Kansas City: Diocese of Kansas City, 2011.

Green, Thomas J. "Clerical Sexual Abuse of Minors: Some Canonical Reflections." *The Jurist* 63 (2003): 366–425

Griffin, Bertram F. "The Reassignment of a Cleric who has been Professionally Evaluated and Treated for Sexual Misconduct with Minors: Canonical Considerations." *The Jurist*, (1991): 326–339.

Hagerty, Barbara Bradley. "Sex Abuse Scandal Catches Up with Religious Orders." *National Public Radio*, December 31, 2007: http://www.npr.org/templates/story/ story.php?storyId=17728112.

Hoye, Daniel E. "Reintegration and Restoration of Exonerated Priests." *Proceedings* 73 (October 2011): 118–129.

Huels, John M. *The Pastoral Companion.* (Quincy, Ill.: Franciscan Press, 1995).

Ingels, Gregory. "Dismissal from the Clerical State: An Examination of the Penal Process." *Studia canonica* 33 (1999): 169–212.

Jenkins, Ronny E. "Jurisprudence in Penal Cases: Select Themes From the Judicial Doctrine of the Tribunal of the Roman Rota." *CLSA Proceedings* 67 (2005): 95–122.

Jenkins, Ronny E. "The Charter and Norms Two Years Later: Towards a Resolution of Recent Canonical Dilemmas." *CLSA Proceedings* 66 (2004): 115–136.

John Jay College Research Team. *The Causes and Context of Sexual Abuse of Minors by Catholic Priests in the United States 1950–2010: A Report Presented to the United States Conference of Catholic Bishops.* (Washington, DC: United States Conference of Catholic Bishops, 2011).

John Jay College. *The Nature and Scope of Sexual Abuse of Minors by Catholic Priests and Deacons in the United States.* Study. (Washington, DC: United States Conference of Catholic Bishops, 2004).

Kaslyn, Robert J. "Accountability of Diocesan Bishops: A Significant Aspect of Ecclesial Communion." *The Jurist* 67 (2007): 109–152.

Kennedy, Eugene & Victor Heckler. *The Catholic Priest in the United States: Psychological Investigations.* (Washington DC: United States Catholic Conference, 1972).

Kinney, Bishop John F. "NCCB Establishes Committee on Sexual Abuse." *Origins* 23, no. 7 (July 1993): 104–105.

Lagges, Patrick. "Elements in the Preliminary Investigation." Edited by Patricia M. Dugan. *Advocacy Vademecum* (Montreal: Wilson & Lefleur, 2006): 153–168.

Lagges, Patrick R. "Canonical Issues of Renumeration and Sustenance for Priests Accused of Sexual Misconduct." *Proceedings* 71 (2009): 150–167.

Lagges, Patrick R. "The Penal Process: The Preliminary Investigation in Light of the Essential Norms of the United States." *Studia Canonica* 38 (2004): 369–410.

McDonough, Elizabeth. "Sanctions in the 1983 Code: Purpose and Procedures; Progress and Problems." *CLSA Proceedings* 52 (1990): 206–221.

McKenna, Kevin. "Canon Law and Civil Law: Working Together for the Common Good." *Canon Law Seminar for Media.* United States Conference of Catholic Bishops, 2010.

Morrisey, Francis G. "Addressing the Issue of Clergy Sexual Abuse." *Studia Canonica* 35 (2001): 403–420.

Morrisey, Francis G. "The Pastoral and Juridical Dimensions of Dismissal from the Clerical State and of Other Penalties for Sexual Misconduct." *CLSA Proceedings* 53 (1991): 221–239.

Morrisey, Francis. "The Preliminary Investigation in Penal Cases: Some of the Better Practices." *The Canonist* 2, no. 2 (2011): 184–198.

Murphy, Edwin J. "Suspension Ex Informata Conscientia." *Canon Law Studies,* (1932): 2–3.

National Review Board for the Protection of Children and Young People. *A Report on the Crisis in the Catholic Church in the United States.* Vol. 71 (Washington, DC: United States Conference of Catholic Bishops, 2004).

National Review Board. *Report of the National Review Board, December 2007.* (Washington, DC: United States Conference of Catholic Bishops, 2007).

O'Connor, James I., ed. *Canon Law Digest.* Vol. VII. Chicago: Chicago Province, S.J., 1975.

O'Reilly, Michael. "Recent Developments in the Laicization of Priests." *The Jurist* 52 (1992): 684–696.

Orsy, Ladislas. "Bishop's Norms: Commentary and Evaluation." *Boston College Law Review* 44 (2003): 999–1029.

Paprocki, Thomas, "As the Pendulum Swings from Charitable Immunity to Bankruptcy, Bringing Iit to Rest with Charitable Viability," 48 *J. Catholic Legal Studies* 1 (2009).

Paulson, Jerome E. "The Clinical and Canonical Considerations in Cases of Pedophilia: The Bishop's Role." *Studia Canonica* 22 (1988): 77–124.

Pilarczyk, Daniel. "Statement of Archbishop Pilarczyk, President of the National Conference of Catholic Bishops on the Sexual Abuse of Children." *Statements of National Conference of Catholic Bishops and the United States Catholic Conference on the Subject of Sexual Abuse of Children by Priests 1988–1992.* (Washington, DC: United States Catholic Conference, 1992).

Pontifical Council for Legislative Texts. *Dignitas Connubii.* (Vatican City: Libreria Editrice Vaticana, 2005).

"Pontificia Commissio Codici Iuris Canonici Recognoscendo." *Communicationes,* (1969): 83.

Pope John Paul II. "Vatican-US Bishops' Committee to Study Applying Canonical Norms." *Origins* 23, no. 7 (July 1993): 102–103

Provost, J.H. "Promoting and Protecting the Rights of Christians: Some Implications for Church Structure." *The Jurist* 46 (1986).

Rabinowitz, Dorothy. "The Trials of Father MacRae." *The Wall Street Journal,* (May 10, 2013).

Renati, Charles G. "Conducting Canonical Investigations and Interviews." *CLSA Proceedings* 67 (2005): 177–196.

Renati, Charles G. "Prescription and Derogation from Prescription in Sexual Abuse of Minor Cases." *The Jurist* 67 (2007): 503–519.

Report of the Grand Jury. MISC. NO. 0009901-2008 (Court of Common Pleas, First Judicial District of Pennsylvania, Philadelphia January 21, 2011).

Robinson, Walter V. "Reinstated Priest: Yes, I'm Angry." Boston Globe, (November 24, 2002).

Rodgers-Melnick, Ann. "Vatican Clears Priest, Wuerl Rejects Verdict." *Pittsburgh Post-Gazette,* (March 21, 1993): A-1+.

Smilinac, Daniel. "Clergy Personnel Files and the Instruction of an Allegation." *CLSA Proceedings,* 2007: 193–202.

Steinfels, Peter. "Giving Healing and Hope to Priests who Molested." *New York Times,* (October 12, 1992): A1+.

Steinfels, Peter. "The Church's Sexual Abuse Crisis." *Commonweal,* April 2002: 13–19.

Strickland, Amy J. "To Protect and Serve: The Relationship Between the Victim Assistance Coordinator and Canonical Personnel." *CLSA Proceedings* (2009): 232–242.

Suprema Sacra Congregatio Sancti Officii. "Crimen Sollicitationis." March 1962.

The 1917 Pio-Benedictine Code of Canon Law. Edited by Edward N. Peters. (San Francisco, CA: Ignatius Press, 2001)

The Boston Globe. *Betrayal: The Crisis in the Catholic Church.* (Boston: Little, Brown and Company, 2002).

United States Conference of Catholic Bishops Ad Hoc Committee on Sexual Abuse. "Efforts to Combat Clergy Sexual Abuse against Minors—Chronology." *Restoring Trust: A Pastoral Response to Sexual Abuse.* (Washington, DC: National Conference of Catholic Bishops, 2002).

United States Conference of Catholic Bishops. *Charter for the Protection of Children and Young People.* (2006).

—— *Diocesan Review Board Resource Booklet.* (Washington, DC: United States Conference of Catholic Bishops, 2008)

United States Conference of Catholic Bishops. "Essential Norms for Diocesan/Eparchial Policies Dealing with Allegations of Sexual Abuse of Minors by Priests or Deacons." *Origins* 32 (June 2004): 415–418.

Ward, Daniel J. "Canonical Advocacy: Practical Representation of a Party." *CLSA Proceedings,* (1993): 98–107.

Ward, Daniel J., OSB. "Sexual Abuse and Exploitation: Canon and Civil Law Issues Concerning Religous." *CLSA* Proceedings 67 (2005).

Woestman, William H. *Papal Allocutions to the Roman Rota.* (Ottawa: Saint Paul University, 1994).

INDEX

Abused and Neglected Child Reporting
    Act (Illinois), 126
accrual date, 63–64, 65, 67
accused clergy
    culpability of the, 273–74
    data regarding, 291–93
    defense under canon law, 267
    delaying final judgment, 395
    denial of accusation by, 348
    exoneration, 375
    guilty verdicts, 377
    investigations wanted by the,
        315–16
    notification of accusations, 328–30
    not proven verdict, 376
    overview, 49–50
    removal of the, 28
    rights under canon law, 334–35,
        346–47, 389
    victim's re-traumatization vs. rights
        of, 357–58, 357n8
    voluntary laicization, 269
    See also priests; religious communities/
        orders
accusers and the canonical process,
    343–52, 343n1, 345n8, 346–47,
    347nn11–12, 395–97
Acta Apostolicae Sedis, 235
adultery, 212
advocates for victims
    Church's victim advocacy, 54–55
    SNAP, 243, 413
advocates/procurators in canon law
    accuser's information, 347–48
    appeals and the, 377–78
    assumptions in canon law regarding,
        392–94, 392n14, 394n15
    CDF information and, 387

discovery and, 363–65, 364n22
    libellus submission and, 360
    overview, 356–57
    priesthood requirement, 354
    prosecutors or charities and, 48
    publication of the acts and, 371–72
    sentences and nondisclosure
        agreements, 374–75
    witnesses and, 368
Alabama, 137
Allen, John, 203
American Catholic Church. See United
    States Catholic Church
American Medical Association (AMA),
    115
American Psychological Association, 135
Anderson, A.C., 413
Anderson, Jeffrey, 52
Anglicans, 407
anti-Catholicism in U.S. society, 223–24
Apostolic Delegate, 164
apostolic nuncio, 52
appeals
    in canon law, 279, 377–78
    civil, 44
    criminal, 78–79
    prosecutor and, 76
    reassignment, 51
"Archdiocesan Commission of Enquiry
    into the Sexual Abuse by Members
    of the Clergy", 414
Arizona, 121–22, 137, 165
asbestos claims, 105–6
assault, 32
assets
    and donor relations, 107–8
    identifying, 40–41
    of parishes, 108–10

auditors in canon law
    conflict of interest and, 355
    evidence and, 365
    investigators status of, 325, 327
    need for, 389
    overview, 327*n*43, 356
    victims and witnesses and the, 268,
        317, 368–69, 370, 391
Australia, 187, 188, 190, 416
Austria, 190–91, 415

bankruptcy
    asset hiding, 4
    assets and donor relations and, 107–8
    assets available for, 40
    considerations of, 27
    costs, 24–25
    delayed reporting and, 16
    diocesan responses, 17–19
    diocesan review boards, 24
    the event, 11–15
    fiscal effects on liabilities of the
        diocese, 25
    income of the diocese, 25–26
    initial reports, 16
    insurer responses, 26
    internal Church disciplinary decisions
        and, 95–96
    law enforcement response, 22–23
    liabilities vs. assets, 26
    news media, 21, 22
    operational effects of, 106–7
    overview of diocese, 103–6
    parish assets, 108–10
    post-event results, 15–16
    prior abuse allegations, 21–22
    remedies, external legal vs. internal
        church, 19–20
    uninsured losses and, 174
    vulnerability of the funds of parishes,
        26–27
Banks, Robert, 419
Baptist, 407
battery, 32
Beal, John, 274, 399–400
Belgium, 10, 77, 191, 293, 420
Benedictines, 297
Benedict XVI, 5, 201, 202–4, 412, 420
    See also Ratzinger's role in abuse crisis
Bernardin, Joseph
    allegations against, 48, 142, 397, 415

effects of allegations against, 136,
    248–49, 250
innovations/policies made by, 243–44,
    286
Berry, Jason, 414
Bertone, Tarcisio, 261
Bierman, Earl, 78
bishops
    abuse cases and external relations of
        the Church, 181–88
    accusers and the, 346
    advocates and, 394
    assignment of priests by, 49
    assumptions regarding, 386–88,
        387*n*6
    bankruptcy fraud and, 112
    on the call to priesthood, 238
    canonically non-defined areas and,
        313–14
    canon law professional community
        and, 194–95
    the *Charter* and Norms, 284–86
    commission for protection of minors
        and, 205
    criminal law system and, 73–74,
        77–80
    defense lawyers and, 56–57
    definition of sexual molestation,
        11–12
    discovery process and, 365–67, 365*n*25
    as employer under state law, 36–38
    functional canonical system and, 403
    good of the community and, 210
    guidelines on abuse, 210
    investigation and pretrial role of the,
        318, 333, 335, 336
    knowledge of sexual abuse and civil
        litigation, 35–36
    lack of accountability for, 388–89,
        389*n*9
    lack of knowledge defense, 162–63
    laicization of priests, 237, 239, 249,
        256–59
    legislators and, 66
    manual regarding handling abuse
        cases and, 240
    misrepresentation torts and, 32
    negligent supervision, 32, 42
    NRB on errors by, 287–88
    parents of victims and, 47–48
    penal trials and, 35

pope and, 200–201, 217
relationship with diocese, 208
relationship with priests, 20, 389
religious communities and, 295, 299–
    300, 300n3, 301, 305, 306
repeat offenders and, 233
role in the canonical system, 386–88,
    387n6
role of diocesan, 50–51
and secular enforcement authorities,
    277–78
settlement decisions by, 43
treatment for abuser clergy and, 155,
    236, 272
varied handling of abuse cases by,
    240–42, 291–92
Vatican relationship to, 52–53
victim contact by, 223, 227, 228,
    246–47
See also canon law and failure to address
    abuse crisis; dioceses; episcopal
    culture; fraud and nondisclosure in
    the assignment of clergy; timeline
    of U.S. sexual abuse crisis
Bishops Conference of England & Wales,
    414
Boston Globe, 182, 282, 286, 417, 419
Boston, Massachusetts
archdiocesan handling of abuse and
    national crisis, 282–83
cardinal's knowledge of abuse, 163, 182
diocesan assets, 178
Geoghan case, 415, 416, 417, 418
Law, Bernard, 39, 182, 282, 283, 417,
    418
news media reports of abuse in, 249,
    417, 419
probation for abuser priests in, 413, 414
settlements in, 178
breach of fiduciary duty, 100–101
Breach of Trust, Breach of Faith, 414
Brennan, Robert L., 422
Brett, Father, 118–19
Bridgeport diocese, 34, 118–19
"Brief Overview of Conference
    Involvement in Assisting Dioceses
    with Child Molestation Claims"
    (USCCB), 414
briefs, 372–73
Brooklyn Jewish community, 407
brothers, religious, 50

Brown, Jerry, 422
Bruni, Frank, 415
Burkett, Elinor, 415

Cafardi, Nicholas, 258–59
California
mandatory reporting in, 130–31, 132,
    133
prison terms for abusers in, 73
reassignment of priests in, 140–41
Sacramento, 165
San Bernadino, 175
San Diego, 105, 112, 175, 420
San Francisco, 175
statute of limitations, 66–67, 68, 157,
    420, 422
Stockton, 105
See also Los Angeles
Camden, New Jersey, 161
Canada, 10, 119, 187–91, 264, 414, 420
Canadian Conference of Catholic Bishops,
    413, 414
"Canonical Delicts Involving Sexual
    Misconduct and Dismissal from the
    Clerical State" (USCCB), 415
canonical investigation and pretrial
    process
accusation as trigger for investigation,
    346
accused cleric's rights, 334–35
administrative process, 338–41
bishops' role in, 318, 336
CDF and, 313, 321, 321n24, 323, 328,
    328n49, 329, 330, 332, 335–42,
    339n79, 340n81, 341n84, 342n86
civil processes vs., 316–18
complaint, 318–20, 319n16
conclusion of, 342
diocesan review board, 330–34,
    332n64, 333n68
discovery during, 363
investigation, 324–28, 324n33,
    326n38, 327nn42–43, 328n48
judicial trial option, 338
notification of the accused, 328–30,
    328n49, 329nn50–51
preliminary investigation, 320–22
prescription, 323–24, 323nn29, 31
reason to conduct investigations,
    314–16, 315nn4–6, 8
sources for, 313–14

canonical penal system limitations and
   weaknesses
   assumptions in the system, 386–97,
      387n6, 389n9, 390n12, 392n14,
      394n15
   canonists experience with penal trials,
      258–59, 263–65, 264n44
   civil law vs. canon law, 383–85
   dismissal, 399–401, 399n18
   inadequacies of the system, 383
   lack of definitive outcomes, 397–99
   laity's perception of the system, 382–
      83, 382n1
   overview, 402–3
   viability of the system, 381–82, 401–2
   victims cooperation in a trial, 266–69
   volume of cases, 385–86
   See also canon law and failure to
      address abuse crisis
canonical penal trials and outcomes
   accusers and, 343–52, 343n1, 345n8,
      346–47, 347nn11–12
   aftermath, 378
   appeals, 377–78, 378n48
   auditor, 356
   canonists experience with penal trials,
      258–59, 263–65, 264n44
   conclusion of evidentiary part of case,
      372
   discouragement of penal trials in
      Canon Law, 270–71
   discovery, 362–66, 363n21, 364n22,
      365n25
   experts, 357
   final statements, 372–73
   joinder of the issues, 361–62,
      362nn17–18, 365
   judges, 355
   notary, 356
   outcome possibilities, 338–42
   overview of trial, 353–54, 379
   penal process, 269–70
   personnel, 354–57
   procedural delays, 358–59
   procurators/advocates, 347–48, 354,
      356–57, 392–94, 392n14, 394n15
   promoter of justice, 355–56
   psychological records, 366–67
   publication of the acts, 371–72, 371n33
   religious communities and, 308
   rendering the decision, 373–74

   start of trial, 359–61, 360n12, 361n15
   verdicts and sentencing, 374–77,
      376n43, 377n45
   victim cooperation and, 266–69
   victims re-traumatization vs. rights of
      accused, 357–58, 357n8
   witnesses, depositions, and hearings,
      367–71, 368n30, 369nn31–32
canon law
   accusers and the canonical process,
      343–52, 343n1, 345n8, 347nn11–12
   as code law, 313, 317, 384–85
   common law vs., 313, 317, 384–85
   conflicts in legal values, 210–11
   current law regarding sexual abuse,
      211–13, 212n32
   due process in, 353–54
   governing structures, 208–9
   overview, 207–8, 209
   parish and diocese relationship under,
      108
   penal aspects of, 209–10
   professional community role, 194–95
   reassignment of priests under, 37
   religious communities and, 298–99, 302
   on sexual abuse of minors, 233
   as standards of conduct for clergy, 164
   Vatican II and, 219
   See also Code of Canon Law; Roman
      Catholic Church's internal
      governance
canon law and failure to address abuse
   crisis
   administrative processes available,
      259–61
   bishops and secular enforcement
      authorities, 277–78
   culpability, 273–74
   cumulative effect, 278–79
   investigations and proofs difficulties,
      265–66
   minor as defined in Canon Law, 271
   overview, 253–54, 279–80
   penal process, 269–70
   priest's rights protection, 261–62
   professional community's role in,
      194–95
   remedies available, 254–59, 259n26
   statute of limitations, 271–73
   treatment used rather than
      punishment, 274–76

Canon Law Society of America, 392n14
cardinals, 74, 78, 200
Carmelites, 175
Carr, Charles, 34
Castrillón Hoyos, Darío, 199
Catechism of the Catholic Church, 415
Catholic Bishops' Conference of England
    & Wales, 416
Catholic Mutual, 88, 174
Catholic schools
    as diocesan assets, 26
    incorporation of, 40
    insurance and, 82
    loss of funds for, 179
    Oblates order, 34
    reassignment of priests at, 42
    religious brothers and, 50
    for religious vocations, 257
    sexual contact with minors in, 14, 24
Causes and Context of Sexual Abuse of
    Minors by Catholic Priests in the
    United States, 1950–2010, 421
CCEO (Code of Canons for the Eastern
    Churches), 303–5, 329, 329n51,
    340, 418
CDF. See Congregation for the Doctrine of
    the Faith
celibacy, 84, 237, 238, 257, 258, 292, 337,
    338, 398
Celibacy in Crisis (Sipe), 418
charitable actions by the Church, 179
charitable immunity from larger
    damages, 161
Charlotte, North Carolina, 78
Charter for the Protection of Children
    and Young People. See Essential
    Norms
Chicago, Illinois, 179
Child Abuse and Neglect Reporting Act
    (California), 130–31, 132, 133
Child Abuse Prevention and Treatment
    Act, 115, 115n7, 129
child pornography, 119, 421
choice of law, 415
Chopko, Mark, 413
Christian Brothers, 297, 414
Church Mutual Insurance Company, 406
Church of Jesus Christ of Latter-Day
    Saints, 406–7
Church. See Roman Catholic Church;
    Roman Catholic Church's internal

governance; United States Catholic
    Church
CICLSAL (Congregation for Institutes of
    Consecrated Life and Societies of
    Apostolic Life) 298, 299, 301, 302,
    303, 307, 308, 309
Cincinnati, Ohio, 78, 127, 176, 422
civil law vs. canon law, 383–85
civil litigation
    appeals, 44
    delays and limitations, 61–69
    discovery and depositions in, 39–40, 64
    employer responsibilities in the church
        context, 35–36
    employer under state law in, 36–38
    failure to report and, 131–34
    identifying assets, 40–41
    individual liability, 31
    judgment, 44–45
    liability of the diocese, 34, 41–42
    news media coverage, 42
    overview, 31–34
    pretrial motions, 41
    role of parishes, 38–39
    settlement discussions pretrial, 43
    trials, 43–44
    See also appeals
clergy abuse litigation patterns
    bankruptcy, 27
    costs, 24–25
    diocesan review boards, 24
    dioceses' responses, 17–19
    the event, 11–15
    fiscal effects on liabilities of the
        diocese, 25
    income of the diocese, 25–26
    initial reports, 16
    insurer responses, 26
    law enforcement response, 22–23
    legislators' roles on limitations
        periods, 27–28
    liabilities vs. assets, 26
    news media, 21, 22
    post-event results, 15–16
    prior abuse allegations, 21–22
    remedies, external legal vs. internal
        church, 19–20
    removal of the accused abuser priests,
        28
    vulnerability of the funds of parishes,
        26–27

clergy sex abuse crisis overview, 3–10
clericalism, 51
Cleveland Middleborough area study, 413
Clinton, William J., 64
CMSM (Conference of Major Superiors of Men), 303–5, 418
Code of Canon Law
  on abuse of minors, 233
  administrative penal process under the, 339–41
  investigations in the, 320, 324–25, 326–27
  on judges qualifications, 389–90
  on judicial discretion, 390–91
  ministerial activity curtailment under the, 333
  minor defined in the, 322
  overview, 207–8, 209
  on presumption of innocence, 362, 362n17
  revision of the, 201, 233–34, 239, 383
  rights of the accused under the, 334–35
  scandal avoidance in the, 224–25
  sovereign immunity and the, 164
  on support of accused clergy, 399
  volume of abuse cases and the, 385–86
  on witnesses, 395–97
  See also canon law and failure to address abuse crisis
Code of Canons for the Eastern Churches (CCEO), 329, 329n51, 340
Cody, John, 184
Colorado, 93, 98, 100
Committee for the Protection of Children and Young People (USCCB), 290
Conference of Major Superiors of Men (CMSM), 303–5, 418
confessional privilege. *See* priest-penitent privilege
Confidential Claimant case (2009), 420
confidentiality/secrecy of canonical courts, 359–60, 378
conflict of interest, 227n45, 355, 393
Congregation for Clergy, 164, 249, 249–50, 258, 260–61, 275
Congregation for Divine Worship and the Discipline of the Sacraments, 249, 258
Congregation for Institutes of Consecrated Life and Societies of

Apostolic Life (CICLSAL), 298, 299, 301, 302, 303, 307, 308, 309
Congregation for the Doctrine of the Faith (CDF)
  accuser and the, 346, 351
  administrative penal process and the, 339, 341
  advocates and the, 392, 394
  case of accused options for the, 336–38
  case of accused submitted to the, 325
  circular letter of 2011, 294, 362n17, 421
  communication with bishops and the, 387
  Crimen Sollicitationis, 197, 234–35, 260, 273
  delays in canonical trials and the, 358
  Delictis Gravioribus, De, 282, 321, 417
  functional canonical system and the, 403
  investigation and pretrial process and the, 313, 321, 321n24, 323, 328, 328n49, 329, 330, 332, 335–42, 339n79, 340n81, 341n84, 342n86
  on judges, 390
  on laicization, 236, 257–58, 261, 261–62
  minors defined by the, 272–73
  on more grave crimes, 417
  notification of accusations to the accused and the, 328, 329
  prescriptive period and the, 323–24
  on priesthood requirement for canonical court, 354
  religious communities and the, 305, 308
  on restricting ministry, 342
  review boards and the, 332
  sovereign immunity and the, 164
  on treatment for abuser priests, 274
  See also Ratzinger's role in abuse crisis; *Sacramentorum sanctitatis tutela*
Conley v. Roman Catholic Archbishop of San Francisco (2000), 133
Connecticut, 34, 96, 117–19, 118–19
conspiracy of silence charges, 152
Constitutional issues
  Church internal discipline, 94–96
  clergy special immunities, 98–99
  damages, 169
  defenses, 98, 162, 419

fiduciary duty, 100–101
malpractice, 99–100
mandatory reporting, 96–98
overview, 93–94
priest-penitent disclosures, 160
statutes of limitations, 101–2
See also due process; First Amendment
corporation law, 34
Corpus Iuris Canonici, 411
costs, investigating and defending older
    abuse claims, 24–25
Council of Elvira, 211, 411
countersuits, 165
courts, reopening legislation and the, 69
Cozzens, Donald, 157
Crimen Sollicitationis, 197, 234–35, 273,
    412
criminal law
    bankruptcy, 112
    canon penal trials vs. criminal trials,
        353–54
    child victims as adults and, 48
    Church's reporting clergy for
        prosecutions, 80
    disclosure and privilege as defense,
        126–27
    disincentives against use of criminal
        charges, 75–76
    insurance and, 89–90
    internal Church workings under,
        95–96
    jury nullification defenses, 80
    overview, 73–74
    process of criminal prosecution, 76–78
    prosecutor's institutional issues, 76
    repeat offenders, 79–80
    reporting requirements, 127–28
    sentencing and appeals, 78–79
    state laws as applied to abuse cases,
        74–75
    statutes of limitations, 57, 67, 69
culpability, 273–74

Dallas Norms. *See* Essential Norms
Dallas, Texas, 42, 141, 175, 249, 416
damages
    canonical damages, 350–51
    caps on, 170–71
    charitable immunity from larger, 161
    church-paid counseling and therapy,
        172

elements of the, 158–59
fiscal impacts of abuse cases on the
    Church, 173–79
juries and, 31
overview, 167
plaintiff's legal fees, 171
prerequisites to damage awards, 167–
    69, 168nn1–2
prerequisites to punitive, 169–70
punitive, 31
reassignment of abuser clergy and,
    148–49
treatment costs and, 31
See also defenses and claims of
    immunity
Daubert hearings, 138, 159
Davenport, Iowa, 105, 419
deacons, 49–50, 285, 297, 303
Decretum Gratiani, 411
defamation, 165
default verdicts, 165–66
defense counsel, 56–57
defenses and claims of immunity
    bishop's lack of knowledge, 162–63
    canonical defenses (culpability), 273–74
    charitable immunity, 161
    Constitutional, 162
    countersuits, 165
    damages, 158–59
    default verdicts, 165–66
    diocesan responses, 157–58, 165
    emotional injury without physical
        harm, 159
    overview, 155–56
    presentation and rebuttal of evidence,
        158
    priest-penitent disclosures privilege,
        160
    reassignment of abuser priests, 150–52
    reporter of abuse, 134
    special immunity for clergy, 98–99
    statute of limitations, 156–57
Delaware
    psychologist's testimony in, 38
    religious communities in, 34
    reporting in, 124
    statute of limitations in, 59, 67, 101,
        107
    Wilmington diocese's abuse files, 421
    Wilmington diocese's bankruptcy, 105,
        111, 420

delays and limitations in abuse cases,
61–69
*Delictis Gravioribus, De. See
Sacramentorum sanctitatis tutela*
(SST)
Demeyer v. Archdiocese of Detroit (1999),
416
Dempsey case (2009), 420
Department of Children and Family
Services (DCFS), 126
depositions, witnesses, and hearings
(canon law)., *See also* witnesses,
depositions, and hearings (canon
law)
Diana, Princess, 278
DiNardo, Larry, 353, 374
Diocese of New Ulm case (2009), 420
dioceses
abuse cases and external relations of
the Church, 181–88
accountability of the, 165
accusers and internal conflicts of,
351–52
administration of, 163–64
assets of, 40–41
assistance for accuser and, 350–51
bankruptcies, 16, 103–12, 171
bishops assigned by the pope to, 200
bishop's role/relationship in, 50–51,
208
canon law professional community
and, 194–95
the *Charter* and Norms, 284–86
civil lawyers role, 226–28
concealment role of, 141–43, 147–48
counseling and therapy for victims
and, 172
Crimen Sollicitationis in, 235
criminal charges and, 73–80
current actions/policies regarding
abuse, 229
defenses of, 157–58, 165
discovery process and the, 363, 363–
66, 365n25
exonerated priests and the, 375
fiscal effects on liabilities of the, 25
fiscal impacts of abuse cases on,
173–79
income of the, 25–26
independence of, 216–17, 216n5
insurance, 81–92

liability of the, 34, 41–42
noncompliance with Church
law, 194
Office for Child and Youth Protection
and, 289–90
overview of responses by the, 17–19,
179
parishes role within, 38–39
relationship with priests, 398
responses to civil litigation, 157–59
review boards, 24, 330–34
staff responding to allegations, 54–55
transfers among, 149–50
varied handling of abuse cases by,
240–42, 291–92
Vatican and, 163–64
witnesses and the, 368
See also bishops; civil litigation;
fraud and nondisclosure in the
assignment of clergy; Vicar for
Clergy
disclosure, 35–36, 365
discovery and depositions in civil
litigation, 33, 39–40, 64, 136
discovery in canon law, 362–66, 363n21,
364n22, 365n25
See also witnesses, depositions, and
hearings (canon law)
Doe v. Holy See (2009), 420
Dolan, Timothy, 112
Dominican Republic, 206, 422
donors to churches, 107–8, 110–12, 176,
179, 382
Doyle, Thomas, 178, 240, 278, 413
Dublin, Ireland, 189, 190
due process
accused priests and, 315
California law and, 130
in canon law, 353–54
delayed lawsuits and, 69
post-arrest, 101
reopening statutes of limitations and,
102
statutes of limitations for, 156
duty, breach of, 100–101, 168
duty of care, 32, 100–101
duty to cooperate, 415

Eller case (2006), 419
emotional injury without physical harm,
159

employers
 clergy-penitent privilege and, 96
 liability vs. clergy abuse liability,
  145–47
 non-Church tort litigation, 34
 responsibility in the church context,
  35–36
 under state law, 32, 36–38
ephebophila, 260
Episcopal Church, 117, 406, 407, 407–8,
 415
Episcopal Conferences, 329
episcopal culture
 accountability of bishops, 217–18
 ambivalence regarding laypersons,
  219–22, 220nn22–24, 221n26
 anti-Catholicism in U.S. society,
  223–24
 changing, 228–29
 deference to bishops, 218–19,
  219nn19–20
 diocesan civil lawyer, 226–28
 diocesan independence, 216–17,
  217nn8–9
 isolation at the top, 222–24
 overview, 17, 215–16, 216n2
 secrecy and scandal avoidance, 224–26
Essential Norms
 accusations covered by the, 345
 on accuser's right to be heard, 348–49
 on active ministry of abusive priests,
  145
 adoption of the, 418
 on apostolic nuncio notification, 52
 audits of diocesan responses to abuse,
  57–58
 bishops accountability under the, 388
 bishop's conforming with the, 187
 Church's stance on reporting and the,
  80
 damages for abuse crisis and the, 184
 diocesan review boards in the, 330–34
 on diocesan staff responding to
  allegations, 54–55
 dismissal under the, 340, 341–42
 following the, 65, 183
 grave delict under, 320–21
 investigations in the, 320, 325, 327
 judges and the, 389
 on law enforcement notification, 52
 minor defined under, 322

news media and the, 185
 notification of accusations to the
  accused in the, 328
 on Office of Children and Youth
  Protection, 289
 one-strike-you're-out policy, 17
 overview, 284–85
 on presumption of innocence, 362
 on psychological evaluations, 366
 public dissemination of the, 22
 reassignment under, 153
 religious communities and the, 303–6,
  304n12, 306, 307, 309, 310
 reporting/disclosure under the, 97,
  152, 293
 on review boards, 24, 330
 sexual abuse of a minor defined in the,
  213
 Vatican and the, 418
 volume of abuse cases and the, 385–86
Establishment Clause, 93–94, 100
Euart, Sharon, 245, 260
Europe, police searches in, 77
Evangelical/Fundamental denominations,
 407
evidence, 96, 123, 158, 168
 See also discovery and depositions in
  civil litigation; discovery in canon
  law; witnesses, depositions, and
  hearings (canon law)
evidence privileges
 civil tort consequences from not
  reporting, 131–34
 conflicts, 121–25, 122n7, 123n13,
  124nn15, 18
 convictions for failure to report,
  130–31
 criminal defense argument, 126–27
 immunity for clergy who report abuse,
  129, 129n45, 134
 penalties for not reporting, 127–29,
  128nn39–40
 penitent privileges, 125–26, 125n19,
  126n23
exoneration in canon law, 375
experts in canon law, 357

FADICA study, 176, 179, 382
Fairbanks, Alaska, 105, 420
Fall River, Massachusetts, 83, 92, 204,
 244

family of victims
    accusations made by, 242–43
    American canonists and, 264
    children's testimony and, 268
    credibility of the, 157
    investigations by the Church and, 314
    NRB recommendations regarding, 289
    response to reported abuse, 14, 16
fiduciary duty, breach of, 32, 93, 100–101,
    415
final judgment, 44–45
final statements in canonical penal trials,
    372–73
Finn, Robert, 119, 421
First Amendment
    bishop's knowledge of abuse and the,
        415
    communications within a church and
        the, 144
    defenses, 98, 162, 419
    doctrinal/internal matters and the, 37,
        41–42, 95
    entanglement issues, 44, 93, 112, 160,
        409
    mandatory reporting and the, 117, 130
    negligent hiring or retention and the,
        100–101
    reassignment of abuser priests and
        the, 150–52
    religious expression under the, 39–40
    special clergy immunities and the,
        98–99
Florida, 94, 204, 417
Foreign Sovereign Immunities Act, 41,
    52, 189
Fortier, Roger, 416
Foundations and Donors Interested in
    Catholic Activities, Inc. (FADICA),
    176, 179, 382
France, 293
Franciscans, 165–66, 175, 297
Francis I, 194n, 197n4, 201, 204–7, 392
Franklin, William, 419
fraud and nondisclosure in the
    assignment of clergy
    conspiracy of silence charges, 152
    data on assignments, 143
    diocesan concealment and, 141–43,
        147–48
    judge's role, 150–53
    jury decisions, 148–49

lawsuits challenging transfers of
    abusers, 139–41
management of transfers, 144–45
traditional employment law, 145–47
transfers among dioceses, 149–50
verdicts and consequences, 152–53
fraudulent concealment, 90–91
Frawley-O'Dea, Mary Gail, 419
freedom of religion, 93–94, 150–53
Frey, William, 408
Fundamental/Evangelical denominations,
    407

Gallager case (1994), 415
Gallup, New Mexico, 105
Gauthe, Gilbert, 78, 239–40, 413
Geoghan, John, 139–40, 276, 415, 416,
    417, 418
Germany, 293
Gibson case (1997), 416
Glenmary Missioners, 422
Gospel of Shame (Burkett and
    Bruni), 415
Greeley, Andrew, 419
Griffin, Bertram, 271
Groer, Hans, 415
Guide One insurance, 406
guilty verdicts, 377

Hannah, Jeff, 406
HBR case (2000), 416
"Healing the Wound of Child Sexual
    Abuse, A Church Response", 416
hearings, depositions, and witnesses
    (canon law). See witnesses,
    depositions, and hearings (canon
    law)
Hodges, Arthur E., 130–31
Holy Family Church case (2009), 420
homosexuality, 139, 234, 292, 411
Horrendum illud, 411
HosannaTabor Evangelical Lutheran Church
    & School v. EEOC (2012), 96
Hutchison ex rel. Hutchison v. Luddy (200),
    134

ICC (International Criminal Court), 421
Idaho, 413
Illinois
    Chicago foster program, 179
    damage awards in, 169

evidence in criminal prosecutions in, 96

First Amendment defenses in, 419

fraudulent concealment in, 416

priest-penitent privilege in, 97, 123

repeat offenders in, 15

reporting requirements in, 126–27

repressed memory in, 420

statute of limitations in, 416

immunities for clergy. *See* defenses and claims of immunity

Indiana, 416

Indianapolis, Indiana, 175, 416

innocence, presumption of, 325, 329, 354, 362

Instruction on the Manner of Proceeding in Cases of Solicitation, 412

Insurance Services Office (ISO), 55, 84, 90, 91, 174

insurers/insurance

 accidental occurrence, 84–85

 age of crimes and contracts, 92

 billing for civil lawsuits, 40

 coverage disputes, 83

 delays in payments by, 40

 denial of coverage, 88

 diocesan lawsuits against carriers, 92

 duty to cooperate, 415

 Episcopal Church claims, 406

 exclusion of coverage for sexual misconduct, 90

 exclusions from coverage after 1987, 91

 final judgment and, 44–45

 liability insurance policies, 55

 limitations on insurance claims timing, 89–90

 low limits of insurance coverage, 87

 old policies, 84, 92

 overview of insurance, 81–83

 pools and retained risk groups, 88–89

 priest's health insurance, 377, 395, 398, 399

 primary and excess coverage carriers, 87

 response overview, 26, 85–87

 settlements and, 44

 sexual abuse reports per year, 406

 tort reform limitations and, 170

 uninsured losses from abuse cases, 174–75

vicarious liability, 90–91

intentional torts, 161, 167

Internal Revenue Service, 162

International Criminal Court (ICC), 421

Internet, 221

In the Name of All That's Holy (Shupe), 415

investigation. *See* canonical investigation and pretrial process

Ireland, 20, 53, 165, 189, 190, 415, 416, 417, 421

Isley case (1995), 415

ISO (Insurance Services Office), 55, 84, 90, 91, 174

Italy, 10, 79, 411, 420

Jehovah's Witnesses, 406–7, 408

Jenkins, Philip, 406

Jesuits, 94–95, 98, 175, 297, 414, 417

Jewish denominations/sects, 406, 407

Jiang, Joseph, 422

John Jay College Report

 on bishops' assumptions regarding treatment, 155

 on bishops' attempted actions, 18

 on bishops' contact with victims, 228

 on Catholic clergy's privileged status, 75

 commissioning of the, 418

 on dioceses' response to NCCB recommendations, 242

 on incidence of reports of cases, 7

 on insurers, 406

 media response to the, 183

 NRB and the, 286, 287

 overview, 290–93

 on priest's refusal of voluntary laicization, 269

 publication date of the, 419

 on responses to abusive priests, 143

 second and more comprehensive report, 421

 on seminarians in the 1950s-1960s, 412

 supplementary report, 419

 on tradition and the Church, 201–2

 on Vatican delay and resistance, 197n5

John Paul II, 258, 415, 417

John XXIII, 201, 233, 258

Jones by Jones decision, 414

judges, canonical
    in the canonical system, 268, 355,
        389–92, 390n12
    in discovery process, 365
    information gathering and witness
        questioning by, 367–71
    judicial discretion, 390–91
    priesthood requirement for, 354
judges, civil
    reassignment of abuser priests role of,
        150–52
    statutes of limitations and, 156
judgment, final, 44–45
juries
    beliefs and practices of a religion and,
        409
    damages and, 31, 36, 157, 170
    news coverage of church and, 75, 165
    past practices of bishops and, 148
    perceptions of, 183
    protection of later victims, 152
    reassignment of priests and, 148–49
    witnesses and, 168
jury nullification defenses, 80

Kansas City, Missouri
    bishop's indictment and conviction in,
        77, 127, 130, 421
    child pornography, 142
    indictment of bishop of, 293
    one intake person in diocese, 325
    priest with child pornography in, 119,
        326, 421
Keating, Frank, 418
Kelley, Robert, 414
Kempe, Henry, 113–14
Kentucky, 52, 78, 418
Kinney, John, 246–47
Kos, Rudolph, 78, 416
Kuhl case (2000), 416

Lafayette, Louisiana, 239–40, 413
Lagges, Patrick, 320
laicization
    administrative, 236, 237, 239, 249,
        256–59
    supervision of abuser during process
        of, 58
    voluntary, 259–60, 269
Larry, DiNardo, 359
Lavigne, Richard, 414

Law, Bernard, 39, 182, 282, 283, 417, 418
law enforcement
    bishops working with, 277–78
    Catholic clergy's privileged status
        with, 75
    error or misconduct, 127
    notification of, 52
    overview of response by, 22–23
    priests and, 218–19
    Vatican on reporting abuse to, 20
lawyers, diocesan civil, 226–28
laypersons
    as advocates, 393
    ambivalence regarding, 219–22,
        220nn22–24, 221n26
    assignment of priests or bishops and,
        144
    on bishop's accountability, 217
    cleric's voluntary return to lay state, 337
    Code of Canon Law on, 209
    cumulative effect in hearing about
        abuse of children, 279
    delays of lawsuits and, 40
    donations by, 39
    lack of episcopal accountability and,
        388
    laity's perception of the penal system,
        382–83, 382n1
    NRB recommendations regarding, 289
    retention of laity in the Church, 33–34
    trust of Church, 279
Lead Us Not into Temptation (Berry), 414
legal fees, plaintiff's, 171
legislators responses to reopening
    limitations, 66–68
legislators role on limitations periods,
    27–28
Lewinsky, Monica, 64
liability, vicarious, 37–38, 90–91
London, Ontario, 420
Lopez, People v. (2008), 75
Los Angeles, California
    archdiocesan assets, 178
    delays in abuse cases in, 65
    evidence in abuse cases, 168
    Jesuits convicted in, 417
    records of clergy abuse in, 421
    settlements in, 82, 175, 420
Louisiana, 12–13, 81, 141, 420
Louisville, Kentucky, 6, 52, 418
Lutherans, 407

Mahony, Roger, 65
Maine, 125, 161, 416
Malicki case (2002), 417
malpractice, clergy, 99–100
Malta, 293
marriage of priests, 235, 257
Martin, Diarmuid, 7
Martinelli v. Bridgeport Roman Catholic Diocesan Corp(1997), 118–19
Maryland, 415
Massachusetts, 73, 79, 94, 97, 161, 170
    See also Boston
media. *See* news media
Memphis, Tennessee, 190
Methodists, 99, 407
Mexico, 142
Michigan, 416
Milwaukee, Wisconsin
    archdiocese assets, 89, 110, 112
    archdiocese bankruptcy, 105, 420
    archdiocese denial of insurance coverage, 83
    archdiocese's booklet on canonical process, 344–45
    bishop's knowledge of abuse, 163
    community reaction in, 185
    fraud by Church in, 158
Minnesota
    archbishop's handling of abuse cases, 422
    employer relationship in, 419
    punitive damages in, 170
    reaction to child's report of abuse in, 14
    St. Paul, 293, 421
    statute of limitations, 420
    verdict awards in, 175
    Winona, 83
minor as defined in canon law, 271, 272, 322
Miranda warnings, 264, 264n44, 328, 330
Mississippi, 98, 124
Missouri, 43, 73, 137, 319, 416, 420, 422
    See also Kansas City
Modo Procedendi in Causis Sollicitationis, De, 412
Moreno, Bishop, 413
Mormons, 406–7
Morrisey, Francis, 269
motions for dismissal, 41, 42

Mouton, Ray, 240, 413
Murphy, Edwin J., 254

National Association of District Attorneys, 13
National Catholic Reporter, 181, 182, 203, 282, 286
National Catholic Risk Retention Group, 88
National Conference of Catholic Bishops (NCCB)
    1990s actions by the, 245–48
    awareness of abuse, 232
    on emotional development of priests, 236
    formation of the, 235
    manual regarding handling abuse cases and the, 240
    recommendations for bishops, 241–42
    Vatican and the, 244–45
    See also United States Conference of Catholic Bishops (USCCB)
National Review Board (NRB)
    on abuse in the 1960s and 1970s, 236
    on attorneys' tactics, 19, 57
    on bishops and religious communities, 299
    on bishops' concern for victims, 267
    bishops cooperation with the, 418
    on bishops talking with victims, 223
    on the Church's failure to address abuse, 74, 141–42, 142–43
    on diocesan civil lawyers, 227
    on lack of accountability for bishops, 388–89
    on NCCB recommendations, 247
    Office for Child and Youth Protection monitored by the, 285
    overview, 286–89
    on religious communities and bishops, 299
    on seminarians screening and training, 237–38
Nature and Scope of the Problem of Sexual Abuse of Minors by Catholic Priests and Deacons in the United States. See John Jay College Report
NCCB. *See* National Conference of Catholic Bishops
Nebraska, 185, 187

negligence, 32, 82, 91, 93, 100–101, 167–69
    See also fraud and nondisclosure in the
        assignment of clergy
New Hampshire, 124, 416
New Jersey, 24, 64, 137, 161
New Mexico, 43, 118, 244
news media
    attacks on victim's parents and the, 157
    Bernardin coverage by the, 248
    on bishop's handling of abuse cases,
        182–83
    on Boston archdiocese, 282–83
    Catholic media on the abuse scandal,
        203–4
    court filings and the, 108
    criminal court proceedings covered by
        the, 78
    Essential Norms and the, 185
    follow-up coverage, 22
    on fraud by Church in Milwaukee, 158
    in Indiana, 416
    in Italy, 420
    juries and coverage of the Church by
        the, 75, 165
    late claims of childhood abuse and the,
        67, 69
    in Louisville, 418
    overview of coverage, 21
    parents of victims and the, 47–48
    pretrial coverage, 33, 42–43
    prosecutor's motives toward the
        Church and the, 48
    role in clergy abuse cases, 55–56
    social media, 221
    in the U.S. coverage of abuse, 202
New York, 98, 99, 417
Nobbs, George Grant, 130–31
nonprofit corporation law, 34, 35
non-Roman Catholic denominations, 8,
    79, 130–31, 405–9
Norms. *See* Essential Norms
North Carolina, 99, 124
notary in canon law, 354, 356
Nothing to Hide (Shaw), 420
NRB. *See* National Review Board
nuns, 50

Oakland, California, 175, 412
Obates, 34, 421
obedience, doctrine of, 52
O'Connell, Anthony, 417

Oddi, Cardinal, 413
Offense of Solicitation (*Crimen
    Sollicitationis*), 234–35, 273, 412
Office for Child and Youth Protection
    (USCCB), 285, 289–90
Ohio, 78, 127, 169, 176, 413, 422
Oklahoma, 124
O'Malley, Seán, 182, 204, 205
Orange County, California, 175
Ordinariates, 304n12
Oregon, 95, 96, 164, 190
    See also Portland, Oregon
O'Sullivan, Eugene, 413

Palm Beach, Florida, 204, 417
parents of victims, 47–48, 157, 158, 279
parishes
    assets of, 40, 45, 108–10
    assignment of priests to, 144
    bankruptcy and assets of, 108–10, 177
    role within a diocese, 38–39
    vulnerability of the funds of, 26–27
participants in the canonical clergy abuse
    case
    accuser, 343
    auditor, 356
    bishop, 318
    CDF, 335
    experts, 357
    investigator, 326
    judges, 355
    notary, 356
    promoter of justice, 355
    witnesses, 367
    See also accused clergy; advocates/
        procurators in canon law
participants in the clergy abuse case
    accused abusers, 49–50
    defense counsel, 56–57
    diocesan bishops, 50–51
    diocesan staff, 54–55
    insurance carriers, 55
    news media, 55–56
    suspended or dismissed priests, 57–58
    Vatican role, 51–53
    Vicar for Clergy, 53–54
    victim advocates and family, 48
    victims, 47–48
Paul II, 236–37
pederasty, 234
pedophilia, 241, 260, 273, 414, 417

Penney, Alphonsus, 414
Pennsylvania, 65, 132, 134–35, 158
  See also Philadelphia
Peter Damien, Saint, 411
Peterson, Michael, 240, 413
Peter's Pence collection, 174
Philadelphia, Pennsylvania
  accusers being misled by archdiocese
    in, 344
  charges against priest in, 422
  delayed claims in, 143
  donations of church members in, 177
  fraudulent concealment in, 37–38
  Grand Jury regarding the archdiocese
    of, 419, 421
  jury conviction of priest in, 421
  mental condition of bishop, 157
  news coverage in, 21, 73–74, 78–79
  reassignment of priests in, 140
  statute of limitations increase and
    victims in, 65
  Vicar for Clergy in, 52–54, 128, 421
  victim cooperation in archdiocese of,
    268
  victims without advocates in, 55
physicians mandatory reporting, 114, 121
Pilarczyk, Daniel, 78, 414
Pius V, 411
Pius XII, 374
plaintiff's legal fees, 171
Plante, Thomas, 292, 418, 420
pleas and prosecutor, 76, 77
Poandl, Robert, 422
Poland, 206
police. See law enforcement
Policies & Procedures for Complaints of
    Sexual Abuse, 413
popes
  bishops and, 200–201, 217, 277
  dismissals and, 337
  sovereign immunity of, 163–64
Porter, James, 92, 244, 414
Portland, Maine, 419
Portland, Oregon, 104, 105, 111, 166,
    179, 419
post-arrest due process, 101
Praesidium, 310
Presbyterians, 79, 99, 407, 408–9
pretrial
  Daubert hearings, 138, 159
  discovery, 33

motions, 41
settlement discussions, 43
  See also canonical investigation and
    pretrial process
priest-penitent privilege
  criminal charges and the, 75
  as defense, 160
  mandatory reporting and the, 96–98
  overextension of the, 79
  See also evidence privileges
priests
  in canonical roles, 354
  Charter and Essential norms and,
    284–85
  criminal law system and, 73–80
  data on sex offending, 4, 418
  dealing with sexual abuse crisis, 195
  decreased numbers of, 257
  employment status under law, 36–38,
    162
  exonerated, 375
  funds/personal wealth of, 35, 40
  guilty verdicts, 377
  immunities for, 98–99
  insistence on concealment, 33
  insurance of, 377, 395, 398, 399
  as judges, 389–90
  laicization, 58, 236, 237, 239, 249,
    256–59
  law enforcement and, 218–19
  leaving the priesthood, 237
  as mandatory reporters, 117–18
  marriage of, 235, 257
  negligent supervision of, 32
  not proven verdicts, 376
  patterns concerning the sexual contact
    event, 11–16
  pensions, 377
  personnel files, 364, 413
  population in the U.S., 412
  pretrial publicity and, 33
  protection of the rights of, 261–62
  relationship with bishops, 20, 389
  relationship with diocese, 398
  rights of, 261–62, 346–47, 389
  solidarity among, 265
  steps to becoming, 49
  suspended or dismissed, 57–58, 416
  suspension or dismissal of, 254–55,
    259–62, 337–38, 399–401, 399n18
  threatening bishops, 51

priests (Cont'd.)
  types of, 49
  See also accused clergy; evidence
    privileges; fraud and nondisclosure
    in the assignment of clergy;
    religious communities/orders;
    treatment for abuser clergy
Priests (Greeley), 419
principal-and-agent relationship, 42, 52
prior abuse allegations, 21–22
Pritzlaff case (1995), 415
Privette, William Edward, 99
Problem of Sexual Molestation by
    Roman Catholic Clergy, The (USCCB),
    413
procurators. See advocates/procurators in
    canon law
"Programme for Action, Final Report of
    the Independent Review on Child
    Protection in the Catholic Church
    in England & Wales" (UK), 417
promoter of justice, 354, 355–56, 362,
    365, 371, 373, 377–78
prosecutors, 76, 77
Protestant denominations, 407
Provost, Jim, 211
psychological records, 366–67
punishment, treatment used rather than,
    274–76
punitive damages, 169–70, 287

Queen, The (movie), 278
Quinn, A.J., 414

Ratigan, Shawn, 421
Ratzinger's role in abuse crisis, 202–4,
    250, 261, 412
  See also Benedict XVI
reasonable person norm, 100–101
reassignments and transfers
  after treatment, 42–43, 147–49, 243
  among dioceses, 149–50
  bankruptcy and, 95
  bishops role in, 50–51
  in Boston, 282–83
  in California, 140–41
  Church hierarchy and, 73
  criminal law and, 73
  freedom of religion and, 150–52
  management of, 144–45
  negligent supervision and, 42

in religious communities, 150, 306–7,
    306n16
under canon law, 37
See also fraud and nondisclosure in the
    assignment of clergy
Reese, Thomas, 74
Re, Giovanni, 418
religious communities/orders
  assets of, 40
  Benedictines, 297
  bishops and, 295, 299–300, 300n3,
    301, 305, 306
  canonical process and, 302
  canonical status of, 298–99
  Carmelites, 175
  Christian Brothers, 297, 414
  in Delaware, 34
  failure to disclose and, 147
  Franciscans, 165–66, 175, 297
  Glenmary Missioners, 422
  Jesuits, 94–95, 98, 175, 297, 414, 417
  leadership/hierarchy in, 49, 50
  membership in, 301–2, 301nn4–6
  non-clerical members of, 307, 307n19
  the Norms and, 303–6, 304n12
  Obates, 34
  overview, 297, 310–11
  penalties available for members of,
    307–9, 308nn21, 23
  proactive efforts of, 310
  Servants of the Paraclete, 244, 411, 413
  settlements with, 175
  sisters, 50, 307n19
  transfers of members, 150, 306–7,
    306n16
  types of religious life, 298
  women's, 50, 220, 220n24, 307n19
religious order members, 57–58, 301–2,
    301nn4–6
remedies, 19–20, 254–59, 259n26
repeat offenders, 15, 79–80, 233, 276
reporting laws (mandated), 80, 96–98,
    113–19, 113n1, 114nn4–6, 115n7,
    116nn16–17, 117nn21, 26–27, 287,
    416
  See also evidence privileges
Report on the Crisis in the Catholic Church
    in the United States (NRB), 287–89,
    419
repressed memory, 67, 68, 118, 135–38,
    156, 416, 420

reputation and privacy, accuser's right to, 349–50

respondeat superior, 34

Restoring Trust (NCCB), 247–48, 415

Rhode Island, 124

RICO claims, 152, 163

Robinson, Paul, 408

Rockville Centre, Suffolk County, New York, 417

Roman Catholic Church
  assets of, 26, 40–41
  Constitution and internal discipline, 94–96
  contingent liability of damages and settlements and the, 103
  costs of investigating and defending older abuse claims, 24–25
  organization of the, 35
  prosecutors and the, 76
  reassignments and transfers and the hierarchy of the, 73
  reporting clergy for criminal prosecutions, 80
  U.S. Constitution and internal discipline of the, 94–95
  U.S. responses vs. non-U.S. responses, 187–91
  See also episcopal culture; United States Catholic Church; Vatican

Roman Catholic Church's internal governance
  canon law professional community, 194–95
  Francis I and, 194*n*, 197*n*4, 204–7
  initial perceptions of the crisis by the Vatican, 196–98, 197*nn*4–5
  managerial accountability conflicts, 199–201, 200*n*11
  organizational norms and mindset, 195–96, 195*n*3
  overview, 193–94, 194*n*2
  Ratzinger's role in abuse crisis, 202–4, 261, 412
  state/international church interaction, 198–99
  traditional and slow nature of the Church, 201–2
  See also canon law

Rossetti, Stephen, 414

Sacramento, California, 165

Sacramentorum sanctitatis tutela (SST)
  bishops, archbishops, and cardinals under the, 200, 388
  dismissal under the, 340
  force of the, 281–82
  on grave crimes, 417
  grave delict under, 320–21
  on investigations, 320, 325
  issuance of the, 250
  on judges, 355, 390
  minor defined under, 322
  notification of accusations to the accused in the, 328
  prescriptive period under, 324
  on prosecution and punishment, 212
  public awareness of the, 210
  update to the, 293–94
  volume of abuse cases and the, 385–86

St. Luke Institute, 246

St. Paul, Minnesota, 293, 421

San Bernadino, California, 175

San Diego, California, 105, 112, 175, 420

San Francisco, California, 175

schools. *See* Catholic schools

Scicluna, Charles, 203, 371

Seattle, Washington, 175

secrecy/confidentiality of canonical courts, 359–60, 378

seminaries/seminarians
  closing, 257
  increased screening and training, 288
  lack of screening and training, 237–39
  minor seminaries, 257
  1950s-1970s, 237–39, 412

sentencing in canon law, 374–75

sentencing in criminal law, 78–79

Servants of the Paraclete's treatment center, 244, 411, 413

settlements
  belated disclosures and, 36
  in Boston, 140
  denials of insurance coverage and, 81
  fiscal impacts of abuse cases on the Church, 173–79
  frustration of the victims and, 65
  impact on the U.S. Catholic Church fiscally, 175–76
  insurance carriers and, 44
  nondisclosure and, 142

settlements (*Cont'd.*)
  pretrial discussions, 43
  See also damages
sexual abuse/molestation definition,
    11–12, 31, 114
*Sexual Abuse of Children in the Roman Catholic
    Archdiocese of Boston, The*, 418
Shanley, Paul, 419
Shaw, Russell, 420
Sheehan v. Oblates of St. Francis de Sales
    (2011), 421
Shupe, Anson, 415, 420
Sipe, A.W. Richard, 74, 418
sisters, religious, 50, 307n19
sixth commandment, 212–13, 239, 321
SNAP (Survivors Network of those
    Abused by Priests), 243, 413
social media, 221
Softcheck case (2006), 419
South Bay Christian Academy, 130
South Bay United Pentecostal Church, 130
sovereign immunity, 163–64, 189
Spoils of the Kingdom (Shupe), 420
Spokane, Washington, 105, 177, 419
SST. *See Sacramentorum sanctitatis tutela*
state law
  conspiracy, 152
  criminal, 74–75
  damages, 169–71
  reporting laws, 96–98, 113–19, 113n1,
    114nn4–6, 115n7, 116nn16–17,
    117nn21, 26–27
  Vatican and, 189
  See also civil litigation; evidence
    privileges; statutes of limitations
"Statement of Episcopal Commitment"
    (USCCB), 418
Statement on Priests and Child Abuse
    (USCCB), 413
Statement on Sexual Abuse of Children
    (USCCB), 413
statutes of limitations
  bankruptcy and, 107, 112
  bishops' responsibility for changes in,
    287
  in California, 157, 420, 422
  canon law (prescription), 271–73,
    323–24, 323nn29, 31
  conspiracy and, 152
  criminal, 418
  defenses, 156–57

  in Delaware, 421
  delays and, 61–69, 101, 155–56
  for fairness and due process, 130
  fraud exception, 420
  legislators' roles on, 27–28
  in Maryland, 415
  in Michigan, 415
  in Minnesota, 420
  reopening of limitation periods, 102
  repressed memory and, 135–38, 136–38
  tolling, 62–63, 136, 157
  in Wisconsin, 158, 419
Steele, Myron, 69
Stockton, California, 105
Stogner v. California (2003), 67, 418
Supreme Sacred Congregation of the Holy
    Office, 234
Survivors Network of those Abused by
    Priests (SNAP), 243, 413
suspension based on the informed
    conscience, 254–55
Swanson case (1997), 416
Synod of Elvira, 211, 411

Talbot, James F., 97–98
Tenantry, Mary, 408
Tennessee, Memphis, 190
Texas, 42, 78, 124, 141, 175, 249, 416
therapy for abuser clergy. *See* treatment
    for abuser clergy
timeline of U.S. sexual abuse crisis
    309–1922, foundations of present law,
    411
  1949, rehabilitation center for priests
    opened, 411
  1950s, 232–33, 412
  1950s–1970s, failure to screen and
    train seminarians, 237–39, 238n22
  1950s -2002, John Jay College Studies,
    290–93
  1960s, 233–35, 412
  1970s, 235–37, 412
  1980s, 239–42, 412–13
  1990s, 243–50, 413–16
  2000–2013, 416–22
  2001, CDF circular letter, 294
  2001,*Sacramentorum sanctitatis tutela*,
    250, 281–82
  2002, John Jay College Studies, 290–93
  2002, USCCB/National Review Board,
    281, 282–90

2010, *Sacramentorum sanctitatis tutela*, 293–94
2011, anticipated canonical legislation, 294–95
2011, CDF Circular Letter, 294
overview, 231–32, 250–51, 295
the victims, 242–43
Today's Parish, 414
tort litigation. *See* civil litigation
"Towards Healing", 416
transfers. *See* reassignments and transfers
treatment for abuser clergy
bishops and, 155, 236, 272
as defense, 152
families of victims and, 242
instead of punishment, 274–76
reassignment after, 42–43, 147–49, 243
records used in penal trials, 366–67
St. Luke Institute, 246
Servants of the Paraclete's treatment center, 244, 411, 413
treatment for victims, 31, 172, 178, 350
trials
civil case, 43–44
criminal vs. canon penal trials, 353–54
See also canonical penal trials and outcomes
Tucson, Arizona, 105, 108, 109, 178, 412, 419
Twenty Eight Suggestions on Sexual Abuse Policies (USCCB), 415

Uniform Laws and Model Acts, 34
United Kingdom, 417
United States
1970s in the, 235
anti-Catholicism in the, 223–24
common law vs. canon law, 210–11
mandatory reporting law, 114–15, 115n7
population of priests in the, 412
sexual abuse (generally) awareness in the, 232
Vatican and the, 189
United States Catholic Church
abuse cases and external relations of the, 181–86
anti-Catholicism in U.S. society and the, 223–24
assets of the, 103

fiscal impacts of abuse cases on the, 173–79
legislation regarding statute of limitation and the, 67–68
responses vs. non-U.S. responses, 187–91
See also canonical penal system limitations and weaknesses; canon law and failure to address abuse crisis; Roman Catholic Church; timeline of U.S. sexual abuse crisis
United States Catholic Conference (USCC), 235, 241, 285, 289–90, 290, 413, 414, 415
United States Conference of Catholic Bishops (USCCB)
authority over bishops, 388–89
awareness and prevention actions, 229
on Church leaders handling of abuse of minors, 73
on the Church preventing abuse, 140
Committee for the Protection of Children and Young People, 290
on concealment of clergy sexual abuse, 51
control of bishops by the, 187, 216
costs of abuse crisis on the, 178
Dallas meeting in 2002, 283–84
damages and the, 41
donations of church members and the, 177
functional canonical system and the, 403
on judges in canonical trials, 359
meetings regarding abuse, 413, 414
merger of USCC and NCCB to form the, 235
offender registry and the, 146–47
Office for Child and Youth Protection, 285, 289–90
recommendations prior to 2002, 157
on removal of abuser priests, 17
on repeat offenders, 80
research by the, 183
rights of clerics and the, 399
role of the, 189
statement on abuse, 413
See also Essential Norms; National Conference of Catholic Bishops (NCCB); United States Catholic Conference (USCC)

United States Constitution. *See* Constitutional issues
United States Department of Health, Education, and Welfare, 114
United States Supreme Court on criminal claim limitation periods, 66–67, 69
USCCB. *See* United States Conference of Catholic Bishops
USCC. *See* United States Catholic Conference

Vatican
    accusers and the, 346
    assets of the, 41
    authority of the, 188–89
    bishop appointments and the, 144, 283
    bishop's authority and the, 277
    bureaucracy, 194n, 197n4, 204–7, 392
    canon law and the, 313, 314
    cardinals exile at the, 78
    Code revisions by the, 294–95
    costs resulting from abuse cases and the, 173–74
    diplomacy and the, 189–90
    Essential Norms and the, 418
    on guidelines regarding abuse, 188
    ICC and the, 421
    initial perceptions of the crisis by the, 196–98, 197nn4–5
    knowledge regarding abuse crisis, 262
    laicization process and the, 58
    Law, Bernard in, 182
    NCCB and the, 244–45
    penal trial convictions overturned by the, 270
    potential claims against the, 420
    on psychological reports use, 367
    removal of priests and the, 261
    on reporting abuse to police, 20
    role in clergy abuse cases, 51–53
    shielding of diocesan funds and the, 112
    sovereign immunity of the pope and officials of the, 163–64
    on suspensions, 416
    symposium on pedophilia, 417
    volume of abuse cases reported to the, 385
    See also Roman Catholic Church
Vatican II, 219, 220, 233–34, 255

verdict and sentencing in canonical penal trials, 374–75
verdicts and consequences
    default verdicts, 165–66
    denials of insurance coverage and, 81
    fiscal impacts of abuse cases on the Church, 173–79
    impact on the U.S. Catholic Church fiscally, 175–76
    overview, 152–53
Vicar for Clergy
    assignment of priests by the, 139, 140, 152
    cover-up by the, 78
    deposition of the, 39
    indictment of Philadelphia, 421
    investigations and the, 326
    negligent supervision by the, 42
    as potential defendant, 53–54
Vicar General, 326
vicarious liability, 37–38, 90–91
victims
    American canonists and, 264
    bishops contact with, 223, 227, 228, 246–47
    in Boston, 282
    canonical process and accusers, 343–52, 343n1, 345n8, 346–47, 347nn11–12
    canon law professionals and the, 195
    coerced silence of, 156, 225–26
    cooperation in a penal trial, 266–69, 395–96
    credibility of the, 157, 396–97
    delay on proof, 64–65
    disbelieving, 128–29
    emotional injury, 32, 159
    investigations by the Church and, 314
    lack of dioceses response and, 228
    NRB recommendations regarding, 288–89
    overview, 47–48
    patterns concerning the sexual contact event, 11–16
    reporting laws, 96–98, 113–19, 113n1, 114nn4–6, 115n7, 116nn16–17, 117nn21, 26–27
    repressed memory, 67, 68, 118, 135–38, 416, 420
    re-traumatizations vs. rights of accused, 357–58, 357n8

secrecy and scandal avoidance of
   Church and, 225–26
settlements and nondisclosure by the,
   142
treatment by dioceses, 242–43
treatment for, 31, 172
VIRTUS program, 85, 89
Voice of Justice, 407
vows, religious, 37, 141, 152, 298, 302

Washington, 42, 105, 175, 177, 419
Wehmeyer, Curtis, 421, 422
Wesolowski, Jozef, 206, 422
West Virginia, 124, 416
Wilmington, Delaware, 105, 111, 420, 421

Winona, Minnesota, 83
Wisconsin, 65, 109, 158, 416, 420
   See also Milwaukee
witnesses, depositions, and hearings
   (canon law), 367–71, 368*n*30,
   369*nn*31–32, 395–97
   See also discovery and depositions in
      civil litigation; discovery in canon
      law
women's religious communities, 50, 220,
   220*n*24, 307*n*19
Wyoming, 124

Yurgel, Robert, 78